DEVIANCE

THE INTERACTIONIST PERSPECTIVE

TEXT AND READINGS IN THE SOCIOLOGY OF DEVIANCE

Earl Rubington
Martin S. Weinberg

RUTGERS UNIVERSITY

The Macmillan Company   NEW YORK
Collier-Macmillan Limited   LONDON

Library of Congress catalog card number: 68–12719

THE MACMILLAN COMPANY, NEW YORK
COLLIER-MACMILLAN CANADA, LTD., TORONTO, ONTARIO

Printed in the United States of America

PREFACE

The purpose of this book is to present students of deviant behavior with the recent work in this rapidly growing field. Along with widespread and growing interest in the field of deviance, there has developed a number of divergent perspectives on the subject itself. The authors decided not to attempt to include them all, but rather to put together more selectively a set of papers that exemplified one way of looking at the general subject of deviant behavior. It is this perspective that we call the interactionist perspective. In this book we do not by any means codify theory and hypotheses from such a perspective. What we do try to do is to fit together a set of papers that makes sense of deviance as somehow being both product and process of social interaction.

This is by no means a new conception in sociology, itself the study of social interaction. But to date the excellent studies of deviance that either set forth or illustrate this general perspective have not been put in one place where they are readily available, and where the general framework they imply is made a little more explicit.

Most of the readings we have selected have been published within the past ten years, mainly in sociological journals. There are a few excerpts from books but, in general, the papers are from journals and are almost evenly divided between theoretical and research papers. We have made a special effort to include the major statements of those sociologists who have more or less shaped interactionist orientations. Though by no means a school in the pejorative sense, nevertheless there is a commonality of viewpoint and attack in the work of such men as Becker, Cicourel, Erikson, Garfinkel, Goffman, Kitsuse, Lemert, Matza, Scheff, and Schur. We have sought to include as much of their work as is relevant to the purposes of this book and as befits its overall design.

Because of the framework in which the papers are organized, and because of their substance, we see the book as having two major uses. As a beginning statement on and collation of the interactionist perspective on deviance, it can be used in courses on deviant behavior that are taught from the same point of view. The second use, typical of the flexibility that text readers have, is that of

iii

adjunct to a course on the same subject but one that is organized from a different point of view. Most of the papers can very easily stand alone on their own merits, and if the book does nothing else but familiarize more readers with these works, it will have fulfilled its task.

New Brunswick, N.J.   E. R.

M. S. W.

GENERAL INTRODUCTION

This book examines the conditions under which deviance emerges, develops, and changes over time. A constant feature of these conditions is social definition. For deviance, in the last analysis, is defined by what people say and do about persons, situations, acts, or events.

In other words, deviance is in the eyes of the beholder. For deviance to become a social fact, somebody must perceive an act, person, situation, or event as a departure from social norms, must categorize that perception, must report the perception to others, must get them to accept this definition of the situation, and must obtain a response that conforms to this definition. Unless all these requirements are met, deviance as a social fact does not come into being.

Once these requirements are met, deviance does become a social reality. Its appearance depends rather heavily on the system of social types that groups employ. These types consist of key terms that describe the deviant as a special kind of person, evaluate him relative to others not singled out for special attention, and prescribe the kinds of conduct now permissible with him. When, for example, undergraduates type a fellow student as a "nut" or a "queer duck," they share a definition of him as a particular kind of person. Subsequently, they organize their relations with him so that their actions will now conform with this understanding of him. And he, in turn, revises his understanding of himself and his actions with them in an attempt to come to terms with this situation.

Deviance, then, is a part of daily life. As a concept affecting the course of that life, it emerges from the interactions that take place between people and the perspectives by which they seek to both understand and control those selfsame interactions. General statements that hold true for the processes of interaction will therefore hold true for deviance, for deviance is but a special case of these processes. Everyday life generates these constructs, which guarantee that interactions will recur in a more or less patterned way. And everyday life is routine and orderly simply because men understand their lives in these same general terms. The basis upon which they join interpretations to conduct is through such typifications of each other.

The Plan of the Book

The selections that follow try to spell out this viewpoint and its processes in greater detail. The first half of the book deals with how people develop a conception of some persons as being different from others, and how they come to act on this definition. Part One deals mainly with primary groups and informal relations and examines how a person is singled out and assigned the status of deviant. Part Two deals with the processes by which agents of social control, working in formal organizations, define persons as deviants according to official categories, and the organized social actions they take on the basis of these shared definitions.

The second half of the book deals with the deviant, how he responds to this typing by others, how he types himself, and how he forms deviant groups. Part Three examines the way in which deviants develop and sustain their own subcultures, how they fashion ways of collectively dealing with the common problem of having been singled out as deviants. Part Four deals with the ways in which a person takes on a deviant identity. It takes up the process of self-typing, whereby a person comes to define himself as a certain kind of person. Then it pays special attention to the transformation of a deviant identity.

The book, it can thus be seen, stresses not so much why a person comes to initiate the actions later to be called deviant, but rather how the person, once exposed to such social typing by others and/or himself, finds that he is routed on a different career than most people. So this book takes relatively little notice of the motivations for deviance, but instead pays closer attention to the sociology of deviance. And that subject quite properly concerns itself with the interactive processes that divide the world into types of people and the effects of these processes on that very world.

CONTENTS

Part One: (Continued)

Part Four: (Continued)

THE SOCIAL DEVIANT

Part One

SOCIOLOGY IS THE ANALYSIS of social relations. Some of its key concepts for carrying out that analysis are culture, social organization, status, norm, group, role, self, and sanctions. Its field of study encompasses how men arrive at a common definition of their situation and how they form themselves into groups on the basis of these definitions. Additional objects of study are the process by which men set down rules of conduct for one another, the social roles they assign to each other, and the manner in which they enforce their rules. Sociology uses its concepts to focus on some of the subjects just noted in its pursuit of one central goal: to explain social order.

A breach of this order is called social deviance. Each presupposes the other. And from studying one, sociologists frequently learn more about the other. This is the special viewpoint of this book. As a book on sociology, it is primarily interested in social order; it takes the position, however, that an examination of social deviance (from a particular perspective to be outlined) is one way of unraveling the mysteries of social order. In turn, of course, as all sciences seek to uncover a pattern of order and regularity behind seeming disorder and chaos, this book also attempts to show that deviance, as a form of social relation in its own right, similarly contains patterned uniformities. Some of these are already known, but many are only suspected, and therefore are hypotheses for future research. The study of social deviance can shed much light on social order in general and, in particular, reveal the paradoxical uniformities that deviance requires in order to exist as a social phenomenon.

There are at least two ways of studying social deviance. The first is the approach of the objectively given; the second, the subjectively problematic. If, for instance, sociologists define deviance as objectively given, they then ask a number of relatively straightforward questions of a society's

1

official records of deviants. On the other hand, if sociologists define deviance as being itself problematic in nature, then the processes of social interaction must be inspected to ascertain the conditions under which deviance comes into being, how it is defined, and what consequences flow from that definition. This book takes the second position. But before outlining that position we will describe and evaluate briefly the first position.

1. *Deviance as the given object.* Men set down rules of conduct and then seek to hold each other to these rules. Departures from the rules upset order and require various measures of enforcement, or in general, some system of social control. Deviance is usually considered any violation of rules and deviants are persons who violate rules. Taking deviance as objectively given, the major questions for inquiry become (a) who is the deviant? (b) how did he become a deviant? (c) why does he continue in deviance despite controls brought to bear on him? (d) what sociocultural conditions are most likely to produce deviants? and (e) how may deviants be best controlled?

The strong point of this position is the sharpness and the simplicity with which it phrases questions. Its weaknesses lie in the perspective giving rise to the questions on the one hand, and the changing and complex world of social reality on the other. In simpler societies, for example, with their small numbers of people, high visibility, low mobility, and elementary moral rules, deviance is easy to identify. In complex modern societies, however, the many possibilities for secret deviance, or persistent patterned violations of norms and rules that go unnoticed, indicate that the position of deviance as objectively given is on unsound ground, for much forbidden behavior today goes unobserved.

In general, it would appear that there is basic agreement in most societies about certain fundamental norms, even if these norms are proscriptions only. For instance, murder, violence, theft, and rape would seem to be universally tabooed. If this is so, one might expect that responses to these deviant acts ought to be uniform. But even to acts of this nature, which presumably evoke universal horror and outrage, there are wide differences in response. Who the criminal is and who his victim is invariably shape responses to deviant behavior. One example of this point comes from a study of homicide. White men who murder Negroes in the South are punished less severely than Negroes who murder white men. Additionally, Negroes who murder other Negroes are punished much less severely than white men who murder other white men.[1]

---

[1] Harold Garfinkel, "Research Note on Inter- and Intra-Racial Homicides," *Social Forces,* **27** (May, 1949), 369–381.

Persons may engage in deviant acts, yet never be assigned a deviant status. Jaywalkers, traffic law violators, and sharp businessmen, to name but three examples, may violate the law, but they are rarely considered criminals. Indeed, one oft-cited study indicates that most people have actually violated legal norms at least once without becoming defined as criminals.[2] If a rule lacks moral support, its violators will not be seen as deviant. With the changes in modern societies, conflict over deviance is more the rule than the exception. And because deviance as often as not arises out of cultural conflict, the question of whether it is objectively given is really moot. Gambling, for instance, is defined as a legal wrong. Yet millions of Americans bet on a variety of events and refuse to regard their actions as morally wrong. Given this conflict, it is quite clear that the millions of people who gamble do not regard themselves as deviant. If anything, they regard laws enjoining gambling as deviant.

2. *Deviance as subjectively problematic.* In this second approach to the study of deviance, major questions of inquiry are less often formulated by the sociologist than by the persons involved. In this conception, it is the actors' definitions of the situation that become the problem. For example, the person who embezzles money from the firm in which he works may never define himself as a thief. He may regard his violation of trust as an instance of "borrowing" and he may fully intend at some point in the future to repay the "loan." The numerous people who take towels from their hotel rooms similarly do not think of themselves as thieves. Thus the sociologist who regards deviance as subjectively problematic pays much less attention to the foregoing questions touched on and instead focuses on questions generated in the interactions between so-called conformists and deviants.

Defining the situation in these more relativistic terms does not mean that the sociologist disregards the social acts of killing, violence, rape, and so forth. But rather than ask why they did it, he focuses on the social definition of deviants. He studies deviance as an interactive process, and this requires him to take the perspective of those who define a person as being a social deviant. He needs to find out (a) what are the circumstances under which a person gets set apart, henceforth to be considered a deviant? (b) how is the person cast into that social role? (c) what actions do others take on the basis of this redefinition of the person? and (d) what value, positive or negative, do they place on the facts of deviance?

Shifting then to the other side of the interaction, the sociologist adopts the perspective of the person adjudged to be a deviant, and considers some

---

[2] James S. Wallerstein and Clement J. Wyle, "Our Law-abiding Lawbreakers," *Probation*, **25** (March–April, 1947), 107–112.

questions such as these: (a) how does a person judged to be a deviant react to this designation? (b) how does he adopt the deviant role that may be set aside for him? (c) what changes in his group memberships result? and (d) to what extent does he realign his self-conception to accord with the deviant role assigned him?

This book presents deviance as subjectively problematic rather than as objectively given. And this means that it looks at deviance from the perspective of defining agents in everyday life and in the world of official agencies of social control. Then, it turns to examine the situation from the viewpoint of the deviant himself. It looks at the changes in his group memberships following his assignment to a deviant role and then it studies the extent to which he comes to regard himself differently.

Instead of looking for answers to deviance in the qualities of a person or in the character of his acts, it is fruitful to make the perception of deviance the problem itself. The primary question then is not, Who is the deviant?, but instead, How does a group define the deviant? Seen in this light deviance becomes a matter of social definition. And this definition often produces the deviant acts. For instance, parents eager to have their children speak well may actually generate social conditions whereby the children become the stutterers the parents do not wish them to become. They define their children's slow (but actually normal) pace of learning how to speak as signs of stuttering. Their anxiety makes them work overly hard teaching their children how to speak without stuttering. Their anxiety, however, eliminates the child's chances of learning how to speak with ease. For each mistake the child makes in the course of talking becomes only further evidence that the child is a stutterer. Whereupon the frightened parents only work harder to teach the child to talk. In actuality, of course, they only succeed in transferring their own speech anxieties to the child, and, in the process, teaching him to talk like the very stutterer they feared he would become. In the course of this interaction process, the parents assigned the child a role as stutterer which he, in time, came to assume.

Role-assignment thus refers to a collective attempt to make sense and to come to terms with a pattern of seemingly deviant acts. So far as they arrive at a shared perspective on this pattern, they have given the acts a social meaning. This exchange of ideas produces a moral judgment. Depending on the harm assumed to be caused by the alleged deviant act, this judgment usually contains an imputation of motives, a definition of the actor as a particular kind of person, and, quite often, a line of action to be taken toward the person designated as a social deviant. In effect, then, group discussions of presumed aberrant conduct yield a group product—

a social definition. This definition consists of a description, an evaluation, and a prescription. For instance, an alcoholic is a person who drinks more than most other people (description); these actions are considered either unhealthy, immoral, or both (evaluation); and persons who come into contact with a person designated as an alcoholic can commiserate, treat, sermonize, or insult him (prescription).

Social definition, then, interprets, classifies, and dictates responses to the actions, real or reported, of another person. And the greater the number of people who share that judgment, the broader the consensus on the deviant. Social definition supplies a group with terms for imparting meaning to actions that frequently seem to make no sense whatsoever. Thus, regardless of the "real motives" or the "real reasons" for the person's conduct, a group now believes it understands the disturbance of social order. It is the group's common understanding of the disturbance, however, that is the basis of the social order it supports and takes for granted.

Social deviants, therefore, are persons who are typed socially in a very special sort of way. They are assigned to certain categories and each category carries with it a stock interpretive accounting for any persons subsumed under its special rubric. For example, a "kook" is a person who is odd, mildly eccentric. The term specifies that his talk or actions are not to be taken too seriously. At the same time, however, it licenses a certain display of either dislike or friendly disrespect in his presence. On the other hand, a person who comes to be defined as a "bad actor" [3] is both odd and severely unpredictable. The term specifies that his talk and actions are to be taken seriously at all times. Thus a person who shows public dislike or disrespect to a "bad actor" does so at great personal risk.

These ideas about deviants as special sorts of persons can have a range of consequences for the people who hold them, as well as for those who are defined by them. In the perspective that takes deviance as being subjectively problematic, this system of moral judgments is considered to precede the identification of the deviant. Accordingly, before we can know who the social deviant is, we must first examine the group and the conditions under which it makes a social judgment; this frequently has fateful consequences for judge and judged alike.

To assess what is subjectively problematic about deviance this Part looks at (a) how persons type social deviants; (b) what kinds of adjustments people make after they have redefined a person in their midst as deviant;

---

[3] This social type is defined as "a mean, malicious, or deceitful person" in Harold Wentworth and Stuart Berg Flexner, *Dictionary of American Slang* (New York: Thomas Y. Crowell, 1960), 13.

(c) what are some of the cultural rules on typing; and (d) how persons sometimes collaborate to exclude from their midst other people whom they have typified as deviants.

The Process of Social Typing

Deviance, as an interactive process, requires that a defining agent perform the work of redefinition upon another person. If successful, the redefinition alters future relations with that person. For this reconstitution to be successful, however, certain requirements must be met. Conditions that initiate typing are first, an uncommon event, and, second, a web of social relations. From what has already been said, however, it is clear that even together these are insufficient to produce social deviants. For if a potential typer sees the uncommon event as actually no more than another aspect of routine, it goes unrecognized as deviant. For instance, marked irritability in a primary group might be seen as the result of the kind of hard work that sustains the group over time. Thus, a housewife expects a tired husband sometimes to act cranky and she "makes allowances" for his irritation. Similarly, a shoe salesman can excuse or never notice marked variation in the behavior of different customers so long as he acts on the principle that "The customer is always right." In many situations people treat unusual behavior as if it were the statistical norm. This is an aspect of what Sumner called conventionalization.[4]

Once the initiating conditions have been met, a social structure for typing the person as deviant can actually come into being. It is possible to fill in the details of this structure of redefinition by answering some of the following questions:

1. Who types whom?
2. On what grounds?
3. In what ways?
4. Before or after what acts, real or imputed?
5. In front of what audiences?
6. With what kinds of effects?

In general, a successful typing occurs when typer, audience, and person singled out for typing understand and ratify the definition in all future interactions that may take place. This means that after typing, all interactions between deviant and witnesses to his identification take the new definition into account. Because both typer and audience share a new understanding of the person, they act on that understanding when in his presence. The person who has been typed, in turn, becomes aware of the

[4] William Graham Sumner, *Folkways* (Boston: Ginn and Company, 1906), 68–69.

new definition that has been placed upon him by members of his group. He too, then, takes this new understanding of himself into account when dealing with them. Thus, the situation between typer, audience, and person singled out for typing undergoes a radical change. The situation for interaction has been radically redefined and all parties subscribe, willingly or otherwise, to this redefinition. When this happens, a social type has been ratified, and a person has been socially reconstituted.

Take the case, for example, of a woman who is rather casual about sexual contacts. Over a period of years, she engages in sex relations more or less promiscuously. If one day she should suggest or hint at receiving a gift for her sexual favors or if one of her friends presents her a gift or some money shortly after the sex act, her status has been redefined. Hereafter, other people may come to think of her as a prostitute and she may, reciprocally, come to think of herself in these same terms. When this happens, casual sex promiscuity has become transmuted into a deviant occupational role.

In general, social types are more apt to be accepted into a group's system of meanings when a high-ranking person does the categorization rather than when a low-ranking person does it. Effective social typing, then, flows down rather than up the social structure. For example, a group of factory workers may designate their foreman as a "company man." But although this is a valid type, it is an ineffective one if they are unable to get the foreman to change his behavior with them. If, for instance, he is unaware of the meaning they place on his actions, or if he is aware of their meaning yet refuses to allow it to influence his dealings with them, the type is valid yet ineffective. By contrast, when both parents induct one of their children into the family scapegoat role, this is an effective social typing because the child is unable not to take their definition of him into account even if he so wishes.

In turn, social typing is more apt to be effective if there is a sense of violation of rules or expectations. For instance, if persons are tacitly expected to turn out only a limited amount of work in certain factories, then a person who is unaware of this informal output norm and goes beyond it will be singled out and treated as a "rate-buster." On the other hand, a person who drinks nine or ten glasses of water a day is unlikely to be singled out for typing and treated as a deviant, primarily because there are few rules if any on drinking water.

Similarly, negative social typing is probably more readily accepted than positive typing. The old adage that "misery loves company" points to the conditions under which persons victimized for one reason or another are both ready, anxious, and willing to believe the worst about other people.

Another reason is simply that more social norms can be defined by infractions than by enactments. Also, typing would seem to be more readily accepted if the acts, real or alleged, suggest that the nonconformity is part of a pattern that will continue despite what other people do. For instance, police officers in college towns expect students to behave uproariously and then, after graduation to become important, influential, and respected citizens. At the same time, they expect slum youth to be vandals, troublemakers, and juvenile delinquents, who in adulthood will become hoodlums or professional criminals. Less apt to pin a negative type on college students who violate certain legal norms, some of these police officers are likely to pin one on slum youth who breached the identical norms. And, finally, typing will be accepted more readily if the audience stands to gain from the new definition. Obviously, calling attention to another person who seems to have broken some rule is often an excellent way of diverting attention from one's own behavior.

The processes of effective typing generally have one of three effects. These are the self-fulfilling prophecy,[5] type-casting, and recasting. In the first case, typing has no basis in reality, but the actions others take on these false beliefs about the person make them real. For example, both white and Negro police officers believe that it is more difficult to arrest a Negro than a white man. As a result, they tend to use more force in arresting Negroes, and in turn to experience more resistance.[6] In type-casting, ratification proceeds so rapidly that interaction between typer, audience, and the person typed becomes a matter of rote. Type-casting, of course, works best when there are fairly well-established deviant roles on which both deviants and conformists alike share a common perspective. For instance, today it seems as if drug addiction has achieved this position. Thus one person could type as a drug addict another person who in turn could accept this role, and any audience would immediately become *en rapport* with the type-caster's subsequent actions and attitudes. In recasting, the last and most difficult, both typer and audience make clear the category in which they have placed the person, but then seek to give him some restricted opportunity to step out of the role. Whenever typers have a maximum of negative information about another person and a controlling relationship with this other person, this is a likely outcome. For instance, the relationship between a probation officer and his charge is clearly of this order. In the first two kinds of typing, typer and audience restrict the per-

---

[5] Robert K. Merton, *Social Theory and Social Structure* (New York: The Free Press of Glencoe, 1957), 421–436.

[6] William M. Kephart, *Racial Factors and Urban Law Enforcement* (Philadelphia: University of Pennsylvania Press, 1957), 116–117.

son's opportunities to disprove the type. In recasting, audience and typer restrict the person's opportunities to confirm the type into which he has been cast.

Accommodation to Deviance

Social deviants, therefore, are persons who have been stamped effectively with a deviant label. And *effectively* here means simply that the label does in fact make a difference in social relations, not only for the person so labeled but also for the person or persons affixing the label. A new set of interpretations is made available for understanding the person adjudged a deviant. And when these interpretations take effect, a person has been socially reconstituted.

This reconstitution of the person as a deviant goes hand in hand with a new status. To be a person is to have a status; and if a group labels one of its number as a deviant then it has assigned that person a new status. Along with that status assignment goes a set of new, or a depreciation of old, rights and duties. With these changes go a new set of expectations about future conduct. That is, in affixing the label, a group usually implies to the person so labeled: "We now expect you to engage in deviant actions." This prediction amounts in some cases to a license to deviate, as when a group may not only tolerate but actually shelter the deviant in their midst. For example, young men in army training groups frequently define one of their number as their mascot and permit him leeway in exhibiting deviant behavior at the same time that they shield him from authorities.[7] More often, however, the prediction licenses the group to treat the person in a special and demeaning way.

Such typing has the effect of reducing uncertainty about persons. Social order is then reestablished when a person is retyped. The pace of events is one of the critical factors in this entire process. If uncommon events appear only gradually and irregularly within the life of a small and intimate group, deviant typing may not take place at all. Even if the uncommon events do place some immediate strain on relationships, members of the group may at first adjust to the strain without judging the person any differently than before the events. But finally, at a critical point in the life of this group, an awareness will develop that things are not what they used to be. In some instances, the person who finally is given the deviant label may have long suspected privately that he was the sort of person who generally is given that designation. In other cases, it may be the other parties who entertained

---

[7] Robert A. Dentler and Kai T. Erikson, "The Functions of Deviance in Groups," *Social Problems,* 7 (Fall, 1959), 98–107.

suspicions. In any case, once members of a group begin to act upon their awareness of the deviant label, the process of accommodation to deviance is usually well underway.

Most, though by no means all, variations in the accommodations people make to deviance can be traced to variations in the social structure of typing discussed above. To the extent that typing flows up rather than down the social structure, typing will not be ratified and accommodations will not be required when (a) the sense of violation is somewhat weak, (b) the type cannot be made out to be completely negative, (c) the illegitimacy of the acts, real or imagined, are of minimal consequence, (d) a pattern of non-conformity cannot be imputed or sustained, and, finally, (e) the audience stands to gain very little by redefining the person. In view of the fact that the possibilities for deviant behavior are actually infinite, it is quite clear that there will be many permutations and combinations in the social structure of typing and the accommodative sequences to deviance that ensue.

The Cultural Rules on Typing

A common factor underlies all processes of typing. That factor is a set of cultural rules for applying the deviant label, for fitting the person to the type.

Once a cloud of suspicion settles around a person, once his identity and character are called into question, others make certain decisions about him in solving future interactional problems. Shorthand descriptions that contain explicit if not implicit evaluations and prescriptions are of immediate use in solving these problems and reducing the uncertainty that surrounds the person in question. Type-casting, as already noted, paves the way for a mutual redefinition of the situation. Typing, like many other social processes, is more apt to work and stick if it goes according to some rules.

A set of cultural rules exists for typing deviants. These rules are not necessarily fully explicated; rather they are tacit, and therefore known usually after the fact. One rule on typing, inferred from many observations, may be summarized as *the greater the social distance between the typer and the person singled out for typing, the broader the type and the quicker it may be applied.*

Because acts required in one society may be forbidden in another, members of an in-group may more freely label as deviants outsiders than fellow insiders. Whether between or within one society, constituents of distinctly different groups need waste no time in assigning members of the other to a deviant category. Within a society, one class may not accord the benefit of doubt to members of another class, but rather may see the others more readily as deviant simply because the others' ways and style of life diverge so markedly from its own. Members of one social class may see a member of a lower one going about his business, actually abiding by the norms of his own class, but because these norms diverge from those of the higher class, the observed person risks being typed as a deviant.

When the focus is on persons acting within family orbits, the risks of being typed as a deviant decrease. A different set of rules for typing exists and the ease with which one can type another as deviant is considerably affected by the ties of intimacy. When the focus shifts to persons acting outside of family orbits, the biases of different cultures can come into play much more readily. The in-group, being ethnocentric, requires much less evidence for assigning nonmembers to a deviant category. Persons already different by reason of class or cultural background can be fitted with greater ease and more social support to a deviant role. Members of the in-group, to a much greater extent, have the protection of their surroundings and may escape cultural bias.

The Role of Third Parties in Exclusion

Cultural familiarity may delay awareness, definition, accommodation, and exclusion. But, in time, all will fail as a screen against expulsion, once a conflict of interests develops within a group. At that point, members stand to gain if one of their number is taken out of the category of the familiar and made out to be a deviant type. Given the strong commitment that persons have to their groups, they are reluctant to set apart one of their own. They are even more reluctant to expel a person from membership. Here again cultural familiarity slows down the social pace of typing deviants. In due time, however, exclusion (after labeling and accommodation have run their course) will come about.

As a conflict of interests develops within a small group, familiarity is cast in doubt, on the one hand, while the unwillingness to label and then exclude a deviant is weakened on the other. A group's familiarity with one of its own is, however, perhaps the greatest barrier against exclusion. As long as the group regards a member in the familiar categories it has developed, and accommodates to the deviance, resistance to exclusion remains comparatively strong. As long as the person's deviant style is accepted and tolerated as part of the group, no movement towards exclusion can succeed. If, however, the viewpoint of nonmembers is taken towards the deviant and if his deviance can be reinterpreted as a growing strain on in-group relationships, the chances of exclusion increase greatly.

Members of the in-group may have to examine one of their own through the eyes of yet another group, or a third party, who is not a member of the group. The weaker the ties within the group and the stronger the potential gains from exclusion, the more likely it is that an insider will accept the case of deviance against another insider. But if ties and potential gains are both strong, then third parties are required either to initiate or to consummate exclusion of a deviant member from the group.

For example, a married man may have strong ties to his family despite the fact that he has become estranged from his wife. Young children in this unit continue to bind husband and wife together as parents, but not as mates. It would take some very powerful outside influence, another woman for instance, to heighten the conflict and the potential gains of exclusion. If the wife is emotionally disturbed, the husband can rely on a psychiatrist as the third party who will sanction at least a temporary, if not permanent, exclusion of the wife from the family unit.

Husbands have also been known to simulate deviance in the family unit in order to provoke their wives into divorcing them. For example, in some states husbands simulate adultery or habitual intemperance in order to give their wives suitable grounds for divorce. Here, of course, the third party that collaborates in the exclusion process is the court of law.

So much by way of introduction to the definition of social deviants. In summary, a violation of rules, real or imputed, activates the process of social typing. Once the deviant typing has been ratified, accommodations follow, usually in a trial-and-error sequence. In the course of time, cultural rules on typing become operative. Finally, third parties will come into play when deviance threatens old, established relationships. At that point, exclusion takes place. We turn to a more detailed consideration of each of these points in the readings that follow.

THE PROCESS OF SOCIAL TYPING

1

Social order depends on the constructs of everyday life. Rules are examples of significant constructs. In the analysis of deviance, rules assume great importance for they constitute the symbolic objects on which the definition of deviance is ultimately grounded. Deviance, in essence, is an implied breach of social rules. A breach, however, does not always produce the conditions whereby defining agents will type a person as deviant.

In the first reading that follows, Becker shows that a number of social conditions must be met before a person is treated as a social deviant. The main condition, of course, is that other people must respond to the label put on the person. The other side of labeling, as it were, is that once a person is typed, his acts are interpreted in accordance with the deviant status to which he has been assigned. In the next excerpt, Tannenbaum shows how this dramatization of evil comes about; a community labels a young person by summarizing all of his acts under one term and then forces him to sustain this redefinition of his person. Kitsuse, in the final selection in this section, shows us the manner in which people impute deviance, type the person, and then act on their social definition of him.

On Labeling Outsiders *

HOWARD S. BECKER

One day an outbreak of wailing and a great commotion told me that a death had occurred somewhere in the neighborhood. I was informed that Kima'i, a young lad of

* Reprinted with permission of The Macmillan Company from *Outsiders: Studies in the Sociology of Deviance* by Howard S. Becker (© The Free Press of Glencoe, a Division of The Macmillan Company, 1963), 10–14, 31–33.

13

my acquaintance, of sixteen or so, had fallen from a coco-nut palm and killed himself. . . . I found that another youth had been severely wounded by some mysterious co-incidence. And at the funeral there was obviously a general feeling of hostility between the village where the boy died and that into which his body was carried for burial.

Only much later was I able to discover the real meaning of these events. The boy had committed suicide. The truth was that he had broken the rules of exogamy, the partner in his crime being his maternal cousin, the daughter of his mother's sister. This had been known and generally disapproved of but nothing was done until the girl's discarded lover, who had wanted to marry her and who felt personally injured, took the initiative. This rival threatened first to use black magic against the guilty youth, but this had not much effect. Then one evening he insulted the culprit in public—accusing him in the hearing of the whole community of incest and hurling at him certain expressions intolerable to a native.

For this there was only one remedy; only one means of escape remained to the unfortunate youth. Next morning he put on festive attire and ornamentation, climbed a coco-nut palm and addressed the community, speaking from among the palm leaves and bidding them farewell. He explained the reasons for his desperate deed and also launched forth a veiled accusation against the man who had driven him to his death, upon which it became the duty of his clansmen to avenge him. Then he wailed aloud, as is the custom, jumped from a palm some sixty feet high and was killed on the spot. There followed a fight within the village in which the rival was wounded; and the quarrel was repeated during the funeral. . . .

If you were to inquire into the matter among the Trobrianders, you would find . . . that the natives show horror at the idea of violating the rules of exogamy and that they believe that sores, disease and even death might follow clan incest. This is the ideal of native law, and in moral matters it is easy and pleasant strictly to adhere to the ideal—when judging the conduct of others or expressing an opinion about conduct in general.

When it comes to the application of morality and ideals to real life, however, things take on a different complexion. In the case described it was obvious that the facts would not tally with the ideal of conduct. Public opinion was neither outraged by the knowledge of the crime to any extent, nor did it react directly—it had to be mobilized by a public statement of the crime and by insults being hurled at the culprit by an interested party. Even then he had to carry out the punishment himself. . . . Probing further into the matter and collecting concrete information, I found that the breach of exogamy —as regards intercourse and not marriage— is by no means a rare occurrence, and public opinion is lenient, though decidedly hypocritical. If the affair is carried on *sub rosa* with a certain amount of decorum, and if no one in particular stirs up trouble— "public opinion" will gossip, but not demand any harsh punishment. If, on the contrary, scandal breaks out—everyone turns against the guilty pair and by ostracism and insults one or the other may be driven to suicide.[1]

Whether an act is deviant . . . depends on how other people react to it. You can commit clan incest and suffer from no more than gossip as long as no one makes a public accusation; but you will be driven to your death if the accusation is made. The point is that the response of other people has to be regarded as problematic. Just because one has committed an infraction of a rule does not mean that others will respond as though this had happened. (Conversely, just because one has not violated a rule does not mean that he may not be treated, in some circumstances, as though he had.)

The degree to which other people will respond to a given act as deviant varies greatly. Several kinds of variation seem

[1] Bronislaw Malinowski, *Crime and Custom in Savage Society* (New York: Humanities Press, 1926), pp. 77–80. Reprinted by permission of Humanities Press and Routledge & Kegan Paul, Ltd.

worth noting. First of all, there is variation over time. A person believed to have committed a given "deviant" act may at one time be responded to much more leniently than he would be at some other time. The occurrence of "drives" against various kinds of deviance illustrates this clearly. At various times, enforcement officials may decide to make an all-out attack on some particular kind of deviance, such as gambling, drug addiction, or homosexuality. It is obviously much more dangerous to engage in one of these activities when a drive is on than at any other time. (In a very interesting study of crime news in Colorado newspapers, Davis found that the amount of crime reported in Colorado newspapers showed very little association with actual changes in the amount of crime taking place in Colorado. And, further, that peoples' estimate of how much increase there had been in crime in Colorado was associated with the increase in the amount of crime news but not with any increase in the amount of crime.)[2]

The degree to which an act will be treated as deviant depends also on who commits the act and who feels he has been harmed by it. Rules tend to be applied more to some persons than others. Studies of juvenile delinquency make the point clearly. Boys from middle-class areas do not get as far in the legal process when they are apprehended as do boys from slum areas. The middle-class boy is less likely, when picked up by the police, to be taken to the station; less likely when taken to the station to be booked; and it is extremely unlikely that he will be convicted and sentenced.[3] This variation occurs even though the original infraction of the rule is the same in the two cases. Similarly, the law is differentially applied to Negroes and whites. It is well known that a Negro believed to have attacked a white woman is much more likely to be punished than a white man who commits the same offense; it is only slightly less well known that a Negro who murders another Negro is much less likely to be punished than a white man who commits murder.[4] This, of course, is one of the main points of Sutherland's analysis of white-collar crime: crimes committed by corporations are almost always prosecuted as civil cases, but the same crime committed by an individual is ordinarily treated as a criminal offense.[5]

Some rules are enforced only when they result in certain consequences. The unmarried mother furnishes a clear example. Vincent [6] points out that illicit sexual relations seldom result in severe punishment or social censure for the offenders. If, however, a girl becomes pregnant as a result of such activities the reaction of others is likely to be severe. (The illicit pregnancy is also an interesting example of the differential enforcement of rules on different categories of people. Vincent notes that unmarried fathers escape the severe censure visited on the mother.)

Why repeat these commonplace observations? Because, taken together, they support the proposition that deviance is

[2] F. James Davis, "Crime News in Colorado Newspapers," *American Journal of Sociology*, LVII (January, 1952), 325–330.

[3] See Albert K. Cohen and James F. Short, Jr., "Juvenile Delinquency," in Robert K. Merton and Robert A. Nisbet, *Contemporary Social Problems* (New York: Harcourt, Brace and World, 1961), p. 87.

[4] See Harold Garfinkel, "Research Note on Inter- and Intra-Racial Homicides," *Social Forces*, 27 (May, 1949), 369–381.

[5] Edwin H. Sutherland, "White Collar Criminality," *American Sociological Review*, V (February, 1940), 1–12.

[6] Clark Vincent, *Unmarried Mothers* (New York: The Free Press of Glencoe, 1961), pp. 3–5.

not a simple quality, present in some kinds of behavior and absent in others. Rather, it is the product of a process which involves responses of other people to the behavior. The same behavior may be an infraction of the rules at one time and not at another; may be an infraction when committed by one person, but not when committed by another; some rules are broken with impunity, others are not. In short, whether a given act is deviant or not depends in part on the nature of the act (that is, whether or not it violates some rule) and in part on what other people do about it.

Some people may object that this is merely a terminological quibble, that one can, after all, define terms any way he wants to and that if some people want to speak of rule-breaking behavior as deviant without reference to the reactions of others they are free to do so. This, of course, is true. Yet it might be worthwhile to refer to such behavior as *rule-breaking behavior* and reserve the term *deviant* for those labeled as deviant by some segment of society. I do not insist that this usage be followed. But it should be clear that insofar as a scientist uses "deviant" to refer to any rule-breaking behavior and takes as his subject of study only those who have been *labeled* deviant, he will be hampered by the disparities between the two categories.

If we take as the object of our attention behavior which comes to be labeled as deviant, we must recognize that we cannot know whether a given act will be categorized as deviant until the response of others has occurred. Deviance is not a quality that lies in behavior itself, but in the interaction between the person who commits an act and those who respond to it. . . .

In any case, being . . . branded as deviant has important consequences for one's further social participation. . . . The most important consequence is a drastic change in the individual's public identity. Committing the improper act and being publicly caught at it place him in a new status. He has been revealed as a different kind of person from the kind he was supposed to be. He is labeled a "fairy," "dope fiend," "nut" or "lunatic," and treated accordingly.

In analyzing the consequences of assuming a deviant identity let us make use of Hughes' distinction between master and auxiliary status traits.[7] Hughes notes that most statuses have one key trait which serves to distinguish those who belong from those who do not. Thus the doctor, whatever else he may be, is a person who has a certificate stating that he has fulfilled certain requirements and is licensed to practice medicine; this is the master trait. As Hughes points out, in our society a doctor is also informally expected to have a number of auxiliary traits: most people expect him to be upper middle class, white, male, and Protestant. When he is not there is a sense that he has in some way failed to fill the bill. Similarly, though skin color is the master status trait determining who is Negro and who is white, Negroes are informally expected to have certain status traits and not to have others; people are surprised and find it anomalous if a Negro turns out to be a doctor or a college professor. People often have the master status trait but lack some of the auxiliary, informally expected characteristics; for example, one may be a doctor but be female or Negro.

Hughes deals with this phenomenon in regard to statuses that are well thought of, desired and desirable (noting that one may have the formal qualifications for

[7] Everett C. Hughes, "Dilemmas and Contradictions of Status," *American Journal of Sociology,* L (March, 1945), 353–359.

entry into a status but be denied full entry because of lack of the proper auxiliary traits), but the same process occurs in the case of deviant statuses. Possession of one deviant trait may have a generalized symbolic value, so that people automatically assume that its bearer possesses other undesirable traits allegedly associated with it.

To be labeled a criminal one need only commit a single criminal offense, and this is all the term formally refers to. Yet the word carries a number of connotations specifying auxiliary traits characteristic of anyone bearing the label. A man who has been convicted of housebreaking and thereby labeled criminal is presumed to be a person likely to break into other houses; the police, in rounding up known offenders for investigation after a crime has been committed, operate on this premise. Further, he is considered likely to commit other kinds of crimes as well, because he has shown himself to be a person without "respect for the law."

Thus, apprehension for one deviant act exposes a person to the likelihood that he will be regarded as deviant or undesirable in other respects.

There is one other element in Hughes' analysis we can borrow with profit: the distinction between master and subordinate statuses.[8] Some statuses, in our society as in others, override all other statuses and have a certain priority. Race is one of these. Membership in the Negro race, as socially defined, will override most other status considerations in most other situations; the fact that one is a physician or middle-class or female will not protect one from being treated as a Negro first and any of these other things second. The status of deviant (depending on the kind of deviance) is this kind of master status. One receives the status as a result of breaking a rule, and the identification proves to be more important than most others. One will be identified as a deviant first, before other identifications are made.

The Dramatization of Evil *

FRANK TANNENBAUM

In the conflict between the young delinquent and the community there develop two opposing definitions of the situation. In the beginning the definition of the situation by the young delinquent may be in the form of play, adventure, excitement, interest, mischief, fun. Breaking windows, annoying people, running around porches, climbing over roofs, stealing from pushcarts, playing truant— all are items of play, adventure, excitement. To the community, however, these activities may and often do take on the form of a nuisance, evil, delinquency, with the demand for control, admonition, chastisement, punishment, police court, truant school. This conflict over the situation is one that arises out of a diver-

[8] *Ibid.*
* Reprinted from *Crime and the Community* by Frank Tannenbaum (New York: Columbia University Press, 1938), pp. 19–20, by permission of the publisher.

gence of values. As the problem develops, the situation gradually becomes redefined. The attitude of the community hardens definitely into a demand for suppression. There is a gradual shift from the definition of the specific acts as evil to a definition of the individual as evil, so that all his acts come to be looked upon with suspicion. In the process of identification his companions, hang-outs, play, speech, income, all his conduct, the personality itself, become subject to scrutiny and question. From the community's point of view, the individual who used to do bad and mischievous things has now become a bad and unredeemable human being. From the individual's point of view there has taken place a similar change. He has gone slowly from a sense of grievance and injustice, of being unduly mistreated and punished, to a recognition that the definition of him as a human being is different from that of other boys in his neighborhood, his school, street, community. This recognition on his part becomes a process of self-identification and integration with the group which shares his activities. It becomes, in part, a process of rationalization; in part, a simple response to a specialized type of stimulus. The young delinquent becomes bad because he is defined as bad and because he is not believed if he is good. There is a persistent demand for consistency in character. The community cannot deal with people whom it cannot define. Reputation is this sort of public definition. Once it is established, then unconsciously all agencies combine to maintain this definition even when they apparently and consciously attempt to deny their own implicit judgment.

The first dramatization of the "evil" which separates the child out of his group for specialized treatment plays a greater role in making the criminal than perhaps any other experience. It cannot be too often emphasized that for the child the whole situation has become different. He now lives in a different world. He has been tagged. A new and hitherto nonexistent environment has been precipitated out for him.

The process of making the criminal, therefore, is a process of tagging, defining, identifying, segregating, describing, emphasizing, making conscious and self-conscious; it becomes a way of stimulating, suggesting, emphasizing, and evoking the very traits that are complained of. If the theory of relation of response to stimulus has any meaning, the entire process of dealing with the young delinquent is mischievous in so far as it identifies him to himself or to the environment as a delinquent person.

The person becomes the thing he is described as being. Nor does it seem to matter whether the valuation is made by those who would punish or by those who would reform. In either case the emphasis is upon the conduct that is disapproved of. The parents or the policeman, the older brother or the court, the probation officer or the juvenile institution, in so far as they rest upon the thing complained of, rest upon a false ground. Their very enthusiasm defeats their aim. The harder they work to reform the evil, the greater the evil grows under their hands. The persistent suggestion, with whatever good intentions, works mischief, because it leads to bringing out the bad behavior that it would suppress. The way out is through a refusal to dramatize the evil. The less said about it the better. The more said about something else, still better.

The hard-drinker who keeps thinking of not drinking is doing what he can to initiate the acts which lead to drinking. He is starting with the stimulus to his habit. To succeed he must find some positive interest or line of action which will inhibit the drinking series and which by instituting another course of action will bring him to his desired end.[1]

The dramatization of the evil therefore tends to precipitate the conflict situation which was first created through some innocent maladjustment. The child's isolation forces him into companionship with other children similarly defined, and the gang becomes his means of escape, his security. The life of the gang gives it special mores, and the attack by the community upon these mores merely overemphasizes the conflict already in existence, and makes it the source of a new series of experiences that lead directly to a criminal career.

In dealing with the delinquent, the criminal, therefore, the important thing to remember is that we are dealing with a human being who is responding normally to the demands, stimuli, approval, expectancy, of the group with whom he is associated.

Societal Reaction to Deviant Behavior *

JOHN I. KITSUSE

Sociological theory and research in the area traditionally known as "social pathology" have been concerned primarily with the classification and analysis of *deviant forms of behavior* and relatively little attention has been given to societal reactions to deviance.[1] In a recent paper, Merton has noted this lack of a "systematic *classification* of the responses of the conventional or conforming members of a group to deviant behavior."[2] Similarly, Cohen has observed that "a sociology of deviant behavior-conformity will have to devise ways of conceptualizing responses to deviant behavior from the standpoint of their relevance to the production or extinction of deviant behavior."[3] In this paper, I shall discuss some of the theoretical and methodological issues posed by the problem of societal reactions to deviant behavior and report on a preliminary attempt to formulate a research design which specifically takes them into account.

I propose to shift the focus of theory and research from the forms of deviant behavior to the *processes by which persons come to be defined as deviant by others*. Such a shift requires that the sociologist view as problematic what he

---

[1] John Dewey, *Human Nature and Conduct*, p. 35. New York, 1922.

* Reprinted from *Social Problems*, Vol. 9, No. 3 (Winter, 1962), pp. 247–256, by permission of the author and *Social Problems*.

[1] A notable exception is the work of Edwin M. Lemert who systematically incorporates the concept of societal reaction in his theory of sociopathic behavior. See *Social Pathology*, McGraw-Hill, New York: 1951.

[2] Robert K. Merton, "Social Conformity, Deviation, and Opportunity-Structures: A Comment on the Contributions of Dubin and Cloward," *American Sociological Review*, 24 (1959), pp. 177–189.

[3] Albert K. Cohen, "The Study of Social Disorganization and Deviant Behavior," in *Sociology Today*, R. Merton, L. Broom, and L. Cottrell, eds., Basic Books: New York, 1959, pp. 465–466.

generally assumes as given—namely, that certain forms of behavior are *per se* deviant and are so defined by the "conventional or conforming members of a group." This assumption is frequently called into question on empirical grounds when the societal reaction to behaviors defined as deviant by the sociologist is non-existent, indifferent, or at most mildly disapproving. For example, in his discussion of "ritualism" as a form of deviant behavior, Merton states that it is not that such behavior is treated by others as deviant which identifies it as deviant "since the overt behavior is institutionally permitted, though not culturally prescribed." [4] Rather, the behavior is deviant because it "clearly represents a departure from the cultural model in which men are obliged to move onward and upward in the social hierarchy." [5] The discrepancy between the theoretically hypothesized and empirically observable societal reaction is also noted by Lemert: "It is fairly easy to think of situations in which serious offenses against laws commanding public respect have only mild penalty or have gone entirely unpunished. Conversely, cases are easily discovered in which a somewhat minor violation of legal rules has provoked surprisingly stringent penalties." [6]

Clearly, the forms of behavior *per se* do not activate the processes of societal reaction which sociologically differentiate deviants from non-deviants. Thus, a central problem for theory and research in the sociology of deviance may be stated as follows: What are the behaviors which are defined by members of the group, community, or society as deviant, and how do those definitions organize and activate the societal reactions by which persons come to be differentiated and treated as deviants? In formulating the problem in this way, the point of view of those who interpret and define behavior as deviant must explicitly be incorporated into a sociological definition of deviance. Accordingly, deviance may be conceived as a process by which the members of a group, community, or society (1) interpret behavior as deviant, (2) define persons who so behave as a certain kind of deviant, and (3) accord them the treatment considered appropriate to such deviants. In the following pages, this conception of deviance and societal reaction will be applied to the processes by which persons come to be defined and treated as homosexuals.

Societal Reactions to "Homosexual Behavior"

As a form of deviant behavior, homosexuality presents a strategically important theoretical and empirical problem for the study of deviance. In the sociological and anthropological literature [7] homosexual behavior and the societal reactions to it are conceptualized within the framework of ascribed sex statuses and the socialization of individuals to those statuses. The ascription of sex statuses is presumed to provide a complex of culturally prescribed roles and behaviors which individuals are expected to

---

[4] Robert K. Merton, *Social Theory and Social Structure,* revised, Free Press: New York, 1957, p. 150.

[5] *Ibid.,* p. 150.

[6] *Op. cit.,* p. 55.

[7] For examples, see Talcott Parsons and Robert F. Bales, *Family Socialization and Interaction Process,* Free Press: New York, 1955, pp. 103–105; Ruth Benedict, "Continuities and Discontinuities in Cultural Conditioning," *Psychiatry,* 1 (1938), pp. 161–167; Abram Kardiner and Associates, *Psychological Frontiers of Society,* Columbia University Press: New York, 1945, pp. 57, 88, etc.; Clifford Kirkpatrick, *The Family,* Ronald Press: New York, 1955, pp. 57–58; Margaret Mead, *Sex and Temperament,* William Morrow: New York, 1955.

learn and perform. Homosexual roles and behaviors are conceived to be "inappropriate" to the individual's ascribed sex status, and thus theoretically they are defined as deviant.

With reference to American society, Allison Davis states: "Sex-typing of behavior and privileges is even more rigid and lasting in our society than is age-typing. Indeed, sexual status and color-caste status are the only life-long forms of rank. In our society, one can escape them in approved fashion only by death. Whereas sexual mobility is somewhat less rare today than formerly, sex-inappropriate behavior, social or physical, is still one of the most severely punished infractions of our social code." [8] In Lemert's terminology, norms concerning sex-appropriate behavior have a high degree of "compulsiveness" and social disapproval of violations is stringent and effective.[9] Homosexuals themselves appear to share this conception of the societal reaction to their behavior, activities, and subculture.[10]

Such a view of homosexuality would lead one to hypothesize that "sex appropriate" (and conversely "sex-inappropriate") behaviors are unambiguously prescribed, deviations from those prescriptions are invariably interpreted as immoral, and the reactions of the conventional and conforming members of the society to such deviations are uniformly severe and effective. The evidence which apparently supports this hypothesis is not difficult to find, particularly with reference to the definition and treatment of male homosexuals. Individuals who are publicly identified as homosexuals are frequently denied the social, economic, and legal rights of "normal" males. Socially they may be treated as objects of amusement, ridicule, scorn, and often fear; economically they may be summarily dismissed from employment; legally they are frequently subject to interrogation and harassment by police.

In citing such evidence, however, it is important to note that the societal reaction to and the differentiation of homosexuals from the "normal" population is a consequence of the fact that the former are "known" to be homosexuals by some individuals, groups or agencies. Thus, within the framework of the present formulation of homosexuality as a form of deviant behavior, the processes by which individuals come to be "known" and treated as sexually deviant will be viewed as problematic and a problem for empirical investigation. I shall not be concerned here with the so-called "latent homosexual" unless he is so defined by others and differentially treated as a consequence of that definition. Nor will I be concerned with the variety of "internal" conflicts which may form the "clinical" picture of the homosexual except insofar as such conflicts are manifested in behavior leading others to conceive of him as a homosexual. In short, I shall proceed on the principle that it is only when individuals are defined and identified by others as homosexuals and accorded the treatment considered "appropriate" for individuals so defined that a homosexual "population" is produced for sociological investigation.[11] With reference to homosexuality, then, the empirical questions are: What

---

[8] Allison Davis, "American Status Systems and the Socialization of the Child," *American Sociological Review,* 6 (1941), p. 350.

[9] *Op. cit.,* Chapter 4.

[10] Evelyn Hooker, "Sequences in Homosexual Identification," read at the meetings of the American Sociological Association, 1960; Donald Webster Cory, *The Homosexual in America,* Greenburg: New York, 1951, esp. Part I.

[11] This principle has been suggested by Harold Garfinkel. See "Some Sociological Concepts and Methods for Psychiatrists," *Psychiatric Research Reports,* 6 (1956), pp. 181–195.

forms of behavior do persons in the social system consider to be "sex-inappropriate," how do they interpret such behaviors, and what are the consequences of those interpretations for their reactions to individuals who are perceived to manifest such behaviors?

In a preliminary attempt to investigate these questions, an interview schedule was constructed [12] and administered to approximately seven hundred individuals, most of whom were college undergraduates. The sample was neither random nor representative of any specified population, and the generalizability of the interview materials is limited except insofar as they are relevant to the previously noted hypothesis that homosexual behavior is uniformly defined, interpreted, and negatively sanctioned. The interview materials will therefore be used for the purpose of illustrating the theory and method of the present conception of deviance and societal reaction.

The objectives of the interview were threefold: It attempted to document (1) the behavior forms which are interpreted as deviant, (2) the processes by which persons who manifest such behaviors are defined and (3) treated as deviant. Thus, in the construction of the interview schedule, what the interviewees considered to be "deviant" behavior, the interpretations of such behavior, and the actions of subjects toward those perceived as deviant were addressed as empirical questions. Labels such as alcoholic, illiterate, illegitimate child, and ex-convict were assumed to be categories employed by persons in everyday life to classify deviants, but the behavioral forms by which they identify individuals as deviants were treated as problematic. "Sexual deviant" was one of ten categories of deviants about which subjects were questioned in the interview. Among the more than seven hundred subjects interviewed, seventy-five stated they had "known" a homosexual and responded to questions concerning their experiences with such individuals. The data presented below are drawn from the protocols of interviews with this group of subjects.

The interview proceeded as follows:

The subject was asked "Have you ever known anyone who was a sexual deviant?" If he questioned the meaning of "deviant," the subject was asked to consider the question using his own meaning of "sexual deviant."

When the subject stated he had known a sexual deviant—a homosexual in this case—as he defined the term, he was asked to think about the most recent incident involving him in an encounter with such a person. He was then asked "When was the first time you noticed (found out) that this person was a homosexual?" followed by "What was the situation? What did you notice about him? How did he behave?" This line of questioning was focused on the interaction between the subject and the alleged deviant to obtain a detailed description of the situation which led the subject to define the person as homosexual. The subject's description of the person's behavior was systematically probed to clarify the terms of his description, particularly those which were interpretive rather than descriptive.

Evidence of Homosexuality

Responses to the question "When was the first time you noticed (found out) that this person was homosexual?" and the related probes suggest that an individual's sexual "normality" may be called into question with reference to two broad categories of evidence. (*a*) *Indirect evi-*

---

[12] The interview schedule and methods were conceived and constructed in consultation with Aaron V. Cicourel.

dence in the form of a rumor, an acquaintance's experience with the individual in question subsequently communicated to the subject, or general reputational information concerning the individual's behavior, associates, and sexual predelictions may be the occasion for suspecting him to be "different." Many subjects reported that they first "found out" or "knew" that the individuals in question were homosexuals through the reports of others or by "reputation." Such information was generally accepted by the subjects without independent verification. Indeed, the information provided a new perspective for their retrospective as well as prospective observations and interpretations of the individuals' behaviors. An example of how hearsay organizes observation and interpretation is the following statement by a 35-year-old male (a draftsman):

I: Then this lieutenant was a homosexual?
S: Yes.
I: How did you find out about it?
S: The guy he approached told me. After that, I watched him. Our company was small and we had a bar for both enlisted men and officers, He would come in and try to be friendly with one or two of the guys.
I: Weren't the other officers friendly?
S: Sure, they would come in for an occasional drink; some of them had been with the company for three years and they would sometimes slap you on the back, but he tried to get over friendly.
I: What do you mean "over friendly"?
S: He had only been there a week. He would try to push himself on a couple of guys—he spent more time with the enlisted personnel than is expected from an officer.

(*b*) *Direct observation* by the subject of the individual's behavior may be the basis for calling the latter's sexual "normality" into question. The descriptions of behavior which subjects took to be indicative of homosexuality varied widely and were often vague. Most frequently the behaviors cited were those *"which everyone knows"* are indications of homosexuality. For example, a 20-year-old male subject reports an encounter with a stranger at a bar:

I: What happened during your conversation?
S: He asked me if I went to college and I said I did. Then he asked me what I was studying. When I told him psychology he appeared very interested.
I: What do you mean "interested"?
S: Well, you know queers really go for this psychology stuff.
I: Then what happened?
S: Ah, let's see. I'm not exactly sure, but somehow we got into an argument about psychology and to prove my point I told him to pick an area of study. Well, he appeared to be very pensive and after a great thought he said, "Okay, let's take homosexuality."
I: What did you make of that?
S: Well, by now I figured the guy was queer so I got the hell outta there.

The responses of other subjects suggest that an individual is particularly suspect when he is observed to behave in a manner which deviates from the *behaviors-held-in-common* among members of the group to which he belongs. For example, a behavior which is presumed to be held-in-common among sailors in the U. S. Navy is intense and active sexual activity. When a sailor does not affirm, at least verbally, his interest in such activity, his competence as a "male" may be called into question. A 22-year-old engineer, recently discharged from the Navy, responds to the "how did you first know" question as follows:

All of a sudden you just get suspicious of something. I began to wonder about him. He didn't go in for leave activities that most sailors go for. You know, girls and high times. He just never was interested and when you have been out at sea for a month or two you're interested. That just wasn't Navy, and he was a career man.

Although the responses of our subjects indicate there are many behavioral gestures which "everyone knows" are indicators of homosexuality in males, there are relatively few such gestures that lead persons to suspect females of homosexuality. Following is an excerpt from a 21-year-old college co-ed whose remarks illustrate this lack of definite indicators *prior* to her labeling of an acquaintance as a homosexual:

I: When was the first time you noticed she was a deviant?

S: I didn't notice it. I thought she had a masculine appearance when I first saw her anyway.

I: What do you mean?

S: Oh, her haircut, her heavy eyebrows. She had a rather husky build.

I: Exactly when did you think she had a masculine appearance?

S: It was long after [the first meeting] that I found out that she was "one."

I: How do you define it?

S: Well, a lesbian. I don't know too much about them. It was _____ who told me about her.

I: Did you notice anything else about her [at the first meeting]?

S: No, because you really don't know unless you're looking for those things.

Unlike "effeminate" appearance and gestures in males, "masculine" appearance in females is apparently less likely to be immediately linked to the suspicion or imputation of homosexuality. The statements of the subject quoted above indicate that although "masculine appearance" is an important element in her conception of a lesbian, its significance did not become apparent to her until a third person told her the girl was homosexual. The remarks of other subjects in our sample who state they have "known" female homosexuals reveal a similar ambiguity in their interpretations of what they describe as indicators of sexual deviance.

A third form of evidence by direct observation is behaviors which the subjects interpreted to be *overt sexual propositions*. Descriptions of such propositions ranged from what the subjects considered to be unmistakable evidence of the person's sexual deviance to ambiguous gestures which they did not attempt to question in the situation. The following is an excerpt from an interview with a 24-year-old male school teacher who recounts an experience in a Korean Army barrack:

I: What questions did he [the alleged homosexual] ask?

S: "How long have you been in Korea?" I told him. "What do you think of these Korean girls?" which I answered, "Not too much because they are dirty." I thought he was probably homesick and wanted someone to talk to. I do not remember what he said then until he said, "How much do you have?" I answered him by saying, "I don't know, about average I guess." Then he said, "Can I feel it just once?" To this I responded with, "Get the hell out of here," and I gave him a shove when he reached for me as he asked the question.

In a number of interviews, the subjects' statements indicate that they interpreted the sequence of the alleged deviants' behavior as progressively inappropriate or peculiar in the course of their interaction with them. The link between such behavior and their judgment that a sexual proposition was being made was frequently established by the subjects' growing realization of its deviant character. A 21-year-old male subject recalls the following experience involving his high school tennis coach who had invited him to dinner:

S: Anyway, when I get there he served dinner, and as I think back on it—I didn't notice it at the time—but I remember that he did act sort of effeminate. Finally he got up to change a record and picked up some of my English themes. Then he brought them over and sat down beside me. He began to explain some of my mistakes in my themes, and in the meantime he slipped his arms around me.

I: Would you say that this was done in a friendly manner or with an intent of hugging you or something?

S: Well, no, it was just a friendly gesture of putting his arm around my shoulder. At that time, I didn't think anything of it, but as he continued to explain my mistakes, he started to rub my back. Then he asked me if I wanted a back rub. So I said, "No! I don't need one." At this time, I began thinking something was funny anyway. So I said that I had to go. . . .

The Imputation of Homosexuality

When a detailed description of the subject's evidence concerning the alleged homosexual was obtained, he was asked, "What did you make of that?" to elicit information about how he interpreted the person's observed or reported behavior. This line of questioning yielded data on the inferential process by which the subject linked his information about the individual to the deviant category "homosexual."

A general pattern revealed by the subjects' responses to this section of the interview schedule is that when an individual's sexual "normality" is called into question, by whatever form of evidence, the imputation of homosexuality is documented by *retrospective interpretations* of the deviant's behavior, a process by which the subject re-interprets the individual's past behavior in the light of the new information concerning his sexual deviance. This process is particularly evident in cases where the prior relationship between the subject and the alleged homosexual was more than a chance encounter or casual acquaintanceship. The subjects indicate that they reviewed their past interactions with the individuals in question, searching for subtle cues and nuances of behavior which might give

further evidence of the alleged deviance. This retrospective reading generally provided the subjects with just such evidence to support the conclusion that "this is what was going on all the time."

Some of the subjects who were interviewed were themselves aware of their retrospective interpretations in defining individuals as sexually deviant. For example, a 23-year-old female graduate student states:

I: Will you tell me more about the situation?

S: Well, their relationship was a continuous one, although I think that it is a friendship now as I don't see them together as I used to; I don't think it is still homosexual. When I see them together, they don't seem to be displaying the affection openly as they did when I first realized the situation.

I: How do you mean "openly"?

S: Well, they would hold each other's hand in public places.

I: And what did you make of this?

S: Well, I really don't know, because I like to hold people's hands, too! I guess I actually didn't see this as directly connected with the situation. What I mean is that, if I hadn't seen that other incident [she had observed the two girls in bed together] I probably wouldn't have thought of it [i.e., hand-holding] very much. . . . Well, actually, there were a few things that I questioned later on that I hadn't thought really very much about. . . . I can remember her being quite affectionate towards me several times when we were in our room together, like putting her arm around my shoulder. Or I remember one time specifically when she asked me for a kiss. I was shocked at the time, but I laughed it off jokingly.

The Interactional Contexts of Societal Reactions

When the description of the alleged deviant's behavior and the subject's interpretations of that behavior were recorded, the subject was asked "What did you do then?" This question was directed toward documenting societal reactions to deviant behavior. Forms of behavior *per se* do not differentiate deviants from non-deviants; it is the responses of the conventional and conforming members of the society who identify and interpret behavior as deviant which sociologically transform persons into deviants. Thus, in the formulation of deviance proposed here, if the subject observes an individual's behavior and defines it as deviant but does not accord him differential treatment as a consequence of that definition, the individual is not sociologically deviant.

The reactions of the subjects to individuals they defined as homosexuals ranged from immediate withdrawal from the scene of interaction and avoidance of further encounters with the alleged deviants to the maintenance of the prior relationship virtually unaltered by the imputation of deviance. The following responses to the question "What did you do then?" illustrate the variation in sanctions directed toward persons defined as homosexuals.

Explicit disapproval and immediate withdrawal: The most negatively toned and clearly articulated reaction reported by our subjects is that of the previously quoted Korean War veteran. It is interesting to note that extreme physical punishment as a reaction to persons defined as homosexuals, a reaction which is commonly verbalized by "normal" males as proper treatment of "queers," is not reported by any of the subjects. When physical force is used, it is invariably in response to the deviant's direct physical overtures, and even then it is relatively mild, e.g., "I gave him a shove when he reached for me."

Explicit disapproval and subsequent withdrawal: In the following excerpt, a 20-year-old male college student describes an encounter with a man whom he met in a coffee shop. In the course of their conversation, the man admitted his homosexuality to the subject. The two left the coffee shop and walked together to the subway station.

I: What happened then?

S: We got to the subway whereupon he suggested that he hail a cab and take me up to Times Square—a distance of almost 40 blocks.

I: Did you agree, and what did you think?

S: Yes, I thought he was just being very nice and I had no qualms about getting in a cab with a homosexual since I was quite sure I could protect myself against any advances in a cab.

I: What happened then?

S: When we had ridden a little distance, he put his hand on my knee, and I promptly removed it saying that it just wasn't right and that I wanted nothing of it. However, after a while, he put his hand back. This time I didn't take it away for a while because I was interested in what he would do. It was the funniest thing—he rubbed and caressed my knee the same way in which I would have done this to a girl. This time I took his hand and hit him across the chest with it, telling him to "cut it out." Finally, we got to Times Square, and I got out.

This example and that provided by the Korean War veteran's reaction to behavior interpreted as overt sexual propositions suggest the possibility that responses to persons suspected of homosexuality or defined as homosexuals on the basis of more indirect evidence of appearance, "confessions," hearsay, reputation, or association will vary within an even wider range of applied sanctions. Indeed, the statements of subjects concerning their responses to persons alleged to be deviant on such evidence indicate that the modal reaction is disapproval, implicitly rather than explicitly communicated, and a restriction of interaction through partial withdrawal and avoidance. It should be noted further that although the subject's silent withdrawal from an established relationship with an alleged deviant may represent a stronger disapproval than an explicitly communicated, physically enforced sanction against a stranger, moral indignation or revulsion is not necessarily communicated to the deviant. The subject's prior relationship with the alleged deviant and the demands of propriety in subsequent interactions with him qualify the form and intensity of the sanctions which are applied. Thus, when the organization of the subject's day-to-day activities "forces" him into interaction with the deviant, expressions of disapproval are frequently constrained and diffused by the rules of deference and demeanor.[13] The following excerpts provide illustrations:

Implicit disapproval and partial withdrawal: A 20-year-old co-ed's reaction to a girl she concluded was a homosexual was expressed as follows:

"Well, I didn't want to be alone with X [the homosexual] because the four of us had two connecting rooms and I was in the room with X. As much as I liked the girl and felt sorry for her, I knew she could really wring me through the wringer. So the rest decided that I should tell her that if she and Y wanted to be homos, to do it somewhere else and not in the room."

No disapproval and relationship sustained: The "live and let live" response to homosexuals, which is implied in the preceding reaction, was not uncommon among the subjects. Some subjects not only affirmed the right of the homosexual to "live his own life" but also reported that their knowledge of the deviance has had little or no effect upon their subsequent relationships with the deviants. In this regard, the mildest reaction, so mild that it might be considered no reaction at all, was that of a 19-year-old male college student:

I: What was your reaction to him?
S: My reactions to him have always been friendly because he seems like a very friendly person. Uh, and he has a very nice sense of humor and I've never been repelled by anything he's said. For one thing, I think he's tremendously interesting because he seems to have such a wide range for background. . . .
I: When was the last time you saw this person?
S: Last night. . . . I was sitting in a restaurant and he walked in with some friends . . . he just stopped in and said hello, and was his usual friendly self.
I: What in particular happened after that?
S: Actually, nothing. He sat down with his friends and we exchanged a few words about the records that were playing on the juke box. But nothing, actually. . . .

The theoretical significance of these data for the conception of deviance and societal reaction presented here is not that the subjects' information is of dubious accuracy or questionable relevance as evidence of homosexuality. Nor is it that the subjects' interpretations of them are unreasonable, unjustifiable, or spurious. They suggest rather that the conceptions of persons in everyday life concerning "sex-appropriate" or "sex-inappropriate" behavior may lead them to interpret a variety of behavioral forms as indications of the same deviation, and the "same" behavioral forms as indications of a variety of deviant as well as "normal" behavior. An individual's sexual "normality" may be made problematic by the interpretations and re-interpretations of his behavior by others, and the interpretive process may be activated by a wide range of situational behaviors which lend new significance to the individual's past and present behavior. His behavior with respect to speech, interests, dress, dating, or relations with other males are not *per se*

---

[13] Erving Goffman, "The Nature of Deference and Demeanor," *American Anthropologist,* 58 (1956), pp. 473–502.

significant in the deviant-defining process. The data suggest that the critical feature of the deviant-defining process is not the behavior of individuals who are defined as deviant, but rather the interpretations others make of their behaviors, whatever those behaviors may be.

With specific reference to homosexuality as a form of deviant behavior, the interview materials suggest that while reactions toward persons defined as homosexuals tend to be negatively toned, they are far from homogeneous as to the forms or intensity of the sanctions invoked and applied. Indeed, reactions which may appear to the sociological observer or to the deviant himself as negative sanctions, such as withdrawal or avoidance, may be expressions of embarrassment, a reluctance to share the burden of the deviant's problems, fear of the deviant, etc., as well as moral indignation or revulsion. In none of the interviews does the subject react with extreme violence, explicitly define or directly accuse the deviant of being a "queer," "fairy," or other terms of opprobrium, nor did any of them initiate legal actions against the deviant. In view of the extreme negative sanctions against homosexuality which are posited on theoretical grounds, the generally mild reactions of our subjects are striking.

The relative absence of extreme and overtly expressed negative sanctions against homosexuals among our subjects may, of course, reflect the higher than average educational level of the sample. A sample of subjects less biased toward the highly educated, middle-class segment of the population than was interviewed in this preliminary study may be expected to reflect a more definite pattern with reference to such negative reactions. We must, therefore, be cautious in generalizing the range of reactions among our subjects to the general population. It is

equally important to note, however, that these data do indicate that reactions to homosexuals in American society are not *societal* in the sense of being uniform within a narrow range; rather, they are significantly conditioned by sub-cultural as well as situational factors. Thus, not only are the processes by which persons come to be defined as homosexuals contingent upon the interpretations of their behavior by others, but also the sanctions imposed and the treatment they are accorded as a consequence of that definition vary widely among conventional members of various sub-cultural groups.

The larger implications of these data are that a sociological theory of deviance must explicitly take into account the variety and range of conceptions held by persons, groups, and agencies within the society concerning any form of behavior. The increasing differentiation of groups, institutions, and sub-cultures in modern society generates a continually changing range of alternatives and tolerance for the expression of sexual as well as other forms of behavior. Consequently, it is difficult if not impossible to theoretically derive a set of *specific behavioral prescriptions* which will in fact be normatively supported, uniformly practiced, and socially enforced by more than a segment of the total population. Under such conditions, it is not the fact that individuals engage in behaviors which diverge from some theoretically posited "institutionalized expectations" or even that such behaviors are defined as deviant by the conventional and conforming members of the society which is of primary significance for the study of deviance. A sociological theory of deviance must focus specifically upon the interactions which not only define behaviors as deviant but also organize and activate the application of sanctions by individuals, groups, or agencies. For in modern society, the socially significant differentiation of deviants from the non-deviant population is increasingly contingent upon circumstances of situation, place, social and personal biography, and the bureaucratically organized activities of agencies of control.[14]

---

[14] For a discussion of such contingencies, see Edwin M. Lemert, *op. cit.*, Chapter 4, and Erving Goffman, "The Moral Career of the Mental Patient," *Psychiatry*, 22 (1959), pp. 123–142.

ACCOMMODATION TO DEVIANCE

2

Deviation from rules, seen or unseen, may well abound without necessarily leading to the construct of deviance. Unless a number of social conditions are met, deviation, seen or unseen, real or imagined, does not come to be socially redefined as deviance.

Given a deviation in their immediate social world, people may not see it at all for a long time. As it slowly begins to take shape before their eyes, a set of options become available to them. They can perceive the developing phenomenon in a number of ways. That is, they can optimize, neutralize, normalize, or pessimize. To optimize is to hope that the deviance will pass away, that the problematic behavior is no more than a transitory episode. To neutralize is to accommodate to the deviance in a way that obscures it. To normalize is to regard deviance as but a special case of normal behavior. And, finally, to pessimize is to accept the worst—thus the deviance may be defined as basically irreversible.

Yarrow, Schwartz, Murphy, and Deasy, in the first of the readings to follow, deal with the efforts of wives to see their mentally ill husbands as healthy. The wives go a long way in normalizing the deviation and not making the deviant assignment. It is only when third parties enter to redefine the situation that they give up normalizing. Sampson, Messinger, and Towne deal with neutralization. They study two types of families that accept deviance as part of the relationship with a family member. Again these acceptances are fairly stable accommodations until both interested and disinterested third parties come on the scene. Joan Jackson, in the final selection, describes in detail the array of responses and accommodations that wives of alcoholics make to their husbands' cycle of deviance.

The Psychological Meaning of Mental Illness in the Family *

MARIAN RADKE YARROW, CHARLOTTE GREEN SCHWARTZ,
HARRIET S. MURPHY, AND LEILA CALHOUN DEASY

The manifestations of mental illness are almost as varied as the spectrum of human behavior. Moreover, they are expressed not only in disturbance and functional impairment for the sick person but also in disruptive interactions with others. The mentally ill person is often, in his illness, a markedly deviant person, though certainly less so than the popular stereotype of the "insane." One wonders what were the initial phases of the impact of mental illness upon those within the ill person's social environment. How were the disorders of illness interpreted and tolerated? What did the patients, prior to hospitalization, communicate of their needs, and how did others—those closest to the ill persons—attempt, psychologically and behaviorally, to cope with the behavior? How did these persons come to be recognized by other family members as needing psychiatric help?

This paper presents an analysis of cognitive and emotional problems encountered by the wife in coping with the mental illness of the husband. It is concerned with the factors which lead to the reorganization of the wife's perceptions of her husband from a *well* man to a man who is mentally sick or in need of hospitalization in a mental hospital. The process whereby the wife attempts to understand and interpret her husband's manifestations of mental illness is best communicated by considering first the concrete details of a single wife's experiences. The findings and interpretations based on the total sample are presented following the case analysis.

Illustrative Case

Robert F., a 35-year-old cab driver, was admitted to Saint Elizabeth's Hospital with a diagnosis of schizophrenia. How did Mr. F. get to the mental hospital? Here is a very condensed version of what his wife told an interviewer a few weeks later.

Mrs. F. related certain events, swift and dramatic, which led directly to the hospitalization. The day before admission, Mr. F. went shopping with his wife, which he never had done before, and expressed worry lest he lose her. This was in her words, "rather strange." (*His behavior is not in keeping with her expectations for him.*) Later that day, Mr. F. thought a TV program was about him and that the set was "after him." "Then I was getting worried." (*She recognizes the bizarre nature of his reactions. She becomes concerned.*)

That night, Mr. F. kept talking. He reproached himself for not working enough to give his wife surprises. Suddenly, he exclaimed he did have a surprise for her—he was going to kill her. "I was petrified and said to him, 'What do you mean?' Then, he began to cry and told me not to let him hurt me and to do for him what I would want him to do for me. I asked him what was wrong. He said he had cancer. . . . He began talk-

* Reprinted from the *Journal of Social Issues*, Vol. 11, No. 4 (1955), pp. 12–24, by permission of the authors and the *Journal*.

ing about his grandfather's mustache and said there was a worm growing out of it." She remembered his watching little worms in the fish bowl and thought his idea came from that. Mr. F. said he had killed his grandfather. He asked Mrs. F. to forgive him and wondered if she were his mother or God. She denied this. He vowed he was being punished for killing people during the war. "I thought maybe . . . worrying about the war so much . . . had gotten the best of him. (*She tries to understand his behavior. She stretches the range of normality to include it.*) I thought he should see a psychiatrist . . . I don't know how to explain it. He was shaking. I knew it was beyond what I could do . . . I was afraid of him . . . I thought he was losing his normal mental attitude and mentality, but I wouldn't say that he was insane or crazy, because he had always bossed me around before . . ." (*She shifts back and forth in thinking his problem is psychiatric and in feeling it is normal behavior that could be accounted for in terms of their own experience.*) Mr. F. talked on through the night. Sometime in the morning, he "seemed to straighten out" and drove his wife to work. (*This behavior tends to balance out the preceding disturbed activities. She quickly returns to a normal referent.*)

At noon, Mr. F. walked into the store where his wife worked as a clerk. "I couldn't make any sense of what he was saying. He kept getting angry because I wouldn't talk to him. . . . Finally, the boss' wife told me to go home." En route, Mr. F. said his male organs were blown up and little seeds covered him. Mrs. F. denied seeing them and announced she planned to call his mother. "He began crying and I had to promise not to. I said, . . . 'Don't you think you should go to a psychiatrist?' and he said, 'No, there is nothing wrong with me.' . . .

Then we came home, and I went to pay a bill . . ." (*Again she considers, but is not fully committed to, the idea that psychiatric help is needed.*)

Back at their apartment, Mr. F. talked of repairing his cab while Mrs. F. thought of returning to work and getting someone to call a doctor. Suddenly, he started chasing her around the apartment and growling like a lion. Mrs. F. screamed, Mr. F. ran out of the apartment, and Mrs. F. slammed and locked the door. "When he started roaring and growling, then I thought he was crazy. That wasn't a human sound. You couldn't say a thing to him . . ." Later, Mrs. F. learned that her husband went to a nearby church, created a scene, and was taken to the hospital by the police. (*Thoroughly threatened, she defines problem as psychiatric.*)

What occurred before these events which precipitated the hospitalization? Going back to their early married life, approximately three years before hospitalization, Mrs. F. told of her husband's irregular work habits and long-standing complaints of severe headaches. "When we were first married, he didn't work much and I didn't worry as long as we could pay the bills." Mrs. F. figured they were just married and wanted to be together a lot. (*Personal norms and expectations are built up.*)

At Thanksgiving, six months after marriage, Mr. F. "got sick and stopped working." During the war he contracted malaria, he explained, which always recurred at that time of year. "He wouldn't get out of bed or eat. . . . He thought he was constipated and he had nightmares. . . . What I noticed most was his perspiring so much. He was crabby. You couldn't get him to go to a doctor. . . . I noticed he was nervous. He's always been a nervous person. . . . Any little thing that would go wrong would upset him—if I didn't get a drawer closed right. . . . His friends are nervous, too. . . . I came to the conclusion that maybe I was happy-go-lucky and everyone else was a bundle of nerves. . . . For a cab driver, he worked hard—most cab drivers loaf. When he felt good, he worked hard. He didn't work so hard when he didn't." (*She adapts to his behavior. The atypical is normalized as his type of personality and appropriate to his subculture.*)

As the months and years went by, Mrs. F. changed jobs frequently, but she worked more regularly than did her husband. He continued to work sporadically, get sick intermittently, appear "nervous and tense" and refrain from seeking medical care. Mrs. F. "couldn't say what was wrong." She had first one idea, then another, about his behavior. "I knew it wasn't right for him to be acting sick like he did." Then, "I was beginning to think he was getting lazy because there wasn't anything I could see." During one period, Mrs. F. surmised he was carrying on with another woman. "I was right on the verge of going, until he explained it wasn't anyone else." (*There is a building up of deviant behavior to a point near her tolerance limits. Her interpretations shift repeatedly.*)

About two and a half years before admission, Mrs. F. began talking to friends about her husband's actions and her lack of success in getting him to a doctor. "I got disgusted and said if he didn't go to a doctor, I would leave him. I got Bill (the owner of Mr. F.'s cab) to talk to him. . . . I begged, threatened, fussed . . ." After that, Mr. F. went to a VA doctor for one visit, overslept for his second appointment and never returned. He said the doctor told him nothing was wrong.

When Mr. F. was well and working, Mrs. F. "never stopped to think about it." "You live from day to day . . . When something isn't nice, I don't think about it. If you stop to think about

things, you can worry yourself sick . . . He said he wished he could live in my world. He'd never seem to be able to put his thinking off the way I do . . ." (*Her mode of operating permits her to tolerate his behavior.*)

Concurrently, other situations confronted Mrs. F. Off and on, Mr. F. talked of a coming revolution as a result of which Negroes and Jews would take over the world. If Mrs. F. argued that she didn't believe it, Mr. F. called her "dumb" and "stupid." "The best thing to do was to change the subject." Eighteen months before admission, Mr. F. began awakening his wife to tell of nightmares about wartime experiences, but she "didn't think about it." Three months later, he decided he wanted to do something besides drive a cab. He worked on an invention but discovered it was patented. Then, he began to write a book about his wartime experiences and science. "If you saw what he wrote, you couldn't see anything wrong with it. . . . He just wasn't making any money." Mrs. F. did think it was "silly" when Mr. F. went to talk to Einstein about his ideas and couldn't understand why he didn't talk to someone in town. Nevertheless, she accompanied him on the trip. (*With the further accumulation of deviant behavior, she becomes less and less able to tolerate it. The perceived seriousness of his condition is attenuated so long as she is able to find something acceptable or understandable in his behavior.*)

Three days before admission, Mr. F. stopped taking baths and changing clothes. Two nights before admission, he awakened his wife to tell her he had just figured out that the book he was writing had nothing to do with science or the world, only with himself. "He said he had been worrying about things for ten years and that writing a book solved what had been worrying him for ten years." Mrs. F. told him to burn his writings if they had nothing to do with science. It was the following morning that Mrs. F. first noticed her husband's behavior as "rather strange."

In the long prelude to Mr. F.'s hospitalization, one can see many of the difficulties which arise for the wife as the husband's behavior no longer conforms and as it strains the limits of the wife's expectations for him. At some stage the wife defines the situation as one requiring help, eventually psychiatric help. Our analysis is concerned primarily with the process of the wife's getting to this stage in interpreting and responding to the husband's behavior. In the preceding case are many reactions which appear as general trends in the data group. These trends can be systematized in terms of the following focal aspects of the process:

1. The wife's threshold for initially discerning a problem depends on the accumulation of various kinds of behavior which are not readily understandable or acceptable to her.
2. This accumulation forces upon the wife the necessity for examining and adjusting expectations for herself and her husband which permit her to account for his behavior.
3. The wife is in an "overlapping" situation, of problem—not problem or of normal—not normal. Her interpretations shift back and forth.
4. Adaptations to the atypical behavior of the husband occur. There is testing and waiting for additional cues in coming to any given interpretation, as in most problem solving. The wife mobilizes strong defenses against the husband's deviant behavior. These defenses take form in such reactions as denying, attenuating, balancing and normalizing the husband's problems.
5. Eventually there is a threshold point at which the perception breaks, when the wife comes to the relatively stable

conclusion that the problem is a psychiatric one and/or that she cannot alone cope with the husband's behavior.

These processes are elaborated in the following analysis of the wives' responses.

Method of Data Collection

Ideally, to study this problem one might like to interview the wives as they struggled with the developing illness. This is precluded, however, by the fact that the problem is not "visible" until psychiatric help is sought. The data, therefore, are the wives' reconstructions of their earlier experiences and accounts of their current reactions during the husband's hospitalization.

It is recognized that recollections of the prehospital period may well include systematic biases, such as distortions, omissions and increased organization and clarity. As a reliability check, a number of wives, just before the husband's discharge from the hospital, were asked again to describe the events and feelings of the prehospital period. In general, the two reports are markedly similar; often details are added and others are elaborated, but events tend to be substantially the same. While this check attests to the consistency of the wives' reporting, it has, of course, the contamination of overlearning which comes from many retellings of these events.

The Beginnings of the Wife's Concern

In the early interviews, the wife was asked to describe the beginnings of the problem which led to her husband's hospitalization. ("Could you tell me when you first noticed that your husband was different?") This question was intended to provide an orientation for the wife to reconstruct the sequence and details of events and feelings which characterized the period preceding hospitalization. The interviewer provided a minimum of structuring in order that the wife's emphases and organization could be obtained.

In retrospect, the wives usually cannot pinpoint the time the husband's problem emerged. Neither can they clearly carve it out from the contexts of the husband's personality and family expectations. The subjective beginnings are seldom localized in a single strange or disturbing reaction on the husband's part but rather in the piling up of behavior and feelings. We have seen this process for Mrs. F. There is a similar accumulation for the majority of wives, although the time periods and kinds of reported behavior vary. Thus, Mrs. Q. verbalizes the impact of a concentration of changes which occur within a period of a few weeks. Her explicit recognition of a problem comes when she adds up this array: her husband stays out late, doesn't eat or sleep, has obscene thoughts, argues with her, hits her, talks continuously, "cannot appreciate the beautiful scene," and "cannot appreciate me or the baby."

The problem behaviors reported by the wives are given in Table 1. They are ordered roughly; the behaviors listed first occurred primarily, but not exclusively, within the family; those later occurred in the more public domain. Whether the behavior is public or private does not seem to be a very significant factor in determining the wife's threshold for perceiving a problem.

TABLE 1
Reported Problem Behavior at Time of the Wife's Initial Concern
and at Time of the Husband's Admission to Hospital

Problem Behavior	Initially		At Hospital Admission	
	Psychotics N	Psycho-neurotics N	Psychotics N	Psycho-neurotics N
Physical problems, complaints, worries	12	5	7	5
Deviations from routines of behavior	17	9	13	9
Expression of inadequacy or hopelessness	4	1	5	2
Nervous, irritable, worried	19	10	18	9
Withdrawal (verbal, physical)	5	1	6	1
Changes or accentuations in personality "traits" (slovenly, deceptive, forgetful)	5	6	7	6
Aggressive or assaultive and suicidal behavior	6	3	10	6
Strange or bizzare thoughts, delusions, hallucinations and strange behavior	11	1	15	2
Excessive drinking	4	7	3	4
Violation of codes of "decency"	3	1	3	2
Number of Respondents	23	10	23	10

There are many indications that these behaviors, now organized as a problem, have occurred many times before. This is especially true where alcoholism, physical complaints or personality "weaknesses" enter the picture. The wives indicate how, earlier, they had assimilated these characteristics into their own expectations in a variety of ways: the characteristics were congruent with their image of their husbands, they fitted their differential standards for men and women (men being less able to stand up to troubles), they had social or environmental justifications, etc.

When and how behavior becomes defined as problematic appears to be a highly individual matter. In some instances, it is when the wife can no longer manage her husband (he will no longer respond to her usual prods); in others, when his behavior destroys the status quo (when her goals and living routines are disorganized); and, in still others,

when she cannot explain his behavior. One can speculate that her level of tolerance for his behavior is a function of her specific personality needs and vulnerabilities, her personal and family value systems and the social supports and prohibitions regarding the husband's symptomatic behavior.

Initial Interpretations of Husband's Problem

Once the behavior is organized as a problem, it tends also to be interpreted as some particular kind of problem. More often than not, however, the husband's difficulties are not seen initially as manifestations of mental illness or even as emotional problems (Table 2).

TABLE 2
Initial Interpretations of the Husband's Behavior

Interpretation	Psychotics N	Psychoneurotics N
Nothing really wrong	3	0
"Character" weakness and "controllable" behavior (lazy, mean, etc.)	6	3
Physical problem	6	0
Normal response to crisis	3	1
Mildly emotionally disturbed	1	2
"Something" seriously wrong	2	2
Serious emotional or mental problem	2	2
Number of Respondents	23	10

Early interpretations often tend to be organized around physical difficulties (18% of cases) or "character" problems (27%). To a very marked degree, these orientations grow out of the wives' longstanding appraisals of their husbands as weak and ineffective or physically sick men. These wives describe their husbands as spoiled, lacking will-power, exaggerating little complaints and acting like babies. This is especially marked where alcoholism complicates the husband's symptomatology. For example, Mrs. Y.,

whose husband was chronically alcoholic, aggressive and threatening to her, "raving," and who "chewed his nails until they almost bled," interprets his difficulty thus: "He was just spoiled rotten. He never outgrew it. He told me when he was a child he could get his own way if he insisted, and he is still that way." This quotation is the prototype of many of its kind.

Some wives, on the other hand, locate the problem in the environment. They expect the husband to change as the environmental crisis subsides. Several wives, while enumerating difficulties and concluding that there is a problem, in the same breath say it is really nothing to be concerned about.

Where the wives interpret the husband's difficulty as emotional in nature, they tend to be inconsistently "judgmental" and "understanding." The psychoneurotics are more often perceived initially by their wives as having emotional problems or as being mentally ill than are the psychotics. This is true even though many more clinical signs (bizarre, confused, delusional, aggressive and disoriented behavior) are reported by the wives of the psychotics than of the psychoneurotics.

Initial interpretations, whatever their content, are seldom held with great confidence by the wives. Many recall their early reactions to their husbands' behaviors as full of puzzling confusion and uncertainty. Something is wrong, they know, but, in general, they stop short of a firm explanation. Thus, Mrs. M. reports, "He was kind of worried. He was kind of worried before, not exactly worried . . ." She thought of his many physical complaints; she "racked" her "brain" and told her husband, "Of course, he didn't feel good." Finally, he stayed home from work with "no special complaints, just blah," and she "began to realize it was more deeply seated."

Changing Perceptions of the Husband's Problem

The fog and uneasiness in the wife's early attempts to understand and cope with the husband's difficulties are followed, typically, by painful psychological struggles to resolve the uncertainties and to change the current situation. Usually, the wife's perceptions of the husband's problems undergo a series of changes before hospitalization is sought or

effected, irrespective of the length of time elapsing between the beginnings of concern and hospitalization.

Viewing these changes macroscopically, three relatively distinct patterns of successive redefinitions of the husband's problems are apparent. One sequence (slightly less than half the cases) is characterized by a progressive intensification; interpretations are altered in a definite direction—toward seeing the problem as mental illness. Mrs. O. illustrates this progression. Initially, she thought her husband was "unsure of himself." "He was worried, too, about getting old." These ideas moved to: "He'd drink to forget. . . . He just didn't have the confidence. . . . He'd forget little things. . . . He'd wear a suit weeks on end if I didn't take it away from him. . . . He'd say nasty things." Then, when Mr. O. seemed "so confused," "to forget all kinds of things . . . where he'd come from . . . to go to work," and made "nasty, cutting remarks all the time," she began to think in terms of a serious personality disturbance. "I did think he knew that something was wrong . . . that he was sick. He was never any different this last while and I couldn't stand it any more. . . . You don't know what a relief it was . . ." (when he was hospitalized). The husband's drinking, his failure to be tidy, his nastiness, etc., lose significance in their own right. They move from emphasis to relief and are recast as signs of "something deeper," something that brought "it" on.

Some wives whose interpretations move in the direction of seeing their husbands as mentally ill hold conceptions of mental illness and of personality that do not permit assigning the husband all aspects of the sick role. Frequently, they use the interpretation of mental illness as an angry epithet or as a threatening prediction for the husband. This is exemplified in such references as: "I told him he should have his head examined," "I called him a half-wit," "I told him if he's not careful, he'll be a mental case." To many of these wives, the hospital is regarded as the "end of the road."

Other wives showing this pattern of change hold conceptions of emotional disturbance which more easily permit them to assign to their husbands the role of patient as the signs of illness become more apparent. They do not as often regard hospitalization in a mental hospital as the "last step." Nevertheless, their feelings toward their husbands may contain components equally as angry and rejecting as those of the wives with the less sophisticated ideas regarding mental illness.

A somewhat different pattern of sequential changes in interpreting the husband's difficulties (about one-fifth of the cases) is to be found among wives who appear to cast around for situationally and momentarily adequate explanations. As the situation changes or as the husband's behavior changes, these wives find reasons and excuses but lack an underlying or synthesizing theory. Successive interpretations tend to bear little relation to one another. Situational factors tend to lead them to seeing their husbands as mentally ill. Immediate, serious and direct physical threats or the influence of others may be the deciding factor. For example, a friend or employer may insist that the husband see a psychiatrist, and the wife goes along with the decision.

A third pattern of successive redefinitions (slightly less than one-third of the cases) revolves around an orientation outside the framework of emotional problems or mental illness. In these cases, the wife's specific explanations change but pivot around a denial that the husband is mentally ill.

A few wives seem not to change their interpretations about their husband's difficulties. They maintain the same explanation throughout the development of his illness, some within the psychiatric framework, others rigidly outside that framework.

Despite the characteristic shiftings in interpretations, in the group as a whole, there tend to be persisting underlying themes in the individual wife's perceptions that remain essentially unaltered. These themes are a function of her systems of thinking about normality and abnormality and about valued and devalued behavior.

The Process of Recognizing the Husband's Problem as Mental Illness

In the total situation confronting the wife, there are a number of factors, apparent in our data, which make it difficult for the wife to recognize and accept the husband's behavior in a mental-emotional-psychiatric framework. Many cross-currents seem to influence the process.

The husband's behavior itself is a fluctuating stimulus. He is not worried and complaining all of the time. His delusions and hallucinations may not persist. His hostility toward the wife may be followed by warm attentiveness. She has, then, the problem of deciding whether his "strange" behavior is significant. The greater saliency of one or the other of his responses at any moment of time depends in some degree upon the behavior sequence which has occurred most recently.

The relationship between husband and wife also supplies a variety of images and contexts which can justify varied conclusions about the husband's current behavior. The wife is likely to adapt to behavior which occurs in their day to day relationships. Therefore, symptomatic reactions which are intensifications of long-standing response patterns become part of the fabric of life and are not easily disentangled as "symptomatic."

Communications between husband and wife regarding the husband's difficulties act sometimes to impede and sometimes to further the process of seeing the difficulties within a psychiatric framework. We have seen both kinds of influences in our data. Mr. and Mrs. F. were quite unable to communicate effectively about Mr. F.'s problems. On the one hand, he counters his wife's urging that he see a doctor with denials that anything is wrong. On the other hand, in his own way through his symptoms, he tries to communicate his problems, but she responds only to his verbalized statements, taking them at face value.

Mr. and Mrs. K. participate together quite differently, examining Mr. K.'s fears that he is being followed by the F.B.I., that their house has been wired and that he is going to be fired. His wife tentatively shares his suspicions. At the same time, they discuss the possibility of paranoid reactions.

The larger social context contributes, too, in the wife's perceptual tug of war. Others with whom she can compare her husband provide contrasts to his deviance, but others (Mr. F.'s nervous friends) also provide parallels to his problems. The "outsiders," seeing less of her husband, often discount the wife's alarm when she presses them for opinions. In other instances, the friend or employer, less adapted to or defended against the husband's symptoms, helps her to define his problem as psychiatric.

This task before the wife, of defining her husband's difficulties, can be conceptualized as an "overlapping" situation (in Lewin's terms), in which the relative potencies of the several effective influences fluctuate. The wife is responding to the various sets of forces simultaneously. Thus, several conclusions or interpretations of the problem are simultaneously "suspended in balance," and they shift back and forth in emphasis and relief. Seldom, however, does she seem to be balancing off clear-cut alternatives, such as physical versus mental. Her complex perceptions (even those of Mrs. F. who is extreme in misperceiving cues) are more "sophisticated" than the casual questioner might be led to conclude.

Thus far, we have ignored the personally threatening aspects of recognizing mental illness in one's spouse, and the defenses which are mobilized to meet this threat. It is assumed that it is threatening to the wife not only to realize that the husband is mentally ill but further to consider her own possible role in the development of the disorder, to give up modes of relating to her husband that may have had satisfactions for her and to see a future as the wife of a mental patient. Our data provide systematic information only on the first aspect of this problem, on the forms of defense against the recognition of the illness. One or more of the following defenses are manifested in three-fourths of our cases.

The most obvious form of defense in the wife's response is the tendency to *normalize* the husband's neurotic and psychotic symptoms. His behavior is explained, justified or made acceptable by seeing it also in herself or by assuring herself that the particular behavior occurs again and again among persons who are not ill. Illustrative of this reaction is the wife who reports her husband's hallucinations and assures herself that this is normal because she herself heard voices when she was in the menopause. Another wife responds to her husband's physical complaints, fears, worries, nightmares, and delusions with "A lot of normal people think there's something wrong when there isn't. I think men are that way; his father is that way."

When behavior cannot be normalized, it can be made to seem less severe or less important in a total picture than an out-

sider might see it. By finding some
grounds for the behavior or something
explainable about it, the wife achieves at
least momentary *attenuation* of the seriousness of it. Thus, Mrs. F. is able to
discount partly the strangeness of her
husband's descriptions of the worms
growing out of his grandfather's mustache
when she recalls his watching the worms
in the fish bowl. There may be attenuation, too, by seeing the behavior as
"momentary" ("You could talk him out
of his ideas.") or by rethinking the problem and seeing it in a different light.

By *balancing* acceptable with unacceptable behavior or "strange" with
"normal" behavior, some wives can conclude that the husband is not seriously
disturbed. Thus, it is very important to
Mrs. R. that her husband kissed her
goodbye before he left for the hospital.
This response cancels out his hostile feelings toward her and the possibility that
he is mentally ill. Similarly, Mrs. V.
reasons that her husband cannot be "out
of his mind" for he had reminded her of
things she must not forget to do when
he went to the hospital.

Defense sometimes amounts to a
thorough-going *denial*. This takes the
form of denying that the behavior perceived can be interpreted in an emotional
or psychiatric framework. In some instances, the wife reports vividly on such
behavior as repeated thoughts of suicide,
efforts to harm her and the like and sums
it up with "I thought it was just a whim."
Other wives bend their efforts toward
proving the implausibility of mental illness.

After the husband is hospitalized, it
might be expected that these denials
would decrease to a negligible level. This
is not wholly the case, however. A breakdown of the wives' interpretations just
following the husband's admission to the
hospital shows that roughly a fifth still

interpret the husband's behavior in another framework than that of a serious
emotional problem or mental illness.
Another fifth ambivalently and sporadically interpret the behavior as an emotional or mental problem. The remainder
hold relatively stable interpretations
within this framework.

After the husband has been hospitalized for some time, many wives reflect
on their earlier tendencies to avoid a
definition of mental illness. Such reactions are almost identically described by
these wives: "I put it out of my mind—
I didn't want to face it—anything but a
mental illness." "Maybe I was aware of
it. But you know you push things away
from you and keep hoping." "Now you
think maybe you should have known
about it. Maybe you should have done
more than you did and that worries me."

Discussion

The findings on the perceptions of
mental illness by the wives of patients
are in line with general findings in studies
of perception. Behavior which is unfamiliar and incongruent and unlikely in
terms of current expectations and needs
will not be readily recognized, and stressful or threatening stimuli will tend to be
misperceived or perceived with difficulty
or delay.

We have attempted to describe the
factors which help the wife maintain a
picture of her husband as normal and
those which push her in the direction
of accepting a psychiatric definition of
his problem. The kind and intensity of
the symptomatic behavior, its persistence
over time, the husband's interpretation
of his problem, interpretations and defining actions of others, including professionals, all play a role. In addition, the
wives come to this experience with different conceptions of psychological processes

and of the nature of emotional illness, itself, as well as with different tolerances for emotional disturbance. As we have seen, there are also many supports in society for maintaining a picture of normality concerning the husband's behavior. Social pressures and expectations not only keep *behavior* in line but to a great extent *perceptions* of behavior as well. . . .

Family Processes and Becoming A Mental Patient * †

HAROLD SAMPSON, SHELDON L. MESSINGER,

AND ROBERT D. TOWNE

Becoming a mental patient is not a simple and direct outcome of "mental illness"; nor is hospitalization in a mental institution, when and if it comes, the automatic result of a professional opinion. Persons who are, by clinical standards, grossly disturbed, severely impaired in their functioning, and even overtly psychotic may remain in the community for long periods without being "recognized" as "mentally ill" and without benefit of psychiatric or other professional attention. It is clear that becoming a mental patient is a socially structured event.[1] The research reported here is directed to increasing our understanding of the nature and significance of this structuring as it mediates the relations between individuals and the more formal means of social control. The research explores (*a*) the relationship between patterns of family means for coping with the deviant behavior of a member who later becomes a mental patient and (*b*) efforts of the future patient or members of his family to secure professional help.

The broad nature of this latter relationship may be inferred from a number of published findings. Yarrow and her colleagues have documented the monumental capacity of family members, before hospitalization, to overlook, minimize, and explain away evidence of profound disturbance in an intimate.[2]

* Reprinted from *American Journal of Sociology*, Vol. 68 (July 1962), 88–96, by permission of The University of Chicago Press and the authors. Copyright 1962 by The University of Chicago Press.

† This report is based on a study carried out by the California Department of Mental Hygiene and partially supported by Grant No. 3M-9124 from the National Institute of Mental Health.

[1] Erving Goffman, in "The Moral Career of the Mental Patient," *Psychiatry*, XXII (May, 1959), 123–42, discusses a variety of "career contingencies" that may intervene between deviant behavior and hospitalization for mental illness. Also see the articles in *Journal of Social Issues*, XI (1955), ed. John A. Clausen and Marian Radke Yarrow, under the general title of "The Impact of Mental Illness on the Family." August B. Hollingshead and Fredrick C. Redlich (*Social Class and Mental Illness: A Community Study* [New York: John Wiley & Sons, Inc., 1958], chap. vi, "Paths to the Psychiatrist") also emphasize this point.

[2] Marian Radke Yarrow, Charlotte Green Schwartz, Harriet S. Murphy, and Leila Calhoun Deasy, "The Psychological Meaning of Mental Illness in the Family," *Journal of*

The post-hospital studies of the Simmons group have suggested that high "tolerance for deviance" in certain types of families is a critical determinant of the likelihood of poorly functioning and sometimes frankly psychotic former patients avoiding rehospitalization.[3] Myers and Roberts found that few mental patients or their families sought or used professional assistance before hospitalization until the problems they encountered became unmanageable.[4] Whitmer and Conover reported that the occasion for hospitalization was ordinarily not recognition of "mental illness" by the patient or his family but inability to cope with disturbed behavior within the family.[5]

These observations and our own permit two inferences. First, both before and after hospitalization some type of accommodative pattern ordinarily evolves between a disturbed person and his family which permits or forces him to remain in the community in spite of severe difficulties. Second, it is the disruption of this pattern which eventually brings a disturbed person to psychiatric attention.[6] An investigation of typical family accommodations to the deviant behavior of future patients, and how these accommodations collapse, should therefore contribute to our understanding of the ways in which individuals and the intimate social networks of which they are members are rendered less and more accessible to institutionalized devices of social control. Specifically, it should provide us with a glimpse of those dynamic family processes which determine a future mental patient's accessibility to community, particularly psychiatric intervention; these same processes determine the accessibility of the family. It should also contribute to our understanding of the meaning of such intervention to the future patient and his family. Such family accommodations pose strategic problems for the persons who constitute and man community remedial facilities. These are problems seldom taken into explicit or systematic account by such persons—problems beyond but related to the pathology of the patient.

We shall be concerned here with two phases in the relationship between the

---

Social Issues, XI (1955), 12–24. Also see Charlotte Green Schwartz, "Perspectives on Deviance—Wives' Definitions of Their Husbands' Mental Illness," *Psychiatry,* XX (August, 1957), 275–91; Hollinghead and Redlich, *op. cit.,* esp. pp. 172–79; and Elaine Cumming and John Cumming, *Closed Ranks* (Cambridge, Mass.: Harvard University Press, 1957), esp. pp. 91–108.

[3] See Ozzie G. Simmons, *After Hospitalization: The Mental Patient and His Family* (Hogg Foundation for Mental Health, n.d.) and the several studies by the Simmons group cited there.

[4] Jerome K. Myers and Bertram H. Roberts, *Family and Class Dynamics* (New York: John Wiley & Sons, Inc., 1959), pp. 213–20. These findings also suggest that lower-class families are better able to contain an extremely disturbed person for long periods of time than are middle-class families; the latter call on outside help more rapidly when "major psychotic decompensation" occurs. This would follow from the argument presented by Talcott Parsons and Renée Fox in "Illness, Therapy, and the Modern Urban American Family," *Journal of Social Issues,* VIII (1953), 31–44.

[5] Carroll A. Whitmer and Glenn C. Conover, "A Study of Critical Incidents in the Hospitalization of the Mentally Ill," *Journal of the National Association of Social Work,* IV (January, 1959), 89–94 (see also Edwin C. Wood, John M. Rakusin, and Emanuel Morse, "Interpersonal Aspects of Psychiatric Hospitalization," *Archives of General Psychiatry,* III [December, 1960], 632–41).

[6] Another inference we have made, and which we discuss elsewhere, is that an important set of effects of community devices of social control pertain to family patterns of accommodation. In important ways, it is through these that individuals are controlled, rather than by direct action (Harold Sampson, Sheldon L. Messinger, and Robert D. Towne, "The Mental Hospital and Family Accommodations" [unpublished manuscript, 1962]).

future patient and his family and with the connections between these phases and the course of events leading to hospitalization. The first phase consists of the evolution of a pattern of accommodation within the family to behavioral deviance on the part of the future patient.[7] The second phase consists in the disruption of this pattern of accommodation. Our observations are derived from a study of seventeen families in which the wife-mother was hospitalized for the first time in a large state mental institution and therein diagnosed as schizophrenic.[8] We established a research relationship with both patient and spouse at the time of admission and continued to see them regularly and frequently throughout hospitalization, and for varying periods extending to more than two years following first release. We conducted about fifty interviews with the members of each marital pair, including typically one or more joint interviews. Other relatives, psychiatrists, physicians, hospital personnel, and other remedial agents who had become involved with the patient or family over the years were also interviewed. Interview materials were supplemented by direct observation at home and in the hospital, and by such medical and social records as we could locate and gain permission to abstract.

These methods, which are described more fully elsewhere,[9] enabled us to reconstruct the vicissitudes of these marital families from courtship through marriage, child-bearing and child-rearing, eventual hospitalization of the wife, and well into the period following the patient's first release. We shall focus here on a longitudinal analysis of two patterns of accommodation which evolved between these women and their families prior to hospitalization and the disruption of these patterns. The patterns are exemplified by eleven and four cases, respectively; two of the seventeen families do not appear to be adequately characterized by either pattern. In order to present the patterns in some detail, our analysis will be developed in terms of selected families exhibiting each type of accommodation. This does not exhaust the empirical variety to be found even in the limited number of cases studied here. In the concluding section, however, emphasis will be placed on common patterns of relationship between future mental patients and their immediate interpersonal communities, as well as on the conditions under which these patterns deteriorate and collapse.

The Uninvolved Husband and Separate Worlds

In the first situation, exemplified by eleven families, the marital partners and

---

[7] This phase emphasizes one side of a complicated reciprocity between family relations and the deviance of family members. We have focused on the other side of this reciprocity —family relations as they sustain and promote deviant behavior—elsewhere (see Robert D. Towne, Sheldon L. Messinger, and Harold Sampson, "Schizophrenia and the Marital Family: Accommodations to Symbiosis," *Family Process* (forthcoming), and Robert D. Towne, Harold Sampson, and Sheldon L. Messinger, "Schizophrenia and the Marital Family: Identification Crises," *Journal of Nervous and Mental Diseases,* CXXXIII [November, 1961], 423–29). There is a large and growing literature on this topic, particularly as it concerns schizophrenia, much of which is referred to in the various citations to be found in *The Etiology of Schizophrenia,* ed. by Don D. Jackson (New York: Basic Books, Inc., 1960).

[8] Detailed characteristics of the families studied may be found in Harold Sampson, Sheldon L. Messinger, and Robert D. Towne, "The Mental Hospital and Marital Family Ties," *Social Problems,* IX (Fall, 1961), 141–55. In two of seventeen cases, a brief psychiatric hospitalization in a county hospital had occurred earlier; in a third case, the woman had been hospitalized in a private sanitarium for one month earlier in the same year she entered the state institution.

[9] *Ibid.*

their children lived together as a relatively independent, self-contained nuclear family, but the marital relationship was characterized by mutual withdrawal and the construction of separate worlds of compensatory involvement. At some point during the marriage, usually quite early, one or both of the partners had experienced extreme dissatisfaction with the marriage. This was ordinarily accompanied by a period of violent, open discord, although in other cases, the dissatisfaction was expressed only indirectly, through reduced communication with the marital partner. Whatever the means of managing the dissatisfaction when it occurred, in each of these families the partners withdrew and each gradually instituted a separate world. The husband became increasingly involved in his work or in other interests outside the marital relationship. The wife became absorbed in private concerns about herself and her children. The partners would rarely go out together, rarely participate together in dealing with personal or family problems, and seldom communicate to each other about their more pressing interests, wishes, and concerns. The marriage would continue in this way for some time without divorce, without separation, and without movement toward greater closeness. The partners had achieved a type of marital accommodation based on interpersonal isolation, emotional distance, and lack of explicit demands upon each other. This accommodation represented an alternative to both divorce and a greater degree of marital integration.

It is a particularly important characteristic of this type of family organization that pathological developments in the wives were for a time self-sustaining. The wife's distress, withdrawal, or deviant behavior did not lead to immediate changes of family life but rather to an intensification of mutual withdrawal. In

this setting, the wives became acutely disturbed or even psychotic, without, for a time, very much affecting the pre-existing pattern of family life. This is exemplified in the following cases:

In the evenings, Mr. Urey worked on his car in the basement while his wife remained upstairs, alone with her sleeping children, engaged in conversations and arguments with imaginary others. This situation continued for at least two years before Mrs. Urey saw a psychiatrist on the recommendation of her family physician. Another two years elapsed before Mrs. Urey was hospitalized. During this period, Mr. Urey became ever less concerned with his wife's behavior, accepting it as a matter of course, and concerned himself with "getting ahead" in his job.

For two years prior to hospitalization, Mrs. Rand was troubled by various somatic complaints, persistent tension, difficulty in sleeping, a vague but disturbing conviction that she was a sinner, and intermittent states of acute panic. Mr. Rand was minimally aware of her distress. He worked up to fourteen hours a day, including weekends, in his store, and eventually a second job took him out of the home three evenings a week. On those infrequent occasions when his wife's worries forced themselves on his attention, he dismissed them curtly as absurd, and turned once again to his own affairs.

In these families the patterned response to distress, withdrawal, or illness in the wife was further withdrawal by the husband, resulting in increasing distance between, and disengagement of, the marital partners. These developments were neither abrupt nor entirely consistent, but the trend of interaction in these families was toward mutual alienation and inaccessibility of each partner to the other. In this situation, early involvement of the wife in a professional treatment situation was limited by her own withdrawal and difficulty in taking the initiative for any sustained course of action in the real world, as well as by the husband's detachment.

This pattern of mutual withdrawal eventually became intolerable to one or the other partner, pressure for a change was brought to bear, and the family suffered an acute crisis. In some cases, pressure for change was initiated by the husband. In other cases, such pressure was initiated by the wife in the form of increasing agitation, somatic and psychic complaints, and repeated verbal and behavioral communications that she was unable to go on. However the pre-hospital crisis was initiated, and whether it signaled a desire for increased or reduced involvement by the initiating partner, the change indicated an incipient collapse of the former pattern of accommodation.

In four of the eleven cases considered here, the pre-hospital crisis was primarily precipitated by a shift in the husband's "tolerance for deviance." In two of these cases, the wives had been chronically and pervasively withdrawn from role performances and at least periodically psychotic. One husband, in the midst of job insecurities and a desire to move to another state to make a new start, pressed his wife to assume more responsibility. Another husband, approaching forty years of age, reassessed his life and decided that the time had come to rid himself of a wife whom he had long considered "a millstone around my neck." These husbands sought medical or psychiatric assistance specifically to exclude their wives from the family; the two wives were passively resistant to hospitalization. The explicit attitude of the husbands was that they wished the hospital to take their wives off their hands.

In the other two cases, the disruption of the earlier accommodation was associated with the establishment, by the husband, of a serious extra-marital liaison. Here, as in the two cases referred to above, there appeared to be no marked change in the wife's conduct prior to this indication of a desire by the husband for total withdrawal.

Virtually identical family processes were apparent in those cases where the manifest illness of the wife was itself the source of pressure for change, the harbinger of the collapse of the prior marital accommodation. The wife's illness intruded itself into family life, at first with limited impact, but then more insistently, like a claim which has not been paid or a message that must be repeated until it is acknowledged. The wife's "complaints" came to be experienced by the husband as, literally, complaints to him, as demands upon him for interest, concern, and involvement. These husbands, however, uniformly initially struggled to preserve the earlier pattern, that is, to maintain uninvolvement in the face of demands which implicitly pressed for their active concern. Thus, as the pre-hospital crisis unfolded, the wife's manifest illness assumed the interpersonal significance of a demand for involvement, and the husband's difficulty in recognizing her as seriously disturbed had the interpersonal significance of a resistance to that demand. The excerpt cited earlier from the Rand case illustrates this process if we add to it the observation that during these two years Mrs. Rand's difficulties recurrently came to the husband's attention in the form of momentary crises which compelled at least the response of curt dismissal.

In this situation, the husband initially assumed a passive or indifferent attitude toward his wife's obtaining professional help. But if she became involved with a psychiatrist, physician, minister, or social worker who took some interest in her life situation, the husband became concerned with the treatment in a negative way. The treatment "wasn't necessary," it "wasn't helping," it "cost too much money." In addition to these deprecations was a hint of alarm that the treatment would challenge the husband's pattern of uninvolvement.[10] For example, Mr. Rand, whose working schedule was mentioned earlier, worried that his wife's psychiatrist might support her complaint that he did not spend enough time at home. Thus the involvement of the wife with a psychiatrically oriented helper was experienced by the husband, at least initially, as a claim upon himself—for money, for concern, and most centrally, for reinvolvement. We have reported elsewhere [11] that there is some basis for this feeling. The treatment process, especially during hospitalization, does tend to induct the husband into the role of the responsible relative, and thereby presses for the reestablishment of reciprocal expectations which had been eroded in the earlier family accommodation.

In most of these cases, these processes led to more extreme deviance on the part of the wife which eventually came to the attention of the larger community, thereby resulting in hospitalization. For example, Mrs. Urey, who had been actively psychotic for some time, was hospitalized only after she set fire to her home. In brief, the wife's distress is at first experienced by the husband as an unwarranted demand for his reinvolvement in the marital relationship, he withdraws further, and her behavior becomes more deviant.

We may conclude this section with a few more general remarks. The pre-hospital crisis, in each of these cases, marked, and was part of, the disruption of a pattern of accommodation which had been established between the marital partners. The disruption was in effect initiated by one of the partners and resisted by the other.[12] The former accommodation and the way in which it came to be disrupted were important determinants of the processes of "recognizing" the wife as mentally ill, of seeking and using professional help, and of moving the wife from the status of a distressed and behaviorally deviant person within the community to that of a mental patient. These processes, in fact, can only be understood within the context of these family patterns. The problems of early intervention in cases of serious mental illness and of effective intervention in the later crises which ordinarily do come to psychiatric attention cannot even be formulated meaningfully without consideration of these interpersonal processes which determine when, why, and how sick persons become psychiatric patients.

The Overinvolved Mother and the Marital Family Triad

In a contrasting situation found in four cases, the marital partners and their children did not establish a relatively self-contained nuclear family. Rather, family life was organized chronically or periodically around the presence of a maternal figure who took over the wife's domestic and child-rearing functions.[13]

This organization of family life was a conjoint solution to interlocking conflicts of the wife, husband, and mother. In brief, these mothers were possessive and intrusive, motivated to perpetuate their

[10] In one case, the psychiatrist urged the husband to seek treatment for himself.

[11] Sampson *et al.*, "The Mental Hospital and Marital Family Ties," *op. cit.*

[12] Wood, Rakusin, and Morse, *op. cit.*, have arrived at a related conclusion on the basis of an analysis of the circumstances of admission of forty-eight patients to a Veterans Administration hospital. "There is also evidence to suggest that hospitalization can for some patients be a way of demanding that those close to them change their behavior, just as it can be an expression by relatives that they are dissatisfied with the patient's behavior."

[13] This person was the wife's mother in three cases, her mother-in-law in the fourth. This distinction is not critical in the present context, and we shall refer to "the wife's mother," etc.

daughters' dependency, and characteristically disposed to assume the "helpful" role in a symbiotic integration with her. The daughters ambivalently pressed for the establishment or maintenance of a dependent relationship with their mothers and struggled to break the inner and outer claims of the maternal attachment. The husbands responded to anxieties of their own about the demands of heterosexual intimacy and marital responsibility, as well as their own ambivalent strivings toward maternal figures, by alternately supporting and protesting the wives' dependence on the maternal figure. The resulting family organization, in which the mother was intermittently or continuously called upon for major assistance, represented an alternative to both a relatively self-contained, independent nuclear family and to marital disruption with the wife returning to live within the parental family.

In direct contrast to the family accommodation described in the preceding section, the wives in "triadic" families did not quietly drift into increasing isolation and autism. Here, sickness or withdrawal by the wife were occasions for intense maternal concern and involvment. This development was ordinarily abetted by the husband. The resulting situation, however, would come to be experienced as threatening by the wife. She would come to view her mother as interfering with her marriage and her fulfilment of her own maternal responsibilities, as restricting her freedom, and as preventing her from growing up. At this point a small but often violent rebellion would ensue, and the husband would now participate with his wife to exclude the mother from family life. Such cycles of reliance on the mother followed by repudiation of her recurred over the years with only minor variations.

This accommodation complicated seeking and using professional help, but in a distinctively different way than in the family setting depicted earlier. Here, the family accommodation included this patterned response to withdrawal, illness, or distress in the wife: the mother replaced the wife in her domestic and child-care functions, and established with the wife a characteristic integration involving a helpless one who needs care and a helpful one who administers it; the husband withdrew to the periphery of the family system, leaving the wife and mother bound in a symbiotic interdependency.

In this patterned response, outside help was not simply superfluous but constituted an actual threat to the existing interdependency of mother and daughter (by implying that it was inadequate, unnecessary, or even harmful), whereas in the type of family accommodation previously described, treatment was experienced as a threat to the husband's uninvolvement; here, treatment was a threat to the mother's involvement.

It was the failure of this family accommodation which led to the wife's contact with the physician or psychiatrist. This failure occurred when, simultaneously, the wife rebelled against the maternal attachment but could not establish with her husband the previously effective alternative of temporary repudiation of that attachment. The following example demonstrates these processes:

Mrs. Yale became anxious, confused, and unable to cope with the demands of daily life in the context of increasing withdrawal by her husband combined with increasing inner and outer pressure for reinvolvement with her mother. Her mother, Mrs. Brown, was living with the marital family, tending the house, caring for the child, and remaining by the side of her troubled daughter night and day. Mr. Yale had become increasingly involved in shared interests with a circle of male friends, and felt disaffected from family life.

Mrs. Brown later characterized this period to the research interviewer: "I think Mary resented me because I tried to help and do things for her. She didn't want me to help with her work. She didn't seem to want me around—sort of resented me. She kept saying she wanted to be on her own and that she didn't have confidence because I was always doing things for her. She even resented me doing the dishes. I just wanted to help out." At this point, Mrs. Brown considered her daughter to be seriously emotionally disturbed, and thought psychiatric help would be advisable.

In such cases, the behavior which led family members to doubt the young woman's sanity consisted of hostility, resentment, and accusatory outbursts directed toward the mother. In these violent outbursts toward the maternal figure, the daughter was indeed "not herself." It was at just this point that the daughter's behavior constituted a disruption of the former family pattern of accommodation and led toward involvement with outside helpers. The mother might now view outside helpers as potential allies in re-establishing the earlier interdependency. The psychiatrist, however, was unlikely to fulfil the mother's expectations in this regard, and then he became an heir to the husband in the triadic situation, a potential rival to the mother-daughter symbiosis.

Shortly after outpatient treatment began, Mrs. Brown took her daughter on an extended vacation which effectively interrupted the treatment, detached the daughter from her incipient attachment to the psychiatrist, and re-established the pattern of mother-daughter interdependency with the husband at the periphery of involvement.

We may summarize, then, certain connections between this type of family accommodation and the use of professional help prior to hospitalization. The initial response of the family to the wife's distress was to attempt to reinstate a familiar pattern: a drawing together of mother and daughter in symbiotic interdependency, and a withdrawal of the husband to the periphery of the family. This accommodation was disrupted by the eruption of the daughter's formerly ego-alien resentment toward her mother, and at this point the latter was likely to view physicians or psychiatrists as potential allies in restoring the former equilibrium. The psychiatrist, however, was unlikely to play this part and became, for the mother, a rival to the interdependency. For the daughter, also, this meaning of treatment invested it with the dangerous promise of a possible separation from the maternal figure. In this drama, the husband was likely to play a relatively passive if not a discouraging role, affording the wife little if any support in what she experienced as a threatening and disloyal involvement outside the family.

The way in which the hospitalization of the wife came about, in the collapse of this family accommodation, also provided contrasts to the processes depicted in the preceding section. As the pre-hospital crisis developed, the wife sought to withdraw from continuing intolerable conflict in the triadic situation. At first, the wife felt impelled to choose between regressive dependency on a maternal figure and the claims of her marital family, but was unable to either relinquish the former or achieve inner and outer support for the latter. Both alternatives were transiently affirmed and repudiated in the period preceding hospitalization, but in time she came to feel alienated from *both* mother and husband, and driven toward increasing *psychic* withdrawal. This process did not resolve her conflicts or remove her from the triadic field, and in time she herself pushed for physical removal.

Thus, in two of the four triadic cases, the wife herself, with a feeling of desperation, explicitly requested hospitalization. In a third case, the disturbed wife was brought to a psychiatrist in the company of both mother and husband, refused to return home with them after the appointment, and was thereupon hospitalized. In the fourth case, the wife was initially co-operative to a hospitalization plan, but equivocation by the husband and psychiatrist delayed action, and the wife gave herself and her daughter an overdose of drugs, thereby precipitating the hospitalization. This last case resembles the most common pattern described in the preceding section, in which the wife is driven to extreme deviance which comes to the attention of the larger community and compels hospitalization. But the secondary pattern, in which a husband takes primary initiative for hospitalizing a reluctant wife because she has become a "millstone around my neck," was entirely absent.

Discussion

The career of the mental patient and his family ordinarily comes to the attention of treatment personnel during the course of an "unmanageable" emergency and fades from view when that emergency is in some way resolved. Prior to this public phase of the crisis, and often again after it, the disturbance of the patient is contained within a community setting. It is the collapse of accommodative patterns *between* the future patient and his interpersonal community which renders the situation unmanageable and ushers in the public phase of the pre-hospital (or rehospitalization) crisis.

Our analysis has been addressed to ways in which two particular organizations of family life have contained pathological processes, to the ways in which these organizations were disrupted, and to the links between family dynamics and recognition of illness, seeking and using professional help, and the circumstances

of mental hospitalization. The analysis carries us beyond the observations that families often "tolerate" deviant behavior, may resist "recognition" that the future patient is seriously disturbed, and may be reluctant to use help, toward a systematic view of "typical" accommodations around deviance and typical patterns of crisis.

It is, of course, by no means evident how typical the patterns we have described may be. Although the analysis is confined to certain marital family organizations and does not entirely exhaust our own empirical materials, we suggest that the presentation does touch upon two common situations encountered in work with the mentally ill and their families. In the first situation, the future patient and his immediate interpersonal community move from each other, effect patterns of uninvolvement, and reciprocate withdrawal by withdrawal. The future patient moves, and is moved, toward exclusion from interpersonal ties and from any meaningful links to a position in communal reality. This situation, as we have seen, is compatible with very high "tolerance for deviant behavior," which may permit an actively psychotic patient to remain *in* the community while not psychosocially *of* it.

The accommodation may be disrupted by a shift in the "tolerance" of the interpersonal community, however determined,[14] or from the side of the future patient by increasing agitation which signals an attempt to break out of inner and outer isolation. Here, hospitalization is a possible route toward further disengagement of the patient from his interpersonal community, or conversely, toward re-establishment of reciprocal expectations compatible with re-engagement. Whatever the outcome, a strategic

---

[14] The determinants may be extraneous to inherent family processes. Thus, in a case not included in the present sample, the movement of a family from farm to city altered the family's capacity to retain a psychotic young man and precipitated his hospitalization.

therapeutic problem is posed by the chronic pattern of mutual disinvolvement and withdrawal.

In the second situation, the future patient and a member of his immediate interpersonal community become locked in mutual involvement, effect patterns of intense interdependency, and reciprocate withdrawal by concern. The future patient moves and is moved toward a bond in which interlocking needs tie the participants together rather than isolate them. This situation is also compatible with high tolerance for deviant behavior, but here because the deviance has become a necessary component of the family integration. It is this type of family process, rather than the first type, which has attracted most psychiatric interest,[15] although there is no reason from our data to suppose that it is the more common.

In the cases observed the disruption of this accommodation took the form of an ego-alien movement by the future patient against the claims of the overwhelming attachment. Here, hospitalization is at once a route of escape from intolerable conflict in the interpersonal community, and a potential pathway toward re-establishing the earlier pattern of accommodation. The strategic therapeutic problem posed is the contrasting one of modification of a chronic pattern of intense involvement.

The observations reported do not yield precise knowledge as to how psychiatric intervention might routinely be brought about early in the development of a serious mental illness, whether or when this is advisable, and how intervention might be more effective later on. The observations indicate, rather, that we must confront these questions in their real complexity, and investigate more closely and persistently than heretofore the characteristic ways in which families cope with severe psychiatric disturbances, the ways in which these intra-family mechanisms are disrupted, and the significance of the family dynamics which form the crucial background of the eventual encounter between patient and clinician.

The Adjustment of the Family to the Crisis of Alcoholism * †

JOAN K. JACKSON

. . . Over a 3-year period, the present investigator has been an active participant in the Alcoholics Anonymous Auxiliary in Seattle. This group is composed partly of women whose husbands are or were members of Alcoholics Anonymous, and

[15] See Jackson (ed.), *op. cit.*

* Reprinted by permission of the author and publisher from *Quarterly Journal of Studies on Alcohol*, Vol. 15 (December 1954), pp. 564–586. Copyright by Journal of Studies on Alcohol, Inc., New Brunswick, N.J.

† From the Department of Psychiatry, University of Washington School of Medicine, Seattle, Washington. This report is part of an alcoholism project at the University of Washington which has been supported by the State of Washington Research Fund under Initiative 171.

partly of women whose husbands are excessive drinkers but have never contacted Alcoholics Anonymous. At a typical meeting one fifth would be the wives of Alcoholics Anonymous members who have been sober for some time; the husbands of another fifth would have recently joined the fellowship; the remainder would be equally divided between those whose husbands were "on and off" the Alcoholics Anonymous program and those whose husbands had as yet not had any contact with Alcoholics Anonymous.

At least an hour and a half of each formal meeting of this group is taken up with a frank discussion of the current family problems of the members. As in other meetings of Alcoholics Anonymous the questions are posed by describing the situation which gives rise to the problem and the answers are a narration of the personal experiences of other wives who have had a similar problem, rather than direct advice. Verbatim shorthand notes have been taken of all discussions, at the request of the group, who also make use of the notes for the group's purposes. Informal contact has been maintained with past and present members. In the past 3 years 50 women have been members of this group.

The families represented by these women are at present in many different stages of adjustment and have passed through several stages during the past few years. The continuous contact over a prolonged period permits generalizations about processes and changes in family adjustments.

In addition, in connection with research on hospitalized alcoholics, many of their wives have been interviewed. The interviews with the hospitalized alcoholics, as with male members of Alcoholics Anonymous, have also provided information on family interactions. Further information has been derived from another group of wives, not connected with Alcoholics Anonymous, and from probation officers, social workers and court officials.

The following presentation is limited insofar as it deals only with families seeking help for the alcoholism of the husband. Other families are known to have solved the problem through divorce, often without having attempted to help the alcoholic member first. Others never seek help and never separate. There were no marked differences between the two groups seeking help, one through the hospital and one through the A.A. Auxiliary. The wives of hospitalized alcoholics gave a history of the family crisis similar to that given by women in the Auxiliary.

A second limitation is that only the families of male alcoholics are dealt with. It is recognized that the findings cannot be generalized to the families of alcoholic women without further research. Due to differences between men and women in their roles in the family as well as in the pattern of drinking, it would be expected that male and female alcoholics would in some ways have a different effect on family structure and function.

A third limitation is imposed for the sake of clarity and brevity: only the accounts of the wives of their attempts to stabilize their family adjustments will be dealt with. For any complete picture, the view of the alcoholic husband would also have to be included.

It must be emphasized that this paper deals with the definitions of the family situations by the wives, rather than with the actual situation. It has been noted that frequently wife and husband do not agree on what has occurred. The degree to which the definition of the situation by the wife or husband correlates with actual behavior is a question which must be left for further research.

The families represented in this study are from the middle and lower classes. The occupations of the husbands prior to excessive drinking include small business owners, salesmen, business executives, skilled and semiskilled workers. Prior to marriage the wives have been nurses, secretaries, teachers, saleswomen, cooks or waitresses. The economic status of the childhood families of these husbands and wives ranged from very wealthy to very poor.

Method

From the records of discussions of the Alcoholics Anonymous Auxiliary, the statements of each wife were extracted and arranged in a time sequence. Notes on informal contacts were added at the point in the sequence where they occurred. The interviews with the wives of hospitalized alcoholics were similarly treated. These working records on individual families were then examined for uniformities of behavior and for regularities in changes over time.

The similarities in the process of adjustment to an alcoholic family member are presented here as stages of variable duration. It should be stressed that only the similarities are dealt with. Although the wives have shared the patterns dealt with here, there have been marked differences in the length of time between stages, in the number of stages passed through up to the present time, and in the relative importance to the family constellation of any one type of behavior. For example, all admitted nagging but the amount of nagging was variable.

When the report of this analysis was completed it was read before a meeting of the Auxiliary with a request for correction of any errors in fact or interpretation. Corrections could be presented either anonymously or publicly from the floor. Only one correction was suggested and has been incorporated. The investigator is convinced that her relationship with the group is such that there would be no reticence about offering corrections.

Throughout her contact with this group her role has been that of one who is being taught, very similar to the role of the new member. The over-all response of the group to the presentation indicated that the members individually felt that they had been portrayed accurately.

The sense of having similar problems and similar experiences is indicated also in the reactions of new members to the Auxiliary's summarization of the notes of their discussions. Copies of these summaries are given to new members, who commonly state that they find it a relief to see that their problems are far from unique and that there are methods which successfully overcome them.

Statement of the Problem

For purposes of this presentation, the family is seen as involved in a cumulative crisis. All family members behave in a manner which they hope will resolve the crisis and permit a return to stability. Each member's action is influenced by his previous personality structure, by his previous role and status in the family group, and by the history of the crisis and its effects on his personality, roles and status up to that point. Action is also influenced by the past effectiveness of that particular action as a means of social control before and during the crisis. The behavior of family members in each phase of the crisis contributes to the form which the crisis takes in the following stages and sets limits on possible behavior in subsequent stages.

Family members are influenced, in addition, by the cultural definitions of alcoholism as evidence of weakness, inadequacy or sinfulness; by the cultural prescriptions for the roles of family members; and by the cultural values of family solidarity, sanctity and self-sufficiency. Alcoholism in the family poses a situation defined by the culture as shameful but for the handling of which there are no prescriptions which are effective or which permit direct action not in conflict with other cultural prescriptions. While in crises such as illness or death the family members can draw on cultural definitions of appropriate behavior for procedures which will terminate the crisis, this is not the case with alcoholism in the family. The cultural view has been that alcoholism is shameful and should not occur. Only recently has any information been offered to guide families in their behavior toward their alcoholic member and, as yet, this information resides more in technical journals than in the media of mass communication. Thus, in facing alcoholism, the family is in an unstructured situation and must find the techniques for handling it through trial and error.

Stages in Family Adjustment to an Alcoholic Member

THE BEGINNING OF THE MARRIAGE At the time marriage was considered, the drinking of most of the men was within socially acceptable limits. In a few cases the men were already alcoholics but managed to hide this from their fiancées. They drank only moderately or not at all when on dates and often avoided friends and relatives who might expose their excessive drinking. The relatives and friends who were introduced to the fiancée were those who had hopes that "marriage would straighten him out" and thus said nothing about the drinking. In a small number of cases the men spoke with their fiancées of their alcoholism. The women had no conception of what alcoholism meant, other than that it involved more than the usual frequency of drinking, and they entered the marriage with little more preparation than if they had known nothing about it.

STAGE 1 Incidents of excessive drinking begin and, although they are sporadic,

place strains on the husband–wife interaction. In attempts to minimize drinking, problems in marital adjustment not related to the drinking are avoided.

STAGE 2 Social isolation of the family begins as incidents of excessive drinking multiply. The increasing isolation magnifies the importance of family interactions and events. Behavior and thought become drinking-centered. Husband–wife adjustment deteriorates and tension rises. The wife begins to feel self-pity and to lose her self-confidence as her behavior fails to stabilize her husband's drinking. There is an attempt still to maintain the original family structure, which is disrupted anew with each episode of drinking, and as a result the children begin to show emotional disturbance.

STAGE 3 The family gives up attempts to control the drinking and begins to behave in a manner geared to relieve tension rather than achieve long-term ends. The disturbance of the children becomes more marked. There is no longer an attempt to support the alcoholic in his roles as husband and father. The wife begins to worry about her own sanity and about her inability to make decisions or act to change the situation.

STAGE 4 The wife takes over control of the family and the husband is seen as a recalcitrant child. Pity and strong protective feelings largely replace the earlier resentment and hostility. The family becomes more stable and organized in a manner to minimize the disruptive behavior of the husband. The self-confidence of the wife begins to be rebuilt.

STAGE 5 The wife separates from her husband if she can resolve the problems and conflicts surrounding this action.

STAGE 6 The wife and children reorganize as a family without the husband.

STAGE 7 The husband achieves sobriety and the family, which had become organized around an alcoholic husband, reorganizes to include a sober father and experiences problems in reinstating him in his former roles.

STAGE 1. ATTEMPTS TO DENY THE PROBLEM

Usually the first experience with drinking as a problem arises in a social situation. The husband drinks in a manner which is inappropriate to the social setting and the expectations of others present. The wife feels embarrassed on the first occasion and humiliated as it occurs more frequently. After several such incidents she and her husband talk over his behavior. The husband either formulates an explanation for the episode and assures her that such behavior will not occur again; or he refuses to discuss it at all. For a time afterward he drinks appropriately and drinking seems to be a problem no longer. The wife looks back on the incidents and feels that she has exaggerated them, feels ashamed of herself for her disloyalty and for her behavior. The husband, in evaluating the incident, feels shame also and vows such episodes will not recur. As a result, both husband and wife attempt to make it up to the other and, for a time, try to play their conceptions of the ideal husband and wife roles, minimizing or avoiding other difficulties which arise in the marriage. They thus create the illusion of a "perfect" marriage.

Eventually another inappropriate drinking episode occurs and the pattern is repeated. The wife worries but takes action only in the situations in which inappropriate drinking occurs, as each long intervening period of acceptable drinking behavior convinces her that a recurrence is unlikely. As time goes on, in attempting to cope with individual episodes, she runs the gamut of possible trial and error behaviors, learning that none is permanently effective.

If she speaks to other people about her husband's drinking, she is usually assured that there is no need for concern, that her husband can control his drinking and that her fears are exaggerated. Some friends possibly admit that his drinking is too heavy and give advice on how they handled similar situations with their husbands. These friends convince her that her problem will be solved as soon as she hits upon the right formula for dealing with her husband's drinking.

During this stage the husband–wife interaction is in no way "abnormal." In a society in which a large proportion of the men drink, most wives have at some time had occasion to be concerned, even though only briefly, with an episode of drinking which they considered inappropriate (7). In a society in which the status of the family depends on that of the husband, the wife feels threatened by any behavior on his part which might lower it. Inappropriate drinking is regarded by her as a threat to the family's reputation and standing in the community. The wife attempts to exert control and often finds herself blocked by the sacredness of drinking behavior to men in America. Drinking is a private matter and not any business of the wife's. On the whole, a man reacts to his wife's suggestion that he has not adequately controlled his drinking with resentment, rebelliousness and a display of emotion which makes rational discussion difficult. The type of husband–wife interaction outlined in this stage has occurred in many American families in which the husband never became an excessive drinker.

STAGE 2. ATTEMPTS TO ELIMINATE THE PROBLEMS

Stage 2 begins when the family experiences social isolation because of the husband's drinking. Invitations to the homes of friends become less frequent. When the couple does visit friends, drinks are not served or are limited, thus emphasizing the reason for exclusion from other social activities of the friendship group. Discussions of drinking begin to be side-stepped awkwardly by friends, the wife and the husband.

By this time the periods of socially acceptable drinking are becoming shorter. The wife, fearing that the full extent of her husband's drinking will become known, begins to withdraw from social participation, hoping to reduce the visibility of his behavior, and thus the threat to family status.

Isolation is further intensified because the family usually acts in accordance with the cultural dictate that it should be self-sufficient and manage to resolve its own problems without recourse to outside aid. Any experiences which they have had with well-meaning outsiders, usually relatives, have tended to strengthen this conviction. The husband has defined such relatives as interfering and the situation has deteriorated rather than improved.

With increasing isolation, the family members begin to lose perspective on their interaction and on their problems. Thrown into closer contact with one another as outside contacts diminish, the behavior of each member assumes exaggerated importance. The drinking behavior becomes the focus of anxiety. Gradually all family difficulties become attributed to it. (For example, the mother who is cross with her children will feel that, if her husband had not been drinking, she would not have been so tense and would not have been angry.) The fear that the full extent of drinking may be discovered mounts steadily; the conceptualization of the consequences of such a discovery becomes increasingly vague and, as a result, more anxiety-provoking. The family feels different from others and alone with its shameful secret.

Attempts to cover up increase. The employer who calls to inquire about the husband's absence from work is given excuses. The wife is afraid to face the consequences of loss of the husband's pay check in addition to her other concerns. Questions from the children are evaded or they are told that their father is ill. The wife lives in terror of the day when the children will be told by others of the nature of the "illness." She is also afraid that the children may describe their father's symptoms to teachers or neighbors. Still feeling that the family must solve its own problems, she keeps her troubles to herself and hesitates to seek outside help. If her husband beats her, she will bear it rather than call in the police. (Indeed, often she has no idea that this is even a possibility.) Her increased isolation has left her without the advice of others as to sources of help in the community. If she knows of them, an agency contact means to her an admission of the complete failure of her family as an independent unit. For the middle-class woman particularly, recourse to social agencies and law-enforcement agencies means a terrifying admission of loss of status.

During this stage, husband and wife are drawing further apart. Each feels resentful of the behavior of the other. When this resentment is expressed, further drinking occurs. When it is not, tension mounts and the next drinking episode is that much more destructive of family relationships. The reasons for drinking are explored frantically. Both husband and wife feel that if only they could discover the reason, all members of the family could gear their behavior to making drinking unnecessary. The discussions become increasingly unproductive, as it is the husband's growing conviction that his wife does not and cannot understand him.

On her part, the wife begins to feel that she is a failure, that she has been unable to fulfill the major cultural obligations of a wife to meet her husband's needs. With her increasing isolation, her sense of worth derives almost entirely from her roles as wife and mother. Each failure to help her husband gnaws away at her sense of adequacy as a person.

Periods of sobriety or socially acceptable drinking still occur. These periods keep the wife from making a permanent or stable adjustment. During them her husband, in his guilt, treats her like a queen. His behavior renews her hope and rekindles positive feelings toward him. Her sense of worth is bolstered temporarily and she grasps desperately at her husband's reassurance that she is really a fine person and not a failure and an unlovable shrew. The periods of sobriety also keep her family from facing the inability of the husband to control his drinking. The inaccuracies of the cultural stereotype of the alcoholic—particularly that he is in a constant state of inebriation—also contribute to the family's rejection of the idea of alcoholism, as the husband seems to demonstrate from time to time that he can control his drinking.

Family efforts to control the husband become desperate. There are no culturally prescribed behavior patterns for handling such a situation and the family is forced to evolve its own techniques. Many different types of behavior are tried but none brings consistent results; there seems to be no way of predicting the consequences of any action that may be taken. All attempts to stabilize or structure the situation to permit consistent behavior fail. Threats of leaving, hiding his liquor away, emptying the bottles down the drain, curtailing his money, are tried in rapid succession, but none is effective. Less punitive methods, as discussing the situation when he is sober, babying him during hangovers, and trying to drink with him to keep him in the home, are attempted and fail. All be-

havior becomes oriented around the drinking, and the thought of family members becomes obsessive on this subject. As no action seems to be successful in achieving its goal, the wife persists in trial-and-error behavior with mounting frustration. Long-term goals recede into the background and become secondary to just keeping the husband from drinking today.

There is still an attempt to maintain the illusion of husband–wife–children roles. When father is sober, the children are expected to give him respect and obedience. The wife also defers to him in his role as head of the household. Each drinking event thus disrupts family functioning anew. The children begin to show emotional disturbances as a result of the inconsistencies of parental behavior. During periods when the husband is drinking the wife tries to shield them from the knowledge and effects of his behavior, at the same time drawing them closer to herself and deriving emotional support from them. In sober periods, the father tries to regain their favor. Due to experiencing directly only pleasant interactions with their father, considerable affection is often felt for him by the children. This affection becomes increasingly difficult for the isolated wife to tolerate, and an additional source of conflict. She feels that she needs and deserves the love and support of her children and, at the same time, she feels it important to maintain the children's picture of their father. She counts on the husband's affection for the children to motivate a cessation of drinking as he comes to realize the effects of his behavior on them.

In this stage, self-pity begins to be felt by the wife, if it has not entered previously. It continues in various degrees throughout the succeeding stages. In an attempt to handle her deepening sense of inadequacy, the wife often tries to convince herself that she is right and her husband wrong, and this also continues through the following stages. At this point the wife often resembles what Whalen (5) describes as "The Sufferer."

STAGE 3. DISORGANIZATION

The wife begins to adopt a "What's the use?" attitude and to accept her husband's drinking as a problem likely to be permanent. Attempts to understand one another become less frequent. Sober periods still engender hope, but hope qualified by skepticism; they bring about a lessening of anxiety and this is defined as happiness.

By this time some customary patterns of husband–wife–children interaction have evolved. Techniques which have had some effectiveness in controlling the husband in the past or in relieving pent-up frustration are used by the wife. She nags, berates or retreats into silence. Husband and wife are both on the alert, the wife watching for increasing irritability and restlessness which mean a recurrence of drinking, and the husband for veiled aspersions on his behavior or character.

The children are increasingly torn in their loyalties as they become tools in the struggle between mother and father. If the children are at an age of comprehension, they have usually learned the true nature of their family situation, either from outsiders or from their mother, who has given up attempts to bolster her husband's position as father. The children are often bewildered but questioning their parents brings no satisfactory answers as the parents themselves do not understand what is happening. Some children become terrified; some have increasing behavior problems within and outside the home; others seem on the surface to accept the situation calmly.[1]

During periods of the husband's drinking, the hostility, resentment and frustrations felt by the couple is allowed expression. Both may resort to violence—the wife in self-defense or because she can find no other outlet for her feelings. In those cases in which the wife retaliates to violence in kind, she feels a mixture of relief and intense shame at having deviated so far from what she conceives to be "the behavior of a normal woman."

When the wife looks at her present behavior, she worries about her "normality." In comparing the person she was in the early years of her marriage with the person she has become, she is frightened. She finds herself nagging and unable to control herself. She resolves to stand up to her husband when he is belligerent but instead finds herself cringing in terror and then despises herself for her lack of courage. If she retaliates with violence, she is filled with self-loathing at behaving in an "unwomanly" manner. She finds herself compulsively searching for bottles, knowing full well that finding them will change nothing, and is worried because she engages in such senseless behavior. She worries about her inability to take constructive action of any kind. She is confused about where her loyalty lies, whether with her husband or her children. She feels she is a failure as a wife, mother and person. She believes she should be strong in the face of adversity and instead feels herself weak.

The wife begins to find herself avoiding sexual contact with her husband when he has been drinking. Sex under these circumstances, she feels, is sex for its own sake rather than an indication of affection for her. Her husband's lack of consideration of her needs to be satisfied leaves her feeling frustrated. The lack of sexual responsiveness reflects her emotional withdrawal from him in other

---

[1] Some effects of alcoholism of the father on children have been discussed by Newell (8).

areas of family life. Her husband, on his part, feels frustrated and rejected; he accuses her of frigidity and this adds to her concern about her adequacy as a woman.[2]

By this time the opening wedge has been inserted into the self-sufficiency of the family. The husband has often been in difficulty with the police and the wife has learned that police protection is available. An emergency has occurred in which the seeking of outside help was the only possible action to take; subsequent calls for aid from outsiders do not require the same degree of urgency before they can be undertaken. However, guilt and a lessening of self-respect and self-confidence accompany this method of resolving emergencies. The husband intensifies these feelings by speaking of the interference of outsiders, or of his night in jail.

In Stage 3 all is chaos. Few problems are met constructively. The husband and wife both feel trapped in an intolerable, unstructured situation which offers no way out. The wife's self-assurance is almost completely gone. She is afraid to take action and afraid to let things remain as they are. Fear is one of the major characteristics of this stage: fear of violence, fear of personality damage to the children, fear for her own sanity, fear that relatives will interfere, and fear that they will not help in an emergency. Added to this, the family feels alone in the world and helpless. The problems, and the behavior of family members in attempting to cope with them, seem so shameful that help from others is unthinkable. They feel that attempts to get help would meet only with rebuff, and

that communication of the situation will engender disgust.

At this point the clinical picture which the wife presents is very similar to what Whalen (5) has described as "The Waverer."

STAGE 4. ATTEMPTS TO REORGANIZE IN SPITE OF THE PROBLEMS

Stage 4 begins when a crisis occurs which necessitates that action be taken. There may be no money or food in the house; the husband may have been violent to the children; or life on the level of Stage 3 may have become intolerable. At this point some wives leave, thus entering directly into Stage 5.

The wife who passes through Stage 4 usually begins to ease her husband out of his family roles. She assumes husband and father roles. This involves strengthening her role as mother and putting aside her role as wife. She becomes the manager of the home, the discipliner of the children, the decision-maker; she becomes somewhat like Whalen's (5) "Controller." She either ignores her husband as much as possible or treats him as her most recalcitrant child. Techniques are worked out for getting control of his pay check, if there still is one, and money is doled out to her husband on the condition of his good behavior. When he drinks, she threatens to leave him, locks him out of the house, refuses to pay his taxi bills, leaves him in jail overnight rather than pay his bail. Where her obligations to her husband conflict with those to her children, she decides in favor of the latter. As she views her husband increasingly as a child, pity and a sense of

[2] It is of interest here that marriage counselors and students of marital adjustment are of the opinion that unhappy marriage results in poor sexual adjustment more often than poor sexual adjustment leads to unhappy marriage. If this proves to be true, it would be expected that most wives of alcoholics would find sex distasteful while their husbands were drinking. The wives of the inactive alcoholics report that their sexual adjustments with their husbands are currently satisfactory; many of those whose husbands are still drinking state that they enjoyed sexual relationships before the alcoholism was established.

being desperately needed by him enter. Her inconsistent behavior toward him, deriving from the lack of predictability inherent in the situation up to now, becomes reinforced by her mixed feelings toward him.

In this stage the husband often tries to set his will against hers in decisions about the children. If the children have been permitted to stay with a friend overnight, he may threaten to create a scene unless they return immediately. He may make almost desperate efforts to gain their affection and respect, his behavior ranging from getting them up in the middle of the night to fondle them, to giving them stiff lectures on children's obligations to fathers. Sometimes he will attempt to align the males of the family with him against the females. He may openly express resentment of the children and become belligerent toward them physically or verbally.

Much of the husband's behavior can be conceptualized as resulting from an increasing awareness of his isolation from the other members of the family and their steady withdrawal of respect and affection. It seems to be a desperate effort to regain what he has lost, but without any clear idea of how this can be accomplished—an effort to change a situation in which everyone is seen as against him; and, in reality, this is becoming more and more true. As the wife has taken over control of the family with some degree of success, he feels, and becomes, less and less necessary to the ongoing activity of the family. There are fewer and fewer roles left for him to play. He becomes aware that members of the family enjoy each other's company without him. When he is home he tries to enter this circle of warmth or to smash it. Either way he isolates himself further. He finds that the children discuss with the mother how to manage him and he sees the children acting on the basis of

their mother's idea of him. The children refuse to pay attention to his demands: they talk back to him in the same way that they talk back to one another, adding pressure on him to assume the role of just another child. All this leaves him frustrated and, as a result, often aggressive or increasingly absent from home.

The children, on the whole, become more settled in their behavior as the wife takes over the family responsibilities. Decisions are made by her and upheld in the face of their father's attempts to interfere. Participation in activities outside the home is encouraged. Their patterns of interaction with their father are supported by the mother. Whereas in earlier stages the children often felt that there were causal connections between their actions and their father's drinking, they now accept his unpredictability. "Well," says a 6-year old, "I'll just have to get used to it. I have a drunken father."

The family is more stabilized in one way but in other ways insecurities are multiplied. Pay checks are received less and less regularly. The violence or withdrawal of the father increases. When he is away the wife worries about automobile accidents or injury in fights, which become more and more probable as time passes. The husband may begin to be seriously ill from time to time; his behavior may become quite bizarre. Both of these signs of increasing illness arouse anxiety in the family.

During this stage hopes may rise high for father's "reform" when he begins to verbalize wishes to stop drinking, admits off and on his inability to stop, and sounds desperate for doing something about his drinking. Now may begin the trek to sanitariums for the middle-class alcoholic, to doctors, or to Alcoholics Anonymous. Where just the promise to stop drinking has failed to revive hope, sobriety through outside agencies has the ability to rekindle it brightly. There is the feeling that at last he is "taking really constructive action." In failure the discouragement is deeper. Here another wedge has been inserted into the self-sufficiency of the family.

By this time the wedges are many. The wife, finding she has managed to bring some semblance of order and stability to her family, while not exactly becoming a self-assured person, has regained some sense of worth which grows a little with each crisis she meets successfully. In addition, the very fact of taking action to stabilize the situation brings relief. On some occasion she may be able to approach social agencies for financial help, often during a period when the husband has temporarily deserted or is incarcerated. She may have gone to the family court; she may have consulted a lawyer about getting a restraining order when the husband was in a particularly belligerent state. She has begun to learn her way around among the many agencies which offer help.

Often she has had a talk with an Alcoholics Anonymous member and has begun to look into what is known about alcoholism. If she has attended a few Alcoholics Anonymous meetings, her sense of shame has been greatly alleviated as she finds so many others in the same boat. Her hopes rise as she meets alcoholics who have stopped drinking, and she feels relieved at being able to discuss her problems openly for the first time with an audience which understands fully. She begins to gain perspective on her problem and learns that she herself is involved in what happens to her husband, and that she must change. She exchanges techniques of management with other wives and receives their support in her decisions.

She learns that her husband is ill rather than merely "ornery," and this often serves to quell for the time being thoughts about leaving him which have begun to germinate as she has gained more self-confidence. She learns that help is available but also that her efforts to push him into help are unavailing. She is not only supported in her recently evolved behavior of thinking first of her family, but now this course also emerges from the realm of the unconceptualized and is set in an accepted rationale. She feels more secure in having a reason and a certainty that the group accepts her as "doing the right thing." When she reports deviations from what the group thinks is the "right way," her reasons are understood; she receives solid support but there is also pressure on her to alter her behavior again toward the acceptable. Blaming and self-pity are actively discouraged. In group discussions she still admits to such feelings but learns to recognize them as they arise and to go beyond them to more productive thinking.

How much her altered behavior changes the family situation is uncertain, but it helps her and gives her security from which to venture forth to further actions of a consistent and constructive type, constructive at least from the point of view of keeping her family on as even a keel as possible in the face of the disruptive influence of the husband. With new friends whom she can use as a sounding board for plans, and with her growing acquaintance with the alternatives and possible patterns of behavior, her thinking ceases to be circular and unproductive. Her anxiety about her own sanity is alleviated as she is reassured by others that they have experienced the same concern and that the remedy is to get her own life and her family under better control. As she accomplishes this, the difference in her feelings about herself convinces her that this is so.

Whether or not she has had a contact with wives of Alcoholics Anonymous members or other wives who have been through a similar experience and have emerged successfully, the very fact of taking hold of her situation and gradually making it more manageable adds to her self-confidence. As her husband is less and less able to care for himself or his family, she begins to feel that he needs her and that without her he would be destroyed. Such a feeling makes it difficult for her to think of leaving him. His almost complete social isolation at this point and his cries for help reinforce this conviction of being needed.

The drinking behavior is no longer hidden. Others obviously know about it, and this becomes accepted by the wife and children. Already isolated and insulated against possible rejection, the wife is often surprised to find that she has exaggerated her fears of what would happen were the situation known. However, the unpredictability of her husband's behavior makes her reluctant to form social relationships which could be violently disrupted or to involve others in the possible consequences of his behavior.

STAGE 5. EFFORTS TO ESCAPE THE PROBLEMS

Stage 5 may be the terminal one for the marriage. In this stage the wife separates from her husband. Sometimes the marriage is reestablished after a period of sobriety, when it appears certain that the husband will not drink again. If he does revert to drinking, the marriage is sometimes finally terminated but with less emotional stress than the first time. If the husband deserts, being no longer able to tolerate his lack of status in his family, Stage 6 may be entered abruptly.

The events precipitating the decision to terminate the marriage may be near-catastrophic, as when there is an attempt by the husband to kill the wife or children, or they may appear trivial to out-siders, being only the last straw to an accumulation of years.

The problems in coming to the decision to terminate the marriage cannot be underestimated. Some of these problems derive from emotional conflicts; some are related to very practical circumstances in the situation; some are precipitated by the conflicting advice of outsiders. With several children dependent on her, the wife must decide whether the present situation is more detrimental to them than future situations she can see arising if she should leave her husband. The question of where the money to live on will come from must be thought out. If she can get a job, will there be enough to provide for child care also while she is away from home? Should the children, who have already experienced such an unsettled life, be separated from her to be cared for by others? If the family still owns its own home, how can she retain control of it? If she leaves, where can she go? What can be done to tide the family over until her first earnings come in? How can she ensure her husband's continued absence from the home and thus be certain of the safety of individuals and property in her absence? These are only a small sample of the practical issues that must be dealt with in trying to think her way through to a decision to terminate the marriage.

Other pressures act on her to impede the decision-making process. "If he would only stay drunk till I carry out what I intend to do," is a frequent statement. When the husband realizes that his wife really means to leave, he frequently sobers up, watches his behavior in the home, plays on her latent and sometimes conscious feelings of her responsibility for the situation, stresses his need for her and that without her he is lost, tears away at any confidence she has that she will be able to manage by herself, and threatens her and the children with injury or with his own suicide if she carries out her intention.

The children, in the meantime, are pulling and pushing on her emotions. They think she is "spineless" to stay but unfair to father's chances for ultimate recovery if she leaves. Relatives, who were earlier alienated in her attempts to shield her family but now know of the situation, do not believe in its full ramifications. They often feel she is exaggerating and persuade her to stay with him. Especially is this true in the case of a "solitary drinker." His drinking has been so well concealed that the relatives have no way of knowing the true nature of the situation. Other relatives, afraid that they will be called on for support, exert pressure to keep the marriage intact and the husband thereby responsible for debts. Relatives who feel she should leave him overplay their hands by berating the husband in such a manner as to evoke her defense of him. This makes conscious the positive aspects of her relationship with him, causing her to waver in her decision. If she consults organized agencies, she often gets conflicting advice. The agencies concerned with the well-being of the family may counsel leaving; those concerned with rehabilitating the husband may press her to stay. In addition, help from public organizations almost always involves delay and is frequently not forthcoming at the point where she needs it most.

The wife must come to terms with her own mixed feelings about her husband, her marriage and herself before she can decide on such a step as breaking up the marriage. She must give up hope that she can be of any help to her husband. She must command enough self-confidence, after years of having it eroded, to be able to face an unknown future and leave the security of an unpalatable but familiar past and present. She must accept that she has failed in her marriage, not an easy thing to do after having devoted years to stopping up the cracks in the family structure as they appeared. Breaking up the marriage involves a complete alteration in the life goals toward which all her behavior has been oriented. It is hard for her to rid herself of the feeling that she married him and he is her responsibility. Having thought and planned for so long on a day-to-day basis, it is difficult to plan for a long-term future.

Her taking over of the family raises her self-confidence but failure to carry through on decisions undermines the new gains that she has made. Vacillation in her decisions tends to exasperate the agencies trying to help her, and she begins to feel that help from them may not be forthcoming if she finally decides to leave.

Some events, however, help her to arrive at a decision. During the absences of her husband she has seen how manageable life can be and how smoothly her family can run. She finds that life goes on without him. The wife who is working comes to feel that "my husband is a luxury I can no longer afford." After a few short-term separations in which she tries out her wings successfully, leaving comes to look more possible. Another step on the path to leaving is the acceptance of the idea that, although she cannot help her husband, she can help her family. She often reaches a state of such emotional isolation from her husband that his behavior no longer disturbs her emotionally but is only something annoying which upsets daily routines and plans.

STAGE 6. REORGANIZATION OF
PART OF THE FAMILY

The wife is without her husband and must reorganize her family on this basis. Substantially the process is similar to that in other divorced families, but with some additions. The divorce rarely cuts her relationships to her husband. Unless she and her family disappear, her husband may make attempts to come back. When drunk, he may endanger her job by calls at her place of work. He may attempt violence against members of the family, or he may contact the children and work to gain their loyalty so that pressure is put on the mother to accept him again. Looking back on her marriage, she forgets the full impact of the problem situation on her and on the children and feels more warmly toward her husband, and these feelings can still be manipulated by him. The wide circulation of information on alcoholism as an illness engenders guilt about having deserted a sick man. Gradually, however, the family becomes reorganized.

STAGE 7. RECOVERY AND REORGANIZATION OF THE WHOLE FAMILY

Stage 7 is entered if the husband achieves sobriety, whether or not separation has preceded. It was pointed out that in earlier stages most of the problems in the marriage were attributed to the alcoholism of the husband, and thus problems in adjustment not related directly to the drinking were unrecognized and unmet. Also, the "sober personality" of the husband was thought of as the "real" personality, with a resulting lack of recognition of other factors involved in his sober behavior, such as remorse and guilt over his actions, leading him to act to the best of his ability like "the ideal husband" when sober. Irritation or other signs of growing tension were viewed as indicators of further drinking, and hence the problems giving rise to them were walked around gingerly rather than faced and resolved. Lack of conflict and lack of drinking were defined as

indicating a perfect adjustment. For the wife and husband facing a sober marriage after many years of an alcoholic marriage, the expectations of what marriage without alcoholism will be are unrealistically idealistic, and the reality of marriage almost inevitably brings disillusionments. The expectation that all would go well and that all problems be resolved with the cessation of the husband's drinking cannot be met and this threatens the marriage from time to time.

The beginning of sobriety for the husband does not bring too great hope to the family at first. They have been through this before but are willing to help him along and stand by him in the new attempt. As the length of sobriety increases, so do the hopes for its permanence and efforts to be of help. The wife at first finds it difficult to think more than in terms of today, waking each morning with fear of what the day will bring and sighing with relief at the end of each sober day.

With the continuation of sobriety, many problems begin to crop up. Mother has for years managed the family, and now father again wishes to be reinstated in his former roles. Usually the first role reestablished is that of breadwinner, and the economic problems of the family begin to be alleviated as debts are gradually paid and there is enough left over for current needs. With the resumption of this role, the husband feels that the family should also accept him at least as a partner in the management of the family. Even if the wife is willing to hand over some of the control of the children, for example, the children often are not able to accept this change easily. Their mother has been both parents for so long that it takes time to get used to the idea of consulting their father on problems and asking for his decisions. Often the father tries too hard to manage this change overnight, and the very pressure put on the children toward this end defeats him. In addition, he is unable to meet many of the demands the children make on him because he has never really become acquainted with them or learned to understand them and is lacking in much necessary background knowledge of their lives.

The wife, who finds it difficult to conceive of her husband as permanently sober, feels an unwillingness to let control slip from her hands. At the same time she realizes that reinstatement of her husband in his family roles is necessary to his sobriety. She also realizes that the closer his involvement in the family the greater the probability of his remaining sober. Yet she remembers events in the past in which his failure to handle his responsibilities was catastrophic to the family. Used to avoiding anything which might upset him, the wife often hesitates to discuss problems openly. At times, if she is successful in helping him to regain his roles as father, she feels resentful of his intrusion into territory she has come to regard as hers. If he makes errors in judgment which affect the family adversely, her former feelings of being his superior may come to the fore and affect her interaction with him. If the children begin to turn to him, she may feel a resurgence of self-pity at being left out and find herself attempting to swing the children back toward herself. Above all, however, she finds herself feeling resentful that some other agency achieved what she and the children could not.

Often the husband makes demands for obedience, for consideration and for pampering which members of the family feel unable to meet. He may become rather euphoric as his sobriety continues and feel superior for a time.

Gradually, however, the drinking problem sinks into the past and marital adjustment at some level is achieved. Even when this has occurred, the drinking problem crops up occasionally, as when the time comes for a decision about whether the children should be permitted to drink. The mother at such times becomes anxious, sees in the child traits which remind her of her husband, worries whether these are the traits which mean future alcoholism. At parties, at first, she is watchful and concerned about whether her husband will take a drink or not. Relatives and friends may, in a party mood, make the husband the center of attention by emphasizing his nondrinking. They may unwittingly cast aspersions on his character by trying to convince him that he can now "drink like a man." Some relatives and friends have gone so far as secretly to "spike" a non-alcoholic drink and then cry "bottoms up!" without realizing the risk of reactivating patterns from the past.

If sobriety has come through Alcoholics Anonymous, the husband frequently throws himself so wholeheartedly into A.A. activities that his wife sees little of him and feels neglected. As she worries less about his drinking, she may press him to cut down on these activities. That this is dangerous, since A.A. activity is correlated with success in Alcoholics Anonymous, has been shown by Lahey (9). Also, the wife discovers that, though she has a sober husband, she is by no means free of alcoholics. In his Twelfth Step work, he may keep the house filled with men he is helping. In the past her husband has avoided self-searching; and now he may become excessively introspective, and it may be difficult for her to deal with this.

If the husband becomes sober through Alcoholics Anonymous and the wife participates actively in groups open to her, the thoughts of what is happening to her, to her husband and to her family will be verbalized and interpreted within the framework of the Alcoholics Anonymous philosophy and the situation will probably be more tolerable and more easily worked out. . . .

Summary

The onset of alcoholism in a family member has been viewed as precipitating a cumulative crisis for the family. Seven critical stages have been delineated. Each stage affects the form which the following one will take. The family finds itself in an unstructured situation which is undefined by the culture. Thus it is forced to evolve techniques of adjustment by trial and error. The unpredictability of the situation, added to its lack of structure, engenders anxiety in family members which gives rise to personality difficulties. Factors in the culture, in the environment and within the family situation prolong the crisis and deter the working out of permanent adjustment patterns. With the arrest of the alcoholism, the crisis enters its final stage. The family attempts to reorganize to include the ex-alcoholic and makes adjustments to the changes which have occurred in him.

It has been suggested that the clinical picture presented by the wife to helping agencies is not only indicative of a type of basic personality structure but also of the stage in family adjustment to an alcoholic. That the wives of alcoholics represent a rather limited number of personality types can be interpreted in two ways, which are not mutually exclusive.

(*a*) That women with certain personality attributes tend to select alcoholics or potential alcoholics as husbands in order to satisfy unconscious personality needs;

(*b*) That women undergoing similar experiences of stress, within similarly unstructured situations, defined by the culture and reacted to by members of the society in such a manner as to place limits on the range of possible behavior, will emerge from this experience showing many similar neurotic personality traits. As the situation evolves some of these personality traits will also change. Changes have been observed in the women studied which correlate with altered family interaction patterns. This hypothesis is supported also by observations on the behavior of individuals in other unstructured situations, in situations involving conflicting goals and loyalties, and in situations in which they were isolated from supporting group interaction. It is congruent also with the theory of reactions to increased and decreased stress.

References

1. MOWER, H. R. A psychocultural analysis of the alcoholic. *Amer. Sociol. Rev.* 5: 546–557, 1940.
2. BACON, S. D. Excessive drinking and the institution of the family. In: Alcohol, Science and Society; Lecture 16. New Haven; *Quarterly Journal of Studies on Alcohol;* 1945.
3. BAKER, S. M. Social case work with inebriates. In: Alcohol, Science and Society; Lecture 27. New Haven; *Quarterly Journal of Studies on Alcohol;* 1945.
4. FUTTERMAN, S. Personality trends in wives of alcoholics. *J. Psychiat. Soc. Work* 23: 37–41, 1953.
5. WHALEN, T. Wives of alcoholics: four types observed in a family service agency. *Quart. J. Stud. Alc.* 14: 632–641, 1953.
6. PRICE, G. M. A study of the wives of

20 alcoholics. *Quart. J. Stud. Alc.* 5: 620–627, 1945.

7. CLUB AND EDUCATIONAL BUREAUS OF NEWSWEEK. Is alcoholism everyone's problem? Platform, N. Y., p. 3, Jan. 1950.

8. NEWELL, N. Alcoholism and the fa-ther-image. *Quart. J. Stud. Alc.* 11: 92–96, 1950.

9. LAHEY, W. W. *A Comparison of Social and Personal Factors Identified with Selected Members of Alcoholics Anonymous.* Master's Thesis; University of Southern California; 1950.

CULTURAL RULES ON TYPING

3

Perceptual bias operates in a number of ways when persons are given the opportunity to play defining agent. Deviations of a similar kind within families of different social classes are experienced differently. Relative tolerance of deviance can be seen in the varying speed with which persons seize on a deviant category to which they can assign the deviating party. When disinterested defining agents (e.g., doctors) confront deviance the meanings they impute often vary with the class backgrounds of the deviators. And when the deviator is a stranger to the prevailing culture, ease in assigning deviant status is immeasurably greater.

In the first reading in this section, Jewell shows us why it was a simple matter to label a displaced young Navaho as psychotic. In the next selection Hollingshead and Redlich make clear that it is easier to find persons "incurable" if their social class backgrounds are distant from that of the psychiatrist.

The pace of labeling is generally slow inside the family. But Mercer indicates that middle class parents are quicker than lower class parents to define their children as mentally retarded, quicker to get third party support in gaining the children's commitment, and more likely to secure longer hospital stays for the youngsters.

A Case of a "Psychotic" Navaho Indian Male * †

DONALD P. JEWELL

. . . The writer had the opportunity recently to make a rather extensive observation of a Navaho Indian institutionalized as a psychotic in a California state mental hospital. By drawing from the literature of Navaho ethnopsychology and the writer's own experience among the Navaho people, it was hoped that the dynamics of the patient's maladjustment would be revealed. It was also anticipated that some sort of psychotherapy would evolve.

This report is a summary of those endeavors to understand and assist the Navaho patient. Cultural and linguistic obstacles prohibited an ideal approach, but enough was accomplished to permit considerable insight into the patient's behavior. There were features about the patient's personality which would not fit harmoniously with concepts of psychiatric symptomatology derived from European culture, those concepts dealing particularly with the dynamics of the patient's diagnosis of catatonic schizophrenia. The unique characteristics of this individual's personality lead, in fact, to the question as to what extent he should be considered psychotic, and whether that consideration should be viewed from Navaho or Anglo perspective.

During his many interviews with the patient, some of them with the aid of a Navaho interpreter, the writer developed an increasing awareness that to call the patient psychotic was an arbitary matter. When this Navaho is referred to as psychotic, then, it is merely because he carried such a diagnosis during his 18 months of hospitalization as a mental patient.

Orientation

Considerable literary attention has been given to the general psychological characteristics of Navaho Indians [3, 5]. These have related psychological findings to ethnological contexts, and so offer a background against which the atypical Navaho individual may be examined.

On the behavioral level, the Navahos are in many ways unique, with respect not only to white people but to other Indian tribes as well. One of their most characteristic traits may be seen in crisis situations. Kluckhohn and Leighton describe it as a passive resistance, the individual masking his fear by quiet unmovingness, an appearance of stoicism. If forced into action, the response is a mechanical, apparently uncomprehending behavior [5, p. 108].

Another form of withdrawal is often expressed in periods of depression, apparently a morbid preoccupation with health [5, p. 110].

* Reprinted from *Human Organization*, *11*, No. 1:32–36 (1952) by permission of the author and The Society for Applied Anthropology.

† This study was undertaken during the writer's internship in Clinical Psychology at Patton State Hospital, Patton, California. The writer wishes to gratefully acknowledge the supervision of this study by Mr. William Walcott, Clinical Psychologist and Supervisor of Interns. This study was made possible by the interest and cooperation of Dr. Otto L. Gericke, Superintendent of the hospital.

These being salient aspects of the typical Navaho personality, the question now arises as to how those traits would be characterized on the psychotic level. Under prolonged psychological stress, what would develop from the stoicism and moods of morbid preoccupation?

In an endeavor to answer this question a survey was made of those mental hospitals which would most likely be caring for Navaho patients. The Bureau of Indian Affairs' policy is not to concentrate Indian patients, but to subsidize their care in whatever hospital they may have been committed. It is thus possible that a few Navahos may be hospitalized some distance from their reservation area of New Mexico, Utah, and Arizona, and have not been located in this survey. It is felt, however, that a survey of those mental hospitals in the Southwest only would be adequate to show general trends. The findings are summarized in the following table.

TABLE 1

**Summary of Survey of Navaho Indian Mental Patients
Hospitalized in Southwestern United States,
Excluding Mental Defectives ***

Diagnosis	*Number*	*Sex and Age* †
Psychosis with syphilis of the C.N.S.	2	1f: 47; 1m: 31
Psychosis with cerebral arteriosclerosis	1	1f: 62
Psychosis due to trauma (organic)	1	1m: 47
Epilepsy	8	6m: 20, 24, 29, 33, 37, 39; 2f: 20, 32
Schizophrenia, simple type	1	1m: 25
Schizophrenia, mixed type	1	1f: 26
Schizophrenia, hebephrenic type	1	1f: 30
Schizophrenia, catatonic type	7	4m: 26, 28, 28, 36; 3f: 20, 30, 38
Depressed state	1	1f: 37
Manic depressive psychosis, manic type	1	1m: 42

* Acknowledgment of the hospitals cooperating in this survey must be regretfully omitted due to the need to protect the identity of the patients.
† f, female; m, male.

Elimination of the organic psychoses leaves one manic, one depressive, and 10 schizophrenics. Of the schizophrenics, seven are catatonic. This is an unusually high incidence of catatonic schizophrenia, and seems to indicate that Navahos are predisposed toward that particular psychosis. This immediately suggests that the above-described stoicism has been carried to pathological extremes, and possibly that the stoicism is actually a transient form of catatonia. It was with this problem in mind that the Navaho patient discussed in this report was studied.

The Patient

The patient was a 26-year-old Navaho male. For purposes of anonymity he will be referred to as Bill. He came to the writer's attention through a survey of Indian patients at the hospital. He was the only Navaho of 13 Indian patients scattered throughout the various wards and cottages, and of the 4,000 general patient population.

The outlook for examination and therapy seemed at first quite discouraging. The patient was in a cottage ordinarily reserved for the most regressed patients.

Unlike most of the others in this cottage, however, he was not there because of repeated failure of such routine therapies as shock treatment, occupational therapy, etc. It was unusual for a patient in his condition, who had been at the hospital for eight months, not to have received at least electric shock treatment.

A preliminary period was spent at the cottage, observing Bill's behavior. He was very withdrawn. Most of his day was spent in inactive sitting or sleeping. He would rouse himself only for eating or attending to other personal needs. He would assist with floor waxing, dish washing, or other activities the attendants might require of him, but in a perfunctory and apathetic manner. His behavior was not patently catatonic, but certainly suggestive of it.

Most of the attendants reported never having heard Bill speak. A few, however, indicated that Bill would occasionally approach them and, in almost unintelligible English, ask if he could go home.

Shortly thereafter Bill was brought to the writer's office where he was greeted in Navaho. Bill responded in that language, glancing briefly at the writer before returning his gaze to the floor.

This closer inspection of Bill revealed occipital flattening, resulting from the cradle board as a child, and the pierced ear lobes of a conservative Navaho. During this first interview he complained about the close hair cuts he received at the hospital, further evidence that he belonged to the old-fashioned, "longhair" conservatives of the reservation.

The interview proceeded very slowly, but gradually a system of communication began to evolve. By utilizing mutually understood Navaho and English words, by means of pantomime, and with the aid of penciled sketches, the system became increasingly refined during the following interviews.

Bill was seen three hours a week for three months. The writer then took an eight months' leave of absence from the hospital, during which time he spent several months in Bill's home area near Shiprock, New Mexico.

While in the Shiprock area, the writer endeavored to locate Bill's family to advise them of the patient's circumstances. Bill had previously drawn a map indicating the approximate location of his family's *hogans* (dwellings), but it proved impossible to find them. The *hogans* were located about 5 miles from the nearest road, and even if a horse and interpreter had been available the chances of locating the specific *hogans* were slight. The situation was complicated by the fact that the family did not have American names and the writer did not know their Navaho names. Missionaries and Bureau of Indian Affairs personnel were consequently given the problem of finding the family but several months elapsed before they were equipped with sufficient information to do so.

Although he could not communicate with Bill's family, the writer succeeded in talking with several Navahos who had known Bill, and in obtaining ecological and further case history material.

Shortly after the writer's return to the hospital a Navaho interpreter was brought in from the Sherman Institute, a large Indian school not far from the hospital. Interviews with the patient through the interpreter corroborated the case history material obtained, and further satisfied the writer in his clinical evaluation of the patient. Both of these areas are separately discussed in the following text.

Case History

The gathering of Bill's history extended over a period of 11 months, and was obtained piecemeal from a variety of sources. In summarizing, however, this material will be integrated for greater coherency.

Bill was born in a part of the reservation noted for being both very conservative and poverty-stricken. Only 50 miles away is the markedly contrasting community of Shiprock, considered to be one of the most acculturated Navaho communities. It is also prospering from recently developed uranium operations in the region.

During his early years Bill saw very little of Shiprock, and was reared in the traditional Navaho way. He was born during an eclipse (it is not known whether of the sun or moon), and was thus destined to take part in a periodic ceremony identified to the writer as the "Breath of Life" sing. The first of this series of ceremonies was held while he was still an infant, the second about six years ago. During the ceremony he inhales the breath of a great deity, and is thus assured of continued good health in the respiratory and vocal organs.

Bill lived with his immediate family until he was 6 years of age. He had only one younger sister at that time, although the family was later to include seven living siblings. He did not become well acquainted with his family, however, as he was given to his grandfather when he was 6 years old. The grandfather, a widower, lived several miles deeper into the reservation and required Bill's assistance as a sheep herder.

Bill worked for his grandfather as a sheep herder until he was 17, except for one interruption when, at the age of 15, he spent 50 days in the Shiprock hospital with a back ailment. Bill reports that the old man never talked to him.

At his grandfather's death Bill went to work for the railroad in Colorado. This was cut short by an illness which confined him to the Navaho Medical Center in Fort Defiance, Arizona. The illness was diagnosed as tuberculosis, pulmonary, moderately advanced. He was in the hospital for eight months and was discharged in the summer of 1944.

Bill returned to railroad employment, and worked in Utah, Oregon, and Nebraska. He was always part of Navaho crews and thus never exposed to acculturative influences. His father and a younger brother were also part of these crews.

Bill returned home for a brief visit in 1949, accompanied by his brother and father. He had saved $1,022. Subsequently, he went to Phoenix, Arizona, to pick cotton, a job that had been found for him by the employment agency at Shiprock. This was his first trip from home without a family member.

The employment at Phoenix did not last long and in December, 1949, on the advice of an Indian friend he went to Barstow, California, seeking railroad employment. At the section camp there his attempt to find work was unsuccessful, and after three days he started by bus back to Phoenix.

On this return trip he stopped for dinner at Colton. A white man he met there promised to obtain railroad employment for him. The stranger said that he required funds for this effort and in some way relieved Bill of his savings which had now dwindled to $725.

Bill returned home penniless, pawned some jewelry, borrowed some money, and returned to Colton to try to find the man who had taken his savings. He also looked for Navahos who might have information about employment. The many hours of waiting around the bus station searching for his man apparently caused suspicion, for he was arrested for vagrancy.

In jail he met some Navahos with whom he went to Barstow after his release. But in Barstow he was still unable to find employment and after six days he was completely out of funds. He started walking toward Phoenix, and was picked up by a man driving a truck. This man gave Bill one day's employment which allowed funds for a return to Barstow and another attempt to find work.

He managed to raise a little money doing odd jobs about the section camp near Barstow, and then returned to San Bernardino on the first lap of his return to Phoenix and home. It occurred to him that if he could get to a hospital, the officials there would send him to a reservation hospital, from whence he would be sent home. This was logical thinking: on the reservations, the hospitals, schools, and trading posts are the major source of assistance in all sorts of troubles.

As this idea occurred to Bill, he noticed

a woman dressed in white whom he took to be a nurse. He approached her and endeavored to explain that he was sick, but his endeavors were misinterpreted and he was taken to jail.

At the county jail Bill was apparently mistaken for a Mexican since a Mexican interpreter had tried to interview him. When the interview failed he was transferred to the psychopathic ward. Interviewed by the medical examiner there, he reportedly demonstrated an anguished appearance and repeated, "Me sick." He was diagnosed as Schizophrenia, Catatonic Type, and delivered to the state mental hospital.

Upon admission to the hospital, Bill was first taken to be a Filipino. The psychiatric admission note indicated that he was, ". . . confused, dull, and preoccupied. He has a look of anguish and appears to be hallucinating. . . . He repeats, 'I don't know.' " He was diagnosed as Dementia Praecox, which was later specified as Hebephrenic Type.

Several months later the psychiatrist on Bill's cottage tested him for *cerea flexibilitas* (waxy flexibility) and, finding it to be present, altered the diagnosis to Catatonic Type.

Eight months after his admittance he was discovered by the writer.

Psychological Aspects

Concomitant with gathering the case history material presented above, endeavors were made to evaluate the patient's intelligence and personality. The lack of culturally unbiased examining techniques made this extremely difficult.

Bill's performance on the various tests that were administered led to a conclusion that his probable I.Q. was in the vicinity of 80. This had to take into consideration the patient's slowness. At best, a Navaho refuses to be put under pressure of time, and to what extent Bill's slowness was cultural rather than psychotically pathological was a question of primary concern.

Bill's apathetic and withdrawn behavior has already been described. For diagnostic purposes, however, this syndrome is confused by cultural factors. It is common for Navahos, with their morbid fear of hospitals, to demonstrate just such a withdrawal patterning [5, pp. 108–109]. It is not known whether or not this would reach a stage of *cerea flexibilitas* or how long this behavior will persist. Accordingly it was concluded that Bill's apparent catatonia should not be accepted as a symptom of schizophrenia until underlying signs of schizophrenic processes could be detected.

During the first interview Bill was given the Draw A Person Test. The figure he drew was indistinct and without facial features and clearly reflected his withdrawal.

On the seventh interview the test was again given. Compared with the earlier attempt, the second drawing clearly reflected an improvement. It probably indicated the therapeutic benefits derived from the extensive individual treatment the patient was receiving.

The second drawing filled the paper, the facial features were portrayed, the arms were extended, and the drawing generally implied those signs which are held to indicate good contact with reality.

Although Bill's second drawing seems to infer considerable personality change, no changes could be observed in his behavior. He continued to appear apathetic and withdrawn. On several occasions he indicated his reluctance to talk because, "me no good this place," pointing to his chest. This suggested the characteristic organ cathexes of schizophrenia. However, the patient's thinking behind this statement was made clear during the later interviews through an interpreter.

Bill was concerned about the fact that he had not completed the second series of the "Breath of Life" ceremony. This matter had gone too long unattended, and he assumed that he must conserve his vocal energies until they could be supplemented by the breath of the deity. He expressed a great need to return home to pursue the ceremony.

In continued endeavor to detect schizophrenic underlay of his apparent catatonia, Bill was given a series of tests, none of which revealed responses normally associated with schizophrenia.

During the early course of the interviews with Bill, although not satisfied that the patient was not psychotic, the writer recommended that the best therapeutic environment for him would be his own home. This recommendation was not acted upon, partly because no one knew where his home was, or how he could be supervised there, but chiefly because he continued to appear catatonic.

Later, as the writer became convinced that the catatonia—if such it could be termed—was not symptomatic of underlying schizophrenia, efforts were renewed to release the patient. The outcome of these endeavors is summarized in the following section.

Outcome

As mentioned earlier, the final interviews with Bill were carried on with the aid of a Navaho interpreter. Bill conversed quite freely with the other Navahos and expressed gratitude at being able to talk to someone in his own language. The conversations did not add much to the history and understanding previously gained, but did offer an opportunity to inquire for the presence of hallucinations, delusions, and more subtle clues of schizophrenic thinking. Unless Bill's anxiety regarding the uncompleted "Breath of Life" ceremony could be considered bizarre, nothing of significance was elicited.

The interpreter's reaction to the interviews represented their most significant outcome. He was a professional interpreter, with vast experience in interviewing Navaho youths in strange environments. He expressed a strong conviction that Bill's behavior and attitudes were not unusual under the circumstances.

The interpreter communicated his feelings to the superintendent of the Sherman Institute who took an immediate and active interest in the case. After several interviews with Bill, satisfied that he could observe nothing about Bill's behavior which could be considered atypical under the circumstances, the superintendent offered to accept him into the flexible program of the Sherman Institute.

Bill was accordingly released under custody of the superintendent and careful plans were made to assure his adjustment at the school. At first, he was quartered in the school hospital, but allowed to participate in the school's social and recreational activities. He was employed with the animal husbandry and gardening program.

The writer's last visit to the Sherman Institute disclosed that Bill's adjustment had been quite rapid. He had put on weight and after about two weeks announced that he "felt right at home, now."

It had been difficult at first, because in spite of all precautions the students had learned something of Bill's past hospitalization. To the Navahos the hospital symbolizes death, and death is particularly abhorrent to them as they have no clearly structured concepts of an afterlife. The students consequently shied away from Bill a little when he arrived, but he has since found acceptance.

He will go back to the reservation in the spring, at the close of the school year, and attend to the unfinished business of the "Breath of Life" ceremony.

Concluding Discussion

In the course of this Navaho's commitment and 18 months of hospitalization, he was routinely examined by several psychiatrists, all of whom concurred with the diagnosis of schizophrenia. Without verbal communication with the patient, diagnosis was necessarily derived from observation of his overt behavior. Diagnosis was apparently confident as the patient was not referred to staff clinic or for psychological testing, the normal procedure with questionable cases.

Most of the psychiatrists' diagnostic observations were based on information received from the attendants of Bill's cottage, who reported the patient's withdrawn and apathetic behavior. Upon closer examination the patient would demonstrate *cerea flexibilitas*. Because of these factors the patient was assumed to be catatonic and hence schizophrenic.

Actually, many of the classic symptoms of catatonia were not present in this patient. He was not markedly stuporous or mute; he was clean in his personal habits and would eat willingly; he tended to doze as he sat rather than stare fixedly into space as does the typical catatonic. The writer, too, examined Bill for *cerea flexibilitas*, but learned later that the patient held grotesque positions because he thought it was expected of him.

With the assumption, however, that the patient's overt behavior could be interpreted as symptomatic of catatonic schizophrenia, it remains to be explained why testing and closer observation did not reveal the underlying ego disintegration which should be expected.

General personality traits of the Navaho people, as briefly reviewed earlier in this paper, could possibly infer a potential for schizophrenic disintegration. Navahos do not have the imaginative activity and the inner control which is so important to adjustment in the Anglo world. The scales are balanced, however, by a defense of rigidity and constriction. In a threatening situation they strive to maintain ego structure by psychic withdrawal.

The few tests that were applicable in examining Bill did not permit a very intensive examination of the dynamics of his withdrawal, but all indications were that he continued to maintain ego strength. He could account for his acts rationally, he performed very well with conceptualization, he maintained orientation for time and place, and could hold in mind simultaneously various aspects of situations or problems. His visuomotor performance exhibited no signs of distorted perspective. Many of his expressions could be considered naive, but hardly bizarre.

The apparent incongruity between the patient's overt behavior and underlying personality dynamics, although not fully understood psychologically, should not be considered as psychotic manifestation. Culturally derived, it can probably be explained as a defense mechanism characterized by an extreme and sustained withdrawal.

To what extent Bill's case may be typical of other Navaho patients diagnosed as catatonic schizophrenia cannot, of course, be proposed. It would be necessary to know if those patients were similarly diagnosed on the basis of overt behavior alone.

It is also unknown to what degree Bill may personify on-reservation Navaho youth. Superficially at least, his history appears quite typical. His lack of school, his years as a sheep herder for his grandfather, his attack of tuberculosis, and his railroad employment are circumstances and events common to many Navahos. His grandfather's apparent lack of affection implies an almost feral existence for the growing boy, but even this situation is not unusual. It is, in fact, difficult to discern some way in which this patient could be atypical as evaluated against his cultural background. Except for his possible low intelligence, he appears to represent a typical Navaho youth, a fact heavy with implication when his 18 months of hospitalization as a mental patient are considered.

The previously cited survey of hospitalized Navaho mental patients shows an amazingly small percentage of the total Navaho population (which is about 65,000). This is probably because few Navahos are currently coming in very close contact with Anglo structure.

Of the catatonic schizophrenics, it would be of value to know more about the details of their admission. If they were referred from the reservation, it probably meant that they were considered psychotic within the Navaho milieu; if, on the other hand, they were referred by agencies off the reservation (as was Bill), it would imply an evaluation derived from Anglo perspective. This will become a more poignant problem with increasing off-reservation movement of the Navaho people. . . .

References

1. V. BARNOUW, "Acculturation and Personality among the Wisconsin Chippewa," *American Anthropologist,* Memoir No. 72, vol. 52, 1950.
2. G. DEVEREUX, *Reality and Dream,* International Universities Press, Inc., New York, 1950.
3. W. HENRY, "The Thematic Apperception Technique in the Study of Culture-Personality Relations," *Genetic Psychology Monographs,* 35:3–135, 1947.
4. C. KLUCKHOHN, "The Influence of Psychiatry on Anthropology in America during the Past One Hundred Years," in *One Hundred Years of American Psychiatry,* J. K. Hall, C. Zilboorg, and E. A. Bunker (eds.), Columbia University Press, New York, 1947, pp. 589–617.
5. C. KLUCKHOHN and D. LEIGHTON, *Children of the People,* Harvard University Press, Cambridge, Mass., 1948.

Social Class and Mental Illness *

AUGUST B. HOLLINGSHEAD AND
FREDRICK C. REDLICH

The case histories of two compulsively promiscuous adolescent females will be drawn upon to illustrate the differential impact of class status on the way in which lay persons and psychiatrists perceive and appraise similar behavior. Both girls came to the attention of the police at about the same time but under very different circumstances. One came from a core group class I family (upper class), the other from a class V family (lower class) broken by the desertion of the father. The class I girl, after one of her frequent drinking and sexual escapades on a weekend away from an exclusive boarding school, became involved in an

* Reprinted from *Social Class and Mental Illness* by August B. Hollingshead and Fredrick C. Redlich (New York: John Wiley and Sons, 1958), pp. 175–76, by permission of the publisher.

automobile accident while drunk. Her family immediately arranged for bail through the influence of a member of an outstanding law firm; a powerful friend telephoned a newspaper contact, and the report of the accident was not published. Within twenty-four hours, the girl was returned to school. In a few weeks the school authorities realized that the girl was pregnant and notified her parents. A psychiatrist was called in for consultation by the parents with the expectation, expressed frankly, that he was to recommend a therapeutic interruption of the pregnancy. He did not see fit to do this and, instead, recommended hospitalization in a psychiatric institution to initiate psychotherapy. The parents, though disappointed that the girl would not have a "therapeutic" abortion, finally consented to hospitalization. In due course, the girl delivered a healthy baby who was placed for adoption. Throughout her stay in the hospital she received intensive psychotherapy and after being discharged continued in treatment with a highly regarded psychoanalyst.

The class V girl was arrested by the police after she was observed having intercourse with four or five sailors from a nearby naval base. At the end of a brief and perfunctory trial, the girl was sentenced to a reform school. After two years there she was paroled as an unpaid domestic. While on parole, she became involved in promiscuous activity, was caught by the police, and sent to the state reformatory for women. She accepted her sentence as deserved "punishment" but created enough disturbance in the reformatory to attract the attention of a guidance officer. This official recommended that a psychiatrist be consulted. The psychiatrist who saw her was impressed by her crudeness and inability to communicate with him on most subjects. He was alienated by the fact that she thought masturbation was "bad," whereas intercourse with many men whom she hardly knew was "O.K." The psychiatrist's recommendation was to return the girl to her regular routine because she was not "able to profit from psychotherapy."

Labeling the Mentally Retarded * †

JANE R. MERCER

   . . .
The clinical perspective is the frame of reference most commonly adopted in studies of mental deficiency, mental illness, drug addiction, and other areas which the students of deviance choose

* Reprinted from "Social System Perspective and Clinical Perspective: Frames of Reference for Understanding Career Patterns of Persons Labelled as Mentally Retarded" by Jane R. Mercer in *Social Problems*, Vol. 13, No. 1 (Summer, 1965), pp. 21–30, 33–34, by permission of the author and *Social Problems*.

† Supported in part by the National Institute of Mental Health, Grant No. 3M-9130: Population Movement of Mental Defectives and Related Physical, Behavioral, Social, and Cultural Factors; and Grant No. MH-5687: Mental Retardation in a Community, Pacific State Hospital, Pomona, California. Appreciation for assistance is expressed to the Western Data Processing Center, Division of the Graduate School of Business Administration, University of California, Los Angeles.

to investigate.[1, 2] This viewpoint is readily identified by several distinguishing characteristics.

First, the investigator accepts as the focus for study those individuals who have been labelled deviant. In so doing, he adopts the values of whatever social system has defined the person as deviant and assumes that its judgments are the valid measure of deviance. . . . Groups in the social structure sharing the values of the core culture tend to accept the labels attached as a consequence of the application of these values without serious questioning. . . .

A second distinguishing characteristic of the clinical perspective is the tendency to perceive deviance as an attribute of the person, as a meaning inherent in his behavior, appearance, or performance. Mental retardation, for example, is viewed as a characteristic of the person, a lack to be explained. This viewpoint results in a quest for etiology. Thus, the clinical perspective is essentially a medical frame of reference, for it sees deviance as individual pathology requiring diagnostic classification and etiological analysis for the purpose of determining proper treatment procedures and probable prognosis.

Three additional characteristics of the clinical perspective are the development of a diagnostic nomenclature, the creation of diagnostic instruments, and the professionalization of the diagnostic function.

When the investigator begins his research with the diagnostic designations assigned by official defining agents, he tends to assume that all individuals placed in a given category are essentially equivalent in respect to their deviance. . . . Individuals assigned to different categories of deviance are compared with each other or with a "normal" population consisting of persons who, for whatever reason, have escaped being labelled. The focus is on the individual.

Another characteristic of the clinical perspective is its assumption that the official definition is somehow the "right" definition. . . .

Finally, when deviance is perceived as individual pathology, social action tends to center upon changing the individual or, that failing, removing him from participation in society. Prevention and cure become the primary social goals. . . .

The social system perspective, on the other hand, attempts to see the definition of an individual's behavior as a function of the values of the social system within which he is being evaluated. The professional definers are studied as one of the most important of the evaluating social systems but within the context of other social systems which may or may not concur with official definitions.

Defining an individual as mentally ill, delinquent, or mentally retarded is viewed as an interpersonal process in which the definer makes a value judgment about the behavior of the persons being defined. . . . Deviation is not seen as a characteristic of the individual or as a meaning inherent in his behavior, but as a socially derived label which may be attached to his behavior by some social systems and not by others.[3]

. . . Thus, it follows that a person may be mentally retarded in one system and not mentally retarded in another. He may change his label by changing his social group. This viewpoint frees us from the necessity of seeing the person as

[1] August B. Hollingshead and Fredrick C. Redlich, *Social Class and Mental Illness*, New York: John Wiley and Sons, 1958, Chapter 11.

[2] H. E. Freeman and O. G. Simmons, "Social Class and Posthospital Performance Levels," *American Sociological Review*, 2 (June, 1959), p. 348.

[3] Howard S. Becker, editor, *The Other Side: Perspectives on Deviance*, New York: The Free Press, 1964.

permanently stigmatized by a deviant label and makes it possible to understand otherwise obscure patterns in the life careers of individuals. . . . The research reported in this paper attempts to answer these questions about a group of persons who shared the common experience of having been labelled retarded by official defining agencies and placed in a public institution for the retarded. . . .

The specific question which this study seeks to investigate within the above framework is: "Why do the families of some individuals take them back home after a period of institutionalization in a hospital for the retarded while other families do not, when, according to official evaluations, these individuals show similar degrees of deviance, that is, have comparable intelligence test scores, and are of equivalent age, sex, ethnic status, and length of hospitalization?" . . .

Method

Two groups of labelled retardates were studied. One group consisted of patients who had been released to their families from a state hospital for the retarded and the other group consisted of a matched group of patients still resident in the hospital at the time of the study.[4]

Specifically, the released group was made up of all patients released to their families during a three year period (1957–59), who had not been readmitted to another institution for the retarded at the time of the study, and who were reported to be living within a one hundred mile radius of the hospital. Only those cases in which the family had assumed responsibility for the patient were in-

cluded. Of the 76 patients who met these qualifications, it was possible to complete interviews with 63 of the families. Six families refused to be interviewed and seven could not be located.

The resident group was selected to match the released group in intelligence quotient, age, sex, ethnic status, and year of admission, other studies having demonstrated that these factors are related to the probability of release.[5]

The matched group of resident patients was selected in the following manner: all patients on the hospital rolls were sorted into two groups by sex, two groups by age, three groups by ethnic status, three groups by intelligence quotient, and two groups by year of admission. All released patients were likewise assigned to the proper category. Resident patients were then chosen at random from within each cell in sufficient numbers to correspond to the number of discharged patients also falling in that cell. Each resident case was required to have a family living within a one hundred mile radius of the hospital. If a case did not meet this requirement, another case was drawn randomly from the appropriate cell until there were an equal number of discharged and resident cases in each cell. Sex distribution in each group was 53 males and 23 females; ethnic distribution, 47 Caucasians, 20 Mexicans, and 9 Negroes.

. . . Table 1 presents the distribution of intelligence quotients, birth years, and years of admission for the interviewed cases. Of the 76 resident cases selected to match the released cases, interviews were completed with 70 families. Two refused to be interviewed and four families could not be located. Using a Kolmogorov-Smirnov Test of two independent samples, we found that all differences

---

[4] Pacific State Hospital, Pomona, California is a state supported hospital for the mentally retarded with a population of approximately 3,000 patients.

[5] G. Tarjan, S. W. Wright, M. Kramer, P. H. Person, Jr., and R. Morgan, "The Natural History of Mental Deficiency in a State Hospital. I: Probabilities of Release and Death by Age, Intelligence Quotients, and Diagnosis," *AMA J. dis. Childr.*, 96 (1958), pp. 64–70.

TABLE 1

Comparison of Interviewed Cases by Birth Year, Intelligence
Quotient, and Year of Admission

Matched Variable	Released (63)	Resident (70)	Significance Level
Birth Year			
Before 1920	4	5	
1921–1930	13	12	
1931–1940	33	34	> .05 [1]
1941–1950	12	17	
1951–1960	1	2	
Intelligence Quotient			
0–9	2	4	
10–19	2	1	
20–29	4	3	
30–39	6	4	> .05 [1]
40–49	13	15	
50–59	14	18	
60–69	19	19	
70 +	3	6	
Year of Admission			
Before 1945	5	9	
1945–1950	20	14	
1951–1956	33	31	> .05 [1]
1957 and later	5	16	

[1] The Kolmogorov-Smirnov Test of two independent samples was used.

between the interviewed groups could be accounted for by chance.

When the 19 non-interviewed cases were compared with the 133 interviewed cases, no significant differences were found in the sex, age, I.Q., or ethnic status of the patients, or the socioeconomic level of the families. . . .

The hospital file for each patient selected for study was searched for relevant data and an interview was held with a family member. In 75 per cent of the cases the mother was interviewed; in 8 per cent the father was interviewed; and in the remaining cases some other relative served as informant. . . .

To clarify the circumstances under which the released group returned to their families, the respondent was asked two questions: "Who was the most important person in getting you to take ————— out of the hospital?" and

"What were the main reasons you decided to have ————— discharged from the hospital?"

In 12 cases the parents reported that someone in the hospital, i.e., a social worker, family care mother, or a ward technician, had first suggested that the patient could be released to the family. In the 51 remaining cases the families were the active agents in release. Reasons given by the families for seeking a discharge are described in Table 2.

It is clear from this table that most of the patients who returned to their families returned because the family made an effort to secure their release. . . .

Findings

SOCIAL STATUS OF RELEASED PATIENTS

Several indices were used to measure the socioeconomic level of the family

TABLE 2
The Release Process as Reported by the Families of
Released Patients

	f	%
Hospital Initiated Releases	12	19
Family Initiated Releases		
Family opposed to placement from beginning	9	14
Parents lonely without patient or need him for some practical reason, e.g., to help with younger children, earn money, etc.	8	13
Patient was unhappy in the hospital. Hospital Failure: Mistreated patient, made him work too hard, etc.	6	9
Hospital Success: Patient improved enough to come home	9	14
Home conditions changed to permit return, e.g., found patient a job, mother's health better, etc.	10	16
Total Released Cases	63	

of each retardate. A socioeconomic index score based on the occupation and education of the head of the household, weighted according to Hollingshead's system, was used as the basic measure. In addition, the interviewer rated the economic status of the street on which the patient's home was located, rated the physical condition of the housing unit, and completed a checklist of equipment present in the household. As can be seen in Table 3, the families of the released

TABLE 3
Socioeconomic Differences Between Patients Released to Their
Families and Those Still Resident in the State Hospital

Socioeconomic Measure		*Released Living at Home (63%)*	*Resident In State Hospital (70%)*	*Significance Level*
Socioeconomic Index	Above Median	36.5	61.4	
Score of Head of	Below Median	61.9	38.6	< .01 [3]
Household	Unknown	1.6	0.0	
Economic Status	Housing Value	29.0	55.1	
of Street [1]	$10,000 and Above			
	Housing Value	71.0	44.9	< .05 [3]
	Less Than $10,000			
Condition of Housing	Run Down	48.4	23.2	
Unit [1]	Average	46.8	57.2	< .05 [3]
	Above Average	4.8	18.8	
Household Equipment	0–2	19.0	11.9	
Scale [1]	3–5	27.6	20.9	< .05 [2]
	6–8	43.1	41.8	
	9–11	10.3	25.4	

[1] Some cases are not included because data were not available.
[2] Test of significance of difference between unrelated means was used.
[3] Chi Square test was used.

patients rated significantly lower than the families of the resident patients on every measure. The heads of the households in the families of released patients had less education and lower level jobs, the family residence was located among less affluent dwellings, the housing unit was in a poorer state of repair, and the dwelling was less elaborately furnished and equipped. Contrary to the pattern found in studies of those placed as mentally ill,[6] it is the "retardate" from lower socioeconomic background who is most likely to be released to his family while higher status "retardates" are more likely to remain in the hospital.

From the clinical perspective, several explanations may be proposed for these differences. It has been found in hospital populations that patients with an I.Q. below 50 are more likely to come from families which represent a cross-section of social levels, while those with an I.Q. between 50 and 70 are more likely to come from low status families.[7] Since persons with higher I.Q.'s have a higher probability of release, this could account for higher rates of release for low status persons. However, in the present study, the tested level of intelligence was equal for both groups, and this hypothesis cannot be used as an explanation.

A second possible explanation from a clinical perspective might be based on the fact that persons who have more physical handicaps tend to be institutionalized for longer periods of time than persons with few handicaps.[8] Should it be found that high status patients have more physical handicaps than low status patients, then this could account for the latter's shorter hospitalization. Data from the present sample were analyzed to determine whether there was a significant relationship between physical handicap and social status. Although released patients tended to have fewer physical handicaps than resident patients, this was irrespective of social status. When high status patients were compared with low status patients, 50% of the high status and 56% of the low status patients had no physical handicaps. A chi square of 1.9 indicates these differences could be accounted for by chance variation.

A third explanation from the clinical perspective may hinge on differences in the diagnostic categories to which retardates of different social status were assigned. . . . A diagnostic label of "familial" or "undifferentiated" ordinarily indicates that the individual has few or no physical stigmata and is essentially normal in body structure. All other categories ordinarily indicate that he has some type of physical symptomatology. Although released patients were more likely to be diagnosed as familial or undifferentiated than resident patients ($x^2 = 7.08$, p $<$ .01), this, like physical handicap, was irrespective of social status. Fifty-seven per cent of the high status retardates, and 69% of the low status retardates were classified as either undifferentiated or familial, a difference which could be accounted for by chance. . . .

DIVERGENT DEFINITIONS

In analyzing social status, four types of situations were identified. The modal category for resident patients was high social status with a smaller number of resident patients coming from low status families. The modal category for released patients was low status with a smaller number of released patients coming from

---

[6] August B. Hollingshead and Fredrick C. Redlich, 1958, *op. cit.*, Chapter 11.

[7] Georges Sabagh, Harvey F. Dingman, George Tarjan, and Stanley W. Wright, "Social Class and Ethnic Status of Patients Admitted to a State Hospital for the Retarded," *Pacific Sociological Review*, 2 (Fall, 1959), pp. 76–80.

[8] G. Tarjan, S. W. Wright, M. Kramer, R. H. Person, Jr., and R. Morgan, 96, 1958, *op. cit.*, pp. 64–70.

higher status families. If we are correct in our hypothesis (that higher release rates for low status patients are related to the fact that the family social system is structurally more distant from the core culture and that its style of life, values, and definitions of the patient are more divergent from official definitions than that of high status families), we would expect the largest differences to occur when high status resident families are compared to low status released families. The two non-modal categories would be expected to fall at some intermediate point. For this reason, the analysis of all subsequent variables has retained these four basic classifications.

Table 4 presents the responses made to three questions asked to determine the extent to which the family concurred in the official label of "retardation," the extent to which they believed the patient's condition amenable to change, and the extent to which they anticipated that the individual could live outside the hospital and, perhaps, fill adult roles. The patterns of the divergent definitions of the situation which emerged for each group are illuminating.

When asked whether *he* believed the patient to be retarded, the high status parent more frequently concurred with the definitions of the official defining agencies while the low status parent was more prone to disagree outright or to be uncertain. This tendency is especially marked when the two modal categories are compared. While 33.3% of the parents of the low status released patients stated that they did not think the patient was retarded and 25.6% were uncertain whether he was retarded, only 4.6% of the parents of high status resident patients felt he was not retarded and 20.9% were uncertain.

When parents were asked whether they believed anything could change the patient's condition, the differences between all groups were significant at the .02 level or beyond. The high status parent was most likely to believe that nothing could change his child's condition, and this was significantly more characteristic of parents whose children were still in the hospital than those who had taken their child from the hospital on both status levels.

When asked what they saw in the future for their child, all groups again differed significantly in the expected direction. The modal, high status group was least optimistic and the modal, low status group, most optimistic about the future. Fully 46% of the parents of the latter group expressed the expectation that their child would get a job, marry, and fulfill the usual adult roles while only 6.9% of the modal high status group responded in this fashion. High status parents, as a group, more frequently see their child playing dependent roles. It is interesting to note that, although a large percentage of parents of released patients believe the patient will be dependent, they demonstrate their willingness to accept responsibility for the retarded child themselves by their responding that they foresee him having a future in which he is dependent at home. Only 9.3% of the high status and 22.2% of the low status parents of the resident patients see this as a future prospect. Release to the family clearly appears to be contingent upon the willingness of the family to accept the patient's dependency, if they do not foresee him assuming independent adult roles.

FACTORS IN THE LABELLING PROCESS

From the social system perspective, retardation is viewed as a label placed upon an individual after someone has evaluated his behavior within a specific set of norms. Retardation is not a meaning necessarily inherent in the behavior

TABLE 4

Patterns of Deviant Definitions

Question	Response Categories	High Status Resident (43) %	High Status Released (23) %	Low Status Resident (27) %	Low Status Released (39) %	Significance Levels — High Status / Low Status	High Status Resident / Low Status Released	High Status Resident / High Status Released	Low Status Resident / Low Status Released
1. We know that many people have told you ___ is retarded but we want to know what you think. Do you think he/she is retarded?	Yes	74.4	47.8	66.6	41.0				
	Uncertain	20.9	39.1	14.8	25.6	< .02 [1]	< .02 [1]	NS [1]	NS [1]
	No	4.6	13.0	18.5	33.3				
2. Do you believe anything can change ___'s condition?	Nothing	74.3	39.0	66.6	33.3				
	Uncertain	2.3	17.3	11.1	38.4	< .02 [2]	< .001 [2]	< .01 [2]	< .01 [2]
	Training, Medical Care, etc.	23.2	43.4	22.2	28.2				
3. What do you see in the future for ___?	Dependent in Institution	83.7	13.0	74.0	2.5				
	Dependent at Home	9.3	60.8	22.2	48.7	< .02 [2]	< .001 [2]	< .001 [2]	< .001 [2]
	Normal Adult Roles	6.9	26.0	3.7	46.1				

[1] The Kolmogorov-Smirnov Test of two independent samples was used.
[2] The Log-Likelihood Ratio Test was used. (Barnett, Wolf, "The Log-Likelihood Ratio Test [The G-Test]; Methods and Tables for a Test of Heterogeneity in Contingency Tables," *Annals of Human Genetics*, Vol. 21, Part 4, June 1957, pp. 397–409.)

of the individual. We have seen that the parents of low status, released patients tend to reject the label of retardation and to be optimistic about the future. We surmised that this divergent definition could well be related to factors in the process by which the child was first categorized as subnormal, such as his age at the time, the type of behavior which was used as a basis for making the evaluation, and the persons doing the labelling. Consequently, parents were asked specifically about these factors. Table 5 records their responses.

Children from lower status families were labelled as mentally subnormal at a significant later age than children from high status families. Seventy-nine per cent of the patients in the high status, modal group were classified as retarded by the age of six while only 36.1 per cent of those in the low status, modal group were identified at such an early age. The largest percentage of low status retardates were first classified after they reached public school age. This indicates that relatives and friends, who are the individuals most likely to observe and evaluate the behavior of young children, seldom saw anything deviant in the early development of lower status children later labelled retarded, but that the primary groups of higher status children did perceive early deviation.

This is related to the responses made when parents were asked what first prompted someone to believe the patient retarded. The modal, high status group reported slow development in 48.8% of the cases and various types of physical symptoms in an additional 20.9%, while only 14.7% and 11.8% of the modal, low status parents gave these responses. On the other hand, 55.9% of the modal, low status group were first labelled because they had problems learning in school, while this was true of only 9.3% of the modal high status group.

When parents were asked who was the most important person influencing them in placing the child in the hospital, a parallel pattern emerged. Medical persons are the most important single group for the modal high status persons while the police and welfare agencies loom very significant in 64.1% of the cases in the modal, low status group. These findings are similar to those of Hollingshead and Redlich in their study of paths to the hospital for the mentally ill.[9] Of additional interest is the fact that the person important in placement differentiates the low status released from the low status resident patient at the .01 level. The resident low status patient's path to the hospital is similar to that of the high status patient and markedly different from released low status persons. When authoritative figures such as police and welfare are primary forces in placement, the patient is more likely to return home.

We interpret these findings to mean that when the family—or persons whose advice is solicited by the family, i.e., medical persons—is "most important" in placing a person in a hospital for the retarded, the primary groups have themselves first defined the individual as a deviant and sought professional counsel. When their own suspicions are supported by official definitions, they are more likely to leave the patient in an institution.

Conversely, when a person is labelled retarded by an authoritative, governmental agency whose advice is not solicited and who, in the case of the police, may be perceived as a punishing agent, the family frequently rejects the official definition of the child as retarded and withdraws him from the institution at the first opportunity. This attitude was

[9] August B. Hollingshead and Fredrick C. Redlich, 1958, *op. cit.,* Chapter 11.

TABLE 5
Factors in the Labeling Process

Question	Response Categories	High Status Resident (43) %	High Status Released (23) %	Low Status Resident (27) %	Low Status Released (39) %	Significance Levels: High Status / Low Status	Resident High / Released Low	Resident High / Released High	Resident Low / Released Low
1. How old was ___ when someone first said he was retarded?	1–2 years	44.1	18.1	23.2	16.7	<.001 [1]	<.02 [1]	NS [1]	NS [1]
	3–6 years	34.8	50.0	30.2	19.4				
	7–10 years	9.3	22.7	11.5	30.5				
	11–14 years	4.6	0.0	11.5	16.7				
	15 or over	6.9	9.1	23.2	16.7				
2. What was there about ___ that made you/them think he/she might be retarded?	Slow Development	48.8	30.4	19.2	14.7	<.005 [2]	<.001 [2]	NS [2]	NS [2]
	Physical Symptoms	20.9	17.3	26.9	11.8				
	Behavioral Problems	20.9	21.7	15.4	17.6				
	Couldn't Learn in School	9.3	30.4	38.5	55.9				
3. Who was the most important person in getting you to place ___ in the hospital?	Family	27.9	43.4	48.1	25.6	<.01 [2]	<.001 [2]	NS [2]	<.01 [2]
	Medical or Psychological Person	37.2	30.4	11.1	2.5				
	Police or Welfare	13.9	17.3	18.5	64.1				
	Schools or Other	20.9	8.6	22.2	7.6				

[1] The Kolmogorov-Smirnov Test of two independent samples was used.

[2] The Log-Likelihood Ratio Test was used. (Barnett, Wolf, The Log-Likelihood Ratio Test [The G-Test]: Methods and Tables for a Test of Heterogeneity in Contingency Tables," *Annals of Human Genetics*, Vol. 21, Part 4, June 1957, pp. 397–409.)

clearly exemplified by one mother who, when asked why the family had taken the child from the hospital, replied, "Why not? He had served his time."

The influence of the police as a factor in labelling the low status person as retarded may actually be greater than that shown in Table 5. Fifty per cent of the low status retardates had some type of police record while only 23 per cent of the high status subnormals were known to the police, a difference significant beyond the .01 level. . . .

Discussion and Conclusions

The life space of the individual may be viewed as a vast network of interlocking social systems through which the person moves during the course of his lifetime. Those systems which exist close to one another in the social structure tend, because of overlapping memberships and frequent communication, to evolve similar patterns of norms. Most individuals are born and live out their lives in a relatively limited segment of this social network and tend to contact mainly social systems which share common norms. When an individual's contacts are restricted to a circumscribed segment of the structure, this gives some stability to the evaluations which are made of his behavior and to the labels which are attached to him.

However, when the person's life career takes him into segments of the social network which are located at a distance from his point of origin, as when a Mexican-American child enters the public school or a Negro child gets picked up by the police, he is then judged by a new and different set of norms. Behavior which was perfectly acceptable in his primary social systems may now be judged as evidence of "mental retardation." At this point, he is caught up in the web of official definitions. However, because he has primary social systems which may not agree with these official labels, he may be able to return to that segment of the social structure which does not label him as deviant after he has fulfilled the minimal requirements of the official system. That is, he can drop out of school or he can "serve his time" in the state hospital and then go home. By changing his location in social space, he can change his label from "retarded" to "not much different from the rest of us." For example, the mother of a Mexican-American, male, adult patient who had been released from the hospital after being committed following an incident in which he allegedly made sexual advances to a young girl, told the author, "There is nothing wrong with Benny. He just can't read or write." Since the mother spoke only broken English, had no formal schooling, and could not read or write, Benny did not appear deviant to her. From her perspective, he didn't have anything wrong with him.

The child from a high status family has no such recourse. His primary social systems lie structurally close to the official social systems and tend to concur on what is acceptable. Definitions of his subnormality appear early in his life and are more universal in all his social groups. He cannot escape the retarded label because all his associates agree that he is a deviant.[10]

In conclusion, tentative answers may be given to the three questions raised earlier in this discussion. "Who sees whom as retarded?" Within the social system perspective, it becomes clear that persons who are clinically similar may be defined quite differently by their pri-

---

[10] Lewis Anthony Dexter, "On the Politics and Sociology of Stupidity in our Society" in *The Other Side: Perspectives on Deviance,* edited by Howard S. Becker, New York: The Free Press, 1964, pp. 37–49.

mary social systems. The person from lower status social systems is less likely to be perceived as mentally subnormal.

"What impact does this differential definition have on the life career of the person?" Apparently, these differential definitions do make a difference because the group which diverges most widely from official definitions is the group in which the most individuals are released from the institution to their families.

Finally, "What are the characteristics of the social systems which diverge most widely from official definitions?" These social systems seem to be characterized by low educational achievement, high levels of dependency, and high concentrations of ethnic minorities.

A social system perspective adds a useful dimension to the label "mental retardation" by its focus on the varied definitions which may be applied to behavior by different groups in society. For those interested in the care and treatment of persons officially labelled as mentally subnormal, it may be beneficial in some cases to seek systematically to relocate such individuals in the social structure in groups which will not define them as deviant. Rather than insisting that a family adopt official definitions of abnormality, we may frequently find it advisable to permit them to continue to view the patient within their own frame of reference and thus make it easier for them to accept him.

THE ROLE OF THIRD PARTIES

4

Deviance is very much an interactive process. Individual and group must take complementary roles in order to make a deviant. Consensus, required here as elsewhere, consists of definition and numbers. Consensus by definition comes about when two or more persons agree to type another person as a deviant in more or less the same terms. Consensus by number comes about when two or more persons combine to take joint action on this now shared definition. Without a coalition, the creation of a social deviant is quite obviously slowed. A defining agent's work improves and goes much more smoothly the more significant third parties he can get on his side.

The two readings that follow exemplify this point in some detail. Goffman points out how inside and outside defining agents collaborate smoothly in a process of reassignment that culminates in hospitalization. Lemert, in his analysis of the exclusion of paranoids, shows that these "difficult persons" apparently cannot be eliminated from social interaction unless people actually do conspire to exclude them.

The Moral Career of the Mental Patient *

ERVING GOFFMAN

Traditionally the term *career* has been reserved for those who expect to enjoy the rises laid out within a respectable profession. The term is coming to be

* Reprinted by special permission of the author and The William Alanson White Psychiatric Foundation, Inc., from *Psychiatry: Journal for the Study of Interpersonal Processes,* Vol. 22 (May, 1959), pp. 123–31. Copyright 1959 by The William Alanson White Psychiatric Foundation, Inc.

used, however, in a broadened sense to refer to any social strand of any person's course through life. The perspective of natural history is taken: unique outcomes are neglected in favor of such changes over time as are basic and common to the members of a social category, although occurring independently to each of them. Such a career is not a thing that can be brilliant or disappointing; it can no more be a success than a failure. In this light, I want to consider the mental patient, drawing mainly upon data collected during a year's participant observation of patient social life in a public mental hospital,[1] wherein an attempt was made to take the patient's point of view.

One value of the concept of career is its two-sidedness. One side is linked to internal matters held dearly and closely, such as image of self and felt identity; the other side concerns official position, jural relations, and style of life, and is part of a publicly accessible institutional complex. The concept of career, then, allows one to move back and forth between the personal and the public, between the self and its significant society,

without having overly to rely for data upon what the person says he thinks he imagines himself to be.

This paper, then, is an exercise in the institutional approach to the study of self. The main concern will be with the *moral* aspects of career—that is, the regular sequence of changes that career entails in the person's self and in his framework of imagery for judging himself and others.[2]

The category "mental patient" itself will be understood in one strictly sociological sense. In this perspective, the psychiatric view of a person becomes significant only in so far as this view itself alters his social fate—an alteration which seems to become fundamental in our society when, and only when, the person is put through the process of hospitalization.[3] I therefore exclude certain neighboring categories: the undiscovered candidates who would be judged "sick" by psychiatric standards but who never come to be viewed as such by themselves or others, although they may cause everyone a great deal of trouble;[4] the office patient whom a psychiatrist feels he can

---

[1] The study was conducted during 1955–56 under the auspices of the Laboratory of Socio-environmental Studies of the National Institute of Mental Health. I am grateful to the Laboratory Chief, John A. Clausen, and to Dr. Winfred Overholser, Superintendent, and the late Dr. Jay Hoffman, then First Assistant Physician of Saint Elizabeth's Hospital, Washington, D. C., for the ideal cooperation they freely provided. A preliminary report is contained in Goffman, "Interpersonal Persuasion," pp. 117–193; in *Group Processes: Transactions of the Third Conference,* edited by Bertram Schaffner; New York, Josiah Macy, Jr. Foundation, 1957. A shorter version of this paper was presented at the Annual Meeting of the American Sociological Society, Washington, D. C., August, 1957.

[2] Material on moral career can be found in early social anthropological work on ceremonies of status transition, and in classic social psychological descriptions of those spectacular changes in one's view of self that can accompany participation in social movements and sects. Recently new kinds of relevant data have been suggested by psychiatric interest in the problem of "identity" and sociological studies of work careers and "adult socialization."

[3] This point has recently been made by Elaine and John Cumming, *Closed Ranks:* Cambridge, Commonwealth Fund, Harvard Univ. Press, 1957; pp. 101–102. "Clinical experience supports the impression that many people define mental illness as 'That condition for which a person is treated in a mental hospital.' . . . Mental illness, it seems, is a condition which afflicts people who must go to a mental institution, but until they do almost anything they do is normal." Leila Deasy has pointed out to me the correspondence here with the situation in white collar crime. Of those who are detected in this activity, only the ones who do not manage to avoid going to prison find themselves accorded the social role of the criminal.

[4] Case records in mental hospitals are just now coming to be exploited to show the incredible amount of trouble a person may cause for himself and others before anyone

handle with drugs or shock on the outside; the mental client who engages in psychotherapeutic relationships. And I include anyone, however robust in temperament, who somehow gets caught up in the heavy machinery of mental hospital servicing. In this way the effects of being treated as a mental patient can be kept quite distinct from the effects upon a person's life of traits a clinician would view as psychopathological.[5] Persons who become mental hospital patients vary widely in the kind and degree of illness that a psychiatrist would impute to them, and in the attributes by which laymen would describe them. But once started on the way, they are confronted by some importantly similar circumstances and respond to these in some importantly similar ways. Since these similarities do not come from mental illness, they would seem to occur in spite of it. It is thus a tribute to the power of social forces that the uniform status of mental patient can not only assure an aggregate of persons a common fate and eventually, because of this, a common character, but that this social reworking can be done upon what is perhaps the most obstinate diversity of human materials that can be brought together by society. Here there lacks only the frequent forming of a protective group-life by ex-patients to illustrate in full the classic cycle of response by which deviant sub-groupings are psychodynamically formed in society.

This general sociological perspective is heavily reinforced by one key finding of sociologically oriented students in mental hospital research. As has been repeatedly shown in the study of nonliterate societies, the awesomeness, distastefulness, and barbarity of a foreign culture can decrease in the degree that the student becomes familiar with the point of view to life that is taken by his subjects. Similarly, the student of mental hospitals can discover that the craziness or "sick behavior" claimed for the mental patient is by and large a product of the claimant's social distance from the situation that the patient is in, and is not primarily a product of mental illness. Whatever the refinements of the various patients' psychiatric diagnoses, and whatever the special ways in which social life on the "inside" is unique, the researcher can find that he is participating in a community not significantly different from any other he has studied.[6] Of course, while restricting himself to the off-ward grounds community of paroled patients, he may feel, as some patients do, that life in the locked wards is bizarre; and while on a locked admissions or convalescent ward, he may feel that chronic "back" wards are socially crazy places. But he need only move his sphere of sympathetic participation to the "worst" ward in the hospital, and this too can come into social focus as a place with a livable and continuously meaningful social world. This in no way denies that he will find a minority in any ward or patient group that continues to seem quite beyond the capacity to follow rules of social organi-

---

begins to think about him psychiatrically, let alone take psychiatric action against him. See John A. Clausen and Marian Radke Yarrow, "Paths to the Mental Hospital," *J. Social Issues* (1955) 11:25–32; August B. Hollingshead and Fredrick C. Redlich, *Social Class and Mental Illness;* New York, Wiley, 1958; pp. 173–174.

[5] An illustration of how this perspective may be taken to all forms of deviancy may be found in Edwin Lemert, *Social Pathology;* New York, McGraw-Hill, 1951; see especially pp. 74–76. A specific application to mental defectives may be found in Stewart E. Perry, "Some Theoretic Problems of Mental Deficiency and Their Action Implications," *Psychiatry* (1954) 17:45–73; see especially p. 68.

[6] Conscientious objectors who voluntarily went to jail sometimes arrived at the same conclusion regarding criminal inmates. See, for example, Alfred Hassler, *Diary of a Self-made Convict;* Chicago, Regnery, 1954; p. 74.

zation, or that the orderly fulfilment of normative expectations in patient society is partly made possible by strategic measures that have somehow come to be institutionalized in mental hospitals.

The career of the mental patient falls popularly and naturalistically into three main phases: the period prior to entering the hospital, which I shall call the *prepatient phase;* the period in the hospital, the *inpatient phase;* the period after discharge from the hospital, should this occur, namely, the *ex-patient phase.*[7] This paper will deal only with the first two phases.

The Prepatient Phase

A relatively small group of prepatients come into the mental hospital willingly, because of their own idea of what will be good for them, or because of wholehearted agreement with the relevant members of their family. Presumably these recruits have found themselves acting in a way which is evidence to them that they are losing their minds or losing control of themselves. This view of oneself would seem to be one of the most pervasively threatening things that can happen to the self in our society, especially since it is likely to occur at a time when the person is in any case sufficiently troubled to exhibit the kind of symptom which he himself can see. As Sullivan described it,

What we discover in the self-system of a person undergoing schizophrenic changes or schizophrenic processes, is then, in its simplest form, an extremely fear-marked puzzlement, consisting of the use of rather generalized and anything but exquisitely refined referential processes in an attempt to cope with what is essentially a failure at being human—a failure at being anything that one could respect as worth being.[8]

Coupled with the person's disintegrative re-evaluation of himself will be the new, almost equally pervasive circumstance of attempting to conceal from others what he takes to be the new fundamental facts about himself, and attempting to discover whether others too have discovered them.[9] Here I want to stress that perception of losing one's mind is based on culturally derived and socially engrained stereotypes as to the significance of symptoms such as hearing voices, losing temporal and spatial orientation, and sensing that one is being followed, and that many of the most spectacular and convincing of these symptoms in some instances psychiatrically signify merely a temporary emotional upset in a stressful situation, however terrifying to the person at the time. Similarly, the anxiety consequent upon this perception of oneself, and the strategies devised to reduce this anxiety, are not a product of abnormal psychology, but would be exhibited by any person socialized into our culture who came to conceive of himself as someone losing his mind. Interestingly, subcultures in American society apparently differ in the amount of ready imagery and encouragement they supply for such self-views, leading to differential rates of *self*-referral; the capacity to take this disintegrative view of oneself without

---

[7] This simple picture is complicated by the somewhat special experience of roughly a third of ex-patients—namely, readmission to the hospital, this being the recidivist or "repatient" phase.

[8] Harry Stack Sullivan, *Clinical Studies in Psychiatry;* edited by Helen Swick Perry, Mary Ladd Gavel, and Martha Gibbon: New York, Norton, 1956; pp. 184–185.

[9] This moral experience can be contrasted with that of a person learning to become a marihuana addict, whose discovery that he can be 'high' and still 'op' effectively without being detected apparently leads to a new level of use. See Howard S. Becker, "Marihuana Use and Social Control," *Social Problems* (1955) 3:35–44; see especially pp. 40–41.

psychiatric prompting seems to be one of the questionable cultural privileges of the upper classes.[10]

For the person who has come to see himself—with whatever justification—as mentally unbalanced, entrance to the mental hospital can sometimes bring relief, perhaps in part because of the sudden transformation in the structure of his basic social situations; instead of being to himself a questionable person trying to maintain a role as a full one, he can become an officially questioned person known to himself to be not so questionable as that. In other cases, hospitalization can make matters worse for the willing patient, confirming by the objective situation what has theretofore been a matter of the private experience of self.

Once the willing prepatient enters the hospital, he may go through the same routine of experiences as do those who enter unwillingly. In any case, it is the latter that I mainly want to consider, since in America at present these are by far the more numerous kind.[11] Their approach to the institution takes one of three classic forms: they come because they have been implored by their family or threatened with the abrogation of family ties unless they go "willingly"; they come by force under police escort; they come under misapprehension purposely induced by others, this last restricted mainly to youthful prepatients.

The prepatient's career may be seen in terms of an extrusory model; he starts out with relationships and rights, and ends up, at the beginning of his hospital stay, with hardly any of either. The moral aspects of this career, then, typically begin with the experience of abandonment, disloyalty, and embitterment. This is the case even though to others it may be obvious that he was in need of treatment, and even though in the hospital he may soon come to agree.

The case histories of most mental patients document offense against some arrangement for face-to-face living—a domestic establishment, a work place, a semipublic organization such as a church or store, a public region such as a street or park. Often there is also a record of some *complainant,* some figure who takes that action against the offender which eventually leads to his hospitalization. This may not be the person who makes the first move, but it is the person who makes what turns out to be the first effective move. Here is the *social* beginning of the patient's career, regardless of where one might locate the psychological beginning of his mental illness.

The kinds of offenses which lead to hospitalization are felt to differ in nature from those which lead to other extrusory consequences—to imprisonment, divorce, loss of job, disownment, regional exile, noninstitutional psychiatric treatment, and so forth. But little seems known about these differentiating factors; and when one studies actual commitments, alternate outcomes frequently appear to have been possible. It seems true, moreover, that for every offense that leads to an effective complaint, there are many psychiatrically similar ones that never do. No action is taken; or action is taken which leads to other extrusory outcomes; or ineffective action is taken, leading to the mere pacifying or putting off of the person who complains. Thus, as Clausen and Yarrow have nicely shown, even offenders who are eventually hospitalized

[10] See footnote 2; Hollingshead and Redlich, p. 187, Table 6, where relative frequency is given of self-referral by social class grouping.

[11] The distinction employed here between willing and unwilling patients cuts across the legal one, of voluntary and committed, since some persons who are glad to come to the mental hospital may be legally committed, and of those who come only because of strong familial pressure, some may sign themselves in as voluntary patients.

are likely to have had a long series of ineffective actions taken against them.[12]

Separating those offenses which could have been used as grounds for hospitalizing the offender from those that are so used, one finds a vast number of what students of occupation call career contingencies.[13] Some of these contingencies in the mental patient's career have been suggested, if not explored, such as socioeconomic status, visibility of the offense, proximity to a mental hospital, amount of treatment facilities available, community regard for the type of treatment given in available hospitals, and so on.[14] For information about other contingencies one must rely on atrocity tales: a psychotic man is tolerated by his wife until she finds herself a boy friend, or by his adult children until they move from a house to an apartment; an alcoholic is sent to a mental hospital because the jail is full, and a drug addict because he declines to avail himself of psychiatric treatment on the outside; a rebellious adolescent daughter can no longer be managed at home because she now threatens to have an open affair with an unsuitable companion; and so on. Correspondingly there is an equally important set of contingencies causing the person to by-pass this fate. And should the person enter the hospital, still another set of contingencies will help determine when he is to obtain a discharge —such as the desire of his family for his return, the availability of a "manageable" job, and so on. The society's official view is that inmates of mental hospitals are there primarily because they are suffering from mental illness. However, in the degree that the "mentally ill" outside hospitals numerically approach or surpass those inside hospitals, one could say that mental patients *distinctively* suffer not from mental illness, but from contingencies.

Career contingencies occur in conjunction with a second feature of the prepatient's career—the *circuit of agents* —and agencies—that participate fatefully in his passage from civilian to patient status.[15] Here is an instance of that increasingly important class of social system whose elements are agents and agencies, which are brought into systemic connection through having to take up and send on the same persons. Some of these agent-roles will be cited now, with the understanding that in any concrete circuit a role may be filled more than once, and a single person may fill more than one of them.

First is the *next-of-relation*—the person whom the prepatient sees as the most available of those upon whom he should be able to most depend in times of trouble; in this instance the last to doubt his sanity and the first to have done everything to save him from the fate which, it transpires, he has been approaching. The patient's next-of-relation is usually his next of kin; the special term is introduced because he need not be. Second is the *complainant,* the person who retrospectively appears to have started the person on his way to the hospital. Third are the *mediators*—the sequence of agents and agencies to which the prepatient is referred and through which he is relayed

[12] Clausen and Yarrow: see footnote 4.

[13] An explicit application of this notion to the field of mental health may be found in Edwin M. Lemert, "Legal Commitment and Social Control," *Sociology and Social Research* (1946) 30:370–378.

[14] For example, Jerome K. Meyers and Leslie Schaffer, "Social Stratification and Psychiatric Practice: A Study of an Outpatient Clinic," *Amer. Sociological Rev.* (1954) 19:307–310. Lemert, see footnote 5; pp. 402–403. *Patients in Mental Institutions, 1941;* Washington, D. C., Department of Commerce, Bureau of the Census, 1941; p. 2.

[15] For one circuit of agents and its bearing on career contingencies, see Oswald Hall, "The Stages of a Medical Career," *Amer. J. Sociology* (1948) 53:327–336.

and processed on his way to the hospital. Here are included police, clergy, general medical practitioners, office psychiatrists, personnel in public clinics, lawyers, social service workers, school teachers, and so on. One of these agents will have the legal mandate to sanction commitment and will exercise it, and so those agents who precede him in the process will be involved in something whose outcome is not yet settled. When the mediators retire from the scene, the prepatient has become an inpatient, and the significant agent has become the hospital administrator.

While the complainant usually takes action in a lay capacity as a citizen, an employer, a neighbor, or a kinsman, mediators tend to be specialists and differ from those they serve in significant ways. They have experience in handling trouble, and some professional distance from what they handle. Except in the case of policemen, and perhaps some clergy, they tend to be more psychiatrically oriented than the lay public, and will see the need for treatment at times when the public does not.[16]

An interesting feature of these roles is the functional effects of their interdigitation. For example, the feelings of the patient will be influenced by whether or not the person who fills the role of complainant also has the role of next-of-relation—an embarrassing combination more prevalent, apparently, in the higher classes than in the lower.[17] Some of these emergent effects will be considered now.[18]

In the prepatient's progress from home to the hospital he may participate as a third person in what he may come to experience as a kind of *alienative coalition*. His next-of-relation presses him into coming to "talk things over" with a medical practitioner, an office psychiatrist, or some other counselor. Disinclination on his part may be met by threatening him with desertion, disownment, or other legal action, or by stressing the joint and explorative nature of the interview. But typically the next-of-relation will have set the interview up, in the sense of selecting the professional, arranging for time, telling the professional something about the case, and so on. This move effectively tends to establish the next-of-relation as the responsible person to whom pertinent findings can be divulged, while effectively establishing the other as the patient. The prepatient often goes to the interview with the understanding that he is going as an equal of someone who is so bound together with him that a third person could not come between them in fundamental matters; this, after all, is one way in which close relationships are defined in our society. Upon arrival at the office the prepatient suddenly finds that he and his next-of-relation have not been accorded the same roles, and apparently that a prior understanding between the professional and the next-of-relation has been put in operation against him. In the extreme but common case the professional first sees the prepatient alone, in the role of examiner and diagnostician, and then sees the next-of-relation alone, in the role of advisor, while carefully avoiding talking things over seriously with them both together.[19] And even in those nonconsultative cases where public officials must

[16] See Cumming, footnote 3; p. 92.

[17] Hollingshead and Redlich, footnote 4; p. 187.

[18] For an analysis of some of these circuit implications for the inpatient, see Leila C. Deasy and Olive W. Quinn, "The Wife of the Mental Patient and the Hospital Psychiatrist," *J. Social Issues* (1955) 11:49–60. An interesting illustration of this kind of analysis may also be found in Alan G. Gowman, "Blindness and the Role of Companion," *Social Problems* (1956) 4:68–75. A general statement may be found in Robert Merton, "The Role Set: Problems in Sociological Theory," *British J. Sociology* (1957) 8:106–120.

[19] I have one case record of a man who claims he thought *he* was taking his wife to see the psychiatrist, not realizing until too late that his wife had made the arrangements.

forcibly extract a person from a family that wants to tolerate him, the next-of-relation is likely to be induced to "go along" with the official action, so that even here the prepatient may feel that an alienative coalition has been formed against him.

The moral experience of being third man in such a coalition is likely to embitter the prepatient, especially since his troubles have already probably led to some estrangement from his next-of-relation. After he enters the hospital, continued visits by his next-of-relation can give the patient the "insight" that his own best interests were being served. But the initial visits may temporarily strengthen his feeling of abandonment; he is likely to beg his visitor to get him out or at least to get him more privileges and to sympathize with the monstrousness of his plight—to which the visitor ordinarily can respond only by trying to maintain a hopeful note, by not "hearing" the requests, or by assuring the patient that the medical authorities know about these things and are doing what is medically best. The visitor then nonchalantly goes back into a world that the patient has learned is incredibly thick with freedom and privileges, causing the patient to feel that his next-of-relation is merely adding a pious gloss to a clear case of traitorous desertion.

The depth to which the patient may feel betrayed by his next-of-relation seems to be increased by the fact that another witnesses his betrayal—a factor which is apparently significant in many three-party situations. An offended person may well act forbearantly and accommodatively toward an offender when the two are alone, choosing peace ahead of justice. The presence of a witness, however, seems to add something to the implica-tions of the offense. For then it is beyond the power of the offended and offender to forget about, erase, or suppress what has happened; the offense has become a public social fact.[20] When the witness is a mental health commission, as is sometimes the case, the witnessed betrayal can verge on a "degradation cere-mony." [21] In such circumstances, the offended patient may feel that some kind of extensive reparative action is required before witnesses, if his honor and social weight are to be restored.

Two other aspects of sensed betrayal should be mentioned. First, those who suggest the possibility of another's entering a mental hospital are not likely to provide a realistic picture of how in fact it may strike him when he arrives. Often he is told that he will get required medical treatment and a rest, and may well be out in a few months or so. In some cases they may thus be concealing what they know, but I think, in general, they will be telling what they see as the truth. For here there is a quite relevant difference between patients and mediating professionals; mediators, more so than the public at large, may conceive of mental hospitals as short-term medical establishments where required rest and attention can be voluntarily obtained, and not as places of coerced exile. When the prepatient finally arrives he is likely to learn quite quickly, quite differently. He then finds that the information given him about life in the hospital has had the effect of his having put up less resistance to entering than he now sees he would have put up had he known the facts. Whatever the intentions of those who participated in his transition from person to patient, he may sense they have in effect "conned" him into his present predicament.

[20] A paraphrase from Kurt Riezler, "The Social Psychology of Shame," *Amer. J. Sociology* (1943) 48:458.
[21] See Harold Garfinkel, "Conditions of Successful Degradation Ceremonies," *Amer. J. Sociology* (1956) 61:420–424.

I am suggesting that the prepatient starts out with at least a portion of the rights, liberties, and satisfactions of the civilian and ends up on a psychiatric ward stripped of almost everything. The question here is *how* this stripping is managed. This is the second aspect of betrayal I want to consider.

As the prepatient may see it, the circuit of significant figures can function as a kind of *betrayal funnel*. Passage from person to patient may be effected through a series of linked stages, each managed by a different agent. While each stage tends to bring a sharp decrease in adult free status, each agent may try to maintain the fiction that no further decrease will occur. He may even manage to turn the prepatient over to the next agent while sustaining this note. Further, through words, cues, and gestures, the prepatient is implicitly asked by the current agent to join with him in sustaining a running line of polite small talk that tactfully avoids the administrative facts of the situation, becoming, with each stage, progressively more at odds with these facts. The spouse would rather not have to cry to get the prepatient to visit a psychiatrist; psychiatrists would rather not have a scene when the prepatient learns that he and his spouse are being seen separately and in different ways; the police infrequently bring a prepatient to the hospital in a strait jacket, finding it much easier all around to give him a cigarette, some kindly words, and freedom to relax in the back seat of the patrol car; and finally, the admitting psychiatrist finds he can do his work better in the relative quiet and luxury of the "admission suite" where, as an incidental consequence, the notion can survive that a mental hospital is indeed a comforting place. If the prepatient heeds all of these implied requests and is reasonably decent about the whole thing, he can travel the whole circuit from home to hospital without forcing anyone to look directly at what is happening or to deal with the raw emotion that his situation might well cause him to express. His showing consideration for those who are moving him toward the hospital allows them to show consideration for him, with the joint result that these interactions can be sustained with some of the protective harmony characteristic of ordinary face-to-face dealings. But should the new patient cast his mind back over the sequence of steps leading to hospitalization, he may feel that everyone's *current* comfort was being busily sustained while his long-range welfare was being undermined. This realization may constitute a moral experience that further separates him for the time from the people on the outside.[22]

I would now like to look at the circuit of career agents from the point of view of the agents themselves. Mediators in the person's transition from civil to patient status—as well as his keepers, once he is in the hospital—have an interest in establishing a responsible next-of-relation as the patient's deputy or *guardian;* should there be no obvious candidate for the role, someone may be sought out and pressed into it. Thus while a person is gradually being transformed into a patient, a next-of-relation is gradually being transformed into a guardian. With a

---

[22] Concentration camp practices provide a good example of the function of the betrayal funnel in inducing cooperation and reducing struggle and fuss, although here the mediators could not be said to be acting in the best interests of the inmates. Police picking up persons from their homes would sometimes joke good-naturedly and offer to wait while coffee was being served. Gas chambers were fitted out like delousing rooms, and victims taking off their clothes were told to note where they were leaving them. The sick, aged, weak, or insane who were selected for extermination were sometimes driven away in Red Cross ambulances to camps referred to by terms such as "observation hospital." See David Boder, *I Did Not Interview the Dead;* Urbana, Univ. of Illinois Press, 1949; p. 81; and Elie A. Cohen, *Human Behavior in the Concentration Camp;* London, Cape, 1954; pp. 32, 37, 107.

guardian on the scene, the whole transition process can be kept tidy. He is likely to be familiar with the prepatient's civil involvements and business, and can tie up loose ends that might otherwise be left to entangle the hospital. Some of the prepatient's abrogated civil rights can be transferred to him, thus helping to sustain the legal fiction that while the prepatient does not actually have his rights he somehow actually has not lost them.

Inpatients commonly sense, at least for a time, that hospitalization is a massive unjust deprivation, and sometimes succeed in convincing a few persons on the outside that this is the case. It often turns out to be useful, then, for those identified with inflicting these deprivations, however justifiably, to be able to point to the cooperation and agreement of someone whose relationship to the patient places him above suspicion, firmly defining him as the person most likely to have the patient's personal interest at heart. If the guardian is satisfied with what is happening to the new inpatient, the world ought to be.[23]

Now it would seem that the greater the legitimate personal stake one party has in another, the better he can take the role of guardian to the other. But the structural arrangements in society which lead to the acknowledged merging of two persons' interests lead to additional consequences. For the person to whom the patient turns for help—for protection against such threats as involuntary commitment—is just the person to whom the mediators and hospital administrators logically turn for authorization. It is understandable, then, that some patients will come to sense, at least for a time, that the closeness of a relationship tells nothing of its trustworthiness.

There are still other functional effects emerging from this complement of roles. If and when the next-of-relation appeals to mediators for help in the trouble he is having with the prepatient, hospitalization may not, in fact, be in his mind. He may not even perceive the prepatient as mentally sick, or, if he does, he may not consistently hold to this view.[24] It is the circuit of mediators, with their greater psychiatric sophistication and their belief in the medical character of mental hospitals, that will often define the situation for the next-of-relation, assuring him that hospitalization is a possible solution and a good one, that it involves no betrayal, but is rather a medical action taken in the best interests of the prepatient. Here the next-of-relation may learn that doing his duty to the prepatient may cause the prepatient to distrust and even hate him for the time. But the fact that this course of action may have had to be pointed out and prescribed by professionals, and be defined by them as a moral duty, relieves the next-of-relation of some of the guilt he may feel.[25] It is a poignant fact that an adult son or daughter may be pressed into the role of mediator, so that the

---

[23] Interviews collected by the Clausen group at NIMH suggest that when a wife comes to be a guardian, the responsibility may disrupt previous distance from in-laws, leading either to a new supportive coalition with them or to a marked withdrawal from them.

[24] For an analysis of these nonpsychiatric kinds of perception, see Marian Radke Yarrow, Charlotte Green Schwartz, Harriet S. Murphy, and Leila Calhoun Deasy, "The Psychological Meaning of Mental Illness in the Family," *J. Social Issues* (1955) 11:12–24; Charlotte Green Schwartz, "Perspectives on Deviance—Wives' Definitions of their Husbands' Mental Illness," *Psychiatry* (1957) 20:275–291.

[25] This guilt-carrying function is found, of course, in other role-complexes. Thus, when a middle-class couple engages in the process of legal separation or divorce, each of their lawyers usually takes the position that his job is to acquaint his client with all of the potential claims and rights, pressing his client into demanding these, in spite of any nicety of feelings about the rights and honorableness of the ex-partner. The client, in all good faith, can then say to self and to the ex-partner that the demands are being made only because the lawyer insists it is best to do so.

hostility that might otherwise be directed against the spouse is passed on to the child.[26]

Once the prepatient is in the hospital, the same guilt-carrying function may become a significant part of the staff's job in regard to the next-of-relation.[27] These reasons for feeling that he himself has not betrayed the patient, even though the patient may then think so, can later provide the next-of-relation with a defensible line to take when visiting the patient in the hospital and a basis for hoping that the relationship can be re-established after its hospital moratorium. And of course this position, when sensed by the patient, can provide him with excuses for the next-of-relation, when and if he comes to look for them.[28]

Thus while the next-of-relation can perform important functions for the mediators and hospital administrators, they in turn can perform important functions for him. One finds, then, an emergent unintended exchange or reciprocation of functions, these functions themselves being often unintended.

The final point I want to consider about the prepatient's moral career is its peculiarly *retroactive* character. Until a person actually arrives at the hospital there usually seems no way of knowing for sure that he is destined to do so, given the determinative role of career contingencies. And until the point of hospitalization is reached, he or others may not conceive of him as a person who is becoming a mental patient. However, since he will be held against his will in the hospital, his next-of-relation and the hospital staff will be in great need of a rationale for the hardships they are sponsoring. The medical elements of the staff will also need evidence that they are still in the trade they were trained for. These problems are eased, no doubt unintentionally, by the case-history construction that is placed on the patient's past life, this having the effect of demonstrating that all along he had been becoming sick, that he finally became very sick, and that if he had not been hospitalized much worse things would have happened to him—all of which, of course, may be true. Incidentally, if the patient wants to make sense out of his stay in the hospital, and, as already suggested, keep alive the possibility of once again conceiving of his next-of-relation as a decent, well-meaning person, then he too will have reason to believe some of this psychiatric work-up of his past.

Here is a very ticklish point for the sociology of careers. An important aspect of every career is the view the person constructs when he looks backward over his progress; in a sense, however, the whole of the prepatient career derives from this reconstruction. The fact of having had a prepatient career, starting with an effective complaint, becomes an important part of the mental patient's orientation, but this part can begin to be played only after hospitalization proves that what he had been having, but no longer has, is a career as a prepatient. . . .

---

[26] Recorded in the Clausen data.

[27] This point is made by Cumming, see footnote 3; p. 129.

[28] There is an interesting contrast here with the moral career of the tuberculosis patient. I am told by Julius Roth that tuberculous patients are likely to come to the hospital willingly, agreeing with their next-of-relation about treatment. Later in their hospital career, when they learn how long they yet have to stay and how depriving and irrational some of the hospital rulings are, they may seek to leave, be advised against this by the staff and by relatives, and only then begin to feel betrayed.

Paranoia and the Dynamics
of Exclusion * †

EDWIN M. LEMERT

One of the few generalizations about psychotic behavior which sociologists have been able to make with a modicum of agreement and assurance is that such behavior is a result or manifestation of a disorder in communication between the individual and society. The generalization, of course, is a large one, and, while it can be illustrated easily with case history materials, the need for its conceptual refinement and detailing of the process by which disruption of communication occurs in the dynamics of mental disorder has for some time been apparent. Among the more carefully reasoned attacks upon this problem is Cameron's formulation of the paranoid pseudocommunity (1).

In essence, the conception of the paranoid pseudocommunity can be stated as follows: [1]

Paranoid persons are those whose inadequate social learning leads them in situations of unusual stress to incompetent social reactions. Out of the fragments of the social behavior of others the paranoid person symbolically organizes a pseudocommunity whose functions he perceives as focused on him. His reactions to this *supposed community* of response which he sees loaded with threat to himself bring him into open conflict with the actual community and lead to his temporary or permanent isolation from its affairs. The "real" community, which is unable to share in his attitudes and reactions, takes action through forcible restraint or retaliation *after* the paranoid person "bursts into defensive or vengeful activity" (1).

That the community to which the paranoid reacts is "pseudo" or without existential reality is made unequivocal by Cameron when he says:

"As he (the paranoid person) begins attributing to others the attitudes which he has towards himself, he unintentionally organizes these others into a functional community, a group unified in their supposed reactions, attitudes and plans with respect to him. He in this way organizes individuals, some of whom are actual persons and some only inferred or imagined, into a whole which satisfies for the time being his immediate need for explanation but which brings no assurance with it, and usually serves to increase his tensions. The community he forms not only fails to correspond to any organization shared by others but actually contradicts this consensus. More than this, the actions ascribed by him to its personnel are not actually performed or maintained by them; *they are united in no common undertaking against him*" (1). (Italics ours.)

The general insightfulness of Cameron's analysis cannot be gainsaid and the usefulness of some of his concepts is easily granted. Yet a serious question

* Reprinted from *Sociometry,* Vol. 25, No. 1 (March, 1962), pp. 2–5, 7–15, 18–20, by permission of the author and the American Sociological Association.

† The research for this paper was in part supported by a grant from the California State Department of Mental Hygiene, arranged with the assistance of Dr. W. A. Oliver, Associate Superintendent of Napa State Hospital, who also helped as a critical consultant and made the facilities of the hospital available.

[1] In a subsequent article Cameron (2) modified his original conception, but not of the social aspects of paranoia, which mainly concern us.

must be raised, based upon empirical inquiry, as to whether in actuality the insidious qualities of the community to which the paranoid reacts are pseudo or a symbolic fabrication. There is an alternative point of view, which is the burden of this paper, namely that, while the paranoid person reacts differentially to his social environment, it is also true that "others" react differentially to him and this reaction commonly if not typically involves covertly organized action and conspiratorial behavior in a very real sense. A further extension of our thesis is that these differential reactions are reciprocals of one another, being interwoven and concatenated at each and all phases of a process of exclusion which arises in a special kind of relationship. Delusions and associated behavior must be understood in a context of exclusion which attenuates this relationship and disrupts communication. . . .

From what has been said thus far, it should be clear that our formulation and analysis will deal primarily with what Tyhurst (8) calls paranoid patterns of behavior rather than with a clinical entity in the classical Kraepelinian sense. Paranoid reactions, paranoid states, paranoid personality disturbances, as well as the seldom-diagnosed "true paranoia," which are found superimposed or associated with a wide variety of individual behavior or "symptoms," all provide a body of data for study so long as they assume priority over other behavior in meaningful social interaction. The elements of behavior upon which paranoid diagnoses are based—delusions, hostility, aggressiveness, suspicion, envy, stubbornness, jealousy, and ideas of reference—are readily comprehended and to some extent empathized by others as social reactions, in contrast to the bizarre, manneristic behavior of schizophrenia or the tempo and affect changes stressed in manic-depressive diagnoses. It is for this

reason that paranoia suggests, more than any other forms of mental disorder, the possibility of fruitful sociological analysis.

Data and Procedure

The first tentative conclusions which are presented here were drawn from a study of factors influencing decisions to commit mentally disordered persons to hospitals, undertaken with the cooperation of the Los Angeles County Department of Health in 1952. This included interviews by means of schedules with members of 44 families in Los Angeles County who were active petitioners in commitment proceedings and the study of 35 case records of public health officer commitments. In 16 of the former cases and in seven of the latter, paranoid symptoms were conspicuously present. In these cases family members and others had plainly accepted or "normalized" paranoid behavior, in some instances longstanding, until other kinds of behavior or exigencies led to critical judgments that "there was something wrong" with the person in question, and, later, that hospitalization was necessary. Furthermore, these critical judgments seemed to signal changes in the family attitudes and behavior towards the affected persons which could be interpreted as contributing in different ways to the form and intensity of the paranoid symptoms.

In 1958 a more refined and hypothesis-directed study was made of eight cases of persons with prominent paranoid characteristics. Four of these had been admitted to the state hospital at Napa, California, where they were diagnosed as paranoid schizophrenic. Two other cases were located and investigated with the assistance of the district attorney in Martinez, California. One of the persons had previously been committed to a California state hospital, and the other had been held on an insanity petition but was freed after a jury trial. Added to these was one so-called "White House case," which had involved threats to a President of the United States, resulting in the person's commitment to St. Elizabeth's Hospital in Washington, D. C. A final case was that of a professional person with a history of chronic job difficulties, who was designated and regarded by his associates as "brash," "queer," "irritating," "hypercritical," and "thoroughly unlikeable."

In a very rough way the cases made up a continuum ranging from one with very elaborate delusions, through those in which fact and misinterpretation were difficult to separate, down to the last case, which comes closer to what some would call paranoid personality disturbance. A requirement for the selection of the cases was that there be no history or evidence of hallucinations and also that the persons be intellectually unimpaired. Seven of the cases were of males, five of whom were over 40 years of age. Three of the persons had been involved in repeated litigations. One man published a small, independent paper devoted to exposures of psychiatry and mental hospitals. Five of the men had been or were associated with organizations, as follows: a small-town high school, a government research bureau, an association of agricultural producers, a university, and a contracting business.

The investigations of the cases were as exhaustive as it was possible to make them, reaching relatives, work associates, employers, attorneys, police, physicians, public officials and any others who played significant roles in the lives of the persons involved. As many as 200 hours each were given to collecting data on some of the cases. Written materials, legal documents, publications and psychiatric histories were studied in addition to the interview data. Our procedure in the large was to adopt an interactional perspective which sensitized us to sociologically relevant behavior underlying or associated with the more apparent and formal contexts of mental disorder. In particular we were concerned to establish the order in which delusions and social exclusion occur and to determine whether exclusion takes conspiratorial form. . . .

The Generic Process of Exclusion

The paranoid process begins with persistent interpersonal difficulties between the individual and his family, or his work associates and superiors, or neighbors, or other persons in the community. These frequently or even typically arise out of bona fide or recognizable issues centering upon some actual or threatened loss of status for the individual. This is related to such things as the death of relatives, loss of a position, loss of professional certification, failure to be promoted, age and physiological life cycle changes, mutilations, and changes in family and marital relationships. The status changes are distinguished by the fact that they leave no alternative acceptable to the individual, from whence comes their "intolerable" or "unendurable" quality. For example: the man trained to be a teacher who loses his certificate, which means he can never teach; or the man of 50 years of age who is faced with loss of a promotion which is a regular order of upward mobility in an organization, who knows that he can't "start over"; or the wife undergoing hysterectomy, which mutilates her image as a woman.

In cases where no dramatic status loss can be discovered, a series of failures often is present, failures which may have been accepted or adjusted to, but with progressive tension as each new status situation is entered. The unendurability of the current status loss, which may appear unimportant to others, is a function of an intensified commitment, in some cases born of an awareness that there is a quota placed on failures in our society. Under some such circumstances, failures have followed the person, and his reputation as a "difficult person" has preceded him. This means that he often has the status of a stranger on trial in each new group he enters, and that the groups or organizations willing to take a chance on him are marginal from the standpoint of their probable tolerance for his actions.

The behavior of the individual—arrogance, insults, presumption of privilege and exploitation of weaknesses in others—initially has a segmental or checkered pattern in that it is confined to status-committing interactions. Outside of these, the person's behavior may be quite acceptable—courteous, considerate, kind, even indulgent. Likewise, other persons and members of groups vary considerably in their tolerance for the relevant behavior, depending on the extent to which it threatens individual and organizational values, impedes functions, or sets in motion embarrassing sequences of social actions. In the early generic period, tolerance by others for the individual's aggressive behavior generally speaking is broad, and it is very likely to be interpreted as a variation of normal behavior, particularly in the absence of biographical knowledge of the person. At most, people observe that "there is something odd about him," or "he must be upset," or "he is just ornery," or "I don't quite understand him" (3).

At some point in the chain of interactions, a new configuration takes place in perceptions others have of the individual, with shifts in figure-ground relations. The individual, as we have already indicated, is an ambiguous figure, comparable to textbook figures of stairs or outlined cubes which reverse themselves when studied intently. From a normal variant the person becomes "unreliable," "un-

trustworthy," "dangerous," or someone with whom others "do not wish to be involved." An illustration nicely apropos of this came out in the reaction of the head of a music department in a university when he granted an interview to a man who had worked for years on a theory to compose music mathematically:

When he asked to be placed on the staff so that he could use the electronic computers of the University *I shifted my ground* . . . when I offered an objection to his theory, he became disturbed, so I changed my reaction to "yes and no."

As is clear from this, once the perceptual reorientation takes place, either as the outcome of continuous interaction or through the receipt of biographical information, interaction changes qualitatively. In our words it becomes *spurious,* distinguished by patronizing, evasion, "humoring," guiding conversation onto selected topics, underreaction, and silence, all calculated either to prevent intense interaction or to protect individual and group values by restricting access to them. When the interaction is between two or more persons in the individual's presence it is cued by a whole repertoire of subtle expressive signs which are meaningful only to them.

The net effects of spurious interaction are to:

1. stop the flow of information to ego;
2. create a discrepancy between expressed ideas and affect among those with whom he interacts;
3. make the situation or the group image an ambiguous one for ego, much as he is for others.

Needless to say this kind of spurious interaction is one of the most difficult for an adult in our society to cope with, because it complicates or makes decisions impossible for him and also because it is morally invidious.[2]

The process from inclusion to exclusion is by no means an even one. Both individuals and members of groups change their perceptions and reactions, and vacillation is common, depending upon the interplay of values, anxieties and guilt on both sides. Members of an excluding group may decide they have been unfair and seek to bring the individual back into their confidence. This overture may be rejected or used by ego as a means of further attack. We have also found that ego may capitulate, sometimes abjectly, to others and seek group re-entry, only to be rejected. In some cases compromises are struck and a partial reintegration of ego into informal social relations is achieved. The direction which informal exclusion takes depends upon ego's reactions, the degree of communication between his interactors, the composition and structure of the informal groups, and the perceptions of "key others" at points of interaction which directly affect ego's status.

Organizational Crisis and Formal Exclusion

Thus far we have discussed exclusion as an informal process. Informal exclusion may take place but leave ego's formal status in an organization intact. So long as this status is preserved and rewards are sufficient to validate it on his terms, an uneasy peace between him and others may prevail. Yet ego's social isolation and his strong commitments make him an unpredictable factor; furthermore the rate of change and internal power struggles, especially in large and complex organizations, means that pre-

conditions of stability may be short lived.

Organizational crises involving a paranoid relationship arise in several ways. The individual may act in ways which arouse intolerable anxieties in others, who demand that "something be done." Again, by going to higher authority or making appeals outside the organization, he may set in motion procedures which leave those in power no other choice than to take action. In some situations ego remains relatively quiescent and does not openly attack the organization. Action against him is set off by growing anxieties or calculated motives of associates— in some cases his immediate superiors. Finally, regular organizational procedures incidental to promotion, retirement or reassignment may precipitate the crisis.

Assuming a critical situation in which the conflict between the individual and members of the organization leads to action to formally exclude him, several possibilities exist. One is the transfer of ego from one department, branch or division of the organization to another, a device frequently resorted to in the armed services or in large corporations. This requires that the individual be persuaded to make the change and that some department will accept him. While this may be accomplished in different ways, not infrequently artifice, withholding information, bribery, or thinly disguised threats figure conspicuously among the means by which the transfer is brought about. Needless to say, there is a limit to which transfers can be employed as a solution to the problem, contingent upon the size of the organization and the previous diffusion of knowledge about the transferee.

Solution number two we call encapsulation, which, in brief, is a reorganiza-

[2] The interaction in some ways is similar to that used with children, particularly the *"enfant terrible."* The function of language in such interaction was studied by Sapir (7) years ago.

tion and redefinition of ego's status. This has the effect of isolating him from the organization and making him directly responsible to one or two superiors who act as his intermediators. The change is often made palatable to ego by enhancing some of the material rewards of his status. He may be nominally promoted or "kicked upstairs," given a larger office, or a separate secretary, or relieved of onerous duties. Sometimes a special status is created for him.

This type of solution often works because it is a kind of formal recognition by the organization of ego's intense commitment to his status and in part a victory for him over his enemies. It bypasses them and puts him into direct communication with higher authority who may communicate with him in a more direct manner. It also relieves his associates of further need to connive against him. This solution is sometimes used to dispose of troublesome corporation executives, high-ranking military officers, and academic *personae non gratae* in universities.

A third variety of solutions to the problem of paranoia in an organization is outright discharge, forced resignation or non-renewal of appointment. Finally, there may be an organized move to have the individual in the paranoid relationship placed on sick leave, or to compel him to take psychiatric treatment. The extreme expression of this is pressure (as on the family) or direct action to have the person commited to a mental hospital.

The order of the enumerated solutions to the paranoid problem in a rough way reflects the amount of risk associated with the alternatives, both as to the probabilities of failure and of damaging repercussions to the organization. Generally, organizations seem to show a good deal of resistance to making or carrying out decisions which require expulsion of the individual or forcing hospitalization, regardless of his mental condition. One reason for this is that the person may have power within the organization, based upon his position, or monopolized skills and information,[3] and unless there is a strong coalition against him the general conservatism of administrative judgments will run in his favor. Herman Wouk's novel of *The Caine Mutiny* dramatizes some of the difficulties of cashiering a person from a position of power in an essentially conservative military organization. An extreme of this conservatism is illustrated by one case in which we found a department head retained in his position in an organization even though he was actively hallucinating as well as expressing paranoid delusions.[4] Another factor working on the individual's side is that discharge of a person in a position of power reflects unfavorably upon those who placed him there. Ingroup solidarity of administrators may be involved, and the methods of the opposition may create sympathy for ego at higher levels.

Even when the person is almost totally excluded and informally isolated within an organization, he may have power outside. This weighs heavily when the external power can be invoked in some way, or when it automatically leads to raising questions as to the internal workings of the organization. This touches upon the more salient reason for reluctance to eject an uncooperative and retaliatory person, even when he is relatively unimportant to the organization. We refer to a kind of negative power derived from the vulnerability of organizations to unfavorable publicity and exposure of their private lives that are likely if the crisis proceeds to formal hearings, case review

---

[3] For a systematic analysis of the organizational difficulties in removing an "unpromotable" person from a position see (5).

[4] One of the cases in the first study.

or litigation. This is an imminent possibility where paranoia exists. If hospital commitment is attempted, there is a possibility that a jury trial will be demanded, which will force leaders of the organization to defend their actions. If the crisis turns into a legal contest of this sort, it is not easy to prove insanity, and there may be damage suits. Even if the facts heavily support the petitioners, such contests can only throw unfavorable light upon the organization.

The Conspiratorial Nature of Exclusion

A conclusion from the foregoing is that organizational vulnerability as well as anticipations of retaliations from the paranoid person lay a functional basis for conspiracy among those seeking to contain or oust him. Probabilities are strong that a coalition will appear within the organization, integrated by a common commitment to oppose the paranoid person. This, the exclusionist group, demands loyalty, solidarity and secrecy from its members; it acts in accord with a common scheme and in varying degrees utilizes techniques of manipulation and misrepresentation.

Conspiracy in rudimentary form can be detected in informal exclusion apart from an organizational crisis. This was illustrated in an office research team in which staff members huddled around a water cooler to discuss the unwanted associate. They also used office telephones to arrange coffee breaks without him and employed symbolic cues in his presence, such as humming the Dragnet theme song when he approached the group. An office rule against extraneous conversation was introduced with the collusion of supervisors, ostensibly for everyone, actually to restrict the behavior of the isolated worker. In another case an interview schedule designed by a researcher was changed at a conference arranged without him. When he sought an explanation at a subsequent conference, his associates pretended to have no knowledge of the changes.

Conspiratorial behavior comes into sharpest focus during organizational crises in which the exclusionists who initiate action become an embattled group. There is a concerted effort to gain consensus for this view, to solidify the group and to halt close interaction with those unwilling to completely join the coalition. Efforts are also made to neutralize those who remain uncommitted but who can't be kept ignorant of the plans afoot. Thus an external appearance of unanimity is given even if it doesn't exist.

Much of the behavior of the group at this time is strategic in nature, with determined calculations as to "what we will do if he does this or that." In one of our cases, a member on a board of trustees spoke of the "game being played" with the person in controversy with them. Planned action may be carried to the length of agreeing upon the exact words to be used when confronted or challenged by the paranoid individual. Above all there is continuous, precise communication among exclusionists, exemplified in one case by mutual exchanging of copies of all letters sent and received from ego.

Concern about secrecy in such groups is revealed by such things as carefully closing doors and lowering of voices when ego is brought under discussion. Meeting places and times may be varied from normal procedures; documents may be filed in unusual places and certain telephones may not be used during a paranoid crisis.

The visibility of the individual's behavior is greatly magnified during this period; often he is the main topic of conversation among the exclusionists, while rumors of the difficulties spread to other groups, which in some cases may be drawn into the controversy. At a certain juncture steps are taken to keep the members of the ingroup continually informed of the individual's movements and, if possible, of his plans. In effect, if not in form, this amounts to spying. Members of one embattled group, for example, hired an outside person unknown to their accuser to take notes on a speech he delivered to enlist a community organization on his side. In another case, a person having an office opening onto that of a department head was persuaded to act as an informant for the nucleus of persons working to depose the head from his position of authority. This group also seriously debated placing an all-night watch in front of their perceived malefactor's house.

Concomitant with the magnified visibility of the paranoid individual, come distortions of his image, most pronounced in the inner coterie of exclusionists. His size, physical strength, cunning, and anecdotes of his outrages are exaggerated, with a central thematic emphasis on the fact that he is dangerous. Some individuals give cause for such beliefs in that previously they have engaged in violence or threats, others do not. One encounters characteristic contradictions in interviews on this point, such as: "No, he has never struck anyone around here—just fought with the policemen at the State Capitol," or "No, I am not afraid of him, but one of these days he will explode."

It can be said parenthetically that the alleged dangerousness of paranoid persons storied in fiction and drama has never been systematically demonstrated. As a matter of fact, the only substantial data on this, from a study of delayed admissions, largely paranoid, to a mental hospital in Norway, disclosed that "neither the paranoiacs nor paranoids have been dangerous, and most not particularly troublesome" (6). Our interpretation of this, as suggested earlier, is that the imputed dangerousness of the paranoid individual does not come from physical fear but from the organizational threat he presents and the need to justify collective action against him.[5]

However, this is not entirely tactical behavior—as is demonstrated by anxieties and tensions which mount among those in the coalition during the more critical phases of their interaction. Participants may develop fears quite analogous to those of classic conspirators. One leader in such a group spoke of the period of the paranoid crisis as a "week of terror," during which he was wracked with insomnia and "had to take his stomach pills." Projection was revealed by a trustee who, during a school crisis occasioned by discharge of an aggressive teacher, stated that he "watched his shadows," and "wondered if all would be well when he returned home at night." Such tensional states, working along with a kind of closure of communication within the group, are both a cause and an effect of amplified group interaction which distorts or symbolically rearranges the image of the person against whom they act.

Once the battle is won by the exclusionists, their version of the individual as dangerous becomes a crystallized rationale for official action. At this point misrepresentation becomes part of a more deliberate manipulation of ego. Gross misstatements, most frequently called "pretexts," become justifiable ways of getting his cooperation, for example, to get him to submit to psychiatric examination or detention preliminary to hospital commitment. This aspect of the process has been effectively detailed by Goffman, with his concept of a "betrayal funnel" through which a patient enters a hospital

[5] *Supra,* p. 3.

(4). We need not elaborate on this, other than to confirm its occurrence in the exclusion process, complicated in our cases by legal strictures and the ubiquitous risk of litigation.

The Growth of Delusion

The general idea that the paranoid person symbolically fabricates the conspiracy against him is in our estimation incorrect or incomplete. Nor can we agree that he lacks insight, as is so frequently claimed. To the contrary, many paranoid persons properly realize that they are being isolated and excluded by concerted interaction, or that they are being manipulated. However, they are at a loss to estimate accurately or realistically the dimensions and form of the coalition arrayed against them.

As channels of communication are closed to the paranoid person, he has no means of getting feedback on consequences of his behavior, which is essential for correcting his interpretations of the social relationships and organization which he must rely on to define his status and give him identity. He can only read overt behavior without the informal context. Although he may properly infer that people are organized against him, he can only use confrontation or formal inquisitorial procedures to try to prove this. The paranoid person must provoke strong feelings in order to receive any kind of meaningful communication from others— hence his accusations, his bluntness, his insults. Ordinarily this is non-deliberate; nevertheless, in one complex case we found the person consciously provoking discussions to get readings from others on his behavior. This man said of himself: "Some people would describe me as very perceptive, others would describe me as very imperceptive."

The need for communication and the identity which goes with it does a good deal to explain the preference of paranoid persons for formal, legalistic, written communications, and the care with which many of them preserve records of their contracts with others. In some ways the resort to litigation is best interpreted as the effort of the individual to compel selected others to interact directly with him as equals, to engineer a situation in which evasion is impossible. The fact that the person is seldom satisfied with the outcome of his letters, his petitions, complaints and writs testifies to their function as devices for establishing contact and interaction with others, as well as "setting the record straight." The wide professional tolerance of lawyers for aggressive behavior in court and the nature of Anglo-Saxon legal institutions, which grew out of a revolt against conspiratorial or star-chamber justice, mean that the individual will be heard. Furthermore his charges must be answered; otherwise he wins by default. Sometimes he wins small victories, even if he loses the big ones. He may earn grudging respect as an adversary, and sometimes shares a kind of legal camaraderie with others in the courts. He gains an identity through notoriety. . . .

Concluding Comment

We have been concerned with a process of social exclusion and with the ways in which it contributes to the development of paranoid patterns of behavior. While the data emphasize the organizational forms of exclusion, we nevertheless believe that these are expressions of a generic process whose correlates will emerge from the study of paranoia in the family and other groups. The differential responses of the individual to the exigencies of organized exclusion are significant in the development of paranoid reactions only insofar as they partially determine the "intolerable" or "unendurable" quality of the status changes confronting him. Idiosyncratic life history factors of the sort stressed in more conventional psychiatric analyses may be involved, but equally important in our estimation are those which inhere in the status changes themselves, age being one of the more salient of these. In either case, once situational intolerability appears, the stage is set for the interactional process we have described.

Our cases, it will be noted, were all people who remained undeteriorated, in contact with others and carrying on militant activities oriented towards recognizable social values and institutions. Generalized suspiciousness in public places and unprovoked aggression against strangers were absent from their experiences. These facts, plus the relative absence of "true paranoia" among mental-hospital populations, leads us to conclude that the "pseudocommunity" associated with random aggression (in Cameron's sense) is a sequel rather than an integral part of paranoid patterns. They are likely products of deterioration and fragmentation of personality appearing, when and if they do, in the paranoid person after long or intense periods of stress and complete social isolation.

References

1. CAMERON, N., "The Paranoid Pseudo-community," *American Journal of Sociology,* 1943, 46, 33–38.
2. CAMERON, N., "The Paranoid Pseudo-community Revisited," *American Journal of Sociology,* 1959, 65, 52–58.
3. CUMMING, E., and J. CUMMING, *Closed Ranks,* Cambridge, Mass.: Harvard Press, 1957, Ch. VI.
4. GOFFMAN, E., "The Moral Career of the Mental Patient," *Psychiatry,* 1959, 22, 127 ff.
5. LEVENSON, B., "Bureaucratic Succession," in *Complex Organizations,* A. Etzioni (ed.), New York: Holt, Rinehart and Winston, 1961, 362–395.
6. ÖDEGARD, Ö., "A Clinical Study of Delayed Admissions to a Mental Hospital," *Mental Hygiene,* 1958, 42, 66–77.
7. SAPIR, E., "Abnormal Types of Speech in Nootka," *Canada Department of Mines, Memoir 62,* 1915, No. 5.
8. TYHURST, J. S., "Paranoid Patterns," in A. H. Leighton, J. A. Clausen, and R. Wilson (eds.), *Explorations in Social Psychiatry,* New York: Basic Books, 1957, Ch. II.

THE PUBLIC REGULATION
OF DEVIANCE

Part Two

ONCE AGENTS of social control take official action against deviants, private regulation of deviance must step aside in favor of its public regulation. And once persons enter the work-flow of public regulation and experience official processing, very frequently ratification, induction into the deviant role, and launching into a deviant career all occur simultaneously. On occasion, a dramatic redefinition of self can occur at that turning-point in life when agents of social control take official action against a person. But what may be and usually is a crisis and an emergency to the person experiencing this official processing is, from the point of view of the official and the agency for which he works, simply a matter of organizational routine.

Processing the deviant is the work of the official agents and the organizations for which they act. The public regulation of deviance is their function. And, as this function is carried out according to an elaborate and frequently precise set of official rules, the controls imposed upon deviants by these agencies differ significantly from those employed by private agents in three important ways. In power, in legitimacy, and in routine, public regulation and private regulation are at opposite poles. Generally, the power of the political state stands behind officials who take action against the deviant; they have the principle of legality supporting them, and their work with deviants is efficient and routine, i.e., carried out in accordance with a stock, official plan. In the operation of private regulation, power is frequently distributed equitably between the deviant and others, the rule of law is irrelevant when people may be strongly committed to opposing norms, and action against the deviant need not take place according to any plan at all.

Analysis of the official plan of action to be taken against deviants in the course of processing is necessary if we are to understand the special perspective that agents of social control adopt towards deviants when they perform their official work on them. This perspective provides them with a schema for typing or retyping the persons they encounter in the course of their work. By means of the agency perspective on deviants, they are able to administer deviance with efficiency, though not necessarily with effectiveness.

Accordingly, this Part takes up (a) the basic premises that underlie the organizational routine of agencies of social control or what we will term "the theory of the office"; (b) the special perspectives that police employ as they perform their official work; (c) the rules agents apply in typing court cases; and (d) the social conditions under which laymen take the perspective of official control agents towards the so-called deviant.

The Theory of the Office

The office developed to solve a problem in social management. A number of strangers typed as deviants have either gotten caught or have given themselves up to public regulation. The theory of the office supplies the answer to the question of what is to be done with them. The theory specifies the number and kinds of establishments that will process these deviants. It goes on to define both the characteristics of its clients and the manner in which they will be admitted, how they will be registered, and the manner in which they will be processed. In essence, then, the theory of the office concerns itself with registry. For in supplying agents with rules for typing (retyping) its special clientele of deviants and with directives for acting on these rules, it succeeds in ordering deviance.

Office theory sets down, then, the principles for the management of social deviance. The failure of personal and informal controls, in part, gave rise to the need for processing an array of persons who appear either unwilling or unable to abide by certain social, moral, legal, or technical rules. The office goes on to specify who shall be designated as the defining agent, how he shall go into official action against some of these persons, and under what conditions he will be permitted to type them as deviants. Once official typing has gotten underway, the deviant career has been launched, frequently in what the office would consider a rite of passage. This deviant career now must be managed in accordance with the theory that the office dictates, administered according to certain routine conceptions. Unless this administration proceeds according to the plan, the deviant career is likely to become inoperative or uncontrollable. However, when administration goes according to plan, the office is handling what it takes to be its usual run of business, its "normal cases."

In the private order, the demand to regularize novelty exists as we have seen in the case of wives who normalize their relations with husbands who are later assigned to the role of mental patients. In the public order, offices regularize according to a specific plan of administrative action. In contrast with families, offices have a set of precise categories to fit people in and a set of prescribed rules for sorting them into these very categories. This is not to say that between official agencies of social control there are no variations in precision or in application of official types. But as between public and private orders, it would seem that the public order, in accordance with the theory of the office operates on the theory, "Better a vague categorization than none at all, and better a rapid than a slow application of the label." Otherwise, novelty cannot be regularized and deviance may well spill over into the routine of the office itself.

The theory of the office thus bureaucratizes deviance. This means that deviants come under the regulation of hierarchy, impersonality, specialization, and systematic formal rules.[1] The theory of the office states how defining agents will arrange themselves in accordance with a vertical line of authority, as well as which of them will issue commands to their clientele of deviants. The theory also dictates who will engage in which tasks (e.g., catching, registering, controlling, studying, and processing of deviants). And finally, it prescribes, often in exquisite detail, the rules for managing deviants.

In this respect, the system by which it will type and categorize its deviant clientele is of crucial importance. These categories become the basis for issuing official reports and for indicating the "rates" at which the office is actually both producing and processing deviants. More important, the system establishes the official perspective by means of which agents of social control will define and deal with the deviants they type. For so long and only so long as these agents type the deviants they encounter in their work, to that extent can the agency manage social deviance. As defining agents act on their perspectives they thus order deviance for the society.

The Police Perspective at Work

Agencies of social control order deviance for society in two ways. First, they regulate it by reducing disorders, apprehending rule violators, and, in general, by enforcing moral rule. Second, they regulate or order it by molding deviance into their routine conceptions and agency terms. So that, in the broadest sense, an agency of social control can best regulate and

---

[1] Peter M. Blau, *Bureaucracy in Modern Society* (New York: Random House, 1956), 19.

administer such deviance as takes place in accordance with agency concepts and rules.

Good examples of this principle are found in police work. If we examine police work, we see that the patrolman is doing exactly what the reasonable man of the law courts does not do. Namely, he is actually looking for trouble. Breaches of public order, signs of property crimes, sudden observable violence in interpersonal relations are three of the major sources of what a policeman would define as *trouble*. The same perspective, of course, is at work in traffic law violations. Trouble, for police officers, is thus defined by the penal code, the law of arrest, and experience on the beat with an assortment of persons whom police define as criminals in advance of court trials.

To meet the problems of violation, police culture has fashioned the conceptions that actually predict violation in advance. Police culture, for example, blends both legal and lay categories of deviant persons. Thus, as police officers go about their work, they categorize persons and uncommon events from this predictive and interpretive perspective. The police, in dealing with persons, thus have in advance a notion of what a suspect ought to look like, what signifies trouble, and how suspects should be categorized officially on a police blotter. In ordering deviance in the dual sense discussed, the police devise and act on a routinized conception of specific types of offenders. These types are assigned argot names and roles, are attributed a modus operandi, and are to be known by their dress, posture, and manner with police. Taken together, all of this constitutes a picture of the deviant as the police perceive him. And so it is that the police, operating as they do with these deviant typifications, go about ordering deviance, in the second sense, as they pursue suspects, as they seek out trouble. They perceive trouble in accordance with their working conceptions of it. It is only in this fashion that they can regularize and manage deviance officially.

The Deviant in Court

Police devise their own typology of deviants from contact with a variety of suspects, and from the stock of ideas on these deviants contained in their occupational culture. It is probably true that interaction with their own comrades-in-arms helps to make these categorical perspectives into social realities. For beliefs have a way of shaping reality, and beliefs acquired from significant others (e.g., members of primary groups, one's boss, one's psychiatrist, one's priest) under conditions of emergency are perhaps strongest when it comes to modifying social reality. The police, to a very great extent, have developed their perspectives on deviants as they collaborate with one another in the difficult task of subduing and bringing them into custody and on the basis of their own personal experience with a range of suspects.

In any case, at some point in the performance of their work, police make contact with the deviant at or near the scene of the violation, alleged or actual. And, when they do, most frequently their concern is with subduing and bringing into custody a person whom they believe is guilty of the crime they will charge him with. By contrast, court personnel employ more abstract categories when dealing with most offenders. For their court roles do not require them to subdue suspects but rather to process them in accordance with the rules of law.

Court processing requires a good deal of interaction (some of it behind the scenes) between judge, prosecuting attorney, defense attorney, bailiff, and, in some cases, juries. But just as the legal system is twice-removed from the scene of the alleged crimes, so are its categories. For instance, where police officers would devise and use a set of terms that focus on the kinds of "bad actors," legal workers tend more to categorize in terms of illegal acts, and in a more abstract sense. What seems important, then, in carrying out the court's work is not so much the actions of persons at the scene of alleged crimes, but rather the extent to which these persons fit the court's ideas of typical offenders. And if, finally, court personnel can arrange trades, negotiations, bargains, and exchanges on the basis of these symbolic properties, to that extent are cases settled more rapidly and deviants processed in accordance with the court's ideas of accepted organizational routine.

Once again, an abstract system of categories steps between persons and facts, with the result that the construction of a set of cases is what is required if the courts are to perform. Justice is served most rapidly to the extent that court personnel can collaborate to make the facts fit their ideas of what cases are supposed to look like.

To a very large extent, this court processing of deviants depends rather heavily on legal terminology, court norms, and routine conceptions of accused persons. Just as the police find it necessary to regularize crisis by fitting suspects into their own system of categories, so does the court find it necessary to regularize court procedure by fitting defendants into the court's notion of "normal cases." In general, "normal cases" refer to the typical recurrent combinations of deviant actions *as court personnel understand them.*

So long as this sifting and sorting of unique individuals into routinely conceived slots goes on, the court can also order, manage and process the deviants that regularly come its way. As courts regularize their cases according to these routine conceptions, some persons somehow manage never to get into court. Others receive lighter sentences, though they are guilty of the identical offenses. The only explanation for these observed variations is that those who do not get into court or who go out with somewhat lighter sentences do not fit the categories into which they have been assigned as well as the other more heavily-sentenced deviants. For courts, like other agencies of social control, come to have standard conceptions on how the people they deal with as duly designated social deviants ought to think, feel, and act.

The Effects of Formal Sanctions

In making deviance part of an organizational routine, police adopt a certain perspective towards the people who come before them in the course of their work. They sift and sort them into categories, in the process typing them as certain kinds of deviants. They then go on to manage these deviants in terms of these categorical perspectives. The result is that the rates of deviant behavior officially recorded on police blotters is as dependent upon the actions of these officials as it is on the actions of the so-called deviants themselves. Of course, there are areas of a city where reported crime rates are higher than others. In these areas, other things equal, police patrol more frequently and in greater numbers. But it is also precisely in these areas that police devote disproportionately more attention to certain categories of persons who fit the "hood" type.

This processing in accordance with routine conceptions does not stop, as we have already noted, in the court. Rather, it continues there, perhaps in a somewhat more sophisticated manner. The results, however, are more or less the same. The shared official perspectives on these categories play a much greater role in the administration of deviance than do the characteristics of the persons who are being processed.

These categories continue to influence the course of interaction after deviants have ceased their relations with official agencies. Laymen frequently acquire their own perspectives on deviants from agents of social control. The fact that a person has had contact with an official agency of social control alters officials' opinions of the person. In time, laymen come to adopt the same viewpoint. Thus it is that experience with official agencies is a dialectical process for agents, the deviants they manage, and members of the general public.

For example, when persons first go to work in official agencies, they begin with a fresh, naive perspective on the kinds of persons their agencies are charged with managing. Police officers, for instance, may start out as rookies, unprejudiced against certain minority groups. Similarly, young criminal lawyers may also begin their work with a commitment to see persons as innocent until proven guilty. In time, they exchange their unique viewpoint for the one dominant in the office in which they work. As they adopt the agency perspective, they acquire a set of simple yet extremely workable categories for defining and responding to the kinds of persons they will regard as official deviants. In this process, "good" names are first exchanged for "bad" names and then later transmuted into agency names. For instance, initial contact with an official agency of social control, such as the police, generally suffices to call into question a person's reputation. Additional contact replaces respect with disesteem and, in time, the agency comes to view the person solely in terms of the kinds of trouble he creates for its own orderly operations.

As we have said, this dialectic does not end with any person's particular experience with a given formal agency of social control. For the very function of a deviant label is to bring a person back into a predictable and orderly routine. As already noted, this is sometimes only the organizational routine. But laymen, similarly, have requirements for signs and information when they make initial contact with strangers. Any information in these strange circumstances can become a sign for assigning status. The ironic results of a person's contact with formal control agencies is that laymen have at hand a ready made perspective for dealing with persons who have just left a hospital or prison.

Once, for instance, it becomes known that a person has been in a prison or a mental hospital, his inmate status is often reactivated. Given information of a person's past contact with formal control agencies, laymen tend to give more weight to that official past than to immediate face-to-face cues. Once he knows of the person's "past," the layman quite naturally withdraws the benefit of the doubt that he automatically accords to people in most ordinary social contacts.

Withdrawing the customary faith and trust, he still views the person who has had contact with an official agency as one who is likely to reactivate the kind of behavior that presumably caused the unfavorable designation in the first place. So it is that experience with formal sanctions has its effects on the perspectives of persons who will come to deal with officially processed deviants. So long as these perspectives remain constant, it seems almost as if a deviant label, once formulated in the social process, continues to exert its influence on people, long after the existential basis for the label has disappeared.

Folk wisdom, shared by conformists and deviants alike, recognizes that once suspicion centers around a person, once his very being and integrity are called into question, it often makes little difference for his future what evidence may have raised the suspicions of others. For now laymen and agents of social control alike recast his role and redefine him as the kind of person who very likely performed the imputed actions or, if not, as certainly the kind who would if given a chance. And once this alchemy gets under way, all combine to devise the category by means of which they and the deviant himself will now order their subsequent relations together, whether they like it or not. Management of deviance, then, turns out to be very largely a matter of reputation control. Once a person makes contact with the agency, what happens to his reputation depends heavily on the perspective the agency adopts towards him. And that perspective may later get adopted by persons who are not acting in the status of formal control agents.

Representatives of official agencies of social control begin to make contact with persons who have been designated as deviants. As private persons, these agents may or may not share common sentiments on assorted social deviants. But, in their official capacity as agents, they are constrained to look upon the deviants whom they encounter in a very special sort of way. They may or may not be aware of the sources of these special constraints. The primary source of this constraint is the office in which they work. If they are to manage deviants on behalf of society, they can best do so if they adopt the perspective of their agencies.

The readings for this section all sound the theme that defining agents have official categories for what they take to be deviance. These agents of social control assume a particular stance when they confront typical deviants in the course of their work. The readings that follow specify some of the sociocultural sources of this moral stance. First, Freidson points out that agencies come to think and work in terms of a defined population. Scheff then suggests a number of propositions that may account for how personnel define and respond to "normal cases." Finally, Cicourel and Kitsuse show how high school counselors find deviants who fit their official categories, thereby producing rates of deviant behavior.

Disability as Social Deviance *

ELIOT FREIDSON

. . . Deviance is a social rather than necessarily behavioral or biological fact.

This seems necessary in light of the fact that possession of a given trait does not

* Reprinted from *Sociology and Rehabilitation,* Marvin B. Sussman, ed. (Cleveland: American Sociological Association, 1966), pp. 82–93, by permission of the author and publisher.

117

always lead to assignment to a given deviant role. Indeed, socially structured biases seem to operate in the identification of deviants and their allocation into deviant roles. This may be understood when we recognize the implications of the fact that the true universe or rate of deviance, whether defined by behavioral or biological criteria, is difficult if not impossible to determine. In a practical sense, deviance consists in cases identified by agents or agencies concerned with controlling it—that is, the deviant is he who gets caught, whether he turns himself in or others do it for him, and the universe of deviance is that population of people delineated or defined by the agencies whose function it is to deal with those who get caught.[1] This seems true not only for "criminals," "perverts," or any other deviants who might be expected to hide themselves in order to avoid punishment, but also for the mentally ill, the blind, the deaf, or whatever. One does not play the role of the deviant until he has been so identified by others or by himself.

Formal control agents have become more and more important in making such identifications. In everyday life, precise delineations of classes of deviance are not made: vague and permissive stereotypes seem to be used, the tendency being in all areas, not merely mental illness,[2] to avoid segregating people into deviant roles in any but the most persistent and extreme cases. Control agencies in our society, however, have the business of defining deviance and must both solicit support for their activities and account for what support they have already gained: if only to account for themselves, they must calculate a general universe. They can, of course, as Me-

chanic feels has been the case for some medical investigation,[3] assume that what they see is in fact the total universe, but if they seek to maintain their level of support without implying that their method of control is ineffective, or if they seek to gain a higher level of support for their work, they are likely to consider the cases they see to be but a hint of the deplorable but as yet undiscovered state of things lying outside. If their orientation is punitive, they seek support to "root out" deviance lying outside their purview; if their orientation is therapeutic, they seek support to "reach out." In either case, they must define a universe outside of themselves.

In the course of defining and classifying the universe which they claim needs their services, all control agencies in effect become responsible for drawing clearer lines than in fact exist either in everyday life or in the processes by which people were originally led into their services, and agencies may come to define people as deviant who would not ordinarily have been so defined. Both professionalism and bureaucratization objectify deviance and reify diagnostic categories. In this sense, while such agencies may not actually *create* deviant roles, they do by the nature of their activities refine and clarify their boundaries and, by assuming responsibility for their control, add elements to the roles that may not have existed previously, and so encourage pulling new people into them.

These are general aspects of what Kitsuse and Cicourel called a "rate-producing process." [4] To this we may add some of the various circumstances responsible for producing different types of "representation" of the universe in the

[1] *Cf.* Becker, *Outsiders,* New York: Free Press, 1963, p. 10.

[2] Elaine Cumming and John Cumming, *Closed Ranks,* Cambridge, Mass.: Harvard University Press, 1957.

[3] David Mechanic, "Some Implications of Illness Behavior for Medical Sampling," *New England Journal of Medicine,* CCLXIX (August 1, 1963), pp. 244–247.

[4] John I. Kitsuse and Aaron V. Cicourel, "A Note on the Uses of Official Statistics," *Social Problems,* XI (Fall 1963), pp. 131–139.

way by which control agencies "root out," "reach out," or "bring to book" their cases and establish the official rate of deviance.

Several circumstances seem especially important in determining how a rate is produced and what its bias will be. First, the degree to which a definition of deviance is so highly specialized that few people feel competent to assign it obviously limits the possibility of identifying cases. Second, the social distance of defining agents from the lay community obviously restricts access to cases to be identified. And the isolation of a defining agency from other agencies or agents also restricts access to possible cases to be identified.

Some agencies seem to find it difficult to make contact with the cases over which they presume jurisdiction. Agencies for the blind, for example, seem to be fairly isolated from others, and their definitions of blindness are comparatively technical, even if arbitrary. To "reach out" to all qualified cases, their discouragingly particularistic definitions must be disseminated to other agencies, running the gamut of independent and critical valuation by such referring experts as school physicians, optometrists, and ophthalmologists. Given reluctance to impute stigma in both cases, a barrier composed of ignorance on the part of some potential referrers and of oversophistication and independence of judgment on the part of others is created by the very specialized character of the agency and discourages the ready transmission of cases. Therefore, the cases

seen are markedly underrepresentative of the universe they presume by their definitions. Fewer people will be labeled "appropriately" than in fact conform to the nominal definition of the deviance.[5] The cases that do come to their attention are likely to be biased toward the most severe social and psychological handicaps, insofar as such can vary independently of visual acuity. In sum, the sampling bias is severe on both quantitative and qualitative grounds, making for disproportionately low rates.

In contrast to such specialized agencies are those that use definitions of deviance that are broad and vague enough to encourage an enormous variety of people to presume tentative identification and referral on the basis of an infinite variety of behavior presumed to be symptomatic. Many agencies devoted to mental illness fall there. Such key functionaries as teachers, social workers, and, to a considerably lesser but nonetheless important degree, policemen and physicians, have been encouraged to use the definition. And it is sufficiently nontechnical that virtually anyone so inclined can feel free to use it. It would follow that, stigma or not, agencies devoted to the control of those declared mentally ill are likely to obtain a fairer approximation of the universe of such cases outside. Indeed, "overrepresentation" can occur in the sense that many "mistaken" labelings are likely to be made, particularly among those segments of the population prone to use the label freely.[6] And insofar as the decision-logic of medical diagnosis described by Scheff [7] is involved in this rate-

[5] Howard S. Becker suggested in a personal communication that the very particularism of an agency can also lead to its gaining a virtual monopoly over dealings with people who fit its definition. An agency may develop the reputation of specializing in all people with a given impairment. People who have no particular difficulty with an impairment but who seek help for other types of difficulties at general, "normal" agencies may find themselves denied service and sent instead to the agency specially devoted to their impairment.

[6] "Overrepresentation" is likely to be greatest among groups prone to the use of the diagnosis. In this sense, the clinical insights of practicing psychiatry are "biased" toward middle-class values because the practitioners see an overrepresentation of the literate and monied class in their "sample."

[7] Thomas J. Scheff, "Decision Rules, Types of Error, and Their Consequences in Medical Diagnosis," *Behavioral Science,* VIII (April 1963), pp. 97–107.

producing process, bias will be toward imputing pathology in cases of doubt just to make sure nothing is missed. This, too, produces "overrepresentation." More people will be labeled than conform to the definition, although in the case of mental illness, the shortage of facilities may mitigate the effect, as may reluctance to impute a stigmatized form of deviance.

Hopefully, these remarks have indicated the serious and interesting problem of analysis to be found in study of the process by which deviance comes to be known and rendered into statistical rates. However, so long as the agent or agency does not publicly label or segregate individuals, only a "rate-producing process" is involved, similar to that which occurs when a new census category is adopted. But if public labeling or visible segregation from which a labeling conclusion can be drawn occurs,[8] the process may

be said to be deviance-producing in that, by labeling the individual, it may organize the responses of the community toward him as a stereotyped deviant. Whereas those around him might never have attained any consensus about his behavior before, each responding to him according to his individual relationship, public labeling establishes a common focus for uniform community responses that carve out a role for him. This lay process of retrospective selection of evidence confirming the label [9] is similar to the process in some official agencies of building up a case history or dossier observed by Goffman: [10] it is not a process by which evidence disconfirming the label is sought out and weighed against that confirming the label, but rather one by which the confirming evidence alone is recorded.

Typification in Rehabilitation Agencies *

THOMAS J. SCHEFF

One particular avenue of research which would move outside of the traditional research perspective in rehabilitation is diagnostic, prognostic, and treatment stereotypes of officials and clients and the ways in which these influence re-

habilitation process. Following Sudnow, this discussion will use the generic term, "normal cases." The discussion will begin with a review of Balint's concepts concerning doctor-patient relationships.

One of Balint's conclusions is that

[8] *Cf.* Becker, *Outsiders, op. cit.,* pp. 122ff. for publicity.

[9] *Cf.* John I. Kitsuse, "Societal Reaction to Deviant Behavior: Problems of Theory and Method," in Becker, *The Other Side,* New York: The Free Press, pp. 87–102.

[10] Erving Goffman, *Asylums,* New York: Anchor Books, 1961.

* Reprinted from "Typification in the Diagnostic Practices of Rehabilitation Agencies" in *Sociology and Rehabilitation,* Marvin B. Sussman, ed. (Cleveland: American Sociological Association, 1966), pp. 139–44, by permission of the author and publisher. Work on this paper was facilitated by grants from the Graduate Research Committee, University of California, Santa Barbara; the Social Science Research Committee, and the Center for the Study of Law and Society, U. of California, Berkeley. Arlene K. Daniels made useful criticisms of an earlier draft.

there is an apostolic function, i.e., that doctors in some ways act as apostles, seeking to proselytize their patients into having the kinds of diseases that the doctor thinks are conceivable in their cases:

Apostolic mission or function means in the first place that every doctor has a vague, but almost unshakably firm, idea of how a patient ought to behave when ill. Although this idea is anything but explicit and concrete, it is immensely powerful, and influences, as we have found, practically every detail of the doctor's work with his patients. *It was almost as if every doctor had revealed knowledge of what was right and what was wrong for patients to expect and to endure, and further, as if he had a sacred duty to convert to his faith all the ignorant and unbelieving among his patients.*[1]

It would be easy to accept Balint's statement concerning apostolic mission as academic hyperbole which is used to make a subtle point concerning physical and psychiatric diagnosis. However, one can also take Balint's statement as literally true, and talk about the kinds of organizations and the kinds of situations in which diagnostic stereotypes are used in classifying clientele and become the base for action.

The literal use of such stereotypes is apparent in Sudnow's "Normal Crimes." [2] Making observations in the public defender's office in the court of a large city, he notes that the effective diagnostic unit for the public defender is the *typical* kind of crime—that is, the crime that is typical for the city that he describes at this time in history. He proceeds to describe burglary, child molestation, assault with a deadly weapon, and so on, in terms of the folklore which exists in the court about these crimes in that particular city. To say that this is folklore is not to say that it is completely or even mostly inaccurate. The point that is made, however, is that the thinking of the public defender is in terms of these stereotypic crimes, and his questioning of the defendant is not so much an attempt to find the particular dimensions and aspects of the situation in which the defendant finds himself, but almost entirely to discover the extent to which this defendant seems to fit into the stereotyped category of criminal which exists in the court.

This discussion will not attempt to repeat details of Sudnow's article. The point that is relevant is that these stereotypes are the functional units which are used by the public defender and, apparently to a large extent, by the public prosecutor also. In carrying out the business of the court, in this particular case, it should be noted that the aim of the public defender in using these stereotypes is not as much an attempt to get an acquittal as to get a reduction of sentence. This technique is therefore a way of maintaining smooth-running operation of the court, without gross violation of either the court's concepts of punishment, on the one hand, or the defendant's rights, on the other.

It seems likely that such diagnostic stereotypes function in many kinds of treatment, control, and welfare agencies. As the functional units in which business gets done, it is important to note, however, that these diagnostic packages are of different importance in different kinds of organizations and situations. In the kind of situation which one might find, say, in the surgical ward of an outstanding hospital, one would assume that diagnostic stereotypes are used as preliminary hypotheses which are retained or rejected on the basis of further investigation—

---

[1] Michael Balint, *The Doctor, His Patient, and the Illness,* New York: International Universities Press, 1957, p. 216.

[2] David Sudnow, "Normal Crimes: Sociological Features of the Penal Code in a Public Defender's Office," *Social Problems,* 12 (Winter 1965), pp. 255–276.

that is, at one pole of the organizational continuum. At the other pole, in the kind of situation which Sudnow describes, these stereotypes are not only first hypotheses, but also the final result of the investigation. That is, there is a tendency to accept these stereotyped descriptions with a very minimal attempt to see if they fit the particular case at hand. Later in this discussion, some propositions will relate the type of situation, the type of organization, and the functional importance of the diagnostic stereotypes.

The idea of "normal cases" would seem to offer an entering wedge for research in the most diverse kinds of agencies. In current medical practice, the dominant perspective is the "doctrine of specific etiology." [3] This perspective, largely an outgrowth of the successful application of the germ theory of disease, gives rise to the stance of "scientific medicine" in which the conceptual model of disease is a determinate system. The four basic components of this system are a single cause, usually a pathogen in the body; a basic lesion; uniform and invariant symptoms; and regularly recurring outcome, usually damage in the body or death, if medical intervention is not forthcoming.

The model of disease in scientific medicine gives rise to "normal cases" in which diagnosis, prognosis, and treatment are somewhat standardized. (Thus diabetes mellitus is a disease in which the basic lesion is glucose intolerance; primary features are nutritional and metabolic disorders and susceptibility to infection; secondary features include retinopathy, coronary heart disease, renal disease, or neuropathy; and treatment is by routine insulin control.) An important compo-nent of this disease model is the application for treatment by the patient, with complaints which are traceable to the disease. (Feinstein uses the term "lanthanic" for patients who have the disease but either do not have complaints, or whose complaints do not result in application for treatment.) [4] Cases in which the disease is present but the symptoms are not, are obvious deviations from the "normal case" and cause difficulties in medical practice and research. Equally troublesome are cases in which the primary and/or secondary features of the disease are present, but in which the basic lesion is absent. Meador has suggested, only half in jest, that such conditions be given specific medical status as "nondiseases." [5]

The concept of "normal cases" is closely connected with the notion that physicians have of "what's going around." That is, in a normal practice, a physician is not exposed to all kinds of the most diverse diseases that are described in medical textbooks, but rather only to a small sample of diseases which come in repeatedly: colds, flu, appendicitis, nervous headaches, low back pain, etc.

Proportionately as the case load increases, or inversely with the amount of time, interest, or knowledge that the physician has, one would expect that these diagnostic stereotypes would play an important role. Some of the atrocity tales of medical practice in the armed services and in industry suggest what can occur. For example, at the extreme, in some medical clinics for trainees in the army, virtually all treatments fall into one or two categories—aspirins for headaches and antihistamines for colds, and possibly a third category—a talk with

---

[3] René Dubose, *Mirage of Health,* Garden City, N.Y.: Doubleday-Anchor, 1961.
[4] Alvan R. Feinstein, "Boolean Algebra and Clinical Taxonomy," *New England Journal of Medicine,* 269 (October 31, 1964), pp. 929–938.
[5] Clifton K. Meador, "The Art and Science of Nondisease," *New England Journal of Medicine,* 272 (January 14, 1965), pp. 92–95.

the commanding officer for the residual category of malingerers.[6]

It is conceivable that the same kinds of conceptual packages would be used in other kinds of treatment, welfare, and control agencies. Surely in rehabilitation agencies, the conceptual units which the working staff uses cover only a rather limited number of contingencies of disability, placement possibilities, and client attitudes. The same minimal working concepts should be evident in such diverse areas as probation and parole, divorce cases, adoption cases, police handling of juveniles, and mental health.

Propositions Concerning Normal Cases

Perhaps the most important characteristic of normal diagnoses, prognoses, and treatments is their validity. How accurate are the stereotypes which agency workers and patients use in considering their situations? One would guess that validity of stereotypes is related to their precision. Other things being equal, the more precise the stereotypes, the more ramified they are in the various characteristics of the client, the situation, and the community, the more accurate one would guess that they would be. The first proposition, therefore, concerns simply the number of the different stereotypes that are used in an agency. One would guess that validity and precision are correlated. That is, the more numerous the stereotypes that are actually used in the agency, the more precise they will be; and the more precise, the more valid they will be.

Proposition #2 concerns the power of clients. Using the term "marginality," in the sense used by Krause, the more marginal the patients, the less numerous, precise, and valid the stereotypes will be. That is, the more the status of the client is inferior to and different from that of the staff, whether because of economic position, ethnicity, race, education, etc., the more inaccurate and final the normal cases will be.[7]

Proposition #3: The less dependent the agent is on the client's good will, the less precise and valid the stereotypes will be. In private practice, where the physician is dependent on the patient for remuneration, one is more likely to find a situation as outlined by Balint, where decision concerning the patient's diagnosis becomes a matter of bargaining.

If the doctor has the opportunity of seeing (patients) in the first phase of their becoming ill, i.e., before they settle down to a definite organized illness, he may observe that these patients, so to speak, offer or propose various illnesses, and that they have to go on offering new illnesses until, between doctor and patient, an agreement can be reached resulting in the acceptance of both of them of one of the illnesses as justified.[8]

This discussion qualifies Balint's formulation by suggesting that bargaining or negotiation is a characteristic of a medical service in which patients are powerful, such that the diagnostic stereotypes of the physician are confronted by the diagnostic stereotypes of the patient, and that the patient has some power to regulate the final diagnosis.

A fourth proposition relates to the body of knowledge in the agency or profession which is handling the clients. One would suspect that the more substantial or scientific the body of knowledge, the less important and the more valid and accurate the conceptual packages. In areas of general medicine, for example, such as pneumonia and syphilis, the kind

---

[6] *Cf.* Philip Roth, "Novotny's Pain," *The New Yorker,* October 27, 1962, pp. 46–56.

[7] Elliott A. Krause, *Factors Related to Length of Mental Hospital Stay,* Community Mental Health Monograph, Massachusetts Department of Mental Health (forthcoming).

[8] Balint, *op. cit.,* p. 18.

of stereotyping process discussed here is relatively unimportant. The same would be true in some areas of physical rehabilitation.

A fifth proposition relates the socialization of the staff member to his use of conceptual packages. A fairly accurate index of socialization into an agency might be the degree to which a staff member uses the diagnostic packages that are prevalent in that agency. This proposition suggests a final proposition which is somewhat more complicated, relating effectiveness of a staff member in diagnosis or prognosis to his use of diagnostic stereotypes. Effectiveness presumably has a curvilinear relationship to knowledge and use of stereotypes. In the beginning, a new staff member would have only theory and little experience to guide him and would find that his handling of clients is time-consuming and

that his diagnoses tend to be inaccurate. As he learns the conceptual packages, he becomes more proficient and more rapid in his work, so that effectiveness increases. The crucial point comes after the time in which he has mastered the diagnostic packages, when the question becomes, is his perceptiveness of client situations and placement opportunities going to remain at his stereotypic level, where it is certainly more effective than it was when he was a novice in the organization? Is it going to become frozen at this stereotypic level, or is he going to go on to begin to use these stereotypes as hypotheses for guiding further investigation on his part? This would appear to be a crucial point in the career of any staff member in an agency, and research considering this crisis would be most beneficial. . . . [9]

The Social Organization of the High School and Deviant Adolescent Careers *

AARON V. CICOUREL AND JOHN I. KITSUSE

. . . Everett C. Hughes has suggested that a study of careers—"of the moving perspective in which persons orient themselves with reference to the social order, and of the typical sequences and con-

catenations of office—may be expected to reveal the nature and 'working constitution' of society." [1] Erving Goffman has applied this conception of career in his analysis of the status of the mental patient

---

[9] Charles Spaulding has suggested the proposition that typification practices in organizations are also a function of hierarchical position: the higher a person in the hierarchy (and therefore, the more removed from organizational routine), the less stereotyped are his typifications.

* Reprinted from a previously unpublished paper by permission of the authors.

[1] E. C. Hughes, "Institutional Office and the Person," *American Journal of Sociology,* November 1937, v. 43, pp. 404–413.

which examines the "moral aspects of career—that is, the regular sequence of changes that career entails in the person's self and in his framework of imagery for judging himself and others."[2] Our usage of the concept of career follows Hughes' lead by focusing on the "working constitution" of social organizations, and like Goffman, we shall direct our attention to the day-to-day interaction between adolescents and others in several organizational settings. We shall not, however be concerned with the consequences of these interactions for the adolescent's self-concept. Rather, we are concerned with the consequences of the daily activities of the organizational personnel for the differentiation of the adolescent population within a given social organization, namely the high school.[3] A central problem here is that of identifying the environment of verbal and nonverbal objects to which such personnel attend and orient their actions.

The conception of adolescent careers as a product of organizational activities refers to decisions that lead to a student's transfer from one high school status to any other within the system. We have applied this conception in two empirical studies, directing investigation to the various ways students come into routine and special contact with school personnel, the basis for singling students out for such contacts, the organizationally structured situations in which such decisions were made, and the organizationally defined actions which follow such decisions vis-a-vis adolescents so classified.[4] The gathering of these data was directed by an understanding of the personnel's conceptions for dealing with adolescents in the routine activities of the organization, and their use of the "vocabulary and syntax of everyday language."[5]

The description of the "vocabulary and syntax" employed by the school personnel, parents, the police, and peer groups identify the variety of social types which are recognized as significant within the different organizations. In Schutz's terms, the social types are the common sense constructs employed by persons in everyday life to interpret and classify adolescent behavior. The consequences of the actions oriented by the application of the social types produce what we have called "adolescent careers." Thus, "adolescent career" is a "construct of the second degree" and may be defined as the product of the social typing, classifying,

---

[2] E. Goffman, "The Moral Career of the Mental Patient," *Psychiatry*, May 1959, v. 22, p. 123. Although Goffman proposes to move back and forth between the patient's conceptions of his self and those of others in the institutional environment, he does not present a conceptually clear way of handling the problem of systematically investigating the socially organized character of the conceptions that "others" have of the mental patient. Clarity in the conceptual formulation of this problem is critical if the organizational features of career-defining interactions are to be distinguished from the variety of interpersonal transactions that the mental patient (or, in the context of the present discussion, the adolescent) encounters in everyday life.

[3] A study of patient selection in a psychiatric out-patient clinic by Garfinkel deals explicitly with the social processes by which a population is differentiated within a social organization. The study is concerned with the socially organized and socially controlled ways in which a patient's transfer from one clinic status to a succeeding one is achieved by the decisions of patients and clinic personnel and thus affect the features of patient load and flow. The study provides a method for investigating the processes by which different rates of deviance are produced in an organizational setting. See *Studies in Ethnomethodology*, Englewood Cliffs, N.J.: Prentice-Hall, 1967. See also A. V. Cicourel, *The Social Organization of Juvenile Justice*, New York: John Wiley & Sons, 1968.

[4] Cf. A. V. Cicourel and J. I. Kitsuse, *The Educational Decision-Makers*, Indianapolis: Bobbs-Merrill, 1963.

[5] A. Schutz, *Collected Papers I: The Problem of Social Reality*, The Hague: Martinus Nijhoff, 1962, pp. 3–47.

and processing of adolescents by the personnel of any social organization or set of organizations.

The focus upon the processing of deviants by social agencies distinguishes the present approach to the study of deviance from those which attempt to explain rates of deviant behavior by investigating the motivational "sources" of deviant behavior, whether they are conceived to be psychological or social structural in origin. From the view of deviance followed here, the motivational processes which presumably lead to deviant behavior are conceptually independent of the social processes by which the members of the social organization *impute* motives and perceive regularities in their construction of the deviant, the grounds for such decisions, and the subsequent treatment of persons so defined.

The first task of the sociologist is to provide for the range of adolescent behaviors observed and interpreted by the personnel of the school and other organizations, and the social processes whereby adolescents come to be defined and classified as social types. The second task is to determine the consequences of such processes for any given adolescent's career within the specified organizations.

The school system may be conceived as an organization which produces, in the course of its activities, a variety of adolescent careers including the delinquent. Because the school occupies a strategic position as a coordinating agency between the activities of the family, the police, and the peer group vis-a-vis adolescents, it also provides a "clearing house" which receives and releases information from and to other agencies concerning adolescents. In the following discussion of the school system as an institutionalized differentiator of adolescent careers, we suggest how the interpretations and actions of parents, police, and peer group may affect the activation, maintenance and alteration of various careers within the high school.

The organizational structure of the school and its activities create a variety of "adolescent problems" which are identified in the vocabulary and syntax of its personnel. The "problems" may be grouped under three rough headings: Those pertaining to (1) the student's academic activities, (2) student infractions of rules of conduct, and (3) the emotional problems of students. School personnel frequently refer to those they consider "academic problems" as "over-achievers," "under-achievers," "normal-achievers," and "opportunity students." Among the labels applied to students in the second category are "trouble-makers," "hoods," and "delinquents." In the third category are students who are considered "nervous," "withdrawn and unsocial," and "isolates." [6] The reader should note that any given student may be the object of several social type designations by the same teacher, by different teachers or by other students. Consequently, it is possible for a student to have several careers concurrently or consecutively within the high school organization.

The typing of students in the three problem areas provides the bases for a variety of careers. Any one of these

---

[6] The reader will note that we have ignored the social type identified by "good student" or "nice kid" who might be considered by the school personnel to have "no problems." The "normal" adolescent would presumably be included in such a category. Our exclusion of this type of student follows from the present formulation which suggests that the so-called "normal" adolescent would be a rare case. We shall attempt to explicate this position in the following discussion of the organizational differentiation of the student population. We do not deny, however, the theoretical and empirical relevance of the "normal" adolescent, for any study of the processes of organizational differentiation would have to address the question of who is considered "normal" and the extent to which such individuals are behaviorally different from those labeled variously deviant.

careers may begin even prior to the student's enrollment in the school. For example, in the highly bureaucratized urban school system, the student's transfer to the high school may be preceded by a biography of records and comments documenting his social as well as academic performance in the elementary and junior high school. A review of such biographies by the admissions personnel of the high school results in a student being typed as an "academic problem," for example, and thus initiates a career of the "academic failure," "drop-out," "slow-learner," etc.

Academic careers. The social typing of the adolescent vis-a-vis his career within the high school often is based on the student's prior biography and the tests administered to the new cohort of freshmen. Students are usually given preliminary counseling on the basis of some personnel's interpretations of the test results and other information, frequently while those students are still in the junior high school. These initial organizational activities may result in the following classification of students: (1) The student may be defined as an "under-achiever" if his test scores are considered higher than his prior achievement measured by course grades. (2) Conversely, if the student is achieving higher than the "ability" his test scores indicate, he may be labeled an "over-achiever." (3) The student may be classified as an "opportunity student" if his record in class and on the entrance tests is consistently poor. (4) The student may be labeled a "normal-achiever." [7]

Concomitant with the social typing with reference to "academic problems" is the classification of students as "college," "vocational," or "business-secretarial" (often designated "commercial") on the basis of their declared choice of curricula. The declaration of this choice may be the outcome of the student's interaction with his parents, with whom he is instructed by the school personnel to consult regarding the decision, and his peers. In the middle and upper-middle income groups, parents, peers, and the student himself frequently assume that college follows high school as a matter of course. It is important to bear in mind, however, that from an organizational point of view, the differentiation of students in this regard is not decided solely by criteria internal to the high school system (e.g., by achievement scores) but is also affected by considerations which may be independent of those which the personnel might consider relevant. For example, parents may insist that their child be placed in an academic program regardless of his prior academic record. Thus, in principle, a student has the right, on the approval of his parents, to choose between the curricula, a right which he, however, may not know he has.

Even where the right is invoked, the classification of the student as an "academic problem" by the school personnel may have major consequences for the organizational processing of his declared choice of curriculum. If an "under-achiever," "over-achiever," or an "opportunity student" declares his decision to follow a college-preparatory curriculum, the counselor may decide that he is "not col-

---

[7] Insofar as school personnel document "academic problems" by the discrepancy between some presumed "objective" measure(s) of the student's ability and his level of performance as indicated by course grades, the process by which the latter are assigned becomes a major contingency in the classification of students as "problems." In this connection, a recent study by William Chambliss suggests that teachers accommodate a student's poor performance when he is viewed as a "right type" of student. See W. J. Chambliss, "Two Gangs: A Study of Societal Responses to Deviance and Deviant Careers," unpublished manuscript.

lege material" or "not adequately motivated" and thus unlikely to successfully complete such a curriculum. In such circumstances, the counselor frequently attempts to persuade the student or his parents to change to the vocational curriculum, or he may refuse to allow the student to enroll in certain elective courses because the courses may be considered "too difficult" for him. On the other hand, a student whose test results and class performance are consistently high but who declares the choice of a non-college curriculum, may be counseled into the college-preparatory courses in case he should change his mind. Our study of the high school suggests, however, that school personnel are more likely to view middle and upper income adolescents as "natural" college prospects than lower income students with comparable academic records.[8]

Such counseling activity may have consequences for the student's family relations as well as those with his peers. When parents are informed of the counselor's advice, either directly by the school or via the student, they may request a conference. In such conferences, parents are advised of their child's performance on achievement tests, the ability group in which he will be placed, and the possible difficulties he may encounter in gaining admission to certain colleges. The counselor may indirectly suggest that the parent's aspiration for the child is "unrealistic" and that his ability is not as great as they may have assumed.

Counseled in this manner, the parents may now be able to "see" that their child has "bad study habits," "he fools around too much," "he hangs around with the wrong crowd," etc. These retrospective interpretations [9] of their child's behavior and activities may be revealed to school personnel along with additional information that "we've had some problems at home" or that "he has had difficulties" in the past and thus add support to the school's interpretation of his "problem." Other parental responses to the interview may take the form of requests that the school "put the pressure on him," give him counseling, find him a tutor, "let us know if there's anything we can do." Organizationally the variety of parental response may lead to the typing of students as "over-anxious," "behavior problem," "rebellious," "ambitious parents," etc.

While the counselor's activities are "officially" advisory in nature, the career consequences of his advice vary with the organizationally defined position of counselors within the school system. In schools where the "search for talent" has stimulated and intensified counseling services, counselors are authorized and in some instances prescribed to control the student's access to alternative courses of action. A student whose record is interpreted by the counselor to indicate low ability but who nevertheless insists on following a college-preparatory curriculum may be assigned by the counselor to courses which do not carry college entrance credit. The consequences of such counselor action often do not become apparent to the student or his parents until he makes application for admission to a college when he is a senior in high school.

The differentiation of students which results from their declaration of curriculum choice have organizational consequences other than those which affect

---

[8] See A. V. Cicourel and J. I. Kitsuse, *op. cit.*

[9] The notion of "retrospective interpretations" is adapted from Karl Mannheim's discussion of the "documentary method." See "On the Interpretation of Weltanschauung," in *Essays on the Sociology of Knowledge*, trans. and ed., by P. Kesckemeti, New York: Oxford University Press, 1952, pp. 53–63. See also Garfinkel's discussion of the documentary method in *Studies on Ethnomethodology*.

his academic career. One of these is that his declaration reduces the probable as well as possible interaction between him and his peers who have elected other curricula. Aside from factors such as differences in interests or socio-economic backgrounds which operate to reduce the interaction between students enrolled in different curricula, the curricula establish routines which separate students ecologically and socially. College preparatory students are enrolled in different courses than their non-college peers, their classrooms are frequently located at opposite ends of the school buildings, their curricula demand different kinds and amounts of study at school as well as at home. Further, the college/non-college differentiation is reflected in the membership of school-sponsored student organizations such as the honor society, language, science, home-making, auto and other course-related clubs.

The differentiations of students in these respects are not merely differences but they are evaluated as socially, culturally, as well as academically significant differences by school personnel. The differential valuation given by school personnel to the college and non-college preparatory curricula is a familiar "problem" in educational philosophy and administration, and one which has been intensified by the "search for talent." The differential valuation is reflected not only in the status hierarchy of teachers (e.g., language and math instructors rank those who teach industrial and home-making courses), but also in the distinctions implicit in the teachers' conceptions of college and non-college preparatory students and their activities. The "brighter," "more ambitious" students from "better family gackgrounds" are enrolled in the college preparatory courses, they belong to the "better groups," and they are engaged in more "worthwhile" activities during and after school hours.

In middle-income urban and suburban communities where parents are strongly oriented to sending their children to college, college preparatory students receive intensive attention from school personnel in the form of counseling them about "academic" and "emotional" problems so as to salvage and develop their talent, i.e., get them into colleges. Thus, the occasions and frequency of interaction between college preparatory students and school personnel may have a significant effect upon the differentiation of their academic as well as other careers from those of the non-college preparatory students within the high school.

Academic careers are continually subject to change as a consequence of the routine review of the student's performance, conducted in most schools after each marking period, and especially after the recording of the final grade for a given semester. On these occasions the student's performance is compared with his tested ability, and marked discrepancies between the two may lead to a re-classification of students with preference to "academic problems." This review may verify the fact that "over-achievers" are now performing more nearly up to their ability, or that "normal-achievers" should be re-classified as "under-achievers," etc.[10]

A student's academic career may also be altered by communications to school personnel from parents or from his peers. A parent may call one of the student's teachers to find out why no homework is assigned, and the teacher may check and find that the student's homework has been copied from one of his friends. This may in turn lead to the referral of the

---

[10] On such occasions considerations such as the student's socio-economic status, his ethnic status, his reputation as a "trouble-maker" can enter the decision-making definitions of academic careers.

student to the principal's office for disciplinary action or to the counselor as an "emotional problem." A friend may report to a teacher or counselor that a student is "real worried" about passing a course. If such a student has been typed previously as an "over-achiever," he may be referred to the counselor, or the teacher may consult his superior about transferring the student to a "less competitive" section. Similarly, the police or juvenile authorities may inform the school about a student's delinquent activities which can lead to changes in his academic status even in the absence of any prior academic difficulties.

Such routine and "special" reviews of the student's performance are the occasions for classifying, confirming, and changing the academic status of students. We do not here impute malevolence or "discrimination" to the actions of counselors, teachers, and other school personnel, for their activities may open as well as close future alternatives for students. The importance of investigating the consequences of the counseling system for the social typing of students which alter their careers is to be found in the counselors' and teachers' conceptions of what constitutes "improvement," "satisfactory performance," "predictable failure," etc. These are sources of data for the investigation of how rates of college-going students, failures, drop-outs, etc. are organizationally produced.

"Delinquent" careers. The social typing of students with reference to infractions of conduct rules may launch students on "delinquent" careers within the high school. Like academic careers, a review of the student's folder or biographical materials received from the junior high school, may lead admissions personnel to alert teachers, counselors, and administrators to his history of "difficulties." The labeling of the student as a "trouble-maker," "truant," "fresh," etc. may pro-

vide the occasion for singling him out for special handling and treatment. For example, he may be more closely supervised, his academic progress more frequently reviewed, his parents requested to come in for conferences, counseling advised, etc. Thus, the student's cumulative folder and the interpretations and actions which may follow from it are important sources of data for the investigation of delinquent as well as academic careers.

Another context of organizational activity which may be consequential for the classification of a student as a "conduct problem" is in the classroom where his behavior may be interpreted by the teacher as "disruptive" and lead her to refer him to the counselor, principal or some other administrator. Official as well as "unofficial" records of such actions leave their organizational traces and subsequent "difficulties" with the student may be interpreted in the light of his organizational history. The student may be disciplined for behavior (or even imputed attitudes) that is overlooked or unnoticed among "good" students, and he may be denied opportunities to participate in extra-curricular athletics, student government activities, school-sponsored recreational programs, etc.

The school personnel's conceptions of the "good" student are particularly relevant for an investigation of the social processes by which adolescents are typed as "conduct problems." Such conceptions may be so general that the adolescent's posture, walk, cut of hair, clothes, use of slang, manner of speech—or indeed, almost any aspect of the so-called "adolescent behavior"—may be the basis for the typing of the student as a "conduct problem." The stylizations of such behaviors are often the characteristics which distinguish peer groups of different socioeconomic backgrounds, interests, academic orientations, etc. and as a consequence, the student's association with peers considered by school personnel to be "rowdies," "serious students," or "active in school activities" may implicitly be taken as indicative of the type of student he is.[11]

Thus, peer group activities and the variety of types which are differentiated by them may have important career-defining consequences. The emphasis on "peer group adjustment" and the conception of the "well-rounded student," which has been promoted virtually as an educational principle in high schools, have made teachers, counselors, and other school personnel aware of and attentive to the variety of social type distinctions made by adolescents themselves. Students may characterize groups as well as individuals as "square" or "jock," "brain," "hippy," "acid heads," "hoody," etc. The evaluation and ranking of such individuals and groups among and between school personnel and adolescents may in some instances concur, in others be quite discrepant. Thus, the "squares" or "brains" may be considered "nice" students by school personnel, but "jerks" by some student groups; "jocks" may be held in high esteem by some students and personnel for their athletic ability, but ignored or deprecated by others. The alignments and realignments of peer groups, and the inclusion and exclusion of students in their activities may therefore become the occasion for parent-school communications, initiating counseling activity, instituting programs of closer supervision, transfer of students from one section to another, etc.

Delinquent careers are particularly sensitive to information from outside as well as from within the system. School attendance being compulsory in most states until the age of 16, the adolescent's school affiliation is (together with the family) one of the first institutions to which his conduct or misconduct is referred. Thus, the school is the agency to which the police, shopkeepers, civic organizations, welfare agencies, as well as parents go with their reports (if not complaints) concerning the actual or suspected delinquency of students.

The consequences for the school of variously delinquent students, whether or not these delinquencies occur within the school, are primarily organizational in contrast to the family's legal responsibility. Delinquent students are viewed by school personnel as "disruptive," "harmful influences," and bad for the "reputation" of the school. This is particularly true when students are "officially" defined and publicized as delinquent by police action. Thus, contacts between the police and adolescents, and the police-school communication which may follow from them, have major significance for the adolescent's career as a delinquent within the school system. When students are particularly troublesome in their misconduct, the school will often initiate police contacts to rid the organization of "trouble-makers" despite a lack of legal violations.

Contacts between the police and adolescents may, of course, occur in a variety of situations and circumstances. The police may act on their own observations of the adolescent's behavior, on complaint from members of the community, on the request from an adolescent's parents, the school, or other social agencies. Police may classify adolescents with whom they come into contact as being of two general types: Those whom they consider "good kids" who rarely cause any trouble, and the "trouble-makers" who constitute the bulk of their contacts with adolescents. Among the "good kids" the

---

[11] The significance of deference, demeanor, and appearance in the processing of juvenile offenders is discussed in Irving Piliavin and Scott Briar, "Police Encounters with Juveniles," *American Journal of Sociology*, Sept. 1964, v. 70, pp. 206–214.

police may differentiate between the "quiet, studious kids who never cause any trouble," and those who might be referred to as "good kids who cut up a little and need to be warned." The police also distinguish between two types of "trouble-makers": Those referred to as "wild kids who need a good kick in the ass," and those considered "real no-good punks" headed for criminal careers.

The conceptions held by the police concerning adolescents may be critical for their interpretations and processing of cases which come to their attention. With reference to a given complaint or observation of adolescent behavior, the police officer's conception of the youth as a "good kid" may lead him to define the behavior as a "prank" attributable to "letting off steam," "spring fever," "high spirits," etc. The adolescent may be dismissed with a strong warning which the officer does not record. Assuming that there is a "reasonable" time lapse, from the officer's point of view, between the incident and any other similar event involving this adolescent, the police contact may be "lost," organizationally speaking. On the other hand, should the police view the youth as a "no-good punk," the adolescent may be processed and thus become an official case subject to various (usually negative) interpretations when he is in "trouble" again.

Many aspects of police activities vis-a-vis adolescents may never affect the career-defining processes of the school system.[12] The contingencies of police-school contacts, however, vary with the policies and practices of police departments in this regard. In large cities, the police may assemble biographies on students containing records of traffic tickets issued to "hot-rodders," warnings for curfew violations, boisterous conduct at drive-in theatres or malt shops, etc. which may not come to the attention of school authorities. But a court hearing usually leads to a probation department report containing a school evaluation. The referral of a student by the school to the police for action, or inquiries to the school by the police in their investigation of a student's activities may be the occasion for an exchange of information leading to the development of a new career for the student within the high school. For example, a student who, until that time, had been considered "loud" or "sullen" may now be typed as a "trouble-maker," "anti-social," "delinquent," etc.

The organization of inter-agency communication is therefore a major source of data for the study of adolescent careers. In smaller towns and suburban communities, police may routinely contact the school for information concerning adolescents who come to their attention. In the more specialized police systems, trained juvenile officers have been added to the staff, and their activities lead to an increasing coordination of the records com-

---

[12] The way in which the youth is processed through juvenile court can be independent of what has transpired prior to his appearance before this agency. Other personnel introduced into the situation such as social workers, judges, psychiatrists, psychologists, and the like, may interpret the youth's behavior quite differently from those who have activated the career-defining process. See P. W. Tappan, *Juvenile Delinquency,* New York: McGraw-Hill, 1949, Chs. 8–15. A juvenile court judge may, on the counsel of a psychologist, psychiatrist, or social worker, dispose of a case in a manner which negates all previous interpretations of the youth's behavior. Thus, the differential conceptions held by the police, social workers, psychiatrists, judges, and so on, may lead to a re-definition of a youth as "disturbed" rather than "wild" or "insecure" and "in need of love" rather than vigorous discipline and "a kick where it hurts." *The behavioral content of a youth's activities, therefore, may not be as critical in such cases as the interpretations which are placed upon it by others.* It is necessary, however, to go beyond this formulation and attempt to specify the behavioral regularities which are identified as relevant by personnel who have day-to-day contact with adolescents.

piled by the school and other community agencies. A development in the coordination of police and school records is the addition to the school personnel of a "security officer" (often a person with some previous experience in police work) to handle problems of traffic and parking violations, infractions of curfew, smoking, and other school rules. Where such personnel are employed, liaison between the school and police may be routinized through the "security officer." To the degree that information concerning students defined as "delinquents" of various types, either by the police or school personnel, is routinely exchanged between the two organizations, the interpretations and actions of one agency can have important consequences for the adolescent's career in both systems.

The organizational actions which chart the course of delinquent careers may have consequences beyond the student's participation in the school system. Should he seek part-time employment after school hours, apply for a job or military service upon leaving the school, the student's record may be used as the basis for unfavorable or qualified letters of recommendation to prospective employers. The student's record may be reviewed when police direct inquiries to the school about some "delinquent" action or his family or peer group may learn about his record when school personnel contact them in the course of investigating cases of stealing, fighting, smoking, vandalism, etc.

The consequences of social typing for differential interpretation and treatment of the behavior of individuals so typed are commonplace and quite obvious. What is not so obvious, and the central concern of this paper, are the interpretive rules utilized by the organizational personnel who decide what forms of behavior and what kinds of evidence warrant actions which define individuals as

deviant within the system. Our description of the organizational actions that may lead to various careers, delinquent and others, is not intended to take issue with the justification of such actions or the bases on which they are taken. The point we are making is theoretical and methodological: In any investigation of how "deviant" and "non-deviant" populations are differentiated within a system, the rules of interpretation employed for evaluating the behavioral elements observed and classified in the day-to-day activities of the personnel must systematically be taken into account.

"Clinical" careers. The personnel available to many high schools include clinically trained persons such as psychiatrists, psychiatric social workers, and clinical psychologists whose primary responsibility is the handling of students who are considered "emotionally disturbed" by teachers, parents, counselors, and others. In such schools, parents and often students are informed of the availability of clinical services as part of their orientation to the high school. Referral to the clinical service is the organizational basis for the activation of clinical careers.

A student may come to the attention of clinical personnel in several ways: (1) The student may have been an "emotional case" in the junior high school, and a recommendation for further treatment may accompany his biographical records to the high school. (2) The fact that a student is undergoing privately financed treatment by a psychiatrist may be communicated to the high school by his therapist or parents. (3) In schools where all students are assigned a counselor, the counselor's routine contacts with his counselees may be the occasion for a referral to clinical personnel. (4) A student's behavior may be viewed as "strange" by teachers in the classroom or on school grounds, by custodial and administrative staff or by other students, any one of whom may initiate the referral process. (5) The student's behavior at home or within the community (e.g., delinquent acts) may lead his parents and the personnel of other agencies to seek information or advice from school clinicians.

The organizational processing of students who are defined as "emotionally disturbed" is likely to be more problematic than in the case of the "academic" or "conduct" problems for several reasons. Unlike the classification of the student as an "academic problem," there is relatively little organizational control over the competence of the person who reports the behavior which is the occasion for initiating the process of classifying a student as "emotionally disturbed." Almost any person within the school as well as outside of it may report that a student has been observed behaving in a "strange," "bizarre," or "crazy" manner. Since the common sense interpretation of such behavior is relative to the observer, there may be considerable disagreement as to the "objectivity" of the observer. Here the classification of the student as "emotionally disturbed" is similar to the "conduct problem."

Unlike the "conduct problem," however, the organizational processing of students whose behaviors are reported to be "strange" in various ways has become professionalized by the activities of counselors, clinical psychologists, psychiatrists and psychiatric social workers. The professional training and theoretical orientation of such personnel may be critical for determining the classification of the

student as a "clinical" case. A psychiatrist or social worker, for example, may interpret the reported behavior and the preliminary interview with the student as indicative of "deep-seated problems," with the implication that he is "sick" and in need of "professional help." On the other hand, a part-time teacher-counselor may interpret the "same facts" as a "situation problem" or as no problem at all.[13]

When such cases come to the attention of counseling personnel, parents may be routinely advised of their child's "difficulties" and a conference suggested. Parental response to such a communication may be critical for the student's career as a "clinical case." If we assume that the parents' conceptions of their child are based on his performance at home, the routine accommodations within the family of a wide variety of behavior may insulate the parents from definitions of those behaviors as "strange," "peculiar," "immature," etc. In the absence of intrusive communications from extra-familial sources such as neighbors, the police, school authorities, and welfare agencies, parental interpretations of their child's behavior as a "problem"—emotional delinquent, or whatever —may be vague or non-existent. Thus, when parents are advised of their child's "difficulties" they may be surprised as well as resentful, hostile, and often belligerent toward the communicating agency's suggestion that he is in need of psychotherapeutic treatment. In the face of such "resistance" parents may be informed that referral of the child to some

---

[13] The current trend toward psychological interpretations of adolescent "problems" of which the organizational provision for clinical services is one reflection, has given impetus to the view among some high school personnel that academic, conduct, and other problems are all reducible to "emotional difficulties." For example, an "under-achiever" might be interpreted by the clinician to be an expression of the student's reaction to "parental conflicts," a "hood" is rebelling against the authority of the school, etc. From an organizational point of view, it is important to investigate whether and how the differentiation of the several problem areas are maintained within the same system. Cf., *The Educational Decision-Makers,* ch. 4.

other agency, e.g., the juvenile courts, may be necessary in order to obtain parental agreement to the counselor's recommendations.

"Family cooperation" is particularly important for the school when a student has been organizationally defined as a "clinical" case. Since the "difficulty" in question may include reports of such behaviors as hysterical weeping, sexual exhibition, use of marijuana or LSD, verbal and physical abuse of school personnel, and the like, the content of the communication itself creates a "touchy" problem in parent-school relations. The current psychological interpretations of such behaviors, furthermore, implicitly if not explicitly attribute major significance to early socialization or "the family situation." Although middle-income parents may be more receptive to such interpretations and their implications for the importance of "family cooperation," the parental response of rejecting them as "nonsense" may be quite frequent, or the parents may ignore the communications altogether. Since parental consent is re-quired in most schools for referring students to psychiatrists or social workers for intensive or "deep" therapy, their rejection of such recommendations precludes the school from officially "treating" the student as a "clinical" case. He may, nevertheless, be classified and recorded officially as a "behavior" or "conduct" problem and assigned to a counselor for more "superficial" counseling for which parental consent may not be required.

The processing of any given type of deviant within an organization may be modified at any point by such factors as parental response to organizational definitions, introduction of information from outside agencies, review of prior records, etc. Empirical investigation of the above remarks must establish the behavioral environment within which exchanges between organizational personnel and adolescents take place in order to pinpoint the verbal and nonverbal properties by which organizational conceptions are initiated or changed vis-a-vis the generation of deviant categories.

POLICE WORK

6

The theory of the office dictates that work with records determines the form the official records will ultimately take. The form in which records are kept and the implicit questions they ask tend to dictate the kinds of answers that case-makers will file in those self-same records. A set of abstractions set down the rules for making concrete human actions meaningful to all those who must make some later use of the record.

Under conditions of close and strained contact with persons, face-to-face work can actually produce a similar set of abstractions for defining, typing, and responding to people who seem to be excellent candidates for deviance. When that experience is mediated through the lenses of an occupational culture, typing of persons as deviants tends to occur almost by rote.

In the three readings that follow, police culture is seen as but a special instance of the office, prescribing the form that interaction will take when police officers come into contact with deviants. Piliavin and Briar show how police officers form a concept of the juvenile delinquent as a "hood," that is a youth who looks and carries himself in a certain truculent manner. The officers, proceeding on this notion, concentrate their attention in certain areas of the city and, on the basis of the social types they work with, help to produce the very trouble their job requires them to quell. Stinchcombe then shows that performing police work in certain public places permits the police to employ certain cultural rules in typing and processing offenders. Then Chambliss and Liell go on to show what happens when police apply these rules in the wrong places. Their analysis of these mistakes in police work shows how routine cases are handled—persons who look poor and who are alleged to have committed minor crimes in public receive very little deference from the police.

Police Encounters with Juveniles * †

IRVING PILIAVIN AND SCOTT BRIAR

As the first of a series of decisions made in the channeling of youthful offenders through the agencies concerned with juvenile justice and corrections, the disposition decisions made by police officers have potentially profound consequences for apprehended juveniles. Thus arrest, the most severe of the dispositions available to police, may not only lead to confinement of the suspected offender but also bring him loss of social status, restriction of educational and employment opportunities, and future harassment by law-enforcement personnel.[1] According to some criminologists, the stigmatization resulting from police apprehension, arrest, and detention actually reinforces deviant behavior.[2] Other authorities have suggested, in fact, that this stigmatization serves as the catalytic agent initiating delinquent careers.[3] Despite their presumed significance, however, little empirical analysis has been reported regarding the factors influencing, or consequences resulting from, police actions with juvenile offenders. Furthermore, while some studies of police encounters with adult offenders have been reported, the extent to which the findings of these investigations pertain to law-enforcement practices with youthful offenders is not known.[4]

The above considerations have led the writers to undertake a longitudinal study of the conditions influencing, and consequences flowing from, police actions with juveniles. In the present paper findings will be presented indicating the influence of certain factors on police actions. Research data consist primarily of notes and records based on nine months' observation of all juvenile officers in one police department.[5] The officers were observed in the course of their regular tours of

* Reprinted from *American Journal of Sociology*, Vol. 69 (September, 1964), pp. 206–214, by permission of the authors and The University of Chicago Press. Copyright 1964 by The University of Chicago Press.

† This study was supported by Grant MH-06328-02, National Institute of Mental Health, United States Public Health Service.

[1] Richard D. Schwartz and Jerome H. Skolnick, "Two Studies of Legal Stigma," *Social Problems*, X (April, 1962), 133–42; Sol Rubin, *Crime and Juvenile Delinquency* (New York: Oceana Publications, 1958); B. F. McSally, "Finding Jobs for Released Offenders," *Federal Probation*, XXIV (June, 1960), 12–17; Harold D. Lasswell and Richard C. Donnelly, "The Continuing Debate over Responsibility: An Introduction to Isolating the Condemnation Sanction," *Yale Law Journal*, LXVIII (April, 1959), 869–99.

[2] Richard A. Cloward and Lloyd E. Ohlin, *Delinquency and Opportunity* (New York: Free Press, 1960), pp. 124–30.

[3] Frank Tannenbaum, *Crime and the Community* (New York: Columbia University Press, 1936), pp. 17–20; Howard S. Becker, *Outsiders: Studies in the Sociology of Deviance* (New York: Free Press of Glencoe, 1963), chaps. i and ii.

[4] For a detailed accounting of police discretionary practices, see Joseph Goldstein, "Police Discretion Not To Invoke the Criminal Process: Low Visibility Decisions in the Administration of Justice," *Yale Law Journal*, LXIX (1960), 543–94; Wayne R. LaFave, "The Police and Non-enforcement of the Law—Part I," *Wisconsin Law Review*, January, 1962, pp. 104–37; S. H. Kadish, "Legal Norms and Discretion in the Police and Sentencing Processes," *Harvard Law Review*, LXXV (March, 1962), 904–31.

[5] Approximately thirty officers were assigned to the Juvenile Bureau in the department studied. While we had an opportunity to observe all officers in the Bureau during the study, our observations were concentrated on those who had been working in the Bureau for one or two years at least. Although two of the officers in the Juvenile Bureau were Negro, we observed these officers on only a few occasions.

duty.[6] While these data do not lend themselves to quantitative assessments of reliability and validity, the candor shown by the officers in their interviews with the investigators and their use of officially frowned-upon practices while under observation provide some assurance that the materials presented below accurately reflect the typical operations and attitudes of the law-enforcement personnel studied.

The setting for the research, a metropolitian police department serving an industrial city with approximately 450,000 inhabitants, was noted within the community it served and among law-enforcement officials elsewhere for the honesty and superior quality of its personnel. Incidents involving criminal activity or brutality by members of the department had been extremely rare during the ten years preceding this study; personnel standards were comparatively high; and an extensive training program was provided to both new and experienced personnel. Juvenile Bureau members, the primary subjects of this investigation, differed somewhat from other members of the department in that they were responsible for delinquency prevention as well as law enforcement, that is, juvenile officers were expected to be knowledgeable about conditions leading to crime and delinquency and to be able to work with community agencies serving known or potential juvenile offenders. Accordingly, in the assignment of personnel to the Juvenile Bureau, consideration was given not only to an officer's devotion to and reliability in law enforcement but also to his commitment to delinquency prevention. Assignment to the Bureau was of advantage to policemen seeking promotions. Consequently, many officers

requested transfer to this unit, and its personnel comprised a highly select group of officers.

In the field, juvenile officers operated essentially as patrol officers. They cruised assigned beats and, although concerned primarily with juvenile offenders, frequently had occasion to apprehend and arrest adults. Confrontations between the officers and juveniles occurred in one of the following three ways, in order of increasing frequency: (1) encounters resulting from officers' spotting officially "wanted" youths; (2) encounters taking place at or near the scene of offenses reported to police headquarters; and (3) encounters occurring as the result of officers' directly observing youths either committing offenses or in "suspicious circumstances." However, the probability that a confrontation would take place between officer and juvenile, or that a particular disposition of an identified offender would be made, was only in part determined by the knowledge that an offense had occurred or that a particular juvenile had committed an offense. The bases for and utilization of non-offenses related criteria by police in accosting and disposing of juveniles are the focuses of the following discussion.

Sanctions for Discretion

In each encounter with juveniles, with the minor exception of officially "wanted" youths,[7] a central task confronting the officer was to decide what official action to take against the boys involved. In making these disposition decisions, officers could select any one of five discrete alternatives:

[6] Although observations were not confined to specific days or work shifts, more observations were made during evenings and weekends because police activity was greatest during these periods.

[7] "Wanted" juveniles usually were placed under arrest or in protective custody, a practice which in effect relieved officers of the responsibility for deciding what to do with these youths.

1. outright release
2. release and submission of a "field interrogation report" briefly describing the circumstances initiating the police-juvenile confrontation
3. "official reprimand" and release to parents or guardian
4. citation to juvenile court
5. arrest and confinement in juvenile hall.

Dispositions 3, 4, and 5 differed from the others in two basic respects. First, with rare exceptions, when an officer chose to reprimand, cite, or arrest a boy, he took the youth to the police station. Second, the reprimanded, cited, or arrested boy acquired an official police "record," that is, his name was officially recorded in Bureau files as a juvenile violator.

Analysis of the distribution of police disposition decisions about juveniles revealed that in virtually every category of offense the full range of official disposition alternatives available to officers was employed. This wide range of discretion resulted primarily from two conditions. First, it reflected the reluctance of officers to expose certain youths to the stigmatization presumed to be associated with official police action. Few juvenile officers believed that correctional agencies serving the community could effectively help delinquents. For some officers this attitude reflected a lack of confidence in rehabilitation techniques; for others, a belief that high case loads and lack of professional training among correctional workers vitiated their efforts at treatment. All officers were agreed, however, that juvenile justice and correctional processes were essentially concerned with apprehension and punishment rather than treatment. Furthermore, all officers believed that some aspects of these proc-

esses (e.g., judicial definition of youths as delinquents and removal of delinquents from the community), as well as some of the possible consequences of these processes (e.g., intimate institutional contact with "hard-core" delinquents, as well as parental, school, and conventional peer disapproval or rejection), could reinforce what previously might have been only a tentative proclivity toward delinquent values and behavior. Consequently, when officers found reason to doubt that a youth being confronted was highly committed toward deviance, they were inclined to treat him with leniency.

Second, and more important, the practice of discretion was sanctioned by police-department policy. Training manuals and departmental bulletins stressed that the disposition of each juvenile offender was not to be based solely on the type of infraction he committed. Thus, while it was departmental policy to "arrest and confine all juveniles who have committed a felony or misdemeanor involving theft, sex offense, battery, possession of dangerous weapons, prowling, peeping, intoxication, incorrigibility, and disturbance of the peace," it was acknowledged that "such considerations as age, attitude and prior criminal record might indicate that a different disposition would be more appropriate." [8] The official justification for discretion in processing juvenile offenders, based on the preventive aims of the Juvenile Bureau, was that each juvenile violator should be dealt with solely on the basis of what was best for him.[9] Unofficially, administrative legitimation of discretion was further justified on the grounds that strict enforcement practices would overcrowd court calendars and detention facilities, as well as dramatically increase juvenile

---

[8] Quoted from a training manual issued by the police department studied in this research.
[9] Presumably this also implied that police action with juveniles was to be determined partly by the offenders' need for correctional services.

crime rates—consequences to be avoided because they would expose the police department to community criticism.[10]

In practice, the official policy justifying use of discretion served as a demand that discretion be exercised. As such, it posed three problems for juvenile officers. First, it represented a departure from the traditional police practice with which the juvenile officers themselves were identified, in the sense that they were expected to justify their juvenile disposition decisions not simply by evidence proving a youth had committed a crime—grounds on which police were officially expected to base their dispositions of non-juvenile offenders [11]—but in the *character* of the youth. Second, in disposing of juvenile offenders, officers were expected, in effect, to make judicial rather than ministerial decisions.[12] Third, the shift from the offense to the offender as the basis for determining the appropriate disposition substantially increased the uncertainty and ambiguity for officers in the situation of apprehension because no explicit rules existed for determining which disposition different types of youths should receive. Despite these problems, officers were constrained to base disposition decisions on the character of the apprehended youth, not only because they wanted to be fair, but because persistent failure to do so could result in judicial criticism, depart-

mental censure, and, they believed, loss of authority with juveniles.[13]

Disposition Criteria

Assessing the character of apprehended offenders posed relatively few difficulties for officers in the case of youths who had committed serious crimes such as robbery, homicide, aggravated assault, grand theft, auto theft, rape, and arson. Officials generally regarded these juveniles as confirmed delinquents simply by virtue of their involvement in offenses of this magnitude.[14] However, the infraction committed did not always suffice to determine the appropriate disposition for some serious offenders; [15] and, in the case of minor offenders, who comprised over 90 per cent of the youths against whom police took action, the violation per se generally played an insignificant role in the choice of disposition. While a number of minor offenders were seen as serious delinquents deserving arrest, many others were perceived either as "good" boys whose offenses were atypical of their customary behavior, as pawns of undesirable associates or, in any case, as boys for whom arrest was regarded as an unwarranted and possibly harmful punishment. Thus, for nearly all minor violators and for some serious delinquents, the assessment of character—the

[10] This was reported by beat officers as well as supervisory and administrative personnel of the Juvenile Bureau.

[11] In actual practice, of course, disposition decisions regarding adult offenders also were influenced by many factors extraneous to the offense per se.

[12] For example, in dealing with adult violators, officers had no disposition alternative comparable to the reprimand-and-release category, a disposition which contained elements of punishment but did not involve mediation by the court.

[13] The concern of officers over possible loss of authority stemmed from their belief that court failure to support arrests by appropriate action would cause policemen to "lose face" in the eyes of juveniles.

[14] It is also likely that the possibility of negative publicity resulting from the failure to arrest such violators—particularly if they became involved in further serious crime—brought about strong administrative pressure for their arrest.

[15] For example, in the year preceding this research, over 30 per cent of the juveniles involved in burglaries and 12 per cent of the juveniles committing auto theft received dispositions other than arrest.

distinction between serious delinquents, "good" boys, misguided youths, and so on—and the dispositions which followed from these assessments were based on youths' personal characteristics and not their offenses.

Despite this dependence of disposition decisions on the personal characteristics of these youths, however, police officers actually had access only to very limited information about boys at the time they had to decide what to do with them. In the field, officers typically had no data concerning the past offense records, school performance, family situation, or personal adjustment of apprehended youths.[16] Furthermore, files at police headquarters provided data only about each boy's prior offense record. Thus both the decision made in the field—whether or not to bring the boy in—and the decision made at the station— which disposition to invoke—were based largely on cues which emerged from the interaction between the officer and the youth, cues from which the officer inferred the youth's character. These cues included the youth's group affiliations, age, race, grooming, dress, and demeanor. Older juveniles, members of known delinquent gangs, Negroes, youths with well-oiled hair, black jackets, and soiled denims or jeans (the presumed uniform of "tough" boys), and boys who in their interactions with officers did not manifest what were

considered to be appropriate signs of respect tended to receive the more severe dispositions.

Other than prior record, the most important of the above cues was a youth's *demeanor*. In the opinion of juvenile patrolmen themselves the demeanor of apprehended juveniles was a major determinant of their decisions for 50–60 per cent of the juvenile cases they processed.[17] A less subjective indication of the association between a youth's demeanor and police disposition is provided by Table 1, which presents the police dispositions for sixty-six youths whose encounters with police were observed in the course of this study.[18] For purposes of this analysis, each youth's demeanor in the encounter was classified as either

TABLE 1
Severity of Police Disposition by Youth's Demeanor

| Severity of Police Disposition | Youth's Demeanor | | |
	Co-opera-tive	Unco-opera-tive	Total
Arrest (most severe)	2	14	16
Citation or official reprimand	4	5	9
Informal reprimand	15	1	16
Admonish and release (least severe)	24	1	25
Total	45	21	66

[16] On occasion, officers apprehended youths whom they personally knew to be prior offenders. This did not occur frequently, however, for several reasons. First, approximately 75 per cent of apprehended youths had no prior official records; second, officers periodically exchanged patrol areas, thus limiting their exposure to, and knowledge about, these areas; and third, patrolmen seldom spent more than three or four years in the juvenile division.

[17] While reliable subgroup estimates were impossible to obtain through observation because of the relatively small number of incidents observed, the importance of demeanor in disposition decisions appeared to be much less significant with known prior offenders.

[18] Systematic data were collected on police encounters with seventy-six juveniles. In ten of these encounters the police concluded that their suspicions were groundless, and consequently the juveniles involved were exonerated; these ten cases were eliminated from this analysis of demeanor. (The total number of encounters observed was considerably more than seventy-six, but systematic data-collection procedures were not instituted until several months after observations began.)

co-operative or unco-operative.[19] The results clearly reveal a marked association between youth demeanor and the severity of police dispositions.

The cues used by police to assess demeanor were fairly simple. Juveniles who were contrite about their infractions, respectful to officers, and fearful of the sanctions that might be employed against them tended to be viewed by patrolmen as basically law-abiding or at least "salvageable." For these youths it was usually assumed that informal or formal reprimand would suffice to guarantee their future conformity. In contrast, youthful offenders who were fractious, obdurate, or who appeared nonchalant in their encounters with patrolmen were likely to be viewed as "would-be tough guys" or "punks" who fully deserved the most severe sanction: arrest. The following excerpts from observation notes illustrate the importance attached to demeanor by police in making disposition decisions.

1. The interrogation of "A" (an 18-year-old upper-lower-class white male accused of statutory rape) was assigned to a police sergeant with long experience on the force. As I sat in his office while we waited for the youth to arrive for questioning, the sergeant expressed his uncertainty as to what he should do with this young man. On the one hand, he could not ignore the fact that an offense had been committed; he had been informed, in fact, that the youth was prepared to confess to the offense. Nor could he overlook the continued pressure from the girl's father (an important political figure) for the police to take severe action against the youth. On the other hand, the sergeant had formed a low opinion of the girl's moral character, and he considered it unfair to charge "A" with statutory rape when the girl was a willing partner to the offense and

might even have been the instigator of it. However, his sense of injustice concerning "A" was tempered by his image of the youth as a "punk," based, he explained, on information he had received that the youth belonged to a certain gang, the members of which were well known to, and disliked by, the police. Nevertheless, as we prepared to leave his office to interview "A," the sergeant was still in doubt as to what he should do with him.

As we walked down the corridor to the interrogation room, the sergeant was stopped by a reporter from the local newspaper. In an excited tone of voice, the reporter explained that his editor was pressing him to get further information about this case. The newspaper had printed some of the facts about the girl's disappearance, and as a consequence the girl's father was threatening suit against the paper for defamation of the girl's character. It would strengthen the newspaper's position, the reporter explained, if the police had information indicating that the girl's associates, particularly the youth the sergeant was about to interrogate, were persons of disreputable character. This stimulus seemed to resolve the sergeant's uncertainty. He told the reporter, "unofficially," that the youth was known to be an undesirable person, citing as evidence his membership in the delinquent gang. Furthermore, the sergeant added that he had evidence that this youth had been intimate with the girl over a period of many months. When the reporter asked if the police were planning to do anything to the youth, the sergeant answered that he intended to charge the youth with statutory rape.

In the interrogation, however, three points quickly emerged which profoundly affected the sergeant's judgment of the youth. First, the youth was polite and co-operative; he consistently addressed the officer as "sir," answered all questions quietly, and signed a statement implicating himself in numerous counts of statutory rape. Second, the youth's

[19] The data used for the classification of demeanor were the written records of observations made by the authors. The classifications were made by an independent judge not associated with this study. In classifying a youth's demeanor as co-operative, or unco-operative, particular attention was paid to: (1) the youth's responses to police officers' questions and requests; (2) the respect and deference—or lack of these qualities—shown by the youth toward police officers; and (3) police officers' assessments of the youth's demeanor.

intentions toward the girl appeared to have been honorable; for example, he said that he wanted to marry her eventually. Third, the youth was not in fact a member of the gang in question. The sergeant's attitude became increasingly sympathetic, and after we left the interrogation room he announced his intention to "get 'A' off the hook," meaning that he wanted to have the charges against "A" reduced or, if possible, dropped.

2. Officers "X" and "Y" brought into the police station a seventeen-year-old white boy who, along with two older companions, had been found in a home having sex relations with a fifteen-year-old girl. The boy responded to police officers' queries slowly and with obvious disregard. It was apparent that his lack of deference toward the officers and his failure to evidence concern about his situation were irritating his questioners. Finally, one of the officers turned to me and, obviously angry, commented that in his view the boy was simply a "stud" interested only in sex, eating, and sleeping. The policemen conjectured that the boy "probably already had knocked up half a dozen girls." The boy ignored these remarks, except for an occasional impassive stare at the patrolmen. Turning to the boy, the officer remarked, "What the hell am I going to do with you?" And again the boy simply returned the officer's gaze. The latter then said, "Well, I guess we'll just have to put you away for a while." An arrest report was then made out and the boy was taken to Juvenile Hall.

Although anger and disgust frequently characterized officers' attitudes toward recalcitrant and impassive juvenile offenders, their manner while processing these youths was typically routine, restrained, and without rancor. While the officers' restraint may have been due in part to their desire to avoid accusation and censure, it also seemed to reflect their inurement to a frequent experience. By and large, only their occasional "needling" or insulting of a boy gave any hint of the underlying resentment and dislike they felt toward many of these youths.[20]

Prejudice in Apprehension and Disposition Decisions

Compared to other youths, Negroes and boys whose appearance matched the delinquent stereotype were more frequently stopped and interrogated by patrolmen—often even in the absence of evidence that an offense had been committed [21]—and usually were given more severe dispositions for the same violations. Our data suggest, however, that these selective apprehension and disposition practices resulted not only from the intrusion of long-held prejudices of individual police officers but also from certain job-related experiences of law-enforcement personnel. First, the tendency for police to give more severe dispositions to Negroes and to youths whose appearance corresponded to that which police associated with delinquents

[20] Officers' animosity toward recalcitrant or aloof offenders appeared to stem from two sources: moral indignation that these juveniles were self-righteous and indifferent about their transgressions, and resentment that these youths failed to accord police the respect they believed they deserved. Since the patrolmen perceived themselves as honestly and impartially performing a vital community function warranting respect and deference from the community at large, they attributed the lack of respect shown them by these juveniles to the latters' immorality.

[21] The clearest evidence for this assertion is provided by the overrepresentation of Negroes among "innocent" juveniles accosted by the police. As noted, of the seventy-six juveniles on whom systematic data were collected, ten were exonerated and released without suspicion. Seven, or two-thirds of these ten "innocent" juveniles were Negro, in contrast to the allegedly "guilty" youths, less than one-third of whom were Negro. The following incident illustrates the operation of this bias: One officer, observing a youth walking along the street, commented that the youth "looks suspicious" and promptly stopped and questioned him. Asked later to explain what aroused his suspicion, the officer explained, "He was a Negro wearing dark glasses at midnight."

partly reflected the fact, observed in this study, that these youths also were much more likely than were other types of boys to exhibit the sort of recalcitrant demeanor which police construed as a sign of the confirmed delinquent. Further, officers assumed, partly on the basis of departmental statistics, that Negroes and juveniles who "look tough" (e.g., who wear chinos, leather jackets, boots, etc.) commit crimes more frequently than do other types of youths.[22] In this sense, the police justified their selective treatment of these youths along epidemiological lines: that is, they were concentrating their attention on those youths whom they believed were most likely to commit delinquent acts. In the words of one highly placed official in the department:

If you know that the bulk of your delinquent problem comes from kids who, say, are from 12 to 14 years of age, when you're out on patrol you are much more likely to be sensitive to the activities of juveniles in this age bracket than older or younger groups. This would be good law enforcement practice. The logic in our case is the same except that our delinquency problem is largely found in the Negro community and it is these youths toward whom we are sensitized.

As regards prejudice per se, eighteen of twenty-seven officers interviewed openly admitted a dislike for Negroes. However, they attributed their dislike to experiences they had, as policemen, with youths from this minority group. The officers reported that Negro boys were much more likely than non-Negroes to "give us a hard time," be unco-operative,

and show no remorse for their transgressions. Recurrent exposure to such attitudes among Negro youth, the officers claimed, generated their antipathy toward Negroes. The following excerpt is typical of the views expressed by these officers:

They (Negroes) have no regard for the law or for the police. They just don't seem to give a damn. Few of them are interested in school or getting ahead. The girls start having illegitimate kids before they are 16 years old and the boys are always "out for kicks." Furthermore, many of these kids try to run you down. They say the damnedest things to you and they seem to have absolutely no respect for you as an adult. I am prejudiced now, but frankly I don't think I was when I began police work.

Implications

It is apparent from the findings presented above that the police officers studied in this research were permitted and even encouraged to exercise immense latitude in disposing of the juveniles they encountered. That is, it was within the officers' discretionary authority, except in extreme limiting cases, to decide which juveniles were to come to the attention of the courts and correctional agencies and thereby be identified officially as delinquents. In exercising this discretion policemen were strongly guided by the demeanor of those who were apprehended, a practice which ultimately led, as seen above, to certain youths, (particularly Negroes[23] and boys dressed in the style of "toughs") being treated more severely than other juveniles for comparable offenses.

---

[22] While police statistics did not permit an analysis of crime rates by appearance, they strongly supported officers' contentions concerning the delinquency rate among Negroes. Of all male juveniles processed by the police department in 1961, for example, 40.2 per cent were Negro and 33.9 per cent were white. These two groups comprised at that time, respectively, about 22.7 per cent and 73.6 per cent of the population in the community studied.

[23] An unco-operative demeanor was presented by more than one-third of the Negro youths but by only one-sixth of the white youths encountered by the police in the course of our observations.

But the relevance of demeanor was not limited only to police disposition practices. Thus, for example, in conjunction with police crime statistics the criterion of demeanor led police to concentrate their surveillance activities in areas frequented or inhabited by Negroes. Furthermore, these youths were accosted more often than others by officers on patrol simply because their skin color identified them as potential troublemakers. These discriminatory practices—and it is important to note that they are discriminatory, even if based on accurate statistical information—may well have self-fulfilling consequences. Thus it is not unlikely that frequent encounters with police, particularly those involving youths innocent of wrongdoing, will increase the hostility of these juveniles toward law-enforcement personnel. It is also not unlikely that the frequency of such encounters will in time reduce their significance in the eyes of apprehended juveniles, thereby leading these youths to regard them as "routine." Such responses to police encounters, however, are those which law-enforcement personnel perceive as indicators of the serious delinquent. They thus serve to vindicate and reinforce officers' prejudices, leading to closer surveillance of Negro districts, more frequent encounters with Negro youths, and so on in a vicious circle. Moreover, the consequences of this chain of events are reflected in police statistics showing a disproportionately high percentage of Negroes among juvenile offenders, thereby providing "objec-tive" justification for concentrating police attention on Negro youths.

To a substantial extent, as we have implied earlier, the discretion practiced by juvenile officers is simply an extension of the juvenile-court philosophy, which holds that in making legal decisions regarding juveniles, more weight should be given to the juvenile's character and life-situation than to his actual offending behavior. The juvenile officer's disposition decisions—and the information he uses as a basis for them—are more akin to the discriminations made by probation officers and other correctional workers than they are to decisions of police officers dealing with non-juvenile offenders. The problem is that such clinical-type decisions are restrained by mechanisms comparable to the principles of due process and the rules of procedure governing police decisions regarding adult offenders. Consequently, prejudicial practices by police officers can escape notice more easily in their dealings with juveniles than with adults.

The observations made in this study serve to underscore the fact that the official delinquent, as distinguished from the juvenile who simply commits a delinquent act, is the product of a social judgment, in this case a judgment made by the police. He is a delinquent because someone in authority has defined him as one, often on the basis of the public face he has presented to officials rather than of the kind of offense he has committed.

The Behavior of Police in Public and Private Places *

ARTHUR L. STINCHCOMBE

Legal institutions in general depend on rare events, such as arrests or civil court cases, to structure the field in which frequent events take place. This makes the operation of legal institutions very difficult to study, except when fairly comparable types of frequent events operate in strikingly different legally structured fields. The institutions of liberty generally, and of legally protected privacy in particular, have the characteristic that rare events, such as a case being thrown out of court because the law of search and seizure has been violated, structure the field in which the everyday activity of police is carried out. The many types of crimes that police deal with are very differently situated with respect to the legal institutions of privacy, as we shall try to demonstrate in the first part of this paper.

Certain statistics on the arrest and conviction rates for different types of crimes as well as pieces of common knowledge can be used to explore the different characteristics of police administrative practice in these different legally structured fields. We will then try to show that police administrative practice with respect to different types of crime varies strikingly and systematically with the relation of the crimes to the legal institutions of privacy. This paper then tries to conduct an empirical study of that kind of "structural effect" on which the regulatory power of the law depends,

namely, an effect on the behavior of many of an action by the courts that specifically applies only to the action of a few.

The order of presentation will be as follows: first I shall outline some well-known characteristics of the legal institutions by which "private places" are defined, and the effects of the growth of large cities on the social structure of "public places." Then I shall outline the relation of certain types of crime to these legal institutions and show how the location of crimes with respect to private and public places affects the organized activities of the police in handling these crimes. Since the police "organization" is made up of organized activities with respect to crime, this is really an indirect approach to studying the effect of social structure on organizational structure. To show this more clearly, in the final part of the section I shall summarize the way that the socially determined activities of police for particular types of crime are organized into police subsections with different characteristics.

Legal Relations of Police Power to Privacy

Most of our daily life is lived in a number of small, bounded social systems, such as families, schools, factories, clubs, etc., that have their own norms, goals, and facilities. The maintenance of the

* Reprinted from "Institutions of Privacy in the Determination of Police Administrative Practice" in *American Journal of Sociology,* Vol. 69 (September, 1963), pp. 150–52, 157–58, by permission of the author and The University of Chicago Press. Copyright 1963 by The University of Chicago Press.

boundaries of these systems is necessary to their free and autonomous development. If agents of the state or strange private citizens could enter these systems arbitrarily and interfere with interaction within them, they cannot develop freely.

The central practical boundaries are such mundane things as walls, doors, window shades, and locks. But in modern society few of these are made to withstand a concerted effort by a group of men to breach them (in contrast to feudal societies, for example). Yet these fragile doors and windows effectively prevent police or private citizens from interfering with our sleep, our classrooms, our toolbenches, or our bars, at least most of the time. This is because a door is a legal entity of great importance: legitimate concerted social efforts to break down a door may only take place on legally defined occasions. These occasions are defined in the law of arrest [1] and the law of search and seizure,[2] and therefore, derivatively, in the criminal law.

The legal defense of doors and walls and windows means that small social systems which have legal possession of a place can maintain *continuous, discretionary* control over who crosses their boundaries. And this discretion may be enforced against agents of the state unless they have legal cause to penetrate the system or are invited in. Whenever such continuous discretionary control is maintained, the law speaks of "private places." The legal existence of "private places," then, is the main source of the capacity of small social systems to maintain their boundaries and determine their own interaction without interference from the outside. The distinctive feature of a modern *liberal* state is that it uses the monopoly of violence (which all modern industrial states have) to guarantee the boundaries of small, autonomous social systems.

The central importance in our society of the private places created in this way is indicated by two facts. First, in Maryland, a state not much less free than others, a man entirely without access to private places is legally unfree:

Every person, not insane, who wanders about in this state and lodges in market houses, market places, or in other public buildings [note that some of these "public buildings" are "private property"] or in barns, outhouses, barracks, or in the open air, without having any lawful occupation in the city, town, or county in which he may so wander, and without having any visible means of support, shall be deemed to be a tramp, and to be guilty of a misdemeanor, and shall be subject to imprisonment, at the discretion of the Court or Justice of the Peace hearing the charge, for a period of not less than thirty days nor more than one year. This section not to apply to Allegany County.[3]

That is, if a man is not a member of some organization or family or other group that has control over a "private place" (which may, of course, be "public property," as for instance a county hospital), then he has to *satisfy a policeman* that his occupation in the area is lawful, and has to make visible his means of support (except in Allegany County). Access to private places is itself sufficient evidence that a man has a legitimate relation to the social structure; without that evidence, special evidence of legitimate occupation has to be provided. "Occupation" here means any legitimate activity, not specifically a job.

The second fact indicating the impor-

---

[1] A good summary of the law of arrest is R. M. Perkins, "The Law of Arrest," *Iowa Law Review*, XXV (1940), 201–89.

[2] See E. W. Machen, Jr., *The Law of Search and Seizure* (Chapel Hill: University of North Carolina Press, 1950).

[3] H. E. Flack (ed.), *The Annotated Code . . . of Maryland, 1951.* Art. 27, Sec. 666.

tance of the legal definition of private places is that unless continuous discretionary control of access to a piece of property is maintained (creating a "private place"), police may freely enter and supervise interaction and arrest without a warrant:

An officer in uniform or in citizen's clothes, may enter any public house, if open, as other people enter, for the purpose of detecting or suppressing crime, and having peaceably entered, may arrest for any offense committed in his presence. [Apparently a common law rule, as cases are cited for authority rather than statutes.] [4]

A man's affairs are never, then, legally free of police supervision except within private places. Police may not legally, of course, forbid actions in public places that are not prohibited by law. But there is a fundamental difference between conducting the affairs of a small social system in such a manner that no crimes committed shall *come to the attention* of the police, and conducting them so that a physically present policeman will approve. In the first case, the problem is to prevent complaints, perhaps by agreement; in the second, the problem is to satisfy the police, rather than other members of the system, that all is as it should be. Few of us ever see a policeman in those places where we spend most of our time; a "tramp" sees one wherever he goes, and the policeman has the discretionary power to "run him in."

Distribution of Private Places and Urban-Rural Police Practice

The concentration of the population into cities concentrates intensively used "public places" within a small geographical area, thus greatly reducing the amount of "public" area per person and making professional control of public places much more economical. At the same time the size and anonymity of the city decrease the chance of small social systems to control the behavior of their members in public. In a small village, activity in public places easily comes to the attention of the family, the priest, the employer, and the peers of the offender. Further, in large cities there are much stronger norms about "deliberately not noticing" the behavior of other people. This means that in cities, much more behavior is *only* inquired into by the police.

That is, in cities it is economically possible to patrol public places, and at the same time it is functionally necessary. City police can therefore depend much more on their own presence and information for the detection of crime (especially certain types of crime) than can a rural police force. To a large degree (except for the patrol of main highways) rural police depend on complaints from people who are injured or know of a crime rather than on their own patrol.

Besides leading to different structural conditions of police practice, intensively used public places pose new problems. The most important are, of course, traffic jams and accidents. But also, extensive traffic creates opportunities for the use of public places for private profit in ways that create a "nuisance." Soliciting for prostitution, begging, street vending, speech-making, all become profitable uses of public places when the traffic gets heavy enough. The control of these "nuisances" is easily done without access to private places, along with other patrol duties.

The increasing predominance of patrol of public places means that policemen act much more on their own initiative. Much or all of the evidence that justifies

---

[4] *Instructions . . . and Digest of the Statutes, Ordinances and Decisions* (Baltimore: Baltimore Police Department, 1939), p. 13.

arrest will be collected by the policeman on the spot. The arrest often need not involve any invasion at all of private places. Consequently these arrests are much more likely than are those in rural areas to be arrests without a warrant, and therefore without prior check by the judiciary, or to be a direct summons to appear in court (as in traffic cases). . . .

. . . The regulation of public places is the central responsibility of patrol police. We may distinguish three main types of public disorder: individual, collective, and structural. Perhaps the ideal type of individual disorder is "drunk and disorderly." By "collective disorder" I refer primarily to riot, parades that get out of hand, and other types of collective behavior, though in unusual circumstances private military groups may create collective disorder. By "structural disorder" I refer especially to the modern phenomenon of the traffic jam. No crowd or individual "wills" a traffic jam.

1. Individual disorder in public places consists mainly of doing things that would be entirely legitimate if done in private, such as getting too drunk to stand up, or sleeping on park benches. Other individual disorder, such as soliciting for prostitution, or begging, may be illegal even if done in private, but is in fact relatively safe there.

This means first of all that there is a good deal of difference in the "commission" of these "crimes" according to the degree of access people have to private places. Homeless men are obviously more likely to commit the crime of vagrancy, which is the crime of being a homeless man. And if they get drunk, homeless men are more likely to have to sleep it off in the street. Since there is a rough correlation between social class and access to private places (particularly *enough* private places to cover most of one's social life), individual public disorder is related to social class even if the behavior of all classes is the same.

The fact that the "commission" of individual disorder is an index of the lack of connection to small social systems results in a main characteristic of these offenders, that they have not the will, the money, the friends, or the reputation to make good use of their legal right to defend themselves. For will depends on social support of intimates; money for defense often comes from the collective resources (or credit) of a small system; friends are products of intimate interaction; and reputation is generally dependent on a guaranty of good behavior by a small system. Those whose ties to small systems are weak are at a disadvantage in all these ways. Hearings before a police court magistrate in these cases are generally purely formalities; it is assumed by all concerned, including the defendant, that the presumed offender is guilty. The only question that remains to be decided is how much *noblesse oblige* the magistrate should show. . . . The conviction rates for these crimes are quite high, and this is not the result of the sterling qualities of the evidence.

The information on which arrest is based is generally collected entirely by the patrolman, and he has a relatively wide degree of discretion about whether behavior constitutes "disorder." Arrests are almost entirely without a warrant. The fact that police information rather than complaint starts the proceedings means that there are no "crimes known to the police" that have not been solved. The FBI has the good sense not to try to report how many people were drunk or disorderly on the streets of the nation during the year. Investigative police are hardly ever involved.

In summary, the substitution of police for small bounded social systems in the government of the streets produces discretionary power in the hands of the police, particularly over population groups that are unlikely to defend themselves vigorously and effectively in court. The arrest is rarely justified to a judicial officer before it takes place, nor afterward except by the word of the policeman. When convictions do not follow on arrest, it is generally due to *noblesse oblige* rather than to defense by the presumed offender. . . .

Mistakes in Police Work

WILLIAM J. CHAMBLISS AND JOHN T. LIELL

In the eyes of the community an individual is not automatically a deviant simply because he has committed one or more "deviant" acts. As Erikson,[1] Kitsuse and Cicourel,[2] and Becker[3] have recently pointed out, becoming a deviant involves not only the deviant act itself but also the reaction of others to it. Thus it is necessary to know the circumstances under which a reaction to the deviance can be expected and to discover the form that the reaction is likely to take.

On this question there is a convergence of interest for at least two traditionally separate areas of inquiry within sociology: the sociology of law and the study of deviant behavior. For those interested in the former, the "others" responding to the deviant acts are usually limited to officials who make decisions in such matters. This official group comprises all in the entire legal system, from the police to the administrators of containing institutions, and includes the prosecutor, the judge, sometimes a jury, and, on occasion, political officials such as the mayor and councilmen.

The study reported here deals with the response of the legal system to the perceived deviation of others. By analyzing a particular case of law enforcement, we intend to identify factors involved in (1) the selection of others as deviant and (2) the development of a policy for dealing with deviant acts.

Locating a Problem

Joe Lord (this is not his real name) arrived in town, a small midwestern community, inconspicuously enough. The police were not forewarned and, at the time of his arrival, he did not, to the best of their knowledge, have a criminal record. Shortly afterward, however, a series of incidents brought him to the attention of officials and culminated in their defining him as a deviant.

In the course of a few years Lord had

* Reprinted from "The Legal Process in the Community Setting" in *Crime and Delinquency*, Vol. 12 (October 1966), pp. 310–17, by permission of the authors and publisher.

[1] Kai T. Erikson, "Notes on the Sociology of Deviance," *Social Problems*, Spring 1962, pp. 307–14.

[2] John Kitsuse, "Societal Reaction to Deviant Behavior: Problems of Theory and Method," *Social Problems*, Winter 1962, pp. 247–56; and John Kitsuse and Aaron Cicourel, "A Note on the Use of Official Statistics," *Social Problems*, Fall 1963, pp. 131–39.

[3] Howard S. Becker, *Outsiders: Studies in the Sociology of Deviance* (New York: Free Press, 1963).

purchased several taverns, all of them catering primarily to a lower-class clientele. He also purchased and resold some property in a transaction described by one official as "shady," apparently because Lord had somehow received advance knowledge that this piece of property was going to be sought by a local bank and that this would raise its price considerably. The town officials did not understand where Lord could have obtained financing for these enterprises; they assumed he was "not the type" to have either investments or enough capital to pay for these "deals." The prosecuting attorney, in an interview, hinted that Lord was being financed by a group of "outsiders."

In addition to the three taverns, Lord also purchased what came to be known as the 713 Club. (This building, located in a lower-class deteriorating area, was two doors away from a home owned by the university in the town and occupied by the university's vice-president. Despite the fact that it was several miles from the campus, this home was of considerable sentimental value to the university, because it had once been the home of the university's president.)

Shortly after this purchase, Joe Lord applied for a liquor license for the 713 Club. At the hearing he was opposed by the university, and by several persons who lived near the club. The secretary of the Board of Trustees was one of three university officials who appeared at the hearing to voice the university's opposition, which was strenuous, organized, and effective. As a result, Joe Lord's application was refused.

Officers of the university were convinced that Joe Lord's taverns frequently served liquor to minors and allowed them to drink to excess on the premises. Other local officials had even more serious reservations about Lord's character. The mayor stated that he first became aware of his activities several years before when Joe Lord was sued by his former wife for failure to pay alimony, a fact also commented upon by one of the deans at the university. The town officials also thought that Joe Lord at times rented rooms for purposes of prostitution, and they suspected him of somehow being involved in selling drugs. Both university and town officials said there was evidence that Lord was involved with a known distributor of drugs from a nearby large city. The information supporting this suspicion was tenuous at best; it was, however, sufficient to arouse fear among the officials, who perceived Joe Lord as a person always "walking a tightrope between legal and illegal activities."

Action

As a result of these suspicions and fears the local officials tacitly agreed, apparently with the complicity of the university, to "do something" about Joe Lord. But "doing something" about him involved some risk. His known activities were, at the worst, minor transgressions (selling liquor to college students), and at best, describable only as "shady" or "on the fringe" of legality. Furthermore, his suspected illegal activities took place in privacy. And finally, Lord had at least a modicum of esteem in the community. He did not enjoy membership in the upper echelons of the community's social life, but he was not readily defined as intrinsically "bad." Thus the officials were faced with the problem of "doing something" about a case that could become a source of trouble for the police themselves. They chose, not surprisingly, to engage in what amounted to a campaign of harassment.

Lord was accused of "keeping a gaming device" (a punch board on which the winning number received a fifth of whiskey [4]) in one of his taverns; he was tried, found guilty, and fined. Next came the refusal of his application for a liquor license for the 713 Club. Then some girls were arrested in a hotel (which was partly owned by Lord) on a charge of "keeping a dive" when they sold a drink of whiskey to a plain-clothes policeman. And finally, some underage students were arrested at Lord's 713 Club, where they were having a private party at which alcoholic drinks were served. This last offense might have been serious enough to drive Lord from town had it not been for some events which were unanticipated by the officials and which, in fact, almost culminated in their own undoing.[5]

One of the fraternities at the university had rented the second floor of the 713 Club for a private party for the night of the Coronation Ball. At eleven o'clock that night, when the party was in progress, the police received a phone call from an unknown person stating that a woman who occupied a third-floor apartment above the 713 Club had had a heart attack. When the police arrived to investigate, they were seen by the students, who thereupon assumed that their party was about to be raided and proceeded to leave the premises by every available means—windows, fire escapes, and stairs.

The mayor, on his way home from visiting friends, heard, on the police radio in his car, the call instructing the police to make the investigation. Recognizing the address as that of Joe Lord's club, the mayor speeded there, parked his car in the adjoining alley, and went into the building just as the students were scurrying from it. (One fleeing student dashing down the alley opened the door of the mayor's car and said to the mayor's wife: "You'd better get the hell out of here fast. The cops are here.")

The police, occupied upstairs, had paid no attention to the students' party. The mayor, however, insisted that the police "stake out" the building. The prosecutor and the police chief were notified that the place was about to be raided.

At 1:00 A.M. ten students joined the party. They danced and had a "couple of drinks." At 1:30 six plain-clothes policemen came into the room and informed the students they were under arrest and that they would all have to "come down to headquarters." The male students were handcuffed (a procedure described by the dean of students as "highly irregular"), taken to the sheriff's office, booked, and held in custody. The boys were placed in cells upstairs in the jail; the girls, one of whom was the Coronation Queen, were put into one large room. A phone call by the girls alerted their sorority and the university to their arrest. Bond was scraped together from the sorority and from a university fund specifically set aside for such purposes. Within a few hours the students were released on bail.

The story of the mass arrest was headlined the next morning in several towns where the students were residents. Special attention was given to the arrest of the Coronation Queen, ironically enough because her father, a well-known public relations man in the state,[6] had

---

[4] That this concern over "keeping a gaming device" did not stem from a consistently puritanical attitude toward gambling in this community is evidenced by the law enforcement agents' tolerance of slot machines and gambling of all kinds in the local fraternal organizations. Virtually all kinds of gambling took place quite openly at the American Legion Stag held annually in the armory.

[5] Two years after these incidents the prosecuting attorney lost the election and the mayor retired from office to take a position with the federal government.

[6] He was also influential in state politics, but not, it must be noted, in the mayor's political party.

previously arranged for national coverage of her coronation. The papers, of course, quickly switched the emphasis away from a routine story to one that featured her arrest at a party described by the police as a "drinking orgy."

The following day her father came down to the university and informed the dean of students and the police that there had been a grievous error. He also informed the local police that if they did not drop the charges he would sue them for false arrest. The local police, the mayor, and the county prosecutor had, of course, not anticipated such a reaction; in fact, they were all somewhat stunned by the publicity. Some rather uncomplimentary remarks were exchanged publicly between university officials and the mayor and between mayor and the prosecutor.

The mayor was the only one to come out of the fracas apparently unscathed. He consistently maintained that the students should be prosecuted and that they should receive their deserved punishment. The prosecutor, on the other hand, maintained that the police would not sign an affidavit showing that they had evidence against the students and that therefore he could not prosecute the case. He even went so far as to place a statement in the local paper for one week that if anyone, citizen or policeman, would sign a complaint and thereby commit himself to testify against the students, he would prosecute.

By this time the university was trying to be as quiet as possible.

There were numerous letters to the editor of the local newspaper, most of which were uncomplimentary to the university and to the prosecutor.

Of the ten students involved, four (those who were not befriended by the Coronation Queen's vociferous and influential father) were placed on probation by the university. All of the girls were placed on probation by their national sorority. The father protested to the sorority headquarters that its action was not justified since "no crime" had been committed by the students.

The whole series of events was described by the dean of students as a "comedy of errors," a statement later denied after rather pointed criticism from the mayor. Ultimately the furor died down.

Discussion

Even in "police state" societies, official agents of social control do not operate with impunity. Accusation, suspicion, and official action depend on more than the mere fact that someone has committed a wrong. For the official agents of formal social control are themselves surveyed and, if their actions do not meet with approval, they are liable to sanctions. In American society the approval which is of considerable importance to law-enforcement agencies comes from "the public," especially from those members of the "legitimate" society who are in a position to influence public opinion. Because of this, law-enforcement agents take measures to protect themselves against the possibility of public reprisal for their actions; they consider whether a given course of action (wherein a member of the community is arrested, tried, and convicted) is likely to arouse public antipathy toward them rather than toward the accused and they devise techniques to reduce the dangers involved in "pointing the finger" at someone. For example, suspected persons are asked to "come downtown" or to "come see the lieutenant" instead of being put "under arrest." Some members of the agency are given special training to handle cases which have the potential of arousing public antipathy toward the law enforcers.

But devious techniques and specially trained personnel afford only partial protection for the agencies. For the vast majority of the accused—vagrants, drunks, streetwalkers—no special care or treatment is required because the likelihood of public arousal is exceedingly small.[7] There are, however, other cases which are potentially troublesome no matter how discreetly they are handled. When a mayor's son steals an automobile or when a high school football coach is found to be engaging with local youth in homosexuality, no amount of discretion and care is going to keep the public eye away from the law-enforcement agencies.

In general, from the standpoint of the police, arrests are "safe" or "risky" according to three variables: the *place* where the offense occurs, the *seriousness* of the offense, and the *reputation* of the persons involved.

Place.—If the offense is committed in a public place, the police have the right to be there (or to enter if they are not present at the time the act is committed) and to make arrests on "reasonable suspicion" without special permission from higher authority. On the other hand, if the event occurs in a private dwelling, the police can enter only if called upon by someone who has a legitimate right to be there, or if given special permission by some higher authority. Thus the arrest is considerably less risky for the law-enforcement agents if the offense occurs in a public rather than a private place.[8]

Seriousness.—Minor transgressions are unlikely to arouse the public's great interest and, therefore, can be handled rather easily by the legal system. Severe offenses, on the other hand, frequently bring attention to law-enforcement activities and may disrupt their smooth functioning.

Reputation.—If both the offender and the offended are persons of low esteem (such as pimps, vagrants, or known criminals), and even if the crime is serious and occurs in private, the law-enforcement agencies have little cause for concern.[9] Public awareness of the arrest and conviction of such persons is likely to be minimal; and even if the public is informed, opposition to whatever the legal system sees fit to do is not likely to be strong.

There is thus a grading of offenses on the "safe-risky" continuum. If the act occurs in public, if the offense is a minor one, and if those involved are of low esteem, the law-enforcement agencies are relatively free to act in whatever way they deem expedient. But if the transgression occurs in private, if it is severe, and if the persons involved are of high esteem, the case must be handled with caution. Wherever possible, the enforcement agencies will avoid taking any action until they are certain that their judgment is correct, and, even when certain, they will act with great discretion. Special police, trained to be mannerly and to project the proper image of the department, will do the investigating. The prosecuting attorney, not one of his assistants, will take the case to court. Persons with a pipeline to public opinion

---

[7] Occasionally, *after* the legal machinery has been put in motion, it appears that an agency misjudged the safety of the accusation. For example, Caryl Chessman would not have proved to be a problem to the legal system had he not written of his troubles and had he not done so *after* the police and the courts had taken action. Quite possibly a different decision might have emerged if he had written his book *before* his trial.

[8] Arthur L. Stinchcombe, "Institutions of Privacy in the Determination of Police Administrative Practice," *American Journal of Sociology,* September 1963, pp. 150–60.

[9] Warden Lewis Edward Lawes's famous assertion that one must be poor and black in America in order to be executed (*Twenty Thousand Years in Sing Sing* [New York: Ray Long & Richard R. Smith, 1932], p. 302) can be viewed as an extension of the legal system's concern for being "safe" in its decisions.

will be cajoled, courted, and perhaps even threatened in order to obtain support for the action of the entire system.

Officially defining someone as deviant, then, is inextricably interwoven with considerations of what the public reaction may be. Most of the cases handled in the legal system pose no great problem. If the transgression is on one extreme, it is handled routinely and with little concern for the rules under which the system is supposed to operate. If the case falls at the other extreme, specially trained personnel are assigned and the system operates with a maximum of attention to the rules. But not all cases fall clearly into one or the other of the extreme categories. We can better understand the dynamics of this process by examining cases which do not fall clearly into one of these categories and then observing the way the official agencies proceed to solve this problem—for example, the case of Joe Lord. Because Lord was seen as deviant but did not fit into either extreme, the persons operating the legal system had to resort to devious means to achieve their goal. That these means backfired points up the fact that the middle-range cases are the ones that cause the legal system the most difficulty.

Where did the legal system go awry in this instance? Specifically, it chose to prosecute where the violation was not serious, where the accused had relatively high esteem, and where the events took place in a semiprivate arena. The error was made primarily by an official who had control over the police but little knowledge of the criteria for making an arrest: the mayor.

All of the law enforcement participants were deceived by their own perspective. They were interested really in "getting" Joe Lord, not the students. Thus the external pressure to "do something" led them to focus their attention not on the particulars of the arrest of the students but rather on the intended consequences of this arrest—the conviction of another party.

Finally, they misjudged the esteem of the students. The mayor, especially, appears to have thought of the students as defenseless. The prosecuting attorney, whose daily operations brought him in closer contact with the university, advised against making the arrests but was overruled by the mayor.

When the furor arose over the arrest, the officials were caught in the middle of a tug-of-war. The townspeople deeply resented the failure to prosecute the students. The university and the students' parents insisted that the students had done "nothing seriously wrong." This conflict created a split among the local officials. The mayor defended the action of the police in arresting the students. The prosecuting attorney maintained that the police had not secured sufficient evidence to make an arrest and it was on this ground that the case was dismissed. The police remained silent throughout.

As a consequence of the support the students received from the university and from influential family members, their esteem generally was perceived as much higher by the police and the other officials after these events than before. The processing agencies came to see more clearly than before that extracommunity influences had to be reckoned with as well as persons' esteem in the immediate community.

But we must now consider the extent to which these findings are generally applicable. Specifically, are considerations of privacy, seriousness, and esteem as relevant for police activities in large cities as they are in small towns?

It is relatively easy for members of the processing agencies to identify the esteem of prospective offenders in the small town; it is a good deal more difficult to do this in a large city. In the city, then, mistakes in judging the esteem of an offender are more likely to occur. The consequence of this complication is not a lessening in the importance of the three variables but an attempt to protect the agencies against reprisals.

In the small town the agencies argued, quibbled, and blamed one another for the fiasco. In an urban setting certain features of the system are designed to avoid such mistakes. The newspapers, for example, are systematically excluded from information dealing with problematic cases until the police are certain of the possible consequences of their actions. Specialists trained in "public relations" are employed. The autonomy of the urban policeman is reduced to protect the police department from possible embarrassment. Higher officials, such as the mayor and the prosecuting attorney, have less direct influence over the police department. Urban police are also more likely to take the status of the offender into account. Membership in or attachment to certain organizations serves as a cue to esteem, as does residence in certain neighborhoods.

What is the impact of professionalization of the police on these considerations? Professionalization implies that the police will be impartial and objective. Does this mean that the importance of such things as esteem will be reduced? In all likelihood it does not. The police and the other legal processing agencies are not supposed to act impartially. The community does not define "crime" as something separated from "criminals." The processing agencies are not expected to react the same way to a boy who steals a car from his father as they do to a boy who steals a car from his neighbor. The fact of the theft is not the sole relevant consideration.

The important thing to note, however, in this selective process is the degree to which organizational considerations determine which individuals will be defined as deviant. Instead of the idealized picture of the police and the courts as a set of agencies that guard the community against transgressors of the law, we find that the police attempt to accomplish their job with a minimum of strain and that this effort leads to the selection of law violators *not* according to legal prescriptions alone but also according to how closely they approximate the ideal case, in which the police gain prestige and run no risk of criticism. Cases such as the one analyzed here emerge as guidelines on how the police will respond to other known deviant acts. Accordingly, it is these organizational considerations that determine who is defined by the community as a deviant. The fact of the deviance itself is a point of only secondary importance. It is the organization's ability to prosecute safely that is of primary consideration in determining both who will be prosecuted and how the prosecution will be accomplished.

THE DEVIANT IN COURT

7

Courts are one of the significant kinds of offices through which many, though by no means all, deviants will wend their way as they follow the stages of their own particular career. Once again the theory of the office reveals how court functionaries will type, define, and deal with the deviants with whom they have to do legal business. And that business can be done in a more orderly and expeditious manner when types fit cases in accordance with the social definitions of court personnel.

Sudnow, reporting on the public defender, shows how cases can be dispatched more readily if they can be fitted to prevailing sociolegal conceptions of what different kinds of criminals are supposed to be like. Cameron shows that prosecuted Negro shoplifters are typed differently, and are more likely to receive jail sentences, than are white shoplifters. Ross describes the conditions under which persons and agents *do not* see certain offenses as crime. Scheff then shows in psychiatric commitment hearings how psychiatrists assume that persons must be legally insane because otherwise their families would not seek to commit them. Given this assumption, they spend little time ascertaining mental status; more often, they ascribe patient status, instead of giving persons a fair chance of achieving that status on their own.

Normal Crimes *

DAVID SUDNOW

Two stances toward the utility of official classificatory schema for criminological research have been debated for years. One position, which might be termed that of the "revisionist" school, has it that the categories of the criminal law, e.g., "burglary," "petty theft," "homicide," etc., are not "homogeneous in respect to causation." [1] From an inspection of penal code descriptions of crimes, it is argued that the way persons seem to be assembled under the auspices of criminal law procedure is such as to produce classes of criminals who are, at least on theoretical grounds, as dissimilar in their social backgrounds and styles of activity as they are similar. The entries in the penal code, this school argues, require revision if sociological use is to be made of categories of crime and a classificatory scheme of etiological relevance is to be developed. Common attempts at such revision have included notions such as "*white collar* crime," and "*systematic* check forger," these conceptions constituting attempts to institute sociologically meaningful specifications which the operations of criminal law procedure and statutory legislation "fail" to achieve.

The other major perspective toward the sociologist's use of official categories and the criminal statistics compiled under their heading derives less from a concern with etiologically useful schema than from an interest in understanding the actual operations of the administrative legal system. Here, the categories of the criminal law are not regarded as useful or not, as objects to be either adopted, adapted, or ignored; rather, they are seen as constituting the basic conceptual equipment with which such people as judges, lawyers, policemen, and probation workers organize their everyday activities. The study of the actual use of official classification systems by actually employed administrative personnel regards the penal code as data, to be preserved intact; its use, both in organizing the work of legal representation, accusation, adjudication, and prognostication, and in compiling tallies of legal occurrences, is to be examined as one would examine any social activity. By sociologically regarding, rather than criticizing, rates of statistics and the categories employed to assemble them, one learns, it is promised,

* Reprinted from "Normal Crimes: Sociological Features of the Penal Code" by David Sudnow in *Social Problems*, Vol. 12 (Winter, 1965), pp. 255–64, 269–70, by permission of the author and *Social Problems*.

This investigation is based on field observations of a Public Defender Office in a metropolitan California community. The research was conducted while the author was associated with the Center for the Study of Law and Society, University of California, Berkeley. I am grateful to the Center for financial support. Erving Goffman, Sheldon Messinger, Harvey Sacks, and Emanuel Schegloff contributed valuable suggestions and criticisms to an earlier draft.

[1] D. R. Cressey, "Criminological Research and the Definition of Crimes," *American Journal of Sociology*, Vol. 61 (No. 6) 1951, p. 548. See also, J. Hall, *Theft, Law and Society*, second edition, Indianapolis: Bobbs-Merrill, 1952; and E. Sutherland, *Principles of Criminology*, New York: Lippincott, 1947, p. 218. An extensive review of "typological developments" is available in D. C. Gibbons and D. L. Garrity, "Some Suggestions for the Development of Etiological and Treatment Theory in Criminology," *Social Forces*, Vol. 38 (No. 1) 1959.

about the "rate producing agencies" and the assembling process.[2]

While the former perspective, the "revisionist" position, has yielded several fruitful products, the latter stance (commonly identified with what is rather loosely known as the "labelling" perspective), has been on the whole more promissory than productive, more programmatic than empirical. The present report will examine the operations of a Public Defender system in an effort to assess the warrant for the continued theoretical and empirical development of the position argued by Kitsuse and Cicourel. It will address the question: what of import for the sociological analysis of legal administration can be learned by describing the actual way the penal code is employed in the daily activities of legal representation? First, I shall consider the "guilty plea" as a way of handling criminal cases, focusing on some features of the penal code as a description of a population of defendants. Then I shall describe the Public Defender operation with special attention to the way defendants are represented. The place of the guilty plea and penal code in this representation will be examined. Lastly, I shall briefly analyze the fashion in which the Public Defender prepares and conducts a "defense." The latter section will attempt to indicate the connection between certain prominent organizational features of the Public Defender system and the penal code's place in the routine operation of that system.

Guilty Pleas, Inclusion, and Normal Crimes

It is a commonly noted fact about the criminal court system generally, that the greatest proportion of cases are "settled" by a guilty plea.[3] In the county from which the following material is drawn, over 80 per cent of all cases "never go to trial." To describe the method of obtaining a guilty plea disposition, essential for the discussion to follow, I must distinguish between what shall be termed "necessarily-included-lesser-offenses" and "situationally-included-lesser-offenses." Of two offenses designated in the penal code, the lesser is considered to be that for which the length of required incarceration is the shorter period of time. *Inclusion* refers to the relation between two or more offenses. The "necessarily-included-lesser-offense" is a strictly legal notion:

Whether a lesser offense is included in the crime charged is a question of law to be determined solely from the definition and corpus delicti of the offense charged and of the lesser offense. . . . If all the elements of the corpus delicti of a lesser crime can be found in a list of all the elements of the offense charged, then only is the lesser included in the greater.[4]

Stated alternatively:

The test in this state of necessarily included offenses is simply that where an offense cannot be committed without necessarily committing another offense, the latter is a necessarily included offense.[5]

The implied negative is put: could Smith have committed A and not B? If the

---

[2] The most thorough statement of this position, borrowing from the writings of Harold Garfinkel, can be found in the recent critical article by J. I. Kitsuse and A. V. Cicourel, "A Note on the Official Use of Statistics," *Social Problems*, Vol. 11, No. 2 (Fall, 1963) pp. 131–139.

[3] See D. J. Newman, "Pleading Guilty for Considerations," 46 *J. Crim. L. C. and P.S.* Also, M. Schwartz, *Cases and Materials on Professional Responsibility and the Administration of Criminal Justice*, San Francisco: Matthew Bender and Co., 1961, esp. pp. 79–105.

[4] C. W. Fricke, *California Criminal Law*, Los Angeles: The Legal Book Store, 1961, p. 41.

[5] People v. Greer, 30 Cal. 2d, 589.

answer is yes, then B is not necessarily included in A. If the answer is no, B is necessarily included. While in a given case a battery might be committed in the course of a robbery, battery is not necessarily included in robbery. Petty theft is necessarily included in robbery but not in burglary. Burglary primarily involves the "intent" to acquire another's goods illegally (e.g., by breaking and entering); the consummation of the act need not occur for burglary to be committed. Theft, like robbery, requires that some item be stolen.

I shall call *lesser* offenses that are not necessarily but "only" *actually* included, "situationally-included-lesser-offenses." By statutory definition, necessarily included offenses are "actually" included. By actual here, I refer to the "way it occurs as a course of action." In the instance of necessary inclusion, the "way it occurs" is irrelevant. With situational inclusion, the "way it occurs" is definitive. In the former case, no particular course of action is referred to. In the latter, the scene and progress of the criminal activity would be analyzed.

The issue of necessary inclusion has special relevance for two procedural matters:

A. A man cannot be charged and/or convicted of two or more crimes any one of which is necessarily included in the others, unless the several crimes occur on separate occasions.

If a murder occurs, the defendant cannot be charged and/or convicted of both "homicide" and "intent to commit a murder," the latter of which is necessarily included in first degree murder. If, however, a defendant "intends to commit a homicide" against one person and commits a "homicide" against another, both offenses may be properly charged. While it is an extremely complex question as to the scope and definition of "in the course of," in most instances the rule is easily applied.

B. The judge cannot instruct the jury to consider as alternative crimes of which to find a defendant guilty, crimes that are not necessarily included in the charged crime or crimes.

If a man is charged with "statutory rape" the judge may instruct the jury to consider as a possible alternative conviction "contributing to the delinquency of a minor," as this offense is necessarily included in "statutory rape." He cannot however suggest that the alternative "intent to commit murder" be considered and the jury cannot find the defendant guilty of this latter crime, unless it is charged as a distinct offense in the complaint.

It is crucial to note that these restrictions apply only to (a) the relation between several charged offenses in a formal allegation, and (b) the alternatives allowable in a jury instruction. At any time before a case "goes to trial," alterations in the charging complaint may be made by the district attorney. The issue of necessary inclusion has no required bearing on (a) what offense(s) will be charged initially by the prosecutor, (b) what the relation is between the charge initially made and "what happened," or (c) what modifications may be made after the initial charge and the relation between initially charged offenses and those charged in modified complaints. It is this latter operation, the modification of the complaint, that is central to the guilty plea disposition.

Complaint alterations are made when a defendant agrees to plead guilty to an offense and thereby avoid a trial. The alteration occurs in the context of a "deal" consisting of an offer from the district attorney to alter the original charge in such a fashion that a lighter sentence will be incurred with a guilty plea than would be the case if the defendant were sentenced on the original charge. In return for this manipulation, the defendant agrees to plead guilty. The arrangement is proposed in this following format: "if you plead guilty to this new lesser offense, you will get less time in prison than if you plead not guilty to the original, greater charge and lose the trial." The decision must then be made whether or not the chances of obtaining complete acquittal at trial are great enough to warrant the risk of a loss and higher sentence if found guilty on the original charge. As we shall see below, it is a major job of the Public Defender, who mediates between the district attorney and the defendant, to convince his "client" that the chances of acquittal are too slight to warrant this risk.

If a man is charged with "drunkenness" and the Public Defender and Public Prosecutor (hereafter P.D. and D.A.) prefer not to have a trial, they seek to have the defendant agree to plead guilty. While it is occasionally possible, particularly with first offenders, for the P.D. to convince the defendant to plead guilty to the originally charged offense, most often it is felt that some "exchange" or "consideration" should be offered, i.e., a lesser offense charged.

To what offense can "drunkenness" be reduced? There is no statutorily designated crime that is necessarily included in the crime of "drunkenness." That is, if any of the statutorily required components of drunk behavior (its corpus delicti) are absent, there remains no offense of which the resultant description is a definition. For drunkenness there is, however, an offense that while not necessarily included is "typically-situationally-included," i.e., "typically" occurs as a feature of the way drunk persons are seen to behave—"disturbing the peace." The range of possible sentences is such that, of the two offenses, "disturbing the

peace" cannot call for as long a prison sentence as "drunkenness." If, in the course of going on a binge, a person does so in such a fashion that "disturbing the peace" may be employed to describe some of his behavior, it would be considered as an alternative offense to offer in return for a guilty plea. A central question for the following analysis will be: in what fashion would he have to behave so that disturbing the peace would be considered a suitable reduction?

If a man is charged with "molesting a minor," there are not any necessarily included lesser offenses with which to charge him. Yet an alternative charge— "loitering around a schoolyard"—is often used as a reduction. As above, and central to our analysis the question is: what would the defendant's behavior be such that "loitering around a schoolyard" would constitute an appropriate alternative?

If a person is charged with "burglary," "petty theft" is not necessarily included. Routinely, however, "petty theft" is employed for reducing the charge of burglary. Again, we shall ask: what is the relation between burglary and petty theft and the *manner in which the former occurs* that warrants this reduction?

Offenses are regularly reduced to other offenses the latter of which are not necessarily or situationally included in the former. As I have already said the determination of whether or not offense X was situationally included in Y involves an analysis of the course of action that constitutes the criminal behavior. I must now turn to examine this mode of behavioral analysis.

When encountering a defendant who is charged with "assault with a deadly weapon," the P.D. asks: "what can this offense be reduced to so as to arrange for a guilty plea?" As the reduction is only to be proposed by the P.D. and accepted or not by the D.A., his question becomes "what reduction will be allowable?" (As shall be seen below, the P.D. and D.A. have institutionalized a common orientation to allowable reductions.) The method of reduction involves, as a general feature, the fact that the particular case in question is scrutinized to decide its membership in a class of similar cases. But *the penal code does not provide the reference for deciding the correspondence between the instant event and the general case; that is, it does not define the classes of offense types.* To decide, for purposes of finding a suitable reduction, if the instant case involves a "burglary," reference is not made to the statutory definition of "burglary." To decide what the situationally included offenses are in the instant case, the instant case is not analyzed as a *statutorily* referable course of action; rather, reference is made to a *non-statutorily* conceived class "burglary" and offenses that are typically situationally included in it, taken as a class of behavioral events. Stated again: in searching an instant case to decide what to *reduce it to,* there is no analysis of the statutorily referable elements of the instant case; instead, its membership in a class of events, the features of which cannot be described by the penal code, must be decided. An example will be useful. If a defendant is charged with burglary and the P.D. is concerned to propose a reduction to a lesser offense, he might search the elements of the burglary at hand to decide what other offenses were committed. The other offenses he might "discover" would be of two sorts: those necessarily and those situationally included. In attempting to decide those other offenses situationally included in the instant event, the instant event might be analyzed as a statutorily referable course of action. Or, as is the case with the P.D., the instant case might be analyzed to decide if it is a "burglary" in common with other "burglaries" con-

ceived of in terms other than those provided by the statute.

Burglaries are routinely reduced to petty theft. If we were to analyze the way burglaries typically occur, petty theft is neither situationally nor necessarily included; when a burglary is committed, money or other goods are seldom illegally removed from some person's body. If we therefore analyzed burglaries, employing the penal code as our reference, and then searched the P.D.'s records to see how burglaries are reduced in the guilty plea, we could not establish a rule that would describe the transformation between the burglary cases statutorily described and the reductions routinely made (i.e., to "petty theft"). The rule must be sought elsewhere, in the character of the non-statutorily defined class of "burglaries," which I shall term *normal burglaries.*

Normal Crimes

In the course of routinely encountering persons charged with "petty theft," "burglary," "assault with a deadly weapon," "rape," "possession of marijuana," etc., the P.D. gains knowledge of the typical manner in which offenses of given classes are committed, the social characteristics of the persons who regularly commit them, the features of the settings in which they occur, the types of victims often involved, and the like. He learns to speak knowledgeably of "burglars," "petty thieves," "drunks," "rapists," "narcos," etc., and to attribute to them personal biographies, modes of usual criminal activity, criminal histories, psychological characteristics, and social backgrounds. The following characterizations are illustrative:

Most ADWs (assault with deadly weapon) start with fights over some girl.

These sex fiends (child molestation cases) usually hang around parks or schoolyards.

But we often get fathers charged with these crimes. Usually the old man is out of work and stays at home when the wife goes to work and he plays around with his little daughter or something. A lot of these cases start when there is some marital trouble and the woman gets mad.

I don't know why most of them don't rob the big stores. They usually break into some cheap department store and steal some crummy item like a $9.95 record player you know.

Kids who start taking this stuff (narcotics) usually start out when some buddy gives them a cigarette and they smoke it for kicks. For some reason they always get caught in their cars, for speeding or something.

They can anticipate that point when persons are likely to get into trouble:

Dope addicts do O.K. until they lose a job or something and get back on the streets and, you know, meet the old boys. Someone tells them where to get some and there they are.

In the springtime, that's when we get all these sex crimes. You know, these kids play out in the schoolyard all day and these old men sit around and watch them jumping up and down. They get their ideas.

The P.D. learns that some kinds of offenders are likely to repeat the same offense while others are not repeat violators or, if they do commit crimes frequently, the crimes vary from occasion to occasion:

You almost never see a check man get caught for anything but checks—only an occasional drunk charge.

Burglars are usually multiple offenders, most times just burglaries or petty thefts. Petty thefts get started for almost anything —joy riding, drinking, all kinds of little things.

These narcos are usually through after the second violation or so. After the first time some stop, but when they start on the heavy stuff, they've had it.

I shall call *normal crimes* those occurrences whose typical features, e.g., the ways they usually occur and the characteristics of persons who commit them (as well as the typical victims and typical scenes), are known and attended to by the P.D. For any of a series of offense types the P.D. can provide some form of proverbial characterization. For example, *burglary* is seen as involving regular violators, no weapons, low-priced items, little property damage, lower class establishments, largely Negro defendants, independent operators, and a non-professional orientation to the crime. *Child molesting* is seen as typically entailing middle-aged strangers or lower class middle-aged fathers (few women), no actual physical penetration or severe tissue damage, mild fondling, petting, and stimulation, bad marriage circumstances, multiple offenders with the same offense repeatedly committed, a child complainant, via the mother, etc. *Narcotics* defendants are usually Negroes, not syndicated, persons who start by using small stuff, hostile with police officers, caught by some form of entrapment technique, etc. *Petty thefts* are about 50-50 Negro-white, unplanned offenses, generally committed on lower class persons and don't get much money, don't often employ weapons, don't make living from thievery, usually younger defendants with long juvenile assaultive records, etc. *Drunkenness* offenders are lower class white and Negro, get drunk on wine and beer, have long histories of repeated drunkenness, don't hold down jobs, are usually arrested on the streets, seldom violate other penal code sections, etc.

Some general features of the normal crime as a way of attending to a category of persons and events may be mentioned:

1. The focus, in these characterizations, is not on particular individuals, but offense types. If asked "What are burglars like?" or "How are burglaries

usually committed?", the P.D. does not feel obliged to refer to particular burglars and burglaries as the material for his answer.

2. The features attributed to offenders and offenses are often not of import for the statutory conception. In burglary, it is "irrelevant" for the statutory determination whether or not much damage was done to the premises (except where, for example, explosives were employed and a new statute could be invoked). Whether a defendant breaks a window or not, destroys property within the house or not, etc., does not affect his statutory classification as a burglar. While for robbery the presence or absence of a weapon sets the degree, whether the weapon is a machine gun or pocket knife is "immaterial." Whether the residence or business establishment in a burglary is located in a higher income area of the city is of no issue for the code requirements. And, generally, the defendant's race, class position, criminal history (in most offenses), personal attributes, and particular style of committing offenses are features specifically not definitive of crimes under the auspices of the penal code. For deciding "Is this a 'burglary' case I have before me," however, the P.D.'s reference to this range of non-statutorily referable personal and social attributes, modes of operation, etc., is crucial for the arrangement of a guilty plea bargain.

3. The features attributed to offenders and offenses are, in their content, specific to the community in which the P.D. works. In other communities and historical periods the lists would presumably differ. Narcotics violators in certain areas, for example, are syndicated in dope rackets or engage in systematic robbery as professional criminals, features which are not commonly encountered (or, at least, evidence for which is not systematically sought) in this community. Burglary in some cities will more often occur at large industrial plants, banking establishments, warehouses, etc. The P.D. refers to the population of defendants in the county as "our defendants" and qualifies his prototypical portrayals and knowledge of the typically operative social structures, "for our county." An older P.D., remembering the "old days," commented:

We used to have a lot more rapes than we do now, and they used to be much more violent. Things are duller now in. . . .

4. Offenses whose normal features are readily attended to are those which are routinely encountered in the courtroom. This feature is related to the last point. For embezzlement, bank robbery, gambling, prostitution, murder, arson, and some other uncommon offenses, the P.D. cannot readily supply anecdotal and proverbial characterizations. While there is some change in the frequencies of offense-type convictions over time, certain offenses are continually more common and others remain stably infrequent. . . . Troubles (are) created for the P.D. when offenses whose features are not readily known occur, and whose typicality is not easily constructed. . . .

5. Offenses are ecologically specified and attended to as normal or not according to the locales within which they are committed. The P.D. learns that burglaries usually occur in such and such areas of the city, petty thefts around this or that park, ADWs in these bars. Ecological patterns are seen as related to socio-economic variables and these in turn to typical modes of criminal and non-criminal activities. Knowing where an offense took place is thus, for the P.D., knowledge of the likely persons involved, the kind of scene in which the offense occurred, and the pattern of activity characteristic of such a place:

Almost all of our ADWs are in the same half a dozen bars. These places are Negro bars where laborers come after hanging around the union halls trying to get some work. Nobody has any money and they drink too much. Tempers are high and almost anything can start happening.

6. One further important feature can be noted at this point. . . . The P.D. office consists of a staff of twelve full time attorneys. Knowledge of the properties of offense types of offenders, i.e., their normal, typical, or familiar attributes, constitutes the mark of any given attorney's competence. A major task in socializing the new P.D. deputy attorney consists in teaching him to recognize these attributes and to come to do so naturally. The achievement of competence as a P.D. is signalled by the gradual acquisition of professional command not simply of local penal code peculiarities and courtroom folklore, but, as importantly, of relevant features of the social structure and criminological wisdom. His grasp of that knowledge over the course of time is a key indication of his expertise. Below, in our brief account of some relevant organizational properties of the P.D. system, we shall have occasion to re-emphasize the competence-attesting aspects of the attorney's proper use of established sociological knowledge. Let us return to the mechanics of the guilty plea procedure as an example of the operation of the notion of normal crimes.

Over the course of their interaction and repeated "bargaining" discussions, the P.D. and D.A. have developed a set of unstated recipes for reducing original charges to lesser offenses. These recipes are specifically appropriate for use in instances of normal crimes and in such instances alone. "Typical" burglaries are reduced to petty theft, "typical" ADWs to simple assault, "typical" child molestation to loitering around a schoolyard, etc. The character of these recipes deserves attention.

The specific content of any reduction, i.e., what particular offense class X offenses will be reduced to, is such that the reduced offense may bear no obvious relation (neither situationally nor necessarily included) to the originally charged offense. The reduction of burglary to petty theft is an example. The important relation between the reduced offense and the original charge is such that the reduction from one to the other is considered "reasonable." At this point we shall only state what seems to be the general principle involved in deciding this reasonableness. The underlying premises cannot be explored at the present time, as that would involve a political analysis beyond the scope of the present report. *Both P.D. and D.A. are concerned to obtain a guilty plea wherever possible and thereby avoid a trial. At the same time, each party is concerned that the defendant "receive his due." The reduction of offense X to Y must be of such a character that the new sentence will depart from the anticipated sentence for the original charge to such a degree that the defendant is likely to plead guilty to the new charge and, at the same time, not so great that the defendant does not "get his due."*

In a homicide, while battery is a necessarily included offense, it will not be considered as a possible reduction. For a conviction of second degree murder a defendant could receive a life sentence in the penitentiary. For a battery conviction he would spend no more than six months in the county jail. In a homicide, however, "felony manslaughter," or "assault with a deadly weapon," whatever their relation to homicide as regards inclusion, would more closely approximate the sentence outcome that could be expected on a trial conviction of second degree murder. These alternatives would be considered. For burglary, a typically situationally included offense might be "disturbing the peace," "breaking and entering" or "destroying public property." "Petty theft," however, constitutes a reasonable lesser alternative to burglary as the sentence for petty theft will often range between six months and one year in the county jail and burglary regularly does not carry higher than two years in the state prison. "Disturbing the peace" would be a thirty-day sentence offense.

While the present purposes make the exposition of this calculus unnecessary, it can be noted and stressed that the particular content of the reduction does not necessarily correspond to a relation between the original and altered charge that could be described in either the terms of necessary or situational inclusion. Whatever the relation between the original and reduced charge, its essential feature resides in the spread between sentence likelihoods and the reasonableness of that spread, i.e., the balance it strikes between the defendant "getting his due" and at the same time "getting something less than he might so that he will plead guilty."

The procedure we want to clarify now, at the risk of some repetition, is the manner in which an instant case is examined to decide its membership in a class of "crimes such as this" (the category *normal crimes*). Let us start with an obvious case, burglary. As the typical reduction for burglary is petty theft and as petty theft is neither situationally nor necessarily included in burglary, the examination of the instant case is clearly not undertaken to decide whether petty theft is an appropriate statutory description. The concern is to establish the relation between the instant burglary and the normal category "burglaries" and, having decided a "sufficient correspondence," to now employ petty theft as the proposed reduction.

In scrutinizing the present burglary case, the P.D. seeks to establish that "this is a burglary just like any other." If that correspondence is not established, regardless of whether or not petty theft in fact was a feature of the way the crime was enacted, the reduction to petty theft would not be proposed. *The propriety of proposing petty theft as a reduction does not derive from its in-fact-existence in the present case, but is warranted or not by the relation of the present burglary to "burglaries," normally conceived.*

In a case of "child molestation" (officially called "lewd conduct with a minor"), the concern is to decide if this is a "typical child molestation case." While "loitering around a schoolyard" is frequently a feature of the way such crimes are instigated, establishing that the present defendant *did in fact loiter around a schoolyard* is secondary to the more general question "Is this a typical child molestation case?" What appears as a contradiction must be clarified by examining the status of "loitering around a schoolyard" as a typical feature of such child molestations. The typical character of "child molesting cases" does not stand or fall on the fact that "loitering around a schoolyard" is a feature of the way they are in fact committed. It is *not* that "loitering around a schoolyard" as a *statutorily referable behavior sequence* is part of typical "child molesting cases" but that "loitering around a schoolyard" as a *socially distinct mode of committing child molestations typifies the way such offenses are enacted.* "Strictly speaking," i.e., under the auspices of the statutory *corpus delicti,* "loitering around a schoolyard," requires *loitering, around,* a *schoolyard;* if one loiters around a ball park or a public recreation area, he "cannot," within a proper reading of the statute, be charged with loitering around a *schoolyard.* Yet "loitering around a schoolyard," as a feature of the typical way such offenses as child molestations are committed, has the status not of a description of the way in *fact* (*fact*, statutorily decided) it occurred or typically occurs, but "the-kind-of-social-activity-typically-associated-with-such-offenses." It is not its statutorily conceived features but its socially relevant attributes that gives "loitering around a schoolyard" its status as a feature of the class "normal child molestations." Whether the defendant loitered around a schoolyard or a ball park, and whether he loitered or "was passing by," "loitering around a schoolyard" as a reduction will be made if the defendant's activity was such that "he was hanging around some public place or another" and "was the kind of guy who hangs around schoolyards." As a component of the class of normal child molestation cases (of the variety where the victim is a stranger), "loitering around a schoolyard" typifies a mode of committing such offenses, the class of "such persons who do such things as hang around schoolyards and the like." A large variety of actual offenses could thus be nonetheless reduced to "loitering" if, as kinds of social activity, "loitering," conceived of as typifying a way of life, pattern of daily activity, social psychological circumstances, etc., characterized the conduct of the defendant. The young P.D. who would object "You can't reduce it to 'loitering'—he didn't really 'loiter,'" would be reprimanded: "Fella, you don't know how to use that term; he might as well have 'loitered'—it's the same kind of case as the others." . . .

The P.D.'s activity is seldom geared to securing acquittals for clients. He and the D.A., as co-workers in the same courts, take it for granted that the persons who come before the courts are guilty of crimes and are to be treated accordingly:

Most of them have records as you can see. Almost all of them have been through our courts before. And the police just don't make mistakes in this town. That's one thing about—, we've got the best police force in the state.

As we shall argue below, the way defendants are "represented" (the station manning rather than assignment of counselors to clients), the way trials are conducted, the way interviews are held and the penal code employed—all of the P.D.'s work is premised on the supposition that people charged with crimes— have committed crimes.

This presupposition makes such first questions as "Why don't you start by telling me where this place was . . ." reasonable questions. When the answer comes: "What place? I don't know what you are talking about," the defendant is taken to be a phony, making an "innocent pitch." The conceivable first question: "Did you do it?", is not asked because it is felt that this gives the defendant the notion that he can try an "innocent pitch":

I never ask them, "did you do it?", because on one hand I know they did and mainly because then they think that they can play games with us. We can always check their records and usually they have a string of offenses. You don't have to, though, because in a day or two they change their story and plead guilty. Except for the stubborn ones.

Of the possible answers to an opening question, bewilderment, the inability to answer or silence are taken to indicate that the defendant is putting the P.D. on. For defendants who refuse to admit anything, the P.D. threatens:

Look, if you don't want to talk, that's your business. I can't help you. All I can say is that if you go to trial on this beef you're going to spend a long time in the joint. When you get ready to tell me the story straight, then we can see what can be done.

If the puzzlement comes because the wrong question is asked, e.g., "There wasn't any fight—that's not the way it happened," the defendant will start to fill in the story. The P.D. awaits to see if, how far, and in what ways the instant case is deviant. If the defendant is charged with burglary and a middle class establishment was burglarized, windows shattered, a large payroll sought after and a gun used, then the reduction to petty theft, generally employed for "normal burglaries," would be more difficult to arrange.

Generally, the P.D. doesn't have to discover the atypical kinds of cases through questioning. Rather, the D.A., in writing the original complaint, provides the P.D. with clues that the typical recipe, given the way the event occurred, will not be allowable. Where the way it occurs is such that it does not resemble normal burglaries and the routinely used penalty would reduce it *too far* commensurate with the way the crime occurred, the D.A. frequently charges various situationally included offenses, indicating to the P.D. that the procedure to employ here is to suggest "dropping" some of the charges, leaving the originally charged greatest offense as it stands.

In the general case he doesn't charge all those offenses that he legally might. He might charge "child molesting" and "loitering around a schoolyard" but typically only the greater charge is made. The D.A. does so so as to provide for a later reduction that will appear particularly lenient in that it seemingly involves a *change* in the charge. Were he to charge both molesting and loitering, he would be obliged, moreover, should the case come to trial, to introduce evidence for both offenses. The D.A. is thus always constrained not to set overly high charges or not situationally included multiple offenses by the possibility that the defendant will not plead guilty to a lesser

offense and the case will go to trial. Of primary importance is that he doesn't charge multiple offenses so that the P.D. will be in the best position vis-à-vis the defendant. He thus charges the first complaint so as to provide for a "setup."

The alteration of charges must be made in open court. The P.D. requests to have a new plea entered:

P.D.: Your honor, in the interests of justice, my client would like to change his plea of not guilty to the charge of burglary and enter a plea of guilty to the charge of petty theft.
Judge: Is this new plea acceptable to the prosecution?
D.A.: Yes, your honor.

The prosecutor knows beforehand that the request will be made, and has agreed in advance to allow it.

I asked a P.D. how they felt about making such requests in open court, i.e., asking for a reduction from one offense to another when the latter is obviously not necessarily included and often (as is the case in burglary-to-petty theft) not situationally included. He summarized the office's feeling:

. . . in the old days, ten or so years ago, we didn't like to do it in front of the judge. What we used to do when we made a deal was that the D.A. would dismiss the original charge and write up a new complaint altogether. That took a lot of time. We had to re-arraign him all over again back in the muni court and everything. Besides, in the same courtroom, everyone used to know what was going on anyway. Now, we just ask for a change of plea to the lesser charge regardless of whether it's included or not. Nobody thinks twice about asking for petty theft on burglary, or drunkenness on car theft, or something like that. It's just the way it's done.

Some restrictions are felt. Assaultive crimes (e.g., ADW, simple assault, attempted murder, etc.) will not be reduced to or from "money offenses" (burglary, robbery, theft) unless the latter involve weapons or some violence. Also, victimless crimes (narcotics, drunkenness) are not reduced to or from assaultive or "money offenses," unless there is some factual relation, e.g., drunkenness with a fight might turn out to be simple assault reduced to drunkenness.

For most cases that come before their courts, the P.D. and D.A. are able to employ reductions that are formulated for handling typical cases. While some burglaries, rapes, narcotics violations and petty thefts are instigated in strange ways and involve atypical facts, some manipulation in the way the initial charge is made can be used to set up a procedure to replace the simple charge-alteration form of reducing. . . .

Court Responses to Shoplifting *

MARY OWEN CAMERON

Store cases: After store officials have made the decision for disposition of a case, shoplifters are either "escorted" from the door with a warning never to return to the store, or they are formally charged and conveyed by the city police in a patrol wagon to the "lockup." Those that are to be prosecuted are usually sent to jail for the night and "booked"; when they can furnish or obtain bond, they are released on bail until trial.

The typical trial averages 5 to 10 minutes and unless the defendant has some sophistication in legal matters, the trial is likely to be over before he realizes that it has begun. In Women's Court especially, confused defendants were—as I observed—propelled away from the judge's bench by court aides or by their attorneys as they asked in a bewildered way what was going to happen to them. And what does happen to the shoplifter who is found guilty seemingly depends on the sex, race, and prior record of the shoplifter, and on the individual predilec-

tions of the judge who sits on the bench.

Of the 110 *adults* from the Store sample who were formally charged with larceny, the outcome of court action is known for 99. Of these 99, 43 per cent were sentenced to jail for periods of from five days to one year; six per cent were fined; 29 per cent were placed on probation; 21 per cent were given token sentences ($1.00 considered paid and one day considered served); and one was discharged without prosecution. None was found "not guilty." But the overall figures conceal the differences found in court action between sentences given to men and to women; to Negro and to white shoplifters. Thirteen per cent of the white women who were tried on the complaint of Lakeside Co., for example, were sentenced to jail, 33 per cent of the Negro women. Thus the likelihood of a Negro woman arrested in the store serving a jail sentence is about six times the likelihood of a white woman (. . . [yet there was a] similar mean and median

* Reprinted with permission of The Macmillan Company from *The Booster and the Snitch* by Mary Owen Cameron. © The Free Press of Glencoe, a Division of the Macmillan Company, 1964.

value of stolen merchandise as between Negro women and white women). In proportion to their numbers at *ime of apprehension, four times as many Negro women as white women were formally charged, and of those formally charged, twice as many Negro women were sentenced to jail.

Seventy per cent of white men tried were sentenced to jail and 75 per cent of Negro men. Men . . . stole merchandise of greater value than women. They were also, in larger number than women, probably commercial thieves.

Court cases: In . . . [a study of court records] differentials similar to those of the Store cases were found in sentences by racial group. Differences are especially striking in the proportions of Negro and white women not found guilty on the one hand, and those actually sentenced to jail on the other. Of white women 16.2 per cent were not found guilty and of Negro women 3.7 per cent. . . . Of white women, 4.1 per cent, and of Negro women 21.8 per cent were sentenced to jail. . . . Of the 21 white women sentenced to jail, 2 (9.5 per cent) were sentenced for 30 days or more. Of the 76 Negro women, 20 (26.3 per cent) were

sentenced for 30 days or more. . . . The differences in the proportion of jail sentences handed down to Negro and white women might have resulted from a greater proportion of commercial shoplifters or "occupational criminals" among Negro women. But, in the small sample of women whose prior court records were ascertained through Police Department records, of 15 white women sentenced to jail, 8 had prior records of arrest, and of 20 Negro women sentenced to jail, 10 had prior records.

The sentences imposed on women shoplifters by different municipal court judges showed considerable variation. Among eight judges who sat at the Women's Court in three years, the range in the proportion of women found "not guilty" ran from 5.0 per cent for one judge to 19.5 per cent for another. Women given "token sentences" by judges ranged from 0 for one judge to 58.4 per cent for another; probation from 10.5 per cent to 62.4 per cent and jail sentences ranged from 3.3 per cent to 31.2 per cent. The idiosyncrasies of judges rotating in the same court have been studied with similar conclusions by others.[1]

Traffic Law Violation: A Folk Crime *

H. LAURENCE ROSS

It may be useful to think of both white-collar crime and traffic law violations as sub-species of folk crime. This category is proposed in order to group together

[1] Smith, R. H. and H. B. Ehrmann. *"The Criminal Courts," Cleveland Survey of Criminal Justice.* Part 1, pp. 76–80. Also, Gaudet, F. J., G. S. Harris, and C. W. St. John. "Individual Differences in the Sentencing Tendencies of Judges," *Journal of Criminal Law, Criminology and Police Science,* 23:811–818, January, 1933.
* Reprinted from *Social Problems,* Vol. 8, No. 3 (Winter, 1960–61), pp. 236–37, by permission of the author and *Social Problems.*

violations of laws that are introduced
to regulate the novel kinds of behavior
that an increasingly advanced technology
and an increasing division of labor generate. It should be noted, as Aubert states
in connection with white-collar crime,
that "the laws . . . are usually not in obvious or apparent harmony with the
mores. They are largely an outcome of
the increased complexity of modern industrial society, a complexity which requires legal control of activities with
long-range and often very indirectly damaging effects." [1]

The characteristics of folk crime are
present in Sutherland's description of
white-collar crime. However, in proposing the more general category of folk
crime, these characteristics are emphasized to the exclusion of Sutherland's
focus on the occupational context of the
act and the white-collar status of the
criminal.

The following propositions are specu-
latively offered concerning folk crime:

(a) Major increments to the complexity
of a society, of which the automobile is a technological example,
create a need for regulation where
none was previously necessary.

(b) Legislation to regulate the conditions
brought about by increasing complexity reclassifies certain prevalent
non-criminal behavior as crime.

(c) Especially where the harmful effect
of the proscribed behavior is indirect or improbable in most instances,
the novel legislation may not be
related to previously existing norms.

(d) Criminal behavior in folk crime is
rooted, not necessarily in lower-class
culture, but in the culture of groups
most affected by the social or technological changes that the legislation attempts to control. White-collar

crime is the special case of folk
crime resulting from legislation regulating business and finance. The
automobile, with its impact on all
social classes, generates more pervasive forms of folk crime.

(e) In particular instances, large numbers of people including those of
high status, will be involved in law
violations related to major social
changes.

(f) The lack of congruence between the
new laws and established mores, the
generally higher social status of the
violators, and the possibly large size
of the group of violators among the
total population, will tend to be associated with preferential treatment
of folk criminals in the public image
and in the judicial process.

Examples of other law violations with
the characteristics of folk crime can be
found in the literature. Among them is
"chiseling" in unemployment compensation. According to Smigel, chiseling
shares with white-collar crime (and traffic
law violation) the following characteristics: the participant is not a professional
criminal, he is not stigmatized as criminal, he may lack criminal intent, and he
is treated differently from "ordinary"
criminals. Smigel notes that the chiseler
differs from the white-collar criminal in
that his action need not be committed in
the course of his occupation, and he may
be found in any social class.

Another example is participation in the
wartime black market. Although Clinard
claims this is white-collar crime, he presents statistics showing that 65 per cent
of the people imprisoned for these violations had less than a high-school education, thus indicating that high social
status need not be involved. Furthermore,
it is obvious that at least the consumers

[1] Vilhelm Aubert, "White Collar Crime and Social Structure," *American Journal of
Sociology*, 58 (Nov., 1952), pp. 263–71.

engaging in black market transactions did not necessarily commit these crimes in the course of their occupations.

In sum, the category of folk crime is proposed as a convenient way of thinking about traffic law violations, white-collar crime, chiseling, black market dealings, and many other illegal actions that have in common a source in social complexity.

As opposed to "ordinary criminals," folk criminals are relatively numerous, unstigmatized, and differentially treated in the legal process. While they tend to be from higher social classes than the typical stigmatized criminal, they need not be predominantly white-collar, and the proscribed acts need not be committed in the course of business. . . .

Screening Mental Patients *

THOMAS J. SCHEFF †

The case for making the societal reaction to deviance a major independent variable in studies of deviant behavior has been succinctly stated by Kitsuse:

A sociological theory of deviance must focus specifically upon the interactions which not only define behaviors as deviant but also organize and activate the application of sanctions by individuals, groups, or agencies. For in modern society, the socially significant differentiation of deviants from the non-deviant population is increasingly contingent upon circumstances of situation, place, social and personal biography, and the bureaucratically organized activities of agencies of control. [1]

In the case of mental disorder, psychiatric diagnosis is one of the crucial steps which "organizes and activates" the societal reaction, since the state is legally empowered to segregate and isolate those persons whom psychiatrists find to be committable because of mental illness.

Recently, however, it has been argued that mental illness may be more usefully considered to be a social status than a disease, since the symptoms of mental illness are vaguely defined and widely distributed, and the definition of behavior as symptomatic of mental illness is usually dependent upon social rather than medical contingencies.[2] Furthermore, the argument continues, the status of the mental patient is more often an ascribed status, with conditions for status entry external to the patient, than an achieved status with conditions for status entry dependent upon the patient's own behavior. According to this argument, the societal reaction is a fundamentally important variable in all stages of a deviant career.

The actual usefulness of a theory of

* Reprinted from "The Societal Reaction to Deviance: Ascriptive Elements in the Psychiatric Screening of Mental Patients in a Midwestern State" in *Social Problems*, Vol. 11, No. 4 (Spring, 1964), pp. 401–13, by permission of the author and *Social Problems*.

† With the assistance of Daniel M. Culver this report is part of a larger study, made possible by a grant from The Advisory Mental Health Committee of Midwestern State. By prior agreement, the state in which the study was conducted is not identified in publications.

[1] John I. Kitsuse, "Societal Reaction to Deviant Behavior: Problems of Theory and Method," *Social Problems*, 9 (Winter, 1962), pp. 247–257.

[2] Edwin M. Lemert, *Social Pathology*, New York: McGraw-Hill, 1951; Erving Goffman, *Asylums*, Chicago: Aldine, 1962.

mental disorder based on the societal reaction is largely an empirical question: to what extent is entry to the status of mental patient independent of the behavior or "condition" of the patient? The present paper will explore this question for one phase of the societal reaction: the legal screening of persons alleged to be mentally ill. This screening represents the official phase of the societal reaction, which occurs after the alleged deviance has been called to the attention of the community by a complainant. This report will make no reference to the initial deviance or other situation which resulted in the complaint, but will deal entirely with procedures used by the courts after the complaint has occurred.

The purpose of the description that follows is to determine the extent of uncertainty that exists concerning new patients' qualifications for involuntary confinement in a mental hospital, and the reactions of the courts to this type of uncertainty. The data presented here indicate that, in the face of uncertainty, there is a strong presumption of illness by the court and the court psychiatrists.[3] In the discussion that follows the presentation of findings, some of the causes, consequences and implications of the presumption of illness are suggested.

The data upon which this report is based were drawn from psychiatrists' ratings of a sample of patients newly admitted to the public mental hospitals in a Midwestern state, official court records, interviews with court officials and psychiatrists, and our observations of psychiatric examinations in four courts. The psychiatrists' ratings of new patients will be considered first.

In order to obtain a rough measure of the incoming patient's qualifications for involuntary confinement, a survey of newly admitted patients was conducted with the cooperation of the hospital psychiatrists. All psychiatrists who made admission examinations in the three large mental hospitals in the state filled out a questionnaire for the first ten consecutive patients they examined in the month of June, 1962. A total of 223 questionnaires were returned by the 25 admission psychiatrists. Although these returns do not constitute a probability sample of all new patients admitted during the year, there were no obvious biases in the drawing of the sample. For this reason, this group of patients will be taken to be typical of the newly admitted patients in Midwestern State.

The two principal legal grounds for involuntary confinement in the United States are the police power of the state (the State's right to protect itself from dangerous persons) and *parens patriae* (the State's right to assist those persons who, because of their own incapacity, may not be able to assist themselves).[4] As a measure of the first ground, the potential dangerousness of the patient, the questionnaire contained this item: "In your opinion, if this patient were released at the present time, is it likely he would harm himself or others?" The psychiatrists were given six options, ranging from Very Likely to Very Unlikely. Their responses were: Very Likely, 5%; Likely, 4%; Somewhat Likely, 14%; Somewhat Unlikely, 20%; Unlikely 37%; Very Unlikely, 18%. Three patients were not rated (1%).

As a measure of the second ground, *parens patriae*, the questionnaire contained the item: "Based on your observa-

[3] For a more general discussion of the presumption of illness in medicine, and some of its possible causes and consequences, see the author's "Decision Rules, Types of Error and Their Consequences in Medical Diagnosis," *Behavioral Science*, 8 (April, 1963), pp. 97–107.

[4] Hugh Allen Ross, "Commitment of the Mentally Ill: Problems of Law and Policy," *Michigan Law Review*, 57 (May, 1959), pp. 945–1018.

tions of the patient's behavior, his present degree of mental impairment is: None ——— Minimal ——— Mild ——— Moderate ——— Severe ———." The psychiatrists' responses were: None, 2%; Minimal, 12%; Mild, 25%; Moderate, 42%; Severe, 17%. Three patients were not rated (1%).

To be clearly qualified for involuntary confinement, a patient should be rated as likely to harm self or others (Very Likely, Likely, or Somewhat Likely) and/or as Severely Mentally Impaired. However, voluntary patients should be excluded from this analysis, since the court is not required to assess their qualifications for confinement. Excluding the 59 voluntary admissions (26% of the sample), leaves a sample of 164 involuntary confined patients. Of these patients, 10 were rated as meeting both qualifications for involuntary confinement, 21 were rated as being severely mentally impaired, but not dangerous, 28 were rated as dangerous but not severely mentally impaired, and 102 were rated as not dangerous nor as severely mentally impaired. (Three patients were not rated.)

According to these ratings, there is considerable uncertainty connected with the screening of newly admitted involuntary patients in the state, since a substantial majority (63%) of the patients did not clearly meet the statutory requirements for involuntary confinement. How does the agency responsible for assessing the qualifications for confinement, the court, react in the large numbers of cases involving uncertainty?

On the one hand, the legal rulings on this point by higher courts are quite clear. They have repeatedly held that there should be a presumption of sanity. The burden of proof of insanity is to be on the petitioners, there must be a preponderance of evidence, and the evidence should be of a "clear and unexceptionable" nature.[5]

On the other hand, existing studies suggest that there is a presumption of illness by mental health officials. In a discussion of the "discrediting" of patients by the hospital staff, based on observations at St. Elizabeth's Hospital, Washington, D. C., Goffman states:

[The patient's case record] is apparently not regularly used to record occasions when the patient showed capacity to cope honorably and effectively with difficult life situations. Nor is the case record typically used to provide a rough average or sampling of his past conduct. [Rather, it extracts] from his whole life course a list of those incidents that have or might have had "symptomatic" significance. . . . I think that most of the information gathered in case records is quite true, although it might seem also to be true that almost anyone's life course could yield up enough denigrating facts to provide grounds for the record's justification of commitment.[6]

Mechanic makes a similar statement in his discussion of two large mental hospitals located in an urban area in California:

In the crowded state or county hospitals, which is the most typical situation, the psychiatrist does not have sufficient time to make a very complete psychiatric diagnosis, nor do his psychiatric tools provide him with the equipment for an expeditious screening of the patient . . .

In the two mental hospitals studied over a period of three months, the investigator never observed a case where the psychiatrist advised the patient that he did not need treatment. Rather, all persons who appeared at the hospital were absorbed into the pa-

---

[5] This is the typical phrasing in cases in the *Dicennial Legal Digest,* found under the heading "Mental Illness."

[6] Goffman, *op. cit.,* pp. 155, 159.

tient population regardless of their ability to function adequately outside the hospital.[7]

A comment by Brown suggests that it is a fairly general understanding among mental health workers that state mental hospitals in the U. S. accept all comers.[8]

Kutner, describing commitment procedures in Chicago in 1962, also reports a strong presumption of illness by the staff of the Cook County Mental Health Clinic:

Certificates are signed as a matter of course by staff physicians after little or no examination . . . The so-called examinations are made on an assembly-line basis, often being completed in two or three minutes, and never taking more than ten minutes. Although psychiatrists agree that it is practically impossible to determine a person's sanity on the basis of such a short and hurried interview, the doctors recommend confinement in 77% of the cases. It appears in practice that the alleged-mentally-ill is presumed to be insane and bears the burden of proving his sanity in the few minutes allotted to him . . .[9]

These citations suggest that mental health officials handle uncertainty by presuming illness. To ascertain if the presumption of illness occurred in Midwestern State, intensive observations of screening procedures were conducted in the four courts with the largest volume of mental cases in the state. These courts were located in the two most populous cities in the state. Before giving the results of these observations, it is necessary to describe the steps in the legal procedures for hospitalization and commitment.

Steps in the Screening of Persons Alleged to Be Mentally Ill

The process of screening can be visualized as containing five steps in Midwestern State:

1. The application for judicial inquiry, made by three citizens. This application is heard by deputy clerks in two of the courts (C and D), by a court reporter in the third court, and by a court commissioner in the fourth court.
2. The intake examination, conducted by a hospital psychiatrist.
3. The psychiatric examination, conducted by two psychiatrists appointed by the court.
4. The interview of the patient by the guardian *ad litem,* a lawyer appointed in three of the courts to represent the patient. (Court A did not use guardians *ad litem.*)
5. The judicial hearing, conducted by a judge.

These five steps take place roughly in the order listed, although in many cases (those cases designated as emergencies) step No. 2, the intake examination, may occur before step No. 1. Steps No. 1 and No. 2 usually take place on the same day or the day after hospitalization. Steps No. 3, No. 4, and No. 5 usually take place within a week of hospitalization. (In courts C and D, however, the judicial hearing is held only once a month.)

This series of steps would seem to provide ample opportunity for the presumption of health, and a thorough assessment, therefore, of the patient's qualifications

[7] David Mechanic, "Some Factors in Identifying and Defining Mental Illness," *Mental Hygiene,* 46 (January, 1962), pp. 66–75.

[8] Esther Lucile Brown, *Newer Dimensions of Patient Care,* Part I, New York: Russell Sage, 1961, p. 60, fn.

[9] Luis Kutner, "The Illusion of Due Process in Commitment Proceedings," *Northwestern University Law Review,* 57 (Sept., 1962), pp. 383–399.

for involuntary confinement, since there are five separate points at which discharge could occur. According to our findings, however, these procedures usually do not serve the function of screening out persons who do not meet statutory requirements. At most of these decision points, in most of the courts, retention of the patient in the hospital was virtually automatic. A notable exception to this pattern was found in one of the three state hospitals; this hospital attempted to use step No. 2, the intake examination, as a screening point to discharge patients that the superintendent described as "illegitimate," i.e., patients who do not qualify for involuntary confinement.[10] In the other two hospitals, however, this examination was perfunctory and virtually never resulted in a finding of health and a recommendation of discharge. In a similar manner, the other steps were largely ceremonial in character. For example, in court B, we observed twenty-two judicial hearings, all of which were conducted perfunctorily and with lightning rapidity. (The mean time of these hearings was 1.6 minutes.) The judge asked each patient two or three routine questions. Whatever the patient answered, however, the judge always ended the hearings and retained the patient in the hospital.

What appeared to be the key role in justifying these procedures was played by step No. 3, the examination by the court-appointed psychiatrists. In our informal discussions of screening with the judges and other court officials, these officials made it clear that although the statutes give the court the responsibility for the

decision to confine or release persons alleged to be mentally ill, they would rarely if ever take the responsibility for releasing a mental patient without a medical recommendation to that effect. The question which is crucial, therefore, for the entire screening process is whether or not the court-appointed psychiatric examiners presume illness. The remainder of the paper will consider this question.

Our observations of 116 judicial hearings raised the question of the adequacy of the psychiatric examination. Eighty-six of the hearings failed to establish that the patients were "mentally ill" (according to the criteria stated by the judges in interviews).[11] Indeed, the behavior and responses of 48 of the patients at the hearings seemed completely unexceptionable. Yet the psychiatric examiners had not recommended the release of a single one of these patients. Examining the court records of 80 additional cases, there was still not a single recommendation for release.

Although the recommendation for treatment of 196 out of 196 consecutive cases strongly suggests that the psychiatric examiners were presuming illness, particularly when we observed 48 of these patients to be responding appropriately, it is conceivable that this is not the case. The observer for this study was not a psychiatrist (he was a first year graduate student in social work) and it is possible that he could have missed evidence of disorder which a psychiatrist might have seen. It was therefore arranged for the observer to be present at a series of psychiatric examinations, in order to determine whether the ex-

[10] Other exceptions occurred as follows: the deputy clerks in courts C and D appeared to exercise some discretion in turning away applications they considered improper or incomplete, at step No. 1; the judge in court D appeared also to perform some screening at step No. 5. For further description of these exceptions see "Rural-Urban Differences in the Judicial Screening of the Mentally Ill in a Midwestern State." (In press)

[11] In interviews with the judges, the following criteria were named: Appropriateness of behavior and speech, understanding of the situation, and orientation.

aminations appeared to be merely formalities or whether, on the other hand, through careful examination and interrogation, the psychiatrists were able to establish illness even in patients whose appearance and responses were not obviously disordered. The observer was instructed to note the examiners' procedures, the criteria they appeared to use in arriving at their decision, and their reaction to uncertainty.

Each of the courts discussed here employs the services of a panel of physicians as medical examiners. The physicians are paid a flat fee of ten dollars per examination, and are usually assigned from three to five patients for each trip to the hospital. In court A, most of the examinations are performed by two psychiatrists, who went to the hospital once a week, seeing from five to ten patients a trip. In courts B, C and D, a panel of local physicians was used. These courts seek to arrange the examinations so that one of the examiners is a psychiatrist, the other a general practitioner. Court B has a list of four such pairs, and appoints each pair for a month at a time. Courts C and D have a similar list, apparently with some of the same names as court B.

To obtain physicians who were representative of the panel used in these courts, we arranged to observe the examinations of the two psychiatrists employed by court A, and one of the four pairs of physicians used in court B, one a psychiatrist, the other a general practitioner. We observed 13 examinations in court A and 13 examinations in court B. The judges in courts C and D refused to give us the names of the physicians on their panels, and we were unable to observe examinations in these courts. (The judge in court D stated that he did not want these physicians harassed in their work, since it was difficult to obtain their services even under the best of circum-

stances.) In addition to observing the examinations by four psychiatrists, three other psychiatrists used by these courts were interviewed.

The medical examiners followed two lines of questioning. One line was to inquire about the circumstances which led to the patient's hospitalization, the other was to ask standard questions to test the patient's orientation and his capacity for abstract thinking by asking him the date, the President, Governor, proverbs, and problems requiring arithmetic calculation. These questions were often asked very rapidly, and the patient was usually allowed only a very brief time to answer.

It should be noted that the psychiatrists in these courts had access to the patient's record (which usually contained the Application for Judicial Inquiry and the hospital chart notes on the patient's behavior), and that several of the psychiatrists stated that they almost always familiarized themselves with this record before making the examination. To the extent that they were familiar with the patient's circumstances from such outside information, it is possible that the psychiatrists were basing their diagnoses of illness less on the rapid and peremptory examination than on this other information. Although this was true to some extent, the importance of the record can easily be exaggerated, both because of the deficiencies in the typical record, and because of the way it is usually utilized by the examiners.

The deficiencies of the typical record were easily discerned in the approximately one hundred applications and hospital charts which the author read. Both the applications and charts were extremely brief and sometimes garbled. Moreover, in some of the cases where the author and interviewer were familiar with the circumstances involved in the hospitalization, it was not clear that the complainant's testimony was any more accurate than the version presented by the patient. Often the original complaint was so paraphrased and condensed that the application seemed to have little meaning.

The attitude of the examiners toward the record was such that even in those cases where the record was ample, it often did not figure prominently in their decision. Disparaging remarks about the quality and usefulness of the record were made by several of the psychiatrists. One of the examiners was apologetic about his use of the record, giving us the impression that he thought that a good psychiatrist would not need to resort to any information outside his own personal examination of the patient. A casual attitude toward the record was openly displayed in 6 of the 26 examinations we observed. In these 6 examinations, the psychiatrist could not (or in 3 cases, did not bother to) locate the record and conducted the examination without it, with one psychiatrist making it a point of pride that he could easily diagnose most cases "blind."

In his observations of the examinations, the interviewer was instructed to rate how well the patient responded by noting his behavior during the interview, whether he answered the orientation and concept questions correctly, and whether he denied and explained the allegations which resulted in his hospitalization. If the patient's behavior during the interview obviously departed from conventional social standards (e.g., in one case the patient refused to speak), if he answered the orientation questions incorrectly, or if he did not deny and explain the petitioners' allegations, the case was rated as meeting the statutory requirements for hospitalization. Of the 26 examinations observed, eight were rated as Criteria Met.

If, on the other hand, the patient's behavior was appropriate, his answers correct, and he denied and explained the petitioners' allegations, the interviewer rated the case as not meeting the statutory criteria. Of the 26 cases, seven were rated as Criteria Not Met. Finally, if the examination was inconclusive, but the interviewer felt that more extensive investigation might have established that the criteria were met, he rated the cases as Criteria Possibly Met. Of the 26 examined, 11 were rated in this way. The interviewer's instructions were that whenever he was in doubt he should avoid using the rating Criteria Not Met.

Even giving the examiners the benefit of the doubt, the interviewer's ratings were that in a substantial majority of the cases he observed, the examination failed to establish that the statutory criteria were met. The relationship between the examiners' recommendations and the interviewer's ratings are shown in the following table.

The interviewer's ratings suggest that the examinations established that the statu-

TABLE 1
Observer's Ratings and Examiners' Recommendations

Observer's Ratings		Criteria Met	Criteria Possibly Met	Criteria Not Met	Total
Examiners' Recommendations	Commitment	7	9	2	18
	30-day Observation	1	2	3	6
	Release	0	0	2	2
	Total	8	11	7	26

tory criteria were met in only eight cases, but the examiners recommended that the patient be retained in the hospital in 24 cases, leaving 16 cases which the interviewer rated as uncertain, and in which retention was recommended by the examiners. The observer also rated the patient's expressed desires regarding staying in the hospital, and the time taken by the examination. The ratings of the patient's desire concerning staying or leaving the hospital were: Leave, 14 cases; Indifferent, 1 case; Stay, 9 cases; and Not Ascertained, 2 cases. In only one of the 14 cases in which the patient wished to leave was the interviewer's rating Criteria Met.

The interviews ranged in length from five minutes to 17 minutes, with the mean time being 10.2 minutes. Most of the interviews were hurried, with the questions of the examiners coming so rapidly that the examiner often interrupted the patient, or one examiner interrupted the other. All of the examiners seemed quite hurried. One psychiatrist, after stating in an interview (before we observed his examinations) that he usually took about thirty minutes, stated:

It's not remunerative. I'm taking a hell of a cut. I can't spend 45 minutes with a patient. I don't have the time, it doesn't pay.

In the examinations that we observed, this physician actually spent 8, 10, 5, 8, 8, 7, 17, and 11 minutes with the patients, or an average of 9.2 minutes.

In these short time periods, it is virtually impossible for the examiner to extend his investigation beyond the standard orientation questions, and a short discussion of the circumstances which brought the patient to the hospital. In those cases where the patient answered the orientation questions correctly, behaved appropriately, and explained his presence at the hospital satisfactorily, the examiners did not attempt to assess the reliability of the petitioner's complaints, or to probe further into the patient's answers. Given the fact that in most of these instances the examiners were faced with borderline cases, that they took little time in the examinations, and that they usually recommended commitment, we can only conclude that their decisions were based largely on a presumption of illness. Supplementary observations reported by the interviewer support this conclusion.

After each examination, the observer asked the examiner to explain the criteria he used in arriving at his decision. The observer also had access to the examiner's official report, so that he could compare what the examiner said about the case with the record of what actually occurred during the interview. This supplementary information supports the conclusion that the examiner's decisions are based on the presumption of illness, and sheds light on the manner in which these decisions are reached:

1. The "evidence" upon which the examiners based their decision to retain often seemed arbitrary.
2. In some cases, the decision to retain was made even when no evidence could be found.
3. Some of the psychiatrists' remarks suggest prejudgment of the cases.
4. Many of the examinations were characterized by carelessness and haste. The first question, concerning the arbitrariness of the psychiatric evidence, will now be considered.

In the weighing of the patient's responses during the interview, the physician appeared not to give the patient credit for the large number of correct answers he gave. In the typical interview, the examiner might ask the patient fifteen or twenty questions: the date, time, place, who is President, Governor, etc., what is

11x10, 11x11, etc., explain "Don't put all your eggs in one basket," "A rolling stone gathers no moss," etc. The examiners appeared to feel that a wrong answer established lack of orientation, even when it was preceded by a series of correct answers. In other words, the examiners do not establish any standard score on the orientation questions, which would give an objective picture of the degree to which the patient answered the questions correctly, but seem at times to search until they find an incorrect answer.

For those questions which were answered incorrectly, it was not always clear whether the incorrect answers were due to the patient's "mental illness," or to the time pressure in the interview, the patient's lack of education, or other causes. Some of the questions used to establish orientation were sufficiently difficult that persons not mentally ill might have difficulty with them. Thus one of the examiners always asked, in a rapid-fire manner: "What year is it? What year was it seven years ago? Seventeen years before that?" etc. Only two of the five patients who were asked this series of questions were able to answer it correctly. However, it is a moot question whether a higher percentage of persons in a household survey would be able to do any better. To my knowledge, none of the orientation questions that are used have been checked in a normal population.

Finally, the interpretations of some of the evidence as showing mental illness seemed capricious. Thus one of the patients, when asked, "In what way are a banana, an orange, and an apple alike?" answered, "They are all something to eat." This answer was used by the examiner in explaining his recommendation to commit. The observer had noted that the patient's behavior and responses seemed appropriate and asked why the recommendation to commit had been

made. The doctor stated that her behavior had been bizarre (possibly referring to her alleged promiscuity), her affect inappropriate ("When she talked about being pregnant, it was without feeling,") and with regard to the question above:

She wasn't able to say a banana and an orange were fruit. She couldn't take it one step further, she had to say it was something to eat.

In other words, this psychiatrist was suggesting that the patient manifested concreteness in her thinking, which is held to be a symptom of mental illness. Yet in her other answers to classification questions, and to proverb interpretations, concreteness was not apparent, suggesting that the examiner's application of this test was arbitrary. In another case, the physician stated that he thought the patient was suspicious and distrustful, because he had asked about the possibility of being represented by counsel at the judicial hearing. The observer felt that these and other similar interpretations might possibly be correct, but that further investigation of the supposedly incorrect responses would be needed to establish that they were manifestations of disorientation.

In several cases where even this type of evidence was not available, the examiners still recommended retention in the hospital. Thus, one examiner, employed by court A stated that he had recommended 30-day observation for a patient whom he had thought *not* to be mentally ill, on the grounds that the patient, a young man, could not get along with his parents, and "might get into trouble." This examiner went on to say:

We always take the conservative side. [Commitment or observation] Suppose a patient should commit suicide. We always make the conservative decision. I had rather play it safe. There's no harm in doing it that way.

It appeared to the observer that "playing safe" meant that even in those cases where the examination established nothing, the psychiatrists did not consider recommending release. Thus in one case the examination had established that the patient had a very good memory, was oriented and spoke quietly and seriously. The observer recorded his discussion with the physician after the examination as follows:

When the doctor told me he was recommending commitment for this patient too (he had also recommended commitment in the two examinations held earlier that day) he laughed because he could see what my next question was going to be. He said, "I already recommended the release of two patients this month." This sounded like it was the maximum amount the way he said it.

Apparently this examiner felt that he had a very limited quota on the number of patients he could recommend for release (less than two percent of those examined).

The language used by these physicians tends to intimate that mental illness was found, even when reporting the opposite. Thus in one case the recommendation stated: "No gross evidence of delusions or hallucinations." This statement is misleading, since not only was there no gross evidence, there was not any evidence, not even the slightest suggestion of delusions or hallucinations, brought out by the interview.

These remarks suggest that the examiners prejudge the cases they examine. Several further comments indicate prejudgment. One physician stated that he thought that most crimes of violence were committed by patients released too early from mental hospitals. (This is an erroneous belief.) [12] He went on to say that he thought that all mental patients should be kept in the hospital at least three months, indicating prejudgment concerning his examinations. Another physician, after a very short interview (8 minutes), told the observer:

On the schizophrenics, I don't bother asking them more questions when I can see they're schizophrenic because *I know what they are going to say.* You could talk to them another half hour and not learn any more.

Another physician, finally, contrasted cases in which the patient's family or others initiated hospitalization ("petition cases," the great majority of cases) with those cases initiated by the court:

The petition cases are pretty *automatic.* If the patient's own family wants to get rid of him you know there is something wrong.

The lack of care which characterized the examinations is evident in the forms on which the examiners make their recommendations. On most of these forms, whole sections have been left unanswered. Others are answered in a peremptory and uninformative way. For example, in the section entitled Physical Examination, the question is asked: "Have you made a physical examination of the patient? State fully what is the present physical condition.", a typical answer is "Yes. Fair.", or, "Is apparently in good health." Since in none of the examinations we observed was the patient actually physically examined, these answers appear to be mere guesses. One

[12] The rate of crimes of violence, or any crime, appears to be less among ex-mental patients than in the general population. Henry Brill and Benjamin Maltzberg, "Statistical Report Based on the Arrest Record of 5354 Ex-patients Released from New York State Mental Hospitals During the Period 1946–48." Mimeo available from the authors; Louis H. Cohen and Henry Freeman, "How Dangerous to the Community Are State Hospital Patients?", *Connecticut State Medical Journal,* 9 (Sept., 1945), pp. 697–700; Donald W. Hastings, "Follow-up Results in Psychiatric Illness," *Amer. Journal of Psychiatry,* 118 (June, 1962), pp. 1078–1086.

of the examiners used regularly in court B, to the question "On what subject or in what way is derangment now manifested?" always wrote in "Is mentally ill." The omissions, and the almost flippant brevity of these forms, together with the arbitrariness, lack of evidence, and prejudicial character of the examinations, discussed above, all support the observer's conclusion that, except in very unusual cases, the psychiatric examiner's recommendation to retain the patient is virtually automatic.

Lest it be thought that these results are unique to a particularly backward Midwestern state, it should be pointed out that this state is noted for its progressive psychiatric practices. It will be recalled that a number of the psychiatrists employed by the court as examiners had finished their psychiatric residencies, which is not always the case in many other states. A still common practice in other states is to employ, as members of the "Lunacy Panel," partially retired physicians with no psychiatric training whatever. This was the case in Stockton, California, in 1959, where the author observed hundreds of hearings at which these physicians were present. It may be indicative of some of the larger issues underlying the question of civil commitment that, in these hearings, the physicians played very little part; the judge controlled the questioning of the relatives and patients, and the hearings were often a model of impartial and thorough investigation.

Discussion:

Ratings of the qualifications for involuntary confinement of patients newly admitted to the public mental hospitals in a Midwestern state, together with observations of judicial hearings and psychiatric examinations by the observer

connected with the present study, both suggest that the decision as to the mental condition of a majority of the patients is an uncertain one. The fact that the courts seldom release patients, and the perfunctory manner in which the legal and medical procedures are carried out, suggest that the judicial decision to retain patients in the hospital for treatment is routine and largely based on the presumption of illness. Three reasons for this presumption will be discussed: financial, ideological, and political.

Our discussions with the examiners indicated that one reason that they perform biased "examinations" is that their rate of pay is determined by the length of time spent with the patient. In recommending retention, the examiners are refraining from interrupting the hospitalization and commitment procedures already in progress, and thereby allowing someone else, usually the hospital, to make the effective decision to release or commit. In order to recommend release, however, they would have to build a case showing why these procedures should be interrupted. Building such a case would take much more time than is presently expended by the examiners, thereby reducing their rate of pay.

A more fundamental reason for the presumption of illness by the examiners, and perhaps the reason why this practice is allowed by the courts, is the interpretation of current psychiatric doctrine by the examiners and court officials. These officials make a number of assumptions, which are now thought to be of doubtful validity:

1. The condition of mentally ill persons deteriorates rapidly without psychiatric assistance.

2. Effective psychiatric treatments exist for most mental illnesses.

3. Unlike surgery, there are no risks in-

volved in involuntary psychiatric treatment: it either helps or is neutral, it can't hurt.

4. Exposing a prospective mental patient to questioning, cross-examination, and other screening procedures exposes him to the unnecessary stigma of trial-like procedures, and may do further damage to his mental condition.

5. There is an element of danger to self or others in most mental illness. It is better to risk unnecessary hospitalization than the harm the patient might do himself or others.

Many psychiatrists and others now argue that none of these assumptions are necessarily correct.

1. The assumption that psychiatric disorders usually get worse without treatment rests on very little other than evidence of an anecdotal character. There is just as much evidence that most acute psychological and emotional upsets are self-terminating.[13]

2. It is still not clear, according to systematic studies evaluating psychotherapy, drugs, etc., that most psychiatric interventions are any more effective, on the average, than no treatment at all.[14]

3. There is very good evidence that involuntary hospitalization and social isolation may affect the patient's life:

his job, his family affairs, etc. There is some evidence that too hasty exposure to psychiatric treatment may convince the patient that he is "sick," prolonging what might have been an otherwise transitory episode.[15]

4. This assumption is correct, as far as it goes. But it is misleading because it fails to consider what occurs when the patient who does not wish to be hospitalized is forcibly treated. Such patients often become extremely indignant and angry, particularly in the case, as often happens, when they are deceived into coming to the hospital on some pretext.

5. The element of danger is usually exaggerated both in amount and degree. In the psychiatric survey of new patients in state mental hospitals, danger to self or others was mentioned in about a fourth of the cases. Furthermore, in those cases where danger is mentioned, it is not always clear that the risks involved are greater than those encountered in ordinary social life. This issue has been discussed by Ross, an attorney:

A truck driver with a mild neurosis who is "accident prone" is probably a greater danger to society than most psychotics; yet, he will not be committed for treatment, even if he would be benefited. The community expects a certain amount of dangerous ac-

---

[13] For a review of epidemiological studies of mental disorder see Richard J. Plunkett and John E. Gordon, *Epidemiology and Mental Illness*, New York: Basic Books, 1960. Most of these studies suggest that at any given point in time, psychiatrists find a substantial proportion of persons in normal populations to be "mentally ill." One interpretation of this finding is that much of the deviance detected in these studies is self-limiting.

[14] For an assessment of the evidence regarding the effectiveness of electroshock, drugs, psychotherapy, and other psychiatric treatments, see H. J. Eysenck, *Handbook of Abnormal Psychology*, New York: Basic Books, 1961, Part III.

[15] For examples from military psychiatry, see Albert J. Glass, "Psychotherapy in the Combat Zone," in *Symposium on Stress*, Washington, D. C., Army Medical Service Graduate School, 1953, and B. L. Bushard, "The U. S. Army's Mental Hygiene Consultation Service," in *Symposium on Preventive and Social Psychiatry*, 15–17 (April, 1957), Washington, D. C.: Walter Reed Army Institute of Research, pp. 431–443. For a discussion of essentially the same problem in the context of a civilian mental hospital, cf. Kai T. Erikson, "Patient Role and Social Uncertainty—A Dilemma of the Mentally Ill," *Psychiatry*, 20 (August, 1957), pp. 263–275.

tivity. I suspect that as a class, drinking drivers are a greater danger than the mentally ill, and yet the drivers are tolerated or punished with small fines rather than indeterminate imprisonment.[16]

From our observations of the medical examinations and other commitment procedures, we formed a very strong impression that the doctrines of danger to self or others, early treatment, and the avoidance of stigma were invoked partly because the officials believed them to be true, and partly because they provided convenient justification for a pre-existing policy of summary action, minimal investigation, avoidance of responsibility and, after the patient is in the hospital, indecisiveness and delay.

The policy of presuming illness is probably both cause and effect of political pressure on the court from the community. The judge, an elected official, runs the risk of being more heavily penalized for erroneously releasing than for erroneously retaining patients. Since the judge personally appoints the panel of psychiatrists to serve as examiners, he can easily transmit the community pressure to them, by failing to reappoint a psychiatrist whose examinations were inconveniently thorough.

Some of the implications of these findings for the sociology of deviant behavior will be briefly summarized. The discussion above, of the reasons that the psychiatrists tend to presume illness, suggests that the motivations of the key decision-makers in the screening process may be significant in determining the extent and direction of the societal reaction. In the case of psychiatric screening of persons alleged to be mentally ill, the social dif-

ferentiation of the deviant from the non-deviant population appears to be materially affected by the financial, ideological, and political position of the psychiatrists, who are in this instance the key agents of social control.

Under these circumstances the character of the societal reaction appears to undergo a marked change from the pattern of denial which occurs in the community. The official societal reaction appears to reverse the presumption of normality reported by the Cummings as a characteristic of informal societal reaction, and instead exaggerates both the amount and degree of deviance.[17] Thus, one extremely important contingency influencing the severity of the societal reaction may be whether or not the original deviance comes to official notice. This paper suggests that in the area of mental disorder, perhaps in contrast to other areas of deviant behavior, if the official societal reaction is invoked, for whatever reason, social differentiation of the deviant from the non-deviant population will usually occur.

Conclusion

This paper has described the screening of patients who were admitted to public mental hospitals in early June, 1962, in a Midwestern state. The data presented here suggest that the screening is usually perfunctory, and that in the crucial screening examination by the court-appointed psychiatrists, there is a presumption of illness. Since most court decisions appear to hinge on the recommendation of these psychiatrists, there appears to be a large element of status

---

[16] Ross, *op. cit.,* p. 962.

[17] Elaine Cumming and John Cumming, *Closed Ranks,* Cambridge, Mass.: Harvard University Press,, 1957, 102; for further discussion of the bipolarization of the societal reaction into denial and labeling, see the author's "The Role of the Mentally Ill and the Dynamics of Mental Disorder: A Research Framework," *Sociometry,* 26 (December, 1963), pp. 436–453.

ascription in the official societal reaction to persons alleged to be mentally ill, as exemplified by the court's actions. This finding points to the importance of lay definitions of mental illness in the community, since the "diagnosis" of mental illness by laymen in the community initiates the official societal reaction, and to the necessity of analyzing social processes connected with the recognition and reaction to the deviant behavior that is called mental illness in our society.

THE EFFECTS OF FORMAL
SANCTIONS

8

The careers that many deviants pursue take them through the correctional cycle from beginning to end. Thus, they are arrested, detained, tried, sentenced, and sent away to prison. Others are similarly processed through a network of health and welfare agencies. Their passage through these agencies is not without its effects even on persons having no contact at all with them while they are housed in those institutions. It is as if there is a culture on deviants, providing the ideas and expectations one ought to have of such persons in advance of any real contact with them. Given these circumstances, cultural interpretations dictate the form that social experiences shall take. For once it is known that a person has made contact with an official agency of social control, regardless of the outcome of that contact, all other people have a license to regard him as a species of permanent deviant.

In the papers that follow, Garfinkel states the necessary and sufficient conditions that must be present before an agent of social control can successfully degrade another person. Goffman then shows the personal effects of degradation in the mental hospital. Schwartz and Skolnick show, in the final paper, that one's deviant status transcends time, place, organizational setting, and indeed, sometimes even truth or falsity. They indicate that would-be employers accept stigma in denying employment even when there is no factual basis for stigma. In doing so, they reveal that laymen can become defining agents long after official agents of social control have ceased their work with deviants.

Conditions of Successful Degradation Ceremonies *

HAROLD GARFINKEL

Any communicative work between persons, whereby the public identity of an actor is transformed into something looked on as lower in the local scheme of social types, will be called a "status degradation ceremony." Some restrictions on this definition may increase its usefulness. The identities referred to must be "total" identities. That is, these identities must refer to persons as "motivational" types rather than as "behavioral" types,[1] not to what a person may be expected to have done or to do (in Parsons' term,[2] to his "performances") but to what the group holds to be the ultimate "grounds" or "reasons" for his performance.[3]

The grounds on which a participant achieves what for him is adequate understanding of why he or another acted as he did are not treated by him in a utilitarian manner. Rather, the correctness of an imputation is decided by the participant in accordance with socially valid and institutionally recommended standards of "preference." With reference to these standards, he makes the crucial distinctions between appearances and reality, truth and falsity, triviality and importance, accident and essence, coincidence

and cause. Taken together, the grounds, as well as the behavior that the grounds make explicable as the other person's conduct, constitute a person's identity. Together, they constitute the other as a social object. Persons identified by means of the ultimate "reasons" for their socially categorized and socially understood behavior will be said to be "totally" identified. The degradation ceremonies here discussed are those that are concerned with the alteration of total identities.

It is proposed that only in societies that are completely demoralized, will an observer be unable to find such ceremonies, since only in total anomie are the conditions of degradation ceremonies lacking. Max Scheler [4] argued that there is no society that does not provide in the very features of its organization the conditions sufficient for inducing shame. It will be treated here as axiomatic that there is no society whose social structure does not provide, in its routine features, the conditions of identity degradation. Just as the structural conditions of shame are universal to all societies by the very fact of their being organized, so the structural conditions of status degradation are uni-

* Reprinted by permission of the author and *The American Journal of Sociology,* Vol. 61 (March, 1956), pp. 420–424. Copyright, 1956, The University of Chicago. All rights reserved.

[1] These terms are borrowed from Alfred Schutz, "Common Sense and Scientific Interpretation of Human Action," *Philosophy and Phenomenological Research,* Vol. XIV, No. 1 (September, 1953).

[2] Talcott Parsons and Edward Shils, "Values, Motives, and Systems of Action," in Parsons and Shils (eds.), *Toward a General Theory of Action* (Cambridge: Harvard University Press, 1951).

[3] Cf. the writings of Kenneth Burke, particularly *Permanence and Change* (Los Altos, Calif.: Hermes Publications, 1954), and *A Grammar of Motives* (New York: Prentice-Hall, Inc., 1945).

[4] Richard Hays Williams, "Scheler's Contributions to the Sociology of Affective Action, with Special Attention to the Problem of Shame," *Philosophy and Phenomenological Research,* Vol. II, No. 3 (March, 1942).

versal to all societies. In this framework the critical question is not whether status degradation occurs or can occur within any given society. Instead, the question is: Starting from any state of a society's organization, what program of communicative tactics will get the work of status degradation done?

First of all, two questions will have to be decided, at least tentatively: *What are we referring to behaviorially when we propose the product of successful degradation work to be a changed total identity?* And *what are we to conceive the work of status degradation to have itself accomplished or to have assumed as the conditions of its success?*

I

Degradation ceremonies fall within the scope of the sociology of moral indignation. Moral indignation is a social affect. Roughly speaking, it is an instance of a class of feelings particular to the more or less organized ways that human beings develop as they live out their lives in one another's company. Shame, guilt, and boredom are further important instances of such affects.

Any affect has its behavioral paradigm. That of shame is found in the withdrawal and covering of the portion of the body that socially defines one's public appearance—prominently, in our society, the eyes and face. The paradigm of shame is found in the phrases that denote removal of the self from public view, i.e., removal from the regard of the publicly identified other: "I could have sunk through the floor; I wanted to run away and hide; I wanted the earth to open up and swallow me." The feeling of guilt finds its paradigm in the behavior of self-abnegation—disgust, the rejection of further contact with or withdrawal from,

and the bodily and symbolic expulsion of the foreign body, as when we cough, blow, gag, vomit, spit, etc.

The paradigm of moral indignation is *public* denunciation. We publicly deliver the curse: "I call upon all men to bear witness that he is not as he appears but is otherwise and *in essence* [5] of a lower species."

The social affects serve various functions both for the person as well as for the collectivity. A prominent function of shame for the person is that of preserving the ego from further onslaughts by withdrawing entirely its contact with the outside. For the collectivity shame is an "individuator." One experiences shame in his own time.

Moral indignation serves to effect the ritual destruction of the person denounced. Unlike shame, which does not bind persons together, moral indignation may reinforce group solidarity. In the market and in politics, a degradation ceremony must be counted as a secular form of communism. Structurally, a degradation ceremony bears close resemblance to ceremonies of investiture and elevation. How such a ceremony may bind persons to the collectivity we shall see when we take up the conditions of a successful denunciation. Our immediate question concerns the meaning of ritual destruction.

In the statement that moral indignation brings about the ritual destruction of the person being denounced, destruction is intended literally. The transformation of identities is the destruction of one social object and the constitution of another. The transformation does not involve the substitution of one identity for another, with the terms of the old one loitering about like the overlooked parts of a fresh assembly, any more than the woman we

---

[5] The man at whose hands a neighbor suffered death becomes a "murderer." The person who passes on information to enemies is really, i.e., "in essence," "in the first place," "all along," "in the final analysis," "originally," an informer.

see in the department-store window that turns out to be a dummy carries with it the possibilities of a woman. It is not that the old object has been overhauled; rather it is replaced by another. One declares, "*Now,* it was otherwise in the first place."

The work of the denunciation effects the recasting of the objective character of the perceived other: The other person becomes in the eyes of his condemners literally a different and *new* person. It is not that the new attributes are added to the old "nucleus." He is not changed, he is reconstituted. The former identity, at best, receives the accent of mere appearance. In the social calculus of reality representations and test, the former identity stands as accidental; the new identity is the "basic reality." What he is now is what, "after all," he was all along.[6]

The public denunciation effects such a transformation of essence by substituting another socially validated motivational scheme for that previously used to name and order the performances of the denounced. It is with reference to this substituted, socially validated motivational scheme as the essential grounds, i.e., the *first principles,* that his performances, past, present, and prospective, according to the witnesses, are to be properly and necessarily understood.[7] Through the interpretive work that respects this rule, the denounced person becomes in the eyes of the witnesses a different person.

II

How can one make a good denunciation?[8]

To be successful, the denunciation must redefine the situations of those that are witnesses to the denunciation work. The denouncer, the party to be denounced (let us call him the "perpetrator"), and the thing that is being blamed on the perpetrator (let us call it the "event") must be transformed as follows:[9]

---

[6] Two themes commonly stand out in the rhetoric of denunciation: (1) the irony between what the denounced appeared to be and what he is seen now really to be where the new motivational scheme is taken as the standard and (2) a re-examination and redefinition of origins of the denounced. For the sociological relevance of the relationship between concerns for essence and concerns for origins see particularly Kenneth Burke, *A Grammar of Motives.*

[7] While constructions like "substantially a something" or "essentially a something" have been banished from the domain of scientific discourse, such constructions have prominent and honored places in the theories of motives, persons, and conduct that are employed in handling the affairs of daily life. Reasons can be given to justify the hypothesis that such constructions may be lost to a group's "terminology of motives" only if the relevance of socially sanctioned theories to practical problems is suspended. This can occur where interpersonal relations are trivial (such as during play) or, more interestingly, under severe demoralization of a system of activities. In such organizational states the frequency of status degradation is low.

[8] Because the paper is short, the risk must be run that, as a result of excluding certain considerations, the treated topics may appear exaggerated. It would be desirable, for example, to take account of the multitude of hedges that will be found against false denunciation; of the rights to denounce; of the differential apportionment of these rights, as well as the ways in which a claim, once staked out, may become a vested interest and may tie into the contests for economic and political advantage. Further, there are questions centering around the appropriate arenas of denunciation. For example, in our society the tribal council has fallen into secondary importance; among lay persons the denunciation has given way to the complaint to the authorities.

[9] These are the effects that the communicative tactics of the denouncer must be designed to accomplish. Put otherwise, in so far as the denouncer's tactics accomplish the reordering of the definitions of the situation of the witnesses to the denunciatory performances, the denouncer will have succeeded in effecting the transformation of the public identity of his victim. The list of conditions of this degrading effect are the determinants of the effect. Viewed in the scheme of a project to be rationally pursued, they are the adequate means. One would have to chose one's tactics for their efficiency in accomplishing these effects.

1. Both event and perpetrator must be removed from the realm of their everyday character and be made to stand as "out of the ordinary."

2. Both event and perpetrator must be placed within a scheme of preferences that shows the following properties:

A. The preferences must not be for event A over event B, but for event of *type* A over event of *type* B. The same typing must be accomplished for the perpetrator. Event and perpetrator must be defined as instances of a uniformity and must be treated as a uniformity throughout the work of the denunciation. The unique, never recurring character of the event or perpetrator should be lost. Similarly, any sense of accident, coincidence, indeterminism, chance, or momentary occurrence must not merely be minimized. Ideally, such measures should be inconceivable; at least they should be made false.

B. The witnesses must appreciate the characteristics of the typed person and event by referring the type to a dialectical counterpart. Ideally, the witnesses should not be able to contemplate the features of the denounced person without reference to the counterconception, as the profanity of an occurrence or a desire or a character trait, for example, is clarified by the references it bears to its opposite, the sacred. The features of the mad-dog murderer reverse the features of the peaceful citizen. The confessions of the Red can be read to teach the meanings of patriotism. There are many contrasts available, and any aggregate of witnesses this side of a complete war of each against all will have a plethora of such schemata for effecting a "familiar," "natural," "proper," ordering of motives, qualities, and other events.

From such contrasts, the following is to be learned. If the denunciation is to take effect, the scheme must not be one in which the witness is allowed to elect the preferred. Rather, the alternatives must be such that the preferred is morally required. Matters must be so arranged that the validity of his choice, its justification, is maintained by the fact that he makes it.[10] The scheme of alternatives must be such as to place constraints upon his making a selection "for a purpose." Nor will the denunciation succeed if the witness is free to look beyond the fact that he makes the selection for evidence that the correct alternative has been chosen, as, for example, by the test of empirical consequences of the choice. The alternatives must be such that, in "choosing," he takes it for granted and beyond any motive for doubt that not choosing can mean only preference for its opposite.

3. The denouncer must so identify himself to the witnesses that during the denunciation they regard him not as a private but as a publicly known person. He must not portray himself as acting according to his personal, unique experiences. He must rather be regarded as acting in his capacity as a public figure, drawing upon communally entertained and verified experience. He must act as a bona fide participant in the tribal relationships to which the witnesses subscribe. What he says must not be regarded as true for him alone, not even in the sense that it can be regarded by denouncer and witnesses as matters upon which they can become agreed. In no case, except in a most ironical sense, can the convention of true-for-reasonable-men be invoked. What the denouncer says must be regarded by the witnesses as true on the grounds of a socially employed metaphysics whereby witnesses

---

[10] Cf. Gregory Bateson and Jurgen Ruesch, *Communication: The Social Matrix of Psychiatry* (New York: W. W. Norton & Co., 1951), pp. 212–27.

assume that witnesses and denouncer are alike in essence.[11]

4. The denouncer must make the dignity of the supra-personal values of the tribe salient and accessible to view, and his denunciation must be delivered in their name.

5. The denouncer must arrange to be invested with the right to speak in the name of these ultimate values. The success of the denunciation will be undermined if, for his authority to denounce, the denouncer invokes the personal interests that he may have acquired by virtue of the wrong done to him or someone else. He must rather use the wrong he has suffered as a tribal member to invoke the authority to speak in the name of these ultimate values.

6. The denouncer must get himself so defined by the witnesses that they locate him as a supporter of these values.

7. Not only must the denouncer fix his distance from the person being denounced, but the witnesses must be made to experience their distance from him also.

8. Finally, the denounced person must be ritually separated from a place in the legitimate order, i.e., he must be defined as standing at a place opposed to it. He must be placed "outside," he must be made "strange."

These are the conditions that must be fulfilled for a successful denunciation. If they are absent, the denunciation will fail. Regardless of the situation when the denouncer enters, if he is to succeed in degrading the other man, it is necessary to introduce these features.[12]

Not all degradation ceremonies are carried on in accordance with publicly prescribed and publicly validated measures. Quarrels which seek the humiliation of the opponent through personal invective may achieve degrading on a limited scale. Comparatively few persons at a time enter into this form of communion, few benefit from it, and the fact of participation does not give the witness a definition of the other that is standardized beyond the particular group or scene of its occurrence.

The devices for effecting degradation

---

[11] For bona fide members it is not that these are the grounds upon which we are agreed but upon which we are *alike,* consubstantial, in origin the same.

[12] Neither of the problems of possible communicative or organizational conditions of their effectiveness have been treated here in systematic fashion. However, the problem of communicative tactics in degradation ceremonies is set in the light of systematically related conceptions. These conceptions may be listed in the following statements:

1. The definition of the situation of the witnesses (for ease of discourse we shall use the letter S) always bears a time qualification.

2. The S at t_2 is a function of the S at t_1. This function is described as an operator that transforms the S at t_1.

3. The operator is conceived as communicative work.

4. For a successful denunciation, it is required that the S at t_2 show specific properties. These have been specified previously.

5. The task of the denouncer is to alter the S's of the witnesses so that these S's will show the specified properties.

6. The "rationality" of the denouncer's tactics, i.e., their adequacy as a means for effecting the set of transformations necessary for effecting the identity transformation, is decided by the rule that the organizational and operational properties of the communicative net (the social system) are determinative of the size of the discrepancy between an intended and an actual effect of the communicative work. Put otherwise, the question is not that of the temporal origin of the situation but always and only how it is altered over time. The view is recommended that the definition of the situation at time 2 is a function of the definition at time 1 where this function consists of the communicative work conceived as a set of operations whereby the altered situation at time 1 is the situation at time 2. In strategy terms the function consists of the program of procedures that a denouncer should follow to effect the change of state S_{t1} *to* S_{t2}. In this paper S_{t1} is treated as an unspecified state.

vary in the feature and effectiveness according to the organization and operation of the system of action in which they occur. In our society the arena of degradation whose product, the redefined person, enjoys the widest transferability between groups has been rationalized, at least as to the institutional measures for carrying it out. The court and its officers have something like a fair monopoly over such ceremonies, and there they have become an occupational routine. This is to be contrasted with degradation undertaken as an immediate kinship and tribal obligation and carried out by those who, unlike our professional degraders in the law courts, acquire both right and obligation to engage in it through being themselves the injured parties or kin to the injured parties.

Factors conditioning the effectiveness of degradation tactics are provided in the organization and operation of the system of action within which the degradation occurs. For example, timing rules that provide for serial or reciprocal "conversations" would have much to do with the kinds of tactics that one might be best advised to use. The tactics advisable for an accused who can answer the charge as soon as it is made are in contrast with those recommended for one who had to wait out the denunciation before replying. Face-to-face contact is a different situation from that wherein the denunciation and reply are conducted by radio and newspaper. Whether the denunciation must be accomplished on a single occasion or is to be carried out over a sequence of "tries," factors like the territorial arrangements and movements of persons at the scene of the denunciation, the numbers of persons involved as accused, degraders, and witnesses, status claims of the contenders, prestige and power allocations among participants, all should influence the outcome.

In short, the factors that condition the success of the work of degradation are those that we point to when we conceive the actions of a number of persons as group-governed. Only some of the more obvious structural variables that may be expected to serve as predictors of the characteristics of denunciatory communicative tactics have been mentioned. They tell us not only how to construct an effective denunciation but also how to render denunciation useless.

The Effects of Inmate Status *

ERVING GOFFMAN

The Inpatient Phase

. . . The last step in the prepatient's career can involve his realization—justified or not—that he has been deserted by society and turned out of relationships by those closest to him. Interestingly enough, the patient, especially a first ad-

* Reprinted by special permission of The William Alanson White Psychiatric Foundation, Inc., and the author from "The Moral Career of the Mental Patient" in *Psychiatry: Journal for the Study of Interpersonal Processes*, Vol. 22 (May, 1959), pp. 131–35. Copyright 1959 by The William Alanson White Psychiatric Foundation, Inc.

mission, may manage to keep himself from coming to the end of this trail, even though in fact he is now in a locked mental hospital ward. On entering the hospital, he may very strongly feel the desire not to be known to anyone as a person who could possibly be reduced to these present circumstances, or as a person who conducted himself in the way he did prior to commitment. Consequently, he may avoid talking to anyone, may stay by himself when possible, and may even be "out of contact" or "manic" so as to avoid ratifying any interaction that presses a politely reciprocal role upon him and opens him up to what he has become in the eyes of others. When the next-of-relation makes an effort to visit, he may be rejected by mutism, or by the patient's refusal to enter the visiting room, these strategies sometimes suggesting that the patient still clings to a remnant of relatedness to those who made up his past, and is protecting this remnant from the final destructiveness of dealing with the new people that they have become.[1]

Usually the patient comes to give up this taxing effort at anonymity, at not-hereness, and begins to present himself for conventional social interaction to the hospital community. Thereafter he withdraws only in special ways—by always using his nickname, by signing his contribution to the patient weekly with his initial only, or by using the innocuous "cover" address tactfully provided by some hospitals; or he withdraws only at special times, when, say, a flock of nursing students makes a passing tour of the ward, or when, paroled to the hospital grounds, he suddenly sees he is about to cross the path of a civilian he happens to know from home. Sometimes this making of oneself available is called "settling down" by the attendants. It marks a new stand openly taken and supported by the patient, and resembles the "coming out" process that occurs in other groupings.[2]

Once the prepatient begins to settle down, the main outlines of his fate tend to follow those of a whole class of segregated establishments—jails, concentration camps, monasteries, work camps, and so on—in which the inmate spends the whole round of life on the grounds, and marches through his regimented day in the immediate company of a group of persons of his own institutional status.[3]

Like the neophyte in many of these "total institutions," the new inpatient finds himself cleanly stripped of many of his accustomed affirmations, satisfactions, and defenses, and is subjected to a rather

---

[1] The inmate's initial strategy of holding himself aloof from ratifying contact may partly account for the relative lack of group-formation among inmates in public mental hospitals, a connection that has been suggested to me by William R. Smith. The desire to avoid personal bonds that would give license to the asking of biographical questions could also be a factor. In mental hospitals, of course, as in prisoner camps, the staff may consciously break up incipient group-formation in order to avoid collective rebellious action and other ward disturbances.

[2] A comparable coming out occurs in the homosexual world, when a person finally comes frankly to present himself to a "gay" gathering not as a tourist but as someone who is "available." See Evelyn Hooker, "A Preliminary Examination of Group Behavior of Homosexuals," *J. Psychology* (1956) 42:217–225; especially p. 221. A good fictionalized treatment may be found in James Baldwin's *Giovanni's Room;* New York, Dial, 1956; pp. 41–63. A familiar instance of the coming out process is no doubt to be found among prepubertal children at the moment one of these actors sidles *back* into a room that had been left in an angered huff and injured *amour-propre*. The phrase itself presumably derives from a *rite-de-passage* ceremony once arranged by upper-class mothers for their daughters. Interestingly enough, in large mental hospitals the patient sometimes symbolizes a complete coming out by his first active participation in the hospital-wide patient dance.

[3] See Goffman, "Characteristics of Total Institutions," pp. 43–84; in *Proceedings of the Symposium of Preventive and Social Psychiatry;* Washington, D. C., Walter Reed Army Institute of Research, 1957.

full set of mortifying experiences: re-striction of free movement; communal living; diffuse authority of a whole echelon of people; and so on. Here one begins to learn about the limited extent to which a conception of oneself can be sustained when the usual setting of sup-ports for it are suddenly removed.

While undergoing these humbling moral experiences, the inpatient learns to orient himself in terms of the "ward sys-tem." [4] In public mental hospitals this usually consists of a series of graded liv-ing arrangements built around wards, ad-ministrative units called services, and parole statuses. The "worst" level involves often nothing but wooden benches to sit on, some quite indifferent food, and a small piece of room to sleep in. The "best" level may involve a room of one's own, ground and town privileges, con-tacts with staff that are relatively undam-aging, and what is seen as good food and ample recreational facilities. For disobey-ing the pervasive house rules, the inmate will receive stringent punishments ex-pressed in terms of loss of privileges; for obedience he will eventually be allowed to reacquire some of the minor satisfactions he took for granted on the outside.

The institutionalization of these radi-cally different levels of living throws light on the implications for self of social set-tings. And this in turn affirms that the self arises not merely out of its possessor's interactions with significant others, but also out of the arrangements that are evolved in an organization for its mem-bers.

There are some settings which the per-son easily discounts as an expression or extension of him. When a tourist goes slumming, he may take pleasure in the situation not because it is a reflection of him but because it so assuredly is not. There are other settings, such as living rooms, which the person manages on his own and employs to influence in a favor-able direction other persons' views of him. And there are still other settings, such as a work place, which express the employee's occupational status, but over which he has no final control, this being exerted, however tactfully, by his em-ployer. Mental hospitals provide an ex-treme instance of this latter possibility. And this is due not merely to their uniquely degraded living levels, but also to the unique way in which significance for self is made explicit to the patient, piercingly, persistently, and thoroughly. Once lodged on a given ward, the patient is firmly instructed that the restrictions and deprivations he encounters are not due to such things as tradition or econ-omy—and hence dissociable from self— but are intentional parts of his treatment, part of his need at the time, and therefore an expression of the state that his self has fallen to. Having every reason to initiate requests for better conditions, he is told that when the staff feels he is "able to manage" or will be "comfortable with" a higher ward level, then appropriate action will be taken. In short, assignment to a given ward is presented not as a reward or punishment, but as an expression of his general level of social functioning, his status as a person. Given the fact that the worst ward levels provide a round of life that inpatients with organic brain damage can easily manage, and that these quite limited human beings are present to prove it, one can appreciate some of the mirror-ing effects of the hospital.[5]

The ward system, then, is an extreme

---

[4] A good description of the ward system may be found in Ivan Belknap, *Human Prob-lems of a State Mental Hospital;* New York, McGraw-Hill, 1956; see especially p. 164.

[5] Here is one way in which mental hospitals can be worse than concentration camps and prisons as places in which to "do" time; in the latter, self-insulation from the sym-bolic implications of the settings may be easier. In fact, self-insulation from hospital settings may be so difficult that patients have to employ devices for this which staff interpret as psychotic symptoms.

instance of how the physical facts of an establishment can be explicitly employed to frame the conception a person takes of himself. In addition, the official psychiatric mandate of mental hospitals gives rise to even more direct, even more blatant, attacks upon the inmate's view of himself. The more "medical" and the more progressive a mental hospital is— the more it attempts to be therapeutic and not merely custodial—the more he may be confronted by high-ranking staff arguing that his past has been a failure, that the cause of this has been within himself, that his attitude to life is wrong, and that if he wants to be a person he will have to change his way of dealing with people and his conceptions of himself. Often the moral value of these verbal assaults will be brought home to him by requiring him to practice taking this psychiatric view of himself in arranged confessional periods, whether in private sessions or group psychotherapy.

Now a general point may be made about the moral career of inpatients which has bearing on many moral careers. Given the stage that any person has reached in a career, one typically finds that he constructs an image of his life course—past, present, and future— which selects, abstracts, and distorts in such a way as to provide him with a view of himself that he can usefully expound in current situations. Quite generally, the

person's line concerning self defensively brings him into appropriate alignment with the basic values of his society, and so may be called an *apologia*. If the person can manage to present a view of his current situation which shows the operation of favorable personal qualities in the past and a favorable destiny awaiting him, it may be called a *success story*. If the facts of a person's past and present are extremely dismal, then about the best he can do is to show that he is not responsible for what has become of him, and the term *sad tale* is appropriate. Interestingly enough, the more the person's past forces him out of apparent alignment with central moral values, the more often he seems compelled to tell his sad tale in any company in which he finds himself. Perhaps he partly responds to the need he feels in others of not having their sense of proper life courses affronted. In any case, it is among convicts, 'winos,' and prostitutes that one seems to obtain sad tales the most readily.[6] It is the vicissitudes of the mental patient's sad tale that I want to consider now.

In the mental hospital, the setting and the house rules press home to the patient that he is, after all, a mental case who has suffered some kind of social collapse on the outside, having failed in some over-all way, and that here he is of little social weight, being hardly capable of acting like a full-fledged person at all. These

[6] In regard to convicts, see Anthony Heckstall-Smith, *Eighteen Months;* London, Wingate, 1954; pp. 52–53. For 'winos' see the discussion in Howard G. Bain, "A Sociological Analysis of the Chicago Skid-Row Lifeway"; unpublished M.A. thesis, Dept. of Sociology, Univ. of Chicago, Sept., 1950; especially "The Rationale of the Skid-Row Drinking Group," pp. 141–146. Bain's neglected thesis is a useful source of material on moral careers. Apparently one of the occupational hazards of prostitution is that clients and other professional contacts sometimes persist in expressing sympathy by asking for a defensible dramatic explanation for the fall from grace. In having to bother to have a sad tale ready, perhaps the prostitute is more to be pitied than damned. Good examples of prostitute sad tales may be found in Sir Henry Mayhew, "Those that Will Not Work," pp. 210–272; in his *London Labour and the London Poor,* Vol. 4; London, Griffin, Bohn, and Cox, 1862. For a contemporary source, see *Women of the Streets,* edited by C. H. Rolph; London, Zecker and Warburg, 1955; especially p. 6. "Almost always, however, after a few comments on the police, the girl would begin to explain how it was that she was in the life, usually in terms of self-justification." Lately, of course, the psychological expert has helped out the profession in the construction of wholly remarkable sad tales. See, for example, Harold Greenwald, *Call Girl;* New York, Ballantine, 1958.

humiliations are likely to be most keenly felt by middle-class patients, since their previous condition of life little immunizes them against such affronts; but all patients feel some downgrading. Just as any normal member of his outside subculture would do, the patient often responds to this situation by attempting to assert a sad tale proving that he is not "sick," that the "little trouble" he did get into was really somebody else's fault, that his past life course had some honor and rectitude, and that the hospital is therefore unjust in forcing the status of mental patient upon him. This self-respecting tendency is heavily institutionalized within the patient society where opening social contacts typically involve the participants' volunteering information about their current ward location and length of stay so far, but not the reasons for their stay—such interaction being conducted in the manner of small talk on the outside.[7] With greater familiarity, each patient usually volunteers relatively acceptable reasons for his hospitalization, at the same time accepting without open immediate question the lines offered by other patients. Such stories as the following are given and overtly accepted.

I was going to night school to get a M.A. degree, and holding down a job in addition, and the load got too much for me.

The others here are sick mentally but I'm suffering from a bad nervous system and that is what is giving me these phobias.

I got here by mistake because of a diabetes diagnosis, and I'll leave in a couple of days. [The patient had been in seven weeks.]

I failed as a child, and later with my wife I reached out for dependency.

My trouble is that I can't work. That's what I'm in for. I had two jobs with a good home and all the money I wanted.[8]

The patient sometimes reinforces these stories by an optimistic definition of his occupational status: A man who managed to obtain an audition as a radio announcer styles himself a radio announcer; another who worked for some months as a copy boy and was then given a job as a reporter on a large trade journal, but fired after three weeks, defines himself as a reporter.

A whole social role in the patient community may be constructed on the basis of these reciprocally sustained fictions. For these face-to-face niceties tend to be qualified by behind-the-back gossip that comes only a degree closer to the 'objective' facts. Here, of course, one can see a classic social function of informal networks of equals: they serve as one another's audience for self-supporting tales —tales that are somewhat more solid than pure fantasy and somewhat thinner than the facts.

But the patient's *apologia* is called forth in a unique setting, for few settings could be so destructive of self-stories except, of course, those stories already constructed along psychiatric lines. And this destructiveness rests on more than the official sheet of paper which attests that the patient is of unsound mind, a danger to himself and others—an attestation, incidentally, which seems to cut deeply into the patient's pride, and into the possibility of his having any.

Certainly the degrading conditions of the hospital setting belie many of the self-stories that are presented by patients;

---

[7] A similar self-protecting rule has been observed in prisons. Thus, Alfred Hassler, *Diary of a Self-Made Convict;* Chicago, Regnery, 1954, in describing a conversation with a fellow-prisoner; "He didn't say much about why he was sentenced, and I didn't ask him, that being the accepted behavior in prison" (p. 76). A novelistic version for the mental hospital may be found in J. Kerkhoff, *How Thin the Veil: A Newspaperman's Story of His Own Mental Crack-up and Recovery;* New York, Greenberg, 1952; p. 27.

[8] From the writer's field notes of informal interaction with patients, transcribed as near verbatim as he was able.

and the very fact of being in the mental hospital is evidence against these tales. And of course, there is not always sufficient patient solidarity to prevent patient discrediting patient, just as there is not always a sufficient number of 'professionalized' attendants to prevent attendant discrediting patient. As one patient informant repeatedly suggested to a fellow patient:

If you're so smart, how come you got your ass in here?

The mental hospital setting, however, is more treacherous still. Staff has much to gain through discreditings of the pa-

tient's story—whatever the felt reason for such discreditings. If the custodial faction in the hospital is to succeed in managing his daily round without complaint or trouble from him, then it will prove useful to be able to point out to him that the claims about himself upon which he rationalizes his demands are false, that he is not what he is claiming to be, and that in fact he is a failure as a person. If the psychiatric faction is to impress upon him its views about his personal make-up, then they must be able to show in detail how their version of his past and their version of his character hold up much better than his own.[9] . . .

Legal Stigma *

RICHARD D. SCHWARTZ AND JEROME H. SKOLNICK

Legal thinking has moved increasingly toward a sociologically meaningful view of the legal system. Sanctions, in particular, have come to be regarded in functional terms.[1] In criminal law, for instance, sanctions are said to be designed to prevent recidivism by rehabilitating, restraining, or executing the offender. They are also said to be intended to deter others from the performance of similar acts and, sometimes, to provide a channel for the expression of retaliatory motives.

In such civil actions as tort or contract, monetary awards may be intended as retributive and deterrent, as in the use of punitive damages, or may be regarded as a *quid pro quo* to compensate the plaintiff for his wrongful loss.

While these goals comprise an integral part of the rationale of law, little is known about the extent to which they are fulfilled in practice. Lawmen do not as a rule make such studies, because their traditions and techniques are not designed

[9] The process of examining a person psychiatrically and then altering or reducing his status in consequence is known in hospital and prison parlance as *bugging,* the assumption being that once you come to the attention of the testers you either will automatically be labeled crazy or the process of testing itself will make you crazy. Thus psychiatric staff are sometimes seen not as *discovering* whether you are sick, but as *making* you sick; and "Don't bug me, man," can mean, "Don't pester me to the point where I'll get upset." Sheldon Messinger has suggested to me that this meaning of bugging is related to the other colloquial meaning, of wiring a room with a secret microphone to collect information usable for discrediting the speaker.

* Reprinted from "Two Studies of Legal Stigma" in *Social Problems*, Vol. 10 (Fall, 1962), pp. 133–38, by permission of the authors and *Social Problems*.

[1] Legal sanctions are defined as changes in life conditions imposed through court action.

for a systematic examination of the operation of the legal system in action, especially outside the courtroom. Thus, when extra-legal consequences—e.g., the social stigma of a prison sentence—are taken into account at all, it is through the discretionary actions of police, prosecutor, judge, and jury. Systematic information on a variety of unanticipated outcomes, those which benefit the accused as well as those which hurt him, might help to inform these decision makers and perhaps lead to changes in substantive law as well. The present paper is an attempt to study the consequences of stigma associated with legal accusation. . . .

The Effects of a Criminal Court Record on the Employment Opportunities of Unskilled Workers

In [a] field experiment, four employment folders were prepared, the same in all respects except for the criminal court record of the applicant. In all of the folders he was described as a thirty-two year old single male of unspecified race, with a high school training in mechanical trades, and a record of successive short term jobs as a kitchen helper, maintenance worker, and handyman. These characteristics are roughly typical of applicants for unskilled hotel jobs in the Catskill resort area of New York State where employment opportunities were tested.[2]

The four folders differed only in the applicant's reported record of criminal court involvement. The first folder indicated that the applicant had been convicted and sentenced for assault; the second, that he had been tried for assault and acquitted; the third, also tried for assault and acquitted, but with a letter from the judge certifying the finding of not guilty and reaffirming the legal presumption of innocence. The fourth folder made no mention of any criminal record.

A sample of one hundred employers was utilized. Each employer was assigned to one of four "treatment" groups.[3] To each employer only one folder was shown; this folder was one of the four kinds mentioned above, the selection of the folder being determined by the treatment group to which the potential employer was assigned. The employer was asked whether he could "use" the man described in the folder. To preserve the reality of the situation and make it a true field experiment, employers were never given any indication that they were participating in an experiment. So far as they knew, a legitimate offer to work was being made in each showing of the folder by the "employment agent."

The experiment was designed to determine what employers would do in fact if confronted with an employment applicant with a criminal record. The questionnaire approach used in earlier studies[4] seemed ill-adapted to the problem, since respondents confronted with hypothetical situations might be particu-

---

[2] The generality of these results remains to be determined. The effects of criminal involvement in the Catskill area are probably diminished, however, by the temporary nature of employment, the generally poor qualifications of the work force, and the excess of demand over supply of unskilled labor there. Accordingly, the employment differences among the four treatment groups found in this study are likely, if anything to be *smaller* than would be expected in industries and areas where workers are more carefully selected.

[3] Employers were not approached in pre-selected random order, due to a misunderstanding of instructions on the part of the law student who carried out the experiment during a three and one-half week period. Because of this flaw in the experimental procedure, the results should be treated with appropriate caution. Thus, chi-squared analysis may not properly be utilized. (For those used to this measure, $P < .05$ for Table 1.)

[4] Sol Rubin, *Crime and Juvenile Delinquency*, New York: Oceana, 1958, pp. 151–56.

larly prone to answer in what they considered a socially acceptable manner. The second alternative—studying job opportunities of individuals who had been involved with the law—would have made it very difficult to find comparable groups of applicants and potential employers. For these reasons, the field experiment reported here was utilized.

Some deception was involved in the study. The "employment agent"—the same individual in all hundred cases—was in fact a law student who was working in the Catskills during the summer of 1959 as an insurance adjuster. In representing himself as being both an adjuster and an employment agent, he was assuming a combination of roles which is not uncommon there. The adjuster role gave him an opportunity to introduce a single application for employment casually and naturally. To the extent that the experiment worked, however, it was inevitable that some employers should be led to believe that they had immediate prospects of filling a job opening. In those instances where an offer to hire was made, the "agent" called a few hours later to say that the applicant had taken another job. The field experimenter attempted in such instances to locate a satisfactory replacement by contacting an employment agency in the area. Because this procedure was used and since the jobs involved were of relatively minor consequence, we believe that the deception caused little economic harm.

As mentioned, each treatment group of twenty-five employers was approached with one type of folder. Responses were dichotomized: those who expressed a willingness to consider the applicant in any way were termed positive; those who made no response or who explicitly refused to consider the candidate were termed negative. Our results consist of comparisons between positive and negative responses, thus defined, for the treatment groups.

Of the twenty-five employers shown the "no record" folder, nine gave positive responses. Subject to reservations arising from chance variations in sampling, we take this as indicative of the "ceiling" of jobs available for this kind of applicant under the given field conditions. Positive responses by these employers may be compared with those in the other treatment groups to obtain an indication of job opportunities lost because of the various legal records.

Of the twenty-five employers approached with the "convict" folder, only one expressed interest in the applicant. This is a rather graphic indication of the effect which a criminal record may have on job opportunities. Care must be exercised, of course, in generalizing the conclusions to other settings. In this context, however, the criminal record made a major difference.

From a theoretical point of view, the finding leads toward the conclusion that conviction constitutes a powerful form of "status degradation" [5] which continues to operate after the time when, according to the generalized theory of justice underlying punishment in our society, the individual's "debt" has been paid. A record of conviction produces a durable if not permanent loss of status. For purposes of effective social control, this state of affairs may heighten the deterrent effect of conviction—though that remains to be established. Any such contribution to social control, however, must be balanced against the barriers imposed upon rehabilitation of the convict. If the ex-prisoner finds difficulty in securing menial kinds of legitimate work, further crime

---

[5] Harold Garfinkel, "Conditions of Successful Degradation Ceremonies," *American Journal of Sociology,* 61 (March, 1956), pp. 420–24.

may become an increasingly attractive alternative.[6]

Another important finding of this study concerns the small number of positive responses elicited by the "accused but acquitted" applicant. Of the twenty-five employers approached with this folder, three offered jobs. Thus, the individual accused but acquitted of assault has almost as much trouble finding even an unskilled job as the one who was not only accused of the same offense, but also convicted.

From a theoretical point of view, this result indicates that permanent lowering of status is not limited to those explicitly singled out by being convicted of a crime. As an ideal outcome of American justice, criminal procedure is supposed to distinguish between the "guilty" and those who have been acquitted. Legally controlled consequences which follow the judgment are consistent with this purpose. Thus, the "guilty" are subject to fine and imprisonment, while those who are acquitted are immune from these sanctions.

But deprivations may be imposed on the acquitted, both before and after victory in court. Before trial, legal rules either permit or require arrest and detention. The suspect may be faced with the expense of an attorney and a bail bond if he is to mitigate these limitations on his privacy and freedom. In addition, some pre-trial deprivations are imposed without formal legal permission. These may include coercive questioning, use of violence, and stigmatization. And, as this study indicates, some deprivations not under the direct control of the legal process may develop or persist after an official decision of acquittal has been made.

Thus two legal principles conflict in practice. On the one hand, "a man is innocent until proven guilty." On the other, the accused is systematically treated as guilty under the administration of criminal law until a functionary or official body—police, magistrate, prosecuting attorney, or trial judge or jury—decides that he is entitled to be

TABLE 1
Effect of Four Types of Legal Folder on Job Opportunities
(in per cent)

	No Record	Acquitted With Letter	Acquitted Without Letter	Convicted	Total
	(N = 25)	(N = 25)	(N = 25)	(N = 25)	(N = 100)
Positive response	36	24	12	4	19
Negative response	64	76	88	96	81
Total	100	100	100	100	100

[6] Severe negative effects of conviction on employment opportunities have been noted by Sol Rubin, *Crime and Juvenile Delinquency*, New York: Oceana, 1958. A further source of employment difficulty is inherent in licensing statutes and security regulations which sometimes preclude convicts from being employed in their pre-conviction occupation or even in the trades which they may have acquired during imprisonment. These effects may, however, be counteracted by bonding arrangements, prison associations, and publicity programs aimed at increasing confidence in, and sympathy for, exconvicts. See also, B. F. McSally, "Finding Jobs for Released Offenders," *Federal Probation*, 24 (June, 1960), pp. 12–17; Harold D. Lasswell and Richard C. Donnelly, "The Continuing Debate over Responsibility: An Introduction to Isolating the Condemnation Sanction," *Yale Law Journal*, 68 (April, 1959), pp. 869–99; Johs Andenaes, "General Prevention—Illusion or Reality?" *J. Criminal Law, Criminology and Police Science*, 43 (July–August, 1952), pp. 176–98.

free. Even then, the results of treating him as guilty persist and may lead to serious consequences.

The conflict could be eased by measures aimed at reducing the deprivations imposed on the accused, before and after acquittal. Some legal attention has been focused on pre-trial deprivations. The provision of bail and counsel, the availability of habeas corpus, limitations on the admissibility of coerced confessions, and civil actions for false arrest are examples of measures aimed at protecting the rights of the accused before trial. Although these are often limited in effectiveness, especially for individuals of lower socioeconomic status, they at least represent some concern with implementing the presumption of innocence at the pre-trial stage.

By contrast, the courts have done little toward alleviating the post-acquittal consequences of legal accusation. One effort along these lines has been employed in the federal courts, however. Where an individual has been accused and exonerated of a crime, he may petition the federal courts for a "Certificate of Innocence" certifying this fact.[7] Possession of such a document might be expected to alleviate post-acquittal deprivations.

Some indication of the effectiveness of such a measure is found in the responses of the final treatment group. Their folder, it will be recalled, contained information on the accusation and acquittal of the applicant, but also included a letter from a judge addressed "To whom it may concern" certifying the applicant's acquittal and reminding the reader of the presumption of innocence. Such a letter might have had a boomerang effect, by reemphasizing the legal involvement of the applicant. It was important, therefore, to determine empirically whether such a communication would improve or harm the chances of employment. Our findings indicate that it increased employment opportunities, since the letter folder elicited six positive responses. Even though this fell short of the nine responses to the "no record" folder, it doubled the number for the "accused but acquitted" and created a significantly greater number of job offers than those elicited by the convicted record. This suggests that the procedure merits consideration as a means of offsetting the occupational loss resulting from accusation. It should be noted, however, that repeated use of this device might reduce its effectiveness.

The results of the experiment are summarized in Table 1. The differences in outcome found there indicate that various types of legal records are systematically related to job opportunities. It seems fair to infer also that the trend of job losses corresponds with the apparent punitive intent of the authorities. Where the man is convicted, that intent is presumably greatest. It is less where he is accused but acquitted and still less where the court makes an effort to emphasize the absence of a finding of guilt. Nevertheless, where the difference in punitive intent is ideally greatest, between conviction and acquittal, the difference in occupational harm is very slight. . . .

[7] 28 United States Code, Secs. 1495, 2513.

DEVIANT SUBCULTURES

Part Three

When persons assigned statuses as deviants associate with one another more frequently than they do with persons in nondeviant statuses, a subculture often develops. These subcultures, like cultures generally, present a common understanding and prescribed ways of thinking, feeling, and acting when in the company of one's own deviant peers and when dealing with representatives of the conventional world. Once these deviant subcultures come into being and flourish, they have consequences for their bearers and conventional outsiders as well.

Part Three examines some of the conditions that give rise to deviant subcultures, how persons enter and are assigned a role in deviant groups, and the effects of deviant social organization. Before examining these questions, however, a few remarks are in order.

Contrary to widespread public opinion, deviance is not unilinear nor does it have fixed and inevitable stages. It is clearly to the advantage of the larger culture, for instance, to foster simplistic notions about the socialization and subsequent life-cycle of deviants. But from what we have already seen, assignment to a deviant status, even when deviance persists, is not always an easy matter. In primary group relations, some persons well aware of the nature and consequences of public disgrace, go out of their way first of all not to notice deviance. Second, if forced to see it, they take evasive action to protect themselves and those others immediately involved in deviance, hoping thereby to forestall a cycle of deviance. Similarly, agents of social control define deviance selectively.

There is then no one natural history of deviance. There are only natural histories. If we examine the hypothetical deviant career, however, its stages are: 1) a person lives in a group where qualities and acts are viewed as deviant; 2) this person is believed to exhibit deviance; 3) he gets typed and assigned deviant status; 4) his actions come to official notice and he becomes an official case in various agencies of social control; 5) this social processing propels him into organized deviant life, and out of conventional life; and 6) finally, as a culmination of this entire process, he redefines himself, assumes the status and performs the deviant role, becoming in the end what everybody said he was at the outset.

This is only one developmental model of deviant socialization as an interactive process. We can reverse the model, however, and probably advance better explanations for at least some varieties of deviance. The model in reverse probably accounts better for professional crime. When reversed, a person defines himself as a certain kind of person, enters a deviant subculture to confirm that identity, comes to official notice, becomes an official case, engages in more persistent and patterned deviations, and reinforces the system of social types by his actions. But other types of deviant careers may well require different developmental models in order to explain them. Given the many varieties of deviant careers, it seems fairly clear that a person might enter the deviance process at any one of the stages just noted only to move forward, backward, or out of the process completely.

Perhaps a visual image here may help. Suppose we think of deviance as an interactive process taking place in the corridor of a building. There is a front and a rear to the building and there are offices off the corridor on both of its sides. Viewed this way, the schema suggests that each portion of the corridor has openings at the front, the rear, and along both sides. These openings can work as entrances or as exits. The following diagram indicates the possible flow of deviance through the corridor.

The Deviance Corridor

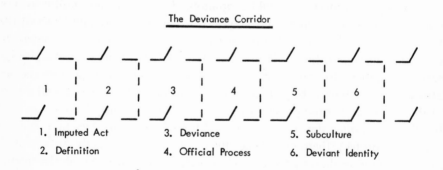

1. Imputed Act   3. Deviance   5. Subculture

2. Definition   4. Official Process   6. Deviant Identity

Traffic flows north, south, east, and west in this corridor. The dotted lines represent the symbolic boundaries marking a person's progress through the corridor. These boundaries, though unseen by all of course, are quite real in their effects. And they are maintained by sentries, some visible, some unseen. Social typing, for example, steers people through the corridor. Defining agents work at each of these symbolic boundaries. And, as we have already seen, agents speed certain candidates further along the corridor and usher others out the side doors or back to where they started from.

At each stage of the traffic flow, the person walking through this corridor is responding to his own actions in terms of the symbols by which others define him, as person and as actor. Who these others are, his relationship to them, and their symbolic definitions are important in affecting the next steps he will take. To a very great extent, it is the actions of these others that create and sustain the deviant career. In addition, the visibility, the frequency, the exposure, the severity of reacting others, and the particular form of deviance shapes the flow, direction, and pace of traffic up and down the corridor.

Stutterers, for example, because of the social definition of stuttering acquire a deviant identity almost immediately at the hands of their parents when these significant figures work desperately to eliminate their faulty speech patterns. The steps or flow would be from 1 through 3. Stutterers break no laws and they sustain no deviant subculture. Delinquents, by contrast, move all the way through the process from 1 through 6 (though not necessarily in that order; see the Kitsuse and Dietrick reading).

There is a tendency to see deviants as lonely and isolated human beings; persons so miserable and so disgraced that they themselves avoid contact with other people. There is another tendency to see them as persons who have banded together in happy company. The first view stems from pity or moral superiority. The second view arises out of fear, ambivalence, and, even in some cases, envy. Both of these views are caricatures. For just as there are no fixed or unilinear stages in the natural history of deviance, neither is it guaranteed that deviants will be more or less happy than so-called conventional people. Finally, it is not guaranteed that once they have been assigned a deviant label that they will automatically seek out or be drawn into a deviant subculture.

The Emergence of Subcultures

A subculture is apt to come into being when a category of persons find themselves suffering a common fate. It is essential, however, for them to be in contact with one another and to find out in the course of communication that they do in fact have common interests. These interests arise generally from their social situation, because they face more or less the same dilemma. The subculture sometimes arises as an unofficial response to official processes.

Now the general dilemma for the persons who ultimately become participants in a deviant subculture is that they seek to continue to engage in the kinds of practices their society labels as deviant, yet avoid social punishment. When enough persons assigned deviant status become aware of their common problems, a deviant subculture emerges.

If the persons are more concerned with activities, the deviant group forms on the basis of a common attraction (see the Cohen reading). If the persons are more concerned with avoiding social punishment and are actually thrust together because of official processes and subsequent deviant status-assignment, the deviant group forms on the basis of exposure to shared social punishment (see the Kitsuse and Dietrick reading). And finally if the persons somehow find themselves together, engaged almost by chance in deviant activities, and form no group either through push or pull, they are viewed as a congeries or pseudo-deviant subculture (see the Yablonsky reading).

Entry and Acculturation

Entry refers to the manner in which the deviant subculture admits and assigns status to novices and acculturation refers to its special processes of socialization. Statuses can be clearly defined or rather loose in character. And induction into these statuses can be intense and highly specialized or casual and off-hand at best. Much of this depends upon the degree of commitment others in the subculture expect from the novice and the extent to which their own safety and welfare depends upon close cooperation with him. Where, for example, a high degree of interdependence is involved in executing deviant activities, as in say pickpocketing, entry and acculturation will be rigorous. Admission, on the other hand, to a Skid Row bottle gang is a relatively simple matter. In this last case, the person need only indicate a willingness to "go in on a bottle." He need only give a few coins to gain admission.

The criminal subculture has a good deal to teach about skills in breaking rules and avoiding detection. Revolutionary movements have more recondite skills and ideology to teach and make somewhat sterner tests of commitment. Since they seek to overthrow the social order, they mount a profound threat against the status quo. Somewhat lower down in their organized concern with issues of entry and acculturation would be drug addicts, homosexuals, and Bohemians.

Subcultures, much like colleges, can be rated on how hard they are to get into and how hard they are to stay in. Here again specific activities, status-assignment, and the subculture itself produce different ratings. If the deviant subculture can obtain a commitment from the novice, he is more apt to remain loyal to its prescriptions. And commitment is greatest where the societal reaction against the newcomer and his particular brand of deviant activity is most severe.

Variations in Deviant Social Organization

While it is true that deviant subcultures instruct their bearers in the arts of deviance, it does not always follow that the practitioners become totally immersed in the deviant way of life. Persons may engage in systematic but solitary deviation, as do certain check forgers. Actually such persons appear to be marginal to all established social organization, conventional or deviant, since the nature of their work requires them to remain pseudonymous and mobile. By way of contrast, certain kinds of Bohemians remain fully outside of conventionality. During the brief heyday of the beat subculture, for instance, beats took vows of voluntary poverty, and spent most of their time on the beat scene. Even these persons, however, in order to "make some bread" found it necessary to engage in commerce with the "square" world.

Variations in deviant communities depend heavily on social visibility. Covert deviants remain underground and perform secretly. Overt deviants perform publicly. These two types of deviant role require different social organizations. Overt deviants more often find themselves totally immersed in unconventional ways. This way of life sets forth a calendar, a daily round of activities, and a circle of intimate acquaintances.

Sanctions that deviants bring against one another are important here. For once persons step inside a deviant way of life, be it completely in the underworld, in the half-world, or secretly within the conventional world, they do not forego social control. Social control exists within the deviant enclave as well as outside. The question remains, then—How well do deviant groups control their members?

The Consequences of Systematic Deviance

The answer comes through looking at how deviant careers evolve within deviant subcultures. Subcultures, like cultures generally, state beliefs, values, and norms. These are supposed to regulate conduct. In turn, these prescriptions get ordered socially. As we have seen, deviants vary in the extent to which they organize their activities and the extent to which they define them by subcultural rules. Some contain many statements on what to believe, think, and feel; others have simpler codes. Again, if one has a relatively tight social organization, another has an amorphous one. Deviants sometimes impute to an organization a degree of solidarity that is largely illusory.

A simple code organized tightly leads to one set of consequences. A complex set of rules organized loosely leads to other consequences. And disorganization can very easily affect deviant subcultures. Thus, if some protect and dignify their constituents, others actually spawn normlessness, induce exploitation, and set deviants against one another.

All of these, of course, constitute important researchable questions. On the basis of present evidence, it does seem, however, that the degree of social organization among most duly qualified social deviants is highly exaggerated, by sociologists and deviants alike. Although this is testimony to the successful workings of conventional socialization, which defines order and social organization as one of the established values and verities of social life, it reveals how persons occasionally might be hoodwinked into an illusory solidarity.

THE RISE OF SUBCULTURES

9

Typing and social differentiation redefine the person as deviant. Experience with official societal reactions punishes at the same time that it sets the person apart. Typing, differentiation, and punishment produce some but not all of the conditions for an organized way of life, the deviant subculture. For instance, a group of persons now categorized in the same way may form a group to live up to its social type while protecting its members from social punishment. Unless, however, additional conditions are met, such a group will not continue to sustain its own deviant lifeways.

The readings that follow deal with some of these conditions. Cohen first lists some of the requirements for the development of subcultures and goes on to point out that unless persons face the same social situation and engage in effective social interaction, no subculture will arise. He then shows how the delinquent subculture emerged. Kitsuse and Dietrick question Cohen's theory and discuss how sanctions help to maintain a subculture. Schur then shows how repressive sociolegal measures guarantee that effective interaction among those with common interests will take place. Matza indicates how it is possible for participants to believe they are actually participating in a subculture, and that the "subculture of delinquency" is really a subterranean tradition in American culture. Yablonsky, in the last reading, shows that often the outsider's notion that a solidified deviant group exists complete with its own code is misleading.

A Theory of Subcultures *

ALBERT K. COHEN

. . . The crucial condition for the emergence of new cultural forms is the existence, *in effective interaction with one another, of a number of actors with*

* Reprinted with permission of The Macmillan Company from *Delinquent Boys* by Albert K. Cohen pp. 59–61, 65–66. Copyright The Free Press, a Corporation 1955.

similar problems of adjustment. These may be the entire membership of a group or only certain members, similarly circumstanced, within the group. Among the conceivable solutions to their problems may be one which is not yet embodied in action and which does not therefore exist as a cultural model. This solution, except for the fact that it does not already carry the social criteria of validity and promise the social rewards of consensus, might well answer more neatly to the problems of this group and appeal to its members more effectively than any of the solutions already institutionalized. For each participant, this solution would be adjustive and adequately motivated provided that he could anticipate a simultaneous and corresponding transformation in the frames of reference of his fellows. Each would welcome a sign from the others that a new departure in this direction would receive approval and support. But how does one *know* whether a gesture toward innovation will strike a responsive and sympathetic chord in others or whether it will elicit hostility, ridicule and punishment? *Potential* concurrence is always problematical and innovation or the impulse to innovate a stimulus for anxiety.

The paradox is resolved when the innovation is broached in such a manner as to elicit from others reactions suggesting their receptivity; and when, at the same time, the innovation occurs by increments so small, tentative and ambiguous as to permit the actor to retreat, if the signs be unfavorable, without having become identified with an unpopular position. Perhaps all social actions have, in addition to their instrumental, communicative and expressive functions, this quality of being *exploratory gestures*. For the actor with problems of adjustment which cannot be resolved within the frame of reference of the established culture, each response of the other to what the actor says and does is a clue to the directions in which change may proceed further in a way congenial to the other and to the direction in which change will lack social support. And if the probing gesture is motivated by tensions common to other participants it is likely to initiate a process of *mutual* exploration and *joint* elaboration of a new solution. My exploratory gesture functions as a cue to you; your exploratory gesture as a cue to me. By a casual, semi-serious, noncommittal or tangential remark I may stick my neck out just a little way, but I will quickly withdraw it unless you, by some sign of affirmation, stick *yours* out. I will permit myself to become progressively committed but only as others, by some visible sign, become likewise committed. The final product, to which we are jointly committed, is likely to be a compromise formation of all the participants to what we may call a cultural process, a formation perhaps unanticipated by any of them. Each actor may contribute something directly to the growing product, but he may also contribute indirectly by encouraging others to advance, inducing them to retreat, and suggesting new avenues to be explored. The product cannot be ascribed to any one of the participants; it is a real "emergent" on a group level. . . .

The emergence of these "group standards" of this shared frame of reference, is the emergence of a new subculture. It is cultural because each actor's participation in this system of norms is influenced by his perception of the same norms in other actors. It is *sub*cultural because the norms are shared only among those actors who stand somehow to profit from them and who find in one another a sympathetic moral climate within which these norms may come to fruition and persist. In this fashion culture is continually being created, re-created and modified wherever individuals sense in one another like needs, generated by like circumstances, not shared generally in the larger social system. Once established, such a subcultural system may persist, but not by sheer inertia. It may achieve a life which outlasts that of the individuals who participated in its creation, but only so long as it continues to serve the needs of those who succeed its creators.

One variant of this cultural process interests us especially because it provides the model for our explanation of the delinquent subculture. Status problems are problems of achieving respect in the eyes of one's fellows. Our ability to achieve status depends upon the criteria of status applied by our fellows, that is, the standards or norms they go by in evaluating people. These criteria are an aspect of their cultural frames of reference. If we lack the characteristics or capacities which give status in terms of these criteria, we are beset by one of the most typical and yet distressing of human problems of adjustment. One solution is for individuals who share such problems to gravitate toward one another and jointly to establish new norms, new criteria of status which define as meritorious the characteristics they *do* possess, the kinds of conduct of which they *are* capable. It is clearly necessary for each participant, if the innovation is to solve his status problem, that these new criteria be shared with others, that the solution be a group and not a private solution. If he "goes it alone" he succeeds only in further estranging himself from his fellows. Such new status criteria would represent new subcultural values different from or even antithetical to those of the larger social system.

The Delinquent Subculture *

ALBERT K. COHEN

. . . I have addressed the question: Why is delinquency disproportionately frequent among lower-class youth, and why does so much of it have no manifest point or utility, but seem rather to proceed from a spirit of pure meanness, negativism, contrariness, and the like? [1] Very briefly summarized, my argument states that young people's self-feelings depend very largely upon how they are judged by others. In this country the stages on which they perform and the situations in which they are judged—most notably, the school situation—are largely dominated by middle-class people, and the standards or measuring rods by which they are judged are those current among middle-class people. They are not, however, exclusively middle-class standards. They express the dominant American value system; they pervade the mass media; and they are also applied, although in a less thoroughgoing way, by "respectable" working-class people. These standards include such criteria as verbal fluency, academic intelligence, high levels

* Reprinted from *Deviance and Control* by Albert K. Cohen, pp. 65–66 © 1966, by permission of the author and Prentice-Hall, Inc., Englewood Cliffs, N.J.
[1] Albert K. Cohen, *Delinquent Boys: The Culture of the Gang* (New York: The Free Press, 1955).

of aspiration, drives for achievement, capacity for sustained effort in the service of long-run goals, the ability to delay gratification, neatness, cleanliness, polished manners, and others. It is also a characteristic of American culture generally—an aspect of its "democratic" ethos—that young people of different origins and backgrounds tend to be judged by the same standards, so that young people of different social class, race, and ethnicity find themselves competing with one another for status and approval under the same set of rules. However, they are not all equally well-equipped for success in this status game. In particular, different patterns of socialization are associated with the different social classes, and middle-class socialization is far more effective in training children for such success than is lower-class socialization. For this and other reasons, lower-class children are more likely to experience failure and humiliation. In brief, they are caught up in a game in which others are typically the winners and they are the losers and the also-rans.

One way they can deal with this problem is to repudiate and withdraw from the game, to refuse to recognize the rules as having any application to them, and to set up new games with their own rules or criteria of status—rules by which they *can* perform satisfactorily. It is not, however, quite that simple. The dominant value system is also, to a degree, *their* value system. They have, to a certain extent, internalized its rules also. They can *tell* themselves that they don't really care about what people think of them, and about the things these people think are important, but their internalized values, even if repressed, threaten always to break through and dilute their satisfaction with the alternative they have chosen. Therefore, to buttress this choice, to protect it from incursions from "the enemy within as well as the enemy without," they resort to reaction-formation. They not only reject the dominant value system, but do so with a vengeance. They "stand it on its head"; they exalt its opposition; they engage in malicious, spiteful, "ornery" behavior of all sorts to demonstrate not only to others, but to themselves as well, their contempt for the game they have rejected. . . .

Critique of Cohen's Theory *

JOHN I. KITSUSE AND DAVID C. DIETRICK

. . . What . . . are the research directives of the theory of the delinquent subculture? When this problem is analyzed, Cohen's methodology presents numerous difficulties, for his theory is an historical construction addressed to the explanation of the *emergence* of an existing subculture and its *present* concentration among the working-class male population. Furthermore, the basic propositions of this

* Reprinted from "Delinquent Boys: A Critique" in *American Sociological Review,* Vol. 24 (April, 1959), pp. 213–15, by permission of the authors and the American Sociological Association.

explanation utilize concepts which require data about the psychological characteristics of past populations.

Cohen's use of the present indicative in the development of his theory is misleading, for the interpretation of the rise of the delinquent subculture requires historical data. It is not that the working-class boy *is* ambivalent about middle-class values; the theory requires only that at some unspecified time when the delinquent subculture emerged, the working-class boy *was* ambivalent about middle-class values.

Subculture Maintenance and Motivation. There is no objection *per se* to a plausible explanation that cannot be tested if the explanation is viewed as an heuristic device for the generating of hypotheses. If then a direct test of Cohen's theory through the measurement of deduced empirical regularities is not possible as a practical matter, is it feasible to approach the problem from a functional point of view? The question may be phrased: what are the necessary conditions for the maintenance of the delinquent subculture? On this question, Cohen's statements are quite explicit. Commenting on the fact that his theory is not concerned with the processes by which one boy becomes delinquent while another does not, Cohen writes:

> We have tried to show that a subculture owes its existence to the fact that it provides a solution to certain problems of adjustment shared among a community of individuals. However, it does not follow that for every individual who participates these problems provide the sole or sufficient source of motivation. Indeed, there may be some participants to whose motivation these problems contribute very little. . . . Our delinquent subculture . . . is not a disembodied set of beliefs and practices but is "carried" and supported by groups with distinctive personnel. A position in this organization or affiliation with this or that particular member may offer other satisfactions which help to account for the participation of certain members but do not help to explain the content of the culture in which they participate.[1]

An implication of this statement is that the maintenance of the delinquent subculture is not wholly dependent upon the motivational structure which explains its emergence. Not *every* individual who participates in the delinquent subculture need be so motivated and, for some, such motivation may be peripheral if not irrelevant. Clearly an investigation of the motivations which lead individuals to participate in the delinquent subculture does not constitute even an indirect test of the theory. For the statement may be read to mean that once the subculture is established, it can be maintained by the behavior of individuals who bring a diverse range of motivations to the gangs which embody the delinquent subculture. Thus, functionally, the delinquent subculture requires another explanation.

The Double Dilemma: Theory and Method. The theoretical significance of Cohen's explanation of the emergence of the delinquent subculture, however, lies precisely in its relevance for an explanation of the maintenance of that subculture. Were this not so, the theory could be dismissed as merely plausible and untestable or as incapable of generating hypotheses about regularities other than the pre-existing "facts" which it explains. We suggest that the statement quoted above presents a methodological dilemma by divorcing the dynamics of the etiology of the delinquent subculture from the dynamics of its maintenance. Cohen is correct of course in asserting that, theoretically, the former does not necessarily

---

[1] Albert K. Cohen, *Delinquent Boys: The Culture of the Gang,* New York: Free Press, 1955.

require the same motivational dynamics as the latter. However, the ambiguity of his statement lies in his implicit concession that *some* of the participants in the subculture must have the characteristic motivational structure posited in the theory.

The research dilemma posed by Cohen's theory is two-fold. Methodologically, the historical method relies upon data concerning the psychological dynamics of a population which are difficult if not impossible to obtain. Theoretically, the motivational dynamics posited as necessary for the *emergence* of the delinquent subculture is considered either (a) independent of the motivational dynamics necessary for the *maintenance* of the subculture, or (b) dependent upon it in some unspecified relationship.

In view of these difficulties, it may be fruitful to turn the problem around and ask: What are the consequences of participation in the delinquent subculture for the motivational structure of the participants? This question places the theory of the delinquent subculture in its proper relation to the value-transmission theories of delinquency, and directs us to examine the heuristic value of Cohen's theory. Viewing his theory from this perspective, the following propositions about the maintenance of the delinquent subculture may be stated:

1. The individual learns the values of the delinquent subculture through his participation in gangs which embody that subculture.

2. The motivations of individuals for participating in such gangs are varied.

3. The malicious, non-utilitarian, and negativistic behavior which is learned through participation in the subculture is met by formal negative sanctions, rejection, and limitation of access to prestigeful status within the middle-class system.

4. Thus, participation in the delinquent subculture creates similar problems for all its participants.

5. The participants' response to the barriers raised to exclude them from status in the middle-class system (that is, the "problem") is a hostile rejection of the standards of "respectable" society and an emphasis upon status within the delinquent gang.

6. The hostile rejection response reinforces the malicious, non-utilitarian, and negativistic norms of the subculture.

The formulation suggested here relates Cohen's explanation of the emergence of the delinquent subculture with an explanation of its maintenance. It hypothesizes that the delinquent subculture persists because, once established, it creates for those who participate in it, the very problems which were the bases for its emergence. It is possible to derive the further hypothesis that the motivational structure of the participants of the subculture displays characteristics similar to those described by Cohen.

Crimes Without Victims *

EDWIN M. SCHUR

. . . Crimes without victims . . . refers essentially to the willing exchange, among adults, of strongly demanded but legally proscribed goods or services. Do prohibitions of this sort, and the social problems to which they are directed (and of which they are a part), constitute a sociologically meaningful category? H. L. A. Hart has asked: "Ought immorality as such to be a crime?" [1] Crimes without victims involve attempts to legislate morality for its own sake; the two conceptions very largely relate to the same thing. From the sociological standpoint, however, reference to the victimless nature of the offense may have certain advantages. It reveals the basis for saying that certain laws are indeed designed merely to legislate morality. It also highlights an important criterion for determining which laws fall into this category—the question: "Is there, in this particular situation, any real victimization?"

Another concept closely related . . . is *dissensus*. With respect to each of the cases examined here, there is a lack of public consensus about the law. However, consensus is similarly lacking in the enactment and execution of other criminal laws, yet not all those instances involve the peculiar characteristics of the deviance situations described here. For instance, not only is there extensive violation of existing income tax laws, but there also appears to be considerable ambivalence in public attitudes toward these statutes (at least toward their specific provisions if not their very existence). But although these laws are not easily or completely enforceable, they do not give rise to the secondary elaboration of deviance. . . . A main point of differentiation seems to be *the element of transaction, or exchange.* Crimes without victims may be limited to those situations in which one person obtains from another, in a fairly direct exchange, a commodity or personal service which is socially disapproved and legally proscribed.

This limitation is admittedly somewhat arbitrary. It can be seen that there are other offenses in which there really is no victim. And if one were solely concerned with straight description, the phrase *exchange crimes* or even *business crimes* (i.e., offenses giving rise to illegal businesses) might be almost as appropriate a label. . . . But, as already mentioned, the concept of victimless crime helps to pinpoint a major criterion for evaluating policies, and this, too, is of concern in this discussion. The limitation of the concept to the exchange situations keeps it from getting out of hand. In a sense, every criminal law represents a societal judgment establishing both an offender and an individual or collective victim. Where there is direct offense by one person against another person or his property, the victim and victimizer are easily identified. On the other hand, in a crime against the state or a crime against morals, the victim becomes more elusive.

* Reprinted from Edwin M. Schur, *Crimes Without Victims: Deviant Behavior and Public Policy,* © 1965, by permission of Prentice-Hall, Inc., Englewood Cliffs, New Jersey, pp. 169–173.
[1] H. L. A. Hart, *Law, Liberty and Morality,* Stanford: Stanford University Press, 1963, p. 4.

215

And when the law specifically insists that a person is a victim even if the facts contradict that contention—for instance, sexual intercourse with a girl "under the age of consent" is statutory rape, even though she consents—the victim element is blurred still further.

In the examples considered here, the "harm" seen in the proscribed transaction seems primarily to be *harm to the participating individuals themselves* (apart from any alleged harm to general morals). Does the term *self-harm,* then, adequately describe the situations being considered? Not quite. In the first place, there is much dispute as to the extent of self-harm actually involved in the various proscribed behaviors. But, beyond that, not all proscriptions of self-harm produce situations of the sort analyzed here. Thus legal attempts to ban suicide or masturbation might seem to establish victimless crime situations in the sense of prohibiting self-harm, but precisely because the offense involves only the lone individual there is little or no basis for any elaboration of the deviance. Perhaps it is *the combination of an exchange transaction and lack of apparent harm* to others that constitutes the core of the victimless crime situation as here defined. Not all "exchange crimes" would qualify, because in some there may be evident harm to others. This is seen in the case of wartime black-market operations, in which the exchange of proscribed but strongly demanded goods between willing sellers and buyers does work patently to the disadvantage of many other individuals. Perhaps it is because the buyer of such goods is attempting to get more than his fair share of commodities desired by a large proportion of the general citizenry that dispassionate observers can easily view his behavior as harmful to society.[2] Of course it must be kept in mind that even

dispassionate analysts will differ in their assessments of the harm involved in particular situations, and indeed there will be some individuals who see distinct harm to others even in the nonvictim situations described. . . .

One feature which seems to characterize all crimes without victims is the unenforceability of the laws surrounding them. Such *unenforceability stems directly from the lack of a complainant* and the consequent difficulty in obtaining evidence. Also significant is the low visibility of these offenses. If for some reason the proscribed exchanges had to occur always in public, enforcement would be far more efficient. Obviously the willing nature of the interpersonal exchange and the privacy in which it can take place are related. Another apparent consequence of privacy and lack of a complainant (combined with public ambivalence about the law) is the invitation to police corruption. Outside of these points, however, there is considerable variation within the category of crimes without victims. A comparison of the three situations analyzed . . . [abortion, homosexuality, and drug addiction] may provide some hints as to the factors determining the expansion of deviance in the victimless crime sphere. . . .

This raises the matter of subculture, the development of which is similarly dependent on the nature and extent of the engagement or involvement required of the particular type of deviant. There is pronounced subcultural development in the cases of homosexuality and drug addiction but none in the case of abortion. (Quite simply, in getting what she is looking for, the woman who has had an abortion has no need for frequent or continuing contact with other abortion-seekers.) Partly, it would seem, the development of a subculture has something to

[2] I am grateful to David Matza for suggesting this point and the general relevance of the black market example.

do with the continuing nature of the deviant behavior. Generally speaking, abortion is a discrete act, which one can easily bracket in time and space. This explanation is too simple, however, for the physician-addict is indeed continuously addicted yet he does not display subcultural involvement. It is not then merely the continuing nature of the basic deviant act that establishes the basis for a subculture but, again, the *need for continuous contact with other like individuals in order for the basic deviant acts to be carried out.* (There are, of course, psychological considerations which—as noted in the specific studies—may well exert some pressure on deviants to come together, even in the absence of practical need.) This assertion still leaves open the question of how and to what extent legal repression affects such need. . . . Perhaps the best example is drug addiction, where it seems clear that the curbing of legitimate supplies tremendously increases the addict's practical need for involvement with other addicts. The role of law in stimulating the development of deviant subculture is less clear in the case of homosexuality. It is interesting to speculate, for example, that the homosexual

subculture would be appreciably weaker if all confirmed homosexuals were free to embark on homosexual marriages without fear of legal interference. . . . It is extremely difficult, in trying to answer such questions, to analyze the effects of legal sanctions apart from the influence of the concurrently existing general social disapproval.

It should be clear from this discussion that deviant self-images and involvement in deviant subcultures are interrelated phenomena. Involvement in such a subculture, however, is not an absolute prerequisite to the development of a deviant self-concept. The physician-addict, for example, may well have a consciousness of his continuing deviance and experience great uneasiness about it, even if he has not become generally alienated and totally self-condemning. Likewise, engagement in deviant or criminal behavior may have a pronounced impact on one's self-concept even when the individual is not involved in continuous behavior patterns that imply taking on a set and deviant role. The guilt feelings of the aborted woman serve to illustrate such possibilities.

The Nature of Delinquent Commitment *

DAVID MATZA

. . . A distinctive feature of the subculture of delinquency is that its beliefs are imbedded in action. This is partially true of all traditions but never as much so as in delinquency. We speak of the delinquent code as if it existed somewhere clearly displayed. There are such patent codes in modern society. Their hallmark is that they are written. The code of delinquency is relatively latent. It is not

* Reprinted from *Delinquency and Drift* by David Matza (New York: John Wiley, 1964), pp. 51–59, 62–64, by permission of the author and publisher.

written, except by sociologists, nor is it even well verbalized. Delinquency is well characterized as a relatively inarticulate oral tradition. Its precepts are neither codified nor formally transmitted. Rather, they are inferred from action which obviously includes speech. An ideology of delinquency in the sense of a coherent viewpoint is implicit in delinquent action, but this ideology is not known to delinquents. They are not conscious of an ideology because they have not bothered to work it out. Thus, they infer ideology from each other. This is the primary relevance of the situation of company. It is that context in which the subculture of delinquency is mutually inferred. Mutual inference is accomplished through concrete verbal directives, hints, sentiments, gestures, and activities. But as long as the subculture is inferred, it is not taught in the usual sense of the term. Instead, it is cued.[1] Each member of the company infers the subculture from the cues of others. The company is in a state of acute mutual dependence since there is no coherent ideology which may be consulted. There are only specific and concrete slogans. But there is no explicit general theory.

The mutual inference is a delinquent subculture. Each member believes that others are committed to their delinquencies. But what about each member, what does he believe of himself? Has he not revealed in a variety of other situations that he is not so committed? Possibly, he is transformed in the situation of company to a committed delinquent by dint of the cues he has received from others. Possibly, however, each member believes himself to be an exception in the company of committed delinquents. The intricate system of cues may be miscues. Since the subculture must be constructed

from the situation of company, it may be misconstructed. But is this not implausible? All that would be necessary to straighten out the mess would be a discussion. The company consists of friends, and surely if delinquency is public, attitudes toward it could similarly become part of the common knowledge. But that does not necessarily follow. In every public, there is the realm of privacy. There are things that are not openly discussed, and thus do not become part of the common knowledge. Frequently, the basis of privacy is *status anxiety*.[2] As such, it may preface a system of shared misunderstanding.

Status anxiety is not likely to attain publicity. Its distinctive feature is that the dissipation of anxiety may occur only through reassurance from those parties whose perceived rebuff initiated anxiety. The anxiety is about status, about how one *stands* within a specific or general company. A person suffering such anxiety may either put the question—how do I stand with you?—or, anticipating rebuff, he may indefinitely postpone it, in which case the anxiety is never dissipated, but instead is expressed in one way or another. Why does the delinquent suffer status anxiety, of what sort, and why does he not put the question?

The situation of delinquent company elicits two related anxieties. One reason for both may be found in an innocent pastime—sounding. Sounding is a daily and almost incessant activity of the delinquent company. But because of its mundane and legal quality, its effects have remained unconsidered. Sounding reflects the delinquent's status anxieties, and it aggravates them by minimizing the likelihood that they will be publicized and thus dissipated.

Sounding . . . is a probing of one's

---

[1] Albert K. Cohen, *Delinquent Boys*, New York: Free Press, 1955, pp. 59–62.
[2] For a more extensive use of a conception of status anxiety with respect to politics, see the essays in Daniel Bell, *The New American Right*, New York: Criterion, 1955.

depth, taking the form of insult. One's depth is never definitively certified. It is sounded almost daily. One's depth is probed along a number of dimensions, but two loom most important. Most sounding is a probing of one's manliness and one's membership. Are you really a man, or just a kid? Are you really one of us, or just faking it? Thus, each delinquent in the situation of company suffers generally from masculinity anxiety and specifically from membership anxiety. He can hardly avoid these anxieties. He is sounded daily by a jury of peers. Note, there is initially nothing different about the substance of delinquent anxiety. Most boys suffer some degree of masculinity and membership anxiety. But sounding which may or may not reflect greater initial anxiety eventuates in either case in an increase in the level of anxiety. Note, also, that the consequence of masculinity and membership anxiety is not delinquency, but only the prevention of publicity regarding the evaluation of delinquent acts. The function of anxiety is the limitation of discussion and common knowledge. Thus, it is a key fact in the emergence of the possibility of mutual misconception culminating in a system of shared misunderstanding. Each thinks others are committed to delinquency.

Why are the questions of masculinity and membership not put? And assuming my answer to be plausible, why does it follow that the question of delinquency is not put? The questions of membership and masculinity are not put because given the history of sounding one can anticipate the following kinds of responses: "Do I really like you? Yea, come here and suck and I'll show you how much I like you." "Are you really a man? Well, I don't know, man; sometimes I think you a kid and sometimes you a fag." The anticipation of these sorts of response make good sense since one excellent way of tem-

porarily alleviating one's own anxiety is the invidious derogation of others. Sounding is both a source of anxiety and a vehicle by which it may be temporarily alleviated.

The question of evaluation of delinquency is not put because it is almost immediately translated into a question of masculinity or membership. "Do I think that stealing a car is a good thing? Man, you a fag or something? Ain't you one of the boys?" The serious discussion of sentiments regarding delinquency is prevented by frivolous replies whose motive is a demonstration of depth and thus a suggestion that a formal sounding is unnecessary. Thus, the delinquent in the situation of company *does not consider* his misdeeds. Instead, he infers the assessments of others from barbed remarks whose basic motive is not an exposition of the subculture but an alleviation of status anxiety. Whatever the motive, however, the function of such remarks is to mislead the delinquent into believing that his subculture is committed to delinquency.

Is the delinquent forever trapped in this comedy of errors? I think not. Moreover, I believe that the ways out may be taken as partial confirmation of what surely seems a strange and implausible hypothesis. . . . The majority of delinquents do not become adult criminals. Among the manifold and complex reasons for the drift out of delinquency is one that is immediately pertinent. The serious evaluation of delinquency does attain publicity but not in the situations of company thus far described. There are two situations of company, one crescive and mundane, the other contrived and esoteric in which the public evaluation of delinquency may occur. Publicity and its implicit potential for correcting possible misconceptions and misunderstandings is commonly a preface to the drift out of delinquency.

The occasion for crescive and mundane

publicity is friendship ideally involving two buddies. Why two? Sounding is a public display of feud. Since the couple is friendly they are not given to feuding except for appearance sake. When they are alone there is no wider company before whom to perform. Public evaluation of delinquency is possible in the situation of isolated couples. Though possible, it is not probable until the anxieties which soundings reflect as well as aggravate subside.

Masculinity anxiety is somewhat reduced when someone becomes a man rather than being a mere aspirant. Boys are less driven to prove manhood unconventionally through deeds or misdeeds when with the passing of time they may effortlessly exhibit the conventional signposts of manhood—physical appearance, the completion of school, job, marriage, and perhaps even children. Adulthood may not in all social circles definitively prove manhood, but it is always good *prima facie* evidence. In a revealing reversal, the incumbent of manhood may exempt himself from the demand to engage in delinquencies emanating from mere aspirants by condescendingly observing that it is, after all, kid stuff. This applies not only to rumbling but also to many forms of theft.

The reduction of membership anxiety is coincident with that of masculinity anxiety. The approach of adulthood is marked by the addition of new affiliations. One is less anxious about membership in the company of peers because there are new alternative affiliations. There were always alternatives but the new ones are more tenable since they are adult. They cannot be slandered as kid stuff and thus dismissed. Work, marriage, and other conventional adult statuses may be considered stupid or "square" but they

are obviously not kid stuff. To that extent they invite affiliation. Their very existence serves to reduce the membership anxiety inherent in the subculture of juvenile delinquency.

Thus, the approach of adulthood converts the possibility of public evaluation of delinquency to a probability. In the majority of cases, pairs of delinquents discover one after the other that they had shared misunderstandings. They had not really been committed to delinquency— it was fun and each thought that others demanded it, but *they* had never really believed in it.[3] However, this does not always happen. A very small proportion may discover that they are in fact committed to their misdeeds. These *decide* to be criminals. A larger proportion never publicly evaluate delinquency and continue through adult life guided by their misconception of the subculture deriving from the system of shared misunderstandings. Each is privately uncommitted but publicly a receiver and transmitter of miscues suggesting commitment. Why does this group maintain its pluralistic ignorance?

There are many contingencies, but the pertinent factors are inherent in the conditions of publicity already described. They are merely the reverse side of the conditions converting the possibility of publicity to a probability: the frequency and intensity of the coupled relationship and the level of status anxiety. It is not the fact of coupling that is crucial but what can be said about delinquency. Everyone or almost everyone in the subculture of delinquency has a close buddy at one time or another. However, friendship varies according to intimacy and frequency. Thus, disliked adherents who less frequently enter into close coupled relationships are less likely than others

---

[3] The couple is the ideal situation of publicity and discovery of misconception, but slightly larger cliques may also undergo this process.

to discover their misconception regarding the subculture of delinquency. But even if one is liked and thus involved in a series of close coupled relationships, the level of status anxiety sets limits on what may be discussed. Normally, the level of both status anxieties is reduced with the approach of adulthood. Sometimes, however, the membership anxiety remains high because the additional affiliations ordinarily inherent in adulthood do not occur. For a variety of reasons some members do not join a woman in marriage; others, and frequently the same members, do not join the labor force. Thus, the membership anxiety persists.

What of masculinity anxiety? Did I not suggest that the approach of adulthood is *prima facie* evidence of masculinity? Ordinarily, this is so but occasionally an additional and weighty piece of evidence may offset whatever reassurance of manhood one may find in the approach of adulthood. Often, the dwindling remnants of the old gang affiliate with younger cohorts. Obviously, this is quite functional in the transmission of the subculture. But what of its effect on the bearded adolescent? The increment of assurance painfully gained through the slow passage of years is cruelly offset by the humiliation of hanging around with mere kids. The level of masculinity anxiety persists or is heightened.[4]

Thus, the persistence of misconceptions ideally depends on the interrelated circumstances of superficial friendship, abstinence from the affiliations of work and marriage, and a chronologic descent into the still densely populated cohorts of the subculture of delinquency. Those who never discover their misconception become criminals, but they never decide to do so. They simply continue the drift into adulthood.

The occasion for contrived and esoteric publicity is commonly called group therapy but more accurately termed guided group interaction.[5] Public evaluation of delinquency may occur in guided group interaction, either in a street or institutional setting. Guided group interaction is pertinent because it may help confirm the initially implausible thesis of shared misunderstandings. The limited success of this technique may derive from the discovery of misconception during the many hours of public discussion. Given this interpretation, it is not insight into self that is the critical contribution of guided group interaction; rather, the discovery of the outlook of others.

The two settings of guided group interaction have offsetting advantages and disadvantages that set limits on its effectiveness. In the institutional setting, two possible ways of interpreting the discovery that others share one's private outlook may interfere with applying the knowledge gained. The participant may feel that his companions in therapy are simply responding in tactical fashion to the situation of incarceration. According to reports on guided group interaction, this feeling is dispelled in the initial stages of the process. These reports are credible if we assume the initially implausible assertion that delinquents are involved in a system of shared misunderstanding in which commitment to delinquency is a common misunderstanding. The reports on the dissipation of doubt are less credi-

---

[4] Other patterns of accommodating to declining gang membership are well described in Richard Cloward and Lloyd Ohlin, *Delinquency and Opportunity,* New York: Free Press, 1960.

[5] See, for instance, Lloyd McCorkle, Albert Elias, and F. Lovell Bixby, *The Highfield Story,* New York: Holt, 1958; and Lamar T. Empey and Jerome Rabow, "The Provo Experiment in Delinquency Rehabilitation," *American Sociological Review,* October 1961, pp. 679–695.

ble, perhaps incredible, if we assume the initially plausible assertion that delinquents are committed to their misdeeds. Being more gullible about reported observations than speculative theory, but also for self-serving reasons, I prefer to assume that the reports on the dissipation of doubt are credible.

But even if the delinquent surrenders the belief that the outlook on delinquency expressed by institutional companions is a tactical response to the situation of incarceration, he is still left with the possibility that his civilian peers are different. This is the fundamental limitation of guided group interaction in an institutional setting.[6] Unless the delinquent assumes the unity of subcultural delinquency—the essential similarity of delinquents throughout a large territory—he may not easily apply his institutional discovery to mates in civil society. He may assume the unity of subcultural delinquency, but that is a risky and not entirely warranted choice. The delinquent is not a trained theorist and the generalization implicit in such a notion may elude him. Moreover, an assumption of the unity of subcultural delinquency flies in the face of the well-known enmities that abound in his world. True, he is confused on the term unity and takes it to mean cooperation rather than like-mindedness. But such equivocation is the stuff of social misconception. Finally, he may be unwilling to hazard the application of his discovery when he returns to his civilian mates. Even if the unity of subcultural delinquency becomes explicit through guidance or intuition, it is, after all, just a theory. The delinquent is surely capable of that observation. He may not be willing to risk his status as man and member to test so undocumented a notion. Thus, the guided group interaction of institutional setting is fundamentally limited in the transfer of discoveries to civilian life.

Guided group interaction, less formal to be sure, may also occur on a street setting. Here, too, the public evaluation of delinquency is not the focused aim of gang work. Here, too, effort is dissipated in a hundred directions. But just as in the institutional setting, public evaluation of delinquency is an almost inevitable by-product of the gang worker's larger enterprise.

The limitations inherent in the street setting are just the reverse of those in the institution. On the street, the limitation derives from the fact that this is *his* company of peers. The obstacle to the public evaluation of delinquency and the subsequent discovery of misconception—status anxiety regarding masculinity and membership—are all here despite the intervention of the street worker. It is the relative absence of masculinity but especially membership anxiety that makes the discovery of misconception easy and rapid in the institutional setting, but also helps account for the frequently premature prognosis of reformation. The situation of incarceration is not simply an extension of the situation of authentic company. Minimal masculinity is demonstrated but one may easily claim the desire to do quick time. Membership anxiety is even less warranted since this is not his company of peers. The pace and ease of attaining public evaluation and the discovery of previously shared misunderstandings is slow and uncertain in the street setting. More of one's investments are here. That is the fundamental disadvantage of the street setting. Its advantage is obvious. Accomplishment of publicity, discovery, and the drift out of delinquency when attained are of more durable consequence than in the institutional setting.

[6] A highly local institution which more or less coincides with the civilian street setting is limited because it quickly confronts the fundamental restriction of the street setting.

In summary, my thesis is that even in the situation of company, commitment to delinquency is a misconception—first of delinquents and later of the sociologists who study them. Instead, there is a system of shared misunderstandings, based on miscues, which leads delinquents to believe that all others situated in their company are committed to their misdeeds. Thus, the situation of company perhaps does not result in a posture toward delinquency radically different from that revealed in the situations previously discussed. If in all situations the delinquent reveals a basic ambivalence toward his behavior, a new conception of his subculture may be warranted. . . .

The continued existence of the subculture is facilitated and perhaps even dependent on support and reinforcement from conventional sources. The subculture is buttressed by beliefs that flourish in influential sectors of the normative order. These views, which include the professional ideology of criminology, psychiatry, and social work, an emergent ideology of leisure, a celebration of the primitive in Bohemia and anthropology, the cult of cowboy masculinity in the mass media, and the persistence of provincial sentiments in insulated sections of metropolis, all reflect at critical points precepts in the subculture of delinquency. But we cannot point to these obscure but consequential similarities unless we first discontinue the current sociological practice of confusing a richly pluralistic American normative system with a simple puritanism. Puritanism or its routinized equivalent, middle-class morality, is one tradition among many in American life. No one has documented its continued dominance. *Les bourgeoises* have undergone such steady and militant attack since an allegedly grubby ascent to power that the persistence of their moral dominance would be quite surprising, except perhaps in the suburbs of Boston.

The morality of the historical bourgeoisie has undergone drastic modification. Moreover, it has encountered moral rivals in the spirit of modern corporate enterprise, the influence of intellectuals in an increasingly educated society, and in the rise of specialized professions of welfare. Moreover, its ancient rival, the sentiments of feudal provincialism, was never more than partially vanquished. Unless the proliferation of important moral traditions in a pluralistic America is understood and granted, the sustenance of the subculture of delinquency by conventional beliefs is implausible. To be consequential, the new traditions and the very old must be in the moral atmosphere of society. They need not reach the adherents of subcultural delinquency in pure and sophisticated form to support and reinforce it. On the contrary, the function of reinforcement and sustenance is best served if these beliefs are grossly vulgarized. But to be consequential, they must in some form be heard by members of the subculture.

The subculture of delinquency receives cultural support from conventional traditions. Moreover, it receives considerable social and personal reinforcement if we conceive of support as a range rather than an attribute. Thus, an apparently tenuous and precarious subculture delicately balanced between crime and convention has an additional source of stability. It is itself a subterranean tradition in American life.

A subterranean tradition is characterized by contemporary adherents linked to the past through local legacies and to the wider social structure by a range of support. It is an ideal case of an integrated subculture. Thus, it is an advancing of the fundamental sociological notion of the *relation* between society and its deviants.

The major contribution of sociology to the understanding of deviance has consisted of two fundamental insights. First, persistent deviance typically is not a solitary enterprise; rather, it best flourishes when it receives group support. Second, deviance typically is not an individual or group innovation; rather, it has a history in particular locales. Thus, according to the sociological view, the deviant is linked to society in minimal form through companies of deviants and through local traditions. When these minimal links appear we speak of a deviant subculture. The view of sociology is extended if additionally we explore the relations between that subculture and the wider cultural system. That extension is the essence of the idea of subterranean analysis. Such analysis requires the exploration of *connections* between localized deviant traditions and the variety of traditions in conventional society. Moreover, subterranean analysis implies an ongoing dialectic among a variety of conventional and deviant viewpoints, and that in the process of exchange each of the traditions is simultaneously stabilized and modified. The paradox of simultaneous stability and modification is the fundamental meaning of cultural pluralism.

Subterranean tradition may be defined by specification of key points along the range of support. It is deviant, which is to say that it is publicly denounced by authorized spokesmen. However, the tradition is viewed with ambivalence in the privacy of contemplation and in intimate publics by most conventional citizens. The spirit and substance of subterranean traditions are familiar and within limits tolerated by broad segments of the adult population. Adolescent immersion in the delinquent tradition, or flirtation with it, is a suitable subject of nostalgic reminiscence and recreation. So popular is the pastime that surviving puritans are sometimes forced to either falsify a biography or ludicrously confuse their innocent naughtiness with the precepts of a subculture which under proper conditions countenances murder. Among youth, conventional versions of subterranean traditions—reasonable facsimiles stripped of the more intolerable aspects —are experienced by broad segments of the population. Teenage culture consists of the frivolous and mindless pursuit of fun and thrill. The experiences encountered in this pursuit ordinarily include many of the juvenile status offenses. Its spirit is a modification of that implicit in the subculture of delinquency. Thus, teenage culture may be conceived as a conventional version, a reasonable facsimile, of subcultural delinquency. Finally, of course, subterranean traditions have bands of adherents. These adherents are the bona fide members of the subculture. They are the carriers of its theory and the perpetrators of its practice.

The Delinquent Gang as a Near-Group *

LEWIS YABLONSKY

This paper is based on four years of research and direct work with some thirty delinquent gangs in New York City. During this period I directed a crime prevention program on the upper West Side of Manhattan for Morningside Heights, Inc., a community social agency sponsored by fourteen major institutions including Columbia University, Barnard, Teacher's College, Union Theological Seminary, and Riverside Church.

Approaches used in data gathering included field study methods, participant observation, role-playing, group interaction analysis, and sociometry. The data were obtained through close daily interaction with gang boys over the four-year period during which I was the director of the project.

Although data were obtained on 30 gangs, the study focused on two, the Balkans and the Egyptian Kings. It was the latter which committed the brutal killing of a polio victim, Michael Farmer, in an upper west side park of New York City. The trial lasted over three months and received nation-wide attention. These two groups were intensively interviewed and contributed heavily to the formulation of a theory of near-groups. In addition to the analysis of the gang's structure, a number of delinquent gang war events produced vital case material.

There is a paucity of available theory based on empirical evidence about the structure of delinquent gangs. Two landmarks in the field are Thrasher's *The Gang* and Whyte's *Street Corner Society*. Some recent publications and controversy focus on the emergence of gangs and their function for gang members. Professor Cohen deals with gangs as sub-cultures organized by working-class boys as a reaction to middle-class values (1). In a recent publication Bloch and Niederhoffer discuss gangs as organizations designed to satisfy the adolescent's striving for the attainment of adult status (2).

Although partial group structuring has been extensively discussed in sociological literature on "groups," "crowds," and "mobs," my gang research revealed that these collectivity constructs did not seem to adequately describe and properly abstract the underlying structural characteristics of the delinquent gang. Consequently, I have attempted here to construct a formulation which would draw together various described social dimensions of the gang under one conceptual scheme. I call this formulation Near-Group Theory.

Near-Group Theory

One way of viewing human collectivities is on a continuum of organization characteristics. At one extreme, we have a highly organized, cohesive, functioning collection of individuals as members of a sociological group. At the other extreme, we have a mob of individuals characterized by anonymity, disturbed leadership, motivated by emotion, and

* Reprinted from *Social Problems,* Vol. 7, No. 2 (Fall, 1959), pp. 108–17, by permission of the author and *Social Problems.* This is a revised version of a paper delivered at The Eastern Sociological Meetings in New York City, April 11, 1959. [A larger version of the theory of near-groups and gang data presented in this paper can be found in *The Violent Gang,* Baltimore, Md.: Penguin Books, 1966.]

in some cases representing a destructive collectivity within the inclusive social system. When these structures are observed in extreme, their form is apparent to the observer. However, in viewing these social structures on a continuum, those formations which tend to be neither quite a cohesive integrated group nor a disturbed mal-functioning mob or crowd are often distorted by observers in one or the other direction.

A central thesis of this paper is that mid-way on the group-mob continuum are collectivities which are neither groups nor mobs. These are structures prevalent enough in a social system to command attention in their own right as constructs for sociological analysis. Near-groups are characterized by some of the following factors: (1) diffuse role definition, (2) limited cohesion, (3) impermanence, (4) minimal consensus of norms, (5) shifting membership, (6) disturbed leadership, and (7) limited definition of membership expectations. These factors characterize the near-group's "normal" structure.

True groups may manifest near-group structure under stress, in transition, or when temporarily disorganized; however, at these times they are moving toward or away from their normative, permanent structure. The near-group manifests its homeostasis in accord with the factors indicated. It never fully becomes a *group* or a *mob*.

The Gang as a Near-Group Pattern

Some recent sociological theory and discourse on gangs suffers from distortions of gang structure to fit a group rather than a near-group conception. Most gang theorizing begins with an automatic assumption that gangs are defined sociological groups. Many of these

misconceived theories about gangs in sociological treatises are derived from the popular and traditional image of gangs held by the general public as reported in the press, rather than as based upon empirical scientific investigation. The following case material reveals the disparities between popular reports of gang war behavior and their organization as revealed by more systematic study.

The official report of a gang fight, which made headlines in New York papers as the biggest in the city's history, detailed a gang war between six gangs over a territorial dispute.[1] The police, social workers, the press, and the public accepted a defined version of groups meeting in battle over territory. Research into this gang war incident, utilizing a near-group concept of gangs, indicates another picture of the situation.

N. Y. Daily News
NIP 200—PUNK FIGHT NEAR COLUMBIA CAMPUS
by Grover Ryder and Jack Smee
A flying squad of 25 cops, alerted by a civilian's tip, broke up the makings of one of the biggest gang rumbles in the city's turbulent teen history last night at the edge of Columbia University campus on Morningside Heights.

N. Y. Herald Tribune
POLICE SEIZE 38, AVERT GANG BATTLE—RIVERSIDE PARK RULE WAS GOAL
Police broke up what they said might have been "a very serious" battle between two juvenile factions last night as they intercepted thirty-eight youths.

N. Y. Times
GANG WAR OVER PARK BROKEN BY POLICE
The West Side police broke up an impending gang fight near Columbia University last night as 200 teen-agers were massing for battle over exclusive rights to the use of Riverside Park.

[1] New York newspaper headlines—June 11, 1955.

N. Y. Journal-American
6-GANG BATTLE FOR PARK AVERTED NEAR GRANT'S TOMB
COPS PATROL TROUBLE SPOT

Police reinforcements today patrolled Morningside Heights to prevent a teen-aged gang war for "control" of Riverside Park.

World-Telegram and Sun
HOODLUM WAR AVERTED AS COPS ACT FAST
38 to 200 Seized near Columbia
by Richard Graf

Fast police action averted what threatened to be one of the biggest street gang fights in the city's history as some 200 hoodlums massed last night on the upper West Side to battle over "exclusive rights" to Riverside Park.

Depth interviews with 40 gang boys, most of whom had been arrested at the scene of the gang fight, revealed a variety of reasons for attendance at the battle. There were also varied perceptions of the event and the gangs involved reported simply in the press as "gangs battling over territory." Some of the following recurring themes were revealed in the gang boys' responses.

Estimates of number of gang boys present varied from 80 to 5,000.

Gang boys interviewed explained their presence at the "battle" as follows:

I didn't have anything to do that night and wanted to see what was going to happen.

Those guys called me a Spic and I was going to get even. [He made this comment even though the "rival" gangs were mostly Puerto Ricans.]

They always picked on us. [The "they" is usually a vague reference.]

I always like a fight; it keeps up my rep.

My father threw me out of the house; I wanted to get somebody and heard about the fight.

The youth who was responsible for "calling on" the gang war—the reputed Balkan Gang leader—presented this version of the event:

That night I was out walkin' my dog about 7:30. Then I saw all these guys coming from different directions. I couldn't figure out what was happening. Then I saw some of the guys I know and I remembered we had called it on for that night.

I never really figured the Politicians [a supposed "brother Gang" he had called] would show.

Another boy added another dimension to "gang war organization":

How did we get our name? Well, when we were in the police station, the cops kept askin' us who we were. Jay was studying history in school—so he said how about The Balkans. Let's call ourselves Balkans. So we told the cops—we're the Balkans—and that was it.

Extensive data revealed this was not a case of two organized groups meeting in battle. The press, public, police, social workers, and others projected group conceptions onto a near-group activity. Most of the youths at the scene of the gang war were, in fact, participating in a kind of mob action. Most had no real concept of belonging to any gang or group; however, they were interested in a situation which might be exciting and possibly a channel for expressing some of their aggressions and hostilities. Although it was not necessarily a defined war, the possibilities of a stabbing or even a killing were high—with a few hundred disturbed and fearful youths milling around in the undefined situation. The gang war was not a social situation of two structured teen-aged armies meeting on a battlefield to act out a defined situation; it was a case of two near-groups in action.

Another boy's participation in this gang war further reveals its structure. The evening of the fight he had nothing to do, heard about this event and decided that he would wander up to see what was going to happen. On his way to the scene of the rumored gang fight he thought it might be a good idea to invite a few friends "just to be on the safe side." This swelled the final number of youths arriving at the scene of the gang fight, since other boys did the same. He denied (and I had no reason to disbelieve him) belonging to either of the gangs and the same applied to his friends. He was arrested at the scene of "battle" for disorderly conduct and weapon-carrying.

I asked him why he had carried a knife and a zip gun on his person when he went to the gang fight if he did not belong to either of the reputed gangs and intended to be merely a "peaceful observer." His response: "Man, I'm not going to a rumble without packin'." The boy took along weapons for self-defense in the event he was attacked. The possibilities of his being attacked in an hysterical situation involving hundreds of youths who had no clear idea of what they were doing at the scene of a gang fight was, of course, great. Therefore, he was correct (within his social framework) in taking along a weapon for self-protection.

These characteristic responses to the situation when multiplied by the numbers of others present characterizes the problem. What may be a confused situation involving many aggressive youths (belonging to near-groups) is often defined as a case of two highly mechanized and organized gang groups battling each other with definition to their activities.

In another "gang war case" which made headlines, a psychotic youth acted out his syndrome by stabbing another youth. When arrested and questioned about committing the offense, the youth stated that he was a member of a gang

carrying out retaliation against another gang, which was out to get him. He attributed his assault to gang affiliation.

The psychotic youth used the malleable near-group, the gang, *as his psychotic syndrome.* Napoleon, God, Christ, and other psychotic syndromes, so popular over the years, may have been replaced on city streets by gang membership. Not only is it a convenient syndrome, but some disturbed youths find their behavior as rational, accepted, and even aggrandized by many representatives of society. Officials such as police officers and social workers, in their interpretation of the incident, often amplify this individual behavior by a youth into a group gang war condition because it is a seemingly more logical explanation of a senseless act.

In the case of the Balkans, the societal response of viewing them as a group rather than a near-group solidified their structure. After the incident, as one leader stated it, "lots more kids wanted to join."

Another gang war event further reveals the near-group structure of the gang. On the night of July 30, 1957, a polio victim named Michael Farmer was beaten and stabbed to death by a gang varyingly known as the Egyptian Kings and the Dragons. The boys who participated in this homicide came from the upper West Side of Manhattan. I had contact with many of these boys prior to the event and was known to others through the community program I directed. Because of this prior relationship the boys cooperated and responded openly when I interviewed them in the institutions where they were being held in custody.[2]

Responses to my interviews indicated

---

[2] The research and interviewing at this time was combined with my role as consultant to the Columbia Broadcasting System. I assisted in the production of a gang war documentary narrated by Edward R. Murrow, entitled "Who Killed Michael Farmer?" The documentary tells the story of the killing through the actual voices of the boys who committed the act.

the near-group nature of the gang. Some of the pertinent responses which reveal this characteristic of the Egyptian King gang structure are somewhat demonstrated by the following comments made by five of the participants in the killing. (These are representative comments selected from over ten hours of recorded interviews.)

I was walking uptown with a couple of friends and we ran into Magician [one of the Egyptian King gang leaders] and them there. They asked us if we wanted to go to a fight, and we said yes. When he asked me if I wanted to go to a fight, I couldn't say no. I mean, I could say no, but for old time's sake, I said yes.

Everyone was pushin' and I pulled out my knife. I saw this face—I never seen it before, so I stabbed it.

He was laying on the ground lookin' up at us. Everyone was kicking, punching, stabbing. I kicked him on the jaw or someplace; then I kicked him in the stomach. That was the least I could do was kick 'im.

They have guys watching you and if you don't stab or hit somebody, they get you later. I hit him over the head with a bat. [Gang youths are unable to articulate specific individuals of the vague "they" who watch over them.]

I don't know how many guys are in the gang. They tell me maybe a hundred or a thousand. I don't know them all. [Each boy interviewed had a different image of the gang.]

These comments and others revealed the gang youths' somewhat different perceptions and rationale of gang war activity. There is a limited consensus of participants as to the nature of gang war situations because the gang structure— the collectivity which defines gang war behavior—is amorphous, diffuse, and malleable.

Despite the fact of gang phenomena taking a diffuse form, theoreticians, social workers, the police, the press, and the public autistically distort gangs and gang behavior toward a gestalt of clarity. The rigid frame of perceiving gangs as groups should shift to the fact of gangs as near-groups. This basic redefinition is necessary if progress is to be made in sociological diagnosis as a foundation for delinquent gang prevention and correction.

The Detached Gang Worker

The detached-worker approach to dealing with gangs on the action level is increasingly employed in large cities and urban areas throughout the country. Simply stated, a professional, usually a social worker, contacts a gang in their milieu on the street corner and attempts to redirect their delinquent patterns into constructive behavior.

Because of the absence of an adequate perceptual framework, such as the near-group concept, detached gang workers deal with gang collectivities as if they were organized like other groups and social organizations. The following principle stated in a New York City Youth Board manual on the detached gang worker approach reveals this point of view:

Participation in a street gang or club, like participation in any natural group, is a part of the growing-up process of adolescence. Such primary group associations possess potentialities for positive growth and development. Through such a group, the individual can gain security and develop positive ways of living with other individuals. Within the structure of his group the individual can develop such characteristics as loyalty, leadership, and community responsibility. . . .

This basic misconception not only produces inaccurate reports and theories about gang structure but causes ineffectual work with gangs on the action level. This problem of projecting group structure onto gangs may be further illuminated by a cursory examination of detached gang-worker projects.

Approaching the gang as a group, when it is not, tends to project onto it a structure which formerly did not exist. The gang worker's usual set of notions about gangs as groups includes some of the following distortions: (1) the gang has a measurable number of members, (2) membership is defined, (3) the role of members is specified, (4) there is a consensus of understood gang norms among gang members, and (5) gang leadership is clear and entails a flow of authority and direction of action.

These expectations often result in a group-fulfilling prophecy. A group may form as a consequence of the gang worker's view. In one case a gang worker approached two reputed gang leaders and told them he would have a bus to take their gang on a trip to the country. This gang had limited organization; however, by travel-time there were 32 gang members ready to go on the trip. The near-group became more organized as a result of the gang worker's misconception.

This gang from a near-group point of view was in reality comprised of a few disturbed youths with rich delusional systems who had need to view themselves as leaders controlling hordes of other gang boys in their fantasy. Other youths reinforce this ill-defined collectivity for a variety of personal reasons and needs. The gang, in fact, had a shifting membership, no clarity as to what membership entailed, and individualized member images of gang size and function.

The detached worker, as an agent of the formal social system, may thus move in on a gang and give a formerly amorphous collectivity structure and purpose through the projection of group structure onto a near-group.

Near-Group Structure

Research into the structure of 30 groups revealed three characteristic levels of membership organization. In the center of the gang, on the first level, are the most psychologically disturbed members—the leaders. It is these youths who require and need the gang most of all. This core of disturbed youths provides the gang's most cohesive force. In a gang of some 30 boys there may be five or six who are central or core members because they desperately need the gang in order to deal with their personal problems of inadequacy. These are youths always working to keep the gang together and in action, always drafting, plotting, and talking gang warfare. They are the center of the near-group activity.

At a second level of near-group organization in the gang, we have youths who claim affiliation to the gang but only participate in it according to their emotional needs at given times. For example, one of the Egyptian Kings reported that if his father had not given him a "bad time" and kicked him out of the house the night of the homicide, he would not have gone to the corner and become involved in the Michael Farmer killing. This second-level gang member's participation in the gang killing was a function of his disturbance on that particular evening. This temporal gang need is a usual occurrence.

At a third level of gang participation, we have peripheral members who will join in with gang activity on occasion, although they seldom identify themselves as members of the gang at times. This type of gang member is illustrated by the youth who went along with the Egyptian Kings on the night of the Farmer killing, as he put it, "for old time's sake." He just happened to be around on that particular evening and went along due to a situational condition. He never really "belonged" to the gang nor was he defined by himself or others as a gang member.

The size of gangs is determined in great measure by the emotional needs of its members at any given point. It is not a measure of actual and live membership. Many of the members exist only on the thought level. In the gang, if the boys feel particularly hemmed in (for paranoid reasons), they will expand the number of their near-group. On the other hand, at other times when they feel secure, the gang's size is reduced to include only those youths known on a face-to-face basis. The research revealed that, unlike an actual group, no member of a near-group can accurately determine the number of its membership at a particular point in time.

For example, most any university department member will tell you the number of other individuals who comprise the faculty of their department. It is apparent that if there are eight members in a department of psychology, each member will know each other member, his role, and the total number of members of the department. In contrast, in examining the size of gangs or near-group participation, the size increases in almost direct relationship to the lack of membership clarity. That is, the second- and third-level members are modified numerically with greater ease than the central members. Third level members are distorted at times to an almost infinite number.

In one interview, a gang leader distorted the size and affiliations of the gang as his emotional state shifted. In an hour interview, the size of his gang varied from 100 members to 4,000, from five brother gangs or alliances to 60, from about ten square blocks of territorial control to include jurisdiction over the five boroughs of New York City, New Jersey, and part of Philadelphia.

Another characteristic of the gang is its lack of role definition. Gang boys exhibit considerable difficulty and contradiction in their roles in the gang. They may say that the gang is organized for protection and that one role of a gang is to fight. How, when, whom, and for what reason he is to fight are seldom clear. The rights, duties, and obligations associated with the gang member's role in the gang varies from gang boy to gang boy.

One gang boy may define himself as a protector of the younger boys in the neighborhood. Another defines his role in the gang as "We are going to get all those guys who call us Spics." Still other gang boys define their participation in the gang as involuntarily forced upon them, through their being "drafted." Moreover, few gang members maintain a consistent function or role within the gang organization.

Definition of membership is vague and indefinite. A youth will say he belongs one day and will quit the next without necessarily telling any other gang member. I would ask one gang boy who came into my office daily whether he was a Balkan. This was comparable to asking him, "How do you feel today?"

Because of limited social ability to assume rights, duties, and obligations in constructive solidified groups, the gang boy attaches himself to a structure which requires limited social ability and can itself be modified to fit his momentary needs. This malleability factor is characteristic of the near-group membership. As roles are building blocks of a group, diffuse role definitions fit in adequately to the near-group which itself has diverse and diffuse objectives and goals. The near-group, unlike a true group, has norms, roles, functions, cohesion, size, and goals which are shaped by the emotional needs of its members.

Gang Leadership Characteristics

Another aspect of near-groups is the factor of self-appointed leadership, usually of a dictatorial, authoritarian type. In interviewing hundreds of gang members one finds that many of them give themselves some role of leadership. For example, in the Egyptian Kings, approximately five boys defined themselves as "war counsellors." It is equally apparent that, except on specific occasions, no one will argue with this self-defined role. Consequently, leadership in the gang may be assumed by practically any member of the gang if he so determines and emotionally needs the power of being a leader at the time. It is not necessary to have his leadership role ratified by his constituents.

Another aspect of leadership in the gang is the procedure of "drafting" or enlisting new members. In many instances, this pattern of coercion to get another youth to join or belong to the gang becomes an end in itself, rather than a means to an end. In short, the process of inducing, coercing, and threatening violence upon another youth, under the guise of getting him to join, is an important gang leader activity. The gang boy is not truly concerned with acquiring another gang member, since the meaning of membership is vague at best; however, acting the power role of a leader forcing another youth to do something against his will becomes meaningful to the "drafter."

Gang Functions

In most groups some function is performed or believed to be performed. The function which it performs may be a constructive one, as in an industrial organization, a P.T.A. group, or a political party. On the other hand, it may be a socially destructive group, such as a drug syndicate, a group of bookies, or a subversive political party. There is usually a consensus of objectives and goals shared by the membership, and their behavior tends to be essentially organized group action.

The structure of a near-group is such that its functions not only vary greatly and shift considerably from time to time, but its primary function is unclear. The gang may on one occasion be organized to protect the neighborhood; on another occasion, to take over a particular territory; and on still another, it may be organized in response to or for the purpose of racial discrimination.

The function of near-groups, moreover, is not one which is clearly understood, known, and communicated among all of its members. There is no consensus in this near-group of goals, objectives, or functions of the collectivity—much near-group behavior is individualistic and flows from emotional disturbance.

A prime function of the gang is to provide a channel to act out hostility and aggression to satisfy the continuing and momentary emotional needs of its members. The gang is a convenient and malleable structure quickly adaptable to the needs of emotionally disturbed youths, who are unable to fulfill the responsibility and demands required for participation in constructive groups. He belongs to the gang because he lacks the social ability to relate to others and to assume responsibility for the relationship, not because the gang gives him a "feeling of belonging."

Because of the gang youth's limited "social ability," he constructs a social organization which enables him to relate and to function at his limited level of performance. In this structure norms are adjusted so that the gang youth can function and achieve despite his limited ability to relate to others.

An example of this is the function of violence in the near-group of the gang. Violence in the gang is highly valued as a means for the achievement of reputation or "rep." This inversion of societal norms is a means for quick upward social mobility in the gang. He can acquire and maintain a position in the gang through establishing a violent reputation.

The following comments by members of the Egyptian Kings illustrate this point:

If I would of got the knife, I would have stabbed him. That would have gave me more of a build-up. People would have respected me for what I've done and things like that. They would say, "There goes a cold killer."

It makes you feel like a big shot. You know some guys think they're big shots and all that. They think, you know, they got the power to do everything they feel like doing.

They say, like, "I wanna stab a guy," and the other guy says, "Oh, I wouldn't dare to do that." You know, he thinks I'm acting like a big shot. That's the way he feels. He probably thinks in his mind, "Oh, he probably won't do that." Then, when we go to a fight, you know, he finds out what I do.

Momentarily, I started to thinking about it inside: den I have my mind made up I'm not going to be in no gang. Then I go on inside. Something comes up den here come all my friends coming to me. Like I said before, I'm intelligent and so forth. They be coming to me—then they talk to me about what they gonna do. Like, "Man, we'll go out here and kill this guy." I say, "Yeah." They kept on talkin' and talkin'. I said, "Man, I just gotta go with you." Myself, I don't want to go, but when they start talkin' about what they gonna do, I say, "So, he isn't gonna take over my rep. I ain't gonna let him be known more than me." And I go ahead just for selfishness.

The near-group of the gang, with its diffuse and malleable structure, can function as a convenient vehicle for the acting out of varied individual needs and problems. For the gang leader it can be a super-powered organization through which (in his phantasy) he dominates and controls "divisions" of thousands of members. For gang members, unable to achieve in more demanding social organizations, swift and sudden violence is a means for quick upward social mobility and the achievement of a reputation. For less disturbed youths, the gang may function as a convenient temporary escape from the dull and rigid requirements of a difficult and demanding society. These are only some of the functions the near-group of the gang performs for its membership.

Near-Group Theory and Social Problems

The concept of the near-group may be of importance in the analysis of other collectivities which reflect and produce social problems. The analysis of other social structures may reveal similar distortions of their organization. To operate on an assumption that individuals in interaction with each other, around some function, with some shared mutual expectation, in a particular normative system as always being a group formation is to project a degree of distortion onto certain types of collectivities. Groups are social structures at one end of a continuum; mobs are social structures at another end; and at the center are near-groups which have some of the characteristics of both, and yet are characterized by factors not found fully in either.

In summary, these factors may include the following:

1. Individualized role definition to fit momentary needs.
2. Diffuse and differential definitions of membership.
3. Emotion-motivated behavior.

4. A decrease of cohesiveness as one moves from the center of the collectivity to the periphery.
5. Limited responsibility and sociability required for membership and belonging.
6. Self-appointed and disturbed leadership.
7. A limited consensus among participants of the collectivities' functions or goals.
8. A shifting and personalized stratification system.
9. Shifting membership.
10. The inclusion in size of phantasy membership.
11. Limited consensus of normative expectations.
12. Norms in conflict with the inclusive social system's prescriptions.

Although the gang was the primary type of near-group appraised in this analysis, there are perhaps other collectivities whose structure is distorted by autistic observers. Their organization might become clearer if subjected to this conceptual scheme. Specifically, in the area of criminal behavior, these might very well include adult gangs varyingly called the "Mafia," the "National Crime Syndicate," and so-called International Crime Cartels. There are indications that these social organizations are comparable in organization to the delinquent gang. They might fit the near-group category

if closely analyzed in this context, rather than aggrandized and distorted by mass media and even Senate Committees.

Other more institutionalized collectivities might fit the near-group pattern. As a possible example, "the family in transition" may not be in transition at all. The family, as a social institution, may be suffering from near-groupism. Moreover, such standardized escape hatches of alcoholism, psychoses, and addictions may be too prosaic for the sophisticated intellectual to utilize in escape from himself. For him, the creation and perpetuation of near-groups requiring limited responsibility and personal commitment may be a more attractive contemporary form for expressing social and personal pathology. The measure of organization or disorganization of an inclusive social system may possibly be assessed by the prevalence of near-group collectivities in its midst. The delinquent gang may be only one type of near-group in American society.

References

1. COHEN, ALBERT K., *Delinquent Boys* (Glencoe: The Free Press, 1955).
2. BLOCH, HERBERT, and ARTHUR NIEDERHOFFER, *The Gang* (New York: The Philosophical Library, 1958).
3. FURMAN, SLYVAN S., *Reaching the Unreached* (New York: Youth Board, 1952).

GETTING INTO DEVIANT GROUPS

10

A person must gain entry into a deviant subculture, a process that is not automatic. He must learn a stock of beliefs, values, norms, and ways of acting that will guarantee continued participation in the group and, at the same time, provide some of the gratifications for being a deviant. He enters the lifeway by one of several routes. Whether he becomes fully committed to the deviant way of life depends partly on the mode of entry, content, and instruction as well as on the nature of the deviant arts practiced.

In the first reading, Wallace discusses three routes into homelessness. Weinberg examines the manner in which people become nudists and the segmental nature of their involvement. Bryan, in the final paper, shows that the apprenticeship into prostitution stems from the secrecy surrounding the occupation rather than its complexity.

Routes to Skid Row *

SAMUEL E. WALLACE

The process of becoming a skid rower is not easy, rapid, or uniform. There are many pitfalls along the way, and the novice must be on the alert ere the Forces of Respectable Society swoop down and snatch up another hapless victim. It is a complex process whose description depends upon one's point of view. To the non-skid rower, the process appears to involve ever-increasing isolation from the

* Reprinted from Samuel E. Wallace, *Skid Row as a Way of Life* (Totowa, N.J.: Bedminster Press, 1965), pp. 163–72. Copyright © 1965, Bedminster Press Incorporated. Reprinted by permission.

larger society accompanied by ever-increasing deviance from its norms. From the point of view of the skid rower, on the other hand, the process is one of increasing participation in the life of the skid row community, and is accompanied by increasing conformity to its norms. In its totality, the process of becoming a skid rower combines both the push out of respectable society with the pull toward the society of skid row. To understand the final product of this process—the completely acculturated skid rower—the investigator must recognize these dual forces of rejection and attraction within the life history of the individual.

The routes to homelessness must first be examined with respect to the person's initial exposure to skid row. Since no one is born into the skid row way of life, it is critical to ask who was the skid rower before he came to skid row? Where did he come from? Where and how did he first meet up with skid row? In short, where are skid row's recruiting offices and who are those attracted to step inside?

Since many are exposed to skid row but nevertheless return to respectable society, a second critical phase in the process occurs at the point of regular participation in the skid row way of life. After having been exposed to skid row, why does a novice continue to take the next step of participation in this deviant community? The reaction of the larger community can only have been against skid row in all its manifestations and yet these negative sanctions fail to stop the fledgling skid rower's pattern of increasing deviance. Exposure followed by participation are the first two stages in the process of becoming a skid rower.

The third and final stage in the process involves conformity to skid row values and the corresponding rejection of the values of the larger society. Just as exposure is not necessarily followed by participation, neither do all who take part in the skid row way of life become full-fledged members of its community. And to understand the entire process, the investigator must be able to account for those who drop out at one point or another between exposure and acculturation.[1]

Throughout the history of the vagrant-skid row subculture, three distinct types of persons appear to have been recruited into the skid row way of life. By far the majority have been drawn from the ranks of those occupations which by their very nature separated men from their fixed places in established society—migratory workers, lumberjacks, soldiers, seamen—occupational itinerants who followed the crops, the seasons, the wars, or the sea.

A second source of recruitment into the skid row way of life has been the welfare client—those displaced and often dispossessed by the crises of war, depression, and natural disaster; those rendered homeless, jobless, and hungry, those who joined bread and soup lines, who sought refuge in municipal shelters and in skid row missions.

The third source of recruits are the skid row *aficionados*, those whose lives and habits made them seek skid row as a kind of sanctuary. The *aficionados* are the wanderers, the alcoholics, the petty criminals, the fringe members of society at large.

The point of entry for the mobile worker usually takes place on the job. The newcomer to one of the temporary, seasonal, or traveling occupations is al-

[1] Howard Becker's recent publication had a significant influence on my own work, an influence which is most gratefully acknowledged. He terms this type of analysis a sequential model. Howard S. Becker. *Outsiders: Studies in the Sociology of Deviance.* Glencoe: Free Press, 1963. See particularly Chapter 2, "Kinds of Deviance: A Sequential Model."

most certain to meet among his fellow laborers some who are already members in good standing of skid row society, who are neither temporarily or even accidentally unattached and homeless, but chronically and permanently without kin or community. In working, eating, talking, drinking, sleeping, and living with confirmed skid rowers on the job, the newcomer to the occupation is exposed to his first taste of skid row subculture. He learns of skid row attitudes toward the community, the employer, the police, the welfare worker—and he learns of their attitudes toward him. To defend himself against the condemnation he experiences in dealing with the outside community, and to adjust to his companions on the job, he gradually begins to enter the world of the skid rower. He may take up the camaraderie of sharing, of heavy drinking, of casual womanizing, and other behavior patterns characteristic of the subculture. When the season's work is finished, or when his voyage is over, or when he simply quits his job, the newcomer may return home, or move directly onto skid row.

When and if he returns home, he faces all the usual problems created by his absence. He has learned, however, that if he does not like living with father, mother, sister, brother, wife or children, he does not have to stay home. He is no longer necessarily or totally committed to the values of home and family life any more than his family is totally committed to accepting him back in their midst. He is now aware of alternative attitudes and an alternative way of life. There are two worlds, he now knows, although he may for the moment feel—with some truth—that he belongs to neither.

It is at this point, and only at this point, that an unsatisfactory home situation becomes relevant in explaining a man's move to skid row. If before he left home he was at constant odds with

his family, he may be less inclined than ever to "put up with it"—now that he knows another way of life complete with a few friends is open to him. Problems at home plus the weakening of family ties brought about by his absence reinforce his sense of isolation, push him further adrift, and help sever the few remaining roots he has in the world of respectable society. The skid row way of life—a life without care, worry, and responsibility, a life with friends, drink, and plenty of time in which to enjoy them—begins to look better and better.

The welfare client's starting point toward skid row is likely to be more direct. He may, for example, when he applies for relief be sent directly to skid row to be fed, housed, and perhaps even clothed by the very same agencies which cater to the needs of the destitute skid rower. When relief agencies are located in the skid row community, the welfare client can hardly avoid coming into contact with the skid rower and his way of life.

During the Depression this was commonplace. A man separated from wife and family because he could no longer support them, or the single person— young or old—with no resources to fall back on when hard times hit, was cared for by welfare agencies who made little or no distinction between him and any other bum, i.e. skid rower. Modern welfare attitudes, policies, and programs have changed the picture considerably. The temporary loss of a man's role as breadwinner no longer necessarily throws him on bread lines, into municipal shelters, or skid row missions. Home relief, housekeeping and institutional care for the aged, the ill, and the infirm or disabled make it possible for more families to stay together even under conditions of extreme financial stress. And welfare agencies no longer are centered in slum or skid row areas. Destitution, therefore, does not automatically bring the welfare client into contact with skid row as it used to.

Destitution, in any case, has never been in and of itself a sufficient explanation for membership in skid row. When destitution came to the mobile worker, he had already met up with the skid row way of life while on one job or another. He was already an initiate if not a full-fledged member of its society. When destitution created a welfare client, it served merely to introduce him to skid row. He made his first contact in the very process of securing relief. Sometimes he stayed on, demoralized or perhaps seduced by a process social workers referred to as "shelterization." Sometimes he fought back, as this letter written at the height of the Depression by several unwilling inhabitants of a Municipal Shelter illustrates:

Sir:
Previous to entering the shelters we considered ourselves to be average contented persons of everyday life . . . After several months . . . we become aware of a change in our mental attitude . . .
Realizing that these conditions will exist for years to come, we are going to leave the shelters no matter what befalls us, because we must get back some sort of normal life again, before we have lost all initiative. The mental strain has become much greater . . .
We cannot understand what crime we have committed that this should be done to us. Certainly a man in our place can claim no country of his own, no society to which he belongs, no flag to inspire him.
So now it is sink or swim. . . .[2]

Skid row *aficionados* are those whose life patterns are inherently deviant and lead them to look for a community where they will find toleration, acceptance, and anonymity. The *aficionado's* pattern of deviancy exists before he makes contact

with skid row, and he may be said to be the only type of skid row recruit truly motivated to disengage himself from society and to seek out the refuge of skid row. The salesman whose drinking gets out of hand looks for a place where his excesses will not embarrass friends and relatives, and where word of it will not leak back to his employer. The wanderer uses skid row as an emergency relief station—an interim residence when he is not "on the road." The alcoholic uses skid row to conceal his compulsive drinking from friends and neighbors. The prostitute, in the last stages of her professional life, uses skid row to pick up a few impoverished clients. The petty racketeer uses skid row to escape identification.

Over the years changes have taken place in the volume of these three points of entry into the skid row community, and along with these changes, the population of skid row has expanded or diminished. Since 1940 the mechanization of agriculture, lumbering, construction, and the decline of the railroads have vastly reduced the number of men employed in mobile occupations. No longer are thousands of men shipped from urban centers like Minneapolis and Chicago to isolated camps to fell trees or maintain railroad tracks. Heavy construction along waterways is now almost completely unionized, and so none of these jobs are available to the homeless man. Within the cities themselves, jobs like shoveling snow, washing dishes, and even street cleaning have been largely replaced by machines. In every single activity which formerly provided the homeless man with work, employment possibilities have either been drastically reduced—if not eliminated—or the labor force has been unionized.

---

[2] Robert W. Beasley. *Care of Destitute Men in Chicago.* Chicago: unpublished M.A. thesis, University of Chicago, 1933. See Appendix B. p. 121.

Even in the field of agricultural labor the homeless man has been displaced not only by machines but by the immigration of Puerto Ricans or the importation of Mexicans. It has also become easier for men to travel with their families and consequently many of these mobile jobs are taken by family units. Finally, average farm wages are so low that many a homeless man prefers to secure whatever relief benefits may be available to him.

The fact that entry into skid row through the world of work has been greatly reduced in both relative and absolute terms when compared with conditions prevailing before World War II has resulted in a decline of the population of most skid rows throughout the United States. An estimate from the Chicago study indicates that the skid row of 1960 is about one-fourth its relative size of 1920.[3]

The Minneapolis data reveal that the relative size of its skid row population has been steadily declining since at least 1940.[4] Data from other major cities in the United States tell a similar story. The skid row population reached its height in absolute numbers and relative proportions in 1935, and since then has declined in relative proportions in nearly every case and in absolute figures in most. Today's population of skid row contains from one-tenth to one-third of persons who entered through the world of work, this proportion varying according to the importance of casual labor in the area surrounding a particular skid row. In general this means a declining proportion from West to East and North to South.

Contact with skid row subculture through welfare agencies and programs has also considerably diminished but in this case because of changes in the policies and practices of welfare agencies rather than because of a decline in the number of relief recipients. Before World War I, skid row and the typically adjacent slums were the centers of welfare activity—when any such organized program existed. The blind, the lame, the ill, and the impoverished were all cared for, if at all, in these locales. When hard times hit the nation, breadlines and soup kitchens were also set up in slums or skid row. Welfare programs such as home relief and institutional care in specialized areas outside the city itself are relatively recent phenomena.

Today the mobile worker has practically vanished from the American scene, and the welfare client no longer need rub shoulders with the skid rower in the process of securing relief. Both these changes have led to a significant decline in the population of all skid rows throughout the country. The *aficionado*-recruit has also been by and large lost to skid row. He seems to find the climate of today's society more temperate toward some, at least, of his proclivities. Nevertheless, those who do find their way to skid row today travel much the same roads as ever though there are a lot fewer travelers and the proportion using one road rather than another may have altered.

[3] Chicago Tenants Relocation Bureau. *The Homeless Man on Skid Row.* Chicago: mimeographed report, 1961.

[4] Theodore Caplow, Keith A. Lovald and Samuel E. Wallace. *A General Report on the Problem of Relocating the Population of the Lower Loop Redevelopment Area.* Minneapolis: Minneapolis Housing and Redevelopment Authority, 1958, p. 22.

Becoming A Nudist * †

MARTIN S. WEINBERG

This paper deals with the interpersonal processes that lead people to contemplate nudism, to visit a nudist camp, and to become nudists. The data came from three sources—101 interviews with nudists in the Chicago area; two successive summers of participant observation in nudist camps; and 617 mailed questionnaires completed by nudists located throughout the United States and Canada.[1]

Prenudist Attitudes Toward Nudism

Most people seldom give much thought to the subject of nudism.[2] Responses in the interviews indicated that nudism is not a prominent object of thought even for many persons who will later become nudists. Thus when nudist members were asked what they had thought of nudism before visiting a camp, 50 percent stated that they had never really given it any thought. Until their initial experience, the interviewees' conceptions of nudism had been vague stereotypes, much like those held by the

general public. In the words of a now active nudist:

I never gave it too much thought. I thought it was a cult—a nut-eating, berry-chewing bunch of vegetarians, doing calisthenics all day, a gymno-physical society. I thought they were carrying health to an extreme, being egomaniacs about their body.

Many of those who had thought about the subject conceived of nudists' camps as more exclusive, luxurious, and expensive than they actually are. Others had different conceptions:

I'm afraid I had the prevailing notion that they were undignified, untidy places populated (a) by the very poor, and (b) by languishing bleached blonds, and (c) by greasy, leering bachelors.

Table 1 sums up the attitudes that nudists reported themselves to have taken before their affiliation.

The Initial Interest in Nudism

If prenudist attitudes are of the nature indicated by Table 1, how does one become interested enough to make a first

* Reprinted by special permission of The William Alanson White Psychiatric Foundation, Inc., from *Psychiatry: Journal for the Study of Interpersonal Processes,* Vol. 29, No. 1 (February, 1966). Copyright 1966 by The William Alanson White Psychiatric Foundation, Inc.

† This investigation was supported in part by a Public Health Service fellowship (No. 7-F1-MH-14, 660-01A1 BEH) from the National Institute of Mental Health, and in part by contributions from Mr. O.B.E. and from the National Nudist Council. I wish to acknowledge my appreciation to the individuals and organizations who helped me in carrying out my research. I am also grateful to John I. Kitsuse for his encouragement, suggestions, and criticisms.

1 Interviews were the primary source of data, and all of the quotations and quantifications in this paper, unless otherwise specified, are drawn from interviews. All known nudists in the vicinity of Chicago were contacted for an interview; the mean interview time was three and one-half hours. Approximately one hundred camps were represented in the interviews and questionnaires. A detailed discussion of my methodology may be found in "Sex, Modesty, and Deviants," Ph.D. Dissertation, Northwestern University, June, 1965.

2 This statement is based on the results of a questionnaire study of social response to nudism.

TABLE 1
Prenudist Attitudes Toward Nudism *

Attitude	Percentage of Interviewees
Positive	35
Live and let live	16
Negative	19
Very negative	1
Does not know	29

* For coding purposes, "positive" was defined as a desire to participate in nudism or to become a nudist. "Live and let live" included those who did not desire participation in nudism, but did not think ill of those who did participate; however, some of these respondents would have imposed social distance from nudists, and some would not.

visit to a nudist camp? As shown in Table 2, the highest percentage of men mentioned magazines as the source of their interest, and the next largest source was

TABLE 2
Source of Initial Interest in Nudism

Source	Male	Female
Magazines	47%	14%
Movies	6	6
Newspapers	6	0
Spouse	0	47
Parents or parents-in-law	2	8
Other person	31	23
Medical advice from physician	0	2
Other source	8	0

other persons (exclusive of parents or parents-in-law). For women, the pattern was different; the highest percentage were first informed about nudism by their husbands. In 78 percent of the families, the husband had been more interested in visiting a camp. In all other cases both spouses had equally wanted to go. There were no cases in which the wife had wanted to go more than the husband.

The fact that the overwhelming majority of women became interested in nudism through their relationships with other people, rather than through the mass media which played such an important part with men, was reflected in the finding that interpersonal trust had to be sustained in order to evoke the women's interest.[3] This was indicated in the content of many interviews. The interviews also indicated that commonsense justifications and "derivations"[4] were important in overcoming the women's anxieties.

The following quotation is from an interview with a woman who became interested in nudism after being informed about it by a male friend. Here she was describing what her feelings would have been prior to that time. (In this quotation, as in others in this paper, *Q* is used to signify a neutral probe by the interviewer that follows the course of the last reply—such as "Could you tell me some more about that?," or "How's that?," or "What do you mean?" Other questions by the interviewer are given in full.)

. . . [Whether or not I would go to a nudist camp would] depend on who asked me. If a friend, I probably would have gone along with it. . . . [*Q*] If an acquaintance, I wouldn't have been interested. [*Q*] I don't know, I think it would depend on who was asking me to go. [*Q*] If it was someone you liked or had confidence in, you'd go along with it. If you didn't think they were morally upright you probably wouldn't have anything to do with it.

A man described how he had persuaded his wife to become interested in nudism:

I expected difficulty with my wife. I presented it to her in a wholesome manner. [*Q*] I had to convince her it was a wholesome thing, and that the people there were

[3] My thanks are due to James L. Wilkins for initially pointing this pattern out in his analysis of the additional data on the response of college students to nudists.

[4] For a discussion of Pareto's concept of derivations, see Talcott Parsons, *The Structure of Social Action* (second edition); Glencoe, Ill., Free Press, 1949; pp. 198 *ff*.

sincere. . . . [Q] That they were sincere in efforts to sunbathe together and had only good purposes in mind when they did that. [Q] All the things that nudism stands for: A healthy body and a cleansed mind by killing sex curiosities.

The anxieties that enter into the anticipation of public nudity were described in the following interview excerpts:

I was nervous. . . . [Q] It's different. It's not a daily practice. . . . I'm heavy, that added to the nervousness.

They said they were ashamed of their builds. They think everyone there is perfection. [Q] They think everyone will look at them.

He [a friend] said he'd never go, but that he could understand it. He saw nothing wrong in it. [Q] He said he wouldn't want other men looking at his wife.

Even though they had enough confidence to make the decision to visit a camp, the respondents did not necessarily anticipate becoming nudists themselves. For many the first trip was merely a joke, a lark, or a new experience, and the main motivation was curiosity. They visited the camp as one might make a trip to the zoo, to see what it was like and what kind of characters would belong to such a group. There was also curiosity, on the part of many of the respondents, about seeing nude members of the opposite sex.

The original thought was that we were going to see a bunch of nuts. It was a joke going out there.

I thought they must be a little nutty. Eccentric. I didn't think there'd be so many normal people. . . . [Q] I felt that people that are nudists are a little bohemian or strange. [Q] I don't feel that way now. I thought we'd be the only sane people there.

I thought it was kind of an adventure. . . . [Q] I like feeling I'm doing something unusual that no one knows about. It's a big secret. . . . [Q] The novelty, the excitement of driving up in the car; no one knew we were going. . . .

Table 3 presents the motivations given by interviewees for their first trip to a nudist camp.

TABLE 3
Motivations for the First Visit to a Nudist Camp

Motivation	Male	Female
Curiosity over what it was like	33%	25%
Sexual curiosity	16	2
To satisfy spouse or relative	2	38
Combination of curiosity and to satisfy spouse	0	13
For relaxation	2	4
For health	12	6
To sunbathe	8	2
To make friends	6	0
Other	21	10

The First Visit

The first trip to camp was frequently accompanied by extreme nervousness. Part of this might be attributed simply to the experience of entering a new group. The visitors did not know the patterns common to the group, and they were uncertain about their acceptance by group members. For example, a nudist said, referring to his participation in a nudist camp in which he was not well known:

I guess I'm a little nervous when I get there, 'cause I'm not recognized as a member of the group.[5]

---

[5] It is this very fact of an established social system, however, that prevents a disruption of social order in nudist camps. Traditions and norms are stabilized, and even neophytes who think of themselves as leader-types are forced to fall into the pattern or be rejected. (For a small-group experiment that studies this phenomenon, see Ferenc Merei, "Group Leadership and Institutionalization," *Human Relations* [1949] 2:23–39.) In another paper I have shown how some of these traditions function to sustain a nonsexual definition of the nudist situation. See Martin S. Weinberg, "Sexual Modesty, Social Meanings, and the Nudist Camp," *Social Problems* (1965) 12:311–318.

But, in the instance of a first visit to a nudist camp, this anxiety on entering a new group was considerably heightened by the unknown nature of the experience that lay ahead. Mead, in his discussion of the "social psychology of the act," has described how people, in planning an action, imaginatively rehearse it and its anticipated consequences.[6] The nudist camp, however, presents a totally unfamiliar situation; the person planning a visit has no past of similar situations, and usually no one has effectively described the situation to him in advance. This gap in effective imagination produces apprehension, anxiety, and nervousness.

[On the trip up] I was very nervous. [*Q*] Because the idea was foreign. [*Q*] . . . The unknown factor. Just seeing a lot of people without clothes on is an unusual situation. Different or new experiences make one nervous.

You're nervous and apprehensive. You don't know what to expect. . . . I was very nervous. . . . I thought of everything under the sun. . . . I didn't know what to expect.

I felt a little inferior at first, because I had no knowledge of nudist camps. . . . I started to enjoy myself, but I couldn't quite feel comfortable. [*Q*] In the nude. In front of a lot of people. A lack of confidence, self-confidence. [*Q*] By not having a complete knowledge. I really didn't know what to expect.

I was afraid of the unknown. I didn't know what to expect. If we had known nudists, I wouldn't have had those fears.

In most instances, the initial nervousness dissipated soon after the newcomer's arrival. Forty-six percent of the interviewees said that they were not nervous at all after arriving at camp. An additional 31 percent felt at ease in less than three hours. Thus most visitors adjusted rapidly to the nudist way of life. Seventy-one percent of those interviewed reported that *no* major adjustment was necessary. Sixteen percent of the residual group reported that undressing for the first time, or becoming used to being nude, was the only adjustment. Of these people who had to adjust, only 15 percent found the adjustment to be difficult.

I really was afraid and shy and I didn't feel too well. We had discussed going, but when the time came to go I couldn't sleep that night. . . . Once we got nude then everything just seemed to come natural. I was surprised at how at ease I felt.

A variety of other response patterns, which I shall not discuss in detail, were characteristic of the initial visit. For example, one pattern related to the visitor's position in the socioeconomic structure of clothed society.[7] Because facilities in many camps are relatively primitive, those used to more comfortable circumstances were likely to be disappointed. One professional man said:

I was disappointed to see it was as rustic and unkept as it was. . . . If people wore clothes and nothing else changed it would be a fourth-class resort. [*Q*] Everything there is shabby and not well cared for.

The Adoption of Nudism as a Way of Life

COACHING AND SOCIAL VALIDATION

The newcomers to camps received no formal indoctrination in the nudist perspective, but acquired it almost imperceptibly as the result of a subtle social process. Informal coaching, either prior

---

[6] Anselm Strauss, editor, *The Social Psychology of George Herbert Mead;* Chicago, Univ. of Chicago Press, 1956; p. xiii.

[7] At the time of the interviews, the interviewers, making a commonsense judgment, placed 54 percent of the nudist respondents in the lower-middle class. This was the modal and median placement.

to or after arrival, appears to have eased adjustment problems.[8]

My husband said the men are gentlemen. He told me I'd have fun, like play in the sun, play games, and swim.

She didn't want to undress. . . . [Q] I tried to talk to her and her husband did; she finally got convinced. [Q] I told her you feel better with them off, and that no one will pay any attention.

The consensus of 95 percent of the interviewees was that, as one of them put it, "Things run along very smoothly when you first become a nudist." Asked if they ever had any doubts that becoming a nudist was the right decision, once they had made up their minds, 77 percent reported that they had never had any doubts. Fourteen percent had doubts at the time of the interview. The following quotations illustrate the process of social validation that tends to quell doubts: [9]

I do and I don't [have doubts], because of my religion. [Q] Nobody knows about it, and I wonder about that. [Q] Whether it's the right thing. But as I read the pamphlets [that is, nudist literature] I realize it's up to the individual. God made Adam and Eve and they had no clothes. You don't have to be ashamed of your body. Some are fat and some are thin, but it doesn't matter; it's your personality that matters. I don't know, if my minister found out, I'd defend it. We don't use bad language. Sometimes I wonder, but down underneath I think it's all right. We've just been taught to hide our bodies. Sometimes I wonder, but then I think what the pamphlets say. [Q: At what time do you have these doubts?] When I'm in church. [Q] Yes, when I get to thinking

about religion. Not very often. Sometimes I just wonder. [Q: Do you ever have these doubts while at camp?] No, I forget about everything. I'm having too much fun. I remind myself that this is something good for the children. My children won't become Peeping Toms or sex maniacs.

[At first] I felt ridiculous. I thought all those people looked so funny. [Q: Why's that?] All your life you've seen people with their clothes on; now they all have them off. After a while, you feel ridiculous with your clothes on. [Q] I liked the people. They were all very nice. They came from nice families. It couldn't just be something anyone would do, or just people from a lower class.

The nudist way of life becomes a different reality, a new world:

It seems like a different world from the world we live in every day. No washing, ironing, worries. You feel so free there. The people are friendly there, interested in each other. But not nosy. You can relax among them more easily than in the city.

And this new reality imposes a different meaning on the everyday life of the outside world:

My daughter told us today the boys and girls don't sit together at school, but it makes no difference to her. Several times they're out playing and the boys get excited when they see their panties. My children don't understand that. They have a different state of mind toward different sexes.

MOTIVES FOR BECOMING A NUDIST

Persons who became nudists—that is, became members of a camp and con-

---

[8] For a discussion of "coaching" relationships, see Anselm Strauss, *Mirrors and Masks: The Search for Identity;* New York: Free Press, 1959; pp. 109–118.

[9] By "social validation," I mean the process by which the subjective comes to be considered objective—that is, true. The views of others (especially those considered to have more extensive knowledge) provide a social yardstick by which to measure truth. Pareto reaches a similar view of objectivity. Note the following statement: ". . . we apply the term 'logical actions' to actions that logically conjoin means to ends not only from the standpoint of the subject performing them, but from the standpoint of other persons who have more extensive knowledge—in other words, to actions that are logical both subjectively and objectively in the sense just explained." See Vilfredo Pareto, *The Mind and Society,* Vol. 1; New York, Harcourt, Brace, 1935; p. 77.

TABLE 4
Comparative Desires of Male and Female Members of Couples to Visit a Nudist Camp *

	Male Wanted To Go More	Male and Female Wanted To Go Equally	Female Wanted To Go More
First visit	79%	21%	0%
Return visits	40	51	9

* Two unmarried couples are included in these data.

ceived of themselves as nudists—usually demonstrated an autonomy of motives,[10] in the sense that their motives for doing so differed from their motives for first visiting a camp. The curiosity that had been the overriding motive for the initial visit was satisfied, and the incentive for affiliating with a nudist group was based on the person's experiences at the camp.[11] It should be noted, however, that the decision was sometimes prompted by the owner's insistence that visitors join if they wished to return. As Table 4 shows, there was a considerable change, after the first visit, in the pattern of male versus female desire to attend the camp.

The following quotations are illustrative of the autonomous motives of respondents for the first and subsequent visits:

[*Q: What was your main reason for wanting to attend camp the first time?*] Curiosity. [*Q*] To see how people behave under such circumstances, and maybe also looking at the girls. [*Q*] Just that it's interesting to see girls in the nude. [*Q: What is the main reason you continue to attend?*] I found it very relaxing. [*Q*] It's more comfortable to swim without a wet suit, and not wearing clothes when it's real warm is more comfortable and relaxing.

[I went up the first time] to satisfy my husband. He wanted me to go and I fought it. But he does a lot for me, so why not do him a favor. [She had told him that people went to nudist camps only for thrills and that she would divorce him before she would go. Although he talked her into it, she cried all the way to camp. Asked why she continued to attend, she looked surprised and replied:] Why, because I thoroughly enjoy it!

This last quotation describes a common pattern for women, which appears also in the following recollection:

[I went the first time] because my husband wanted me to go. [*Q: What is the main reason that you continue to attend?*] Because we had fun . . . and we met a lot of nice people.

The interviewees were asked what they liked most about nudism, with the results shown in Table 5. Three of the benefits cited are of special sociological interest—the concept of nudist freedom, the family-centered nature of the recreation, and the emphasis on friendliness and sociability.

"FREEDOM" Echoing the nudist ideology, many respondents mentioned "freedom"—using the term in various contexts—as a major benefit. There were varied definitions of this freedom and its meaning for the participant. Some defined it in terms of free body action, of being unhindered by clothing.

Nudism . . . gives me an opportunity to be in the sunshine and fresh air. Also to take a swim nude gives me free expression of body. [*Q*] I'm not hindered by clothes, a freedom of body movement, and I can feel the water all over my body.

Nothing was binding; no socks, no tight belt, nothing clothing-wise touching me.

You don't have garter belts or bras. Your body can breathe.

[10] This concept was developed by Gordon Allport, "The Functional Autonomy of Motives," *Amer. J. Psychology* (1937) 50:141–156.
[11] Attendance is usually confined to summer weekends, and sexual curiosity may arise again between seasons.

TABLE 5
What Interviewees Liked Most about Nudism

	Percent of Sample Mentioning the Item
Friendliness, sociability	60%
Relaxation, getting away from the city	47
Enjoyment of outdoors and sports	36
Freedom	31
Sunbathing	26
Physical health	26
Children becoming informed about the human body	11
Mental health	8
Economical vacations	4
Family recreation, keeping family together	4
Seeing people nude	1
Other aspects	15

With perspiration your clothes start to bind and you develop rashes. [Q] You just feel more relaxed when you're nude, and more comfortable from hot, sticky clothing.

Others interpreted freedom from clothing in a different way:

Freedom from a convention of society. It's a relief to get away from it. [Q] A physical relief in that wearing clothes is something you must do. I hate wearing a choking tie at a dinner party, but I have to because it is a society convention.

You don't have to dress appropriate for the occasion. You aren't looking for the smartest slacks and sports clothes.

The freedom. . . . You don't have to worry about the way you're dressed. You don't try to outdo someone with a thirty-dollar bathing suit.

For others, freedom meant the absence of routine and restraint:

A nudist camp has a lot more freedom [than a summer resort]. You do just as you want. . . . [Q] Just to do what you want to do,

there is nothing you have to do. At a resort you have to participate in activities.

The freedom. [Q] You can do as you please. [Q] I can read or just lay in the sun.

The freedom. [Q] You can go any place you want in the camp. You can walk anywhere nude.

The range of conceptions of freedom can be indicated by the following examples:

I felt free in the water. No one staring at you.

I like the complete freedom of . . . expression. With nudist people, I find them more frank and outspoken, not two-faced. You don't have to be cagey and worry about saying the wrong thing.

Feeling free with your body. [Q] I can't really explain it. Feeling more confident, I guess.

The varying constructions of nudist freedom support Schutz's model of man as a commonsense actor.[12] According to Schutz, man lives very naively in his world; clear and distinct experiences are mixed with vague conjectures, and "cookbook" descriptions of experiences are uncritically adopted from others. When these standard descriptions are vague, and are called into question—for example, by an interviewer who asks what is meant by "freedom"—a wide variety of constructions is elicited from respondents. Nudists, as devotees to a "cause," resemble other commonsense actors in their frequent inability to understand their stock answers critically.

FAMILY COHESION   As shown in Table 5, some respondents gave, as the feature of nudism they like most, its function in providing family recreation. One of the interview sample expressed this as follows:

Nudism tends to keep the family together. In the nonnudist society the family tends to

---

[12] See Alfred Schutz, "The Dimensions of the Social World," in *Collected Papers, II: Studies in Social Theory,* edited by Arvid Broderson; The Hague, Martinus Nijhoff, 1964; pp. 48 *ff.*

split into different organizations; all have different interests. You can still do different things in camp, but you still have a common interest. And all your plans are made together.

One would expect that nudism would lead to family cohesiveness, as a result of this common interest, and also as a result of a tendency for the family members to conceal their nudist involvements in their dealings with the outside world. (In regard to the element of secrecy, Simmel has pointed out how a group's intensified seclusion results in heightened cohesiveness.[13]) Participation in nudism did not, however, always lead to increased family cohesiveness. For example, if one spouse did not appreciate the experience, the family's continued participation resulted in increased strain. And although nudist ideology claims that nudist participation brings the family closer together, 78 percent of the interviewees, and 82 percent of the questionnaire respondents, reported no change in their family relationships.

RELATIONSHIPS WITH OTHERS Friendliness and sociability were the characteristics of the nudist experience mentioned most often by interviewees. In addition, nudists extended the concept of "family" to include fellow nudists; they cited a "togetherness" that is rare in the clothed society. Some insight into this cohesiveness was displayed in the following remarks by an interviewee:

Camaraderie and congeniality . . . comes in any minority group that supports an unpopular position. [Q] Feelings develop by these in-groups because you are brought together by one idea which you share. On the street you may run into people you share no ideas with.

The interviewees were asked how the camp situation would change if everything remained constant except that clothes were required. Most of them anticipated that their bond would be dissolved.

They would lose the common bond. They have a bond that automatically is a bond. They are in a minority. They are glad you're here. You are welcome there; they're glad you're one of us.

I think the people would be less friendly. When you're all nude you feel the same as them. You all came here to be nude. . . . [Q] Everybody feels the other is the same; you have something in common to be doing this unusual thing.

A number of interviewees, supporting the nudist contention that social distinctions diminish in the nudist camp, believed that class distinctions would reappear if clothing were donned.[14] A 19-year-old respondent cited both class and age distinctions:

You would have . . . your classes, and age. [Q] I wouldn't feel as close to B and G. There is a great age difference. Knowing them this way, though, gives us a common bond. You just don't think about their ages or anything else about them.

Several blue-collar workers remarked that one of the things they liked about nudism was that, without their uniforms or customary clothes, they and their families could associate with a better class of people. Status striving decreases with the removal of these important props of impression management.

[If everyone in the camp wore clothes] everything I detest about country clubs I've seen would immediately become manifest. Namely: (1) social climbing with all its ac-

13 Kurt H. Wolff, *The Sociology of Georg Simmel;* New York: Free Press, 1950; see Part IV.
14 For discussions of clothes as "sign equipment," see Erving Goffman, "Symbols of Class Status," *British J. Sociology* (1951) 2:294–304; and *The Presentation of Self in Everyday Life;* Garden City, N.Y., Doubleday, 1959; pp. 24 ff. Also see Gregory Stone, "Appearance and the Self," in *Human Behavior and Social Processes: An Interactionist Approach,* edited by Arnold Rose; Boston, Houghton Mifflin, 1962; pp. 86–118.

companying insincerity and ostentation; (2) wolves tracking down virgins; (3) highly formalized activities such as golf; (4) gambling and drinking; (5) embarrassment of having to swim under the appraising gaze of a gallery full of people sipping cocktails. This is the paradox, the curious thing; it doesn't embarrass me to swim at . . . [a nudist camp] whereas I can't be coaxed into the swimming pool at the country club in my hometown. [Q] I think that the reason is the fact that so much in that country club is so calculated to make tableaux or pictures, in which only the young and the handsome can really be a part. That's terribly true.

Another interviewee, when asked what he liked most about social nudism, replied:

It is the best way to relax. [Q] Once you take your clothes off, people are on the same basis. [Q] Everyone is a person. There are no distinctions between a doctor or a mechanic because of clothing. [Q] . . . It's hard to describe. It's just that all have an equal basis, no distinctions because of clothing. That helps you to relax.

Although these statements may be somewhat idealized, the nudist camp does effectively break down patterns common to country clubs, resorts, and other settings in the outside society. Sex, class, and power lose much of their relevance in the nudist camp, and the suspension of the barriers they create effects a greater unity among the participants. This is not to say, however, that there is no social hierarchy—a point to which I shall return shortly.

The suspension of clothing modesty reinforces the atmosphere of "one big family" in another way. Clothing modesty is a *ceremony* of everyday life that sustains a nonintimate definition of relationships, and with its voluntary suspension relationships are usually defined as closer in character. However, for this to occur, trust must not be called into question,

and each person must take for granted that he is differentiated from other social objects. Camp relationships usually meet these conditions. For example, they are differentiated from relationships elsewhere; being undressed in front of others is still out of the ordinary, since nudists do not appear nude among outsiders.

The social effect was significant enough to prompt members to describe the nudist way of life as a discovery that had brought new meaning to their lives. The experience provided many of them with "a sense of belonging." As one respondent put it:

. . . you feel like you're part of a whole family. You feel very close. That's how I feel.

The feeling of being part of "one big family" was, of course, more common to the smaller camps. But even in the large camps, participants in camp activities felt themselves to be a *part* of a special group.

As I have suggested, however, the "togetherness" of nudists is exaggerated. Personality clashes, cliques, and intergroup disagreements exist, and social stratification remains in evidence. In the words of an unmarried neophyte:

Sometimes I think there is a hierarchy at . . . [a large nudist camp]. [Q] In any organization there are cliques. [Q] These cliques I believe are formed by seniority. [Q] Those who have been there the longest. [Q: What makes you think this?] Something that is in the air. [Q] Just an impression you get. It's hard to say; it's just a feeling. [Q] As a newcomer I felt not at ease. [Q] There is an air of suspicion; people are not really friendly. [Q] They are not really unfriendly, just suspicious, I suppose, of single men. . . . They suspect single men are coming for Peeping Tom purposes. [Q] Just to see the nude women. . . . Single men, I think, are the lowest class at camp.

This attitude was borne out in the interviews with other single men; rarely did they describe nudism in *gemeinschaft-lich* terms. The meaning of a person's experiences still depends on his position in the system.

Furthermore, it is doubtful that many people find a Utopia in nudism. The nudists interviewed were asked how seriously they felt that they would be affected if nudist camps were closed. As Table 6

TABLE 6
The Degree to Which the Closing of Nudist Camps Would Affect Interviewees *

Closing Camps Would Affect Respondent	Percent of Respondents
Very much	43
Somewhat	26
Not too much	17
Not at all	13

* Vague categories, such as those presented in this table, were occasionally used for their descriptive value in grossly delineating some point. In this case, respondents were asked to classify themselves (after completing their open-end response). In other cases, the coders used a large group of indicators in constructing such gross scales. Although these scales lacked intrinsic rigor, reliability between coders was high.

shows, 30 percent of the interviewees considered that they would be relatively unaffected. When they were asked to identify their three best friends, almost half of the interviewees did not name another nudist.[15] Table 7 details this information, as well as the degree of social involvement with other nudists, as rated by coders.

Nudists and the Clothed Society

Nudists envision themselves as being labeled deviant by members of the clothed society. In both the interviews and the questionnaires, the respondents were asked to conceptualize the view of nudists taken by the general public, and by their parents. No consistent difference was found between the views of the two groups, as described by the nudists.[16] Approximately one-third of the respondents conceptualized a live-and-let-live attitude on the part of parents and public. Two-thirds conceptualized a negative or very negative attitude.

They think we're fanatics. [Q] That we go overboard on something. That we're out of line.

If I went by what the guys say at work, you'd have to be pretty crazy, off your head a little bit. [Q] They think you almost have to be . . . a sex fiend or something like that. They think there's sex orgies, or wife-swapping, or something.

They think we're a bunch of nuts. [Q] They just think that anyone who runs around without clothes is nuts. If they stopped to investigate, they'd find we weren't.

People think the body should be clothed and not exposed at any time. They associate that with vulgarity, indecency, and abnormality. [Q] Vulgarity is something that is unacceptable to the general public. [Q] Indecency in this respect would be exposing portions of the body which normally we hide. [Q] Abnormality? Well, the general public feels it's abnormal for the body to be undressed around other people, in a social group.

[15] Although 59 percent of the interviewees had been nudists for over two years, and 27 percent of this group had been nudists for over ten years, involvement did not appear to be particularly high. Also, an estimated 17 percent of the membership drops out every year.

[16] Although a positive versus negative differentiation of parents and general public was not found, there was a difference in the character of the typifications involved. In the case of parents, the typifications were derived from a history of experiences with an acting personality and were relatively concrete. In contrast, typifications of the general public were highly anonymous. Because such a collectivity could never be experienced directly, there was a much larger region of taken-for-granteds. This is due to the great number of substrata typifications underlying the general whole. This phenomenon is discussed by Alfred Schutz (see footnote 12).

TABLE 7
Social Involvement of Interviewees with Other Nudists *
Degree of Social Involvement

Best Friends Who Are Nudists	Very Low	Moderately Low	Neither High Nor Low	Moderately High	Very High	Totals	
None	13	9	12	5	7	46	(47%)
One	3	2	6	9	5	25	(26%)
Two		1	3	3	10	17	(18%)
Three					9	9	(9%)
Total	16	12	21	17	31	97	(100%)
	(16%)	(12%)	(22%)	(18%)	(32%)		

* The data on the number of best friends who are nudists were drawn from the replies of interviewees. The degree of social involvement was rated by coders on the basis of the following instructions: Code the degree of social involvement with nudists throughout the year on the basis of answers to Question 40 (b and c). Think of this as a scale or continuum: (1) Very low involvement (no contact at all); (2) moderately low involvement (just write or phone occasionally); (3) neither low nor high involvement (get together every couple of months—or attend New Year's party or splash party together); (4) moderately high involvement (visit once a month); (5) very high involvement (visit every week or two).

The fact that nudists were able to participate in a group which they viewed as stigmatized (and also the sense of belonging they claimed to have found in nudism) suggested that nudists might be isolated in the larger society. If they were isolated they could more easily participate in such a deviant group, being insulated from social controls.

A comparison of nudist interviewees with a sample of the general population [17] did show the nudists to fall substantially below the general population in frequency of informal association,[18] as shown in Table 8. Further, while members of the general population got together most often with relatives, nudists got together most often with friends,[19] as Table 9

TABLE 8
Frequency of Informal Group Participation

	Nudists	General Population
At least twice a week	17%	30%
Every 4 or 5 days	4	35
Once a week	12	16
Less often or never	67	19

indicates. The fact that 34 percent of the nudist sample got together with relatives less than once a month may reflect a considerable insulation from informal controls, since it is relatives who would probably provide the greatest pressure in inhibiting participation in such deviant groups.[20]

The degree to which nudists were iso-

[17] In this comparison, Axelrod's data on a sample of the general population in the Detroit area were used. See Morris Axelrod, "Urban Structure and Social Participation," *Amer. Sociol. Review* (1956) 21:13–18.

[18] A major limitation in this comparison, however, is that Axelrod has collapsed frequencies of association that are less than once a week into the category of "less often or never."

[19] Axelrod finds this greater participation with friends only for members of his sample with high income or high educational or social status.

[20] Also the absolute frequency of association with friends includes association with nudist friends. This reduces the apparent social-control function of their friendship associations.

Curiously, members of the nudist sample belonged to more formal organizations than did members of Axelrod's sample of the general population. The comparison was as follows: Membership in no group—general population, 37 percent; nudists, 18 percent. One group—general population, 31 percent; nudists, 27 percent. Two groups—general population, 16 percent; nudists, 19 percent.

TABLE 9

Frequency of Association with Several Types of Informal Groups

	Relatives		*Friends*		*Neighbors*		*Co-workers*	
	Nudists	*General Popula- tion*	*Nudists*	*General Popula- tion*	*Nudists*	*General Popula- tion*	*Nudists*	*General Popula- tion*
At least once a week	38%	51%	49%	29%	26%	30%	17%	13%
A few times a month	16	13	21	20	11	9	10	8
About once a month	11	13	8	19	6	9	7	15
Less often	34	23	20	32	56	52	63	65

lated in the clothed society was found to be related to the length of time they had been nudists. As shown in Table 10, the

TABLE 10

Social Isolation of Nudists According to Their Length of Time in Nudism

Degree of Social Isolation *	*Years in Nudism*			
	1–2	*3–5*	*6–9*	*10 and Over*
Moderately or very isolated	22%	38%	44%	54%
Neither iso- lated nor active	39	31	25	35
Very or mod- erately active	39	31	32	12

* As rated by coders.

longer a person had been in nudism, the more likely he was to be isolated. This may be interpreted in different ways. For example, there may be a tendency to become more isolated with continued participation, perhaps to avoid sanctions. (Yet, in regard to formal organizations nudists did *not* drop out or become less active.) Or, in the past it is likely that nudism was considered even more deviant than it is today and therefore it may have appealed primarily to more isolated types of people.

Regardless of which interpretation is correct, as previously discussed many nudists found a sense of belonging in nudism.[21]

People are lonely. It gives them a sense of belonging.

Until I started going out . . . [to camp] I never felt like I was part of a crowd. But I do out there. I was surprised. [Q] Well, like I said, I was never part of a crowd . . . I had friends, but never outstanding. My wife and I were [camp] King and Queen.

However, while the nudist experience helps solve this life problem for some, it creates this same problem for others. For the latter group, nudism may only ease the problem that it creates—that is, the isolation that results from concealing one's affiliation with a deviant group.[22]

[21] Some nudists also viewed themselves as members of an elite, superior to clothed society because they had suspended the body taboo.

[22] For a discussion of information control, see Erving Goffman, *Stigma: The Management of Spoiled Identity;* Englewood Cliffs, N. J., Prentice-Hall, 1963; pp. 41–104.

Apprenticeships in Prostitution *

JAMES H. BRYAN

. . . This paper provides some detailed, albeit preliminary, information concerning induction and training in a particular type of deviant career: prostitution, at the call girl level. It describes the order of events, and their surrounding structure, which future call girls experience in entering their occupation.

The respondents in this study were 33 prostitutes, all currently or previously working in the Los Angeles area. They ranged in age from 18 to 32, most being in their mid-twenties. None of the interviewees were obtained through official law enforcement agencies, but seven were found within the context of a neuropsychiatric hospital. The remaining respondents were gathered primarily through individual referrals from previous participants in the study. There were no obvious differences between the "psychiatric sample" and the other interviewees on the data to be reported.

All subjects in the sample were call girls. That is, they typically obtained their clients by individual referrals, primarily by telephone, and enacted the sexual contract in their own or their clients' place of residence or employment. They did not initiate contact with their customers in bars, streets, or houses of prostitution, although they might meet their customers at any number of locations by prearrangement. The minimum fee charged per sexual encounter was $20.00. As an adjunct to the call girl interviews, three pimps and two "call boys" were interviewed as well.[1]

Approximately two thirds of the sample were what are sometimes known as "outlaw broads"; that is, they were not under the supervision of a pimp when interviewed. There is evidence that the majority of pimps who were aware of the study prohibited the girls under their direction from participating in it. It should be noted that many members of the sample belonged to one or another clique; their individually expressed opinions may not be independent. . . .

The Entrance

I had been thinking about it [becoming a call girl] before a lot. . . . Thinking about wanting to do it, but I had no connections. Had I not had a connection, I probably wouldn't have started working. . . . I thought about starting out. . . . Once I tried it [without a contact]. . . . I met this guy at a bar and I tried to make him pay me, but the thing is, you can't do it that way because they are romantically interested in you, and they don't think that it is on that kind of basis. You can't all of a sudden come up and want money for it, you have to be known beforehand. . . . I think that is what holds a lot of girls back who might work. I think I might have started a year sooner had I had a connection. You seem to make one contact or another . . . if it's another girl or a pimp or just someone who will set you up and get you a client. . . .

* Reprinted from *Social Problems,* Vol. 12, No. 3 (Winter, 1965), pp. 287–297, by permission of the author and *Social Problems.*

[1] This definition departs somewhat from that offered by Clinard. He defines the call girl as one dependent upon an organization for recruiting patrons and one who typically works in lower-class hotels. The present sample is best described by Clinard's category high-class independent professional prostitute. M. D. Clinard, *Sociology of Deviant Behavior,* New York: Rinehart & Co., Inc., 1957.

You can't just, say, get an apartment and get a phone in and everything and say, "Well, I'm gonna start business," because you gotta get clients from somewhere. There has to be a contact.

Immediately prior to entrance into the occupation, all but one girl had personal contact with someone professionally involved in call girl activities (pimps or other call girls). The one exception had contact with a customer of call girls. While various occupational groups (e.g., photographers) seem to be peripherally involved, often unwittingly, with the call girl, there was no report of individuals involved in such occupations being contacts for new recruits. The novice's initial contact is someone at the level at which she will eventually enter the occupation: not a street-walker, but a call girl; not a pimp who manages girls out of a house of prostitution, but a pimp who manages call girls.

Approximately half of the girls reported that their initial contact for entrance into the profession was another "working girl." The nature of these relationships is quite variable. In some cases, the girls have been long standing friends. Other initial contacts involved sexual relationships between a Lesbian and the novice. Most, however, had known each other less than a year, and did not appear to have a very close relationship, either in the sense of time spent together or of biographical information exchanged. The relationship may begin with the aspiring call girl soliciting the contact. That is, if a professional is known to others as a call girl, she will be sought out and approached by females who are strangers: [2]

I haven't ever gone out and looked for one. All of these have fell right into my hands. . . . They turned themselves out. . . . They come to me for help.

Whatever their relationship, whenever the professional agrees to aid the beginner, she also, it appears, implicitly assumes responsibility for training her. This is evidenced by the fact that only one such female contact referred the aspirant to another girl for any type of help. Data are not available as to the reason for this unusual referral.

If the original contact was not another call girl but a pimp, a much different relationship is developed and the career follows a somewhat different course. The relationship between pimp and girl is typically one of lovers, not friends:

. . . because I love him very much. Obviously, I'm doing this mostly for him. . . . I'd do anything for him. I'm not just saying I will, I am. . . . [After discussing his affair with another woman] I just decided that I knew what he was when I decided to do this for him and I decided I had two choices— either accept it or not, and I accepted it, and I have no excuse.

Occasionally, however, a strictly business relationship will be formed:

Right now I am buying properties, and as soon as I can afford it, I am buying stocks. . . . It is strictly a business deal. This man and I are friends, our relationship ends there. He handles all the money, he is making all the investments and I trust him. We have a legal document drawn up which states that half the investments are mine, half of them his, so I am protected.

Whether the relationship is love or business, the pimp solicits the new girl.[3]

---

[2] A point also made in the autobiographical account of a retired call girl, Virginia McManus, *Not For Love*, New York: Dell Publishing Co., Inc., 1960, p. 160.

[3] Two of the pimps denied that this was very often so and maintained that the girls will solicit them. The degree to which they are solicited seems to depend upon the nature and extent of their reputations. It is difficult to judge the accuracy of these reports as there appears to be a strong taboo against admitting to such solicitation.

It is usually agreed that the male will have an important managerial role in the course of the girl's career, and that both will enjoy the gains from the girl's activities for an indefinite period:

Actually a pimp has to have complete control or else its like trouble with him. Because if a pimp doesn't, if she is not madly in love with him or something in some way, a pimp won't keep a girl.

Once the girl agrees to function as a call girl, the male, like his female counterpart, undertakes the training of the girl, or refers the girl to another call girl for training. Either course seems equally probable. Referrals, when employed, are typically to friends and, in some cases, wives or ex-wives.

Although the data are limited, it appears that the pimp retains his dominance over the trainee even when the latter is being trained by a call girl. The girl trainer remains deferential to the pimp's wishes regarding the novice.

Apprenticeship

Once a contact is acquired and the decision to become a call girl made, the recruit moves to the next stage in the career sequence: the apprenticeship period. The structure of the apprenticeship will be described, followed by a description of the content most frequently communicated during this period.

The apprenticeship is typically served under the direction of another call girl, but may occasionally be supervised by a pimp. Twenty-four girls in the sample initially worked under the supervision of other girls. The classroom is, like the future place of work, an apartment. The apprentice typically serves in the trainer's apartment, either temporarily residing with the trainer or commuting there almost daily. The novice rarely serves her apprenticeship in such places as a house of prostitution, motel, or on the street. It is also infrequent that the girl is transported out of her own city to serve an apprenticeship. Although the data are not extensive, the number of girls being trained simultaneously by a particular trainer has rarely been reported to be greater than three. Girls sometimes report spending up to eight months in training, but the average stay seems to be two or three months. The trainer controls all referrals and appointments, novices seemingly not having much control over the type of sexual contact made or the circumstances surrounding the enactment of the contract.

The structure of training under the direction of a pimp seems similar, though information is more limited. The girls are trained in an apartment in the city they intend to work and for a short period of time. There is some evidence that the pimp and the novice often do not share the same apartment as might the novice and the girl trainer. There appear to be two reasons for the separation of pimp and girl. First, it is not uncommonly thought that cues which suggest the presence of other men displease the girl's customers:

Well, I would never let them know that I had a lover, which is something that you never ever let a john know, because this makes them very reticent to give you money, because they think you are going to go and spend it with your lover, which is what usually happens.

(Interestingly, the work of Winick suggests that such prejudices may not actually be held by many customers.) [4] Secondly, the legal repercussions are much greater, of course, for the pimp who lives

[4] C. Winick, "Prostitutes' Clients' Perception of the Prostitute and Themselves," *International Journal of Social Psychiatry*, 8 (1961–62), pp. 289–297.

with his girl than for two girls rooming together. As one pimp of 19 years experience puts it:

It is because of the law. There is a law that is called the illegal cohabitation that they rarely use unless the man becomes big in stature. If he is a big man in the hustling world, the law then employs any means at their command. . . .

Because of the convenience in separation of housing, it is quite likely that the pimp is less directly involved with the day-to-day training of the girls than the call girl trainer.

The content of the training period seems to consist of two broad, interrelated dimensions, one philosophical, the other interpersonal. The former refers to the imparting of a value structure, the latter to "do's" and "don'ts" of relating to customers and, secondarily, to other "working girls" and pimps. The latter teaching is perhaps best described by the concept of a short range perspective. That is, most of the "do's" and "don'ts" pertain to ideas and actions that the call girl uses in problematic situations.[5] Not all girls absorb these teachings, and those who do incorporate them in varying degrees.

Insofar as a value structure is transmitted it is that of maximizing gains while minimizing effort, even if this requires transgressions of either a legal or moral nature. Frequently, it is postulated that people, particularly men, are corrupt or easily corruptible, that all social relationships are but a reflection of a "con," and that prostitution is simply a more honest or at least no more dishonest act than the everyday behavior of "squares." Furthermore, not only are "johns" basically exploitative, but they are easily exploited; hence they are, in some respects, stupid. As explained by a pimp:

. . . [in the hustling world] the trick or the john is known as a fool . . . this is not the truth. . . . He [the younger pimp] would teach his woman that a trick was a fool.

Since the male is corrupt, or honest only because he lacks the opportunity to be corrupt, then it is only appropriate that he be exploited as he exploits.

Girls first start making their "scores"—say one guy keeps them for a while or maybe she gets, you know, three or four grand out of him, say a car or a coat. These are your scores. . . .

The general assumption that man is corrupt is empirically confirmed when the married male betrays his wife, when the moralist, secular or religious, betrays his publicly stated values, or when the "john" "stiffs" (cheats) the girl. An example of the latter is described by a girl as she reflects upon her disillusionment during her training period.

It is pretty rough when you are starting out. You get stiffed a lot of times. . . . Oh sure. They'll take advantage of you anytime they can. And I'm a trusting soul, I really am. I'll believe anybody till they prove different. I've made a lot of mistakes that way. You get to the point, well, Christ, what the heck can I believe in people, they tell me one thing and here's what they do to me.

Values such as fairness with other working girls, or fidelity to a pimp, may occasionally be taught. To quote a pimp:

So when you ask me if I teach a kind of basic philosophy, I would say that you could say that. Because you try to teach them in an amoral way that there is a right and wrong way as pertains to this game . . . and then you teach them that when working with other girls to try to treat the other girl fairly because a woman's worst enemy in the street [used in both a literal and figurative sense] is the other woman and only by

[5] H. S. Becker, Blanche Geer, E. C. Hughes, and A. L. Strauss, *Boys In White,* Chicago: University of Chicago Press, 1961.

treating the other women decently can she expect to get along. . . . Therefore the basic philosophy I guess would consist of a form of honesty, a form of sincerity and complete fidelity to her man [pimp].

It should be noted, however, that behavior based on enlightened self-interest with concomitant exploitation is not limited to customer relationships. Interviewees frequently mentioned a pervasive feeling of distrust between trainer and trainee, and such incidents as thefts or betrayal of confidences are occasionally reported and chronically guarded against.

Even though there may be considerable pressure upon the girl to accept this value structure, many of them (perhaps the majority of the sample) reject it.

People have told me that I wasn't turned out, but turned loose instead. . . . Someone who is turned out is turned out to believe in a certain code of behavior, and this involves having a pimp, for one thing. It also involves never experiencing anything but hatred or revulsion for "tricks" for another thing. It involves always getting the money in front [before the sexual act] and a million little things that are very strictly adhered to by those in the "in group," which I am not. . . . Never being nice or pleasant to a trick unless you are doing it for the money, getting more money. [How did you learn that?] It was explained to me over a period of about six months. I learned that you were doing it to make money for yourself so that you could have nice things and security. . . . [Who would teach you this?] [The trainer] would teach me this.[6]

It seems reasonable to assume that the value structure serves, in general, to create in-group solidarity and to alienate the girl from "square" society, and that

this structure serves the political advantage of the trainer and the economic gains of the trainee more than it allays the personal anxieties of either. In fact, failure to adopt these values at the outset does not appear to be correlated with much personal distress.[7] As one girl describes her education experiences:

Some moral code. We're taught, as a culture . . . it's there and after awhile you live, breathe, and eat it. Now, what makes you go completely against everything that's inside you, everything that you have been taught, and the whole society, to do things like this?

Good empirical evidence, however, concerning the functions and effectiveness of this value structure with regard to subjective comfort is lacking.

A series of deductions derived from the premises indicated above serve to provide, in part, the "rules" of interpersonal contact with the customer. Each customer is to be seen as a "mark," and "pitches" are to be made.

[Did you have a standard pitch?] It's sort of amusing. I used to listen to my girl friend [trainer]. She was the greatest at this telephone type of situation. She would call up and cry and say that people had come to her door. . . . She'd cry and she'd complain and she'd say "I have a bad check at the liquor store, and they sent the police over," and really . . . a girl has a story she tells the man. . . . Anything, you know, so he'll help her out. Either it's the rent or she needs a car, or doctor's bills, or any number of things.

Any unnecessary interaction with the customer is typically frowned upon, and the trainee will receive exhortations to be

---

[6] The statements made by prostitutes to previous investigators and mental helpers may have been parroting this particular value structure and perhaps have misled previous investigators into making the assumption that "all whores hate men." While space prohibits a complete presentation of the data, neither our questionnaire nor interview data suggest that this is a predominant attitude among call girls.

[7] There is, from the present study, little support for the hypothesis of Reckless concerning the association of experience trauma and guilt with abruptness of entry into the occupation. W. C. Reckless, *The Crime Problem,* New York: Appleton-Century-Crofts, Inc., 1950.

quick about her business. One girl in her fourth week of work explains:

[What are some of the other don't's that you have learned about?] Don't take so much time. . . . The idea is to get rid of them as quickly as possible.

Other content taught concerns specific information about specific customers.

. . . she would go around the bar and say, now look at that man over there, he's this way and that way, and this is what he would like and these are what his problems are. . . .

. . . she would teach me what the men wanted and how much to get, what to say when I got there . . . just a line to hand them.

Training may also include proprieties concerning consuming alcohol and drugs, when and how to obtain the fee, how to converse with the customers and, occasionally, physical and sexual hygiene. As a girl trainer explains:

First of all, impress cleanliness. Because, on the whole, the majority of girls, I would say, I don't believe there are any cleaner women walking the streets, because they've got to be aware of any type of body odor. . . . You teach them to French [fellatio] and how to talk to men.

[Do they [pimps] teach you during the turning out period how to make a telephone call?] Oh, usually, yes. They don't teach you, they just tell you how to do it and you do it with your good common sense, but if you have trouble, they tell you more about it.

Interestingly, the specific act of telephoning a client is often distressing to the novice and is of importance in her training. Unfortunately for the girl, it is an act she must perform with regularity as she does considerable soliciting.[8] One suspects that such behavior is embarrass-

ing for her because it is an unaccustomed role for her to play—she has so recently come from a culture where young women do *not* telephone men for dates. Inappropriate sex-role behavior seems to produce greater personal distress than does appropriate sex-role behavior even when it is morally reprehensible.

Well, it is rather difficult to get on the telephone, when you've never worked before, and talk to a man about a subject like that, and it is very new to you.

What is omitted from the training should be noted as well. There seems to be little instruction concerning sexual techniques as such, even though the previous sexual experience of the trainee may have been quite limited. What instruction there is typically revolves around the practice of fellatio. There seems to be some encouragement not to experience sexual orgasms with the client, though this may be quite variable with the trainer.

. . . and sometimes, I don't know if it's a set rule or maybe it's an unspoken rule, you don't enjoy your dates.

Yes, he did [teach attitudes]. He taught me to be cold. . . .

It should be stressed that, if the girls originally accepted such instructions and values, many of them, at least at the time of interviewing, verbalized a rejection of these values and reported behavior which departed considerably from the interpersonal rules stipulated as "correct" by their trainers. Some experience orgasms with the customer, some show considerable affect toward "johns," others remain drunk or "high" throughout the contact.[9] While there seems to be general agreement as to what the rules of interpersonal conduct are, there appears to be consid-

---

[8] The topic of solicitation will be dealt with in a forthcoming paper.

[9] In the unpublished paper referred to above, Pomeroy has indicated that, of 31 call girls interviewed, only 23% reported never experiencing orgasms with customers.

erable variation in the adoption of such rules.

A variety of methods are employed to communicate the content described above. The trainer may arrange to eavesdrop on the interactions of girl and client and then discuss the interaction with her. One trainer, for example, listened through a closed door to the interaction of a new girl with a customer, then immediately after he left, discussed, in a rather heated way, methods by which his exit may have been facilitated. A pimp relates:

The best way to do this [teaching conversation] is, in the beginning, when the phone rings, for instance . . . is to listen to what she says and then check and see how big a trick he is and then correct her from there. . . . with everyone of them [trainees] I would make it a point to see two guys to see how they [the girls] operate.

In one case a girl reported that her pimp left a written list of rules pertaining to relating to "johns." Direct teaching, however, seems to be uncommon. The bulk of whatever learning takes place seems to take place through observation.

It's hard to tell you, because we learn through observations.
But I watched her and listened to what her bit was on the telephone.

To summarize, the structure of the apprenticeship period seems quite standard. The novice receives her training either from a pimp or from another more experienced call girl, more often the latter. She serves her initial two to eight months of work under the trainer's supervision and often serves this period in the trainer's apartment. The trainer assumes responsibility for arranging contacts and negotiating the type and place of the sexual encounter.

The content of the training pertains both to a general philosophical stance and to some specifics (usually not sexual) of

interpersonal behavior with customers and colleagues. The philosophy is one of exploiting the exploiters (customers) by whatever means necessary and defining the colleagues of the call girl as being intelligent, self-interested and, in certain important respects, basically honest individuals. The interpersonal techniques addressed during the learning period consist primarily of "pitches," telephone conversations, personal and occasionally sexual hygiene, prohibitions against alcohol and dope while with a "john," how and when to obtain the fee, and specifics concerning the sexual habits of particular customers. Specific sexual techniques are very rarely taught. The current sample included a considerable number of girls who, although capable of articulating this value structure, were not particularly inclined to adopt it.

Contacts and Contracts

While the imparting of ideologies and proprieties to the prospective call girl is emphasized during the apprenticeship period, it appears that the primary function of the apprenticeship, at least for the trainee, is building a clientele. Since this latter function limits the degree of occupational socialization, the process of developing the clientele and the arrangements made between trainer and trainee will be discussed.

Lists ("books") with the names and telephone numbers of customers are available for purchase from other call girls or pimps, but such books are often considered unreliable. While it is also true that an occasional pimp will refer customers to girls, this does not appear to be a frequent practice. The most frequent method of obtaining such names seems to be through contacts developed during the apprenticeship. The trainer refers customers to the apprentice and oversees the latter in terms of her responsibility and adequacy in dealing with the customer. For referring the customer, the trainer receives forty to fifty per cent of the total price agreed upon in the contract negotiated by the trainer and customer.[10] The trainer and trainees further agree, most often explicitly, on the apprentice's "right" to obtain and to use, on further occasions, information necessary for arranging another sexual contract with the "john" without the obligation of further "kick-back" to the trainer. That is, if she can obtain the name and telephone number of the customer, she can negotiate another contract without fee-splitting. During this period, then, the girl is not only introduced to other working colleagues (pimps and girls alike) but also develops a clientele.

There are two obvious advantages for a call girl in assuming the trainer role. First, since there seems to be an abundant demand for new girls, and since certain service requirements demand more than one girl, even the well established call girl chronically confronts the necessity for making referrals. It is then reasonable to assume that the extra profit derived from the fee-splitting activities, together with the added conveniences of having a girl "on call," allows the trainer to profit considerably from this arrangement. Secondly, contacts with customers are reputedly extremely difficult to maintain if services are not rendered on demand. Thus, the adoption of the trainer role enables the girl to maintain contacts with "fickle" customers under circumstances where she may wish a respite from the sexual encounter without terminating the contacts necessary for re-entry into the call girl role. It is also possible that the

financial gains may conceivably be much greater for most trainers than for most call girls, but this is a moot point.

A final aspect of the apprenticeship period that should be noted is the novice's income. It is possible for the novice, under the supervision of a competent and efficient trainer, to earn a great deal of money, or at least to get a favorable glimpse of the great financial possibilities of the occupation and, in effect, be heavily rewarded for her decision to enter it. Even though the novice may be inexperienced in both the sexual and interpersonal techniques of prostitution, her novelty on the market gives her an immediate advantage over her more experienced competitors. It seems quite likely that the new girl, irrespective of her particular physical or mental qualities, has considerable drawing power because she provides new sexual experience to the customer. Early success and financial reward may well provide considerable incentive to continue in the occupation.

A final word is needed regarding the position of the pimp vis-à-vis the call girl during the apprenticeship period. While some pimps assume the responsibility for training the girl personally, as indicated above, as many send the novice to another girl. The most apparent reason for such referral is that it facilitates the development of the "book." Purposes of training appear to be secondary for two reasons: (1) The pimp often lacks direct contact with the customers, so he personally cannot aid directly in the development of the girl's clientele; (2) When the pimp withdraws his girl from the training context, it is rarely because she has obtained adequate knowledge of the pro-

[10] The fee-splitting arrangement is quite common at all levels of career activity. For example, cooperative activity between two girls is often required for a particular type of sexual contract. In these cases, the girl who has contracted with the customer will contact a colleague, usually a friend, and will obtain 40%–50% of the latter's earnings. There is suggestive evidence that fee-splitting activities vary according to geographical areas and that Los Angeles is unique for both its fee-splitting patterns and the rigidity of its fee-splitting structure.

fession. This is not to say that all pimps are totally unconcerned with the type of knowledge being imparted to the girl. Rather, the primary concern of the pimp is the girl's developing a clientele, not learning the techniques of sex or conversation.

The apprenticeship period usually ends abruptly, not smoothly. Its termination may be but a reflection of interpersonal difficulties between trainer and trainee, novice and pimp, or between two novices. Occasionally termination of training is brought about through the novice's discovery and subsequent theft of the trainer's "book." Quite frequently, the termination is due to the novice's developing a sufficient trade or other business opportunities. The point is, however, that no respondent has reported that the final disruption of the apprenticeship was the result of the completion of adequate training. While disruptions of this relationship may be due to personal or impersonal events, termination is not directly due to the development of sufficient skills.

Discussion and Summary

On the basis of interviews with 33 call girls in the Los Angeles area, information was obtained about entrance into the call girl occupation and the initial training period or apprenticeship therein.

The novice call girl is acclimated to her new job primarily by being thoroughly immersed in the call girl subculture, where she learns the trade through imitation as much as through explicit tutoring. The outstanding concern at this stage is the development of a sizeable and lucrative clientele. The specific skills and values which are acquired dur-

ing this period are rather simple and quickly learned.

In spite of the girl's protests and their extensive folklore, the art of prostitution, at least at this level, seems to be technically a low-level skill. That is, it seems to be an occupation which requires little formal knowledge or practice for its successful pursuit and appears best categorized as an unskilled job. Evidence for this point comes from two separate sources. First, there seems to be little technical training during this period, and the training seems of little importance to the career progress. Length or type of training does not appear correlated with success (i.e., money earned, lack of subjective distress, minimum fee per "trick," etc.). Secondly, the termination of the apprenticeship period is often brought about for reasons unrelated to training. It seems that the need for an apprenticeship period is created more by the secrecy surrounding the rendering or the utilization of the call girl service than by the complexity of the role. In fact, it is reasonable to assume that the complexity of the job confronting a street-walker may be considerably greater than that confronting a call girl. The tasks of avoiding the police, sampling among strangers for potential customers, and arrangements for the completion of the sexual contract not only require different skills on the part of the street-walker, but are performances requiring a higher degree of professional "know-how" than is generally required of the call girl.[11]

As a pimp who manages both call girls and "high class" street-walkers explains:

The girl that goes out into the street is the sharper of the two, because she is capable

---

[11] Needless to say, however, all of the sample of call girls who were asked for status hierarchies of prostitution felt that the street-walker had both less status and a less complex job. It *may* well be that the verbal exchange required of the call girl requires greater knowledge than that required of a street-walker, but the non-verbal skills required of the street-walker may be considerably greater than those of the call girl.

of handling herself in the street, getting around the law, picking out the trick that is not absolutely psycho . . . and capable of getting along in the street. . . . The street-walker, as you term her, is really a prima donna of the prostitutes . . . her field is unlimited, she goes to all of the top places so she meets the top people. . . .

The fact that the enactment of the call girl role requires little training, and the introduction of the girl to clients and colleagues alike is rather rapid, gives little time or incentive for adequate occupational socialization. It is perhaps for this reason rather than, for example, reasons related to personality factors, that occupational instability is great and cultural homogeneity small.

In closing, while it appears that there is a rather well defined apprenticeship period in the career of the call girl, it seems that it is the secrecy rather than the complexity of the occupation which generates such a period. While there is good evidence that initial contacts, primarily with other "working girls," are necessary for entrance into this career, there seems no reason, at this point, to assume that the primary intent of the participants in training is anything but the development of an adequate clientele.

LEARNING DEVIANT NORMS

11

The content of any deviant subculture is usually a variation on and sometimes a caricature of the dominant cultural tradition. And, on occasion, it may exist in direct opposition to that tradition. Internally, the deviant group must instruct recruits in its distinctive tradition, be it variation on, caricature of, or opposition to the dominant culture. The deviant group must teach the novice the skills, beliefs, values, and norms that it upholds. Moreover, it must teach the more general perspectives that underlie this culture. If the subculture is an opponent of the dominant cultural tradition, the group must also work at sustaining its ideas and beliefs against the countervailing influences of the dominant culture.

Becker, in the first paper, shows how the process of socialization works with first-time marihuana users. Wallace reveals the process by which homeless men, once they have entered Skid Row, begin to take on its special culture. In the third paper, Weinberg describes the norms that are acquired in the nudist camp and how they sustain the group's perspective. Simmons examines specifically the techniques that a deviant group must use to help sustain its own peculiar system of beliefs. In the final paper, Bryan shows that call girls, who practice an unskilled trade in private, who have easy access to the occupation, and whose instruction is cursory, are unlikely to become totally committed to the ideology of prostitution.

Becoming a Marihuana User *

HOWARD S. BECKER

The novice does not ordinarily get high the first time he smokes marihuana, and several attempts are usually necessary to induce this state. One explanation of

* Reprinted with permission of The Macmillan Company from *Outsiders: Studies in the Sociology of Deviance* by Howard S. Becker. © The Free Press of Glencoe, a Division of The Macmillan Company, 1963, pp. 46–58.

this may be that the drug is not smoked "properly," that is, in a way that insures sufficient dosage to produce real symptoms of intoxication. Most users agree that it cannot be smoked like tobacco if one is to get high:

Take in a lot of air, you know, and . . . I don't know how to describe it, you don't smoke it like a cigarette, you draw in a lot of air and get it deep down in your system and then keep it there. Keep it there as long as you can.

Without the use of some such technique [1] the drug will produce no effects, and the user will be unable to get high:

The trouble with people like that [who are not able to get high] is that they're just not smoking it right, that's all there is to it. Either they're not holding it down long enough, or they're getting too much air and not enough smoke, or the other way around or something like that. A lot of people just don't smoke it right, so naturally nothing's gonna happen.

If nothing happens, it is manifestly impossible for the user to develop a conception of the drug as an object which can be used for pleasure, and use will therefore not continue. The first step in the sequence of events that must occur if the person is to become a user is that he must learn to use the proper smoking technique so that his use of the drug will produce effects in terms of which his conception of it can change.

Such a change is, as might be expected, a result of the individual's participation in groups in which marihuana is used. In them the individual learns the proper way to smoke the drug. This may occur through direct teaching:

I was smoking like I did an ordinary cigarette. He said, "No, don't do it like that." He said, "Suck it, you know, draw in and

hold it in your lungs till you . . . for a period of time."

I said, "Is there any limit of time to hold it?"

He said, "No, just till you feel that you want to let it out, let it out." So I did that three or four times.

Many new users are ashamed to admit ignorance and, pretending to know already, must learn through the more indirect means of observation and imitation:

I came on like I had turned on [smoked marihuana] many times before, you know. I didn't want to seem like a punk to this cat. See, like I didn't know the first thing about it—how to smoke it, or what was going to happen, or what. I just watched him like a hawk—I didn't take my eyes off him for a second, because I wanted to do everything just as he did it. I watched how he held it, how he smoked it, and everything. Then when he gave it to me I just came on cool, as though I knew exactly what the score was. I held it like he did and took a poke just the way he did.

No one I interviewed continued marihuana use for pleasure without learning a technique that supplied sufficient dosage for the effects of the drug to appear. Only when this was learned was it possible for a conception of the drug as an object which could be used for pleasure to emerge. Without such a conception marihuana use was considered meaningless and did not continue.

Learning to Perceive the Effects

Even after he learns the proper smoking technique, the new user may not get high and thus not form a conception of the drug as something which can be used for pleasure. A remark made by a user suggested the reason for this difficulty in

---

[1] A pharmacologist notes that this ritual is in fact an extremely efficient way of getting the drug into the blood stream. See R. P. Walton, *Marihuana: America's New Drug Problem* (Philadelphia: J. B. Lippincott, 1938), p. 48.

getting high and pointed to the next necessary step on the road to being a user:

As a matter of fact, I've seen a guy who was high out of his mind and didn't know it.

[How can that be, man?]

Well, it's pretty strange, I'll grant you that, but I've seen it. This guy got on with me, claiming that he'd never got high, one of those guys, and he got completely stoned. And he kept insisting that he wasn't high. So I had to prove to him that he was.

What does this mean? It suggests that being high consists of two elements: the presence of symptoms caused by marihuana use and the recognition of these symptoms and their connection by the user with his use of the drug. It is not enough, that is, that the effects be present; alone, they do not automatically provide the experience of being high. The user must be able to point them out to himself and consciously connect them with having smoked marihuana before he can have this experience. Otherwise, no matter what actual effects are produced, he considers that the drug has had no effect on him: "I figured it either had no effect on me or other people were exaggerating its effect on them, you know. I thought it was probably psychological, see." Such persons believe the whole thing is an illusion and that the wish to be high leads the user to deceive himself into believing that something is happening when, in fact, nothing is. They do not continue marihuana use, feeling that "it does nothing" for them.

Typically, however, the novice has faith (developed from his observation of users who do get high) that the drug actually will produce some new experience and continues to experiment with it until it does. His failure to get high worries him, and he is likely to ask more experienced users or provoke comments from them about it. In such conversations he is made aware of specific details of his experience which he may not have noticed or may have noticed but failed to identify as symptoms of being high:

I didn't get high the first time. . . . I don't think I held it in long enough. I probably let it out, you know, you're a little afraid. The second time I wasn't sure, and he [smoking companion] told me, like I asked him for some of the symptoms or something, how would I know, you know. . . . So he told me to sit on a stool. I sat on—I think I sat on a bar stool—and he said, "Let your feet hang," and then when I got down my feet were real cold, you know.

And I started feeling it, you know. That was the first time. And then about a week after that, sometime pretty close to it, I really got on. That was the first time I got on a big laughing kick, you know. Then I really knew I was on.

One symptom of being high is an intense hunger. In the next case the novice becomes aware of this and gets high for the first time:

They were just laughing the hell out of me because like I was eating so much. I just scoffed [ate] so much food, and they were just laughing at me, you know. Sometimes I'd be looking at them, you know, wondering why they're laughing, you know, not knowing what I was doing. [Well, did they tell you why they were laughing eventually?] Yeah, yeah, I come back, "Hey, man, what's happening?" Like, you know, like I'd ask, "What's happening?" and all of a sudden I feel weird, you know. "Man, you're on, you know. You're on pot [high on marihuana]." I said, "No, am I?" Like I don't know what's happening.

The learning may occur in more indirect ways:

I heard little remarks that were made by other people. Somebody said, "My legs are rubbery," and I can't remember all the remarks that were made because I was very attentively listening for all these cues for what I was supposed to feel like.

The novice, then, eager to have this feeling, picks up from other users some concrete referents of the term "high" and applies these notions to his own experience. The new concepts make it possible for him to locate these symptoms among his own sensations and to point out to himself a "something different" in his experience that he connects with drug use. It is only when he can do this that he is high. In the next case, the contrast between two successive experiences of a user makes clear the crucial importance of the awareness of the symptoms in being high and re-emphasizes the important role of interaction with other users in acquiring the concepts that make this awareness possible:

[Did you get high the first time you turned on?] Yeah, sure. Although, come to think of it, I guess I really didn't. I mean, like that first time it was more or less of a mild drunk. I was happy, I guess, you know what I mean. But I didn't really know I was high, you know what I mean. It was only after the second time I got high that I realized I was high the first time. Then I knew that something different was happening.

[How did you know that?] How did I know? If what happened to me that night would of happened to you, you would've known, believe me. We played the first tune for almost two hours—one tune! Imagine, man! We got on the stand and played this one tune, we started at nine o'clock. When we got finished I looked at my watch, it's a quarter to eleven. Almost two hours on one tune. And it didn't seem like anything. I mean, you know, it does that to you. It's like you have much more time or something. Anyway, when I saw that, man, it was too much. I knew I must really be high or something if anything like that could happen. See, and then they explained to me that that's what it did to you, you had a different sense of time and everything. So I realized that that's what it was. I knew then.

Like the first time, I probably felt that way, you know, but I didn't know what's happening.

It is only when the novice becomes able to get high in this sense that he will continue to use marihuana for pleasure. In every case in which use continued, the user had acquired the necessary concepts with which to express to himself the fact that he was experiencing new sensations caused by the drug. That is, for use to continue, it is necessary not only to use the drug so as to produce effects but also to learn to perceive these effects when they occur. In this way marihuana acquires meaning for the user as an object which can be used for pleasure.

With increasing experience the user develops a greater appreciation of the drug's effects; he continues to learn to get high. He examines succeeding experiences closely, looking for new effects, making sure the old ones are still there. Out of this there grows a stable set of categories for experiencing the drug's effects whose presence enables the user to get high with ease.

Users, as they acquire this set of categories, become connoisseurs. Like experts in fine wines, they can specify where a particular plant was grown and what time of year it was harvested. Although it is usually not possible to know whether these attributions are correct, it is true that they distinguish between batches of marihuana, not only according to strength, but also with respect to the different kinds of symptoms produced.

The ability to perceive the drug's effects must be maintained if use is to continue; if it is lost, marihuana use ceases. Two kinds of evidence support this statement. First, people who become heavy users of alcohol, barbiturates, or opiates do not continue to smoke marihuana, largely because they lose the ability to distinguish between its effects and those of the other drugs.[2] They no longer know whether the marihuana gets them high. Second, in those few cases in which an individual uses marihuana in such quantities that he is always high, he is apt to feel the drug has no effect on him, since the essential element of a noticeable difference between feeling high and feeling normal is missing. In such a situation, use is likely to be given up completely, but temporarily, in order that the user may once again be able to perceive the difference.

Learning to Enjoy the Effects

One more step is necessary if the user who has now learned to get high is to continue use. He must learn to enjoy the effects he has just learned to experience. Marihuana-produced sensations are not automatically or necessarily pleasurable. The taste for such experience is a socially acquired one, not different in kind from acquired tastes for oysters or dry martinis. The user feels dizzy, thirsty; his scalp tingles; he misjudges time and distances. Are these things pleasurable? He isn't sure. If he is to continue marihuana use, he must decide that they are. Otherwise, getting high, while a real enough experience, will be an unpleasant one he would rather avoid.

The effects of the drug, when first perceived, may be physically unpleasant or at least ambiguous:

It started taking effect, and I didn't know what was happening, you know, what it was, and I was very sick. I walked around the room, walking around the room trying to get off, you know; it just scared me at first, you know. I wasn't used to that kind of feeling.

In addition, the novice's naïve interpretation of what is happening to him may further confuse and frighten him, particularly if he decides, as many do, that he is going insane:

I felt I was insane, you know. Everything people done to me just wigged me. I couldn't hold a conversation, and my mind would be wandering, and I was always thinking, oh, I don't know, weird things, like hearing music different. . . . I get the feeling that I can't talk to anyone. I'll goof completely.

Given these typically frightening and unpleasant first experiences, the beginner will not continue use unless he learns to redefine the sensations as pleasurable:

It was offered to me, and I tried it. I'll tell you one thing. I never did enjoy it at all. I mean it was just nothing that I could enjoy. [Well, did you get high when you turned on?] Oh, yeah, I got definite feelings from it. But I didn't enjoy them. I mean I got plenty of reactions, but they were mostly reactions of fear. [You were frightened?] Yes. I didn't enjoy it. I couldn't seem to relax with it, you know. If you can't relax with a thing, you can't enjoy it, I don't think.

In other cases the first experiences were also definitely unpleasant, but the person did become a marihuana user. This occurred, however, only after a later experience enabled him to redefine the sensations as pleasurable:

[This man's first experience was extremely unpleasant, involving distortion of spatial relationships and sounds, violent thirst, and panic produced by these symptoms.] After the first time I didn't turn on for about, I'd say, ten months to a year. . . . It wasn't a moral thing; it was because I'd gotten so frightened, bein' so high. An' I didn't want to go through that again, I mean, my reac-

[2] "Smokers have repeatedly stated that the consumption of whiskey while smoking negates the potency of the drug. They find it very difficult to get 'high' while drinking whiskey and because of that smokers will not drink while using the 'weed.'" (New York City Mayor's Committee on Marihuana, *The Marihuana Problem in the City of New York*, Lancaster, Pa.: Jacques Cattell Press, 1944, p. 13.)

tion was, "Well, if this is what they call bein' high, I don't dig [like] it." . . . So I didn't turn on for a year almost, accounta that. . . .

Well, my friends started, an' consequently I started again. But I didn't have any more, I didn't have that same initial reaction, after I started turning on again.

[In interaction with his friends he became able to find pleasure in the effects of the drug and eventually became a regular user.]

In no case will use continue without a redefinition of the effects as enjoyable.

This redefinition occurs, typically, in interaction with more experienced users who, in a number of ways, teach the novice to find pleasure in this experience which is at first so frightening.[3] They may reassure him as to the temporary character of the unpleasant sensations and minimize their seriousness, at the same time calling attention to the more enjoyable aspects. An experienced user describes how he handles newcomers to marihuana use:

Well, they get pretty high sometimes. The average person isn't ready for that, and it is a little frightening to them sometimes. I mean, they've been high on lush [alcohol], and they get higher that way than they've ever been before, and they don't know what's happening to them. Because they think they're going to keep going up, up, up till they lose their minds or begin doing weird things or something. You have to like reassure them, explain to them that they're not really flipping or anything, that they're gonna be all right. You have to just talk them out of being afraid. Keep talking to them, reassuring, telling them it's all right. And come on with your own story, you know: "The same thing happened to me. You'll get to like that after awhile." Keep coming on like that; pretty soon you talk them out of being scared. And besides they see you doing it and nothing horrible is hap-

pening to you, so that gives them more confidence.

The more experienced user may also teach the novice to regulate the amount he smokes more carefully, so as to avoid any severely uncomfortable symptoms while retaining the pleasant ones. Finally, he teaches the new user that he can "get to like it after awhile." He teaches him to regard those ambiguous experiences formerly defined as unpleasant as enjoyable. The older user in the following incident is a person whose tastes have shifted in this way, and his remarks have the effect of helping others to make a similar redefinition:

A new user had her first experience of the effects of marihuana and became frightened and hysterical. She "felt like she was half in and half out of the room" and experienced a number of alarming physical symptoms. One of the more experienced users present said, "She's dragged because she's high like that. I'd give anything to get that high myself. I haven't been that high in years."

In short, what was once frightening and distasteful becomes, after a taste for it is built up, pleasant, desired, and sought after. Enjoyment is introduced by the favorable definition of the experience that one acquires from others. Without this, use will not continue, for marihuana will not be for the user an object he can use for pleasure.

In addition to being a necessary step in becoming a user, this represents an important condition for continued use. It is quite common for experienced users suddenly to have an unpleasant or frightening experience, which they cannot define as pleasurable, either because they have used a larger amount of marihuana than usual or because the marihuana they

[3] Sol Charen and Luis Perelman, "Personality Studies of Marihuana Addicts," *American Journal of Psychiatry*, CII (March, 1946), p. 679.

have used turns out to be of a higher quality than they expected. The user has sensations which go beyond any conception he has of what being high is and is in much the same situation as the novice, uncomfortable and frightened. He may blame it on an overdose and simply be more careful in the future. But he may make this the occasion for a rethinking of his attitude toward the drug and decide that it no longer can give him pleasure. When this occurs and is not followed by a redefinition of the drug as capable of producing pleasure, use will cease.

The likelihood of such a redefinition occurring depends on the degree of the individual's participation with other users. Where this participation is intensive, the individual is quickly talked out of his feeling against marihuana use. In the next case, on the other hand, the experience was very disturbing, and the aftermath of the incident cut the person's participation with other users to almost zero. Use stopped for three years and began again only when a combination of circumstances, important among which was a resumption of ties with users, made possible a redefinition of the nature of the drug:

It was too much, like I only made about four pokes, and I couldn't even get it out of my mouth, I was so high, and I got real flipped. In the basement, you know, I just couldn't stay in there anymore. My heart was pounding real hard, you know, and I was going out of my mind; I thought I was losing my mind completely. So I cut out of this basement, and this other guy, he's out of his mind, told me, "Don't, don't leave me, man. Stay here." And I couldn't.

I walked outside, and it was five below zero, and I thought I was dying, and I had my coat open; I was sweating, I was perspiring. My whole insides were all . . . , and I walked about two blocks away, and I fainted behind a bush. I don't know how long I laid there. I woke up, and I was feel-

ing the worst, I can't describe it at all, so I made it to a bowling alley, man, and I was trying to act normal, I was trying to shoot pool, you know, trying to act real normal, and I couldn't lay and I couldn't stand up and I couldn't sit down, and I went up and laid down where some guys that spot pins lay down, and that didn't help me, and I went down to a doctor's office. I was going to go in there and tell the doctor to put me out of my misery . . . because my heart was pounding so hard, you know. . . . So then all week end I started flipping, seeing things there and going through hell, you know, all kinds of abnormal things. . . . I just quit for a long time then.

[He went to a doctor who defined the symptoms for him as those of a nervous breakdown caused by "nerves" and "worries." Although he was no longer using marihuana, he had some recurrences of the symptoms which led him to suspect that "it was all his nerves."] So I just stopped worrying, you know; so it was about thirty-six months later I started making it again. I'd just take a few pokes, you know. [He first resumed use in the company of the same user-friend with whom he had been involved in the original incident.]

A person, then, cannot begin to use marihuana for pleasure, or continue its use for pleasure, unless he learns to define its effects as enjoyable, unless it becomes and remains an object he conceives of as capable of producing pleasure.

In summary, an individual will be able to use marihuana for pleasure only when he goes through a process of learning to conceive of it as an object which can be used in this way. No one becomes a user without (1) learning to smoke the drug in a way which will produce real effects; (2) learning to recognize the effects and connect them with drug use (learning, in other words, to get high); and (3) learning to enjoy the sensations he perceives. In the course of this process he develops a disposition or motivation to use marihuana which was not and could not have been present when he began use, for it involves and depends on conceptions of the drug which could only grow out of the kind of actual experience detailed above. On completion of this process he is willing and able to use marihuana for pleasure.

He has learned, in short, to answer "Yes" to the question: "Is it fun?" The direction his further use of the drug takes depends on his being able to continue to answer "Yes" to this question and, in addition, on his being able to answer "Yes" to other questions which arise as he becomes aware of the implications of the fact that society disapproves of the practice: "Is it expedient?" "Is it moral?" Once he has acquired the ability to get enjoyment by using the drug, use will continue to be possible for him. Considerations of morality and expediency, occasioned by the reactions of society, may interfere and inhibit use, but use continues to be a possibility in terms of his conception of the drug. The act becomes impossible only when the ability to enjoy the experience of being high is lost, through a change in the user's conception of the drug occasioned by certain kinds of experience with it.

The Skid Row Subculture *

SAMUEL E. WALLACE

. . . Once each of . . . [the] three types of recruit has made initial contact with skid row, the slow process of socialization into the subculture begins. What started perhaps as a temporary way of life induced by hard times or personal problems becomes permanent, and another person is "lost" to the world of Respectable Society. The newcomer now has to learn how to behave toward other members of the skid row community. He is in their world now, and to adjust to that world he must come to terms with its venerable citizens.

He learns the proper names for things, and this vocabulary helps structure the subcultural society for him. It conveys the attitudes and values of the skid row community, and proper use of the skid row language quickly identifies one as a genuine insider. Conversely, to be ignorant of the skid row idiom tags one as "not in the know," an outsider, one of "them." A major socializing force in the subculture, skid row argot partly traces its heritage back to Elizabethan cant, some of it originating as a matter of record at least as far back as 1535. Partly, skid row argot borrows from underworld slang, and is further enriched by some of the lingo of the skid rower's world of work. Many words and expressions speak for themselves, while others need translation.

The newcomer's increasing socialization into skid row subculture is paralleled by his increasing isolation from society. His family loses contact with him. His

* Reprinted from Samuel E. Wallace, *Skid Row as a Way of Life* (Totowa, N.J.: Bedminster Press, 1965), pp. 172–177. Copyright © 1965, Bedminster Press Incorporated. Reprinted by permission.

friends in the outside world are gradually replaced by those living on skid row. His neighbors have become the men who lie in the adjoining bunks rather than those who live in the house next door. His work colleagues are now fellow skid rowers. He soon acquires his own social worker.

As the newcomer withdraws from the outside world, his education in these customs, mores, and patterns of behavior essential to life in the larger community ceases. From the viewpoint of respectable society, the skid rower becomes de-socialized [1]—that is, educated outside the mainstream of American society and unfit to live within it. Even the fledgling skid rower, for example, has lived so long in an all male world that he has forgotten how to communicate with women.

Now, how shall I ask one of these girls for a dance? No need of introductions, that much I knew. Which would be best, "C'mon kid, let's prance this out?" Or, "May I have this dance?" How I wished these girls were men. I could talk to the men. The formula was simple; noun or pronoun, obscene adjective; verb, obscene verb; object, obscene adjective. All similes had reference to hell on the unemphatic levels—hot as hell, cold as hell, pretty as hell. On the emphatic levels you used excreta or sexual organs as a basis for comparison.
But these girls! [2]

At some point in his process of alienation and de-socialization from the outside world, and its parallel process of socialization into the skid row subculture, the apprentice skid rower is labeled a deviant —a skid rower. This label may be affixed to him when he comes into contact with

welfare workers, when he attempts to get a job, or when he is simply observed while walking through areas outside skid row. If he is publicly and officially labeled a deviant through arrest, sentence, and incarceration, the newcomer's socialization is vastly intensified since those he lives with in jail and in the workhouse are also members of the skid row community. He spends all day long eating, working, and talking with his fellow community members and returns to skid row with a more intimate knowledge of its way of life. The public label of deviance also adds to the credentials he needs for admittance into the in-group on skid row.

When I returned to the Lower Loop [skid row], I saw many of my former jail and workhouse inmates. Although we may not have talked with each other during our confinement, they now greeted me and were much more friendly than before I had been arrested and jailed. Several introduced me to their friends, often remarking that we had just returned from a "rest in the country." One asked me if I wanted some "pot," [marijuana], another wanted to share his woman with me, and a third wanted me to go with him to L.A. [3]

Once he has been labeled a deviant, self-awareness is forced upon the individual. He must face the fact that he is now indeed on skid row. The same label increases his separation from the wider society and at the same time urges him to enter into ever closer participation with those similarly isolated. Thus is he pushed into still further deviance, additional arrests, workhouse socialization, and more complete isolation until he is finally and

---

[1] I prefer this term to the one sometimes used—undersocialization—since the latter seems to indicate social inadequacy whereas the former is linked to the individual's increasing isolation. The term de-socialization helps indicate the departure from the world of middle class respectability which is accompanied by entry into the skid row community. Whether termed undersocialization or de-socialization, however, it is only a part of the process of making a skid rower.
[2] William Edge. *The Main Stem.* New York: Vanguard, 1927. p. 127.
[3] Samuel E. Wallace. *Participant Observation Journal.* Minneapolis: unpublished research report, University of Minnesota, Department of Sociology, 1958.

completely a full-fledged member of the deviant community. Sooner or later private self-acceptance of the deviant label must inevitably follow public recognition, and thus this greatest of all barriers to reform is erected: he now thinks of himself as a skid rower.

Self-acceptance of membership in a deviant community may be announced to the world in a variety of subtle and yet critical ways. The person may begin by neglecting his appearance. When he is hard up he may sell his clothes, or even worse, his razor, and "when a fellow decides to sell his razor he is about to commit an act that severs the jugular vein of his respectability." [4]

In order to accomplish this change in self-image without destroying himself—in order to defend himself against accepting the outsiders' view of him—the person must make full use of all the subcultural attitudes he has learned. The

newcomer is now a full-fledged member of skid row.

How I changed . . . I had developed the strange fears of the migratory worker. I feared policemen above all things. I felt like an outcast of society, a man to whom good things are permanently denied. I was so accustomed to coarse words and nasty living quarters that I mistrusted, almost to the point of being psychopathic, good meals, clean blankets, a pleasant room. Perhaps I realized this more keenly because of Charlie. He had not developed the cautions and apprehensions of a proletarian. He was a free American with civil rights of which he felt quite confident.

I looked at Charlie. I was thinking, too damn goodlooking for a migratory worker, attracts too much attention. Talks about the wrong thing on the job. On the job a fellow ought not talk about books and theories and things. Ought to talk about the same thing as other workers—whiskey, women, jobs, flophouses.[5]

Sexual Modesty and the Nudist Camp *

MARTIN S. WEINBERG

Deviant sub-systems have norms that permit, organize, and control the behavior which defines them as deviant. The nudist camp is an example of such a deviant sub-system, nudists being defined as deviant by their disregard for clothing when in the presence of others, particularly members of the opposite sex. This paper will describe the normative system of the

nudist camp, its consequences for sustaining the definition of the situation common to this group, and the way it maintains those interaction patterns this sub-system shares with the outside society.

The general sociological framework to be used emphasizes the study of "social meanings" as a salient subject for understanding the realm of social organization.

---

[4] Andress Floyd. *My Monks of Vagabondia.* New Jersey: Self Master Press Union, 1913. p. 39.

[5] Edge, *op. cit.* pp. 152–153.

* Reprinted from *Social Problems*, Vol. 12, No. 3 (Winter, 1965), pp. 311–18, by permission of *Social Problems.*

Such an approach was set forth by Weber:[1] in order to understand social organization it is not sufficient to look at stable and recurrent patterns of social behavior alone; one also must look at the subjective meanings attached to behavior, i.e., those meanings by which social behavior is oriented in its course. The assumption underlying this focus is that stable social meanings are products of a social standardization process, being controlled by the "molds" which social organization imposes on patterns of sociation.[2]

The institutionalized patterns of sexual modesty will be viewed as an aspect of social organization, with attention given to the social meanings linked to normative breaches, i.e., immodesty. A study of the deviant case of social nudists will then be presented, illustrating how members of this social system are re-socialized in the meaning attributed to one form of immodesty. It is hoped that this study will contribute to a better understanding of the nature and essence of sexual mod-

esty, as well as to the general processes of social organization.

Modesty and Meanings

Modesty is a form of reserve. Sexual modesty is sexual reserve (or a communication of non-availability for sexual interaction). This quality of meaning results from the social actor's following the dictates of sexual propriety—the commonsense constructs of proper or "decent" behavior. From the point of view of this paper, sexual modesty is thus defined as an institutionalized pattern of social interaction.[3] It imposes a pattern of tension management by which social control is maintained over the sexual interests latent in any heterosexual encounter.

In the sexual realm, acts of immodesty take the following basic forms, all of them communicating a boldness or lack of inhibition: (1) verbal communications; and (2) non-verbal communications,[4] which typically are differentiated into (a) a display of body or bodily func-

---

[1] Max Weber, *The Theory of Social and Economic Organization,* Glencoe: The Free Press, 1947, pp. 88ff. Also see: Alfred Schutz, *Collected Papers I: The Problem of Social Reality,* The Hague: Martinus Nijhoff, 1962, p. 59. Schutz insists that in considering these social meanings the sociologist develop "constructs of the second degree" out of the meaning constructs which typically guide the social actor. That is, the sociologist should abstract his more generalized model of social order out of the "order" which channels individual actors in their social behavior.

[2] Cf. Harold Garfinkel, "The Routine Grounds of Everyday Activities," *Social Problems,* 3 (Winter, 1964), p. 237.

[3] An "institutionalized pattern of social interaction" will be defined as an organized way of doing something: a formal, legitimized, recognized, established, and stabilized way in which an aspect of behavior is expected to be performed. (Cf. Robert Bierstedt, *The Social Order,* New York: McGraw-Hill Book Co., Inc., 1957, pp. 299ff.)

Modesty may additionally be viewed as a pattern of deference, i.e. conducting oneself with good demeanor is in general a way of showing deference to those present (Cf. Erving Goffman, "The Nature of Deference and Demeanor," *American Anthropologist,* 58 (June, 1956), p. 492). This could be labeled "deference through non-initiation" of sexual overtures. This interpretation of modesty leads us to inequalities in the social structure, since patterns of deference point to the relative positions of the actor and alter in the social hierarchy. Therefore, as women gain more equality in the social structure we would expect the "double standard" of modesty to decline—i.e., women gain more rights to "initiate" or suspend patterns of deference.

A more extreme degree of deference may, however, lead to immodesty rather than modesty. This is "deference through subservience." Thus women who dress or act immodestly solely for the benefit of the male may also demonstrate deference. Deference through both non-initiation and subservience should decrease with equalization of the social structure.

[4] See Erving Goffman, *The Presentation of Self in Everyday Life,* New York: Doubleday and Co., Inc., 1959.

tions, and (b) other forms of erotic overture (e.g., the way one actor looks at another).

Common-sense definitions assume an interrelationship between verbal and nonverbal expressions of immodesty. Rightly or wrongly, most men regard a woman who will curse in their presence—that is, use the proscribed four letter words—as a woman who will suit action to her language.[5] At one time this imputation went so far that if a woman talked about the "legs" of a table or the "breast" of a chicken, she was immediately typed as being immodest and unrefined.[6] The preceding examples illustrate, respectively, two meanings commonly attributed to immodest acts: (1) the act may be perceived as communicating sexual availability; and (2) the act may be perceived as a projection of bad breeding. These types are not mutually exclusive, but they do seem most typically differentiated by the blatancy of display.

Immodest acts may also be analytically differentiated along the dimension of "commission—omission."[7] That is, acts may be classified as immodest because of one's active performance of an act, or because of one's passiveness or failure to manage effectively an impression of restraint in regard to another's immodest act. Thus, the girl who stares at a nude man is defined as immodest, as well as the girl who displays herself nude; the girl who listens to "dirty" jokes (and, if unable to escape the social gathering, fails to display inattention), as well as the girl who tells them; the girl who allows herself to be grabbed, as well as the girl who does the grabbing. Although it may appear contradictory to define passiveness as nullifying reserve, this may be clarified by viewing such an omission as invalidating an impression of sexual reserve (i.e., non-availability for sexual interaction).

Hypothesis and Method

The manifest function of sexual modesty (i.e., those consequences evaluated by common-sense rationality) is maintenance of social control over latent sexual interests. Common-sense conceptions of modesty also put most emphasis on the covering of the body when in the presence of the opposite sex for the performance of this function.[8] Considerations of a breakdown in clothing modesty bring forth images of rampant sexual interest, promiscuity, embarrassment, jealousy, and shame.

TABLE 1
Typology of Immodest Behavior

Act of:	Display of Body	Verbal Expression	Erotic Overtures
Commission	Shows 1-1	Says 1-2	Does 1-3
Omission	Looks at 2-1	Listens to 2-2	Allows 2-3

[5] Shailer Upton Lawton and Jules Archer, *Sexual Conduct of the Teen-Ager,* New York: Spectrolux Corporation, 1951, p. 111.
[6] Alexander M. Gow, *Good Morals and Gentle Manners for Schools and Families,* New York: American Book Co., 1873.
[7] Weber, *op. cit.,* p. 88; Schutz, *op. cit.,* pp. 66ff.
[8] See Lawrence Langner, *The Importance of Wearing Clothes,* New York: Hastings House, 1959; René Guyon, *The Ethics of Sexual Acts,* New York: Blue Ribbon Books, 1941; Havelock Ellis, *Studies in the Psychology of Sex,* Vol. 1, Philadelphia: F. A. Davis Co., 1930.

Social nudists (i.e., those who practice nudism in a nudist camp) are thus defined as "deviants" by their disregard for body covering, falling in cell 1-1 of our typology of immodesty. The remainder of the paper will discuss an empirical study of this group of systematic deviants.[9] The following general hypothesis provided the foundation for this research:

If nudists effectively change the societal definition of the situation regarding nudity, and are also able to maintain the forms of modesty pertaining to the other cells of our typology, then social control over latent sexual interests will still be maintained.

If we take as given that the nudist camp only changes the definition of one of our cells of immodesty, then when other forms of modesty are not maintained the indubitableness or taken-for-grantedness of the changed definition of the situation (regarding nudity) will be called into question.[10]

For an examination of this hypothesis, three nudist camps located near the Chicago metropolitan area were contacted, and readily agreed to be the objects of research. Field work was undertaken in these camps over the course of one summer. During the period of participant observation, nudist members were asked to fill out cards which requested their name and address, so that they could be contacted at a later date for purposes of an interview. These formalized interviews were a supplement to the more exploratory field work, serving as a systematic technique by which to gather the specific data desired. Although nudists tend to be wary of revealing personal data such as last name or address, rapport was high and, when given a promise of confiden-

tiality, very few refused to fill out these sample cards.

After the observational data were organized, an interview schedule was constructed. Selection of respondents was limited to those living within a hundred mile radius of Chicago; a total of one hundred and one interviews were completed.[11]

The Nudist Camp

The ideology of the nudist camp provides a new definition of the situation regarding nudity, which in effect maintains that:

1. nudism and sexuality are unrelated
2. there is nothing shameful about exposing the human body
3. the abandonment of clothes can lead to a feeling of freedom and natural pleasure
4. nude activities, especially full bodily exposure to the sun, leads to a feeling of physical, mental and spiritual well-being.

These definitions are sustained by nudists to a remarkable degree, illustrating the extent to which adult socialization can function in changing long-maintained meanings; in this case regarding the exposure of one's nude body in heterosexual situations. The tremendous emphasis on covering the sexual areas, and the relation between nudism and sexuality which exists in the outside society, however, suggests that the nudist definition of the situation might, at times, be quite easily called into question. The results of the field work and formal interviews indicate

[9] For a discussion of the concept "systematic deviation," see Edwin Lemert, *Social Pathology*, New York: McGraw-Hill, 1951, p. 44.
[10] See Schutz, *op. cit.*, pp. 94–95, for a summary discussion of the process by which presuppositions get called into question.
[11] Many of the nudists interviewed had attended or held membership in a number of different camps. Thus, experiences from at least twenty camps provided concurrent data for our conclusions.

S

Learning Deviant Norms **275**

how the social organization of the nudist camp has developed a system of norms that contributes to sustaining the official definition of the situation. Since the major concern of this paper is modesty, we will restrict our discussion to the first two declarations of nudist ideology (i.e., that nudism and sexuality are unrelated, and that there is nothing shameful about exposing the human body). These are also the elements which lead to the classification of nudists as deviant. The normative proscriptions which contribute to the maintenance of this definition of the situation will be described.

Organizational Precautions. Organizational precautions are initially taken in the requirements for admission to a nudist camp. Most camps do not allow unmarried individuals, especially single men, or allow only a small quota of singles. Those camps that do allow male-singles may charge up to thirty-five per cent higher rates for the single's membership than is charged for the membership of an entire family. This is intended to discourage single memberships but, since the cost is still relatively low in comparison to other resorts, this measure is not very effective. It seems to do little more than create resentment among the singles. By giving formal organizational backing to the definition that singles are not especially desirable, it also might be related to the social segregation of single and married members that is evident in nudist camps.

An overabundance of single men is recognized by the organization as threatening the definition of nudism that is maintained. The presence of singles at the camp is suspected to be for purposes other than the "nudist way of life" (e.g., to gape at the women). Such a view may call into question the denied relation between nudity and sexuality.

Certification by the camp owner is also required before anyone is admitted on the camp grounds. This is sometimes supplemented by three letters of recommendation in regard to the character of the applicant. This is a precaution against admitting those "social types" which might conceivably discredit the ideology of the movement.

A limit is sometimes set on the number of trial visits which can be made to the camp; that is, visits made without membership in some camp or inter-camp organization. In addition, a limit is usually set on the length of time one is allowed to maintain himself clothed. These rules function to weed out those guests whose sincere acceptance of the "nudist" definition of the situation is questionable.

Norms Regarding Interpersonal Behavior. Norms regarding patterns of interpersonal behavior are also functional for the maintenance of the organization's system of meanings. The existence of these norms, however, should be recognized as formally acknowledging that the nudist definition of the situation could become problematic unless precautions were taken.

No staring. This rule functions to prevent any overt signs of "overinvolvement." In the words of a non-nudist who is involved in the publication of a nudist magazine, "They all look up to the heavens and never look below." This pattern of civil inattention [12] is most exaggerated among the females, who manage the impression that there is absolutely no concern or awareness that the male body is in an unclothed state. Women often recount how they expect everyone will look at them when they are nude, only to find that no one communicates any impression of concern when they finally do get up their nerve and undress. One woman told the writer:

[12] See Erving Goffman, *Behavior in Public Places,* New York: The Free Press, 1963, p. 84.

"I got so mad because my husband wanted me to undress in front of other men that I just pulled my clothes right off thinking everyone would look at me." She was amazed (and somewhat disappointed) when no one did. Thus, even though nudists are immodest in their behavior by "showing" their bodies, which falls in cell 1-1 of our typology of immodesty, they are not immodest in the sense of cell 2-1 of our table. "Looking at" immodesty is controlled; external constraints prohibit staring.

(Have you ever observed or heard about anyone staring at someone's body while at camp?) [13] I've heard stories—particularly about men that stare. Since I heard these stories, I tried not to, and even done away with my sunglasses after someone said, half joking, that I hide behind sunglasses to stare. Towards the end of the summer I stopped wearing sunglasses. And you know what, it was a child who told me this.

No sex talk. Sex talk, or telling "dirty" jokes, is not common in the nudist camp. The owner of one of the most widely known camps in the Midwest told the writer: "It is usually expected that members of a nudist camp will not talk about sex, politics, or religion." Or in the words of one single-male: "It is taboo to make sexual remarks here." Verbal immodesty was not experienced by the writer during his period of field work. Interview respondents who mentioned that they had discussed or talked about sex qualified this by stating that such talk was restricted to close friends, was of a "scientific" nature or, if a joke, was of a "cute" sort. Verbal immodesty, represented in the second column of our typology of immodesty, is not common to the nudist camp.

When respondents were asked what they would think of someone who breached this norm, they indicated that such behavior would cast doubt on the actor's acceptance of the nudist definition of the situation:

One would expect to hear less of that at camp than at other places. (Why's that?) Because you expect that the members are screened in their *attitude for nudism*—and this isn't one who prefers sexual jokes.

They probably don't belong there. They're there to see what they can find to observe. (What do you mean?) Well, their mind isn't on being a nudist, but to see so-and-so nude.

Body contact is taboo. Although the degree to which this rule is enforced varies among camps, there is at least some degree of informal enforcement. Nudists mention that one is particularly careful not to brush against anyone or have any body contact, because of the way it might be interpreted. The following quotation illustrates the interpersonal precautions taken:

I stay clear of the opposite sex. They're so sensitive, they imagine things.

One respondent felt that this taboo was simply a common-sense form of modesty:

Suppose one had a desire to knock one off or feel his wife-—modesty or a sense of protocol prohibits you from doing this.

When asked to conceptualize a breakdown in this form of modesty, a common response was:

They are in the wrong place. (How's that?) That's not part of nudism. (Could you tell me some more about that?) I think they are there for some sort of sex thrill. They are certainly not there to enjoy the sun.

If any photographs are taken for publication in a nudist magazine, the subjects are allowed to have only limited body contact. As one female nudist said: "We don't want anyone to think we're immoral." Outsiders' interpretations of body contact among nudists would cast doubt

---

[13] Interview questions and probes have been placed in parentheses.

on the nudist definition of the situation or the characteristics set forth as the "nudist way of life."

A correlate of the body contact taboo is the prohibition of dancing in the nude. This is verbalized by nudist actors as a separate rule, and it is often the object of jest by members. This indication of "organizational strain" can be interpreted as an instance in which the existence of the rule itself brings into question the nudist definition of the situation, i.e., that there is no relationship between nudism and sexuality. The following remark acknowledges this: "This reflects a contradiction in our beliefs. But it's self protection. One incident and we'd be closed." Others define dancing in the nude as an erotic overture which would incite sexual arousal. Such rationalizations are common to the group.

Returning to our typology of immodesty, it can be seen that incitements heightening latent sexual interest that would fall in column three of the typology (i.e., "doing" behavior), are to some extent controlled by prohibiting body contact.

Alcoholic beverages are not allowed in American camps. This rule also functions in controlling any breakdown in inhibitions which could lead to "aggressive-erotic" overtures (column three of immodesty). Even those respondents who told the writer that they had "snuck a beer" before going to bed went on to say, however, that they fully favored the rule. The following quotation is representative of nudists' thoughts:

Anyone who drinks in camp is jeopardizing their membership and they shouldn't. Anyone who drinks in camp could get reckless. (How's that?) Well, when guys and girls drink they're a lot bolder—they might get fresh with someone else's girl. That's why it isn't permitted, I guess.

Rules regarding photography. Taking photographs in a nudist camp is a sensitive matter. Unless the individual is an official photographer (i.e., one photographing for the nudist magazines), the photographer's definition of the situation is sometimes suspect, especially when one hears such remarks as the following: "Do you think you could open your legs a little more?"

There may be a general restriction on the use of cameras and, when cameras are allowed, it is expected that no pictures will be taken without the subject's permission. Members especially tend to blame the misuse of cameras on single men. As one nudist said: "You always see the singles poppin' around out of nowhere snappin' pictures." In general, however, control is maintained, and any infractions which might exist are not blatant or obvious. Any overindulgence in taking photographs would communicate an over-involvement in the nude state of the alters and bring doubt on the denied connection between nudism and sexuality. This, like staring, would fall in cell 2-1 of our typology of immodesty; like staring, it is controlled by the norms of the nudist camp.

The official photographers who are taking pictures for nudist magazines recognize the impression communicated by forms of immodesty other than nudity, i.e., for the communication of sexuality. In regard to the erotic overtures of column three of our typology, the following statement of an official photographer is relevant: "I never let a girl look straight at the camera. It looks too suggestive. I always have her look off to the side."

Accentuation of the body is suspect as being incongruent with the ideology of nudism. The internalization of the previously discussed principles of nudist ideology would be called into question by such accentuation. Thus, one woman who had shaved her pubic area was labeled as disgusting by those members who talked to the writer about it. Women who blatantly sit in an "unladylike" manner are similarly typed. In the words of one female nudist:

It's no more nice to do than when you are dressed. I would assume they have a purpose. (What's that?) Maybe to draw someone's attention sexually. I'd think it's bad behavior and it's one thing that shouldn't be done, especially in a nudist camp. (Why's that?) Because it could lead to trouble or some misfortune. (Could you tell me some more about that?) It could bring up some trouble or disturbance among those who noticed it. It would not be appreciated by "true nudists."

Unnatural attempts at covering any area of the body are similarly ridiculed, since they call into question the actor's acceptance of the definition that there is no shame in exposing any area of the human body. If such behavior occurs early in one's nudist career, however, it is responded to mostly with smiles. The actor is seen as not yet able to get over the initial difficulty of disposing of "outsiders' " definitions.

Communal toilets are also related to the ideological view that there is nothing shameful about the human body or its bodily functions. Although all camps do not have communal toilets, the large camp at which the writer spent the majority of his time did have such a facility, which was labeled "Little Girls Room and Little Boys Too." The stalls were provided with three-quarter length doors. The existence of this combined facility helped, however, to sustain the nudist definition of the situation by the element of consistency: if you are not ashamed of any part of your body, or of any of its natural body functions, why do you need separate toilets? Thus, even the physical ecology of the nudist camp is designed in a way that will be consistent with the organization's definition of modesty.

Consequences of a Breakdown in Clothing Modesty

In the introductory section of this paper it was stated that common-sense actors anticipate breakdowns in clothing modesty to result in rampant sexual interest, promiscuity, embarrassment, jealousy, and shame. The field work and interview data from this study, however, indicate that such occurrences are not common to the nudist camp. The social organization of the nudist camp provides a system of meanings and norms that negate these consequences.

Conclusions

Our results make possible some general conclusions regarding modesty: (1) Covering the body through the use of clothes is not a necessary condition for a pattern of modesty to exist, nor is it required for tension management and social control of latent sexual interests. Sexual interests are very adequately controlled in nudist camps; in fact, those who have visited nudist camps agree that sexual interests are controlled to a much greater extent than they are on the outside. Clothes are also not a sufficient condition for a pattern of modesty; the manipulation of clothes and fashion in stimulating sexual interest is widely recognized. (2) Except for clothing immodesty, which represents one cell of our typology of immodesty, all other forms of modesty are maintained in a nudist camp (e.g., not looking, not saying, not communicating erotic overtures). This suggests that the latter proscriptions are entirely adequate in achieving the functions of modesty when definitions regarding the exposure of the body are changed. (3) When deviance from the institutionalized patterns of modesty is limited to one cell of our typology (i.e., clothing is dispensed with), and the definition of the situation is changed, the typically expected consequence of such a breakdown in this normative pattern does not occur. Rampant sexual interest, promiscuity, embarrassment, jealousy, and shame were not found to be typical in the nudist camp.

Maintaining Deviant Beliefs *

J. L. SIMMONS

The present paper explores some selected aspects of a belief system shared by a small group of "mystics" located in southeastern United States. Its major concern is the means through which these divergent beliefs are maintained in the face of a disbelieving society.

Data for the report were gathered from intimate association and many lengthy conversations with a prominent member of the group and from much briefer conversations with four other members. Pamphlets and newsletters of the group were also examined. Observations from a number of other fringe groups have also been drawn upon.

The concept "belief system" is here defined as the set of notions with which individuals and groups interpret the physical and social reality around them and within themselves. No classification of these notions, such as the psychoanalytic one of conscious vs. unconscious, or Parsons' distinction among cognitive, expressive, and evaluative symbols [1] will be made here since it is neither feasible nor necessary for the purposes of this paper. The term "system" will call the reader's attention to the important fact that beliefs do not exist as a heap of disconnected items, but are related into some kind of "coherent" and "consistent" pattern.

The Espers

The group, which we will call Esper, has its headquarters in a semi-isolated mountainous area of Georgia. This location was picked partly for its relative seclusion and for the natural protection it would afford in the event of a nuclear war. Several members have sold their business and properties in other locations to settle here permanently. The buildings and grounds are extensive, including housing for perhaps two hundred people, ample garden space, springs, and so forth. Several other fringe groups which share many beliefs with Esper are located within a few miles and there seem to be institutional and informal ties with these other groups. However, multiple membership seems to be relatively rare. The ties seem to be based on shared beliefs, admiration of the same fringe heroes, shared knowledge of fringe literature, and similar attitudes of suspicion and

* Reprinted from "On Maintaining Deviant Belief Systems: A Case Study" in *Social Problems*, Vol. 11, No. 3 (Winter, 1964), pp. 250–56, by permission of the author and *Social Problems*.
[1] Talcott Parsons, *The Social System*, New York: Free Press, 1951, pp. 326–383.

benevolent contempt toward the culture at large.

The writer was unable to get exact figures on the size of membership of Esper. Estimates clustered around fifty full members and perhaps half a hundred marginal associates. About twenty-five of these lived in or near the headquarters and most other members lived in eastern United States. There were over three hundred subscribers to the Esper monthly newsletter; subscription price was five dollars per year. Membership dues were thirty dollars the first year and five dollars per year thereafter. The two other major sources of income for the organization and its salaried members were fees for the use of cabins, boats, etc., and fees charged for courses of training in psychic powers. Individual members made other monies through faith-healing, the practice of "natural" medicine, "reading" of an individual's psyche through photographs and signatures, etc.

At this point the reader may wonder about the possibility of fraud, the cynical manipulation of the membership by a few individuals for financial gain. The writer sought evidence for this possibility but concluded that there was no deliberate hoaxing involved. A number of the members earned their living through "mystic" work but their incomes would be judged barely above subsistence level by ordinary American standards. The Elmer Gantry type of personality seemed conspicuously absent and the leaders seemed to believe in what they were doing.

Members ranged in age from fourteen into the seventies and seemed to include roughly as many women as men. In some cases entire families were members but in other cases only one or two individuals from a family would be Espers.

The educational level of the group seemed average at best. However, the group was unmistakably far above average in amount and variety of reading. This included fringe literature, such as books and magazines on flying saucers, hypnotism, mythology, the health food publications of Rodale Press, the writings of Mary Baker Eddy, Pak Subud, and J. B. Rhine. Many of the members were also consumers of popular magazines, general paperback books, and "serious literature."

Most members seem to have had atypical life-histories. These included experiences such as loss of one or both parents, atypical relations with parents, parents who were themselves members of fringe groups, interaction with unusual significant others, and abnormal work-histories.

Such atypical life-histories, combined with breadth of reading, produce broad, though unsystematic, knowledge of the world. Among Espers and similar fringe groups, one may easily meet individuals acquainted with the Sanskrit poets, Norse mythology, medieval painting or German Idealist philosophy. However, they tend not to be "cultured" in the sense of having a broad scholarship in the humanities. They also seem to lack the rigor or critical ability which formal education tends to produce. Members seemed to be most inadequate in appraising the reliability of sources and in the forms of logical argument. At the same time, they possessed an inquiring attitude and openness of mind which would probably have delighted Bacon.

Espers interpret happenings in ways which would seem fantastic to the ordinary layman. Their view of human nature is an echo of the Hindu conception that Man is a creature blinded by external events, who is largely unaware of his real makeup or potentialities. Most of man's "spiritual" life goes on independently of the conscious individual and largely without his awareness. The world is peopled with disembodied spirits, good and bad, and with psychic manifestations of the living. All men possess psychic powers, at least in rudimentary form, and these may be cultivated and formally trained. Telepathy, clairvoyance, telekinesis, communication with spirits, reincarnation, mystical intuition, dowsing, the manipulation of events through faith and magical procedures such as pagan Hawaiian *hunna,* are real and everyday occurrences to the Espers and similar groups. Espers and similar groups are adamant in their disagreement with the world-view presented in conventional scientific and historical writings. Mystic enlightenment is considered a more valid source of knowledge than the techniques of science.

The Maintenance of Esper Beliefs

The reader may wonder how individuals can continue to accept the truth of such a "crazy" belief system. For one who has been socialized into conventional American culture it may seem incredible that anyone could believe such things in the face of so much contrary evidence. As we explore some of the processes involved in confirming and maintaining Esper beliefs, it may become apparent that *all* belief systems are to some extent arbitrary and that the same mechanisms are involved in maintaining them.

The concept of the self-fulfilling prophecy, first advanced by W. I. Thomas, is particularly useful in this exploration.[2]

First, as Bruner has pointed out,[3] we tend to select that part of the total influx of incoming sense perceptions which is congruent with our expectations. This may even involve the active supplying of perceptions which are "not really there,"

as in the case of geometric illusions. Also, most situations are only semi-structured, so that the individual has some degrees of freedom in structuring them to come true.

Examples may clarify these points. I was sitting in a coffee shop with my main Esper informant when a young woman sat down at a table within conversation distance from us. Her hair was a neutral brown and short-cut, her features angular and her hands long and thin. The most striking aspect of her physical appearance was the bright shade of her lipstick and matching nail polish. My informant leaned forward with some agitation and told me in a low voice that she was a hunting demon who drained men of their psychic energy and left them empty hulks. Her true nature was reflected in her aura which he could plainly read. His distress seemed genuine when he asked me to extend psychic protection over him. A few minutes later a young man joined her at the table and we were able to overhear their conversation. They talked for perhaps three-quarters of an hour before leaving. A content analysis of the girl's conversation would reveal statements describing a wide variety of attitudes toward different social objects. But after they had gone, my informant cited, as corroboration of his judgment, only those statements which might bespeak a manipulative attitude toward the world. Other statements, which expressed admiration for certain people, an appreciation of music, and sympathy for the plight of the American Negro, seem to have been ignored by the Esper.

The second aspect of the self-fulfilling prophecy is more subtle, but it is a process which the writer has seen many times with Espers and other fringe group

[2] W. I. Thomas, "The Definition of the Situation," in Lewis Coser and Bernard Rosenberg, editors, *Sociological Theory,* New York: Macmillan, 1957, pp. 209–211.
[3] Jerome Bruner, "Social Psychology and Perception," in Eleanor Maccoby, *et al.,* editors, *Readings in Social Psychology,* 3rd Ed., New York: Holt, 1958, pp. 85–94.

members. It might be described by the following paradigm:

A. Ego makes an inference about alter.
B. Ego acts toward alter in terms of this inference.
C. Alter makes inferences about ego in terms of this action.
D. Alter tends to react toward ego in terms of his action.
E. Thus ego's inferences tend to be confirmed by alter's reaction.

This paradigm is merely a slight modification of many social psychological models of the interpersonal process,[4] but the self-fulfilling aspect of it seems often to be missed. If a situation is rigidly structured, the self-fulfilling aspect will, of course, be limited, i.e., it would be difficult to interpret and confirm a minister's actions at a funeral as a sexual advance. But, as Kuhn has pointed out,[5] all situations are to some extent flexible so that the actors have some freedom in defining them.

To choose an example among many possible ones, my informant rented a room for several days from a middle-aged woman. After seeing her only briefly, and before he had spoken with her, he "intuited" that she was a warm accepting person who was filled with psychic strength and goodness. When he first talked with her a couple of hours later, his manner was far more friendly and patronizing than usual. He showed interest in her collection of antiques, asked about her children, and ended up by saying he felt she was a wonderful person and he wanted to rent from her, partly because they would have a chance to talk together. During the next few days, the writer had a chance to question other tenants and neighbors about the landlady. They described a fairly caustic gossiper who was unreasonably strict about the use of electricity, and of her property and grounds. Her attitude toward the writer was taciturn. But she responded graciously to my informant's open friendliness. She sought him out to talk with on several occasions, she inquired if there was enough light in his room for late reading and supplied him with a table lamp, etc. In her behavior toward him, my informant's intuition certainly seemed correct.

It seems a safe generalization that no individual can maintain beliefs when a large amount of contrary evidence is *perceived*. This is perhaps why the layman finds it difficult to see how fringers can believe "all that crazy stuff" (or why the Russian people are so easily "duped" by Communist propaganda) when common sense so easily shows them wrong. The important point is that "common sense" varies rather arbitrarily from group to group.

Extending some notions developed by Rokeach, *et al.*,[6] we may say that groups and total cultures build up belief systems which tend toward a fairly coherent and consistent portrait of the world. To what extent do these portraits represent faithfully the "real world"? In past intellectual history, these judgments have usually been made ethnocentrically, in terms of the judge's own portrait. Now the institution of science has attempted to set up criteria for evaluating beliefs about reality which will be free of such biases.

Physics and engineering may have advanced to the point that assertions about building a bridge can be readily tested for their realism. But in the behavioral sciences the variance as yet unaccounted for is still so large that it is difficult to

---

[4] A classic statement of such a model is Cooley's "looking-glass self," C. H. Cooley, *Human Nature and the Social Order*, New York: Scribner, 1902, p. 184.
[5] Lecture by Manford Kuhn.
[6] Milton Rokeach, *The Open and Closed Mind*, New York: Basic Books, 1960, pp. 31–71.

invalidate almost any assertion about human behavior conclusively.

To put it another way, confirming evidence for particular beliefs about social reality are sought and *found* because most situations are ambiguous enough to allow them to be *interpreted as* confirming evidence. We need not bring in fringe groups as examples, since this seems to be a more widespread mechanism. For instance, any Russian offer for disarmament is automatically interpreted as a propaganda move by the American press. Lack of information makes this interpretation possible, whether it truly and always represents the real motives of the Russian government or not. In fact, it is difficult to imagine what action the Communists might take which would be accepted as an honest move for peace by our people. It is also probably true that the Russians interpret any actions of ours similarly.[7]

It is difficult to break into this circle of confirmation, to re-educate an individual who is firmly entrenched in a particular belief system, because situations are *defined* by the very notions ego is seeking to confirm and alter is seeking to discredit. For instance, Espers define man as a spiritual being who possesses a psychic aura from which certain inferences can be made about his *spiritual* nature. One cannot demonstrate that individuals do not have psychic auras; in fact, it is ironic that modern science, with its sensitive devices for measuring organic electrical fields, has indirectly lent support to the Esper argument. Fringe group members have often cited such evidence in support of their claims, although the scientific findings are freely interpreted.

A further means by which the Esper is able to maintain his beliefs is through differential association and differential identification with Espers and relative insulation from non-Espers.[8] As an interacting group, Espers provide support for the individual member in his view of the world. As a number of fringe group members have put it, they feel they can be themselves only with kindred fringers. Members feel they are "at home" because they share a common language with which they can communicate about their views and problems to alters who share their meanings.

Communication within the group provides further confirming evidence for the belief system. For instance, several Espers will be able to "read" a given individual's psychic aura. In considering such confirmation through consensus, the reader might recall that many tests of validity in science rest directly or indirectly on intersubjective agreement. Thus, a psychiatric staff reaches agreement on the Oedipal conflict of a patient and a group of similarly trained sociologists agree that certain items measure "anomia." Often an individual's judgment is not accepted until he has been socialized into the group and has learned the processes for arriving at the "right" answer. This provides the group with a rationale for saying that those who disagree are not competent to judge. Thus the Espers explained that the ordinary layman could not read psychic auras because he had not been trained to do so and because he was not in touch with his own spiritual powers.

With regard to this communication of shared meanings, we might note an incident which occurred several times when Espers were dealing with non-Espers. Those who were tolerant toward Esper views were, in every case the writer was able to observe, judged to be psychic

---

[7] For a provocative discussion of this point cf. Erich Fromm, *May Man Prevail?* New York: Anchor, 1961.

[8] For a recent summary statement of the principles underlying this point cf. Daniel Glaser, "The Differential Association Theory of Crime," in Arnold Rose, editor, *Human Behavior and Social Processes,* Boston, Houghton-Mifflin, 1962, pp. 425–443.

themselves. Those who were indifferent or positively rejecting might be judged to be psychic themselves but if they were, they were judged to be evil. The Espers seemed to be unaware of this "latent criterion" for judging non-Espers.

Finally, Espers and similar fringe groups are aided in maintaining their beliefs by the ambivalence of the larger culture toward them. In our culture, a mystical worldview is a well established counter-theme to the more predominant rationalism and pragmatism. In describing Puerto Rican spiritualism Rogler and Hollingshead have noted, "if you ever talk to a Puerto Rican who says he doesn't believe in Spirits, you know what that means? It means you haven't talked to him long enough." [9] Tales of psychic happenings and of individuals gifted with extra-sensory perception are widely, although informally, told in our culture and a large number of Americans have perhaps been half-convinced that "there is something behind them" at one time or another. This ambivalence tends to soften the disbelief and verbal rejection by the non-fringe member when interacting with the mystic. The writer has questioned many non-fringe group members on their attitudes toward Espers and similar groups and the most frequent reply has been that, although they are a bit "crackpot," there may be something to their notions.

Fringe group members are usually keenly aware of the fact that the larger culture disagrees with their view of the world, however, and often adopt a defensive judgment of the layman as unenlightened. This judgment makes it easier for the fringe group member to disregard the rejection and derision of the unbeliever.

The Changing of Beliefs

In general, there seem to be only two kinds of argument one can make against a particular belief system.

1. Grant the "postulates" of the system and argue deductively that some notions are incompatible with others, or that the chain of reasoning in going from "premise" to "consequent" is questionable. (The words in quotation marks are not used in their strict formal logic meaning, but rather in the looser sense of a suggestive analogy.) For instance, Espers embrace the belief that man's future is his own to manipulate, but also notions of foreseeing an inexorable future (precognition), and of strict causal determinism. (This inconsistency should have a familiar ring to the social scientist.)

2. Point out events in the real world which challenge the beliefs. The major difficulty here is that both parties must have some minimum of agreement about what these events of reality are. Everyone must make some concessions to reality or he will not survive as an individual or group. As Kluckhohn has pointed out,[10] no culture has norms about jumping over trees. But here again one must be very cautious lest he dub his own culturally learned views as necessary orientations toward external reality. There actually are cultures with beliefs about the possibility of physical levitation over trees and the projection of the astral body through space.

But if there is a minimum of consensus about what goes on in the real world, one can question beliefs in terms of these happenings. For instance, Espers believe in reincarnation and they also recognize that the human and animal population of the world is increasing. Juxtaposing these

[9] Lloyd Rogler and August Hollingshead, "The Puerto Rican Spiritualist as a Psychiatrist," *American Journal of Sociology*, Vol. 67 (July, 1961), p. 21.
[10] Clyde Kluckhohn, *Mirror for Man,* New York: McGraw-Hill, 1949, p. 20.

two beliefs, the writer asked three Espers, where do more souls for the greater number of living bodies come from? The Espers recognized the inconsistency between the empirical fact of population growth and their belief in reincarnation and admitted that they could give no answer. My informant became quite interested in the question; he bought some books on Eastern religions and also planned to ask other Espers when he returned to the headquarters. (The writer may have unwittingly introduced a chain of events which will result in innovations in the Esper belief system.)

One other point should be made about confirming evidence for beliefs. To the extent that the beliefs are untestable, either because they are tautological or because they are non-empirical, they are safe from the challenge of empirical events.[11] Just how much of a given belief system is untestable in principle remains to be demonstrated, but the proportion may be fairly large.

Conclusions

This paper has been concerned with the means employed by deviant groups in maintaining their beliefs in the face of a divergent and more or less disapproving larger society. The generaliza-

tions were drawn from the study of a small group of "mystics" and from observation of a number of other fringe groups.

The following processes or "mechanisms" facilitate the maintenance of divergent beliefs:

1. Selective attention to those perceptions which are congruent with one's beliefs.
2. Active structuring of social situations so that their outcomes support one's beliefs.
3. *Interpretation* of ambiguous evidence as confirming one's beliefs.
4. Differential association and identification with those who share one's beliefs, coupled with relative isolation from and disparagement of those whose beliefs differ.
5. Ambivalence of the divergent larger culture toward one's beliefs.

These processes increase the difficulty of challenging a given belief system. A belief system may be thrown into question by pointing out major inconsistencies within it. Also, if both parties agree on certain "facts" these facts may be shown to contradict some of the beliefs. However, to the extent that the beliefs are non-empirical or non-testable, they remain value-premises which are susceptible only to the persuasion of competing value-premises.

---

11 Parsons, *op. cit.,* pp. 359–367.

Occupational Ideologies and Individual Attitudes of Call Girls *

JAMES H. BRYAN

Students of deviance emphasize the importance of group perspectives and values and socialization into them in the development and maintenance of deviant behavior. They agree that when behavior is stigmatized, the deviant group will propagate attitudes and moralities counter to dominant cultural values.[1] While individual deviants are thought to vary in their degree of socialization, professionals are said to be developed.[2] The ideologies of deviant groups, according to Becker, "tend to contain a general repudiation of conventional moral rules, conventional institutions, and the entire conventional world." [3] Further, students agree that deviant groups stress in-group loyalties and minimize the moral nature of their transgressions.[4]

Few data have been collected which assess the impact of professional perspectives upon the individual deviant, the degree to which ideology is incorporated into the personal belief system. The present study was concerned, therefore, with the ideological stance of the professional prostitute and its impact upon the individual practitioners.

While it is commonly thought that prostitutes' ideologies play an important role in the continuation of their behavior, these beliefs have rested as much on faith as on fact.[5] The perspectives of prostitutes have generally been ignored in favor of motivational states and, when not ignored, are often inferred from very limited samples or anecdotal material.[6] Among those so concerned, Hirschi, in an excellent review of the available autobiographical material, indicated that the ideology of the prostitute contains justifications based upon functionalistic premises (prostitution is needed) and impugning the "squares' " integrity (they are prostitutes

* Reprinted from *Social Problems*, Vol. 13, No. 4 (Spring, 1966), pp. 441–50, by permission of the author and *Social Problems*.

[1] H. S. Becker, *Outsiders: Studies in the Sociology of Deviance*, New York: The Free Press of Glencoe, 1963; H. S. Becker (ed), *The Other Side*, New York: The Free Press of Glencoe, 1964; M. B. Clinard, *Sociology of Deviant Behavior*, New York: Rinehart and Company, 1957; D. R. Cressey, "Social Psychological Theory for Using Deviants to Control Deviation," *Report of Proceedings, Conference on the Use of a Social Problem in Coping with the Problem*, Norco, California, July, 1963. See also E. Goffman, *Stigma*, Englewood Cliffs, N.J.: Prentice-Hall, 1963; Evelyn Hooker, "The Homosexual Community," *Proceedings, XIVth International Congress of Applied Psychology*, 1961; M. B. Ray, "The Cycle of Abstinence and Relapse among Heroin Addicts," Becker, *The Other Side, op. cit.;* T. J. Scheff, "The Role of the Mentally Ill and the Dynamics of Mental Disorder: A Research Framework," *Sociometry*, 26 (1963), pp. 436–453.

[2] Goffman, *op. cit.*

[3] H. S. Becker, *Outsiders, op. cit.*, pp. 38–39.

[4] See, for example, G. Sykes and D. Matza, "Techniques of Neutralization: A Theory of Delinquency," *American Sociological Review*, 22 (1957), pp. 664–670.

[5] As an example, see M. B. Clinard, *op. cit.;* W. C. Reckless, *The Crime Problem*, New York: Appleton-Century-Crofts, 1950.

[6] For a brief review of the hypothesized motive forces affecting prostitution, see J. H. Bryan, "Apprenticeships in Prostitution," *Social Problems*, 12 (1965), pp. 287–297; for an extended review see V. L. Bullough, "Prostitution and Behavioral Research: A Biographical Essay," *Journal of History of Behavioral Science*, 1 (1965), pp. 244–251.

themselves).[7] Ross, on the basis of interviews with three respondents directly involved with both prostitution and other "hustling" activities, indicated the belief that at least the more professional prostitutes emphasized the value of "craftiness" and in-group loyalties.[8]

Unfortunately, albeit understandably, there are no available data which directly relate attitudes of the individual prostitute to the perspectives of the group in question. It has not yet been demonstrated that such occupationally endorsed values have an impact at the individual level. More importantly, because of the restricted number of respondents heretofore employed and the necessarily limited nature of the controls under which the data have been collected, inferences concerning the values customarily associated with the occupation of prostitution are necessarily suspect. It is well known that such inferences may be unreliable, reliable but invalid, or valid but method specific. To the degree that inferences concerning such ideologies lead to valid predictions, there is evidence that such inferences are correct and that such occupational socialization has occurred. Conversely, the failure of such predictions suggests that either the original inferences were incorrect or that such perspectives have little impact upon the individual actor.

Assuming, however, that individuals acquire occupational ideologies during socialization, it nonetheless remains to be demonstrated that such ideologies are related to *sustained* acts of prostitution. Indeed, to assert that occupationally sanctioned ideologies are important in sustaining deviant behavior requires as minimal evidence correlational data relating time in the deviant behavior to the presence or absence of such views. As yet, no such data exist.

The present study had two purposes: 1) to assess the relationship between an occupational perspective and individually endorsed attitudes toward relevant objects; and 2) to examine the relationship between such attitudes and opportunities for socialization as measured by length of time in prostitution.

Method

The respondents were 52 active or previously active prostitutes who volunteered to be interviewed, who were not paid, and who, with one exception, defined themselves as "call girls."[9] No member of the sample was under the supervision of a police agency; eight were outpatients in a psychiatric hospital. The respondents ranged in age from 18–40, the average being 22. Their average length of time as an active prostitute was 27 months. The informants obtained their clients through individual referrals, primarily by telephone, and the sexual contract was enacted in their or the clients' place of residence or employment. The respondents did not initiate contact with their customers in bars, streets, or houses of prostitution, although they might meet by pre-arrangement at such locations. With five exceptions, the minimum fee ever charged by the girl per sexual encounter was $20. This suggests that the respondents were, in fact, "upper class" prostitutes. Of the five exceptions, all had charged no less than $10 per sexual contract and all but one at the time of interview had eventually set a price of $20. Thirty-nine of the respondents worked primarily in Los Angeles, six in Chicago, three in Las Vegas, and one each in San

---

[7] T. Hirschi, "The Professional Prostitute," *Berkeley Journal of Sociology,* 7 (1962), pp. 33–49.

[8] H. L. Ross, "The 'Hustler' in Chicago," *Journal of Student Research,* 1 (1959), pp. 13–19.

[9] The single exception met all other criteria.

Francisco and Miami. Many of the respondents, however, worked in more than one city.

All but two interviews were, with the respondent's prior knowledge, tape recorded. Most interviews were conducted at the girl's place of work and/or residence. Interviews were semi-structured and employed open-ended questions.

The Ideology

While the data pertaining to ideologies are necessarily impressionistic, certain roughly specifiable criteria were used to select that material relevant to occupational perspectives. First, of course, the material was used by the girls in such a manner as to explain and justify the occupation of prostitution. For example, responses to such questions as "What are the advantages of prostitution for society [self]?" and "Should prostitution be legalized [why]?" were heavily relied upon, as they repeatedly elicited such stereotyped justifying answers. Additionally, such responses had to be known to the majority of respondents. Considerable consensus existed, for example, in response to the above-mentioned questions. Certain views also were repeatedly attributed to or given by members considered "pro," part of the "in-group," of those who had been in the profession for a lengthy period. For example, and not infrequently, a respondent would indicate how one should perceive, feel, or act, if one were to be a real professional. Hence attributed professional views, if there was agreement as to their nature, were used as the basis for inferring occupationally sanctioned ideologies.

A major element in the occupational perspective, indicated by virtually all respondents, was that prostitution served important social functions because of man's extensive and varied sexual needs, protecting both individuals and social institutions alike from destructive ruptures.

We girls see, like I guess you call them perverts of some sort, you know, little freaky people and if they didn't have girls to come to like us that are able to handle them and make it a nice thing, there would be so many rapes and . . . nutty people really.

I think that a lot less rapes and murders if it were (legalized).

I believe that there should be more prostitution houses and what have you, and then we wouldn't have so many of these perverted idiots, sex maniacs, all sorts of weird people running around.

Marriages are thought to be more enduring because of prostitution!

I could say that a prostitute has held more marriages together as part of their profession than any divorce counselor.

Respondents also commonly indicated that prostitutes serve as important psychotherapeutic agents, giving comfort, insight, and satisfaction to those men too embarrassed, lonely, or isolated to obtain interpersonal gratification in other ways.

I don't regret doing it because I feel I help people. A lot of men that come over to see me don't come over for sex. They come over for companionship, someone to talk to. . . . They talk about sex. . . . A lot of them have problems.

While the foregoing positions are commonly stated, the professional, as opposed to the novice, holds additional views. Both trainers and professionals appear to encourage a view that makes exploitation of the "john" less morally reprehensible. The customer is exploitative, hence should be exploited. Customers are to be cultivated through extensive contacts, such that repeated "scores" can be made, often to the customer's disadvantage. The professional also tends to devalue men in general. Interestingly, this position is often felt to be the natural outcome of sustained acts of prostitution so that extensive experience with customers is thought to produce the "hard and cold" girl who has developed a "very crude attitude toward it [the professional]" and ends being "bitter and hating men [clients]." Of the conceptions of the consequences of being a prostitute held by the girls, this is perhaps the one that produces the most personal anxiety.

The prostitute should see her customers as exploitative, cutting each corner of the financial contract, and herself as a potential victim: "So he [trainer] taught me to get my money out in front a lot of times . . . [if] you accept clothes from them, they'll buy you a $10.00 dress and the whole deal is worth fifty."

In addition, girls recognize occupationally-sanctioned attitudes toward women and colleagues alike. They sometimes say that the "in-group" is unique, special, more honest: "I feel that people in the life are more honest with themselves and with others."

Occasionally the trainer will exhort the novice to join the "in-group." As one prostitute of two weeks explains her reaction to her trainer's exhortations to "Get with it; do what we do": "It has to do with being a swinger or hip. Going out and more or less cheating on your boyfriend or carousing around with a fast crowd and looking hot. . . . I won't do it."

Another view, popular at both the novice and professional level, is that interpersonal relationships between the sexes are, in essence, acts of prostitution. This position stems from the assumption that within such relationships gains are often derived from intentional manipulations, deceptions, and sex. The housewife then is no less guilty than the prostitute: ". . . actually all women are whores in my opinion whether they get married for it or whatever it is. There are just different ways of being a whore."

The square's hypocrisy may be further compounded by envy. "They [the public] resent them because the working girl [call girl] can do things that other women can't do."

In sum, the professional perspective argues that customers can and should be exploited, that the role of the prostitute is no more immoral than the role of the "square," and that colleagues are more honest and helpful than women outside the profession. Furthermore, since it is a necessary, indeed therapeutic, practice, prostitution should not be stigmatized, and one should not look down upon oneself for being a prostitute. These simple rules may, perhaps, justify exploitation, sustain what cooperative behavior is necessary for occupational functioning, and reduce both public and personal stigma, real or potential, attached to the actor.

Individual Attitudes

Given these perspectives, the issue remains as to how much impact they have upon the individual respondent. The interview material suggests that individual respondents do not, in fact, personally endorse the above-mentioned perspectives. While the respondents know them, they do not believe them. For example, many of the individual respondents, not surprisingly, refuse to stereotype the customer: "I've never found two alike." Or stereotyping may be more benign than that suggested by the occupation's ideology: "Most of them are very, very nice people, like overly nice." Reality soon appears to break down the ideology, occasionally to the discomfort of the actor: "Even though they're tricks, and I hate tricks, they are still people and they have as many hang-ups a lot of times as I do, therefore, I have been able to empathize with them in most cases which is bad when you try to take somebody for all they're worth. It gives you guilt feelings."

Not infrequently, personal friendships with customers are reported: "Some of them are nice clients who become very good friends of mine." On the other hand, while friendships are formed with "squares," personal disputations with colleagues are frequent. Speaking of her colleagues, one call girl says that most "could cut your throat." Respondents frequently mentioned that they had been robbed, conned, or otherwise exploited by their call girl friends. Interpersonal distrust between call girls appears to be considerable. While respondents tend to deny that they or their fellow workers fulfill the usual conceptions of the tight-skirted, hip swinging, customer-rolling street-walker, they do characteristically indicate that their relationships with other call girls are marked by interpersonal conflict, disloyalties, and mutual exploitation.

To more formally assess individually endorsed attitudes, the last 28 respondents, all currently active in prostitution, were administered a rating scale. Each was asked to rate, on the semantic differential (to be described below), herself, other call girls, women-in-general, "johns," and men-in-general.[10] If occupational socialization occurred, then individually held attitudes toward such groups should be predictable from the occupational ideology. The three audiences of primary concern were: self, "johns," and other working girls. These groups were chosen as they appeared relevant to the girls' occupational success and because occupationally-supported perspectives pertaining to them existed. If occupational socialization does occur, then, on the basis of the described ideology, we can predict that the distribution of attitudes toward these groups would not only not be random, but that

particular groups would be more favorably evaluated than others. If the ideological justifications have the effect of reducing the girls' personal distress, the self should be rated, relative to other groups, as more worthwhile. Conversely, due to the johns' "perverted" sexual nature and economic avarice, they should be held in relatively low esteem. The call girl colleague, a necessary adjunct to the daily round of affairs for most call girls, should be held in greater esteem than the customer. In addition to these groups, girls were also asked to rate women-in-general and men-in-general. These ratings allow us to avoid confounding attitudes toward specific groups with those toward a specific gender. Additionally, in light of the perspective that all women are in spirit if not in practice prostitutes, the latter ratings also served as an additional test of the effects of socialization.

The respondent rated each group on the following nine bi-polar items: good-bad, cruel-kind, valuable-worthless, fast-slow, passive-active, dull-sharp, hard-soft, large-small, weak-strong. These nine items have been shown previously to load on one of three factors subsequently labelled evaluation, activity, potency.[11] The first three items load heavily on evaluation, the next three on activity, and the remaining on the potency dimension. The respondent indicated her rating by checking one of seven spaces spatially separating the bi-polar units of the item. For example, ratings were made by checking one of seven spaces separating the word good from the word bad. If the respondent thought the group in question was good, she checked the space closest to the word good. This procedure was followed for each of the items.

Since it is well known that single items

---

[10] For a description of the procedure, see C. E. Osgood, G. J. Suci, and P. H. Tannenbaum, *The Measurement of Meaning*, Urbana, Ill.: University of Illinois Press, 1957.

[11] C. E. Osgood, *et al.*, *op. cit.*

TABLE 1
Analysis of Variance of Semantic Differential Ratings

Source	df	SS	MS	Error Term	F
Groups (G)	4	187.31	46.83	Ss × G	3.303 *
Dimension (D)	2	254.957	127.48	Ss × D	8.66 **
G × D	8	282.233	35.28	Ss × G × D	5.378 **
Subjects (Ss)	27	605.817	22.44		
Ss × G	108	1531.623	14.18		
Ss × D	54	794.776	14.72		
Ss × G × D	216	1418.03	6.56		
Total		5074.75			

* p < .05.
** p < .01.

on such scales may not be highly reliable, ratings on items loading heavily on one dimension were summed for each respondent and treated as the primary score for that dimension. For example, the ratings of a particular group on the items good-bad, cruel-kind, and valuable-worthless were summed, thus forming the evaluative ratings on that specific group. Since there were three items per dimension, each item having a one to seven scale, summed scores could range only from three to 21 on any one dimension. Scoring was such that the higher the score, the greater the attributed dimension. For example, high scores on the evaluative factor indicated high esteem.

In the present study, the dimension of primary concern was the evaluative factor, because occupational ideologies appear to deal with stereotypes having clear-cut implications for the evaluative rather than activity or potency dimensions. The latter dimensions were included, however, so as to provide evidence that discriminations were being made in the ratings along these dimensions.

In order to assess whether the respondents held differential attitudes toward the several groups rated, variance for correlated measures was analyzed.[12] The results of the analysis are presented in Table 1.

Mean ratings of the groups were reliably different. Respondents did discriminate between groups as evidenced by the significant main effect for groups. The significant main effect of dimensions further indicates that when ratings of the groups are combined, ratings are reliably different across each dimension. Clusters of items were being responded to differentially. The significant interaction of groups by dimensions indicates that groups were rated differently on the different dimensions. The latter finding is of importance because it makes untenable the suggestion that general test-taking habits or artifacts (halo effects, position rating habits, etc.) could account for the results. If, for example, halo effects were operating, differential ratings of groups across such dimensions would not be expected. In sum, then, respondents discriminated, in their ratings, both across different groups and dimensions.

The mean ratings of the groups, within a particular dimension, are presented in Table 2. Since there were no significant mean differences between the ratings of the potency for any of the groups, these results are not presented.

[12] B. J. Winer, *Statistical Principles in Experimental Design,* New York: McGraw-Hill, 1962.

TABLE 2
Mean Rating of Groups on the Evaluative and Activity Dimensions

	Self	Johns	Men	Women	Call Girls
Evaluation	14.78	14.18	13.78	13.10	11.96
Activity	14.71	11.39	13.11	11.53	14.18

The Newman-Keuls analysis was employed to test mean differences in ratings across groups.[13] By this method, each mean rating of a particular group is compared to the mean ratings of all other groups and tested for statistical significance.

While mean differences were found in the ratings of the groups, the rank ordering of the groups on the basis of evaluative ratings was not predictable from the occupational ideology. While the call girl rated herself significantly more worthwhile than her colleagues, her ratings of self did not differ, on the evaluative dimension, from her ratings of men-in-general, women-in-general, or "johns." Only call girls were rated as being significantly less worthwhile than the self. Further, the only other group that was rated reliably as being more worthwhile than call girls were "johns." Indeed, customers were evaluated by the call girl as being as worthwhile as herself, and as significantly better than her colleagues. This particular ranking could not be predicted from knowledge of occupational

beliefs. The ratings of men-in-general and of women-in-general fell just short of being reliably different from ratings of call girls.

In passing, it might be noted that call girls rate themselves as being significantly more active than either "johns" or "women-in-general." These findings suggest that "johns" are seen as more passive than most males, and that self is busier and more active than most women.

The impact of the socialization aside, if the prostitute is exposed to some sort of uniform ideological training, then attitudes toward these groups, whatever their various nature, should be correlated with opportunities for learning. One, admittedly crude, measure of such opportunity is the time the respondent has been working as a prostitute. During the course of the interview each respondent was asked how many months she had been working as a prostitute, and this estimate was then correlated with ratings of the groups for each dimension. These correlations are presented in Table 3.

As can be seen, the only significant

TABLE 3
Product-moment Correlations of Semantic Differential Ratings and Time in the Occupation

	Evaluation	Activity	Potency
Self	−.09	.02	−.20
Other Call Girls	.04	.09	.11
Women	.19	.19	−.16
Johns	.19	.33	.09
Men	.46 *	.06	−.13

* $p < .05$.

13 B. J. Winer, *op. cit.*

correlation is the positive correlation found between time in the profession and esteem of men-in-general. This correlation may well be a result of chance. If it is not, however, the position held by at least some girls, that one becomes hard, cold, and hateful of men, is clearly refuted. At least for girls who stay in the profession, the current ratings do not indicate such attitudes.

Discussion

While the data indicate that there are differential attitudes toward the relevant audiences, correct predictions as to their nature were not deduced from knowledge of the occupational ideology. The respondents know the ideology but they do not endorse it. It is, of course, possible that the description of the occupational perspective may be incorrect, but the consensus in both the scientific and lay literature suggests otherwise. Assuming that the occupationally sanctioned ideology is as described, why do so many know the perspectives and yet not adopt them privately?

It seems reasonable to assume that such ideologies serve a variety of purposes for both the individual prostitute and her related audiences, and do so with varying importance over time. For example, the belief that in-group affiliations are more real, warm, honest, and right than other relationships provides for more cooperative and consequently more lucrative business, isolates the novice from influences hostile to prostitute activities, and provides a group in which passing and duplicity are not required of the actor. Additionally, the myth of man's exploitative nature suits not only the economic aspirations of the novice, but also those of her trainer.[14] The belief that women are hypocrites and that prostitution provides a valuable social service may not only reduce moral conflicts, but serve additionally as a defense against public stigma. It has heretofore been assumed, however, that the functions of these perspectives are served with equal efficiency across the individual prostitute's career span. It appears more likely, in light of the current data, that such orientations are learned during the initial few months of her career and during her apprenticeship period and are taught directly by the trainer. While the professional ideology is learned and perhaps serves a function during this apprenticeship period, it is doubtful that it remains of equal importance throughout the call girl's career.

Once entrance into prostitution has been accomplished, there are many reasons to reject such beliefs. First, prostitution at the call girl level, particularly for pimpless and madamless girls as in this study, is loosely organized. While training periods do exist, the training appears more oriented toward the acquisition of skills than ideology. Cooperative interaction with colleagues is required for only short periods of time and usually within restricted circumstances.[15] For example, the most frequent activity of this nature is that of "putting on a show." This refers to two girls simulating homosexual activities while the customer observes. These activities, however, frequently last a short time. Additionally, many girls are usually available to a particular prostitute for this purpose, each being an actor of equal utility. No critical dependence upon particular individuals is developed.

The everyday interaction of the call girl with her colleagues dramatically belies notions concerning her good char-

[14] J. H. Bryan, *op. cit.*
[15] J. H. Bryan, *op. cit.*

acter. Respondents are suspicious of one another, being less concerned with competition than simple exploitation.[16] Interview data, as well as personal observation, demonstrate that extensive disloyalty and exploitation characterize the interpersonal relationships among call girls. As one girl suggests: "But yet there's never a real close friendship. . . . I mean they will do anything for each other. But still at times when they're taking pills and things, they'll go against you . . . they'll slit your throat at times."

If the adoption of counter-moralities is a function of public visibility and stigma, as is often implied, could it be that prostitution is, in fact, not heavily burdened with reproach? The finding of J. Nunnally that the general public holds in higher esteem the mental hospital attendant than the psychoanalyst makes any *a priori* assumption of stigma or status somewhat suspect.[17] Furthermore, despite general cultural sanctions, the everyday life of the call girl is to a great extent designed to avoid public revelation, and is generally successful in this effort. Unlike the effeminate male homosexual, the arm-marked heroin addict, or the physically disabled, the call girl carries no tell-tale insignia of her occupational status. Nor is she forced into the job market where biographies are demanded and accounts may be checked. Moreover, much of the interaction of "john" with girl is specifically oriented toward the reduction of the stigma attached to both roles, each pretending that the other is

fulfilling a role more obscure than that which is apparent. While role definitions (whore and "john") are rare, when they do occur they are delicately put, stemming from motives more benevolent than otherwise. The call girl rarely experiences moral condemnation through interpersonal relations, thus reducing the need for justification. This may further lessen the impact of attempts at occupational socialization.

In accounting for the evaluative rankings found, the most parsimonious explanation is that they reflect the general culturally supported double standard. While Nunnally, using semantic differential techniques, failed to find women rating the "average man" as being better than the "average woman," McKee and Sherriffs found, using a variety of rating techniques, that women college students consistently rated men as being superior or "more worthy" than females.[18] A plausible hunch, then, is that such ranking might well be found in any randomly selected representative sample of this age group.

In light of the commonplace assumption by the psychological professions that the prostitute must be emotionally disturbed, it is of interest to note that if such emotional disturbance is present, it is not reflected in at least one measure of self-esteem.[19] When compared to the self-ratings of Nunnally's sample, chosen to be representative of the U.S. population on the usual demographic variables, call girls' self-ratings on the dimensions of goodness are only slightly

[16] W. C. Reckless, *op. cit.* has suggested that competition disrupts group cohesiveness among streetwalkers. Competition appears to play a minor role in determining relationships among call girls.

[17] J. C. Nunnally, *Popular Conceptions of Mental Health*, New York: Holt, Rinehart and Winston, 1961.

[18] J. P. McKee and A. C. Sherriffs, "The Differential Evaluation of Males and Females," *Journal of Personality*, 25 (1957), pp. 356–371.

[19] H. Greenwald, *The Call Girl*, New York: Ballantine Books, 1960. See also review by V. L. Bullough, *op. cit.*

below those of his sample.[20] Indeed, the group as a whole fails to identify with their colleagues, each supposing herself to be more worthwhile than the others.

Whatever the reasons, however, it appears that prostitution, at this level, does not require extensive socialization of its members, nor do the members require such socialization for its continuing practice. While stereotypes exist, they play a limited role in the individually held perspectives of the pimpless or independent call girl. Whether independence of the socialization model is due to the lack of cohesiveness of the occupation, the personality of the participants, or the absence of severe stigma, cannot be deduced from the present data.

If the absence of occupational socialization is, in fact, the result of the lack of stigma, then further support is given those hypotheses concerning the role of stigma in producing counter-moralities of deviant groups.

No evidence has been gathered which suggests that specific attitudes toward relevant audiences are related to the continuing practice of prostitution. The effects of such activity upon the attitudes of the participants remain to be determined.

---

[20] Ruth C. Wylie has provided an excellent review of the theoretical and methodological difficulties pertaining to self theories and measurement: *The Self Concept,* Lincoln, Nebraska: University of Nebraska Press, 1961.

SYSTEMATIC DEVIANCE: THE EFFECTS OF VARIATION

12

All deviance is not necessarily systematic. Only when deviance persists, is patterned, and when the deviant takes into account that others are aware of his deviant role, can we rightfully say that deviance is systematic. In addition, not all systematic deviance is socially organized. Many kinds of deviants practice in private, as it were, or as solitary individuals. Solitary deviance differs in some very important respects from socially organized deviance. And in turn, the manner in which deviant statuses and roles are organized according to deviant beliefs, values, and norms, affects the manner in which a person pursues his deviant career. For whereas the social organization of some deviant careers makes for a reasonable degree of gratification, others are so organized as to only increase rather than decrease the stigma and punishment their members experience over time.

Cloward and Ohlin, in the first reading, describe three varieties of delinquent subculture. Leznoff and Westley compare the style of life and world-views of overt and covert homosexuals. Finally, Rubington shows how conformity to bottle drinking norms varies with certain organizational and territorial conditions.

Varieties of Delinquent Subcultures *

RICHARD A. CLOWARD AND LLOYD E. OHLIN

There appear to be three major types of delinquent subculture typically encoun-tered among adolescent males in lower-class areas of large urban centers. One is

* Reprinted with permission of The Macmillan Company from *Delinquency and Opportunity* by Richard A. Cloward and Lloyd E. Ohlin, pp. 20–27. © The Free Press, a Corporation 1960.

based principally upon criminal values; its members are organized primarily for the pursuit of material gain by such illegal means as extortion, fraud, and theft. In the second, violence is the keynote; its members pursue status ("rep") through the manipulation of force or threat of force. These are the "warrior" groups that attract so much attention in the press. Finally, there are subcultures which emphasize the consumption of drugs. The participants in these drug subcultures have become alienated from conventional roles, such as those required in the family or the occupational world. They have withdrawn into a restricted world in which the ultimate value consists in the "kick." We call these three subcultural forms "criminal," "conflict," and "retreatist," respectively.[1]

These shorthand terms simply denote the *principal* orientation of each form of adaptation from the perspective of the dominant social order; although one can find many examples of subcultures that fit accurately into one of these three categories, subcultures frequently appear in somewhat mixed form. Thus members of a predominantly conflict subculture may also on occasion engage in systematic theft; members of a criminal subculture may sometimes do combat in the streets with rival gangs. But this should not obscure the fact that these subcultures tend to exhibit essentially different orientations.

The extent to which the delinquent subculture organizes and controls a participant's allegiance varies from one member to another. Some members of the gang are almost totally immersed in the perspectives of the subculture and bring them into play in all their contacts; others segregate this aspect of their lives and maintain other roles in the family, school, and church. The chances are relatively slight, however, that an adolescent can successfully segregate delinquent and conforming roles for a long period of time. Pressures emanate from the subculture leading its members to adopt unfavorable attitudes toward parents, school teachers, policemen, and other adults in the conventional world. When he is apprehended for delinquent acts, the possibility of the delinquent's maintaining distinctly separate role involvements breaks down, and he is confronted with the necessity of choosing between law-abiding and delinquent styles of life. Since family, welfare, religious, educational, law-enforcement, and correctional institutions are arrayed against the appeal of his delinquent associates, the decision is a difficult one, frequently requiring either complete acceptance or complete rejection of one or the other system of obligations.[2]

At any one point in time, however, the extent to which the norms of the delinquent subculture control behavior will vary from one member to another. Accordingly, descriptions of these subcultures must be stated in terms of the fully indoctrinated member rather than the average member. Only in this way can the distinctiveness of delinquent styles of life be made clear. It is with this understanding that we offer the following brief empirical characterizations of the three main types of delinquent subculture.

[1] It should be understood that these terms characterize these delinquent modes of adaptation from the reference position of conventional society; they do not necessarily reflect the attitudes of members of the subcultures. Thus the term "retreatist" does not necessarily reflect the attitude of the "cat." Far from thinking of himself as being in retreat, he defines himself as among the elect.

[2] Tannenbaum summarizes the community's role in this process of alienation by the phrase "dramatization of evil" (Frank Tannenbaum, *Crime and the Community* [New York: Columbia University Press, 1938], pp. 19–21).

The Criminal Pattern

The most extensive documentation in the sociological literature of delinquent behavior patterns in lower-class culture describes a tradition which integrates youthful delinquency with adult criminality.[3] In the central value orientation of youths participating in this tradition, delinquent and criminal behavior is accepted as a means of achieving success-goals. The dominant criteria of in-group evaluation stress achievement, the use of skill and knowledge to get results. In this culture, prestige is allocated to those who achieve material gain and power through avenues defined as illegitimate by the larger society. From the very young to the very old, the successful "haul"—which quickly transforms the penniless into a man of means—is an ever-present vision of the possible and desirable. Although one may also achieve material success through the routine practice of theft or fraud, the "big score" remains the symbolic image of quick success.

The means by which a member of a criminal subculture achieves success are clearly defined for the aspirant. At a young age, he learns to admire and respect older criminals and to adopt the "right guy" as his role-model. Delinquent episodes help him to acquire mastery of the techniques and orientation of the criminal world and to learn how to cooperate successfully with others in criminal enterprises. He exhibits hostility and distrust toward representatives of the larger society. He regards members of the conventional world as "suckers," his natural victims, to be exploited when possible. He sees successful people in the conventional world as having a "racket" —e.g., big businessmen have huge expense accounts, politicians get graft, etc. This attitude successfully neutralizes controlling effect of conventional norms. Toward the in-group the "right guy" maintains relationships of loyalty, honesty, and trustworthiness. He must prove himself reliable and dependable in his contacts with his criminal associates although he has no such obligations toward the out-group of noncriminals.

One of the best ways of assuring success in the criminal world is to cultivate appropriate "connections." As a youngster, this means running with a clique composed of other "right guys" and promoting an apprenticeship or some other favored relationship with older and successful offenders. Close and dependable ties with income-producing outlets for stolen goods, such as the wagon peddler, the junkman, and the fence, are especially useful. Furthermore, these intermediaries encourage and protect the young delinquent in a criminal way of life by giving him a jaundiced perspective on the private morality of many functionaries in conventional society. As he matures, the young delinquent becomes acquainted with a new world made up of predatory bondsmen, shady lawyers, crooked policemen, grafting politicians, dishonest businessmen, and corrupt jailers. Through "connections" with occupants of these half-legitimate, half-illegitimate roles and with "big shots" in the underworld, the aspiring criminal validates and assures his freedom of movement in a world made safe for crime.

[3] See esp. C. R. Shaw, *The Jack Roller* (Chicago: University of Chicago Press, 1930); Shaw, *The Natural History of a Delinquent Career* (Chicago: University of Chicago Press, 1940); Shaw and H. D. McKay, *Juvenile Delinquency and Urban Areas* (Chicago: University of Chicago Press, 1942); E. H. Sutherland, ed., *The Professional Thief* (Chicago: University of Chicago Press, 1937); Sutherland, *Principles of Criminology*, 4th ed. (Philadelphia: J. P. Lippincott Co., 1947); and Sutherland, *White Collar Crime* (New York: Dryden Press, 1949).

The Conflict Pattern [4]

The role-model in the conflict pattern of lower-class culture is the "bopper" who swaggers with his gang, fights with weapons to win a wary respect from other gangs, and compels a fearful deference from the conventional adult world by his unpredictable and destructive assaults on persons and property. To other gang members, however, the key qualities of the bopper are those of the successful warrior. His performance must reveal a willingness to defend his personal integrity and the honor of the gang. He must do this with great courage and displays of fearlessness in the face of personal danger.

The immediate aim in the world of fighting gangs is to acquire a reputation for toughness and destructive violence. A "rep" assures not only respectful behavior from peers and threatened adults but also admiration for the physical strength and masculinity which it symbolizes. It represents a way of securing access to the scarce resources for adolescent pleasure and opportunity in underprivileged areas.

Above all things, the bopper is valued for his "heart." He does not "chicken out," even when confronted by superior force. He never defaults in the face of a personal insult or a challenge to the integrity of his gang. The code of the bopper is that of the warrior who places great stress on courage, the defense of his group, and the maintenance of honor.

Relationships between bopping gang members and the adult world are severely attenuated. The term that the bopper uses most frequently to characterize his relationships with adults is "weak." He is unable to find appropriate role-models that can designate for him a structure of opportunities leading to adult success. He views himself as isolated and the adult world as indifferent. The commitments of adults are to their own interests and not to his. Their explanations of why he should behave differently are "weak," as are their efforts to help him.

Confronted by the apparent indifference and insincerity of the adult world, the ideal bopper seeks to win by coercion the attention and opportunities he lacks and cannot otherwise attract. In recent years the street-gang worker who deals with the fighting gang on its own "turf" has come to symbolize not only a recognition by conventional adult society of the gang's toughness but also a concession of opportunities formerly denied. Through the alchemy of competition between gangs, this gesture of attention by the adult world to the "worst" gangs is transformed into a mark of prestige. Thus does the manipulation of violence convert indifference into accommodation and attention into status.

The Retreatist Pattern

Retreatism may include a variety of expressive, sensual, or consummatory experiences, alone or in a group. In this analysis, we are interested only in those experiences that involve the use of drugs and that are supported by a subculture. We have adopted these limitations in

---

[4] For descriptions of conflict groups, see Harrison Salisbury, *The Shook-up Generation* (New York: Harper & Bros., 1958); *Reaching the Unreached*, a Publication of the New York City Youth Board, 1952; C. K. Myers, *Light the Dark Streets* (Greenwich, Conn.: Seabury Press, 1957); Walter Bernstein, "The Cherubs Are Rumbling," *The New Yorker*, Sept. 21, 1957; Sam Glane, "Juvenile Gangs in East Side Los Angeles," *Focus*, Vol. 29 (Sept. 1959), pp. 136–41; Dale Kramer and Madeline Karr, *Teen-Age Gangs* (New York: Henry Holt, 1953); S. V. Jones, "The Cougars—Life with a Brooklyn Gang," *Harper's*, Vol. 209 (Nov. 1954), pp. 35–43; P. C. Crawford, D. I. Malamud, and J. R. Dumpson, *Working with Teen-Age Gangs* (New York Welfare Council, 1950); Dan Wakefield, "The Gang That Went Good," *Harper's*, Vol. 216 (June 1958), pp. 36–43.

order to maintain our focus on subcultural formations which are clearly recognized as delinquent, as drug use by adolescents is. The retreatist preoccupation with expressive experiences creates many varieties of "hipster" cult among lower-class adolescents which foster patterns of deviant but not necessarily delinquent conduct.

Subcultural drug-users in lower-class areas perceive themselves as culturally and socially detached from the life-style and everyday preoccupations of members of the conventional world. The following characterization of the "cat" culture, observed by Finestone in a lower-class Negro area in Chicago, describes drug use in the more general context of "hipsterism." [5] Thus it should not be assumed that this description in every respect fits drug cultures found elsewhere. We have drawn heavily on Finestone's observations, however, because they provide the best descriptions available of the social world in which lower-class adolescent drug cultures typically arise.

The dominant feature of the retreatist subculture of the "cat" lies in the continuous pursuit of the "kick." Every cat has a kick—alcohol, marijuana, addicting drugs, unusual sexual experiences, hot jazz, cool jazz, or any combination of these. Whatever its content, the kick is a search for ecstatic experiences. The retreatist strives for an intense awareness of living and a sense of pleasure that is "out of this world." In extreme form, he seeks an almost spiritual and mystical knowledge that is experienced when one comes to know "it" at the height of one's kick. The past and the future recede in the time perspective of the cat, since complete awareness in present experience is the essence of the kick.

The successful cat has a lucrative "hustle" which contrasts sharply with the routine and discipline required in the ordinary occupational tasks of conventional society. The many varieties of the hustle are characterized by a rejection of violence or force and a preference for manipulating, persuading, outwitting, or "conning" others to obtain resources for experiencing the kick. The cat begs, borrows, steals, or engages in some petty con-game. He caters to the illegitimate cravings of others by peddling drugs or working as a pimp. A highly exploitative attitude toward women permits the cat to view pimping as a prestige source of income. Through the labor of "chicks" engaged in prostitution or shoplifting, he can live in idleness and concentrate his entire attention on organizing, scheduling, and experiencing the esthetic pleasure of the kick. The hustle of the cat is secondary to his interest in the kick. In this respect the cat differs from his fellow delinquents in the criminal subculture, for whom income-producing activity is a primary concern.

The ideal cat's appearance, demeanor, and taste can best be characterized as "cool." The cat seeks to exhibit a highly developed and sophisticated taste for clothes. In his demeanor, he struggles to reveal a self-assured and unruffled manner, thereby emphasizing his aloofness and "superiority" to the "squares." He develops a colorful, discriminating vocabulary and ritualized gestures which express his sense of difference from the conventional world and his solidarity with the retreatist subculture.

The word "cool" also best describes the sense of apartness and detachment which the retreatist experiences in his relationships with the conventional world. His reference group is the "society of cats," an "elite" group in which he becomes isolated from conventional society. Within this group, a new order of goals

[5] Harold Finestone, "Cats, Kicks and Color," *Social Problems,* Vol. 5 (July 1957), pp. 3–13.

and criteria of achievement are created. The cat does not seek to impose this system of values on the world of the squares. Instead, he strives for status and deference within the society of cats by cultivating the kick and the hustle. Thus the retreatist subculture provides avenues to success-goals, to the social admiration and the sense of well-being or oneness with the world which the members feel are otherwise beyond their reach.

Overt and Covert Homosexuals *

MAURICE LEZNOFF AND WILLIAM A. WESTLEY

The significance of homosexuality in our society has been minimized and obscured by the force of social taboo. Yet there is evidence that homosexuals are distributed throughout all geographical areas and socio-economic strata.[1] Furthermore, the subjection of homosexuals to legal punishments and social condemnation has produced a complex structure of concealed social relations which merit sociological investigation. The psychological isolation of the homosexual from society, his dependence upon other deviants for the satisfaction of sexual needs and self-expression, the crystallization of social roles and behavior patterns within the deviant group, the reciprocal obligations and demands within the homosexual community, and their significance for the larger society in which they occur, are but a few of the areas of theoretical interest to the sociologist.

In this paper we shall confine our discussion to the social organization of one homosexual community and its constituent social groups: their function, etiology, and interrelationships.

The report is based upon an intensive study of 60 homosexuals in a large Canadian city. The data consist of four-hour interviews with 40 homosexuals and briefer interviews with 20 others.[2] In addition, the data include information based on the observation of many homo-

* Reprinted from "The Homosexual Community" in *Social Problems,* Vol. 3, No. 4 (April, 1956), pp. 257–263, by permission of the authors and *Social Problems.* The authors are indebted to the Canadian Social Science Research Council and to the McGill University Research Fund for grants in support of this study.

[1] Kinsey reports that 37 per cent of the total male population have at least some overt homosexual experience to the point of orgasm between adolescence and old age; 30 per cent of all males have at least incidental homosexual experience or reactions over at least a three year period between the ages of 16 and 55; 25 per cent of the male population have more than incidental homosexual experience or reactions for at least three years between the ages of 16 and 55; 18 per cent of the males have at least as much of the homosexual as the heterosexual in their histories for at least three years between the ages of 16 and 55; 4 per cent of the white males are exclusively homosexual throughout their lives, after the onset of adolescence. Homosexual practices are reported among all occupational groups with the percentage for professionals approximately 50 per cent lower than those of other groups. Further confirmation of the distribution of homosexuals among all social strata was obtained from police files and the testimony of homosexuals.

[2] Access to this homosexual community was obtained through a client at a social welfare agency.

sexual parties and gatherings in bars and restaurants, and a series of 30 letters written by one homosexual to another.

Functions of Homosexual Groups

The primary function of the homosexual group is psychological in that it provides a social context within which the homosexual can find acceptance as a homosexual and collective support for his deviant tendencies. Most homosexuals fear detection and are often insecure and anxious because of this. The following statement illustrates this:

The thought that you are "gay" is always with you and you know it's there even when other people don't. You also think to yourself that certain of your mannerisms and your ways of expression are liable to give you away. That means that there is always a certain amount of strain. I don't say that it's a relief to get away from normal people, but there isn't the liberty that you feel in a gay crowd. When I associate with normal people I prefer very small groups of them. I don't like large groups and I think I try to avoid them when I can. You know, the only time when I really forget I'm gay is when I'm in a gay crowd.

To relieve this anxiety the deviant seeks collective support and social acceptance. Since the homosexual group provides the only social context in which homosexuality is normal, deviant practices moral, and homosexual responses rewarded, the homosexual develops a deep emotional involvement with his group, tending toward a ready acceptance of its norms and dictates, and subjection to its behavior patterns. The regularity with which he seeks the company of his group is a clear expression of this dependency.

A prohibition against sexual relation-

ships within the group, in a manner suggestive of the incest taboo, indicates the extent to which the group culture is oriented to this function. The quotation which follows is indicative of this taboo:

As far as I know, people who hang around with each other don't have affairs. The people who are friends don't sleep with each other. I can't tell you why that is, but they just don't. Unless you are married [3] you have sex with strangers mostly. I think if you have sex with a friend it will destroy the friendship. I think that in the inner mind we all respect high moral standards, and none of us want to feel low in the eyes of anybody else. It's always easier to get along with your gay friends if there has been no sex. Mind you, you might have sex with somebody you just met and then he might become your friend. But you won't have sex with him any more as soon as he joins the same gang you hang around with.

Within these groups the narration of sexual experiences and gossip about the sexual exploits of others is a major form of recreation. The narration of sexual experiences functions to allocate prestige among the members because of the high evaluation placed upon physical attraction and sexual prowess. Yet it creates hostility and sexual rivalry. The intense involvement of homosexuals in the results of this sexual competition is illustrated in the following statement which was overheard in a restaurant:

Who wouldn't blow up. That bitch is trying to get her [4] clutches into Richard. She can't leave anybody alone. I wouldn't be surprised if she ended up with a knife in her back. I don't mean to say I'm threatening her. But she's not going to get away with that stuff forever . . . playing kneesies under the table all night long. I had to get her away from Richard. That lousy bitch. From now on she better keep away from me.

---

[3] A stable social and sexual relationship between two homosexuals is frequently referred to as "marriage."

[4] The substitution of the female for the male pronoun is a common practice within homosexual groups.

An additional function is the provision of a social situation in which the members can dramatize their adherence to homosexual values. Thus, the gossip about sex, the adoption and exaggeration of feminine behavior, and the affectation of speech, represent a way of affirming that homosexuality is frankly accepted and has the collective support of the group. The extreme but not uncommon instance of this is the homosexual institution of the "drag" in which the members of the group dress and make themselves up as women. A good description of a drag is contained in the following letter:

Well, doll, last night was one to remember. Raymond of B. (city) gave me a letter of introduction to one of the local belles. He 'phoned yesterday and we arranged to go out in the evening. Met at my room and proceeded to the Frederick Hotel where I was introduced to my new acquaintances. It was decided to hold a party afterwards, Chez Norman, my new acquaintance. He told me they were supposed to be discontinued but we were going ahead in my honor. And in drag. One queen about 45–50 who is a window dresser brought some materials of fine nylon net, 2 yards wide and changing color across the width from yellow to flaming orange. There must have been about 25 yds. Well, he made his entrance wearing nothing but his shorts and this stuff wound around him and proceeded to do an exotic dance. Included in the costume was a blond wig from one of the store mannequins and artificial tropical fruits. It was something to see. It was very ludicrous to begin with and much more so when you realize that he is by no means graceful and has so much hair on him that I am smooth by comparison. Throughout the evening he kept on making variations of the costume—each becoming briefer until he was down to nothing. Really!

Another one, very slim, put on a pair of falsies, a turban hat to hide short hair, and a dress with a wide flair skirt. Other than hair on the chest which showed, the effect of femininity was so convincing (even his heels) that I promptly lost interest. Actually produced a beautiful effect—the kind of woman I would like if I could. Beautiful dancer, and performed all evening. Later borrowed some of the nylon net of the old queen and did a dance with flowing material and wearing *nothing,* but nothing else.

There were only three of us not in drag, including yrs. truly. But when it came time to leave (not alone, I might add) I couldn't resist flinging about my coat a fox fur which happened to be lying around. Really, my dear, it was quite an affair.

These functions reflect the common needs and problems which homosexuals face in hostile society.

Etiology: The Evasion of Social Controls

In our society, homosexuality is defined both legally and socially as a criminal and depraved practice and the homosexual is threatened by powerful legal and social sanctions such as imprisonment, physical violence (1), social and occupational ostracism, and ridicule. Therefore, all homosexuals face the problem of evading social controls. They do this in two predominant ways.

Some pass for heterosexuals on the job and in most of their social relationships. They mix regularly with heterosexuals for business, entertainment, and other social activities. They avoid situations and persons publicly recognized as homosexual for they fear that discovery will threaten their career and expose them to sanctions. This is illustrated in the following statement of a lawyer:

I know a few people who don't care. They are really pitiful. They are either people who are in very insignificant positions or they are in good positions but are independent. I know of one who is in the retail business. He doesn't care. A lot of the artists don't care. For that reason I have never cultivated the friendship of artists. I just don't get along with anybody who doesn't care. That's why I really can't give you information about those who don't. It's just that I can't afford to get to know them very well, and I try to avoid them. Sometimes personal friends become this way. Then there is a mutual rejection of the friendship. From my point of view I am just no longer interested when they adopt that kind of attitude. From their point of view it means completely living outside of society and they are no longer interested in people who they consider hypocrites.

Others openly admit and practice homosexuality. They usually work in occupations where the homosexual is tolerated, withdraw from uncompromising heterosexual groups, and confine most of their social life to homosexual circles. This attitude is expressed in the following statement by a hairdresser:

Rosenstein can go to hell as far as I care. She works you to the bone if she can get away with it. She told me I run around the place like a regular pansy. So I told her I am a pansy and if she doesn't like it she can get somebody else to do her dirty work for her. I knew she wouldn't fire me. All the ladies ask for me and I don't have to pretend to nobody.

While the problem of evasion is common to all homosexuals, the mechanisms of evasion present various alternatives. Most homosexuals find themselves compelled to conform outwardly to societal demands. They are conscious of their social position within society and seek such satisfactions as occupational mobility and prestige. They endeavor to retain intimate associations within the heterosexual community, and fear recognition as a status threat. Such homosexuals rely upon secrecy and the concealment of their deviant practices. They will therefore be referred to as "secret" homosexuals. A minority retreat from the demands of society and renounce societal goals. Such individuals will be referred to as "overt" homosexuals.

The mode of adaptation is largely de-

pendent upon the extent to which identification as a homosexual is a status threat. While economic status cannot be equated with social status, the individual's position within the work world represents the most significant single factor in the prestige scale. Therefore, the extent to which homosexuality is tolerated in various occupations determines to a great extent the mode of evasion chosen by the homosexual. Thus, there are many occupations, of which the professions are an obvious example, where homosexuals are not tolerated. In other areas, the particular occupation may have traditionally accepted homosexual linkages in the popular image or be of such low rank as to permit homosexuals to function on the job. The artist, the interior decorator, and the hairdresser exemplify the former type; such positions as counter man or bell-hop, the latter. Thus we find a rough relationship between form of evasion and occupation. The overt homosexual tends to fit into an occupation of low status rank; the secret homosexual into an occupation with a relatively high status rank. The relationship is shown in Table 1.

Distinctions Between the Secret and Overt Groups

The chief distinctions between homosexual groups correspond to the differences in the general modes of evading social controls which homosexuals have developed. Thus, secret and overt homosexuals form distinctive groups.

The distinctions between these groups are maintained by the secret homosexuals who fear identification and refuse to associate with overt homosexuals. This statement by a secret homosexual is illustrative:

If someone who is gay wanted to be spiteful they could say something in the wrong quarter. Nobody who cared about himself

TABLE 1
Occupation of 40 Secret and
Overt Homosexuals *

Occupation *	Secret **	Overt	Total
Professional and Managerial	13	0	13
Clerical and Sales	9	4	13
Craftsmen	2	1	3
Operatives	1	1	2
Service	0	6	6
Artists	0	3	3
Totals	25	15	40

* Except for artists the categories and ranking are those established by the National Opinion Research Center. (2) Artists have been listed as a separate category because they often represent a group which is apart from the status structure of the community.

** The secret homosexuals gave the following reasons for concealment: (a) desire to avoid social ridicule—22 cases; (b) fear of dismissal from the job, or where self-employed, inability to get clients—20 cases; (c) a desire to protect others such as family or friends—18 cases.

would say anything. The trouble is that some don't care. I make it a rule to avoid anybody who is perfectly open about himself. It's easy not to become friendly with those people but it's hard to avoid them entirely. You certainly don't want to snub them because that might make them antagonistic. You just don't call them or see them at social gatherings. But you do meet them at bars and that's where you can be introduced to them. If they remember you and continue to say hello to you on the street, you have to acknowledge them or they might feel that you are trying to snub them.

As a result of this social distance a certain amount of reciprocal hostility has developed between the members of secret and overt groups. This hostility helps maintain the social distance and distinctions between these groups. This is demonstrated in the following statements by

an overt and a secret homosexual respectively:

I know some of them because sometimes they stoop down and have an affair with somebody from our gang. They even come to a party over at Robert's once in a while but they never hang around for very long and then you don't see them again. They go over to the Red Room sometimes but we don't have much to say to each other and the same thing happens when we go over to the Burning Flame.[5] We just might say hello. But sometimes they will cruise us and try to take someone home to bed. I think you could say we mix sexually but not socially.

There are some people who I don't like and I wish these people didn't know about me. Then there are the people I don't know too well: people who are obvious or what I uncharitably call the riff-raff. I have always attempted to avoid them and I avoid them now. It is inevitable that you bump into a lot of people you would rather not know. Homosexuals are very democratic people. To achieve their own ends they overlook a lot they wouldn't overlook in other fields. People are bound to each other like a link of a chain. You try to avoid being a link in this chain by carefully choosing.

This poses serious problems for the homosexual who is socially mobile. He is forced to change his primary group affiliations within the homosexual community.

The following statement by the manager of an appliance shop shows how the homosexual tends to change his orientation from "overt" to "secret" as he becomes upwardly mobile.

My promotions have made me more conscious of the gang I hang around with. You see, for the first time in my life I have a job that I would really like to keep and where I can have a pretty secure future. I realize that if word were to get around that I am gay I would probably lose my job. I don't see why that should be, because I

[5] The Burning Flame refers to a bar which tended to draw its clientele from secret homosexuals; the Red Room was the acknowledged gathering place of overt homosexuals.

know that I'm the same person gay or not. But still that's the way it works. I don't want to hang around with Robert [6] any more or any of the people who are like Robert. I don't mind seeing them once in a while at somebody's house, but I won't be seen with them on the street any more.

Both types of groups were identified and observed in the course of this research. Each group consisted of fourteen members. The descriptions which follow are based on the study of these groups.

SECRET GROUPS

The secret homosexuals form groups which consist of a loose amalgamation of small cliques. Interaction within the cliques is frequent, with members meeting at each other's homes and in bars and restaurants. The clique's structure is a product of the diverse interests and occupations and of the desire to limit homosexual contacts which characterize secret homosexuals. The clique unites its several members in common specialized interests apart from the larger group.

The following chart shows the clique structure and occupational composition of a secret homosexual group.

A secret homosexual group is generally characterized by: (a) informal standards of admission; (b) discretion in the manner in which homosexuality is practiced; (c) an attempt at concealment; (d) partial rather than complete involvement in the homosexual world.

OVERT GROUPS

Overt homosexuals gather in cohesive social groups which become the dominant focus of their lives. These groups are openly homosexual in character. The members make little effort to conceal their deviation, spend almost all their free time with the group, and tend to regard their other activities as peripheral.

These groups generally draw their members from persons of low socioeconomic status who have jobs where concealment is not a prerequisite. Table 2 presents the occupational composition of the overt group identified in this study.

TABLE 2
Occupational Composition of an Overt Homosexual Group

Occcupation	Frequency
Manager of appliance shop *	1
School teacher	1
Hospital attendant	1
Hairdresser	4
Sales clerk	2
Foundry worker	1
Baker	1
Salesman	1
Waiter	1
Cashier	1
Total	14

* This individual had just been promoted and was beginning to leave the group. Both he and the school teacher retained for a time their affiliation with an overt group while at the same time concealing their homosexuality at work.

Clique A.	Clique B.	Clique C.	Clique D.
Lawyer	Clerk-bookkeeper	Stenographer	Accountant
Personnel Manager	Auditing clerk	Store Manager	Interior Decorator
University student	Assistant Office	Manager of	
Economist	Manager	Statistical Dept.	
	University student		
	Secretary		

[6] Robert is the leader of an overt group of which the respondent was a member at the time he was contacted.

The members of the group met daily either at a bar, a restaurant, or at the house of the acknowledged leader or "queen." [7] They spent their time in endless gossip about the sexual affairs of the members or other homosexuals known to them. Often they would go to bars and restaurants in the attempt to make a "pick-up," or spend the evening "cruising" individually or in groups of two's and three's.

The queen seems to characterize only "overt" groups. Functionally, the role of the queen is very important in the life of these groups. He provides a place where the group may gather and where its individual members may have their "affairs." He helps finance members in distress, functions as an intermediary in making sexual contacts, partially controls the entrance of new members, and warns the members of hoodlums who would prey upon them. Generally the queen is an older homosexual who has had wide experience in the homosexual world.

The following statement about the queen by a member of the overt group provides insight into the functioning of the queen and tells something of the way in which the individuals relate to him.

A queen really means the leader of the group. You see how that is in a small town where there are not many people who are gay and willing to admit it. She knows who's who and what's what. She will know every gay person in town and will arrange things just the way Roberta does.[8] The queen is always somebody pretty old and pretty much out of the game as far as getting anything for herself is concerned. But she doesn't have anything else to do, so she spends all her time on this. I don't know of any queen as commercial as Roberta. But that's because Roberta is so goddam crude. I know

the queen in Hillsburg and she was a perfect lady if I ever saw one. She knows everything. She used to make quite a bit but it was always in the form of getting invitations for dinner or as a present. You feel grateful to somebody who does something for you and you pay off. It's like a debt.

Overt groups are characterized by: (a) no particular standards of admission; (b) unselfconscious and unrestrained practice of homosexuality; (c) little or no concealment; (d) high degree of social isolation with little involvement in heterosexual activities; (e) little concern with identification as a status threat or the sanctions of heterosexual society.

The Homosexual Community

The diverse secret and overt homosexuals are linked together either through bonds of sex or of friendship. Within the primary group, the emphasis upon friendship rather than sex serves to eliminate excessive sexual competition and preserves group unity. However, this creates a sexual interdependency upon those outside the group with important social consequences.

In the first place, it forces the secret homosexual out into the open in an attempt to solicit sexual partners. He thus frequents the known homosexual meeting places within the city such as specific bars, hotel lobbies, street corners, and lavatories. These activities make him an increasingly familiar figure within the homosexual world.

Secondly, this solicitation leads to the interaction of secret and overt homosexuals on a sexual as opposed to a social basis. While these contacts occur in a spirit of anonymity, an approach to the

[7] Our data with respect to the prevalence of this role are incomplete. However, homosexuals regularly refer to the queens of other cities, suggesting that the practice is widespread.

[8] The adoption of feminine names is a widespread practice among all homosexuals interviewed.

other often requires an exchange of confidences.

Thirdly, this sexual interdependency increases the anxiety of secret homosexuals since it forces them to contact the overt ones whom they fear as a threat to their security.

Thus, it is the casual and promiscuous sexual contacts between the members of different categories of evasion (i.e. the secret and the overt) which weld the city's homosexuals into a community.

Conclusion

The homosexual community thus consists of a large number of distinctive groups within which friendship binds the members together in a strong and relatively enduring bond and between which the members are linked by tenuous but repeated sexual contacts. The result is that homosexuals within the city tend to know or know of each other, to recognize a number of common interests and common moral norms, and to interact on the basis of antagonistic cooperation. This community is in turn linked with other homosexual communities in Canada and the United States, chiefly through the geographical mobility of its members.[9]

References

1. WILLIAM A. WESTLEY. "Violence and the Police," *American Journal of Sociology*, 59 (July, 1953).
2. National Opinion Research Center, *Opinion News*, 9 (September, 1947), 3–13.

Variations in Bottle-Gang Controls *

EARL RUBINGTON

Those who practice deviance openly in groups face internal and external controls. Overt deviants, in addition to managing their own deviant careers, have to screen their activities from conformists and regulate both their own conduct and that of other similar deviants.

Theory states that the solution to these problems comes from a deviant subculture.[1] Such a subculture teaches skills, supplies a more favorable self-image, sets down rules for dealing with others, deviant or conformist, and justifies deviant behavior by a special ideology.

Deviant subcultures, however, supply ideas on social actions; they do not guarantee that prescribed actions will take place. It becomes necessary then to ask how well deviant beliefs, values, and norms are honored in practice, the extent to which conformity to deviant norms produces rewards, and exactly how deviants control one another.

This paper raises questions on social

[9] The queen of the overt group studied maintained an address book containing the names of approximately 3,000 homosexuals scattered across North America.

* Somewhat revised version of a paper presented at the 62nd annual meetings of the American Sociological Association, San Francisco, California, August 31, 1967.

[1] Howard S. Becker, *Outsiders: Studies in the Sociology of Deviance* (New York: The Free Press of Glencoe, 1963), pp. 37–39; Albert K. Cohen, *Delinquent Boys: The Culture of the Gang* (Glencoe: The Free Press, 1955), pp. 49–72.

control in deviant groups. The group to be considered here, the "bottle gang," is relevant since it meets three conditions. Bottle gangs are public, not private in character; their members have more contacts with persons like themselves than with conformists; and their members participate in Skid Row subculture. Rules and sanctions are the major concerns here. The central question is: How well does the bottle gang regulate interaction and activity, and screen both from outsiders?

To answer the question this paper (a) gives a description of a typical East Coast bottle gang; (b) abstracts the rules and functions of the gang; (c) discusses typical breaches and their sanctions; and (d) posits a set of conditions that may account for differences in social control in East Coast and West Coast bottle gangs.

The general argument of this paper is that control in the deviant group rests in part on the number of overt deviants who are visible and known to one another, in part on whether they have a territory and sufficient resources for engaging in deviant activities and interaction, and in part on the nature of their contact with authorities. To the extent that public deviants are more or less left to themselves to control their activities, to that extent will the amount of public deviance be within tolerable limits. But, given high visibility of deviance, frequent attempts at external control will combine with ineffective internal controls to produce a lessened tolerance of deviant behavior.

The Bottle Gang

Bottle gang refers to the typical form of street drinking in which indigent, unattached men engage. The men appear to be heavy drinkers by conventional standards and are usually said to be "alco-holics," "bums," "drunks" or "winos." Generally they meet on the street, pool meager funds, send a member to a package store to buy an inexpensive bottle of fortified wine, share the bottle in some public place (e.g., alley, doorstep, park, or street corner, in rooming-house areas, urban slums, or Skid Row quarter), and split up once the bottle is emptied.

Setting and Methods

Maple City, the setting for the present study, is an East Coast city of some 165,000, with no definable Skid Row quarter. Institutions and establishments catering to homeless men are scattered around the center of the city in various pockets. All are in walking distance, rather than being concentrated as they would be on a typical Skid Row. Lodging houses, rooming-houses, second-hand clothing stores that sell wine, restaurants and taverns catering to the homeless, missions and shelters all radiate out from the center of the city. Important public places for local and transient homeless are the King Street Mission and a grassy common in the center of the city called the Big Green. The present study relies on anthropological methods of field work. The data come from informants, direct observation, and participation, in that order.

A Typical Bottle Gang

The setting assumed for the portrait to follow is the Big Green in Maple City during mild weather in mid-afternoon. The Green is within easy walking distance of the King Street Mission, several package stores, rooming-houses, employment agency, police station, and important street-corner hangouts. There are six stages in the bottle-gang cycle: salutation, negotiation, procurement, consumption, affirmation, and dispersal.

1. *Salutation.* Potential bottle-gang participants come into each other's view on the various paths that criss-cross the Green. Once in each other's presence, they acknowledge their mutual awareness. Each has worked together, drunk together at some time, or is known to a set of mutual acquaintances. They sit down on a bench, pass the time of day, and share information about "the boys." After a brief exchange of news both prepare to negotiate.

2. *Negotiation.* By now, each has read the signs that the other is "on the prowl" (that is, searching for a drink). Typically, one begins the negotiation by saying that he has a certain amount of money that he is willing to contribute towards the purchase of a bottle of wine. He may say, for example: "I have 18 cents; how much are you holding?" The other, if interested, reports his holdings. Generally, they will be "short" the "price of a bottle" (a half-pint of wine generally retails for fifty cents). The initiator collects the money, announces how much more they need, and leads them to others. The leader asks if they wish to "go in on a bottle." If they are still short, a brief excursion in panhandling will be necessary until the price is collected.

3. *Procurement.* When the little group has collected enough money ("made the price" or "scored"), they are now ready to get a bottle and drink it together. The leader picks one of the men to buy the bottle. Buying the bottle is called "making the run" and the buyer is called "the runner." The runner should be a person who is neither too shabbily dressed nor acutely intoxicated, and who is dependable; i.e., that is, if given money, he can be trusted to return with a bottle. While the runner leaves on his errand, the remainder of the gang take seats on a bench and await his return.

4. *Consumption.* The runner returns with the wine (usually Muscatel), con-cealed on his person. The bottle, still in the brown bag the clerk wrapped it in, is inside his belt, under his jacket or in his back pocket. He gives the bag to the leader. The leader looks up and down the pathways of the Big Green, peels the plastic seal, uncaps the bottle, takes two short drinks, and then passes the bottle, still in the brown bag, to the runner. The runner takes two short drinks, then passes the bottle to one of the other men. After the bottle has made its full circle around the gang, the last one to drink from it returns it to the leader. He pockets the bottle, still in the brown bag. After the first round, the men sit back on their bench, light up cigarettes and talk. All during the phases of consumption, each looks up and down the walkways for police officers or outsiders who might jeopardize the activity. All drink surreptitiously.

5. *Affirmation.* The leader, as donor-host, sets style, tone, and topics of talk. There is little talk on personal troubles, much on others' troubles. All make negative comments on outsiders. All compliment the leader on how well or how fast he promoted "bottle money," praise the runner for his speed, and compare and contrast, usually favorably, the ease and sociability of the present gang with others they have been in. The phrase, "you're all right," is heard frequently. In addition, all claim that when they have it, they share with others, and, when it comes to "making the run," they can always be counted on to come back.

6. *Dispersal.* The leader decides when the next round takes place. Again the bottle circles through the small group, traveling the same route as before. Each man takes the customary two drinks. In time, the bottle is emptied. With that, the gang is ready to disband. The man holding the empty bottle, still in its brown paper bag, gets up and disposes of it in a nearby trash container or puts it under

the bench. The rest announce their plans, and then leave. Any or all are free to activate the cycle of bottle-drinking; if so, the gang remains intact. Sometimes, one member will decide to "treat" the rest to a bottle. At other times, the cycle will begin with negotiation and run on through to dispersal.

Rules and Functions

Tacit rules for each stage are as follows:

1. *Salutation*
   a. Never snub drinking "buddies."
   b. Say hello to friends and acquaintances alike.
   c. Always be ready to pass the time of day with an equal.
2. *Negotiation*
   a. Be as ready to offer a drink as you are to accept one.
   b. Show your money and be willing to share it.
   c. Buy or work your way into a bottle gang; don't chisel in.
3. *Procurement*
   a. Make the run quickly, but not obviously.
   b. Have faith in the runner; wait patiently and be discreet.
4. *Consumption*
   a. Let the leader split the seal and drink.
   b. Wait your turn, then match his drinks.
   c. Take two and pass the bottle.
   d. Don't show the world you're drinking.
5. *Affirmation*
   a. Follow the leader in talk and action.
   b. Praise him, the runner, and your partners.
   c. Criticize persons known to have broken gang rules.
6. *Dispersal*
   a. Duck the empty.

b. Say goodbye and go when the going's good.

Functions for each stage in the cycle are as follows:

1. *Salutation*
   a. Ready greetings cement past ties and open up chances of future ones.
   b. Opening ceremonies signify inclusion in an in-group, thereby reducing pains of stigma.
2. *Negotiation*
   a. Assigns one status as a suitable drinking companion, opens up a role in a face-to-face group, no matter how deviant, stigmatized, or short-lived it may be.
   b. Makes it possible to tailor a small budget and a large need for alcoholic drinks to a wider number of drinking encounters throughout the day.
3. *Procurement*
   a. Reduces the visibility of the bottle-gang's activities.
   b. Awaiting the runner's return helps to create a drinking-centered drama.
4. *Consumption*
   a. Satisfies the need for alcohol and drinking company.
   b. Reduces the tension and anxiety brought on while awaiting the runner's return.
5. *Affirmation*
   a. Ratifies one's identity as a person and one's solidarity with gang members present in the immediate situation.
   b. Signifies that each is a "good man" and a good drinking partner.
6. *Dispersal*
   a. Disposing of the empty bottle removes evidence and cuts down risks of exposure.
   b. Shows respect for decency and public order and signifies the gang is about to break up.
   c. Signifies that all rights and duties are at an end. The contract has been

fulfilled. All are now free of each other's company, for the time being.

Whether transitory or permanent in character, whether composed of transient or regular participants, the bottle gang seems ideally suited to the needs of indigent alcoholics. Participation in bottle gangs stretches meager funds so that men get the maximum amount of alcohol possible for their money. For instance, a two-ounce shot of whiskey in a bar costs forty cents. For one-fourth of that amount contributed towards a group bottle, a man can get almost as much absolute alcohol, now in the form of wine.

Participation in bottle gangs increases the range of acquaintance given the easy entry rules. In turn, participation in the simple ritual of the bottle gang gives one status and membership in a group. The exchange is made possible by the display of elementary social skills. Some men, indeed, simply trade presence rights for drinking rights.

Finally, as all become more deeply involved in a drinking-centered existence, statuses and roles, beliefs and norms coalesce around this axis of life. In the process, the usual urban complexities change in meaning and shrink in scope. Now obvious social failures can sustain a life which is to be understood in terms of the metaphors of deviant social drinking with all of its rewards and punishments. Obtaining and maintaining a supply of drinks in accordance with a set of rules provides a schedule, a calendar, a routine, and a morality all its own. The net effect of this life-style is to deny failure in the pursuit of drink in company.

Breaches and Sanctions

It would seem that such a well-designed social form as the bottle gang, so nicely suited to the conditions of the homeless alcoholic life as it is, should not produce many problems of social control. Given the fixity of its ritual, the limited skills required in the activity, the few and simple roles in the interaction, there ought to be few strains. In turn, the brevity of the encounter so nicely tuned to the Skid Row demand on non-involvement, seems, on its face, a guarantee of efficiency.

Yet this most elementary form of the deviant drinking life has more than its share of deviance and problems in social control. If informants are to be believed, deviance rather than conformity characterizes most stages of the bottle-gang cycle. There appear to be an abundance of breaches of the rules at all of the six stages; in addition, there seems to be either erratic, unpredictable application of sanctions on the one hand, and, on the other, actual failure to apply sanctions. In addition to failures to solve internal problems of control, there is the obvious failure of either screening activities from other drinking men as well as from the police. So that in the first instance, the internal peace and flow of interaction in the gang is upset, while in the second instance the very life of the gang is suddenly aborted.

A brief catalogue of the infraction of bottle-gang rules coupled with the ideal sanction and the frequency of its application follows.

1. Salutation breaches consist mainly of saying hello to a person as if he is known when in fact both served time in jail but were never formally introduced. The sanction here is exclusion but it is rarely applied.

2. Negotiation breaches are all instances of attempts at illicit entry into a bottle gang. Illicit entries take the form of inducing an obligation, trying to obtain repayment for a past obligation, or partial evasion of entry rules. Some hover in the vicinity hoping to be invited to share a drink from the bottle; others sim-

ulate tremors. Some offer a drink from their own bottle, particularly when it only has a drop or two left. Others insist on repayment for drinks that one of the members of the gang owe them. Finally, a person may go in on the bottle, yet not really put up as much money as he could have afforded. The ideal sanction, of course, is to exclude all of these men from getting in on the current bottle; this is done but almost at random. All are typed by the manner in which they sought entry and these labels become a part of their reputation. The generic term for all is "chiseler" or "moocher." Those who stand at the periphery of the drinking group are called "merchants," "lap dogs," or "waiters." One who feigns tremors, the signs of acute withdrawal symptoms, is called an "actor" and a man who does not contribute as much as he might is called a "hold-out artist." Labeling is the predictable sanction, but not exclusion. This is always more or less a matter of chance. For instance, if a gang member can persuade the gang to invite in the person to whom the particular gang member is obligated to, he gains while they lose. For in the future, the person whom he paid off with the group's bottle need not feel any obligations to repay the favor. The other members of the gang would lose out, should they comply with this request, since they would only be helping one of their number pay off a debt without incurring an obligation to return their favor.

3. Procurement breaches include a failure to return with the bottle, returning very slowly, or returning with a bottle from which the runner has already drunk himself or/and has offered a few "pulls" at the bottle to people to whom he owes some drinks. Sometimes failure to return is due to accident, loss of memory,

or police arrest. In this last case just as in the one of giving drinks to others not in the gang, the runner has violated cover-up rules. He became socially visible [2] with consequences for the gang. Sometimes failure to return was by intention; the runner kept the bottle for himself. In view of the difficulty of knowing what really happened the gang generally labels the man as untrustworthy; e.g., he is a "Dick Smith," he is a person who "went South with the bottle." This label is disseminated and meant to exclude him from future drinking encounters. Again, the label is much more likely to be applied than the sanction by the current as well as future gang-members.

4. A person breaches consumption rules by drinking too fast, too much, or too obviously from the bottle. Here the gang can tell the person about his failings. Later he will get a label for his troubles, but once again there is a marked reluctance to actually apply sanctions against such a person. On the other hand, if his drinking is so blatant as to call attention of the police, he is a little more apt to be excluded from subsequent gangs. But all is markedly contingent on a host of other factors.

5. Affirmation violations include incorrect talk or actions. Here some men talk out of turn, on the wrong subjects, or become argumentative or experts on uninteresting subjects. Their talk earns them appropriate labels; again whether they will be kept out of subsequent gangs by men who know their label is problematic. Exclusion in the future is a little more likely in the case of those men who "act up" either by fighting with the gang or by engaging in antics. Either calls attention of the police or disrupts the gang and sometimes does both. These men are all labeled as "performers,"

---

2 Howard M. Bahr suggests that increased social visibility may be a general consequence of the dispersion of homeless men in his "The Gradual Disappearance of Skid Row," *Social Problems,* XV (Summer 1967), 41–45.

"wacks," "characters," "nuts," "psychos," "jail bait," etc. and they are avoided in the future whenever possible.

6. Dispersal violations include continuing to call attention to one's self or the activities of the gang or being ostentatious in hiding the empty bottle. In addition, they include illicit ways of continuing the drinking episode at the expense of one of the members. Some beg, or "con" money from the men present for their own drinking. Others sometimes try to rob, steal, or just beat up members thought to have some money. The more violent ones do get labeled and their reputations become widely known. Exclusion does take place; the sanction is much more apt to be applied against them.

Discussion

The East Coast bottle gang reported in this study seems characterized by simple rules, and extreme variability in both conformity and sanctions on deviance. Some plausible hypotheses accounting for these variations in social control can be derived by contrasting these bottle gangs with those reported for the West Coast. There appear to be differences in both ecology and social organization in both areas and these differences may explain the variance. Ecology includes numbers, territory, resources, and the deviance contract with authorities. Social organization encompasses types of drinking patterns and experiences in bottle gangs. First we shall deal with ecology, next with social organization.

1. *Numbers.* West Coast Skid Rows concentrate a relatively large number of men who are in close contact with one another. Maple City bottle-gang drinkers are much fewer in number and are scattered around the city. Given the same meager resources and strong desires to drink, West Coast Skid Row men have access to a greater number of potential gangs. In turn, they need to invest less, while participating in a greater number of different gangs throughout the day. In Maple City, the smaller the number, the poorer the chances of getting in on a bottle. Needing more money to get into fewer gangs poses problems for a slender budget. This situation is more apt to encourage holding out, scheming, attempts to chisel into gangs, etc.

2. *Territory.* Having an established territory, the West Coast bottle-gang participant goes relatively unnoticed in contrast to his Maple City counterpart. The Maple City bottle-gang drinker needs to move around much more, thereby increasing his exposure to police, citizens who may lodge a complaint, and other men also searching for a drink. On a West Coast Skid Row his actions would go unnoticed, due principally to the fact that his actions would be undistinguished from many others in the vicinity. Lack of a territory increases social visibility in Maple City just as its presence decreases it on West Coast Skid Rows. Increased exposure is a problem in particular in encouraging illegal entry into bottle gangs.

3. *Resources.* Again there are more resources on a Skid Row than off it for bottle-gang participants. Panhandling, a way of getting money for a bottle, is less noticed, more tolerated on rather than off Skid Row. In addition, package stores and other liquor outlets are plentiful in the neighborhood. By contrast, when a man "makes the run" in Maple City he enters enemy territory. Again his activity becomes visible to those he would prefer did not see it.

4. *The Deviance Contract.* Police have a contract with Skid Row men. They agree to make predictable expeditions into the territory to arrest a certain number of agreed-upon violations of public order. Hence, West Coast Skid Rows are subjected to less surveillance. This per-

mits more relaxed, leisurely, and less tense interaction in street-corner bottle gangs. In contrast, Maple City men must maintain constant vigilance on their activities; many claim to suffer from the "cop horrors." The result is surreptitious drinking, gulping drinks rapidly, and conveying this tension to all members of the gang. This concern with avoiding exposure to external controls weakens internal controls in the Maple City bottle gang.

Social organization, along with ecology, affects bottle-gang controls. A city that has a Skid Row has a way of life for homeless men.[3] A social organization, replete with statuses and roles results from the manner in which they follow Skid Row culture. A homeless alcoholic community exists in Maple City but dispersion reduces the chances of maintaining those stable patterns of interaction that sustain a subculture. As a result, drinking patterns and experience with bottle gangs are two major factors affecting the presence or absence of bottle-gang controls.

1. *Drinking patterns.* The Skid Row social system of heavy drinkers is based on sifting out and sorting types of drinking patterns. As in any status system, the attempt is always to maintain status homogeneity wherever possible. Maple City bottle drinkers do not participate in such a well-ordered social system; as a result, heterogeneity is more likely. The consequences for social control can be seen clearly in the case of drinking patterns. "Plateau drinkers," for instance, make ideal bottle-gang drinkers, since they seek only to maintain a certain level of alcohol in the blood stream over

the course of any given day.[4] "Blitz drinkers,"[5] on the other hand, seek to drink as much as they can and as fast as they can in order to get drunk and stay drunk. These men make the poorest bottle-gang participants. Nevertheless poverty and need drives them into bottle gangs. It is only a short time before the deviant style of drinking upsets the ritual of the bottle gang. Heterogeneity happens more often in Maple City bottle gangs than on West Coast Skid Row gangs. Similarly, because of the greater need for companions, there is a greater tendency to waive admission requirements. Hence, persons who have bad reputations of one kind or another will still be accepted in the Maple City bottle gang. This is less likely on the West Coast Skid Row scene.

2. *Experience in bottle gangs.* The evidence suggests that the more extensive the experience in bottle gangs on the West Coast, the more conformist the gang member is. On the other hand, the Maple City material suggests that the more extensive the gang member's experience, the more deviant he is (that is, primarily, in the sense of violating gang rules). These two notions on individual gang-member experience are related to responses to deviant behavior in these gangs. For violations of gang norms and their punishments seem to be reversed for both coasts in the following ways:

a. Violations of bottle-gang norms are less likely to happen on the West Coast, but if they should occur, they are more apt to be punished. There, rules and sanctions are interdependent.

b. Violations of bottle-gang norms are more apt to happen on the East Coast, but if they do occur, they are more apt

[3] Samuel E. Wallace, *Skid Row as a Way of Life* (Totowa, New Jersey: Bedminster Press, 1965).
[4] Robert Straus and Raymond G. McCarthy, "Nonaddictive Pathological Drinking Patterns of Homeless Men," *Quarterly Journal of Studies on Alcohol*, XII (December 1951), 601–611.
[5] Richard J. Kingham, "Alcoholism and the Reinforcement Theory of Learning," *Quarterly Journal of Studies on Alcohol*, XIX (June 1958), 320–330.

to go unpunished. Rules and sanctions are relatively independent.

More experienced bottle-gang drinkers on both the West Coast and in Maple City are aware of these relationships between breaches and sanctions, and each acts upon his knowledge to sustain the status quo. But they do so in different ways, though for perhaps the same reasons. Given the relationship between rules and sanctions in their own experience, seasoned West Coast bottle gang drinkers take conformity for granted, thus need to state the rules on how to drink in a bottle gang less frequently. Affirmation of its rules, sentiments, and sanctions are less often required. On the other hand because of unpredictable relations between rules and sanctions in Maple City bottle gangs, seasoned participants talk about gang rules at great length, affirm them and the sentiments attaching to them, and continually point to the sanctions for failing to abide by the rules. They continually point to the failure of others to obey gang rules while simultaneously proclaiming their own loyalty and dependability.

The net effect of their talk is to provide all participants, but most particularly the newcomer, with an illusory sense of a social order replete with definite rules and sanctions. Those experienced members who wish to can gain the conformity of others while they themselves deviate in secret. In time, with increased experience in gangs, the level of suspicion and distrust rises with the knowledge that so many violators go unpunished. It becomes clear that non-conformity is frequently rewarded much more and, at much less cost than conformity. As each comes to see more clearly that his own self-interest comes to lie more and more in non-conformity, he in turn comes to expect more violations of bottle-gang norms from his partners. This only triggers more talk about the rules, about loyalty to them, and about the necessity for punishing violators.

When, as happens so very frequently in this impoverished setting, the need to drink increases inversely with the resources for getting drinks, sanctions become a luxury. For to the extent that past violators may become current donor-hosts, if not men who will actually treat one to a desperately needed drink, it behooves bottle-gang drinkers to be tolerant of behavior that deviates from their own norms. Most, because of their need and their poverty, do not feel that they are in a position to apply sanctions against those who have broken any of the rules. Such control as may come about can only be of a symbolic character. The incessant talk about how others have breached the rules is, on occasion, a plea that the same thing will not happen in the immediate drinking group.

Control in East Coast bottle gangs, such as it is, rests more on talking about rules and sanctions than in taking action on either. This suggests that any deviant subculture is only as good as the organizational conditions that surround it. Because of the tenuous organizational conditions surrounding Maple City homeless men, bottle-gang drinking there is more precarious and less internally controlled than it is for participants in such gangs on the Skid Rows of the West Coast.

DEVIANT IDENTITY

Part Four

HOW CERTAIN ACTIONS are evaluated by self and others depends also on whether the behavior is or is not fitting to the person's status and assigned role. Doctors, for example, are accorded the right to examine unclothed humans because of their professional status. When enacting status norms, they are expected to confine their examinations to medical rather than sexual purposes. And, in executing their duties, they usually see themselves as healers, an assessment that the general public largely shares. In the case of the doctor, status, behavior, and self-image dovetail nicely. Thus, problems of identity rarely arise. When, on the other hand, actions, status, and self fit poorly, we may expect to find identity problems.

Doctors receive a good deal of cultural support in being the kinds of persons they are supposed to be. For this reason, if no other, they should have few problems with identity. Deviants, on the other hand, usually occupy culturally unsupported statuses, if not outright illegitimate ones. Consequently, they can be expected to have considerably more problems with identity. For with or without cultural support, all human beings must establish an identity. Thus, in studying how deviants deal with problems of identity, we learn how all people act when their identities are at stake.

This part, then, takes up deviant identity. We ask, first of all, what are the elements of identity, and then consider the relation of a person's audience to his identity, the social mechanisms that help a person to sustain his identity, and the conditions under which a person is most likely to change his deviant identity.

The Elements of Identity

Identity results from operations that people go through when they wish to answer the question: "Who am I?" There is a private set of operations

317

as well as a public set. The private set yields one's sense of personal identity whereas the public operations produce one's social identity, or how one thinks other people answer the question one has raised about himself. It is important to see that there need not necessarily be any consistency between the personal and the social identity. Astute social deviants, for instance, anxious to practice their specialty in private know full well how to present signs and symbols that will give them a social identity quite distinct from their personal identity. Frequently, for example, secret homosexuals working in all-male groups find it necessary to join in conversations that ridicule or condemn homosexuality. In so doing, they obtain, at least in this group, a social identification as heterosexual.

It is clear, on the other hand, that as the number of statuses a person occupies increases, as his role-performances multiply, and as his self-conceptions extend over different times, places, and circumstances, the matter of making personal identity square with social identity becomes more difficult. This issue is complex enough even for so-called conformists. It is infinitely more complex for certain varieties of deviants, particularly those who follow a career in secret deviance.

In certain kinds of deviant behavior, personal identity more easily follows from social identity. When personal identity does not follow from social identity, this is generally a more active way of settling the personal identity question; and it is more apt to produce overt conflict in identities, particularly when the deviant asserts the importance of his personal identity over the social identity others would claim for him. When the deviant finds it wiser to accept the social identity others have publicly attributed to him, this is generally a more passive style of settling the question of personal identity, and is less apt to produce overt conflict in identities.

Observation of social interaction in certain situations indicates how comedies of error come about when the social and personal identities fail to jibe. For many, if not most kinds of interaction, people need to know who the other person is and what he is in order for them to know who and what they themselves are and how they are to act. Whenever, for instance, a person finds himself mistaken for someone else, he gets a glimpse of how important such classification is. If he is taken for an important person, for a moment he may even toy with the idea of masquerading as that person. On the other hand, if people mistake him for a disgraced person, he will be quick to deny the identity and point out the mistake. To do this, he indignantly produces his social credentials, showing signs that prove conclusively (he hopes) that the other people are mistaken.

Self-casters, like impostors, con men, and spies, assume social identities that all of their off-duty statuses, roles, and selves, if made known, would discredit. Other-casters, like stage directors, public relations men, and hostesses, put social identities on other persons that the true personal assortment of statuses, roles, and selves of these other persons similarly do not support. These social fictions succeed when people give one another the benefit of the doubt.

In a complex urban society where many people engage in a wide assortment of social contacts with other people, the chances of being cast or of casting one's self as a new and different kind of person comes up all the time. The fact that many people are not symbolized as being certain kinds of persons even though they give off the signs produces the recurrent charges of "phoniness." Conventional persons have these problems often. The word *phoney* is in their vocabulary. A deviant's struggles with social authenticity are understandably a little harder. Sorting out statuses, roles, and selves and making them fit in a more or less coherent whole is a definite problem. When these statuses, roles, and selves have both social and cultural support, as with the doctor, a simple and integrated social identity is possible, but when that support is lacking or ambiguous, some very real problems of identity develop. Managing this problem is sufficient in many cases to produce the very deceit that is presumed to be a trait of so many social deviants.

Other things equal, of course, a social identity as a conforming sort of person is generally to be preferred to a deviant social identity. Hence the need for duplicity on the part of most, if not all, deviants. The steady practice of duplicity, however, has effects on personal identity as well as social identity. Duplicity usually has two possible outcomes. It may make it possible to knit together one's repertory of statuses, roles, and selves into a plausible whole, in which case the person comes to believe the story about himself he has invented and told to other people. Or the strain of duplicity is so great that he must ultimately give it up. Lemert points out, for example, that the interactional strains of being a systematic check forger can be reduced by being caught and sent to prison. The need to assume many legitimate social roles and to sustain the social identities that go with these roles taxes the forger heavily. For impersonations are not easy. In a very real sense, being a "phoney" imposes severe strains. Hence, in one of the many paradoxes of social life, imprisonment actually solves the identity problems of the forger. For in prison, at least, he is not hard put to sustain his social identity. The strains the systematic check forger confronts typify the kinds of identity problems that many social deviants must come to terms with one way or another.

Audience and Identity

Audiences certify a person's identity. Audiences will decide if the signs and symbols coalesce in the required manner. When they do, the situation has been defined. In some cases, it means they will accept a person into their midst. In others, it means they want no more to do with the person of that particular kind. This last eventuality is particularly troublesome for some deviants. For ordinarily, being excluded from the so-called conventional social world would be thought sufficient grounds for admission into the half-world or the underworld. Frequently, however, the underworld has its own system of crediting social identity. Only when an in-group audience, therefore, passes on a person's identity can he be certain that he will be accepted as the kind of person he now thinks himself to be.

A marginal deviant, then, is one who has been excluded from the conventional world and at the same time has been denied admission and certification in a deviant subculture. There are a number of persons who fall into this category. An example of a marginal deviant would be a "reformed drunk," a social type recognized mainly among certain types of alcoholics. The reformed drunk is currently sober and intolerant of drinking and he usually believes that he owes his sobriety to no one but himself. These attitudes are not shared by conventional people or by most alcoholics. He is out of both worlds. When he comes into contact with either of these worlds the signs and symbols he puts forth are not accepted.

The marginal deviant teaches us the importance of audiences in shaping and sustaining deviant identity. The person assigned deviant status, whether through push or pull, comes into contact with similar persons. These associations provide the basis for settling on real or imaginary role-models. In the course of increased association with similarly situated deviants, the novice more and more comes to define situations in their terms. He begins to appraise his status, his role, and his sense of self mainly through their eyes. To the extent that he aspires to membership, he will learn their rules and try to abide by them. He engages in simple imitative maneuvers that they, as significant others, appraise. In time, he can look at his actions and appraise them in their terms even though the significant others are now absent. When this change occurs, they have become an effective audience for him.

Sustaining a Deviant Identity

It is not sufficient, however, merely to have adopted an effective audience. To sustain a new identity the person has to make the signs and symbols his own. He has to be able to deliver deviant behavior, so to speak, when others require it of him as well as when he wishes to. These actions must be certified first by them and then by himself. Put another way, if he fails to learn from his teachers he is in jeopardy of being called inauthentic. This means that he might be accepted only among those groups that have vague ideas on what appropriate behavior for persons occupying his deviant status ought to be.

Sometimes there are mistaken assumptions about one's audience. For instance, young sailors returning from their first voyage may believe that they are expected to get drunk and tattooed on their first leave. Many fear the experience of getting tattooed but dread more the risks of being ridiculed by their peers. Because none discusses his private fears (a good example of pluralistic ignorance), each presents himself to his buddies as seeking the experience rather than secretly fearing it. Thus it is that social identities so frequently take precedence over personal ones. Sometimes attempts at being a deviant fail because of the correct assumptions the audience makes about the person who seeks to establish a new social identity. Many audiences will just refuse to reinforce a tryout in deviance. No matter how hard the person tries to become a bona fide deviant, there is no effective audience to reward his actions and to confirm his self-typing. Sometimes faulty performances will suffice to exclude recognition. The jack-of-all-trades offender,[1] for instance, probably never gained admittance into more skillful criminal circles because of his ineptitude or some shared judgment that he did not look the part of a seasoned professional criminal. Many debuts in deviance fail when audiences, conformist and deviant alike, agree that the person making the debut has obviously miscast himself in the role. As the saying goes, "He just does not look the part."

Some deviant statuses imply more than one audience. In turn, each audience demands a different and sometimes contradictory role from the incumbents. In this case, there are problems of identity that can only be resolved if the deviant is clear about which audience he is confronting and which role they require of him.

Similarly, deviants may choose among deviant identities as well as audiences. This means, among other things, that there can be spurious identities in deviant groups as well as in conformist groups. For example, some epileptics try to pass as alcoholics. This simulation shows an appreciation of social typing and the way most people rank behavioral deviations. People view alcoholic convulsions as undesirable events, yet some people regard epileptic ones as being worse. Many epileptics, aware of this ranking of deviant social types, impersonate the least stigmatized of the two.

---

[1] Julian Roebuck and Ronald Johnson, "The Jack-of-All-Trades Offender," *Crime and Delinquency*, **8** (April, 1962), 172–181.

As long as the counterfeit alcoholic makes only casual contact with other bona fide alcoholics, his secret is safe. Sober situations, such as meetings of Alcoholics Anonymous, are the safest for presenting one's self to alcoholics, as well as nonalcoholic audiences, as yet another alcoholic.

To sustain a deviant identity, then, it becomes necessary to think, feel, and act in the manner of persons similarly defined. Some social conditions are more conducive to this than others. For example, total involvement with deviants and avoidance of contact with so-called nondeviants will facilitate learning the appropriate deviant identity and perspective. For those deviations that require discipline and training, such as pickpocketing or safe-cracking, the person must spend a good deal of time practicing the arts and receiving much social coaching. Playing before a deviant audience in a deviant setting, for instance, makes it much easier to cast off residual conformity and to throw one's self deeper into sustained deviant activity. Given these optimum conditions, a deviant identity is more easily sustained.

The Transformation of Deviant Identity

Certain types of deviants, as already suggested, experience much trouble sustaining a deviant identity. The strain of fitting statuses, roles, and selves together in a coherent manner is either (a) too great or (b) not worth the effort. In the first case, certification seems unattainable, and the person experiences no interior peace, no real self-acceptance. In the second case, his certification is no blessing, but actually a curse. The neurotic homosexual is a good example of the first case. The full-blown addict is a good example of the second. Failure or success in certification comes to the same end. The homosexual wishes to resolve his unconscious conflicts whereas the addict wants to give up his addiction. When both types become aware of this aspect of their lives, both face the kind of identity crisis that may well become the turning-point in a deviant career.

It is not necessarily true, however, that all social deviants are miserable and unhappy and wish to change their style of life. Although the ideology of the dominant culture implies that this is nearly always the case, the facts are quite otherwise. An unknown but substantial number of secret deviants of many types would probably disagree with the conventional attitude that they are unhappy. Successful concealment ensures continued practice of their deviant specialty. In so doing, they sustain a different social identity in the conventional world. This is as true for successful professional criminals as it is for secret homosexuals.

A profound identity crisis thus becomes one of the necessary conditions for the transformation of deviant identity. Without this crisis, renunciation of deviance is most unlikely. Without this crisis, incumbents of deviant status find little reason to change their lives. Pangs of remorse along with continued, if not increasing, punishments for discovery of secret deviance sometimes produce the crisis. When they do, the person contemplates making some radical changes in his life. If the mechanisms that have been sustaining deviant identity have been working too well, the person can resign himself to his fate. Usually, however, these mechanisms show signs of breaking down. Their breakdown only adds to the crisis of identity.

Enough has been said thus far to indicate that assuming and maintaining a deviant identity is not an easy matter. Renouncing one is even more difficult. Even if a person experiences an extreme identity crisis he may not succeed in transforming his deviant identity. Three factors imperil successful transformation. They are: lack of practice in conventional roles, continued suspicion from conformists, and pressure from fellow-deviants to return to the fold.

Time spent in deviance is time spent away from conformity. Legitimate skills fall into disuse. Thus, for example, the alcoholic toolmaker who returns to his craft after having been away from it a decade or more because of heavy drinking generally finds it impossible to pick up where he left off. Difficulties in hiring exconvicts reveal the continued suspicion and disapproval that deviants arouse in conformists. Exconvicts, on or off parole, find it hard to find steady work because of their criminal records. And finally there are pressures from deviant peers to resume the activity dropped at incarceration or hospitalization. Thus the drug addict, on release from a hospital, finds many addicts suddenly in his presence, ready, willing, and anxious to obtain a fix for him, frequently free.

If the deviant who wants to give up his deviant status, role, and identity, joins a primary group with similar intentions, his chances of resolving the identity crisis in favor of a more conforming social identity increase. The best-known example of such a primary group is Alcoholics Anonymous. The aspirant to conventionality is assisted by receiving rewards for making these changes from persons in the same situation and by their confirming his new self-in-transition. When these conditions are met, transforming a deviant identity is encouraged. Many deviants would be more willing to return to conformity if these social and cultural supports were present to help them make a comeback. But such supports, for the moment, are in rather short supply. Hence, we should expect to find more deviants justifying their identity rather than seeking to transform it.

THE DEVIANT AND HIS AUDIENCE

13

To be a deviant, a person needs an effective audience of significant others, a perspective on deviance, and an identity as a deviant. Problems of being a deviant, of course, are not all solved in quite the same way. Deviants obtain, sustain, and change their identities in various ways. An effective audience of deviant others provides the perspective for examining one's credentials as a bona fide deviant and for improving in the practice of deviant arts and crafts. Association with deviant others makes available role models, people with whom one may wish to identify. In the course of this association, the novice can acquire a new status, role, and self. Once all this has been successfully accomplished, it can be truly said that the deviant identity has been established.

In the first selection to follow, Klapp outlines the dynamics of self-typing as it is related to one's audience. Glaser next shows how a deviant can take on a new identity in the course of modeling his actions after another member of a deviant group. Then Korn and McCorkle describe the spurious social conditions in which people engage in certain actions because they believe others expect it of them. Cameron shows how the amateur shoplifter, on being caught, generally foregoes future store stealing because she and her effective audiences do not identify her with the thieving type. Then, in the final paper, Erikson shows the role problems a mental patient faces in trying to live up to the expectations of both public and psychiatric audiences.

Dynamics of Self-Typing *

ORRIN E. KLAPP

. . . Our relations with strangers depend almost entirely on superficial cues provided by dress, hair-do, facial expression, tone of voice, vocabulary, and props such

* Reprinted from Orrin E. Klapp, *Heroes, Villains, and Fools: The Changing American Character* (Englewood Cliffs, N.J.: Prentice-Hall, Inc., 1962), pp. 2–5, by permission of the author and publisher.

as cigarette holders. A person may also type himself by friends, style of life, or conspicuous public roles. In any case he has great freedom to create his type by manipulating cues, so long as people do not know him well enough to "have his number" and put him into an inescapable category. Once so categorized, he can change his social identity only by moving on. . . .

All kinds of deviant behavior, I believe, are processes of self-typing—the deviant is not just being antisocial, aggressive, etc. We may well adopt the premise that everyone in modern society is vitally interested in creating a type for himself, the deviant no less than the Philistine. Self-typing gives psychological content to the quest of status. Indeed, the desire to be a type of person may be, consciously or unconsciously, what makes us desire a particular status (more than money, that is, and the other externals). The deviate may have a status-problem (let us say he is a homosexual) because he is typing himself in a manner that causes people to deny him a satisfactory status; if he were willing or able to conform to a normal type, he would have no difficulty keeping his status. Or, if he found a world that would allow him to be the type he wanted to be, he would have no status-problem because the other statuses denied him would not matter.

I might summarize this by saying that "finding oneself" is, in my opinion, to a large extent building a type for oneself —whether it is a type donated by some group or created by individual effort. (It is always a question how much a type can be built without collaboration.) A person who is not sure of his type is not sure of who he is, of what roles are appropriate for him. A person has "found himself" when he has established a type in his own mind which is satisfying to

him (it is possible to dislike one's type) and which gives people the assurance that they know him well. If we accept this premise of finding oneself, we cannot attempt to make predictions about people, analyze their problems, still less understand society as a whole, without knowing a lot more about the types with which individuals identify and which comprise a kind of structure for the entire society. Personality-typing is less a matter of measuring "traits" than of finding out how people type themselves, and to what degree their actual qualities and behavior agree with their self-styled type. Part of this process involves considering a person's role as a strategy of presenting himself to others.[1]

The effort to type oneself, of course, also includes the effort to type others. We are continually creating, as it were, the other fellow. A common kind of conversation in almost any company is characterizing people by what they have been doing or what is being said about them.

Social relationships hinge upon fitting the other into a category that makes it possible to deal with him successfully. We normally try to put a person into a pigeonhole of the same scheme from which our own self was derived—I don't mean attribute our self-image to him but make both images belong to the same system. The other fellow is trying to bring us into his scheme (which may be the same or different from our own). Thus, when Americans come together, they type each other variously as good Joes, smart operators, heels, easy marks, and so on. They may disagree in using the same system (Mr. X thinks Z is a such-and-such, but Y thinks Z is a so-and-so). But when persons have different type systems (Mexican-American, Frenchman-American, and so on) the result is likely to be more frustrating, unless they happen to

[1] Erving Goffman, *The Presentation of Self in Everyday Life* (University of Edinburgh Social Science Research Centre, Monograph No. 2, 1958).

be familiar with each other's systems and to have worked out certain equivalents for themselves. (We know little enough about the American social typology at present, let alone how much it is equivalent to the Mexican, German, Russian, and so on.) When persons have inadequate relationships because of different type systems you have what is properly called stereotyping. But social typing within the same system is useful and fairly accurate; it is needed in a mobile society where status is insecure, identities are uncertain,[2] and people do not know one another well; it does what a personnel file might do: provides us with a convenient *précis* of the one with whom we wish to deal.

It is impossible, except conceptually, to separate this typing of others from the typing of oneself, because by the theories of Charles H. Cooley and George H. Mead and modern reference-group theory, the other *as we type him* is a key to our construct of our self. We find ourselves by the responses of others (Harry Stack Sullivan calls it consensual validation); but it is not simply the response of the other that makes our self but the way we see ourselves in his eyes as we have typed him. Without knowing what kind of fellow the other is, we cannot know what significance to attach to his approval or disapproval, how to rate ourselves by him. We cannot, then, without knowing him, know who we are.

Role Models and Differential Association *

DANIEL GLASER

. . . Slightly paraphrased, Sutherland's last formulation of his theory [1] is as follows: Criminal behavior is learned in interaction with others, principally in intimate personal groups. That which is learned includes techniques, attitudes, and rationalizations. Whether a person's motives and drives are criminal or noncriminal is a function of whether the legal codes have been defined by those around him in a manner favorable to their observance or to their violation. Most people encounter a mixture of these two types of influence. A person will be-

come criminal if his associations result in an excess of definitions favorable to violation of law over definitions unfavorable to violation of law. The influence of such differential association is a function of its frequency, duration, priority, and intensity, in one direction or another. Both criminal and noncriminal behavior is acquired in such association by the same learning mechanisms, and both satisfy the same general human needs and values; but differential association determines the extent to which a person's experience promotes learning and motiva-

[2] See Anselm L. Strauss, *Mirrors and Masks* (New York: The Free Press, 1959).
* Reprinted by permission of the author and publisher from "The Sociological Approach to Crime and Correction" from a symposium, Crime and Correction, in *Law and Contemporary Problems*, Vol. 23, No. 4 (Autumn, 1958), pp. 688–693, published by the Duke University School of Law, Durham, N. C. Copyright, 1959, by Duke University.
[1] First set forth in Edwin H. Sutherland, *Principles of Criminology* 5–7 (3d ed. 1939).

tion by criminal rather than noncriminal influences.

Sutherland seems to have formulated this theory as a way in which the many actual and alleged correlates of crime, such as poverty, family conflicts, personality disturbance, and slum residence, could be causally related to crime. These conditions, to be factors in the criminality of an individual, must so affect his social relationships as to promote his being influenced by criminals and restrict the influence of noncriminal persons on him. Attention to the social relationships of each person studied, however, would also explain why such correlates of crime as family conflict and poverty also may, in some cases, support noncriminal ambitions. From the standpoint of Sutherland's theory, any correlate of crime must be shown to affect an individual's learning experience if it is to be thought of as having a causative function in his criminality. Sutherland's critics generally overlook this integrating function of his theory and the broad sense in which he uses the phrase "differential association." They misrepresent him when they suggest that he predicted that criminality would result with mechanical certainty in any individual whose contacts with criminals exceed contacts with noncriminals.

Essentially, Sutherland set forth a broad point of view for approaching an understanding of criminals, rather than a simple formula for predicting crime. In modern social-psychological terms, what he seems to have had in mind might more aptly be labeled "differential identification," "differential reference," or even "differential learning." It involves a conception of crime as a subclass of the totality of all deliberate human action, as something to be explained as other so-called "voluntary" behavior is explained. It is based on a social-psychological con-

ception of deliberate action as guided by the actors in accordance with the way in which they have learned to rationalize their actions. Such an approach to understanding behavior is convergent with many developments in psychology and sociology. It is a deterministic conception of crime, since it ascribes a person's anticipations to his learning experience; yet, it is consistent with the legal conception of crime as wilful, for it focuses on decision-making as a phenomenon to be studied. This approach contrasts sharply with explanations for crime in terms of biological drives, unconscious motivation, or pressure of external forces, since such explanations do not as completely trace the connection between the alleged causes and specific, consciously-directed criminal acts.[2]

Sutherland presented his theory in highly abstract form and apart from its illustration. His illustrative chapters on "processes in criminal behavior" and "behavior systems in crime" cogently described the ways in which professional criminals become enculturated in crime, but he did not illustrate the influence of associations opposing crime. This neglect probably reflects the fact that it has been much easier to study criminals than noncriminals, for criminals may be studied conveniently when they are in custody or under supervision. Noncriminals are more difficult to study, as a rule, and ex-criminals are most difficult (for they seek to hide their past); yet, studying these people may be essential for a more useful understanding of crime. Thus, the most available applications of Sutherland's theory make it appear to be merely the old enculturation explanation for crime, even though its abstract formulation suggests that it might also be a frame of reference for theoretically connecting correlated conditions with specific crimes

---

[2] George M. Kelly, *The Psychology of Personal Constructs* (1955); A. R. Lindesmith and Anselm Strauss, *Social Psychology* (2d ed. 1956).

and for the analysis of noncriminal behavior and correctional processes.

Recent Theoretical Emphasis

No more adequate general theory of crime causation has replaced differential association. Several recent developments, however, suggest some of the ways in which such a theory would modify the heritage from Sutherland. The criminology which now seems to be emerging in sociology is one focused on change and operating with a more complex conception of the criminal than that involved in earlier theories. These developments reflect long-term trends in general sociological theory, and they are convergent with some new emphases in the other behavioral sciences. Notable among these trends are: (1) attention to all reference groups—not just membership groups—in tracing social influences on individual behavior; [and] (2) the interpretation of motivation as the way in which a person's representation of the behavioral alternatives which he perceives affects his self-conception and his anticipations. . . .

By "reference groups," we designate any persons or groups from whose standpoint an individual evaluates himself and others. These include both groups in which he is a member and groups to which he does not belong, but to which he aspires, or which, for other reasons, provide the standpoint from which he views his own situation. The enculturation approach to crime grew out of the study of the influence of groups on the behavior of their members. Reference-group theory helps to account for much of the behavior of individuals who deviate

from the expectations of their membership groups, for this theory focuses our attention on all of the groups to which these individuals are oriented. The general conditions under which a person is most likely to evaluate his behavior from the standpoint of groups to which he does not belong include: (1) when the other groups have higher status than his own group; (2) when he is an isolate or a failure in his own group; or (3) when change in group affiliation is not strongly counter to the traditions of his society.[3]

While the term "reference group" is fairly new and the analysis of behavior by tracing the influence both of membership and nonmembership groups receives more emphasis now than formerly, such a common-sense idea is by no means completely new. Early students of the gang, while centering their attention on the influence of that group, also noted that most juvenile delinquents drifted out of gang affiliations and became law-abiding members of society in late adolescence and young adulthood if they became interested in marriage or acquired steady employment. The latter interests involve change of reference from their peers exclusively to older persons of legitimate professions and to stable family members.[4] The Tannenbaum and Sutherland enculturation analyses were significant in showing how the transition from enculturation in delinquent gangs to identification with conventional groups becomes unlikely when extensive involvement in criminal groups alienates a youth from conventional circles and increases his ties with professional criminals. Unfortunately, the effects of being caught and prosecuted may be to make criminals

---

[3] *Cf.* Robert K. Merton, *Social Theory and Social Structure*, cc. 9 and 10 (2d ed. 1957); Turner, "Role-taking, Role-standpoint and Reference Group Behavior," 61 *Am. J. Sociology* 316 (1956), reprinted in L. A. Coser and B. Rosenberg, *Sociological Theory* 272 (1957).
[4] *Cf.* W. F. Whyte, *Street Corner Society* (1943).

the only group to which a youth will aspire. But the task of corrections may be said to be the promotion of noncriminal reference groups; a prisoner is rehabilitated when this promotion is successful.

The study of the *non*delinquent in high-delinquency areas has been undertaken on an extensive basis in recent years by persons of diverse academic background. The outstanding finding, expressed in general terms, is that the youth who avoids extreme enculturation in delinquency, despite extensive contact with delinquents, generally is the youth who maintains strong bonds with a noncriminal family. Reckless sees the influence of noncriminal figures as giving such a youth a conception of himself as "good" which "insulates" him from all situations in which he may be encouraged to be delinquent.[5] This is consistent with psychoanalytic interpretation: the family gives the boy a strong conventional superego—that is, conscience. The problem for criminological theory is to handle adequately the fact that everyone in our society is exposed to multiple influences, some making for criminality and some making for conventionality, some from membership groups and some from perceived groups in which one is not a fully-accepted member. An understanding of behavior change, from noncriminal to criminal and vice versa, requires a theory of behavior which accounts for human inconsistency and, therefore, permits some prediction and control of the range of this inconsistency.

Several preliminary explorations and formulations of a theory of behavior change and inconsistency have been undertaken by sociologists in terms of analysis of motivation and decision-making in individual behavior. One of Sutherland's students, Cressey, posed a crucial problem for differential association theory: How does one explain the conduct of persons who reach adulthood as highly conventional persons and, therefore, are placed in positions of financial trust, but suddenly violate such trust by embezzlement? Cressey's interviews with 133 embezzlers and his examination of life histories on over 200 other cases of embezzlement led him to an explanation which seemed to fit every case.[6] He found, first, that trusted persons committed embezzlement only when faced by a financial problem which they could not divulge to others. Nevertheless, he found that in spite of need and opportunity for the crime, the offense was never committed until the embezzler had developed a rationalization which legitimated the offense to him. When frustrated humans perceive a solution to their problems, they seem unable to grasp the solution until they can represent it to themselves in such a manner as to permit them to maintain a favorable conception of themselves. In Cressey's cases, differential association in terms of membership affiliations rarely seemed to explain this reinterpretation of criminal behavior. A shift of perspective, often by taking the standpoint of new reference groups, was needed to change the trustworthy person into an embezzler.

In view of the evidence that most delinquent youth have some acceptance of conventional values, Gresham M. Sykes and David Matza suggest that delinquents

---

[5] *Cf.* Reckless, Dinitz, and Kay, "The Self Component in Potential Delinquency and Potential Non-Delinquency," 22 *Am. Sociological Rev.* 566 (1957); S. and E. Glueck, *Unraveling Juvenile Delinquency* 281 (1950). One of the most sophisticated analyses of the extent of family influence on delinquency is Jackson Toby's statistical analysis of court and census data, "The Differential Impact of Family Disorganization," 22 *Am. Sociological Rev.* 505 (1957).

[6] Donald R. Cressey, *Other People's Money* (1953).

must "neutralize" their conventional ties and moral scruples before they can commit delinquency.[7] They illustrate as common "techniques of neutralization" a variety of rationalizations, such as blaming the theft on pressures from bad parents or on misfortune, defining the victim as a worthless person who deserves to be victimized, justifying the offense in terms of loyalty to a friend, or noting the faults of those who condemn the delinquency. The process of rationalization reconciles crime or delinquency with conventionality; it permits a person to maintain a favorable conception of himself, while acting in ways which others see as inconsistent with a favorable self-conception. In this analysis of motivation by the verbal representation of the world with which a person justifies his behavior, sociologists are converging with many psychologists.[8] This seems to be individualistic analysis of behavior, but the so-called "symbolic interactionist" viewpoint is gaining acceptance, and it sees individual human thought as essentially a social interaction process: the individual "talks to himself" in thinking and reacts to his own words and gestures in "working himself" into an emotional state in much the same manner as he does in discussion or in emotional interaction with others.[9]

The Reluctant Robbers *

RICHARD R. KORN AND LLOYD W. MC CORKLE

The significance of the interpersonal context of motivation is underscored by the next example to be cited. In his classic work, *The Gang,* Thrasher writes about a group of college students, who, one night, for reasons which none of them could explain, suddenly decided to rob a post-office. Thrasher presents the story in the form of a verbatim report by one of the participants.

> We three college students—Mac, Art, and Tom—were rooming together while attending V—— University, one of the oldest colleges in the South. On the day of our crime all three of us spent over three hours in the library—really working. That was on

[7] Sykes and Matza, "Techniques of Neutralization: A Theory of Delinquency," 22 *Am. Sociological Rev.* 664 (1957). These authors, unfortunately, neglect the influence of delinquent subcultures in transmitting and reinforcing these very techniques of neutralization which permit delinquents to adhere simultaneously to delinquent and nondelinquent cultures. Thus, these authors may exaggerate the incompatibility of their views with those propounded in Albert K. Cohen, *Delinquent Boys: The Culture of the Gang* (1955).

[8] For psychological formulation, see Kelly, *op. cit. supra* note 2. Considerable convergence with the multiple-reference and rationalization analysis of sociologists also is apparent in the psychoanalytic work, Fritz Redl and David Wineman, *Children Who Hate* (1951).

[9] *Cf.* Lindesmith and Strauss, *op. cit. supra* note 2; Anselm Strauss, *The Social Psychology of George Herbert Mead* (1956); George H. Mead, *Mind, Self, and Society* (1934).

Sunday and our crime was committed at 1:30 that night (or rather Monday morning).

The conversation began with a remark about the numerous recent bank failures in the state, probably stimulated by one of us glancing at a map of the state. It then shifted to discussion of a local bank that had closed its doors the day before. Tom, who worked at the post-office occasionally as special mail clerk, happened to mention that a sack containing a large amount of money had been received at the post-office that afternoon, consigned to a local bank that feared a run.

The conversation then turned to the careless way in which the money was handled at the office—a plain canvas sack thrown into an open safe. We discussed the ease with which a thief could get into the building and steal the money. Tom drew a plan showing the desk at which the only clerk worked and the location of the only gun in the office. At first the conversation was entirely confined to how easily criminals might manage to steal the money. Somehow it shifted to a personal basis: as to how easily we might get the money. This shift came so naturally that even the next morning we were unable to decide when and by whom the first vital remark had been made.

A possible plan was discussed as to how we might steal the package. Tom could go to the office and gain admittance on the pretense of looking for an important letter. Then Art and I, masked and armed, could rush in, tie Tom and the clerk, and make off with the package. We had lost sight of the fact that the package contained money. We were simply discussing the possibility of playing an exciting prank with no thought of actually committing it. We had played many harmless pranks and had discussed them in much the same way before; but the knowledge that there was danger in this prank made it a subject to linger over.

After about an hour and a half of talk, I started to take off my shoes. As I unlaced them, I thought of how it looked as if I were the one to kill our interesting project. I foolishly said something to the effect that if Tom was going down town, I thought I would write a letter that was already over-

due. Tom was anxiously awaiting a letter that should be in that night. He suggested that I go down also as it was a very decent night. I consented and Art decided to join us. I sat down and wrote the letter—meanwhile we continued our talk about the money package.

My letter finished, something seemed to change. We found further inaction impossible: we had either to rob the post-office or go to bed. Tom brought out his two guns; I hunted up a couple of regular plain handkerchiefs, and Art added some rope to the assortment. At the time we were still individually and collectively playing a game with ourselves. Each of us expected one of the other two to give the thing the horse laugh and suggest going to bed and letting the letters wait till morning. But it seemed that we forgot everything—our position in school, our families and friends, the danger to us and to our folks. Our only thought was to carry out that prank. We all made our preparations more or less mechanically. Our minds were in a daze.

Putting on our regular overcoats and caps, we left the rooms quietly. On the way down town we passed the night patrolman without any really serious qualms. Tom entered the post-office as was his usual custom, being a sub-clerk, and Art and I crept up to the rear door. Tom appeared at a window with his hat, a signal that there were no reasons why our plan would not be effective. At the door, in full illumination of a light, we arranged our handkerchiefs over our faces and took our guns out of our pockets. We were ready.

"Have you enough guts to go through with this thing?" I asked, turning to Art, who was behind me.

"If you have," he answered.

Frankly I felt that I had gone far enough, but for some unknown reason I did not throw out a remark that would have ended it all then and there. And Art didn't. He later said that he was just too scared to suggest anything. We were both, it seems, in a sort of daze.

Tom opened the door and we followed our plan out to the end. There was no active resistance by the regular night man.

Then after we left the office with thousands of dollars in our hands we did not realize all that it meant. Our first words were not about getting the money. They were about the fact that our prank (and it was still that to us) had been successful. When we reached our rooms, having hidden the money in an abandoned dredger, the seriousness of the thing began to penetrate our minds. For an hour or so we lay quietly and finally settled on a plan that seemed safe in returning the money without making our identity known. Then I went to sleep.[1]

This incident, reported by one of the participants, describes a cooperative group activity directed toward a criminal object. What is interesting about the incident is that none of the participants was a criminal, that each was secretly opposed to the undertaking, and that all were personally disinterested in the goal. Why, then, did they do it?

The narrative suggests several clues. In the first place, each was reluctant to occupy the humiliating role of the one who "backs out." Apparently, then, though each was afraid, the prospect of humiliation was more threatening. Moreover, in order to avoid the appearance of reluctance, each found it necessary to keep up the pretense of his own willingness—at the same time nourishing the secret hope that *somebody else* would realize that things were going too far and back out. At this point it is probable that each still felt that the others were merely testing him, and that nobody really intended to go through with it. Then, as preparations advanced, the security of this belief began to wane and each boy began to believe that the others might not be fooling after all. This served to isolate each in the intolerable position of the only one who would be chicken-hearted. When the illusion of group daring reaches this level of mutual deception, there could be no turning back. In this manner, with the

need to conceal their mounting anxiety forcing them to shows of increased bravado, the boys literally pushed each other over the threshold of fantasy into the criminal act.

Thus there arose a situation of group motivation, based on an illusion and contrary to the actual wishes of each participant. A condition of group motivation exists *when each member is behaving in accordance with the same interpretation of what is expected of him*—whether or not this is in accord with his own wishes and regardless of the correctness of the interpretation. Each of the unwilling bandits was behaving *as if* the others were expecting him to participate. (Actually, they were hoping he would back out.) The illusion went further: though each personally dreaded participating, each was eventually convinced that the others were willing. The curious thing was that none of the group, at any point, put any direct pressure on the others to go along. Each was coerced by a similar image of what the others expected and each dreaded an imagined group reaction.

What was it that committed each to conform to this imaginary expectation in violation of his own wishes? A tentative answer might be that conformity involved certain psychological rewards; nonconformity, certain penalties. Apparently, in the mutual roles in which they found themselves *the way each boy felt about himself was dependent on how he imagined the others were feeling about him*.

Here again, the group authority was exercised by each member over himself. The strength of this authority was related to the extent to which each one's self-evaluation was open to influence by the real or imagined attitudes of the others. Each was intent on fulfilling the expectations of his role, on conforming to its

[1] Frederic M. Thrasher, *The Gang* (Chicago: The University of Chicago Press, 1936), pp. 300–303.

conceived requirements. The behavioral requirements of the role were, as it turned out, secondary, since none of the boys actually desired to engage in the activity itself. Thus the commitment was not to the *act* or to the *goal* of the act (the money), but rather to the *group expecta-* *tions*—which, in the given situation, ordained that each take the role of a fearless, daring character. In another situation the usages of this group might have cast the members in different roles, ordaining different responses.

Identity and the Shoplifter *

MARY OWEN CAMERON

It seems probable that most adult pilferers start their careers as children or adolescents in groups where the techniques of successful pilfering are learned from other more experienced children. Later as group activity is abandoned some of the group members continue the practices they learned as adolescents. The lavish displays of merchandise which department stores exhibit to encourage "impulse buying" are, for the experienced pilferer, there for the taking.

Adult women pilferers, generally belonging to families of rather modest income, enter department stores with a strong sense of the limitations of their household budgets. They do not steal merchandise which they can rationalize purchasing: household supplies, husband's clothes, children's wear. But beautiful and luxury goods for their personal use can be purchased legitimately only if some other member of the family is deprived. Although pilferers often have guilt feelings about their thefts, it still seems to them less wrong to steal from a rich store than to take from the family budget. Pilferers seem to be, thus, narcis-

sistic individuals in that they steal for their own personal use, but, on the other hand, they do not use the limited family income for their own luxury goods.

Pilferers differ in one outstanding respect, at least, from other thieves: They generally do not think of themselves as thieves. In fact, even when arrested, they resist strongly being pushed to admit their behavior is theft. This became very clear as I observed a number of interrogations of shoplifters by the store detective staff, and it was supported in conversations with the detectives who drew on their own wider experience. It is quite often difficult for the store staff to convince the arrested person that he has actually been arrested, even when the detectives show their licenses and badges. Again and again store police explain to pilferers that they are under arrest as thieves, that they will, in the normal course of events, be taken in a police van to jail, held in jail until bond is raised, and tried in a court before a judge and sentenced. Much of the interview time of store detectives is devoted to establishing this point; in making the pilferer understand that what

* Reprinted with permission of The Macmillan Company from *The Booster and the Snitch* by Mary Owen Cameron, pp. 159–166. © The Free Press of Glencoe, a Division of The Macmillan Company 1964.

happens to him from the time of his arrest is a legal question, but it is still a question for decision, first of all, by the store staff.

Store detectives use the naivete of pilferers as an assistance in arrest procedures while the pilferer is in the presence of legitimate customers on the floor of the store. The most tactful approach possible is used. The store detective will say, for example, "I represent the store office, and I'm afraid the office will have to see what's in your shopping bag. Would you care to come with me, please?" If the pilferer protests, the detective adds, "You wouldn't want to be embarrassed in front of all these people, would you? In the office we can talk things over in private."

Edwards states that the method of making an arrest is important in preventing excitement and even disorder.

A gentle approach will usually disarm any shoplifter, amateur or professional, while a rough seizure or loud accusation may immediately put him on the defensive. At other times it may result in a nervous or hysterical condition accompanied by an involuntary discharge which may be embarrassing to both the arrestor and the arrested.[1]

Inbau adds the thought that the gentle approach is helpful too in forestalling suits for false arrest.

The finesse with which defendant accosts plaintiff is a definite factor also affecting the temper with which the court approaches a case. The defendant acting in good faith with probable cause, whose attitude is quiet, non-threatening, and deferential to the plaintiff's feelings can weather an honest mistake much more cheaply than otherwise. At the most it may induce a court to find there was no imprisonment at all. At the least, it will relieve defendant of punitive damages and reduce the amount of actual damages.[2]

The "deference" of the arresting detective combined with the already existing rationalizations of the pilferer sustain in him the belief that whereas his behavior might be reprehensible, the objects taken were, after all, not of great value; he would be glad to pay for them and be on his way. "Yes, I took the dress," one woman sobbed as she was being closely interrogated, "but that doesn't mean I'm a thief."

Arrest forces the pilferer to think of himself as a thief. The interrogation procedure of the store is specifically and consciously aimed at breaking down any illusions the shoplifter may have that his behavior is regarded as merely "naughty" or "bad." The breakdown of illusions is, to the store detective staff, both a goal in itself and a means of establishing the fact that each innocent-appearing pilferer, is not in fact, a professional thief "putting on an act." In the interrogation the shoplifter is searched for other stolen merchandise and for identification papers. Pockets and pocketbooks are thoroughly examined. All papers, letters, tickets, bills, etc., are read in detail in spite of considerable protest from the arrested person. Each person is made to explain everything he has with him. If suspect items such as public locker keys, pawn tickets, etc., are found, he will have to explain very thoroughly indeed and agree to have the locker examined and the pawned merchandise seen to avoid formal charge. In any event, once name, address, and occupation have been established (and for women, the maiden name and names in other marriages), the file of names and identifying material of all persons who have, in the past years, been arrested in any of the State Street department stores is consulted. The shoplifter is questioned at length if similarities of

---

[1] Loren Edwards, *Shoplifting and Shrinkage Protection for Stores* (Springfield, Ill.: Charles C. Thomas, 1958), p. 134.

[2] Inbau, Fred E., "Protection and Recapture of Merchandise from Shoplifters," *Illinois Law Review*. Vol. 46, No. 6, 1952.

names or other identifying data are encountered.

While identification and prior record are being checked, store detectives, persons in charge of refunds, and even experienced sales clerks may be summoned to look at the arrested person to determine if he has been previously suspected of stealing merchandise or has been noted as behaving suspiciously.

In the course of all this investigation, it becomes increasingly clear to the pilferer that he is considered a thief and is in imminent danger of being hauled into court and publicly exhibited as such. This realization is often accompanied by a dramatic change in attitudes and by severe emotional disturbance. Occasionally even hysterical semi-attempts at suicide result.

The professional shoplifter who has been arrested and knows he is recognized, on the other hand, behaves quite differently. He does, of course, make every effort possible to talk his way out of the situation. But once he finds that this is impossible, he accepts jail and its inconveniences as a normal hazard of his trade.

"This is a nightmare," said one woman pilferer who had been formally charged with stealing an expensive handbag. "It can't be happening to me! Why, oh why can't I wake up and find that it isn't so," she cried later as she waited at a store exit, accompanied by a city and a store policeman, for the city police van to arrive. "Whatever will I do? Please make it go away," she pleaded with the officer. "I'll be disgraced forever. I can never look anyone in the face again."

Pilferers expect no "in-group" support for their behavior. As they become aware of the possible serious consequences of their arrest (trial, jail, etc.), pilferers obviously feel isolated from all supporting

relationships. Store detectives report that the most frequent question women ask is, "Will my husband have to know about this?" Men, they say, express immediate fear that their employers will be informed of their arrest when questions about employment are raised. Children are apprehensive of parental reaction. Edwards says,

The composure of juveniles being detained has never ceased to amaze me, that is, until notified that they must tell a parent of their misdemeanor. Then the tears flow and pleadings begin. The interviewer must be firm in his denial that notification will "kill" the parent, and he must sell the child on the idea that any deviation from accepted practice must be discussed with the person most interested in his welfare.[3]

Pilferers feel that if their family or friends learn about their arrest they will be thoroughly disgraced. The fear, shame, and remorse expressed by arrested pilferers could not be other than genuine and a reflection of their appraisal of the attitudes they believe others will take toward them. One woman was observed who, thoroughly shaken as the realization of her predicament began to appear to her, interrupted her protestations of innocence from time to time, overwhelmed at the thought of how some particular person in her "in-group" would react to her arrest. Her conversation with the interrogator ran somewhat as follows: "I didn't intend to take the dress. I just wanted to see it in daylight. [She had stuffed it into a shopping bag and carried it out of the store.] Oh, what will my husband do? I *did* intend to pay for it. It's all a mistake. Oh, my God, what will my mother say! I'll be glad to pay for it. See, I've got the money with me. Oh, my children! They can't find out I've been *arrested!* I'd never be able to face them again."

Pilferers not only expect no in-group

[3] Edwards, *op. cit.*, pp. 135–136.

support, but they feel that they have literally *no* one to turn to. The problem of being embroiled in a wholly unfamiliar legal situation is obviously not only frightening but unexpected. Apparently they had anticipated being reprimanded; they had not anticipated being searched by a licensed detective, identified, etc., and on the whole, placed in a position in which the burden of argument for keeping out of jail is theirs.

The contrast in behavior between the pilferer and the recognized and self-admitted thief is striking. The experienced thief either already knows what to do or knows precisely where and how to find out. His emotional reactions may involve anger directed at himself or at features in the situation around him, but he is not at a loss for reactions. He follows the prescribed modes of behavior, and knows, either because of prior experience or through the vicarious experiences of acquaintances, what arrest involves by way of obligations and rights. He has some familiarity with bonding practice and either already has or knows how to find a lawyer who will act for him.

Because the adult pilferer does not think of himself, prior to his arrest, as a thief and can conceive of no in-group support for himself in that role, his arrest forces him to reject the role (at least insofar as department store shoplifting is concerned). The arrest procedure, even though not followed by prosecution, is in itself sufficient to cause him to rede-fine his situation. He is, of course, informed that subsequent arrest by any store will be followed by immediate prosecution and probably by a considerable jail sentence. But since this does not act as a deterrent to the self-admitted thief nor could this kind of admonition deter the compulsive neurotic, neither the fear of punishment nor the objective severity of the punishment in itself is the crucial point in relation to the change from criminal to law-abiding behavior. Rather the threat to the person's system of values and prestige relationships is involved. Social scientists who have investigated criminal activities which have subcultural support are unanimous in pointing out the persistence of criminal activity, the high rate of recidivism and the resistance to reform shown by law violators. Pilfering seems to be the other side of the coin. Not having the support of a criminal subculture, pilferers are very "reformable" individuals. If the findings of this study are substantiated by studies of other offenses in which the offenders are similarly without support of a criminal subculture, there would be a strong argument in favor of keeping pilferers out of jail lest they receive there the kinds of knowledge and emotional support they need to become "successful" commercial thieves. Crime prevention would seem best achieved by helping the law violators retain their self-image of respectability while making it clear to them that a second offense will really mean disgrace.

Patient Role and Social Uncertainty *

KAI T. ERIKSON

The concept of role has become widely used in the field of mental health to relate the behavior of mental patients to the social setting of their illness. The literature in which this concept has appeared, however, has been largely concerned with the specialized culture of the mental hospital—the formal and informal structures of ward life—almost as if the universe to which a patient relates when he enacts a "patient role" is neatly contained within hospital walls.[1] To the sociologist, who generally uses the concept of role in a broader social context, this tends to place a one-sided emphasis on the institution itself as the essential focus of the patient's social life.

When a person enters a mental hospital for treatment, to be sure, he abandons many of the social ties which anchored him to a definite place in society. However, the act of becoming a mental patient effects a fundamental *change* in the person's relationship to the ongoing processes of society, not a complete withdrawal from them; and while the forms of his participation are altered, he remains acutely sensitive to outer influences. Even in the relative isolation of the hospital ward, then, the patient's behavior to some extent articulates his relationship to the larger society and reflects the social position which he feels is reserved for him in its organizational structure. It is this aspect of the role of the patient which the present paper will consider.

Definitions

Role usually is used to designate a set of behaviors or values about behavior which is commonly considered appropriate for persons occupying given statuses or positions in society. For the purposes of this paper, it will be useful to consider that the acquisition of roles by a person involves two basic processes: *role-validation* and *role-commitment*. Role-validation takes place when a community 'gives' a person certain expectations to live up to, providing him with distinct notions as to the conduct it considers appropriate or valid for him in his position.[2] Role-commitment is the complementary process whereby a per-

* Reprinted by special permission of The William Alanson White Psychiatric Foundation from *Psychiatry: Journal for the Study of Interpersonal Processes,* Vol. 20 (August, 1957), pp. 263–68, by permission of the author and The William Alanson White Psychiatric Foundation. The writer would like to thank Nelson N. Foote, formerly director of the Family Study Center, for the opportunity to do this study and for many helpful criticisms.
[1] See, for example, the following: J. F. Bateman and H. W. Dunham, "The State Hospital as a Specialized Community Experience," *Amer. J. Psychiatry* (1948) 105:445–448; William Caudill, Fredrick C. Redlich, Helen R. Gilmore, and Eugene B. Brody, "Social Structure and Interaction Processes on a Psychiatric Ward," *Amer. J. Orthopsychiatry* (1952) 22:314–334; George Devereux, "The Social Structure of the Hospital as a Factor in Total Therapy," *Amer. J. Orthopsychiatry* (1949) 19:493–500; Howard Rowland, "Interaction Processes in a State Mental Hospital," *Psychiatry* (1938) 1:323–337; Alfred Stanton and Morris S. Schwartz, "Medical Opinion and the Social Context in the Mental Hospital," *Psychiatry* (1949) 12:243–249; Stanton and Schwartz, *The Mental Hospital;* New York, Basic Books, 1954.

[2] Validation, it might be pointed out, is meant to be more than a community's attempt to impose its moral preferences upon members. The community may validate certain behavior as appropriate for certain individuals even while remaining completely outraged by

son adopts certain styles of behavior as his own, committing himself to role themes that best represent the kind of person he assumes himself to be, and best reflect the social position he considers himself to occupy.

Normally, of course, these processes take place simultaneously and are seldom overtly distinguished in the relationship between the person and his community. The person learns to accept the image that the group holds up to him as a more-or-less accurate reflection of himself, is able to accept as his own the position which the group provides for him, and thus becomes more or less committed to the behavior values which the group poses as valid for him. The merit of making a distinction between these two processes, then, is solely to visualize what happens in marginal situations in which conflict does occur—in which the person develops behavior patterns which the community regards as invalid for him, or the community entertains expectations which the person feels unable to realize. Sociologists, traditional specialists in this aspect of deviance, have generally been more concerned with the process of validation than that of commitment, concentrating on the mechanisms which groups employ to persuade individuals that roles validated for them deserve their personal commitment.

In so doing, sociologists have largely overlooked the extent to which a person can *engineer* a change in the role expectations held in his behalf, rather than passively waiting for others to 'allocate' or 'assign' roles to him. This he does by being so persistent in his commitment to certain modes of behavior, and so convincing in his portrayal of them, that the community is persuaded to accept these modes as the basis for a new set of expectations on its part.

Thus the process by which persons acquire a recognized role may, at times, involve long and delicate negotiations between the individual and his community. The individual presents himself in behavior styles that express his personal sense of identity and continuity; [3] the group validates role models for him that fit its own functional needs. [4] The negotiation is concluded when a mutually satisfactory definition of the individual is reached and a position established for him in the group structure—or when the issue becomes stalemated and suppressive sanctions against deviance are called into play.

The argument to be presented here is that such a negotiation is likely to follow a mental patient's admission to a mental hospital, particularly if he does not qualify as a "certified" patient with a circumscribed disease. In accepting hospitalization, the patient is often caught in the pull of divergent sets of expectations: on the one hand, he is exposed to psychiatry's demand that he make a whole-hearted commitment to the process of treatment, and, on the other, he is confronted by a larger society which is often unwilling to validate these commitments. He is left, then, with no consistent and durable social role, with no clear-cut social models upon which to fashion his behavior. The patient is thus often persuaded by the logic of psychiatric institutions to attempt to engineer validation in the role this society provides for the *medical* patient—in which, to be sure,

---

it. By naming a criminal "habitual" or "confirmed," for instance, people declare their intention of punishing him, not because his conduct violates their expectations or is "unlike" him, but precisely because it *is* like him and is thus the valid way for him to act.

[3] See, in this connection, Erik H. Erikson, "The Problem of Ego Identity," *J. Amer. Psychoanal. Assn.* (1956) 4:56–121.

[4] See Talcott Parsons, *The Social System;* New York, The Free Press, 1951.

distinctly psychotic patients are presumed to belong. To establish his eligibility for this conventional role, the mental patient must negotiate, using his illness as an instrumentality. He must present his illness to others in a form which they recognize as legitimate, perhaps even exaggerating his portrayal of those behaviors which qualify medical patients for their role. In having to do so, the argument continues, he is often left with little choice but to become sicker or more chronically sick.

The Patient

This section is based primarily on data collected in a small, "open" psychiatric hospital which offered analytically oriented psychotherapy for a fairly selective group of patients. Diagnoses in this population ranged, for the most part, from the severe psychoneuroses to borderline psychoses. The institutional setting lacked the scheduled rigidity of closed hospital routines and allowed for an unusual degree of personal initiative. Since the patients received almost daily individual therapy and were, in a certain respect, volunteers for treatment who recognized the implications of their patienthood, they could hardly be considered representative of the average ward population. But the experienced clinician will be able to determine to what extent generalizations made from observation of this group apply to patients in custodial institutions, whose contacts with the outside world are more limited. No doubt many of the same social forces act upon patients in any hospital situation, even where behavior is more strictly routinized and confined within the limiting boundaries of a closed ward so that it may seem to reflect the common setting in which it took place rather than the common motivations which produced it. Thus it is possible that the uniqueness of the therapeutic setting

in which these observations took place simply affords a more spontaneous picture of social forces operating in any psychiatric hospital.

While doing some sociological work in this setting, the writer took a brief inventory of behavior themes which seemed characteristic of the patient group and which appeared to be among the central motifs of the patients' role behavior.

One may begin by noting certain contradictions implicit in the very act of becoming a mental patient. By accepting hospitalization, the patient makes a contractual agreement to cooperate in a therapeutic partnership: he agrees to want and to appreciate treatment, to be realistic about his need for help, to volunteer relevant information, and to act as reliably as possible upon the recommendations of his therapist. Yet it is widely considered a condition of his illness that he is unable to make meaningful contact with any reality, therapeutic or otherwise. In the grip of these discrepant expectations, his behavior is likely to be a curious mixture of the active and the passive, a mosaic of acts which tend to confirm his competence and acts which tend to dramatize his helplessness. He must test the limits of his own uncertain controls and look for consistent expectations to guide him, as the following fragment from a case history illustrates:

One of the outstanding characteristics of this patient is his absolute uncertainty about his illness and what is expected of him in the institution and in therapy. He is uncertain whether he actively produces his hysterical states or whether they come upon him without his being able to do anything about them. He does not know whether he is supposed to show his symptoms or suppress them, to "let go" of his impulses and act out or to exert active self-control and "put the lid on." He is afraid that if he does the former, he is psychotic and will be considered too sick for the open institutional setting here; if he does the latter, he will be a pretending psychopath and considered too well to continue treatment here at all. He does not know what he should expect from himself, from other patients, from his sickness, from other people he knows, or even from his therapist. Perhaps his most crucial problem at the moment is to define for himself what are the conditions of his stay here as a patient.

This fragment sums up the bewildering social situation in which the patient must act, and it is not difficult to understand how the final assumption of a consistent social role might represent to him a clarification and partial adjustment. To demonstrate this, I shall try to isolate a few strands of behavior from this complicated fabric.

All children are taught in this culture that it is impolite to stare at or make reference to the infirmities of cripples. So it is interesting to note that the generous impulse of outsiders to overlook a patient's less visible infirmities is likely to put the patient in an instant state of alarm, and to bring urgent assurances on his part that he is severely sick and in serious need of treatment. Patients often bring this topic into conversation on scant provocation and continue to talk about it even when fairly vigorous attempts are made by visitors to change the subject. The patient is likely to describe this as "accepting the realities of his illness," by which he means that he frankly admits the seriousness of his sickness and refuses to take refuge in some convenient defense that might deny it. Yet to the observer it often appears that this is an attempt to convince *others* of these realities as well as to remind himself, as if he were afraid they would be overlooked entirely. The patient seems to feel it crucial that his illness be accepted as a fundamental fact about himself, the premise on which he enters into relations with others.

Side by side with this severe "honesty," the patient can develop a considerable degree of responsibility in carrying out the therapeutic recommendations of his therapist. And if the hospital tries to foster the patient's social initiative, he may respond with resources that even the therapist did not know were at his disposal. Such initiative is usually in evidence only during certain hospital activities and sometimes appears to belie the very weaknesses which the patient, at other times, displays so insistently. Patients at the hospital in question, for instance, have organized and produced dramatic plays before outside audiences, performing with a skill that surprised professional dramatic observers, and succeeding even when the therapists themselves had severe reservations about the outcome. At a prizewinning performance in a neighboring city, some of the audience were and remained under the impression that the players were members of the medical staff rather than patients of the institution.

Yet as one records this accomplishment, it must be noted that such positive efforts can sometimes be as deceptive as they are surprising, and that, at times, they can produce negative undercurrents that threaten to cancel out the accomplishment altogether. In reporting on the plays performed at the hospital, one journalist noted this. He said that the patients produce and act in plays before paying audiences with a competence which, according to Clifford Odets, who saw one of his plays so performed, is equal to that of any good amateur group. At the same time, the reporter said, one of the doctors had remarked ruefully, "I was very upset when one of my patients, after doing a fine job in the play, went back to the patients' dormitory and tried to set fire to it."

The example is extreme, but it illustrates the conflict a patient encounters in committing himself to positive and constructive activity. Like Penelope, who wove a cloak by day only to unravel it at night, the mental patient often portrays the insecurity of his position by staging, after every advance of this kind, a dramatic retreat into impulsivity and destruction.

Thus at once the patient accepts responsibility for a type of performance rarely asked of the average person, yet is unable to control actions which, in the light of the earlier accomplishment, would seem to be well within his realm of mastery. This seeming paradox is a recurring motif that runs through the whole complex of the patient's role behavior. As has been shown in the case abstract that introduced this section, the patient has potentialities for activity and passivity, for resourcefulness and helplessness, in any given area of action. To organize these into a coherent role pattern, it seems, the patient partitions his hospital world into areas where he considers one or the other of these potential responses specifically appropriate.

In some decisive situations, as has been described, the patient faces his hospital life with remarkable initiative. Yet in others, an overwhelming theme of helplessness seems to dominate his behavior. He is likely to insist, in terms far stronger than the situation would appear to necessitate, that he is unable to control his behavior and must be given a wide license for conduct that is certainly unconventional according to the values prevalent outside the hospital. A patient was asked, "Why did you do that?" His answer, "How should I know? If I knew these things, I wouldn't be here," reflects the values thus emerging in the patient role pattern. Patients have been heard comforting one another by saying, "Of course you can't do it." This process of "giving up defenses" is, of course, presumed to be essential for successful treatment, particularly in intensive analytic therapy, and a certain license for impulsivity and act-

ing out seems to be part of much of psychotherapy in general. But the patient often seems to reserve his right for such license with what appear to be unnecessary claims that he "can't help it."

One might add that whereas clinical evidence indicates that patients often feel a strong guilt at "having let others down," the values of the patient group seldom allow its overt expression—and even supply convenient channels for its projection elsewhere. It is not uncommon for patients to bitterly indict their parents, often for the same weakness they themselves "can't help," sometimes talking as if a kind of deliberate conspiracy was involved in the events that led to their own illness. The weakness of this logic seems evident even to those who use it most persistently, which again indicates that the social usages which allow its expression must have an important social function to the patient group. If a little harsh, it may be one way to deny one's responsibility for being sick, while nevertheless accounting for one's illness in terms that are current outside the hospital walls.

The point is that most of the persons a patient encounters in the hospital, certainly the other patients, are perfectly willing to acknowledge that ego deficiencies are not his "fault" and that he is often compelled to act without the benefit of sufficient controls. To what audience, then, does he address his continual protest that he has the *right* to some license and can't help the fact that he is sick? Largely, one begins to think, these assertions are broadcast not to the audience assembled in the confined orbit of the hospital at all—but to the omnipresent public which, as shall be seen, fails to validate his commitment to therapy. To assume that hospital walls or the implicit ideology of psychiatric institutions protect the patient from this audience would be an unfortunate oversight. The image of the public audience is firmly incorporated within the patient himself, and this image is constantly reinforced by newspapers, movies, radio, and television. The specialized values which psychiatry introduces into the hospital setting cannot entirely overcome the fact that the patient remains sensitive to current public notions about mental illness, and, on certain levels of awareness, even shares them in substance.

What does the outside audience ask of the patient—and its internalized image make him ask of himself? Essentially, he is asked to justify his voluntary retirement to a hospital by demonstrating that he *needs* it, by displaying a distinct illness requiring highly specialized help. The reason for a person's therapy in a residential setting is obviously the wish on everybody's part that he develop adjustive initiative. Yet if large parts of society doubt his claim to illness when he appears to have a certain competence— when, for instance, he rehearses healthy modes of behavior on or off the stage— he is left in the exposed position of one who has to *look* incompetent even while learning to become the exact opposite. A few minutes before going on the stage, a patient-actor announced, "It is a tradition here that the show *never* goes on!" This tradition is of particular interest because it has no basis in fact whatever. The show in question did go on, as had all of its predecessors. Yet even in the act of positive accomplishment the patient feels it important to repeat that failure is the norm among mental patients, for he always anticipates the question, "Look here, if you can do these things so well, why are you here?"

This prominent theme of helplessness which runs through the patient's verbal and behavioral repertoire again reasserts the basic paradox. For while much of the time he may display a passivity that almost suggests disability, he shows a certain ingenuity in organizing his passive behavior strategically; he can put considerable energy into maneuvers which show him to be helpless; in short, he can go to ample expense to give the impression of one who has nothing to expend. This does not imply, of course, that the patient is deliberately staging a deceptive performance. On the contrary, it suggests that the psychological needs which motivate such behavior are as compelling, in a certain way, as those considered to be anchored somewhere in the dynamics and genetics of his illness, and, in fact, tend to reinforce them.

In the absence of clear-cut organic symptoms, a "real" illness which "can't be helped" is the most precious commodity such patients have in their bargaining with society for a stable patient role. It is the most substantial credential available in their application for equal rights with the medical patient, and as such, may come to have an important social value to them. The fatal logic of this may be that the patient will find his social situation better structured for him if he gives in to his illness and helps others to create an unofficial hospital structure which supports the perpetuation of patienthood. . . .

SUSTAINING DEVIANT IDENTITY

14

Once a deviant identity has been assumed, problems of sustaining it arise. Whether or not the person is happy with the self he presents to others, it behooves him to see whether or not self-role integration is the better part of social wisdom. With deviant peers, this is frequently but not always wise. With conventional others, it is definitely not advisable. In either case, techniques must be devised for coping with this invariant contingency in any deviant career. The manner in which the problem is solved has real consequences for how long the person stays in the career, how he fares while in it, and whether and how he is able to terminate it.

In the first of the readings that follow, Goffman teaches us that being an established deviant requires one also to fend off nondeviants and this is usually done, he argues, by managing the information other people have about one's identity. Jackman, O'Toole, and Geis point out that prostitutes sustain their personal identities in different ways according to whether they are isolates, live in the criminal world, or in a dual world. Kaplan, Boyd, and Bloom describe the methods that patients in a mental hospital use to maintain their self-esteem. Sykes and Matza offer a general discussion of how persons neutralize the effects that conventional values could have on their self-conceptions. Reiss, in a specific case, demonstrates how teenage youths can engage in homosexual activity without ever finding it necessary to identify themselves as homosexuals. The separation between self and role that their peers require enables them to retain their heterosexual identity. Lemert, in the last paper, shows how the nature of the systematic check forger's work requires him to assume more roles than he has selves for, with obvious severe consequences for his personal identity.

Management of Spoiled Identity *

ERVING GOFFMAN

The Discredited and the Discreditable

When there is a discrepancy between an individual's actual social identity and his virtual one, it is possible for this fact to be known to us before we normals contact him, or to be quite evident when he presents himself before us. He is a discredited person. . . . We are likely to give no open recognition to what is discrediting of him, and while this work of careful disattention is being done, the situation can become tense, uncertain, and ambiguous for all participants, especially the stigmatized one.

The cooperation of a stigmatized person with normals in acting as if his known differentness were irrelevant and not attended to is one main possibility in the life of such a person. However, when his differentness is not immediately apparent, and is not known beforehand (or at least known by him to be known to the others), when in fact his is a discreditable, not a discredited, person, then the second main possibility in his life is to be found. The issue is not that of managing tension generated during social contacts, but rather that of managing information about his failing. To display or not to display; to tell or not to tell; to let on or not to let on; to lie or not to lie; and in each case, to whom, how, when, and where. For example, while the mental patient is in the hospital, and when he is with adult members of his own family, he is faced with being treated tactfully as if he were sane when there is known to be some doubt, even though he may not have any; or he is treated as insane, when he knows this is not just. But for the ex-mental patient the problem can be quite different; it is not that he must face prejudice against himself, but rather that he must face unwitting acceptance of himself by individuals who are prejudiced against persons of the kind he can be revealed to be. Wherever he goes his behavior will falsely confirm for the other that they are in the company of what in effect they demand but may discover they haven't obtained, namely, a mentally untainted person like themselves. By intention or in effect the ex-mental patient conceals information about his real social identity, receiving and accepting treatment based on false suppositions concerning himself. It is this second general issue, the management of undisclosed discrediting information about self, that I am focusing on in these notes, in brief, "passing." The concealment of creditable facts—reverse passing—of course occurs, but is not relevant here.[1]

* Reprinted from Erving Goffman, *Stigma: Notes on the Management of Spoiled Identity*, pp. 41–48, © 1963. Reprinted by permission of Prentice-Hall, Inc., Englewood Cliffs, New Jersey.

[1] For one instance of reverse passing, see "H. E. R. Cules," "Ghost-Writer and Failure," in P. Toynbee, ed., *Underdogs* (London: Weidenfeld and Nicolson, 1961), Chap. 2, pp. 30–39. There are many other examples. I knew a physician who was careful to refrain from using external symbols of her status, such as car-license tags, her only evidence of profession being an identification carried in her wallet. When faced with a public accident in which medical service was already being rendered the victim, or in which the victim was past helping, she would, upon examining the victim at a distance from the circle around him, quietly go her way without announcing her competence. In these situations she was what might be called a female impersonator.

Social Information

The information of most relevance in the study of stigma has certain properties. It is information about an individual. It is about his more or less abiding characteristics, as opposed to the moods, feelings, or intents that he might have at a particular moment.[2] The information, as well as the sign through which it is conveyed, is reflexive and embodied; that is, it is conveyed by the very person it is about, and conveyed through bodily expression in the immediate presence of those who receive the expression. Information possessing all of these properties I will here call "social." Some signs that convey social information may be frequently and steadily available, and routinely sought and received; these signs may be called "symbols."

The social information conveyed by any particular symbol may merely confirm what other signs tells us about the individual, filling out our image of him in a redundant and unproblematic way. Some lapel buttons, attesting the social club membership, are examples, as are male wedding rings in some contexts. However, the social information conveyed by a symbol can establish a special claim to prestige, honor, or desirable class position—a claim that might not otherwise be presented or, if otherwise presented, then not automatically granted. Such a sign is popularly called a "status symbol," although the term "prestige symbol" might be more accurate, the former term being more suitably employed when a well-organized social position of some kind is the referent. Prestige symbols can be contrasted to *stigma symbols,* namely, signs which are especially effective in drawing attention to a debasing identity discrepancy, breaking up what would otherwise be a coherent overall picture, with a consequent reduction in our valuation of the individual. The shaved head of female collaborators in World War II is an example, as is an habitual solecism through which someone affecting middle class manner and dress repeatedly employs a word incorrectly or repeatedly mispronounces it.

In addition to prestige symbols and stigma symbols, one further possibility is to be found, namely, a sign that tends —in fact or hope—to break up an otherwise coherent picture but in this case in a positive direction desired by the actor, not so much establishing a new claim as throwing severe doubt on the validity of the virtual one. I shall refer here to *disidentifiers.* One example is the "good English" of an educated northern Negro visiting the South;[3] another is the turban and mustache affected by some urban lower class Negroes.[4] A study of illiterates provides another illustration:

Therefore, when goal orientation is pronounced or imperative and there exists a high probability that definition as illiterate is a bar to the achievement of the goal, the illiterate is likely to try to "pass" as literate. . . . The popularity in the group studied of windowpane lenses with heavy horn frames ("bop glasses") may be viewed as an attempt to emulate the stereotype of the businessman-teacher-young intellectual and especially the high status jazz musician.[5]

[2] The difference between mood information and other kinds of information is treated in G. Stone, "Appearance and the Self," in A. Rose, *Human Behavior and Social Processes* (Boston: Houghton Mifflin, 1962), pp. 86–118. See also E. Goffman, *The Presentation of Self in Everyday Life* (New York: Doubleday & Co., Anchor Books, 1959), pp. 24–25.
[3] G. J. Fleming, "My Most Humiliating Jim Crow Experience," *Negro Digest* (June, 1954), pp. 67–68.
[4] B. Wolfe, "Ecstatic in Blackface," *Modern Review*, III (1950), p. 204.
[5] H. Freeman and G. Kassebaum, "The Illiterate in America," *Social Forces*, XXXIV (1956), p. 372.

A New York specialist in the arts of vagrancy provides still another illustration:

After seven-thirty in the evening, in order to read a book in Grand Central or Penn Station, a person either has to wear horn-rimmed glasses or look exceptionally prosperous. Anyone else is apt to come under surveillance. On the other hand, newspaper readers never seem to attract attention and even the seediest vagrant can sit in Grand Central all night without being molested if he continues to read a paper.[6]

Note that in this discussion of prestige symbols, stigma symbols, and disidentifiers, signs have been considered which routinely convey social information. These symbols must be distinguished from fugitive signs that have not been institutionalized as information carriers. When such signs make claims to prestige, one can call them points; when they discredit tacit claims, one can call them slips.

Some signs carrying social information, being present, first of all, for other reasons, have only an overlay of informational function. There are stigma symbols that provide examples: the wrist markings which disclose that an individual has attempted suicide; the arm pock marks of drug addicts; the handcuffed wrists of convicts in transit;[7] or black eyes when worn in public by females, as a writer on prostitution suggests:

"Outside [the prison where she now is] I'd be in the soup with it. Well, you know how it is: the law sees a chick with a shiner figures she's up to something. Bull figures maybe in the life. Next thing trails her around. Then maybe bang! busted." [8]

Other signs are designed by man solely for the purpose of conveying social information, as in the case of insignia of military rank. It should be added that the significance of the underlay of a sign can become reduced over time, becoming, at the extreme, merely vestigial, even while the informational function of the activity remains constant or increases in importance. Further, a sign that appears to be present for non-informational reasons may sometimes be manufactured with malice aforethought solely because of its informing function, as when dueling scars were carefully planned and inflicted.

Signs conveying social information vary according to whether or not they are congenital, and, if not, whether, once employed, they become a permanent part of the person. (Skin color is congenital; a brand mark or maiming is permanent but not congenital; a convict's head-shave is neither congenital nor permanent.) More important, impermanent signs solely employed to convey social information may or may not be employed against the will of the informant; when they are, they tend to be stigma symbols.[9] Later it will

---

[6] E. Love, *Subways Are for Sleeping* (New York: Harcourt, Brace & World, 1957), p. 28.

[7] A. Heckstall-Smith, *Eighteen Months* (London: Allan Wingate, 1954), p. 43.

[8] T. Rubin, *In the Life* (New York: The Macmillan Company, 1961), p. 69.

[9] In his *American Notes*, written on the basis of his 1842 trip, Dickens records in his chapter on slavery some pages of quotations from local newspapers regarding lost and found slaves. The identifications contained in these advertisements provide a full range of identifying signs. First, there are relatively stable features of the body that in context can incidentally provide partial or full positive identification: age, sex, and scarrings (these resulting from shot and knife wounds, from accidents, and from lashings). Self-admitted name is also provided, though usually, of course, only the first name. Finally, stigma symbols are often cited, notably branded initials and cropped ears. These symbols communicate the social identity of slave but, unlike iron bands around the neck or leg, also communicate something more narrow than that, namely, ownership by a particular master. Authorities then had two concerns about an apprehended Negro: whether or not he was a runaway slave, and, if he was, to whom did he belong.

be necessary to consider stigma symbols that are voluntarily employed.

It is possible for signs which mean one thing to one group to mean something else to another group, the same category being designated but differently characterized. For example, the shoulder patches that prison officials require escape-prone prisoners to wear [10] can come to mean one thing to guards, in general negative, while being a mark of pride for the wearer relative to his fellow prisoners. The uniform of an officer may be a matter of pride to some, to be worn on every possible occasion; for other officers, weekends may represent a time when they can exercise their choice and wear mufti, passing as civilians. Similarly, while the obligation to wear the school cap in town may be seen as a privilege by some boys, as will the obligation to wear a uniform on leave by "other ranks," still there will be wearers who feel that the social information conveyed thereby is a means of ensuring control and discipline over them when they are off duty and off the premises.[11] So, too, during the eighteen hundreds in California, the absence of a pigtail (queue) on a Chinese man signified for Occidentals a degree of acculturation, but to fellow-Chinese a question would be raised as to respectability—specifically, whether or not the individual had served a term in prison where cutting off of the queue was obliga-

tory; loss of queue was for a time, then, very strongly resisted.[12]

Signs carrying social information vary of course as to reliability. Distended capillaries on the cheek and nose, sometimes called "venous stigmata" with more aptness than meant, can be and are taken as indicating alcoholic excess. However, teetotalers can exhibit the same symbol for other physiological reasons, thereby giving rise to suspicions about themselves which aren't justified, but with which they must deal nonetheless.

A final point about social information must be raised; it has to do with the informing character of the "with" relationship in our society. To be "with" someone is to arrive at a social occasion in his company, walk with him down a street, be a member of his party in a restaurant, and so forth. The issue is that in certain circumstances the social identity of those an individual is with can be used as a source of information concerning his own social identity, the assumption being that he is what the others are. The extreme, perhaps, is the situation in criminal circles: a person wanted for arrest can legally contaminate anyone he is seen with, subjecting them to arrest on suspicion. (A person for whom there is a warrant is therefore said "to have smallpox," and his criminal disease is said to be "catching.") [13] In any case, an analysis of how people manage the information

[10] See G. Dendrickson and F. Thomas, *The Truth About Dartmoor* (London: Victor Gollancz, 1954), p. 55, and F. Norman, *Bang to Rights* (London: Secker and Warburg, 1958), p. 125. The use of this type of symbol is well presented in E. Kogon, *The Theory and Practice of Hell* (New York: Berkley Publishing Corp., n.d.), pp. 41–42, where he specifies the markings used in concentration camps to identify differentially political prisoners, second offenders, criminals, Jehovah's Witnesses, "shiftless elements," Gypsies, Jews, "race defilers," foreign nationals (according to nation), feeble-minded, and so forth. Slaves on the Roman slave market also were often labeled as to nationality; see M. Gordon, "The Nationality of Slaves Under the Early Roman Empire," in M. I. Finley, ed., *Slavery in Classical Antiquity* (Cambridge: Heffer, 1960), p. 171.

[11] T. H. Pear, *Personality, Appearance and Speech* (London: George Allen and Unwin, 1957), p. 58.

[12] A. McLeod, *Pigtails and Gold Dust* (Caldwell, Idaho: Caxton Printers, 1947), p. 28. At times religious-historical significance was also attached to wearing the queue; see *ibid.,* p. 204.

[13] See D. Maurer, *The Big Con* (New York: Pocket Books, 1949), p. 298.

they convey about themselves will have to consider how they deal with the contingencies of being seen "with" particular others.

The Self-Image of the Prostitute *

NORMAN R. JACKMAN, RICHARD O'TOOLE,
AND GILBERT GEIS

Sexual behavior represents one of the most sensitive areas in American life. Within this sphere, professional promiscuity on the part of females stands as a striking deviation from what a large segment of the society declares to be acceptable sexual performance. Prostitutes are undoubtedly well aware of the prevailing social attitudes toward their behavior. It would seem, therefore, that these women develop a set of beliefs which counteract the social anathema attached to their way of life. This set of beliefs allows them to continue their behavior and to face and retaliate against persons who share the dominant and negative social values toward them.

Analyses of prostitution have generally employed a socioeconomic or a psychological frame of reference. The socioeconomic approach has ranged from Marxist [1] through ecological [2] to sophisticated structural-functional interpretations.[3] Other attempts at causal explanations have stressed mobility [4] and have concentrated on detailed life histories.[5] In addition, there is a wide range of psychoanalytical approaches, including those on frigidity,[6] Oedipal fixation,[7] maternal rejection,[8] homosexuality,[9] "so-

* Reprinted from *The Sociological Quarterly*, Vol. 4 (Spring, 1963), pp. 150–160, by permission of the authors and *Quarterly*. The authors are indebted to the Oklahoma City and the Norman Police Departments for their co-operation. Police Inspector E. B. Giddens, Oklahoma City, was extremely helpful in arranging interviews with prostitutes held on vagrancy and disorderly conduct charges. Inspector Giddens clearly expressed to the investigators and the respondents the right of any prisoner to refuse to be interviewed. Our thanks are also extended to the personnel of the vice squad and the matrons of the Oklahoma City jail. Officer Terry Sharp, Norman Police Department, and Robert Bristow contributed as graduate students to this research. Acknowledgment is also due the Faculty Research Fund of the University of Oklahoma for partial financial aid.

[1] W. A. Bonger, *Criminality and Economic Conditions* (Boston: Little, Brown, 1916), pp. 321–56.

[2] Robert E. Park and Ernest W. Burgess, *Introduction to the Science of Sociology* (Chicago: Univ. of Chicago Press, 1921); Park, Burgess, and Roderick D. McKenzie, *The City* (Chicago: Univ. of Chicago Press, 1925); Nels Anderson, *The Hobo: The Sociology of the Homeless Man* (Chicago: Univ. of Chicago Press, 1923); Walter C. Reckless, *Vice in Chicago* (Chicago: Univ. of Chicago Press, 1933).

[3] Kingsley Davis, "The Sociology of Prostitution," *American Sociological Review*, 2:744–55 (Oct., 1937).

[4] Edwin M. Lemert, *Social Pathology* (New York: McGraw-Hill, 1951), p. 233.

[5] W. I. Thomas, *The Unadjusted Girl* (Boston: Little, Brown, 1924).

[6] Karl Abraham, *Selected Papers on Psycho-Analysis* (London: Hogarth Press, 1927), p. 361.

[7] Edward Glover, "The Abnormality of Prostitution," in A. M. Krich, ed., *Women* (New York: Dell, 1953), pp. 247–73; and Glover, *The Psychopathology of Prostitution* (London: Institute for the Study and Treatment of Delinquency, 1957).

[8] Harold Greenwald, *The Call Girl* (New York: Ballantine Books, 1958), p. 94.

[9] Frank S. Caprio, *Female Homosexuality* (New York: Citadel, 1954).

cial-existential" castration,[10] and restrictive ego-ideals combined with revenge motives.[11] Nowhere in the literature is there more than a hint of the manner in which the prostitute forms and supports her self-image.[12]

Two questions appear to be central to the problem of the prostitute's self-identity. First, since most Americans scorn prostitutes and these dominant social values travel throughout the society, how are women recruited to prostitution? Second, since a high degree of conformity to the dominant, middle-class American society is considered necessary for the maintenance of self-esteem, how do prostitutes rationalize their violation of a dominant social norm?

Interview Phase

Fifteen prostitutes were interviewed for periods averaging two hours each. Thirteen interviews were obtained while these women were held in the city jail awaiting the results of clinical tests. Two other women were interviewed in night clubs.[13]

Open-ended questions were employed for interviewing. The questions were used only to get the respondents to talk: everything they said was recorded and subsequently coded. Standard profile questions were asked (name, age, education, marital status, number, sex, and age of children, religion, etc.) followed by a series of questions organized around certain principal topics. These were (*a*) account of career, (*b*) self-conception, (*c*) group identifications, and (*d*) role expectations. Specific but unformalized questions were asked in each of these major areas, such as childhood experiences, recruitment to prostitution, attitudes toward clients, police, neighbors, etc., relationships with parents, husbands, children, relatives, other prostitutes, etc., attitudes toward work, future hopes, fears and plans, modes, fantasies, daydreams, and recreation.[14]

Analysis of the Data

The three following propositions concerning the formation and the structure of the self-image of the prostitute emerged from the data.

1. *The . . . isolated girl in urban society comes* [more readily] *to define as acceptable, patterns of behavior condemned by general social values.* . . . Evidence indicated that the respondents were alienated from their parents following a break with the father toward whom they all expressed extreme hostility. After their introduction to prostitution, many of them became reconciled with their mothers, though they all maintained that they had kept knowledge of their activities from the mother:

I would go through hell for my mother, but my father is a bastard. Every time my mother got pregnant [respondent has five

[10] T. Agoston, "Some Psychological Aspects of Prostitution; The Pseudo-Personality," *International Journal of Psycho-Analysis,* 26:62–67 (1945).

[11] Helen Deutsch, *The Psychology of Women* (New York: Grune and Stratton, 1944), vol. 1.

[12] Cf. David W. Maurer, "Prostitutes and Criminal Argots," *American Journal of Sociology,* 44:546–50 (Jan., 1939). On rationalization by juvenile delinquents, see Gresham M. Sykes and David Matza, "Techniques of Neutralization: A Theory of Delinquency," *American Sociological Review,* 22:664–70 (Dec., 1957).

[13] During the jail interviews only the investigating team was present. In two night club interviews patrol car officers were also present but not in a position to hear the conversation.

[14] We were not concerned with the literal "truth" of respondents' statements. We accepted the statements at their face value since we were concerned with the prostitutes' self-image, however fantastic. Where pertinent, however, we have employed police records for validation or further information.

siblings] my father went out with other women.

My parents were divorced when I was eight. I lived with relatives and in an orphan home until I was thirteen and then I went to live with my mother. . . . My father was cruel to me. . . . I hated my father and stepfather. . . . I was glad when my father died. . . .

My father was a carpenter and a gambler. . . . He always treated me like I was strictly from age two. But I got along good with my mother.

Alienation during the period of entrance into prostitution was indicated by the respondents' statements that they associated with people who meant little to them, or that they had no friends at all. In every case they felt that they stood alone against a hostile or indifferent world, though some of them were introduced to semi-criminal groups with which in time they came to identify themselves.

I ran around with a girl who started and so I started, too. She had a lot of friends. . . . I got to know a lot of people in the hustling racket.

I just been runnin' around with rum-dums all my life, I guess. . . . There was a fellow once in San Antone—I came in off a box car, believe it or not, and I met him in a honky-tonk.

I was hanging 'round bars in Tulsa just looking for kicks. I had no place to go, like. It was strictly from hunger, man.

I figgered it was easy money—prostitution. . . . Nobody cared what I did anyway, and I knew a fellow who would set it up for me.

2. *The general social values, nevertheless, have some impact on the isolated individual. Therefore, the violation of these values must be rationalized by the individual.* The violation of sexual values is justified in two ways: (*a*) Everyone

is rotten. Hence prostitutes are no worse than other people, and they are less hypocritical. (*b*) Society doesn't really scorn prostitutes. Every prostitute interviewed expressed some degree of guilt feeling about her activity. This attitude ranged from mild expressions of guilt to statements like the following.

I will rot in hell for what I am doing. If you don't know what you are doing is sinful, then it is not so bad. But it is an unpardonable sin if you know what you are doing is sinful and keep on sinning.

My father told me two things: "Don't ever become a prostitute and don't marry a nigger."

Several respondents reflected in their defensive attitudes their imputation of middle-class disapproval on the part of the interviewers. These responses took the form of an attack on men or women, the world in general, or they reflected the attitude that prostitution did not mean a person was bad.

Men are . . . shrimps. Show me the man that's worth killing and I'll do the job.

Little chippies in bars give it away for a couple of beers.

This business doesn't keep you from having good children. Religion is right. It's a good thing. What we do doesn't affect religious feelings—being a wife, mother, housewife.

Other people look down on you. Deep down inside it hurts, but you ignore it . . . biggest majority are nice people. Several of the vice squad men hold the squad car door open for me [when they arrest her].

3. *The rationalization by prostitutes violating social taboos against commercial sex behavior takes the form of exaggerating other values,[15] particularly those of financial success, and for some the unselfish assumption of the financial burden*

---

[15] Gresham M. Sykes and David Matza, *loc. cit.*

of people dependent upon them. Support for these justifications is found through reference groups, real or fictional, whose values the prostitute internalizes and thus is able to act in a consistent and "normal" manner. The behavior of prostitutes is not abnormal given the norms of those groups with which they identify themselves.

We identified two principal types of reference group orientations: one we labeled the *criminal world contraculture* and the other *dual worlds,* the world of prostitution and the middle-class world of American society.

The criminal world contraculture. The principal characteristic of this type of prostitute is a strong identification with criminals and with those on the edge of the criminal world—Hobohemians. Yinger argues for the use of the concept *contraculture* for this type of group identification:

. . . I suggest the use of the term contra-culture wherever the normative system of a group contains, as a primary element, a theme of conflict with the values of the total society where personality variables are directly involved in the development and maintenance of the group's values, and wherever its norms can be understood only by reference to the relationships of the group to a surrounding dominant culture.[16]

This group had the greatest contempt for middle-class, "proper" people, whom they felt to be dull, frightened, and hypocritical. On the other hand, they made some attempt to justify their behavior by appealing to such dominant social values as financial success, their ability to move in "big business" circles, and being good mothers.

One respondent in this group said that prostitution was a means to secure money for her husband and herself so

that they could lead an exciting life. Her husband is her procurer, and the group with which they associate is composed of people connected with prostitution. They are heavy drinkers, and many of them are addicts. They appear to be carefree and irresponsible, deciding at a moment's notice to go off on trips together. A vice squad officer related an incident wherein this group decided to dig a swimming pool in a back yard. They dug intermittently for several weeks, but finally gave up the project and left on a trip.

Another respondent stated that she liked the easy money. She had gotten tired of working twelve to fourteen hours a day as a waitress.

Another respondent displayed a great deal of satisfaction from claiming to be a big spender, wearing good clothes, and going to expensive restaurants and night clubs. She also associated with a semi-criminal group. She bragged about X,

. . . a very wealthy businessman who pays me twenty-five to thirty dollars an evening just for my company. He takes me to the best places in town for dinner and dancing, and buys me expensive gifts. And I've never been in bed with the man! He told me that I mingled well with the finest people. He said once, "You act like a lady." She also mentioned a boy friend who was in trouble with the Kansas City police.

This respondent, the only one in the criminal subculture who had children, stated that she was "a good mother" who visited her children regularly. However, her account of the break-up of her first marriage indicated that this self-evaluation, as well as the characterization that she acted like a lady, might be questioned.

My husband started running around. I wanted to make him leave so I could keep the children. I cut him off, cursed him, and

[16] J. Milton Yinger, "Contraculture and Subculture," *American Sociological Review,* 25:625–35 (Oct., 1960).

cut him with a knife, but I couldn't make him go.

Her children lived with her first husband and his second wife. When she visited her children once, she told her ex-husband that his present wife, "had better be good to my kids or I'll stomp her in a mudhole."

The final respondent in this group also stressed the luxurious life she leads as a prostitute and aligned herself with a criminal group. Like the second respondent she stressed her claim to association with the "best" people in the city and her attendance at social functions where such people gather. A vice squad officer said that she had been arrested while they were investigating a tip that she was harboring a criminal who was a known drug peddler.

These four respondents were generally friendly in their feelings toward their clients and middle-class society in general. As indicated above, they maintained with considerable pride that they associated with the best people. Toward their clients they expressed some ambivalence:

Most of my clients are nice guys. . . . Most of them are married. . . . I like older men because younger men look down on you.

Some men take it out on you because they feel guilt about cheating on their wives. . . . I don't hold it against married men for going to prostitutes. Actually, it teaches them the values of affection because prostitutes are so cold. . . . All in all they are pretty nice.

Dual worlds. The five cases which fell into this category were characterized by a strong identification with their families and a rejection of the world of prostitutes which they were in, but not of. Two of the respondents claimed to be supporting their husbands and children, while the other two lived alone and claimed to be supporting children in other states whom they visited occasionally. The two married prostitutes said that their husbands acted as procurers for them, but for no other women. This group strongly and consistently expressed middle-class values. Unlike those in the criminal subculture, they never swore or used obscene words. They sought constantly to assure the interviewers that they were excellent mothers who made great sacrifices for their husbands, children, and relatives. They professed religious beliefs, and the two married respondents claimed that their associates (with the exception of their husbands) were not prostitutes or criminals. The two single prostitutes said that they associated with no one except their families whom they visited occasionally in another town. They resisted questions about their clients and other aspects of the business of prostitution. In short, they have seemingly dichotomized their world successfully by depersonalizing their prostitute roles and living almost entirely in the dominant world of American middle-class values.

Sherif and Cantril have noted that the ego can be dissociated from the self under certain extreme situations, and they illustrated this concept with a reference to the autobiography of a London prostitute who wrote, "I have moments when I realize that I am a person to no one. . . . The act of sex I could go through because *I hardly seemed to be taking part in it. . . . Indeed, it was scarcely happening even to me: It was happening to something lying on a bed that had a vague connection with me. . . .*" [17]

All of the respondents reported a certain amount of dissociation in their initial commercial experience. What would seem to distinguish the *dual worlds* groups from

[17] Muzafer Sherif and Hadley Cantril, *The Psychology of Ego-Involvements* (New York: Wiley, 1947), p. 387.

other groups was that this initial dissociation was continued and strengthened. The other two groups reported varying degrees of dissociation or none at all, some respondents claiming that they occasionally participated emotionally in the sex act and enjoyed it. Because of their middle-class moral values most of the *dual worlds* group avoided the topic of sex completely. The members of this group had successfully repressed their prostitute role and justified it as a self-sacrificing necessity to support those who were helpless and dependent upon them.

One of the married prostitutes in this group said that when she became pregnant her husband left her. She became a prostitute to support herself and her child. Her present husband is an unemployed tile-setter. She apologized for her husband by saying that there isn't too much demand for tile-setters. She claimed that she was supporting six persons and herself.

They don't know what I do for a living, except my husband. I see my little girl often. About once a week. I don't work weekends so I can go see her.

. . . My sister just got a job, but she's not on her feet yet. She has a tiny baby. Her husband is in the penitentiary. [Embarrassed laugh.]

The other married prostitute also claimed to be supporting an unemployed husband, two children, and her mother. Her mother takes care of her children and none of them knows that she is a prostitute:

I think that I am a good mother who takes care of her children. I love my family very much. I have a normal family life other than being a prostitute. I hope that my husband can find a job and gets to working steadily again so I can be an ordinary housewife.

Of the single prostitutes in this group, one had five children by a previous marriage and the other had never been married. The first strongly identified herself with her children, while the second strongly identified herself with her parents. Neither of them associated intimately with other people. Both claimed they had become prostitutes in order to care for their children or their parents.

I am very proud of my family. Even though the mother is a prostitute it doesn't reflect on her family—this business doesn't keep you from having good children. I keep my children in the best private schools and colleges in Texas. One of them married very well. They don't know what I do.

The respondent who identified herself with her parents maintained that her father had given her the best of everything as a child, but she had failed to live up to his expectations because she was too much like him. Nevertheless, she helped both parents financially:

My parents are the most wonderful people alive. I like 'em both but my mother is easier to get along with. Dad and I fight like cats and dogs. Both alike. He thinks I'm two years old. He said, "I knew the day you was born you'd be just like me." He's got suspicious of my work, but not my mother. She had an operation—cancer of the brain. I gave him [father] four hundred dollars and three hundred more after I came back from Chicago. He said, "Myra, I know what you're doing, but for God's sake don't let your mother know."

All four respondents in the *dual worlds* category expressed middle-class values:

I have some friends, some are married women, and some work.

My husband and I run around with other couples where the wife isn't a prostitute.

I got lots of friends not even connected with hustling. Went with a Kansas City dick for a long time.

I don't associate with hustling people. Half their husbands are in McAlester [state penitentiary] or the county jail.

Alienation. The six respondents who fell into this group were characterized by feelings of normlessness, apathy, lack of direction or future goal orientation. They identified themselves with no one and felt their lives to be empty and meaningless. Two of them were young: one an eighteen-year-old who was new to the profession, and the other a nineteen-year-old who had been a prostitute for one year. It is possible that the newest recruit's sense of alienation will become modified as she becomes less a stranger to her environment. The third respondent had been a prostitute for ten years. The length of time in prostitution is evidently not a factor in alienation, however, since the second youngest respondent in this group had been a prostitute for one year, and the prostitute with the longest record (eleven years) seemed to be well integrated in a criminal subculture. As noted above, all of this group dissociated themselves from the sex act.

Their conditions of alienation may be summarized by the following selected quotations:

I been in this racket ten years, I guess it's too late to get out. . . . I got no future; I been married four times and that's enough. . . . I don't care. I spent a hundred and fifty dollars over the weekend on drinking and gambling. I can't save. But I kicked the habit cold turkey. [Another respondent in the *dual worlds* category, who knew this prostitute, said: "Hustling's got the best of Jerry. She's drunk all the time. Girls like that are weak. They got no will power."] I got no friends; everybody's rotten, anymore. Women are as bad as men. Women ain't worth a damn. I'm usually too drunk to know what's going on [sex act].

I live by myself and have no friends. I just sleep and hustle at the night club. No, TV shows and books just bore me. Daydreams? Why daydream when you can't be out doing the things you daydream about? . . . Just before you came in, I was out standing in the rain watching the world cry because it's

been so screwed up by all the bastards in it. [This respondent was interviewed in a night club.]

I was drunk when I was arrested—had been drinking for several days. I was too drunk to care. I don't live with anybody. I don't know anyone in this town, except the porter [procurer]. My parents don't care about me, they put me in an Indian boarding school and I ran away from it. Drinking is very bad. I've been so bad I decided I might as well go all the way. I used to walk around town late at night and once a porter from one of the hotels stopped me and tried to get me to start working. He asked me twice. I felt it didn't matter. I was sober when I started, but I had to get drunk to finish it.

Summary and Conclusions

The present study is mainly heuristic. We have been concerned with the problem of self-respect. Assuming that commercialized sexual activity is condemned by general social norms in the United States, how do prostitutes maintain a consistent self-image?

The interviews with fifteen prostitutes provided us with data which we feel are related to these questions. The interviews provided support for the following propositions:

1. The . . . isolated individual in the urban society comes [more readily] to define as acceptable, patterns of behavior condemned by general social values. . . .
2. The general social values have some impact on the isolated individual. Therefore, the violation of these values must be rationalized by the individual.
3. The rationalizations by prostitutes violating sexual taboos against commercial sex behavior take the form of exaggerating other values, particularly those of financial success, and for some the unselfish assumption of the financial burden of people dependent

upon them. Two types of reference group orientation important for self-justification were identified: the *criminal world* and the *dual worlds* categories. A third category of alienated individuals was discerned. . . .

Patient Culture and the Evaluation of Self * †

HOWARD B. KAPLAN, INA BOYD, AND
SAMUEL E. BLOOM

A variety of studies of mental hospitals and wards have described features of the social structure which tend to induce stress in patients, and their response to such stress. Among these features are intrastaff conflicts, overlapping lines of authority, institutional change, lack of clarity of role definition, conflicting values, and inadequate communication of values between patients and staff.[1] In this paper we shall describe some patterned responses of patient groups to the stresses associated with changes in their self-concepts and self-evaluations which derive from two factors: the therapeutic process itself and the negative image of "the mental patient."

It has been observed that patient groups can function so as to resist institutional values or to effect a more constructive adaptation to the dominant institutional culture.[2] Various deviant patterns—including collective disturbance, withdrawal, physical assault, and

* Reprinted by special permission of the authors and The William Alanson White Psychiatric Foundation, Inc., from *Psychiatry: Journal for the Study of Interpersonal Processes*, Vol. 27 (May, 1964), pp. 116–26. Copyright 1964 by The William Alanson White Psychiatric Foundation, Inc.

† Revision of a paper read at the annual meeting of the American Sociological Association, August, 1963. This research was supported by a grant from the Hogg Foundation for Mental Health and by the Veterans Administration Hospital, Houston, Texas.

1 Alfred H. Stanton and Morris S. Schwartz, *The Mental Hospital;* New York, Basic Books, 1954. Elaine and John Cumming, "The Locus of Power in a Large Mental Hospital," *Psychiatry* (1956) 19:361–369. Jules Henry, "The Formal Social Structure of a Psychiatric Hospital," *Psychiatry* (1954) 17:139–151. Harvey L. Smith, "Two Lines of Authority: The Hospital's Dilemma," *Modern Hospital* (1955) 84(March):59–64. John and Elaine Cumming, "Social Equilibrium and Social Change in the Large Mental Hospital," pp. 49–72, and Charlotte Green Schwartz, "Problems for Psychiatric Nurses in Playing a New Role on a Mental Hospital Ward," pp. 402–426, in *The Patient and the Mental Hospital,* edited by Milton Greenblatt, Daniel J. Levinson, and Richard H. Williams; Glencoe, Ill., Free Press, 1957. LaVerne F. Irvine and S. Joel Deery, III, "An Investigation of Problem Areas Relating to the Therapeutic Community Concept," *Mental Hygiene* (1961) 45:367–373. Robert N. Rapoport, Rhona Rapoport, and Irving Rosow, *Community as Doctor;* London, Tavistock Publications, 1959. William Caudill and others, "Social Structure and Interaction Processes on a Psychiatric Ward," *Amer. J. Orthopsychiatry* (1952) 22:314–334.

2 Norman A. Polansky, Robert B. White, and Stuart C. Miller, "Determinants of the Role-Image of the Patient in a Psychiatric Hospital," in *The Patient and the Mental Hospital* (see footnote 1); p. 401.

duplicity—have been observed to be, in large measure, generated by informal patient group processes.[3] On the other hand, several investigators have described patterned responses of patient groups that have served the therapeutic purposes of the system. Caudill and his colleagues have observed that the patient culture provided informal pressures to conform to staff values, and that patient cliques functioned to increase social interaction, to act as mutual therapy groups, and to provide opportunities for "letting off steam." [4] Rosenberg reported that a patient-council group functioned to prevent extreme withdrawal by certain patients.[5] Fox described several patterns of patients' behavior on a metabolic ward that served to reduce the tension associated with their chronic disabilities.[6] Dunham and Weinberg interpreted the patient culture as providing the new patient with techniques for adjusting to other patients and to hospital life in general, and as facilitating the release of improved patients.[7] Similarly, in an earlier report, we identified two types of patient cliques that were described as functioning to support staff values, to socialize new patients, and to provide the patients with a means of withdrawing from dependence on institutional values preparatory to discharge.[8]

In general, then, patient groups tend to generate patterned responses to stress. These patterns may be deviant in the sense that they subvert the institutionalized values, or they may be congruent with the system's therapeutic goals. While many sources of strain are to be found in any type of organization and are not uniquely associated with mental hospitals and psychiatric wards, the two tension-inducing factors discussed here are specific to these settings since they derive from the nature of the therapeutic process itself, and the public and institutional image of the mentally ill. These experiences are intimately related to the very core of the patients' self-image and, in the absence of counteracting influences, tend to generate or confirm a negative self-evaluation.

Concerning the influence of treatment, it is in the nature of standard methods of psychodynamic therapy to uncover and interpret the characterologic defenses of the patient. He is forced to expose and to question modes of adaptation which, as imperfect as they may be, constitute the means whereby he maintains an acceptable identity.[9] The exposure of these defenses and the release of underlying conflicts constitute anxiety-generating experiences.[10] It is not surprising, therefore, that the patient in individual psy-

---

[3] William Caudill and Edward Stainbrook, "Some Covert Effects of Communication Difficulties in a Psychiatric Hospital," *Psychiatry* (1954) 17:27–40. William Caudill, "Social Processes in a Collective Disturbance on a Psychiatric Ward," pp. 438–471, and David A. Hamburg, "Therapeutic Aspects of Communication and Administrative Policy in the Psychiatric Section of a General Hospital," pp. 91–107, in *The Patient and the Mental Hospital* (see footnote 1). Erving Goffman, *Asylums;* Garden City, N.Y., Doubleday, 1961. See also Stanton and Schwartz, in footnote 1.

[4] See Caudill, in footnote 1.

[5] Larry Rosenberg, "Social Status and Participation among a Group of Chronic Schizophrenics," *Human Relations* (1962) 15:365–377.

[6] Renée C. Fox, *Experiment Perilous;* Glencoe, Ill., Free Press, 1959.

[7] H. Warren Dunham and S. Kirson Weinberg, *The Culture of the State Mental Hospital;* Detroit, Wayne State Univ. Press, 1960.

[8] Samuel W. Bloom, Ina Boyd, and Howard B. Kaplan, "Emotional Illness and Interaction Process: A Study of Patient Groups," *Social Forces* (1962) 41 (December): 135–141.

[9] Lewis R. Wolberg, *The Technique of Psychotherapy;* New York, Grune & Stratton, 1954; p. 463.

[10] Milton Greenblatt, "The Psychiatrist as Social System Clinician," in *The Patient and the Mental Hospital* (see footnote 1); p. 318.

chotherapy often interprets therapy as an "attack on his philosophy of life, as an assault on his secret wishes and expectations." [11] Similarly, in hospitals which attempt to create "a therapeutic community," the "total knowledge" aspect of the program is sometimes interpreted as "making its participants especially vulnerable and it is sometimes difficult for the patient to feel that he is being helped rather than 'attacked.' " [12]

The second specific source of stress for the mental patient is the severely negative aspect of public and institutional attitudes toward mental illness. The stigma attached to his status is attested to by the public reaction of "isolation and denial," [13] and by reports of the families of mental patients. [14] Very often, the stigma is intensified by hospital routine and the attitudes that are ascribed to the staff. The "stripping process" which deprives the patient of many of the personal possessions which symbolize his identity, and the staff attitudes which are interpreted as autocratic or condescending are experienced by the patient as an "assault upon the self." [15] These experiences often lead to feelings of inferiority and guilt. The patient comes to recognize that by being "mentally ill" he possesses an attribute that is defined as a social stigma. Associated with this awareness is a loss in self-esteem that may adversely affect the course of the treatment process. [16]

Procedure

The setting. [17]—The patients studied were the occupants of an open male psychiatric ward, one of nine psychiatric wards in the general Veterans Administration hospital in Houston, Texas. The ward, consisting of some 46 beds, was thought of as an experimental ward where new methods of patient care could be tried prior to adoption by other wards.

The ward philosophy can be characterized as that of the "therapeutic community" outlined by Maxwell Jones. [18] It emphasized a democratic and humane orientation. Such innovations in this hospital as the intensive use of group psychotherapy and patient government can be traced to this philosophy.

The ward staff consisted of a psychiatrist, psychologist, social worker, nurse, and three aides. In addition, a psychiatric resident and two psychologists participated as group therapy leaders. The hospital departments of occupational, correctional, industrial, and educational therapy were also utilized by the ward routinely.

The patients were selected for the ward on the assumption that they would benefit sufficiently from the program to become candidates for discharge within a short period of time (up to six months). The average length of hospitalization during the course of the study was 66.8 days. As would be expected, the monthly

---

[11] See footnote 9.

[12] Maxwell Jones and Robert Rapoport, "The Absorption of New Doctors into a Therapeutic Community," in *The Patient and the Mental Hospital* (see footnote 1); p. 252.

[13] Elaine and John Cumming, *Closed Ranks;* Cambridge, Mass., Harvard Univ. Press, 1957.

[14] Howard E. Freeman and Ozzie G. Simmons, "Feeling of Stigma Among Relatives of Former Mental Patients," *Social Problems* (1961) 8:312–321. John A. Clausen and Marian R. Yarrow, "The Impact of Mental Illness on the Family," *J. Social Issues* (1955) 11(4):3–67.

[15] See Goffman, in footnote 3.

[16] Erving Goffman, in *The Patient and the Mental Hospital* (see footnote 1); p. 507. Enid Mills, *Living with Mental Illness;* London, Routledge and Paul, 1962.

[17] A more detailed description of the setting is presented in Bloom, Boyd, and Kaplan (see footnote 8).

[18] Maxwell Jones, *The Therapeutic Community;* New York, Basic Books, 1953.

turnover was relatively high. For the seven months of the study the mean *monthly* turnover (number of discharges during a given month in proportion to the average daily patient load) was .43.

Eighty percent of the patients were diagnosed as anxiety or depressive reactions, fourteen percent as personality disorders, and some six percent as psychotic disorders. However, the more severe psychotics were accepted on the ward only after they were judged to be capable of participating in a program which required them to monitor their own behavior to a large extent.

This ward, then, possesses characteristics which sharply delineate it from other wards in this hospital as well as from other institutional settings. The predominantly neurotic patient population participated in an open ward with an active treatment program and a high staff-patient ratio. The patients were well aware of the possibility of "improvement" as evidenced by the relatively high turnover. This situation is in sharp contrast to those of long-term or low activity treatment settings, some of which are discussed below.

Data.—A daily diary was kept by a graduate sociology student acting as a participant observer throughout a period of seven months. For the first month he lived on the ward on a twenty-four hour basis and for the next six months on an eight-hour daytime basis.

The observer was known to the patients as a student observer but after a brief period of time was fully accepted by the other patients, having successfully adopted their manners, attitudes, and dress, and having participated in all major activities, including work assignments and group therapy.

The observer was instructed to record, with as much detail as possible, the content and circumstances of the patients' conversations and other activities. The following report is based upon a content analysis of these notes supplemented by those of the authors in their regular observations of the various ward activities.[19]

Analysis.—The analysis was originally initiated for the purpose of discerning the major mechanisms of social control utilized by patient groups as modes of adaptation to a variety of stresses associated with the hospital experience. The following observations, however, specifically focus upon those mechanisms that relate to the strains induced by: (1) the nature of the therapeutic process, and (2) the public and institutional evaluation of the mentally ill.

The Therapeutic Process

On this psychiatric ward, as on others,[20] the majority of the patients are socialized to recognize that they "have problems" and "need help," and that in order to achieve therapeutic progress it is necessary to attack the defensive patterns which they utilize to maintain an acceptable self-image. They learn that they are members of a "therapeutic community" in which each person should become intimately involved with the problems of his fellow patients. However, the patients also wish to escape the pressures associated with these injunctions. They feel a need to define the patient role in such a way that they can live with their "character-defenses left reasonably

---

[19] The authors in the course of their duties as sociological consultants (HBK, SWB) or Chief of the open wards (IB) regularly participated in staff conferences, attended group therapy sessions and ward government meetings, and periodically observed informal patient activities.

[20] See, for example, Jones, in footnote 18, and Caudill, in footnote 1.

unchallenged, and with minimal constant tension in adaptation." [21]

On the present ward, the patients have adapted to this conflict, in part, by an appeal to two general principles: (1) the division of the patient life space into mutually exclusive "therapeutic" and "nontherapeutic" spheres; and (2) the invoking of the principle of therapeutic primacy in those situations that are not so easily defined.

Therapeutic versus nontherapeutic spheres.—A number of related norms defining the patient status are apparently devoted to the strict separation of the "sick role" and its attendant stresses from the relatively tension-free activities of "everyday life." This bifurcation of the patients' experiences is accomplished by explicitly defining the therapeutic situation as being confined to particular times, places, and role-partners. In all other situations the obligations ordinarily associated with the sick role are not applicable.

Specifically, a therapeutic definition of the situation is confined to those circumstances: (1) when staff members are present; (2) that occur within group therapy rooms; and (3) that involve interaction between members of the same therapy group.

First, the patients express a desire to have staff members present at all purportedly therapeutic activities. In keeping with the philosophy of the therapeutic community, and in an attempt to allow the patients a measure of responsibility, many such activities are administered by the patients. These include ward government meetings and discussions following showings of documentary movies. These activities are notably more successful when staff members are present. Characteristically, the patients verbalize their sentiments by stating that while, for example, patient leadership of the discussions following movies is a "good idea" they still prefer the staff members "to be there in the audience." Their physical presence signals the therapeutic relevance of the situation.

A number of attitudes relating to the social distance between the patients and staff appear to serve the same function. In general, the patients seem to favor the maintenance of a "professional" relationship as symbolized by distinctive titles and garb. On one occasion, during a ward government meeting, the physician asked the patients to give their opinions concerning the possible introduction of the practice of calling doctors by their first names. The great majority of the patients expressed opposition to this proposal. On other occasions they expressed similar strong resistance to suggestions that the staff members dispense with their white coats and instead wear "everyday" clothing.

It is suggested that the intensity of affect associated with these attitudes is an indication of a need for the patients to clearly differentiate between professional (therapeutic) and nonprofessional relationships. Regardless of any other functions that may be implicit in the sentiments, the *identifiable* presence of staff members serves as a visual cue to signify the appropriateness of therapeutic norms in the situation.

A second type of differentiating cue is provided by specific locations. The most significant of these are the group therapy rooms. On this ward, all patients are assigned to one of several groups which meet regularly for purposes of group psychotherapy. Group methods of treatment are highly valued and individual patient-therapist consultations are relatively rare occurrences.

Each group is assigned to its own

[21] See footnote 2.

group therapy room with its own group leader. The rooms serve as intimate retreats for the members as well as the loci for the regularly scheduled therapy sessions.

A host of affectively laden norms relate to appropriate behavior with respect to the group room. The privacy of these groups must be profoundly respected by all patients and, indeed, except on rare occasions, the members of a group will refrain from entering another group's room with invitation. Violations of these norms are severely criticized. The stringency of the sanctions is accounted for by the fact that the room is associated with therapeutic activities even at times other than scheduled sessions. Whenever a patient wants to discuss some of his problems, he seeks out some group members and proceeds with them to their group room. Any other members who happen to be present cease their individual activities and join in the discussion. The most intimate revelations concerning group members' problems are often made during such spontaneous sessions. The room thus symbolizes for the patients the activity performed therein. It represents a spatial cue for the appropriateness of therapeutic norms.

A third element in the differentiating process relates to interpatient activity. As one would expect from the above, the norms applying to interactions between patients who are members of the same therapy group are different from those regulating the interpatient behavior of persons who are not members of the same group, whether or not the interaction occurs within the confines of the group room.

It is a convention on the ward that personal problems should be discussed with members of one's own group rather than with any patient at random. A re-

lated norm forbids the discussion of any observed group interaction with anyone but the appropriate group or staff members. If any of a group's members are questioned about another member by an "outsider" the questions are ignored. A newcomer who has not yet been properly socialized will be immediately informed of his breach of good conduct if he inappropriately discusses group activities. The emphasis on the confidential nature of group interaction precludes the comparison of group activities, techniques, and therapists to such an extent that the patients will often comment that were it not for the presence of friends in other groups, they would not even be aware of the existence of those groups.

These three sets of norms constitute, for the patients, an adequate definition of the therapeutic situation. The explicit identification of therapeutic interaction as occurring in the presence of or with staff members, in group therapy rooms, or between members of the same therapy group, serves, at the same time, to distinguish all other categories of activity in an equally specific set of terms. The patient's "nontherapeutic" activities tend to be perceived as "normal living," in which the norms are more typically those which apply outside the institution. It would appear that this part of patient life functions to relieve some of the strain inherent in the therapeutic process. It provides a relatively tension-free period in which the patient can escape from the feeling of "assault upon self."

The patients' bifurcation of their experience into therapeutic and nontherapeutic spheres is analogous to a form of resistance reported for individual psychotherapy. Wolberg has stated that a patient will sometimes dissociate the treatment hour from his other life experiences.[22] While he will freely discuss

---

[22] See footnote 9; pp. 467–468.

his interpersonal relationships, the patient does not see how the content of the treatment hour relates to his normal way of life. He, thus, "will lead a dual existence and seemingly be unable to fill the chasm between what happens in treatment and his experiences outside of treatment."[23] However, there is a major difference between this dissociation process in individual treatment and the differentiating process that takes place on the ward.[24] In the ward, the division of the patient's experience is made in such a way that the therapeutic part *includes* informal group interaction and any benefits that may derive from this experience.

Other studies suggest further comparisons, but again with important differences. Goffman has suggested that in the large state mental hospital the patients respond to the regimentation, to the coercive staff behavior, and, in general, to the assault upon the self by an adaptation characterized by duplicity.[25] The patient does strive to do what the staff wishes, but, unlike the patients on this ward, he does so in a defensive and opportunistic maneuver to avoid punishment and gain privileges. He secretly opposes the staff values and, in the patient society, finds a separate system of values and an organized pattern of relationships which allow him to preserve his self-respect. This suggests a method of by-

passing therapy rather than, as we have observed, a social means for supporting and sustaining the therapeutic function.

A quite different picture is presented by Caudill and his associates, who reported that patients did not clearly distinguish between therapeutic and non-therapeutic relationships.[26] However, this particular study was done in a small private teaching hospital with a psychoanalytic orientation. A heavy emphasis was placed on the daily "hour" in which each patient saw his therapist. The patient, under these conditions, may not feel the same kind of "assault upon self" which is so widely reported in larger, public hospitals.[27]

Therapeutic primacy.—On the present ward the patients, in the therapeutic sphere of their experiences, fully accept the fact of their illness and the value of the therapeutic process, unlike the *apparent* acceptance described by Goffman.[28] Indeed, in situations that are so ambiguously structured that they may be interpreted from either the therapeutic or nontherapeutic perspective, the patients will invoke the principle of therapeutic primacy. That is, they assign legitimate priority to therapeutic values and definitions of the situation.

Many personal affronts between patients are interpreted from this point of view. They are rationalized as "under-

[23] See footnote 9; p. 468.

[24] Another interesting manifestation of this mechanism is in the case of the hospital-physician—that is, the physician in charge of the total treatment of the psychiatric patient in the hospital. The physician often perceives a conflict between his psychotherapeutic and administrative orientations. He tends to resolve his dilemma by a discrete division of his role so that he directs his psychological insights toward the problems brought to him as "a kind of psychotherapist" and deals in an "administrative" manner "with the patient's day-to-day affairs in living in the hospital, his activities, medications, privileges, etc." Irving Kartus and Herbert J. Schlesinger, "The Psychiatric Hospital-Physician and His Patient," in *The Patient and the Mental Hospital* (see footnote 1); p. 291.

[25] See Goffman, in footnote 3.

[26] See Caudill, in footnote 1.

[27] The lack of an institutionalized differentiation may result from the failure of the institution to provide for any formally organized patient activities other than the individual patient-physician conference.

Although the authors did not so interpret it, the "social clique" may have served as an attempt at just such a differentiation.

[28] See Goffman, in footnote 3.

standable" in view of the man's illness. On one occasion, for example, patient A became disturbed about the sudden aloofness of patient B, with whom he had associated rather intimately since B's appearance on the ward. Although A at first seemed uncertain as to whether this behavior should be interpreted as a personal affront, he eventually accepted the explanation that the new attitude was a "symptom" of B's illness.

Similar observations were interpreted by Caudill as a general tendency toward "the muting of outerworld distinctions." [29] We are suggesting that this phenomenon is more specific than Caudill implied. It is one of the processes whereby a highly volatile social system maintains its stability.

Just as a patient can accept an affront because of the "illness" of the accuser, by the same principle of therapeutic primacy he can more easily accept criticism since it would ultimately benefit him to be informed of his shortcomings. Thus, a patient might be accused of "homesteading" ("living off" the VA beyond the time he is receiving therapeutic benefits, or without motivation to get well) or "not leveling" (being secretive or dishonest in the communication of personal data during group therapy). On the rare occasions when a patient rebels against such criticism, the group will deny his right to feelings of indignation. This is illustrated by the following incident.

Certain of the therapy groups often met in the absence of the group leader. On one such occasion group member C angrily announced that there was an "informer" in the group who had told the ward physician that C was not participating enough in the group therapy sessions. While under other circumstances (nontherapeutic) it would be a violation of the group norm to "inform" to the authorities,[30] in this instance the group countenanced the activity and instructed C that such behavior on his part *should* be brought to the attention of the physician for C's own good and that, indeed, several of the group members had done so.

The principle of therapeutic primacy serves to protect the patients' self-conception in two ways. First, by asserting the priority of the therapeutic values, the patients implicity recognize another set of values (nontherapeutic) which we have already interpreted as having a defensive function. Second, the impact of insults and criticism upon the self-esteem of patients is softened by their being interpreted as due to the illness of the other patient, rather than as personally intended.

Evaluation of the Mentally Ill

A second type of threat to the patient's self-evaluation is derived from his perception of the negative attitudes toward the mentally ill displayed by the general public and the hospital staff. Concern over the stigma attached to the status of mental patient is most evident in newly arrived patients and in those whose release is imminent. In the context of therapeutic discussions the patients discuss "the outside" with feelings of foreboding and resignation. They fear that they will be set apart as mentally incompetent in their hometowns, and often express their intentions of "explaining" their hospitalization in terms of somatic

---

[29] See Caudill, in footnote 1; p. 317.

[30] On the present ward incidents of petty thievery, for example, are not regarded as therapeutically relevant and are not reported to the staff. On other wards (see Stanton and Schwartz, in footnote 1) the patients *are* socialized to regard such matters as significant in relationship to the progress of the patient.

complaints. The patients accept the "fact" that with a record of psychiatric hospitalization they are limited to lower salaries and restricted from "moving up."

Similar attitudes are attributed to the hospital personnel. In addition to certain regulations which the patients interpret as implying that the patients are irresponsible and even potentially dangerous, the behavior of the clerical staff communicates the same sentiments. The patients often observed, sometimes humorously, that the secretaries manifest great fright on those occasions when they happen to find themselves alone with the patients in their offices.

The perceived public and institutional derogation of his status represents one horn of a dilemma for the patient. On the one hand he experiences great pressures to accept the fact of his illness and the therapeutic potential of the hospital. However, by becoming a patient his self-image is threatened insofar as he recognizes the prevailing negative attitudes toward his illness.

The patients, thus, experience a conflict similar to that described above in connection with the therapeutic process. If they are to achieve maximum therapeutic benefits from their experience, they must resolve this conflict in a way that permits acceptance of the fact of their patienthood while minimizing the stress occasioned by the perceived disparagement of their status.

Among the patterns of patient behavior that apparently function to mitigate this stress are those that: (1) assert the commonality of illness among the total patient population, (2) favorably compare their situation with those of less privileged patient groups, (3) deny the superiority of the staff and extra-institutional population, (4) emphasize any rewards that might attach to the position of "mental patient," and (5) confine their temporal orientation to the immediate present.

The assertion of the commonality of illness.—The patients continually assert that each of them has severe problems. Indeed, the full acceptance of a patient into the group is contingent upon his admission that he has a "problem." This is illustrated by the case of the participant observer. During a group therapy session, his extensive revelation of several personal problems met with quite positive responses on the part of the other group members. One patient commented, "Seems like Bob is really getting into the group now." Another member stated that on the first day he had been hostile toward the observer because of seeing a "successful well person" but that he now "felt much better" toward the observer.

A good deal of criticism is aimed at any patient who even implicitly denies that he has emotional problems. On one occasion a therapy group considered a suggestion by the therapist that the whole group should sign up for the Human Relations Training Laboratory program which is offered on another ward. Patient D stated that he did not need it since he had always "gotten along real well with people." Patient E became quite angry with D, interpreting the remark as implying that D was not as disturbed as the other patients: "You must have had some problems with people or you wouldn't be here in Cuckoo College."

This emphasis upon the commonality of their problems functions to provide mutual support among the patients, and facilitates their acceptance of a stigmatized social position.

The judgment of other patients as more unfavorably situated.—The patients and procedures on locked wards are the objects of derisive humor and criticism. The facial expressions, walk, and incoherent verbalizations of these patients are ridiculed. The locked ward represents, for the patients on our open ward, "the bottom," and is seen as having nontherapeutic value. The open-ward patients view their own situation as more favorable since, relative to the locked ward, they experience greater freedom and such beneficent procedures as group therapy and ward government. Furthermore, they distinguish between themselves, who have "problems," and those on the locked ward, who are "nuts," "buggy," "crazy," or "sick." The occasional presence on their own ward of a more severely disturbed patient serves to reinforce this distinction.

The denial of the superiority of the staff and extrahospital population.—The denial of the superiority of "outsiders" often takes the form of hostile humor. Thus, a patient who was experiencing difficulty in threading the film into the projector commented, "This projector is like a lot of ministers I have known—not worth a Goddamn." Again, during an informal break in a group therapy session the patients' barbs were aimed at the hypocrisy of successful businessmen and public officials.

Such hostility is most apparent following direct contact with representatives of the outside world. For example, one of the therapy groups volunteered to appear before an unmarried adult church group as part of a discussion of psychotherapeutic methods. For days following the presentation the patients aimed humorous barbs at the manners, morals, and "psychic instability" of the audience, accompanied by such remarks as, "They're in worse shape than we are."

Similarly, the staff members often become objects of deflating humor. Most particularly, they are alleged to be involved in illicit sexual relationships or to be almost pathologically interested in sexual material.

In attributing such "faults" to the staff and public, the patients deny the significance of the stigma associated with their own status by detracting from the source of the negative judgments.

Emphasis of the rewarding aspects of the status.—The most frequent comment about advantages concerns the monetary evaluation of the aid which they receive: "The kind of help we're getting [in the hospital] would cost us a fortune on the outside." In addition, the patients point to the protective nature of the hospitalization experience, in that they are temporarily relieved from a variety of obligations, financial and otherwise.

The patients will often go to great lengths to ascribe "benefits" to their position. For example, some point to the advantage they hold in interpersonal conflict since their opponents, believing the patients to be crazy, fear inequitable reprisals. Others state that their position gives them a degree of immunity from the police. That is, they are treated more leniently when it becomes known that they are psychiatric patients at the VA hospital.

In general, by emphasizing any rewards associated with their situation, the patients are enabled to counteract, in some measure, the effects of occupying a status that they perceive as disgraceful.

Confinement of temporal orientation to the immediate present.—In the "nontherapeutic" sphere of their existence, the patients' conversations tend to focus perfunctorily upon the activities and relationships of their immediate environment. Any references to the past are for the most part limited to tales of their sexual or pugilistic prowess. Their allusions to the future take the form of communal daydreams in which, for example, they will be "kept" in luxury by their women, or collectively make a down payment on a yacht and travel around the world.

Such temporal isolation precludes their consideration of the negative consequences of being psychiatrically hospitalized. In the "nontherapeutic" area he is thus simultaneously protected from the dangers to his self-esteem deriving from the therapeutic process and from the public and institutional image of the mentally ill. However, even within the therapeutic sphere, the patients may utilize the other defenses described above. By asserting the commonality of their problem, favorably comparing their state of being with patients on the locked wards, emphasizing the rewards associated with their position, and denying the superiority of their "accusers," the patients mitigate the stigma associated with their position and are consequently better able to accept their patienthood and the attendant stresses of the formal therapeutic process.

It has been suggested that among the goals of a therapeutic milieu is the provision of experiences that enable the patient to accept his illness, reduce his distortion of reality, gain insight into his illness, meaningfully and realistically communicate with others, reduce his anxiety, and increase his self-esteem.[31] However, very often the hospitalization experience is such that in gaining some of these goals, the patient is unable to achieve others. Specifically, many features of the patients' new environment may have important consequences for his self-concept or identity and his self-esteem. In accepting his illness the patient may come to recognize himself as occupying a status that is the object of derogatory attitudes by nonpatients.[32] In the course of treatment, by trying to gain insight into the causes of their illness, many patients "experience changes and upsets of inner balances on which an

identity of sorts was based." [33] Furthermore, the very fact of interaction between patients may lead to mutual rejection or disturbance.[34] In short, the patient's experience in the hospital may result in a confusion of his identity, a loss of self-esteem, and a consequent increase in anxiety.

Stated another way, the patient often finds himself torn between conflicting desires. In order to "get well," as he wishes, he must accept a stigmatized or deviant status and subject himself to a stress-inducing therapeutic process. But he would like to adapt to the demands of the hospital with a minimum of tension. We have observed that certain of the normative patterns constituting the patient culture serve as a systematic, if unrecognized, attempt to resolve this conflict.

First, in effectively differentiating their activities, the patients are able to submit to the stress of the therapy they recognize as necessary; they find surcease in the "normal living" activities that are relatively free from the tensions associated with the therapeutic process and with occupancy of a stigmatized status.

Second, the assignment of legitimate priority to therapeutic values permits the patient to maintain his self-esteem when affronted by another patient.

In effect, these patterns of behavior define two patient roles: When interacting with staff members or members of his therapy group, the patient seems to believe he should be honest, express his feelings, give up his defenses, accept constructive criticism, and so forth. When interacting with patients who are not members of his therapy group, he seems to believe that his behavior should be

[31] Morris S. Schwartz, "What Is a Therapeutic Milieu?," in *The Patient and the Mental Hospital* (see footnote 1); p. 131.
[32] Erving Goffman, in *The Patient and the Mental Hospital* (see footnote 1); p. 507.
[33] See footnote 2; p. 384.
[34] See footnote 31; p. 140.

affectively neutral and that he should avoid stress-inducing circumstances.

Finally, another grouping of mechanisms relates to the stigma of patienthood. In the "nontherapeutic" sphere, a pattern of temporal isolation precludes consideration of the public judgments of the patients' deviant status. In the "therapeutic" sphere, the patients respond to the awareness of their stigma with a system of patterned responses (commonality of their "problem," better situation than other patients, advantages of their position, and denial of nonpatient superiority).

The mechanisms which we have described above are certainly not unique to the setting in which they were observed. Parsons, for example, described how two of them may be utilized to minimize conflict in social situations where contradictory demands are made upon the participants.[35] The first involves the scheduling of activities so that different norms are appropriate at different times, in different places, and with different people. The second concerns the institutionalization of a system of priorities so that one obligation may have a claim to precedence over another. These mechanisms correspond to the patterns we have identified as differentiation between "therapeutic" and "nontherapeutic" spheres, and the principle of "therapeutic primacy." Similarly, the patterns of patient reactions to the public and institutional image of the mentally ill are not unlike those social processes that Goffman observes among "normal deviants,"[36] and that Thibaut

and Kelley describe for "nonvoluntary relationships."[37]

These mechanisms serve important integrating functions in such relationships, just as they do in those of the patient. We have interpreted the patient's responses primarily with respect to his identity and self-esteem. The way in which he conceives of and evaluates himself is a central concern in his treatment. It is hoped that in the course of hospitalization, the patient will develop an identity that will permit him to adjust to the demands of the outside world in a satisfying way. However, he must first adjust to the demands of his *current* environment. If these demands result in a confused identity and a loss of self-esteem, the patient's reactions may impede his therapeutic progress. However, if the current environment provides the patient with an opportunity to maintain a satisfying self-image he may achieve maximum benefits from the formal therapeutic activities.

The patterned responses of the patients that we have observed apparently function in just this way. The patient culture has partially structured the environment so that one part enables its members to maintain a temporarily satisfying identity—offering the patient "a haven from society to permit him to regain his equilibrium"[38]—while the other part enjoins them to create a more enduring and satisfying self-concept which will permit them to function effectively as members of society.

The patterns that comprise the patient

[35] Talcott Parsons, *The Social System;* Glencoe, Ill., Free Press, 1951; pp. 302–303.
[36] Erving Goffman, in *The Patient and the Mental Hospital* (see footnote 1); pp. 507–510. The term "normal deviants" refers to people who occupy stigmatized status but who, otherwise, are psychologically and culturally "normal" (p. 508).
[37] John W. Thibaut and Harold Kelley, *The Social Psychology of Groups;* New York, Wiley, 1961; pp. 169–187. "Relationships are said to be *nonvoluntary* when an individual is constrained to a relationship in which his outcomes are relatively poor and/or is excluded from alternative relationships in which his outcomes are relatively good" (p. 186).
[38] Milton Greenblatt and Theodore Lidz, "Some Dimensions of the Problem," in *The Patient and the Mental Hospital;* p. 501.

culture arise in response to the patient's needs. Those who have formal responsibility for the milieu should be aware of how these patterns function before any purposive changes, such as formally structuring the more informal aspects of patient life, are instituted. Furthermore, such awareness may provide the staff with clues to other sources of stress in the system and suggest changes that *would* make the ward a more effective therapeutic milieu.

On Neutralizing Delinquent Self-Images *

GRESHAM M. SYKES AND DAVID MATZA

The Denial of Responsibility. In so far as the delinquent can define himself as lacking responsibility for his deviant actions, the disapproval of self or others is sharply reduced in effectiveness as a restraining influence. As Justice Holmes has said, even a dog distinguishes between being stumbled over and being kicked, and modern society is no less careful to draw a line between injuries that are unintentional, i.e., where responsibility is lacking, and those that are intentional. As a technique of neutralization, however, the denial of responsibility extends much further than the claim that deviant acts are an "accident" or some similar negation of personal accountability. It may also be asserted that delinquent acts are due to forces outside of the individual and beyond his control such as unloving parents, bad companions, or a slum neighborhood. In effect, the delinquent approaches a "billiard ball" conception of himself in which he sees himself as helplessly propelled into new situations.

From a psychodynamic viewpoint, this orientation toward one's own actions may represent a profound alienation from self, but it is important to stress the fact that interpretations of responsibility are cultural constructs and not merely idiosyncratic beliefs. The similarity between this mode of justifying illegal behavior assumed by the delinquent and the implications of a "sociological" frame of reference or a "humane" jurisprudence is readily apparent.[1] It is not the validity of this orientation that concerns us here, but its function of deflecting blame attached to violations of social norms and its relative independence of a particular personality structure.[2] By learning to view himself as more acted upon than acting, the delinquent prepares the way for deviance from the dominant normative system without the necessity of a frontal assault on the norms themselves.

The Denial of Injury. A second major technique of neutralization centers on the injury or harm involved in the delinquent

* Reprinted from "Techniques of Neutralization: A Theory of Delinquency" in *American Sociological Review*, Vol. 22 (December, 1957), pp. 667–670, by permission of the authors and publisher.

[1] A number of observers have wryly noted that many delinquents seem to show a surprising awareness of sociological and psychological explanations for their behavior and are quick to point out the causal role of their poor environment.

[2] It is possible, of course, that certain personality structures can accept some techniques of neutralization more readily than others, but this question remains largely unexplored.

act. The criminal law has long made a distinction between crimes which are *mala in se* and *mala prohibita*—that is between acts that are wrong in themselves and acts that are illegal but not immoral—and the delinquent can make the same kind of distinction in evaluating the wrongfulness of his behavior. For the delinquent, however, wrongfulness may turn on the question of whether or not anyone has clearly been hurt by his deviance, and this matter is open to a variety of interpretations. Vandalism, for example, may be defined by the delinquent simply as "mischief"—after all, it may be claimed, the persons whose property has been destroyed can well afford it. Similarly, auto theft may be viewed as "borrowing," and gang fighting may be seen as a private quarrel, an agreed upon duel between two willing parties, and thus of no concern to the community at large. We are not suggesting that this technique of neutralization, labelled the denial of injury, involves an explicit dialetic. Rather, we are arguing that the delinquent frequently, and in a hazy fashion, feels that his behavior does not really cause any great harm despite the fact that it runs counter to law. Just as the link between the individual and his acts may be broken by the denial of responsibility, so may the link between acts and their consequences be broken by the denial of injury. Since society sometimes agrees with the delinquent, e.g., in matters such as truancy, "pranks," and so on, it merely reaffirms the idea that the delinquent's neutralization of social controls by means of qualifying the norms is an extension of common practice rather than a gesture of complete opposition.

The Denial of the Victim. Even if the delinquent accepts the responsibility for his deviant actions and is willing to admit that his deviant actions involve an injury or hurt, the moral indignation of self and others may be neutralized by an insistence that the injury is not wrong in light of the circumstances. The injury, it may be claimed, is not really an injury; rather, it is a form of rightful retaliation or punishment. By a subtle alchemy the delinquent moves himself into the position of an avenger and the victim is transformed into a wrong-doer. Assaults on homosexuals or suspected homosexuals, attacks on members of minority groups who are said to have gotten "out of place," vandalism as revenge on an unfair teacher or school official, thefts from a "crooked" store owner—all may be hurts inflicted on a transgressor, in the eyes of the delinquent. As Orwell has pointed out, the type of criminal admired by the general public has probably changed over the course of years and Raffles no longer serves as a hero; [3] but Robin Hood, and his latter day derivatives such as the tough detective seeking justice outside the law, still capture the popular imagination, and the delinquent may view his acts as part of a similar role.

To deny the existence of the victim, then, by transforming him into a person deserving injury is an extreme form of a phenomenon we have mentioned before, namely, the delinquent's recognition of appropriate and inappropriate targets for his delinquent acts. In addition, however, the existence of the victim may be denied for the delinquent, in a somewhat different sense, by the circumstances of the delinquent act itself. Insofar as the victim is physically absent, unknown, or a vague abstraction (as is often the case in delinquent acts committed against property), the awareness of the victim's existence is weakened. Internalized norms and anticipations of the reactions of others must somehow be activated, if they are to serve

---

[3] George Orwell, *Dickens, Dali, and Others,* New York: Reynal, 1946.

as guides for behavior; and it is possible that a diminished awareness of the victim plays an important part in determining whether or not this process is set in motion.

The Condemnation of the Condemners. A fourth technique of neutralization would appear to involve a condemnation of the condemners or, as McCorkle and Korn have phrased it, a rejection of the rejectors.[4] The delinquent shifts the focus of attention from his own deviant acts to the motives and behavior of those who disapprove of his violations. His condemners, he may claim, are hypocrites, deviants in disguise, or impelled by personal spite. This orientation toward the conforming world may be of particular importance when it hardens into a bitter cynicism directed against those assigned the task of enforcing or expressing the norms of the dominant society. Police, it may be said, are corrupt, stupid, and brutal. Teachers always show favoritism and parents always "take it out" on their children. By a slight extension, the rewards of conformity—such as material success—become a matter of pull or luck, thus decreasing still further the stature of those who stand on the side of the law-abiding. The validity of this jaundiced viewpoint is not so important as its function in turning back or deflecting the negative sanctions attached to violations of the norms. The delinquent, in effect, has changed the subject of the conversation in the dialogue between his own deviant impulses and the reactions of others; and by attacking others, the wrongfulness of his own behavior is more easily repressed or lost to view.

The Appeal to Higher Loyalties. Fifth, and last, internal and external social controls may be neutralized by sacrificing the demands of the larger society for the demands of the small social groups to which the delinquent belongs such as the sibling pair, the gang, or the friendship clique. It is important to note that the delinquent does not necessarily repudiate the imperatives of the dominant normative system, despite his failure to follow them. Rather, the delinquent may see himself as caught up in a dilemma that must be resolved, unfortunately, at the cost of violating the law. One aspect of this situation has been studied by Stouffer and Toby in their research on the conflict between particularistic and universalistic demands, between the claims of friendship and general social obligations, and their results suggest that "it is possible to classify people according to a predisposition to select one or the other horn of a dilemma in role conflict."[5] For our purposes, however, the most important point is that deviation from certain norms may occur not because the norms are rejected but because other norms, held to be more pressing or involving a higher loyalty, are accorded precedence. Indeed, it is the fact that both sets of norms are believed in that gives meaning to our concepts of dilemma and role conflict.

The conflict between the claims of friendship and the claims of law, or a similar dilemma, has of course long been recognized by the social scientist (and the novelist) as a common human problem. If the juvenile delinquent frequently resolves his dilemma by insisting that he must "always help a buddy" or "never squeal on a friend," even when it throws him into serious difficulties with the dominant social order, his choice remains familiar to the supposedly law-abiding.

[4] Lloyd W. McCorkle and Richard Korn, "Resocialization Within Walls," *The Annals of the American Academy of Political and Social Science*, 293 (May, 1954), pp. 88–98.
[5] See Samuel A. Stouffer and Jackson Toby, "Role Conflict and Personality," in *Toward a General Theory of Action*, edited by Talcott Parsons and Edward A. Shils, Cambridge: Harvard University Press, 1951, p. 494.

The delinquent is unusual, perhaps, in the extent to which he is able to see the fact that he acts in behalf of the smaller social groups to which he belongs as a justification for violations of society's norms, but it is a matter of degree rather than of kind.

"I didn't mean it." "I didn't really hurt anybody." "They had it coming to them." "Everybody's picking on me." "I didn't do it for myself." These slogans or their variants, we hypothesize, prepare the juvenile for delinquent acts. These "definitions of the situation" represent tangential or glancing blows at the dominant normative system rather than the creation of an opposing ideology; and they are extensions of patterns of thought prevalent in society rather than something created *de novo*.

Techniques of neutralization may not be powerful enough to fully shield the individual from the force of his own internalized values and the reactions of conforming others, for as we have pointed out, juvenile delinquents often appear to suffer from feelings of guilt and shame when called into account for their deviant behavior. And some delinquents may be so isolated from the world of conformity that techniques of neutralization need not be called into play. Nonetheless, we would argue that techniques of neutralization are critical in lessening the effectiveness of social controls and that they lie behind a large share of delinquent behavior. Empirical research in this area is scattered and fragmentary at the present time, but the work of Redl,[6] Cressey,[7] and others has supplied a body of significant data that has done much to clarify the theoretical issues and enlarge the fund of supporting evidence. Two lines of investigation seem to be critical at this stage. First, there is need for more knowledge concerning the differential distribution of techniques of neutralization, as operative patterns of thought, by age, sex, social class, ethnic group, etc. On *a priori* grounds it might be assumed that these justifications for deviance will be more readily seized by segments of society for whom a discrepancy between common social ideals and social practice is most apparent. It is also possible however, that the habit of "bending" the dominant normative system—if not "breaking" it—cuts across our cruder social categories and is to be traced primarily to patterns of social interaction within the familial circle. Second, there is need for a greater understanding of the internal structure of techniques of neutralization, as a system of beliefs and attitudes, and its relationship to various types of delinquent behavior. Certain techniques of neutralization would appear to be better adapted to particular deviant acts than to others, as we have suggested, for example, in the case of offenses against property and the denial of the victim. But the issue remains far from clear and stands in need of more information.

In any case, techniques of neutralization appear to offer a promising line of research in enlarging and systematizing the theoretical grasp of juvenile delinquency. As more information is uncovered concerning techniques of neutralization, their origins, and their consequences, both juvenile delinquency in particular, and deviation from normative systems in general may be illuminated.

---

[6] See Fritz Redl and David Wineman, *Children Who Hate,* New York: The Free Press, 1956.

[7] See D. R. Cressey, *Other People's Money,* New York: The Free Press, 1953.

The Social Integration of Queers and Peers *

ALBERT J. REISS, JR.

. . . An attempt is made in this paper to describe the sexual relation between "delinquent peers" and "adult queers" and to account for its social organization. This transaction is one form of homosexual prostitution between a young male and an adult male fellator. The adult male client pays a delinquent boy prostitute a sum of money in order to be allowed to act as a fellator. The transaction is limited to fellation and is one in which the boy develops no self-conception as a homosexual person or sexual deviator, although he perceives adult male clients as sexual deviators, "queers" or "gay boys." . . .

The Data

Information on the sexual transaction and its social organization was gathered mostly by interviews, partly by social observation of their meeting places. Though there are limitations to inferring social organization from interview data (particularly when the organization arises through behavior that is negatively sanctioned in the larger society), they provide a convenient basis for exploration.

Sex histories were gathered from 18.6 per cent of the 1008 boys between the ages of 12 and 17 who were interviewed in the Nashville, Tennessee, SMA for an investigation of adolescent conforming and deviating behavior. These represent all of the interviews of one of the interviewers during a two-month period, together with interviews with all Nashville boys incarcerated at the Tennessee State Training School for Boys. . . .

How Peers and Queers Meet

Meetings between adult male fellators and delinquent boys are easily made, because both know how and where to meet within the community space. Those within the common culture know that contact can be established within a relatively short period of time, if it is wished. The fact that meetings between peers and queers can be made easily is mute evidence of the organized understandings which prevail between the two populations.

There are a large number of places where the boys meet their clients, the fellators. Many of these points are known to all boys regardless of where they reside in the metropolitan area. This is particularly true of the central city locations where the largest number of contact points are found within a small territorial area. Each community area of the city, and certain fringe areas, inhabited by substantial numbers of lower-class persons, also have their meeting places, generally known only to the boys residing in the area.

Queers and peers typically establish contact in public or quasi-public places. Major points of contact include street corners, public parks, men's toilets in public or quasi-public places such as those in transportation depots, parks or hotels, and "second" and "third-run"

* Reprinted from *Social Problems*, Vol. 9, No. 2 (Fall, 1961), pp. 102, 104, 106–109, 112–119, by permission of the author and *Social Problems*.

movie houses (open around the clock and permitting sitting through shows). Bars are seldom points of contact, perhaps largely because they are plied by older male hustlers who lie outside the peer culture and groups, and because bar proprietors will not risk the presence of under-age boys.

There are a number of prescribed modes for establishing contact in these situations. They permit the boys and fellators to communicate intent to one another privately despite the public character of the situation. The major form of establishing contact is the "cruise," with the fellator passing "queer-corners" or locations until his effort is recognized by one of the boys. A boy can then signal—usually by nodding his head, a hand gesticulation signifying OK, following, or responding to commonly understood introductions such as "You got the time?" —that he is prepared to undertake the transaction. Entrepreneur and client then move to a place where the sexual activity is consummated, usually a place affording privacy, protection and hasty exit. "Dolly," a three-time loser at the State Training School, describes one of these prescribed forms for making contact:

"Well, like at the bus station, you go to the bathroom and stand there pretendin' like . . . and they're standin' there pretendin' like . . . and then they motions their head and walks out and you follow them, and you go some place. Either they's got a car, or you go to one of them hotels near the depot or some place like that . . . most any place."

Frequently contact between boys and fellators is established when the boy is hitchhiking. This is particularly true for boys' first contacts of this nature. Since lower-class boys are more likely than middle-class ones to hitch rides within a city, particularly at night when such contacts are most frequently made, they perhaps are most often solicited in this manner.

The experienced boy who knows a "lot of queers," may phone known fellators directly from a public phone, and some fellators try to establish continued contact with boys by giving them their phone numbers. However, the boys seldom use this means of contact for reasons inherent in their orientation toward the transaction, as we shall see below.

We shall now examine how the transaction is facilitated by these types of situations and the prescribed modes of contact and communication. One of the characteristics of all these contact situations is that they provide a *rationale* for the presence of *both* peers and queers in the *same* situation or place. This rationale is necessary for both parties, for were there high visibility to the presence of either and no ready explanation for it, contact and communication would be far more difficult. Public and quasi-public facilities provide situations which account for the presence of most persons since there is relatively little social control over the establishment of contacts. There is, of course, some risk to the boys and the fellators in making contact in these situations since they are generally known to the police. The Morals Squad may have "stake-outs," but this is one of the calculated risks and the communication network carries information about their tactics.

A most important element in furnishing a rationale is that these meeting places must account for the presence of delinquent boys of essentially lower-class dress and appearance who make contact with fellators of almost any class level. This is true despite the fact that the social settings which fellators ordinarily choose to establish contact generally vary according to the class level of the fellators. Fellators of high social class generally make contact by "cruising" past street-corners, in parks, or the men's rooms in "better" hotels, while those from the lower class are likely to select the public bath or transportation depot. There apparently is some general equation of the class position of boys and fellators in the peer-queer transaction. The large majority of fellators in the delinquent peer-queer transaction probably are from the lower class ("apes"). But it is difficult to be certain about the class position of the fellator clients since no study was made of this population.

The absence of data from the fellator population poses difficulties in interpreting the contact relationship. Many fellators involved with delinquent boys do not appear to participate in any overt or covert homosexual groups, such as the organized homosexual community of the "gay world."[1] The "gay world" is the most visible form of organized homosexuality since it is an organized community, but it probably encompasses only a small proportion of all homosexual contact. Even among those in the organized homosexual community, evidence suggests that the homosexual members seek sexual gratification outside their group with persons who are essentially anonymous to them. Excluding homosexual married couples, Leznoff and Westley maintain that there is ". . . a prohibition against sexual relationships

within the group . . ."[2] Ross indicates that young male prostitutes are chosen, among other reasons, for the fact that they protect the identity of the client.[3] Both of these factors tend to coerce many male fellators to choose an anonymous contact situation.

It is clear that these contact situations not only provide a rationale for the presence of the parties to the transaction but a guarantee of anonymity. The guarantee does not necessarily restrict social visibility as both the boys and the fellators may recognize cues (including, but not necessarily, those of gesture and dress) which lead to mutual role identification.[4] But anonymity is guaranteed in at least two senses; anonymity of presence is assured in the situation and their personal identity in the community is protected unless disclosed by choice.

There presumably are a variety of reasons for the requirement of anonymity. For many, a homosexual relationship must remain a secret since their other relationships in the community—families, business relationships, etc.—must be protected. Leznoff and Westley refer to these men as the "secret" as contrasted with the "overt" homosexuals,[5] and in the organized "gay world," they are known as "closet fags." For some, there is also a necessity for protecting identity to avoid blackmail.[6] Although none of the peer hustlers reported resorting to

[1] See, for example, Maurice Leznoff and William A. Westley, "The Homosexual Community," *Social Problems,* 4 (April, 1956), pp. 257–263.
[2] *Ibid.,* p. 258.
[3] H. Laurence Ross, "The 'Hustler' in Chicago," *The Journal of Student Research,* 1 (September, 1959), p. 15.
[4] The cues which lead to the queer-peer transaction can be subtle ones. The literature on adult male homosexuality makes it clear that adult males who participate in homosexual behavior are not generally socially visible to the public by manner and dress. Cf., Jess Stearn, *The Sixth Man,* New York: Macfadden Publications, 1962, Chapters 1 and 3.
[5] *Op. cit.,* pp. 260–261.
[6] Ross notes that, failing in the con-man role, some hustlers resort to extortion and blackmail since they provide higher income. See Ross, *op. cit.,* p. 16. Sutherland discusses extortion and blackmail of homosexuals as part of the practice of professional thieves. The "muzzle" or "mouse" is part of the role of the professional thief. See Edwin Sutherland, *The Professional Thief,* Chicago: University of Chicago Press, 1937, pp. 78–81. See also the chapter on "Blackmail" in Jess Stearn, *op. cit.,* Chapter 16.

blackmail, the adult male fellator may nonetheless hold such an expectation, particularly if he is older or of high social class. Lower-class ones, by contrast, are more likely to face the threat of violence from adolescent boys since they more often frequent situations where they are likely to contact "rough trade." [7] The kind of situation in which the delinquent peer-queer contact is made and the sexual relationship consummated tends to minimize the possibility of violence.

Not all male fellators protect their anonymity; some will let a boy have their phone number and a few "keep a boy." Still, most fellators want to meet boys where they are least likely to be victimized, although boys sometimes roll queers by selecting a meeting place where by prearrangement, their friends can meet them and help roll the queer, steal his car, or commit other acts of violence. Boys generally know that fellators are vulnerable in that they can't report their victimization. Parenthetically, it might be mentioned that these boys are not usually aware of their own institutional invulnerability to arrest. An adolescent boy is peculiarly invulnerable to arrest even when found with a fellator since the mores define the boy as exploited.[8]

Situations of personal contact between adolescent boys and adult male fellators also provide important ways to *communicate intent* or to carry out the transaction *without* making the contact particularly visible to others. The wall writings in many of these places are not without their primitive communication value, e.g., "show it hard," and places such as a public restroom provide a modus operandi. The entrepreneur and his customer in fact can meet with little more than an exchange of non-verbal gestures, transact their business with a minimum of

verbal communication and part without a knowledge of one another's identity. In most cases, boys report "almost nothing" was said. The sexual transaction may occur with the only formal transaction being payment to the boy. . . .

Norms Governing the Transaction

Does the peer society have any norms about personal relations with fellators? Or, does it simply induct a boy into a relationship by teaching him how to effect the transaction? The answer is that there appear to be several clear-cut norms about the relations between peers and queers, even though there is some deviation from them.

The first major norm is that *a boy must undertake the relationship with a queer solely as a way of making money; sexual gratification cannot be actively sought as a goal in the relationship.* This norm does not preclude a boy from sexual gratification by the act; he simply must not seek this as a goal. Put another way, a boy cannot admit that he failed to get money from the transaction unless he used violence toward the fellator and he cannot admit that he sought it as a means of sexual gratification.

The importance of making money in motivating a boy to the peer-queer transaction is succinctly stated by Dewey H.:

This guy in the Rex Theatre came over and sat down next to me when I was 11 or 12, and he started to fool with me. I got over and sat down another place and he came over and asked me, didn't I want to and he'd pay me five bucks. I figured it was *easy money* so I went with him . . . I didn't do it before that. That wan't too long after I'd moved to South Nashville. I was a pretty good boy before that . . . not

[7] Jess Stearn, *op. cit.,* p. 47.

[8] Albert J. Reiss, Jr., "Sex Offenses: The Marginal Status of the Adolescent," *Law and Contemporary Problems,* 25 (Spring, 1960), pp. 322–324 and 326–327.

real good, but I never ran with a crowd that got into trouble before that. But, I met a lot of 'em there. (Why do you run with queers?) It's *easy money* . . . like I could go out and break into a place when I'm broke and get money that way . . . but that's harder and *you take a bigger risk* . . . with a queer it's *easy money.*

Dewey's comments reveal two important motivating factors in getting money from queers, both suggested by the expression, "easy money." First, the money is easy in that it can be made quickly. Some boys reported that when they needed money for a date or a night out, they obtained it within an hour through the sexual transaction with a queer. All a boy has to do is go to a place where he will be contacted, wait around, get picked up, carried to a place where the sexual transaction occurs, and in a relatively short period of time he obtains the money for his service.

It is easy money in another and more important sense for many of these boys. Boys who undertake the peer-queer transaction are generally members of career-oriented delinquent groups. Rejecting the limited opportunities for making money by legitimate means or finding them inaccessible, their opportunities to make money by illegitimate means may also be limited or the risk may be great. Theft is an available means, but it is more difficult and involves greater risk than the peer-queer transaction. Delinquent boys are not unaware of the risks they take. Under most circumstances, delinquents may calculate an act of stealing as "worth the risk." There are occasions, however, when the risk is calculated as too great. These occasions occur when the "heat" is on the boy or when he can least afford to run the risk of being picked up by the police, as is the case following a pickup by the police, being put on probation or parole, or being warned that incarceration will

follow the next violation. At such times, boys particularly calculate whether they can afford to take the risk. Gerald L., describing a continuing relationship with a fellator who gave him his phone number, reflects Dewey's attitude toward minimizing risk in the peer-queer transaction: "So twic'd after that when I was gettin' real low and couldn't risk stealin' and gettin' caught, I called him and he took me out and blowed me." Here is profit with no investment of capital and a minimum of risk in social, if not in psychological, terms.

The element of risk coupled with the wish for "easy money" enters into our understanding of the peer-queer relationship in another way. From a sociological point of view, the peer-queer sexual transaction occurs between two major types of deviators—"delinquents" and "queers." Both types of deviators risk negative sanctions for their deviant acts. The more often one has been arrested or incarcerated, the more punitive the sanctions from the larger social system for both types of deviators. At some point, therefore, both calculate risks and seek to minimize them, at least in the very short-run. Each then becomes a means for the other to minimize risk.

When the delinquent boy is confronted with a situation in which he wants money and risks little in getting it, how is he to get it without working? Illegitimate activities frequently provide the "best" opportunity for easy money. These activities often are restricted in kind and number for adolescents and the risk of negative sanctions is high. Under such circumstances, the service offered a queer is a chance to make easy money with a minimum of risk.

Opportunities for sexual gratification are limited for the adult male fellator, particularly if he wishes to minimize the risk of detection in locating patrons, to avoid personal involvement and to get his gratification when he wishes it. The choice of a lower-class male, precisely because of his class position somewhat reduces the risk. If the lower-class male also is a delinquent, the risk is minimized to an even greater degree.

This is not to say that the parties take equal risks in the situation. Of the two, the fellator perhaps is less able to minimize his risk since he still risks violence from his patron, but much less so if a set of expectations arise which control the use of violence as well. The boy is most able to minimize his risk since he is likely to be defined as "exploited" in the situation if caught.

Under special circumstances, boys may substitute other gratifications for the goal of money, provided that these gratifications do not include sexual gratification as a major goal. These special circumstances are the case where an entire gang will "make a night (or time) of it" with one or more adult male fellators. Under these circumstances, everyone is excepted from the subcultural expectations about making money from the fellator because everyone participates and there is no reason for everyone (or anyone) to make money. For the group to substitute being given a "good time" by a "queer" for the prescribed financial transaction is, of course, the exception which proves the rule.

Several examples of group exemption from the prescribed norm of a financial gain were discovered. Danny S., leader of the Black Aces, tells of his gang's group experiences with queers: "There's this one gay who takes us to the Colonial Motel out on Dickerson Pike . . . usually it's a bunch of us boys and we all get drunk and get blowed by this queer . . . we don't get any money then . . . it's more a drinking party." The Black Aces are a fighting gang and place great stress on physical prowess, particularly boxing. All of its members have done time more than once at the State Training School. During one of these periods, the school employed a boxing instructor whom the boys identified as "a queer," but the boys had great respect for him since he taught them how to box and was a game fighter. Danny refers to him in accepting terms: "He's a real good guy. He's fought with us once or twice and we drink with him when we run into him. . . . He's taken us up to Miter Dam a coupla times; he's got a cabin up there on the creek and he blows us. . . . But mostly we just drink and have a real good time." These examples illustrate the instrumental orientation of the gang members. If the expense of the gang members getting drunk and having a good time are borne by a "queer," each member is released from the obligation to receive cash. The relationship in this case represents an exchange of services rather than that of money for a service.

The second major norm operating in the relationship is that *the sexual transaction must be limited to mouth-genital fellation. No other sexual acts are generally tolerated.*[9] The adult male fellator must deport himself in such a way as to re-enforce the instrumental aspects of the role relationship and to insure affective neutrality.[10] For the adult male fellator

[9] It is not altogether clear why mouth-genital fellation is the only sexual act which is tolerated in the peer-queer transaction. The act seems to conform to the more "masculine" aspects of the role than do most, but not all possible alternatives. Ross has suggested to me that it also involves less bodily contact and therefore may be less threatening to the peers' self-definitions. One possible explanation therefore for the exclusiveness of the relationship to this act is that it is the most masculine alternative involving the least threat to peers' self-definition as nonhustler and nonhomosexual.

[10] Talcott Parsons in *The Social System* (New York: The Free Press, 1951, Chapter III) discusses this kind of role as ". . . the segregation of specific instrumental performances, both from expressive orientations other than the specifically appropriate rewards and from other components of the instrumental complex." (p. 87).

to violate the boy's expectation of "getting blowed," as the boys refer to the act, is to risk violence and loss of service. Whether or not the boys actually use violent means as often as they say they do when expectations are violated, there is no way of knowing with precision. Nevertheless, whenever boys reported they used violent means, they always reported some violation of the subcultural expectations. Likewise, they never reported a violation of the subcultural expectations which was not followed by the use of violent means, unless it was clearly held up as an exception. Bobby A. expresses the boys' point of view on the use of violent means in the following exchange: "How much did you usually get?" "Around five dollars; if they didn't give that much, I'd beat their head in." "Did they ever want you to do anything besides blow you?" "Yeh, sometimes . . . like they want me to blow them, but I'd tell them to go to hell and maybe beat them up."

Boys are very averse to being thought of in a queer role or engaging in acts of fellation. The act of fellation is defined as a "queer" act. Most boys were asked whether they would engage in such behavior. All but those who had the status of "punks" denied they had engaged in behavior associated with the queer role. Asking a boy whether he is a fellator meets with strong denial and often with open hostility. This could be interpreted as defensive behavior against latent homosexuality. Whether or not this is the case, strong denial could be expected because the question goes counter to the subcultural definitions of the peer role in the transaction.

A few boys on occasion apparently permit the fellator to perform other sexual acts. These boys, it is guessed, are quite infrequent in a delinquent peer population. Were their acts known to the members of the group, they would soon be defined as outside the delinquent peer society. Despite the limitation of the peer-queer sexual transaction to mouth-genital fellation, there are other sexual transactions which the peer group permits members to perform under special circumstances. They are, for example, permitted to perform the *male* roles in "crimes against nature," such as in pederasty ("cornholing" to the boys), bestiality (sometimes referred to as buggery) and carnal copulation with a man involving no orifice (referred to as "slick-legging" among the boys) provided that the partner is roughly of the same age and not a member of the group and provided also that the boys are confined to the single-sex society of incarcerated delinquent boys. Under no circumstances, however, is the female role in carnal copulation acceptable in any form. It is taboo. Boys who accept the female role in sexual transactions occupy the lowest status position among delinquents. They are "punks."

The third major norm operating on the relationship is that *both peers and queers, as participants, should remain affectively neutral during the transaction.* Boys within the peer society define the ideal form of the role with the fellator as one in which the boy is the entrepreneur and the queer is viewed as purchasing a service. The service is a business deal where a sexual transaction is purchased for an agreed upon amount of money. In the typical case, the boy is neither expected to enjoy or be repulsed by the sexual transaction; mouth-genital fellation is accepted as a service offered in exchange for a fee. It should be kept in mind that self-gratification is permitted in the sexual act. Only the motivation to sexual gratification in the transaction is tabooed. But self-gratification must occur without displaying either positive or negative affect toward the queer. In the prescribed form of the role relationship, the boy sells a service for profit and the queer is to accept it without show of emotion.

The case of Thurman L., one of three brothers who are usually in trouble with the law, illustrates some aspects of the expected pattern of affective neutrality. Thurman has had a continuing relationship with a queer, a type of relationship in which it would be anticipated that affective neutrality would be difficult to maintain. This relationship continued, in fact, with a 21 year old "gay" until the man was "sent to the pen." When queried about his relationship with this man and why he went with him, Thurman replied:

Don't know . . . money and stuff like that I guess. (What do you mean? . . . stuff like that?) Oh, clothes. . . . (He ever bought you any clothes?) Sure, by this one gay. . . . (You mind being blowed?) No. (You like it?) Don't care one way or the other. I don't like it, and I don't not like it. (You like this one gay?) Nope, can't say that I liked anythin' about him. (How come you do it then?) Well, the money for one thing. . . . I need that. (You enjoy it some?) Can't say I do or don't.

More typical than Thurman's expression of affective neutrality is the boy who accepts it as "OK" or, "It's all right; I don't mind it." Most frequent of all is some variant of the statement: "It's OK, but I like the money best of all." The definition of affective neutrality fundamentally requires only that there be no positive emotional commitment to the queer *as a person*. The relationship must be essentially an impersonal one, even though the pure form of the business relationship may seldom be attained. Thus, it is possible for a boy to admit self-gratification without admitting any emotional commitment to the homosexual partner.

Although the peer group prescribes affective neutrality toward the queer in the peer-queer transaction, queers must be regarded as low prestige persons, held in low esteem, and the queer role is taboo. The queer is most commonly regarded as

"crazy, I guess." Some boys take a more rationalistic view "They're just like that, I guess" or, "They're just born that way." While there are circumstances under which one is permitted to like a particular fellator, as in the case of all prejudices attached to devalued status, the person who is liked must be the exception which states the rule. Though in many cases both the boy and the fellator are of very low class origins, and in many cases both are altogether repulsive in appearance, cleanliness and dress by middle-class standards, these are not the standards of comparison used by the boys. The deviation of the queers from the boy's norms of masculine behavior places the fellator in the lowest possible status, even "beneath contempt." If the fellator violates the expected affective relationship in the transaction, he may be treated not only with violence but with contempt as well. The seller of the service ultimately reserves the right to set the conditions for his patrons.

Some boys find it difficult to be emotionally neutral toward the queer role and its occupants; they are either personally offended or affronted by the behavior of queers. JDC is an instance of a boy who is personally offended by their behavior; yet he is unable to use violence even when expectations governing the transaction are violated. He does not rely very much on the peer-queer relationship as a source of income. JDC expresses his view: "I don't really go for that like some guys; I just do it when I go along with the crowd. . . . You know. . . . That, and when I do it for money. . . . And I go along. . . . But . . . I hate queers. They embarrass me." "How?" "Well, like you'll be in the lobby at the theatre, and they'll come up and pat your ass or your prick right in front of everybody. I just can't go for that—not me." Most of the boys wouldn't either, but they would have resorted to violent means in this situation.

Two principal types of boys maintain a continuing relationship with a known queer. A few boys develop such relationships to insure a steady income. While this is permitted within peer society for a short period of time, boys who undertake it for extended periods of time do so with some risk, since in the words of the boys, "queers can be got too easy." The boy who is affectively involved with a queer or his role is downgraded in status to a position, "Ain't no better'n a queer." There are also a few boys affectively committed to a continuing relationship with an adult male homosexual. Such boys usually form a strong dependency relationship with him and are kept much as the cabin boys of old. This type of boy is clearly outside the peer society of delinquents and is isolated from participation in gang activity. The sociometric pattern for such boys is one of choice into more than one gang, none of which is reciprocated.

Street-hustlers are also downgraded within the peer society, generally having reputations as "punk kids." The street-hustler pretty much "goes it alone." Only a few street-hustlers were interviewed for this study. None of them was a member of an organized delinquent group. The sociometric pattern for each, together with his history of delinquent activity, placed them in the classification of nonconforming isolates.

A fourth major norm operating on the peer-queer relationship serves as a primary factor in stabilizing the system. This norm holds that *violence must not be used so long as the relationship conforms to the shared set of expectations between queers and peers.* So long as the fellator conforms to the norms governing the transaction in the peer-queer society, he runs little risk of violence from the boys.

The main reason, perhaps, for this norm is that uncontrolled violence is potentially disruptive of any organized system. All

organized social systems must control violence. If the fellator clients were repeatedly the objects of violence, the system as it has been described could not exist. Most boys who share the common expectations of the peer-queer relationship do not use violent means unless the expectations are violated. To use violence, of course, is to become affectively involved and therefore another prescription of the relationship is violated.

It is not known whether adult male fellators who are the clients of delinquent entrepreneurs share the boys' definition of the norm regarding the use of violence. They may, therefore, violate expectations of the peer society through ignorance of the system rather than from any attempt to go beyond the set of shared expectations.

There are several ways the fellator can violate the expectations of boys. The first concerns money: refusal to pay or paying too little may bring violence from most boys. Fellators may also violate peer expectations by attempting to go beyond the mouth-genital sexual act. If such an attempt is made, he is usually made an object of aggression as in the following excerpt from Dolly's sex history:

(You like it?) It's OK. I don't mind it. It feels OK. (They ever try anything else on you?) They usually just blow and that's all. (Any ever try anything else on you?) Oh sure, but we really fix 'em. I just hit 'em on the head or roll 'em . . . throw 'em out of the car. . . . Once a gay tried that and we rolled him and threw him out of the car. Then we took the car and stripped it (laughs with glee).

Another way the fellator violates a boy's expectations is to introduce considerable affect into the relationship. It appears that affect is least acceptable in two forms, both of which could be seen as "attacks on his masculinity." In one form, the queer violates the affective neutrality requirement by treating the adolescent boy as if he were a girl or in a girl's role during the sexual transaction, as for example, by speaking to him in affectionate terms such as "sweetie." There are many reasons why the feminine sex role is unacceptable to these lower-class boys, including the fact that such boys place considerable emphasis on being "tough" and masculine. Walter Miller, for example, observes that:

. . . The almost compulsive lower class concern with "masculinity" derives from a type of compulsive reaction-formation. A concern over homosexuality runs like a persistent thread through lower class culture—manifested by the institutionalized practice of "baiting queers," often accompanied by violent physical attacks, an expressed contempt for "softness" or frills, and the use of the local term for "homosexual" as a general pejorative epithet (e.g., higher class individuals or upwardly mobile peers are frequently characterized as "fags" or "queers").[11]

Miller sees violence as part of a reaction-formation against the matriarchal lower-class household where the father often is absent. For this reason, he suggests, many lower-class boys find it difficult to identify with a male role, and the "collective" reaction-formation is a cultural emphasis on masculinity. Violence toward queers is seen as a consequence of this conflict. Data from our interviews suggest that among career-oriented delinquents, violation of the affective-neutrality requirement in the peer-queer relationship is at least as important in precipitating violence toward "queers." There are, of course, gangs which were not studied in this investigation which "queer-bait" for the express purposes of "rolling the queer."

The other form in which the fellator may violate the affective neutrality requirement is to approach the boy and make suggestive advances to him when he is with his age-mates, either with girls or with his peer group when he is not located for "business." In either case, the sexual advances suggest that the boy is not engaged in a business relationship within the normative expectations of the system, but that he has sexual motivation as well. The delinquent boy is expected to control the relationship with his customers. He is the entrepreneur "looking" for easy money or at the very least he must appear as being merely receptive to business; this means that he is receptive only in certain situations and under certain circumstances. He is not in business when he is with girls and he is not a businessman when he is cast in a female role. To be cast in a female role before peers is highly unacceptable, as the following account suggests:

This gay comes up to me in the lobby of the Empress when we was standin' around and starts feelin' me up and callin' me Sweetie and like that . . . and, I just couldn't take none of that there . . . what was he makin' out like I was a queer or somethin' . . . so I jumps him right then and there and we like to of knocked his teeth out.

The sexual advance is even less acceptable when a girl is involved:

I was walkin' down the street with my steady girl when this gay drives by that I'd been with once before and he whistles at me and calls, "hi Sweetie." . . . And, was I mad . . . so I went down to where the boys was and we laid for him and beat on him 'til he like to a never come to . . . ain't gonna take nothin' like that off'n a queer.

In both of these instances, not only is the boys' masculinity under attack, but the affective neutrality requirement of the business transaction is violated. The queer's behavior is particularly unac-

---

[11] Walter Miller, "Lower-Class Culture as a Generating Milieu of Gang Delinquency," *The Journal of Social Issues,* 14 (1958), No. 3, p. 9.

ceptable, however, because it occurs in a peer setting where the crucial condition is the maintenance of the boy's status within the group. A lower-class boy cannot afford to be cast in less than a highly masculine role before lower-class girls nor risk definition as a queer before peers. His role within his peer group is under threat even if he suffers *no* anxiety about masculinity. Not only the boy himself but his peers perceive such behavior as violating role expectations and join him in violent acts toward the fellator to protect the group's integrity and status.

If violence generally occurs only when one of the major peer norms has been violated, it would also seem to follow that *violence is a means of enforcing the peer entrepreneurial norms of the system*. Violence or the threat of violence is thus used to keep adult male fellators in line with the boys' expectations in his customer role. It represents social control, a punishment meted out to the fellator who violates the cultural expectation. Only so long as the fellator seeks gratification from lower-class boys in a casual pick-up or continuing relationship where he pays money for a "blow-job," is he reasonably free from acts of violence.

There is another, and perhaps more important reason for the use of violence when the peer defined norms of the peer-queer relationship are violated. The formally prescribed roles for peers and queers are basically the roles involved in all institutionalized forms of prostitution, the prostitute and the client. But in most forms of prostitution, whether male or female, the hustlers perceive of themselves in hustler roles, and furthermore the male hustlers also develop a conception of themselves as homosexual whereas *the peer hustler in the peer-queer relationship develops no conception of himself either as prostitute or as homosexual.*

The fellator risks violence, therefore, if he threatens the boy's self-conception by suggesting that the boy may be homosexual and treats him as if he were.

Violence seems to function, then, in two basic ways for the peers. On the one hand, it integrates their norms and expectations by controlling and combatting behavior which violates them. On the other hand, it protects the boy's self-identity as nonhomosexual and reinforces his self-conception as "masculine."

The other norms of the peer society governing the peer-queer transaction also function to prevent boys in the peer-queer society from defining themselves as homosexual. The prescriptions that the goal is money, that sexual gratification is not to be sought as an end in the relationship, that affective neutrality be maintained toward the fellator and that only mouth-genital fellation is permitted, all tend to insulate the boy from a homosexual self-definition. So long as he conforms to these expectations, *his "significant others" will not define him as homosexual;* and this is perhaps the most crucial factor in his own self-definition. The peers define one as homosexual not on the basis of homosexual *behavior* as such, but on the basis of participation in the homosexual *role,* the "queer" role. The reactions of the larger society, in defining the *behavior* as homosexual is unimportant in their own self-definition. What is important to them is the reactions of their peers to violation of peer group norms which define roles in the peer-queer transaction.

The Check Forger and His Identity *

EDWIN M. LEMERT

. . . Check forgery, in contrast to crimes such as assault, robbery, or burglary, is distinguished by its low social visibility. At the time the bogus check is passed there is nothing in the act which reveals that it is deviant or criminal. No special tools or equipment are needed for the crime, as with burglary, nor is any special setting required for the action, as is true with the "store" or the front of a bank, where the confidence man activates his fraudulent enterprises. Furthermore, there are few or no cues in interaction which give feedback to the forger from the victim nor from his own overt responses to indicate that he is behaving contrary to expectations; only later does the act become so defined and then never in direct interaction between the forger and his victim. Here is deviant behavior whose manifest or "existential" qualities do not differentiate or identify the person as a deviant.

Studies of the characteristics of check forgers based upon samples of those in jails, prisons, or on probation show considerable heterogeneity. However, it can be said that in general they more nearly resemble the general middle-class population than they do the populations of jails and prisons. They tend to be native white in origin, male, and much older than other criminals when they commit their first crimes—somewhere in their late 20's or early 30's. Their intelligence averages much higher than that of other criminals and they equal or surpass the general population in years of education completed. Skilled, clerical, professional,

and managerial occupations are at least as fully represented among forgers as in the general population, perhaps more so. An impressive small minority have come from prestigeful, wealthy families, or those in which siblings have achieved social eminence, although considerable discounting of forgers' claims on this point is necessary. A high percentage of forgers have been long-time residents in the communities in which they committed their first offenses, but relatively few have lived in so-called "delinquency areas." Forgers are less likely than other criminals to have had a record of delinquency in their youth.

Prior socialization as delinquents or criminals is insufficient to explain the crimes of a large per cent, or even the majority, of persons who pass bad checks. Many have acquired and lived a considerable part of their early adult lives according to conventional middle-class morality. Typically they tend to express aversion to the idea of using violence in interpersonal dealings for whatever purpose. At the same time it must be said that an occasional person comes into forgery via the criminal route—the "short" con man turned forger, or the "old pro" burglar fallen on hard times, who has turned to passing bad checks for a livelihood. . . .

Pseudonymity

Once a check forger passes a series of worthless checks, the central fact of his existence becomes the threat of arrest.

* Reprinted from Edwin M. Lemert, *Human Deviance, Social Problems, and Social Control*, pp. 119–120, 121–124, 124–126, 131–132, © 1967. Reprinted by permission of Prentice-Hall, Inc., Englewood Cliffs, N.J.

382

The business community through the police is strongly organized against the check forger, and when his checks appear, a number of procedures are activated. The more checks he has outstanding the more intensified and widespread are the efforts to apprehend him. Nearly all of these procedures have to do with identification, for once the check forger is identified as working in an area, apprehension and arrest quickly follow. Consequently if he is to survive as a forger he must develop and use techniques which prevent his identification.

Other criminals anticipate and adapt to the threat of arrest through anonymity, e.g., the burglar who works at night, or the bank robbers who work swiftly, sometimes wearing masks, which will confuse witnesses and make subsequent identification difficult or impossible. The confidence man manipulates his victims so that they often remain unaware they have been duped, or so that they fear to go to the police. The check forger cannot use these alternatives as a defense against arrest because he must work during daylight hours and face large numbers of victims who require identification before they will cash his checks. While the forger might "cool out" a few victims in the manner of the con man, he can't psychologically disarm them all, nor can he employ the "fix" with any great degree of success. The district attorney usually has stacks of checks in evidence and numerous complainants ready to testify against him when he is arrested. The check forger by necessity relies upon pseudonyms as the preferred solution to his technical problem.

In a very literal sense the check forger becomes a real life actor, deliberately assuming a variety of roles and identities which both facilitate the cashing of checks and conceal his former or, if preferred, his "real" identity. Thus he may become a spurious customer in a supermarket, a guilty husband purportedly buying his wife a gift, an out-of-town real estate buyer, a corporation executive seeking to set up a branch office, an army officer on leave, or even an investigator for the Department of Internal Revenue.

The systematic forger's problem is the selection or fabrication of roles rather than the learning of new roles. His role models are occupational or leisure time roles of conventional society. Their distinctive quality is their high degree of superficiality.[1] While they require some acting ability, it is of a low order and easily learned. Such roles, as Goffman [2] suggests, are easily put together in response to situational cues from "bits and pieces of performances" which are already in the repertoire of most people.

Some negative learning is done by forgers in jail or prison, in the sense of things not to do, through listening to the stories of other check criminals. This is reflected in an adage followed by some, of "never try another man's stunt." While check forgers are responding to what they expect of others and what others expect of them, they do so in order to maintain deception and avoid arrest. Their behavior is fundamentally more in the nature of strategy or a swiftly moving game than it is a formal or constituted pattern. In this sense it is generically similar to that of the confidence man, representing, however, a lower order of creativity and strategy.

Mobility

While the check man employs pseudonyms to avoid exposure when passing

---

[1] One forger reported using 285 names during his career. He also argued that the less documentary identification used the less suspicion aroused in the victim. Leonard Hart, "You're a Sucker If You Cash My Check," *Colliers*, February 7, 1953.

[2] Erving Goffman, *The Presentation of the Self in Everyday Life* (New York: Doubleday Anchor, 1959), pp. 72 ff.

his worthless checks, he cannot simply don a different or innocuous identity afterward; he must move on, out of the vicinity of his crime or crimes. This, of course, can be said for other kinds of crimes, but mobility is more or less "built in" the check forger's situation largely because he preys upon resident business-men, rather than on transients, as do pickpockets or con men.[3] His mobility is shaped by continual awareness of the time required to deposit checks, clear them, and communicate notification of non-payment to law enforcement and business protective agencies. In large part his daily activities are geared to the tempo and rhythms of banking and business, which demarcate the length of time he can pass checks and remain in a given area, ending in a critical interval dur-ing which danger of arrest is ubiquitous.[4] Experienced check forgers develop an almost intuitive sense of these points in time which punctuate their periodic movements.

The movements of the systematic check passer take on a circularity of ac-tion and motivation in the sense that their mobility begets more mobility. When queried as to why they stay on the move, check forgers usually explain that it is expensive to travel, and also that if they are to impress their businessmen-victims they must appear to have a bank account appropriate to the checks they cash.[5]

When you're moving around like that you've got to put up a front and look the part. You can't cash checks if you look seedy. How can I impress a clerk that I'm a busi-nessman with a fat bank account if I don't have good quality clothes and stay in better hotels and drive an expensive make of car (rented).

The result of their high levels of ex-penditure is that forgers usually cash numerous checks in order to defray costs of constant travel and to maintain their prosperous style of life. The local "spreads" of checks stir strong indigna-tion in the business community and quickly mobilize law enforcement people, sensing of which becomes the forger's motivation to move frequently. This sug-gests one of the main reasons why some check forgers speak of being caught up in something they can't stop.

Seclusiveness

The vulnerability of the forger to rec-ognition and identification impels him away from unnecessary contacts with other persons. Furthermore he must, if he is to remain free from arrest, keep himself from progressive involvement in social relationships, for with intimate in-terchange of experiences there comes the danger of inadvertent as well as delib-erate exposure by others. Free and un-guarded interaction, even with persons whom he likes and trusts, becomes an indulgence.

The forger's seclusiveness, in large part a learned response of wariness, is rein-forced by his high mobility, which neces-sarily makes his contacts and interactions of short-lived variety; he simply does not have the time to build up close relation-ships with the people he meets. His rela-

[3] Sheldon Messinger thoughtfully suggests that this factor prevents the forger from setting up accommodative relationships with police which are the basis of the fix, by which pro-fessional thieves protect themselves—personal communication.

[4] In one case, a forger traced his itinerary for the author. It uncovered a nine-months period, during which he worked in 25 cities between Oakland, California, and Atlanta, Georgia, never remaining longer than two weeks in each.

[5] This is only partially revealing of the motivation of the forger; it will become apparent that he also needs large amounts of money to underwrite the kinds of recreation or activi-ties he pursues to relieve his tensions and sense of loneliness.

tionships or social activities tend to be those which he can enter and leave quickly, with a minimum of commitment; the roles he enacts apart from the passing of his checks are for the most part casual in nature. In addition to this role selectivity he learns to avoid specific forms of behavior likely to lead beyond casual interaction.

The forger often meets people in settings where drinking is expected behavior, yet he must take care not to drink to the point of intoxication for fear of letting slip revealing or inconsistent facts about himself. If he gets drunk he is likely to do it alone, but this is risky, too, for he might be picked up on a drunk charge and be exposed by a routine fingerprint check. If the forger gambles it is likely to be at a crowded race track or casino, not at a friendly poker game.

The preference for seclusiveness puts its stamp upon the sexual participation of the forger. He is more limited than other criminals in seeking erotic pleasures; for he seldom has a common law wife or a regular traveling companion. Prostitutes are not in keeping with his pseudonyms of respectability, and association with them may lead to unwanted brushes with the police. When he picks up a girl he is apt to be discriminating in his choice, and typically he will treat her lavishly, but seldom will he give her his true name. In this role, as in others, he remains an actor, although at times the temptation to be otherwise is great. . . .

The Growth of Anxiety

An unavoidable conclusion seems to be that the more successfully the forger plays his roles the greater becomes his anxiety. The more checks he has outstanding the greater is his perception of the danger of arrest, and hence the greater his necessity to move on and devise new identities which conceal his previous behavior. The mounting sense of strain is made real to the forger by occasional "close calls" in which he barely escapes identification and arrest. As the anxiety magnifies it is reflected in jumpiness, stomach upsets, and other physical disturbances. A few check forgers develop acute symptoms, such as stomach ulcers.

My routine ran like this: I usually picked my city, then after I arrived I opened a savings account with cash. That's on Monday. On Tuesday I deposited some checks to my account, no good, of course. Wednesday I deposited another check and then drew out part of the account in cash. Then I left town. I worked this all over California, depositing maybe $50,000 altogether in I don't know how many banks. I suppose I got about $10,000 in cash. By this time the ulcers kicked up and I laid off in a resort.

Anxiety serves to amplify the suspiciousness of the forger; in some instances it is aggravated into a paranoid-like state, called the "bull horrors" by professional criminals. This is what it implies—abnormal fear of the police. In this state any unusual behavior of a victim, or a chance knock on a hotel room door, may be taken by the forger to mean that he has been discovered or that detectives have arrived to arrest him. At this point it is clear that the symbolic process has been affected; anxiety has begun to distort or interfere with the forger's ability to take over or realistically appraise the responses of others to his actions.

Cooler or highly experienced forgers may be able to objectify the sources of their anxiety and symbolize it in the jargon of the professional criminal as "heat." As one forger put it, "The checks get hot, not me." As a solution to their psychic problems some forgers take a vacation, or "lay off at a resort." In this setting they continue to use a pseudonym but refrain from passing checks during the interim. This has the merit of reducing anxiety attributable to the fear of being recognized by victims or police, but it does not solve what by now has usually become an identity problem. In any event, contingencies or the need for more money are apt to cut short these palliative respites.

Personal Crisis

Detectives, police, and the check forgers themselves all agree that arrest is inevitable for the person who persists in passing bad checks for any length of time. A few check men manage to evade detection for several years, and one is known to have foiled the FBI for ten years, but these are the rare exceptions which prove the rule. Efficiently organized police work and fortuitous events undeniably have much to do with the forger's ultimate downfall, but from the point of view adopted here, these are constant factors with which he contends. That with which he is unable to cope is a kind of massive personal crisis which inheres in the prolonged enactment of his spurious roles.

That the forger reaches a dead end in his motivation can be inferred from the circumstances and attendant behavior at the time of the arrest. While a number of systematic forgers are apprehended entirely by chance or by police efforts, an impressive number of others engineer their own downfalls. For example, some phone the police or a parole officer and tell them where they can be found. Closely akin are those who foreclose their current criminal careers rather simply by remaining where they are, knowing full well that police or detectives will soon catch up with them, to find them in a resigned mood awaiting their arrival.[6] Still other forgers, like fabled animals wending back to their mythical graveyard to die, return to their home community, there either to court arrest or to arrange for the inevitable in familiar surroundings. In more complex cases an otherwise accomplished check man makes a mistake, knowing at the time that it is a mistake which probably will land him in jail or prison.

After a weekend of drinking and sleeping with this girl I had known before, I woke up in my room at the Mark Hopkins with a hangover and no money left. I had one check left from those I had been passing in the city. It was over two weeks since I had started passing this series and knew I shouldn't try to cash this one. But I did anyway—and now here I am at Folsom.

When queried as to reasons for their sometimes open, sometimes oblique surrenders to detectives or other law enforcement agents, check forgers frequently refer to a cumulative state of apathy or sense of psychic exhaustion,[7] expressed in such statements as the following:

---

[6] One check man, who spent much of his free time in bars, sensed that bartenders had been alerted to his presence in the area. He brought about his arrest in a bar simply by talking a little louder than was his custom. The owner overheard him and phoned the police.

[7] An appropriate descriptive term for this state is not easily found. It resembles the indifference to the threat of death which appeared among some inmates of Nazi concentration camps, as a response to "provisional detention without a time limit." See Bruno Bettelheim, "Individual and Mass Behavior in Extreme Situations," *Journal of Abnormal and Social Psychology*, 38 (1948), p. 434; Elie Cohen, *Human Behavior in the Concentration Camp* (New York: W. W. Norton & Company, Inc., 1953), p. 129. The reaction also suggests the idea of a "breaking point" or limits of effective response under stress. See Eli Ginzberg, *et al.*, *The Ineffective Soldier* (New York: Columbia University Press, 1959). Something of "acute depersonalization" also seems involved. See Paul Schilder, *The Image and Appearance of the Human Body* (London: Kegan Paul, Trench, Trubner and Co., 1935).

After that I began to appreciate what a heck of a job it is to pass checks.

In Seattle I got just plain tired of cashing checks.

The thrill I got from passing checks was gone.

I reached a point where I didn't care whether I stayed in Balboa or went to jail.

It's the same thing over and over again; you get tired of running.

It gets to be more and more of an effort.

You have a sense of being caught in something you can't stop.

One meaning that can be readily assigned to such statements is that, assuming satisfactions or rewards of the forger's activities remain unchanged or constant, their costs of acquisition in terms of effort and expenditure of psychic energy (anxiety) increase to a prohibitive point. What started out as "easy" check passing becomes more and more work or sheer labor, until that game is no longer worth the effort.

A second, less apparent implication of the sense of apathy which finally overwhelms the highly mobile check forger was suggested by a thoughtful older inmate of San Quentin prison, who had in his lifetime been both con man and a notorious utterer of very large checks. His interpretation was simply that during the course of a check passing spree, "You come to realize that kind of life has a false structure to it." This in sociological terms speaks of the inherent difficulty of establishing and maintaining identity by reference to purely extrinsic rewards. To admit this is for the forger in effect to admit that the roles he plays, or his way of life, make impossible a stable identity or the validation of a self ideal. An excerpt from an older published autobiog-raphy of a forger states the problem clearly.[8]

I could not rid myself of the crying need for the sense of security which social recognition and contact with one's fellows, and their approval furnishes. I was lonely and frightened and wanted to be where there was someone who knew me as I had been before.

Identity Crises and Negative Identity

The foregoing argues strongly that the personal crisis of the systematic forger stems less from a moral dilemma than it does from the erosion of identity. So conceived, his problem resides in a neutral component or dimension of the self, namely the sense of separateness and relationship to others, which is assumed to have its own consequences for behavior apart from substantive social value, "good or bad," assigned to it.[9] In a sense the forger fails because he succeeds; he is able to fend off or evade self-degradative consequences of his actions but in so doing he rejects forms of interaction necessary to convert his rewards in positive, status-specific self-evaluations. In time he reaches a point at which he can no longer define himself in relation to others on any basis. The self becomes amorphous, without boundaries; the identity substructure is lost. Apathy replaces motivation, and in phenomenological terms, "life" or "this way of life" is no longer worth living. This is the common prelude to the forger's arrest.

There is, of course, an adaptive aspect to the psychic surrender which precedes or attends the forger's almost casual entry into legal custody, which can be seen quite clearly in the sense of relief which is experienced at the time and also later

---

[8] Roger Benton, *Where Do I Go From Here* (New York: L. Furman, 1936), p. 80.
[9] A conception approximating this distinction can be found in D. L. Burnham, "Identity Definition and Role Demand in Hospital Careers of Schizophrenic Patients," *Psychiatry*, 24 (1961), pp. 96–122.

in jail. From a moral perspective, the forger is "being brought to justice"; he "pays his debt to society." However, from the perspective of this chapter, his apathy or carelessness and subsequent arrest function to end his anxiety which is the subjective aspect of the organized "hue and cry" of modern crime detection. More importantly, they solve his identity problem; arrest immediately assigns the forger an identity, undesirable though it may be, as a jail or prison inmate. In effect, he receives or chooses a *negative identity*,[10] which despite its invidious qualities, is nearest and most real to him. At this juncture he is much like the actor who prefers bad publicity to none at all, or the youth who is willing to be a scapegoat for the group rather than not be part of the group at all.

---

[10] Erik H. Erikson, "The Problem of Ego Identity," in *Identity and Anxiety*, ed. M. R. Stein, *et al.* (New York: Free Press of Glencoe, Inc., 1960), pp. 60–62.

TRANSFORMING DEVIANT IDENTITY

15

Some deviant careers, over the course of time, prove to be more punishing than rewarding. Persons whose deviant acts make them victims of themselves (e.g., alcoholism and drug addiction) are more apt than other deviants to make efforts to rid themselves of deviant status, role, and identity. Stopping a deviant career in midpassage is no easy matter. The conditions for a successful transformation of deviant identity are austere and not easy to come by. Unless there are advancing degrees of integration of self and role, group support from deviants and conformists alike, and legitimate places in which to practice conventionality, transformation is less likely.

The final three selections deal with success and failure in the transformation of the deviant identity. Rubington shows that when the number of legitimate statuses open to a recovered alcoholic dwindles as his sober identity solidifies, the risk of relapse rises. Ray similarly reveals that deviant identities that remain long after the behavior has changed complicate the transformation of addict identity. Volkman and Cressey then show how Synanon meets the primary group conditions for successfully changing addict identity.

An Alcoholic's Relapse *

EARL RUBINGTON

Treatment ideology states: for the alcoholic, prolonged abstinence without personality change is unlikely. Since alcoholism exists in a web of ambiva-

* Reprinted from "Grady 'Breaks Out': A Case Study of an Alcoholic's Relapse" in *Social Problems*, Vol. 11, No. 4 (Spring, 1964), pp. 372–380, by permission of *Social Problems*.

lence, conflicts—social, cultural, and psychological—are endemic in relations alcoholics sustain with non-alcoholics and alcoholics alike. Consequently, when conflicts persist and cumulate, alcoholics who have not changed will dissolve all conflicts by drinking again.

We present here case materials which suggest that absence of personality change and presence of persistent and cumulating conflicts need not necessarily lead to resumption of drinking. Our materials imply that some relapses may be viewed as aborted social relationships. These relationships, as are all relationships, are held together by a set of bonds. If these bonds—the "unwritten contract" as it were—include rules and roles for resolving conflicts, abstinence may be prolonged without modification of personality. Under the terms of these relationships, one alcoholic role partner will relapse if and only if the other party has breached the contract.

Since the data on which this study is based were collected in a rather unique setting, the generality of the findings is obviously restricted. The materials to be presented depict the changing and shifting pattern of relationships which one homeless alcoholic sustained with a number of other alcoholics variously situated in and around a halfway house for chronic drunkenness offenders for a period of some two and a half years. Nevertheless, we feel that the conceptual scheme through which this case of prolonged abstinence and sudden relapse will be interpreted can be extended more widely.

Social Setting and Methods of Research

An east coast state commission on alcoholism established Shelter House [1] for the purpose of rehabilitating chronic drunkenness offenders. Shelter House pursues this goal by attempting to break offenders' ties to drinking and drinking groups. When its members conform with and then internalize abstinence norms, enduring periods of sobriety are likely. When sobriety occurs, staff and members alike speak of someone as "getting the program." Though few can specify how Shelter House works, all agree that a member "gets the program through association." A director and a staff of four, all recovered alcoholics and members of Alcoholics Anonymous, operate the program, simultaneously discharging administrative and rehabilitative duties. That staff are all recovered alcoholics is said to reduce communication barriers; that members are all chronic drunkenness offenders is said to increase sociability.

Compliance with a simple set of rules, particularly the abstinence norm, is taken by staff to mean that a member is "getting the program." While residents, members agree to refrain from drinking, attend mandatory counseling and group discussions on alcoholism, attend meals, observe curfew, obtain outside employment, pay $21 weekly for room and board, and perform housekeeping and maintenance details as assigned. Ninety days' residence suffices for maximum benefit; members who "complete the course" are called "graduates" and are encouraged to maintain close contact with Shelter House and/or join Alcoholics Anonymous to prolong their sobriety.

Three aspects of social organization, sources of most of the conflicts which beset Shelter House staff and members alike, need to be borne in mind. First, Shelter House staff as state employees sought to impose AA norms in a residential treatment facility on recalcitrant

---

[1] Names of all persons and places referred to in this paper are fictitious.

clients; secondly, by leasing space within the King Street Mission, Shelter House was in conflict with the mission over rules and scarce resources, and in competition with a facility likewise devoted to the rehabilitation of homeless alcoholics; and third, location in the mission increased chances of contact with homeless alcoholics who were currently drinking.

Our case materials stem from a field study [2] of the social organization of Shelter House. A major concern of the study was the observation and classification of conflicts and analysis of the means by which different Shelter House persons dealt with these conflicts as their own situations changed over time. A crucial case bearing on conflicts, their resolution, and changes over time was that of Windy Grady. Grady came into Shelter House to regain his sobriety, completed the 90-day residential treatment program, and "graduated" into a private room in the King Street Mission. Since Shelter House leased space within the mission, Grady stayed in contact with the halfway house. During his post-Shelter House career Grady was a mission resident holding outside employment, then a resident though unemployed, and finally both mission resident and employee. After almost ten months as night watchman and some 29 months since his last drinking episode, Grady "broke out." [3]

In view of the fact that Grady evinced none of the personality change that conduces to prolonged abstinence, how was it possible for him to stay sober as long as he did? And, when he finally did relapse, what social conditions made continued abstinence for him in the King Street Mission-Shelter House milieu no longer tenable? To answer these questions, this study examines certain observed changes occurring over time in Grady's situation. Materials on his case can be ordered in a five-part chronology: his pre-Shelter House role as chronic drunkenness offender, his career as member, and the three phases of mission residency culminating in relapse. We turn now to this chronology.

The "Loner" Role: Grady as Chronic Drunkenness Offender

Prior to entering Shelter House, Grady was a well-known though not necessarily well-liked member of Maple City's homeless alcoholic community. He was well-acquainted with both bottle gang and tavern norms, yet conducted himself primarily as a "loner." He had many acquaintances and few friends in this community; nevertheless, because he observed appropriate decorum, he never lacked for drinks when in need.[4] For example, while working as a truck driver, he stopped regularly at a local tavern where he customarily stood several rounds of drinks for the house, thus ensuring himself of reciprocity. Both garrulous and domineering, Grady claimed to have been on all the major Skid Rows throughout the country and to have drunk more than most people. A bona fide offender, Maple City police listed his name in their special "red book" of men who had compiled

---

[2] The study was carried out by means of participant-observation. During its course, the investigator assumed all of the roles in field work which Ray Gold describes in his valuable paper, "Roles in Sociological Field Observation," *Social Forces*, 36 (March 1958), pp. 217–23.

[3] Skid Row argot for relapse.

[4] For studies of drinking ritual among homeless alcoholics, see Joan K. Jackson and Ralph Connor, "The Skid Road Alcoholic," *Quarterly Journal of Studies on Alcohol*, 14 (September, 1953), pp. 468–86; W. Jack Peterson and Milton A. Maxwell, "The Skid Road 'Wino,'" *Social Problems*, 5 (Spring, 1958), pp. 308–16; and James F. Rooney, "Group Processes among Skid Row Winos: A Reevaluation of the Undersocialization Hypothesis," *Quarterly Journal of Studies on Alcohol*, 22 (September, 1961), pp. 444–60.

more than fifty arrests for public drunkenness. The fact that he had a son on the local police force did not endear Grady to his fellow-offenders.

Grady had been a Maple City resident all his life, had married and raised a large family. Then he separated from his wife and began drinking heavily. After several years of heavy drinking and homelessness, he contracted tuberculosis. He spent 29 months in a tuberculosis sanatorium only to resume drinking after discharge. Some time later, a physician at the Maple City out-patient alcoholism clinic referred him to Shelter House. Out of respect for this physician, Grady now an alcoholic in his early fifties, investigated the halfway house located inside the heavily stigmatized King Street Mission and decided to affiliate.

The "Company Man" Role: Grady as Shelter House Member

Grady explicitly rejected the illness conception of alcoholism; in his own words, "alcoholism is no more than a falsified (sic) habit." Unlike others, he had drunk because he wanted to, not because he needed to. And like most offenders who entered Shelter House, he disdained Alcoholics Anonymous and thought anyone who "told his story" at an AA meeting was shameless, "phony," or both. Dissatisfied with the effects of his own drinking, however, he had resolved to regain his self-respect and to show "some people" that he could do it. Compliance with the Shelter House regimen seemed a sensible way of attaining these goals.

Though Grady was a member of the same heavily stigmatized social category as his fellow Shelter House residents, sociability was not thereby promoted. Though Shelter House staff were all recovered alcoholics, barriers to communication persisted. Grady came to dislike many of his fellow members when they failed either to comply with Shelter House rules or come to his assistance. He performed assigned details regularly without complaint, unlike most Shelter House members, and attended all group discussions as required. Though he enjoyed some of these discussions, he never revealed any of his "personal business" at these meetings or to his counselor, Ralph Gray. He disapproved of all staff counselors, particularly Gray. Grady deferred to only two persons in the building, James Sterling, Shelter House's director, and Bill James, the King Street Mission's director, himself a member of Alcoholics Anonymous, personal friend and sponsor of Sterling in AA.

In short, Grady had assumed the role of "company man" [5] soon after his admission to Shelter House. His commitment, however, was to Sterling and Sterling's organization, Shelter House, rather than to the moral beliefs and practices implicit in Shelter House norms. Though loyal to Shelter House, abstinence held different meanings for him than it did for the counseling staff.

Grady's work history while a Shelter House member had three phases: during the early part of his membership he worked at "spot jobs" (day labor), for the middle period he drew unemployment compensation, and during the last third of his membership, he worked for Security Service, guarding a local firearms plant. Significantly, when a counselor on duty had suggested he take a dishwashing job, he refused, saying "you don't send a doctor to do a butcher's job." In addition, he was the first member of the halfway

---

[5] A "company man" contacts staff frequently and supports their values while restricting contacts with fellow-members and rejecting their values. For a detailed discussion of the other roles by which members coped with Shelter House conflicts (e.g., "regular guy," "mixer," and "loner"), see Earl Rubington, "The Reformed Drunk," unpublished paper.

house to request and receive seconds during an evening meal.

The "Graduate" Role: Grady as Mission Resident

When the investigator first became acquainted with Grady, he was a "graduate," occupying a private room in the mission, maintaining contact with Shelter House staff and members as well as mission staff and members. Grady continued to work nights as a guard for Security Service and spent much of his leisure time in the Shelter House sector of the mission. Sterling had given him permission to make use of all Shelter House facilities. Grady drank coffee in the Shelter House dining room and, again with Sterling's permission, filled his thermos jug with its coffee every day before leaving for work. Because numerous homeless alcoholics had begun frequenting the dining room, Sterling set down a rule that "outsiders" would not be permitted to use these facilities. "Outsiders," often ex-Shelter House members, drank coffee, ate Shelter House lunches, visited, and solicited staff and members alike for funds. When Ralph Gray, Grady's former counselor, sought to enforce this rule, Grady told him flatly that Sterling had said that Grady could use any and all Shelter House facilities whenever he wished. Some time later, when Charlie Bragg, a Shelter House member, criticized Grady for drinking Shelter House coffee and eating its food, Grady informed Bragg that he had Sterling's permission.

About this same time, Grady overslept one afternoon and arrived late for work. His foreman, knowing he was an alcoholic, accused him of drinking. Grady became incensed at this accusation and only James' efforts at peacemaking forestalled a rupture. James arranged Grady's transfer to another plant and Sterling himself helped Grady move his belongings to the new plant. At the new plant, Grady became friendly with its president and spoke often of his association with him.

By now, Grady had become an articulate critic of the "bums," his favorite term for most Shelter House members and those transients who used the mission dormitory. Though a past master of the art of "ripping up the back"—derogatory comments made about a person soon after he leaves a small gathering [6]—he was still able to participate in conversation and coffee-drinking with Shelter House staff and members, acting the well-informed and dominating person whenever possible, save in the presence of either James or Sterling. "Bums," according to Grady, "are no good to themselves, and no good to anyone else." He saw them as selfish, jealous, and anxious to drag everyone down to their own level. Most of them had come into Shelter House for what they could get out of it rather than to "straighten out" as he had done. Though Grady thought of Shelter House as a "wonderful place," he revealed little of the personality change which ideology sees as requisite for continued abstinence. In AA terms, Grady was "dry," but not "sober." A characteristic indicator of this state is intolerance of "drunks." Other than not drinking, he was the same man he had always been.

The "Traditional" Role: Grady as Unemployed Mission Resident

After eight months as guard, Grady quit and drew unemployment compensation. He had already amassed a fairly large bank account, obtained a wardrobe, and bought a car which he parked across

---

[6] For a systematic analysis of comparable phenomena see Erving Goffman, "The Treatment of the Absent," *The Presentation of Self in Everyday Life,* New York: Doubleday Anchor Books, 1959, pp. 170–175.

the street from the mission. The car stood there as a symbol to Maple City's homeless alcoholics that Grady was "doin' good." On several occasions, Grady had taken the investigator to his room to display his wardrobe, radio and other properties, to report how he had reestablished credit with downtown merchants, and to contrast himself with the "bums." While unemployed, he ran errands for James, Sterling, and some Shelter House counselors. He continued to use the Shelter House facilities but now made some attempts to make himself useful. He made coffee in the morning for Shelter House and cleaned the tables in the dining room after coffee-drinking sessions.

He celebrated his "anniversary" [7] marking one year's sobriety during this period with five other Shelter House graduates in the Alumni Club. The conduct of its members only confirmed his negative opinions of the "bums." However, since only twelve per cent of Shelter House members had ever become graduates, Grady was an important person in this setting. And since only a handful of these graduates were able to extend their sobriety after separation from Shelter House, Grady became a cynosure in the Shelter House-King Street Mission milieu.

The "Reformed Drunk" Role: Grady as Mission Employee

When the mission's night watchman got drunk, James fired him and offered the post to Grady. Grady accepted and announced his appointment proudly to the investigator in the Alumni Club quarters, saying that he was now to be "night superintendent" [8] of the building. Besides supervising transients in the dormitory at night, Grady mopped mission offices, checked doors, answered phones, and watched the building. In addition, Grady was responsible for keeping noise levels down in the Shelter House lounge and in the Alumni Club while religious services were taking place upstairs in the mission's chapel. Performing these latter duties required the exercise of authority over Shelter House counselors and members.

Grady had made a few overtures towards reconciliation with assorted members of his family. Most of these overtures had ended in rebuff from his point of view. Shelter House had done more for his reformation than his "own people," he felt. When, mid-way during his career as night watchman, Sterling retired as director of Shelter House, Grady felt even more isolated. These changing events together with his own response to them gained for Grady the reputation of "reformed drunk" [9] not only in Shelter House but throughout the entire Maple City homeless alcoholic community. He was brusque in handling transients, many of whom had known him before, in jail or "on the street." Many sought preferential treatment from him because of past associations; he denied all requests vigorously. On King Street, he changed his policy, refusing money to the ubiquitous

---

[7] Many AA groups have ceremonies marking years of abstinence.

[8] Most mission personnel had always referred to Grady's new post as the "night man." The Skid Row term for the post was "crumb boss," so named because the person had charge of delousing operations. The Shelter House cook, who was praying along with a lot of other people that Grady would get drunk, sarcastically labeled him the "security officer."

[9] Shelter House staff and members, King Street Mission personnel, and members of Maple City's homeless alcoholic community all agree that a "reformed drunk" receives help in regaining his sobriety and later claims to have "sobered up on his own," is intolerant of drink, drinkers, and drunkenness, refuses help to fellow-alcoholics and, upon relapsing, runs for help to the very people whom he snubbed when sober. For a fuller discussion of this social type, see Rubington, *op. cit.*

panhandlers. While he was working to become known as a "tough giver," members of the homeless alcoholic community he had left were saying that if Grady ever "broke out" he would never be allowed to share in a group bottle again.

The Trash Bucket Incident: Breach of the Unwritten Contract

A series of seemingly trivial disputes had begun soon after Grady assumed the night watchman's post. As his circle of relations shifted, strains mounted and conflicts rose. As a mission employee, Grady was now entitled to free room and board. He now ate with mission personnel in their sector of the kitchen and drank coffee from the mission's urn, rather than from the Shelter House urn. Sharing access to mission facilities made possible the first dispute. For example, soon after Grady had become night watchman, James had to settle an argument between Grady and another mission employee over which TV program would be seen in the mission's lounge. A little later, Grady usurped James' space in the cramped mission parking lot; when James reproved him, Grady asked where he was supposed to park his car. James advised Grady to park his car across the street in the municipal parking lot and said the mission would foot the bill. Soon afterwards, there were two brushes with Charles Goodwin, a Shelter House counselor. Both times, Goodwin sought to park his car in the mission lot early in the morning. To park, Grady would first have to unlock the alley gate for him; Grady refused both times since he was eating at the time. Though he offered his keys to Goodwin, the counselor insisted that Grady open the gate for him personally. Finally, Herlihy, the assistant director of the mission, advocated a more benign policy in the handling of tran-

sients. He wanted Grady to give transients more time for showering and to provide them with clean towels. Grady saw Herlihy as infringing his rights as night watchman and felt that all these disputes were signs of "friction."

In all these disputes, Grady approached James, protesting the indignities in his situation as he viewed them. James always listened patiently, advised tolerance, then rewarded him with a small raise. Implicit in these patterned encounters was the threat of Grady's quitting. This pattern of resolving disputes continued for ten months until the trash bucket incident. One evening, Herlihy reminded Grady to empty the trash bucket. Grady refused angrily and conveyed his annoyance and intentions of quitting in a note to the associate director of the mission, Mrs. O'Brien. James saw the note and said: "Well, if he wants to, let him. Maybe it'll teach him a lesson." The following day, Grady got drunk, after 29 months of abstinence.

Folk and Scientific Interpretation of Relapse

Though little systematic study of relapse exists, folk and scientific interpretations abound. Alcoholics themselves, their associates, employers, clinicians and researchers alike all seek to endow relapses with some meaning. Their interpretations usually fall into one of the following five classes.

1. *"Researching":* When an alcoholic, after a period of abstinence, resumes drinking with the intent of experiencing the pleasant, cathartic effects of alcohol, this is called "researching." Whether the alcoholic seeks to avoid the unpleasant consequences of heavy drinking or disregards them entirely, most persons view his resumption of drinking as an attempt "to drink normally."

2. *"Alcoholic Psychology":* In this,

the most popular view of relapse, resumption of drinking is a predictable occurrence, depending for its regularity on some widely accepted notions of alcoholic personality. Given their low frustration tolerance and high need to reduce anxiety almost immediately, alcoholics, in this view, resort to alcohol at the first sight of stress.

3. *"Strains of Sobriety":* Use of alcohol as a means of coping with intolerable withdrawal distress explains this class of relapses. In the short run, alcoholics handle both psychic and physiological tensions brought on by withdrawal by resuming drinking.[10] In their own words, "what makes you sick, makes you well." And, in the long run, a life without alcohol has no meaning for many alcoholics.

4. *"Pattern of Sobriety":* Jackson Smith [11] and his colleagues have described what they call the "pattern of sobriety." Relapse, according to them, is a predictable aspect of a regular abstinence-relapse cycle. Family members, associates, employers, and clinicians recognize the typical signs which precede a drinking bout; in some instances, the alcoholic himself may be aware of the pattern. In this pattern, the alcoholic builds up interaction credits for his renunciation of alcohol. All role-partners are aware of the sacrifice he is making; periodic indulgence is granted, given the gravity of the sacrifice he has made. The stability of the abstinence-relapse cycle in many instances is quite marked and the pattern persists over a period of years.

5. *"Strains of Society":* In this, the most popular sociological view, alcoholics relapse when felt difficulties in meeting role obligations mount and cumulate. When conflict in norms and roles reaches the breaking point, the alcoholic evades social norms, withdraws, and dissolves all conflicts by drinking again.

Both Shelter House and the King Street Mission were settings in which relapse was a frequent occurrence. Shelter House staff and membership alike, for instance, had little difficulty in assigning particular relapses to one of these five interpretive classes. Implicit in all of these interpretations was the notion that without personality change, abstinence could not be prolonged. Yet Grady's relapse, occurring in a setting in which relapses were generally accounted for in the above terms, poses problems for these accepted interpretations.

Counselors, Shelter House members and King Street Mission staff were all agreed on two major points. It was quite clear that Grady had undergone little if any personality change; if anything, abstinence had made his heart grow harder. At the same time, all informants had placed his relapse in the "strains of society" class, though few had given consideration to the key questions. Social strains had existed from the moment Grady had entered Shelter House and had only grown in a cumulative spiral culminating in his relapse after 29 months. Given his personality as viewed by most others, Grady was an excellent candidate for relapse, a man who ought to have succumbed to mounting cross-pressures long before his ultimate relapse. To know why Grady finally "broke out," it becomes important to find out what kept him sober over a long and stressful period. In un-

---

[10] Lindesmith has defined a drug addict as a person who knows that relief from withdrawal distress can only come from another dose of the drug itself. See Alfred D. Lindesmith, *Opiate Addiction,* (Bloomington, Indiana: Principia Press, 1947). For a systematic application of these ideas to alcohol addiction, see Robert F. Bales, *The "Fixation Factor" in Alcohol Addiction: An Hypothesis Derived from a Comparative Study of Irish and Jewish Social Norms,* unpublished Ph.D. dissertation, Harvard University, 1944.

[11] See Jackson A. Smith, Howard Herrick, and Lester H. Rudy, "Patterns of Sobriety in the Alcoholic," *Diseases of the Nervous System,* 21 (November, 1960), pp. 622–5.

derstanding his case, we may come to a better grasp of why men in similar circumstances actually relapsed a lot sooner than he did.

Grady's relapse is rightfully classified as falling in the "strains of society" category. But his is a special instance of this category. For like all homeless alcoholics who had become members of Shelter House, social strains were unavoidable, changing and cumulative.[12] If we view the process of social rehabilitation as part of a social game, the question of rules becomes paramount. Grady, in common with his fellow chronic drunkenness offenders, faced a set of cumulative social strains. Unlike most of them, however, he had recourse to an umpire who decided all disputes arising in this game in his favor. Alcoholics in the process of rehabilitation who undergo personality change have less need of umpires in resolving conflicts; those who undergo no personality change very likely will confront as many if not more conflicts and strains. Without an intermediary, the probability is high that resumption of drinking will take place when these strains are deemed illegitimate. Yet Grady, in the anomic situation of the marginal ex-alcoholic, was able to remain sober in the face of mounting strains primarily because of an intermediary who managed social disputes for him.

Interpretation of Grady's Relapse

Grady's situation reflects, on the one hand, some of the problems implicit in paternalistic mission culture and, on the other, the problems of marginality for recovered homeless alcoholics, particularly those who had been "loners" on Skid Row. Because sobriety, Shelter House's paramount objective, was a scarce commodity, Grady had actually become a "big fish in a little pond." Since Grady symbolized success, both James and Sterling indulged him. Both men had adapted the AA sponsor-protege model [13] to their relations with Grady. Primarily, these efforts were in behalf of shoring up and maintaining Grady's sobriety.

As more and more doors to the conventional community closed, Grady came to rely more upon his contacts with these two men as signs of his official redemption. He had cut himself off from any possible social rewards from other homeless alcoholics; as he put it, "living with the bums" had taught him a lesson. Praise from them had no meaning for him whatsoever while efforts which both James and Sterling made on his behalf justified his existence. After Sterling retired as director of Shelter House, only James was left to him as a source of self-respect. Grady's redemption, however, as a person of some moral worth rested solely on those concrete efforts which James made on his behalf and, in a social world fraught with conflicts, these efforts consisted primarily in the resolution of conflicts.

Once Sterling had retired and Grady had become night watchman, strains mounted and cumulated in a vicious circle. Being forced to work with and associate with persons he considered his moral inferiors, being placed in situations which required him to antagonize rather than please clients, only forced home the discrepancy between Grady's self-concept and social reality. Just as alcoholics turn repeatedly to drinking when similar discrepancies prove unbearable, Grady

---

[12] For a discussion of social strains facing heroin addicts comparable to those confronting Shelter House members, see Marsh Ray, "The Cycle of Abstinence and Relapse among Heroin Addicts," *Social Problems*, 9 (Fall, 1961), pp. 132–40.

[13] For an excellent discussion of this model, see Freed Bales, "Types of Social Structure as Factors in 'Cures' for Alcohol Addiction," *Applied Anthropology*, 1 (April–June, 1942), pp. 1–13.

turned to James for resolution of all disputes arising out of these discrepancies, and James, bound to this relation as benefactor and sponsor, never failed him until the trash bucket incident. At that point, when he failed to manage the dispute in the expected manner, Grady's social world collapsed for him. James' sudden refusal to arbitrate breached the premises of their unwritten contract. In the words of one informant, Grady had left himself with no "out" and had no alternative save to get drunk. James' failure to arbitrate sundered the bonds of this relationship.

Summary and Conclusions

Treatment ideology, whether of the professional or Alcoholics Anonymous variety, implies that prolonged abstinence without personality change is unlikely. Nevertheless, countless alcoholics both in and out of Alcoholics Anonymous have obtained their sobriety without personality change.[14] The question arises: how is sobriety possible without the personality change which treatment ideology deems indispensable?

Grady's case sheds light on this important question. Those social settings in which alcoholics seek to practice abstinence can be characterized by degree of social strain and by presence or absence of umpires. Given low strain and personality change, abstinence seems rather likely. Without personality change, abstinence seems likely only under two social conditions: when strains are minimal, or when strains are maximal and umpires are present. Grady's case exemplifies the second condition most clearly.

Abstinence Cycles and Heroin Addicts *

MARSH B. RAY

Those who study persons addicted to opium and its derivatives are confronted by the following paradox: A cure from physiological dependence on opiates may be secured within a relatively short period, and carefully controlled studies indicate that use of these drugs does not cause psychosis, organic intellectual deterioration, or any permanent impairment of intellectual function.[1] But, despite these facts, addicts display a high rate of recidivism. On the other hand, while the rate of recidivism is high, addicts continually and repeatedly seek cure. It is difficult to obtain definitive data concerning the number of cures the addict takes, but

---

[14] Bales, *op. cit.,* argues that Alcoholics Anonymous is not so much an organizational vehicle for personality change as a set of relationships by which alcoholics can continue to act as they always have without the need for drinking.

* Reprinted from *Social Problems,* Vol. 9, No. 2 (Fall, 1961), pp. 132–40, by permission of the author and *Social Problems.*

[1] See as examples: C. Knight Aldrich, "The Relationship of the Concept Formation Test to Drug Addiction and Intelligence," *Journal of Nervous and Mental Diseases,* 100 (July, 1944), pp. 30–34; Margaret E. Hall, "Mental and Physical Efficiency of Women Drug Addicts," *Journal of Abnormal and Social Psychology,* 33 (July, 1938), pp. 332–345; A. Z. Pfeffer and Dorothy Cleck, "Chronic Psychoses and Addiction to Morphine," *Archives of Neurology and Psychiatry,* 56 (December, 1946), pp. 665–672.

various studies of institutional admissions indicate that it is relatively high,[2] and there are many attempts at home cure that go unrecorded.

This paper reports on a study [3] of abstinence and relapse in which attention is focused on the way the addict or abstainer orders and makes meaningful the objects of his experience, including himself as an object,[4] during the critical periods of cure and of relapse and the related sense of identity or of social isolation the addict feels as he interacts with significant others. It is especially concerned with describing and analyzing the characteristic ways the addict or abstainer defines the social situations he encounters during these periods and responds to the status dilemmas he experiences in them.

Secondary Status Characteristics of Addicts

The social world of addiction contains a loose system of organizational and cultural elements, including a special language or argot, certain artifacts, a commodity market and pricing system, a system of stratification, and ethical codes. The addict's commitment to these values gives him a status and an identity.[5] In addition to these direct links to the world

of addiction, becoming an addict means that one assumes a number of secondary status characteristics in accordance with the definitions the society has of this activity.[6] Some of these are set forth in federal and local laws and statutes, others are defined by the stereotypic thinking of members of the larger society about the causes and consequences of drug use.

The addict's incarceration in correctional institutions has specific meanings which he finds reflected in the attitudes adopted toward him by members of non-addict society and by his fellow addicts. Additionally, as his habit grows and the demands for drugs get beyond any legitimate means of supply, his own activities in satisfying his increased craving give him direct experiential evidence of the criminal aspects of self. These meanings of self as a criminal become internalized as he begins to apply criminal argot to his activities and institutional experiences. Thus shop-lifting becomes "boosting," the correctional settings become "joints," and the guards in such institutions become "screws."

The popular notion that the addict is somehow psychologically inadequate is supported by many authorities in the field. In addition, support and definition is supplied by the very nature of the insti-

---

[2] Michael J. Pescor, *A Statistical Analysis of the Clinical Records of Hospitalized Drug Addicts,* Supplement No. 143 to the Public Health Reports, United States Public Health Service (Washington: Government Printing Office, 1943), p. 24; Victor H. Vogel, "Treatment of the Narcotic Addict by the U. S. Public Health Service," *Federal Probation,* 12 (June, 1948), pp. 45–50.

[3] The basic data consisted of case histories collected in repeated depth interviews with 17 addicts and abstainers over a two year period. During this time several of the active addicts became abstainers and vice-versa. Additional material was gathered while the author worked for a year as a social worker in a rehabilitation program for addicts.

[4] "Object" is employed here in the sense intended by George Herbert Mead in his development of the concept in *Mind, Self and Society* (Chicago: University of Chicago Press, 1934), Part III, pp. 135–226. Two earlier studies have applied this kind of thinking in studying the behavior of addicts, see: L. Guy Brown, "The Sociological Implications of Drug Addiction," *Journal of Educational Sociology,* 4 (February, 1931), pp. 358–369, and Alfred R. Lindesmith, *Opiate Addiction* (Bloomington, Indiana: Principia Press, 1947).

[5] Marsh B. Ray, "Cure and Relapse Among Heroin Addicts" (unpublished M.A. thesis, Department of Sociology, University of Chicago, 1958).

[6] For a general discussion of the important role that auxiliary status characteristics play in social situations, see Everett C. Hughes, "Dilemmas and Contradictions in Status," *American Journal of Sociology,* 50 (March, 1945), pp. 253–259.

tution in which drug addicts are usually treated and have a large part of their experience since even the names of these institutions fix this definition of addiction. For example, one of the out-patient clinics for the treatment of addicts in Chicago was located at Illinois Neuropsychiatric Institute, and the connotations of Bellevue Hospital in New York City, another treatment center for addicts, are socially well established. Then, too, the composition of the staff in treatment centers contributes substantially to the image of the addict as mentally ill, for the personnel are primarily psychiatrists, psychologists, and psychiatric social workers. How such a definition of self was brought forcefully home to one addict is illustrated in the following quotation:

When I got down to the hospital, I was interviewed by different doctors and one of them told me, "you now have one mark against you as crazy for having been down here." I hadn't known it was a crazy house. You know regular people [non-addicts] think this too.

Finally, as the addict's habit grows and almost all of his thoughts and efforts are directed toward supplying himself with drugs, he becomes careless about his personal appearance and cleanliness. Consequently non-addicts think of him as a "bum" and, because he persists in his use of drugs, conclude that he lacks "will power," is perhaps "degenerate," and is likely to contaminate others.

The addict is aware that he is judged in terms of these various secondary social definitions, and while he may attempt to reject them, it is difficult if not impossible to do so when much of his interpersonal and institutional experience serves to ratify these definitions. They assume importance because they are the medium of exchange in social transactions with the addict and non-addict world in which the addict identifies himself as an object and judges himself in relation to addict and non-addict values. Such experiences are socially disjunctive and become the basis for motivated acts.

The Inception of Cure

An episode of cure begins in the private thoughts of the addict rather than in his overt behavior. These deliberations develop as a result of experience in specific situations of interaction with important others that cause the addict to experience social stress, to develop some feeling of alienation from or dissatisfaction with his present identity, and to call it into question and examine it in all of its implications and ramifications. In these situations the addict engages in private self-debate in which he juxtaposes the values and social relationships which have become immediate and concrete through his addiction with those that are sometimes only half remembered or only imperfectly perceived.

I think that my mother knew that I was addicted because she had heard rumors around the neighborhood. Around that time [when he first began to think about cure] she had been telling me that I looked like a "bum," and that my hair was down the back of my neck and that I was dirty. I had known this too but had shoved it down in the back of my mind somewhere. She used to tell me that to look like this wasn't at all like me. I always wanted to look presentable and her saying this really hurt. At that time I was going to [college] and I wanted to look my best. I always looked at myself as the clever one—the "mystery man"—outwitting the "dolts." I always thought that no one knew, that when I was in my room they thought I was studying my books when actually I wasn't studying at all.

After mother said those things I did a lot of thinking. I often used to sit around my room and think about it and even look at myself in the mirror and I could see that it was true. What is it called . . . ? When you take yourself out of a situation and look at yourself . . . ? "Self appraisal" . . . I guess that's it. Well I did this about my appearance and about the deterioration of my character. I didn't like it because I didn't want anything to be master over me because this was contrary to my character. I used to sit and look at that infinitesimal bit of powder. I felt it changed my personality somehow.

I used to try staying in but I would get sick. But because I had money I couldn't maintain it [withstand the demands of the withdrawal sickness] and when the pain got unbearable, at least to me it was unbearable, I would go out again. I wanted to be independent of it. I knew then that if I continued I would have to resort to stealing to maintain my habit and this I couldn't tolerate because it was contrary to my character. The others were robbing and stealing but I couldn't be a part of that. I first talked with my uncle about it because my mother was alive then and I thought she would crack up and maybe not understand the problem. I didn't want to be reprimanded, I knew I'd done wrong. I had been through a lot and felt I wanted to be rid of the thing. He was very understanding about it and didn't criticize me. He just talked with me about going to the hospital and said he thought this would be the best way to do it.

In the above example, the meanings of the complex of secondary status characteristics of the addict identity when used as self referents in bringing this identity into question is shown in dramatic fashion.

But the social psychological prerequisites to the inception of an episode of abstinence need not precede physical withdrawal of the drug. It is frequently the case that following the enforced withdrawal that begins a period of confinement in a correctional institution or hospital, the addict engages in self debate in which the self in all of its ramifications emerges as an object and is brought under scrutiny. Such institutional situations constrain the addict's perspectives about himself and have a dual character. On

the one hand, they serve to ratify a secondary status characteristic, while on the other, as addicts interact with older inmates of jails and hospitals, they provide daily concrete models of what life may be like in later years as a consequence of continued use of drugs.

On occasion, however, the addict group itself, rather than non-addict society, provides the socially disjunctive experience that motivates the addict to abstain, although the non-addict world and its values are still the reference point. An addict who had been addicted for several years and had had several involuntary cures in correctional institutions describes such an experience as follows:

When I first started using we were all buddies, but later we started "burning" each other. One guy would say, "Well, I'll go 'cop'" [buy drugs]. Then he'd take the "bread" [money] and he'd never come back. I kicked one time because of that. I didn't have no more money and I got disgusted. First I started to swear him up and down but then my inner conscience got started and I said maybe he got "busted" [arrested]. Then I said, "Aw, to hell with him and to hell with all junkies—they're all the same." So I went home and I tried to read a couple of comic books to keep my mind off it. I was very sick but after a couple of days I kicked.

While the above situation may not be typical, it illustrates the same process to be observed in the other examples—a disruption of the social ordering of experience that has become familiar, a calling into question of the addict identity, and the rejection of this identity and the values associated with it. The more typical situations that evoke such conduct would appear to involve a non-addict or some concrete aspect of the non-addict world as the catalytic agent.

The Addict Self in Transition

The addict who has successfully completed withdrawal is no longer faced with the need to take drugs in order to avert the disaster of withdrawal sickness, and now enters a period which might best be characterized as a "running struggle" with his problems of social identity. He could not have taken such a drastic step had he not developed some series of expectations concerning the nature of his future relationships with social others. His anticipations concerning these situations may or may not be realistic; what matters is that he has them and that the imagery he holds regarding himself and his potentialities is a strong motivating force in his continued abstinence. Above all, he appears to desire ratification by significant others of his newly developing identity, and in his interactions during an episode of abstinence he expects to secure it.

In the early phases of an episode of cure, the abstainer manifests considerable ambivalence about where he stands in addict and non-addict groups, and in discussions of addiction and addicts, he may indicate his ambivalence through his alternate use of the pronouns "we" and "they" and thus his alternate membership in addict and non-addict society. He may also indicate his ambivalence through other nuances of language and choice of words. Later, during a successful episode of abstinence, the ex-addict indicates his non-membership in the addict group through categorizations that place addicts clearly in the third person, and he places his own addiction and matters pertaining to it in the past tense. For example, he is likely to preface a remark with the phrase "When I was an addict. . . ." But of equal or greater importance is the fact that the ex-addict who is successful in remaining abstinent relates to new groups of people, participates in their experience, and to some extent begins to evaluate the conduct of his former associates (and perhaps his own when he was an addict) in terms of the values of the new group.

I see the guys around now quite often and sometimes we talk for a while but I don't feel that I am anything like them anymore and I always leave before they "make up" [take drugs]. I tell them, "You know what you are doing but if you keep on you'll just go to jail like I did." I don't feel that they are wrong to be using but just that I'm luckier than they are because I have goals. It's funny, I used to call them "squares" for not using and now they call me "square" for not using. They think that they are "hip" and they are always talking about the old days. That makes me realize how far I've come. But it makes me want to keep away from them, too, because they always use the same old vocabulary—talking about "squares" and being "hip."

Thus, while some abstainers do not deny the right of others to use drugs if they choose, they clearly indicate that addiction is no longer a personally meaningful area of social experience for them. In the above illustration the abstainer is using this experience as something of a "sounding board" for his newly developed identity. Of particular note is the considerable loss of meaning in the old symbols through which he previously ordered his experience and his concern with one of the inevitable consequences of drug use. This is a common experience for those who have maintained abstinence for any length of time.

During the later stages of the formation of an abstainer identity, the ex-addict begins to perceive a difference in his relations with significant others, particularly with members of his family. Undoubtedly their attitudes, in turn, undergo modification and change as a result of his apparent continued abstinence, and they arrive at this judgment by observing his cleanliness and attention to personal neatness, his steady employment, and his re-subscription to other values of non-addict society. The ex-addict is very much aware of these attitudinal differences and uses them further to bolster his conception of himself as an abstainer.

Lots of times I don't even feel like I ever took dope. I feel released not to be dependent on it. I think how nice it is to be natural without having to rely on dope to make me feel good. See, when I was a "junkie" I lost a lot of respect. My father wouldn't talk to me and I was filthy. I have to build up that respect again. I do a lot of things with my family now and my father talks to me again. It's like at parties that my relatives give, now they are always running up to me and giving me a drink and showing me a lot of attention. Before they wouldn't even talk to me. See, I used to feel lonely because my life was dependent on stuff and I felt different from regular people. See, "junkies" and regular people are two different things. I used to feel that I was out of place with my relatives when I was on junk. I didn't want to walk with them on the street and do things with them. Now I do things with them all the time like go to the show and joke with them and I go to church with my uncle. I just kept saying to myself that "junkies" are not my people. My relatives don't say things behind my back now and I am gaining their respect slow but sure.

In this illustration there may be observed a budding sense of social insight characteristic of abstainers in this period of their development. Another characteristic feature is the recognition that subscription to non-addict values must be grounded in action—in playing the role of non-addict in participation with non-addicts and thus sharing in their values and perspectives.

The Process of Relapse

The tendency toward relapse develops out of the meanings of the abstainer's experience in social situations when he develops an image of himself as socially different from non-addicts, and relapse occurs when he redefines himself as an addict. When his social expectations and the expectations of others with whom he interacts are not met, social stress develops and he is required to re-examine the meaningfulness of his experience in non-addict society and in so doing question his identity as an abstainer. This type of experience promotes a mental realignment with addict values and standards and may be observed in the abstainer's thoughts about himself in covert social situations, in his direct interpersonal relations with active addicts, and in his experience with representatives of non-addict society. It is in these various settings that his developing sense of self as an abstainer is put to the test.

Experiences with other addicts that promote relapse. Re-addiction most frequently occurs during the period immediately following the physical withdrawal of the drug—the period described earlier as a time of "running struggle" with identity problems for the ex-addict. It is at this point, when the old values and old meanings he experienced as an addict are still immediate and the new ordering of his experience without narcotics is not well established, that the ex-addict seems most vulnerable to relapse. Sometimes the experiences that provoke the questioning of identity that precedes relapse occur within the confines of the very institution where the addict has gone to seek cure. The social expectations of other addicts in the hospital are of vital importance in creating an atmosphere in which identification with the values of non-addict society is difficult to maintain.

[The last time we talked you said that you would like to tell me about your experiences in the hospital. What were they like?]

Well, during the first time I was at the

hospital most of the fellows seemed to hate [to give] the "square" impression, not hate it exactly but refuse to admit [to] it. My own feelings were that everyone should have been a little different in expressing themselves that I would like to accept the extreme opposite. But I felt that I would have disagreements about this with the fellow inmates. They thought I was a very queer or peculiar person that constantly showed disagreement about the problem as they saw it. I never did reach an understanding with them about the problem.

But addicts do not always relapse on first contact with members of the old group. In fact, there is nothing to indicate that addicts relapse only as a result of association. Instead, contacts may go on for some time during which the ex-addict carries on much private self debate, feeling at one point that he is socially closer to addicts and at another that his real interest lies in future new identities on which he has decided. Typically he may also call to mind the reason he undertook cure in the first place and question the rationality of relapsing. An interesting example of the dilemma and ambivalence experienced under these circumstances and the partial acceding to social pressures from the addict group by applying the definitions of that group to one's own conduct are the experiences of another addict.

[He had entered the hospital "with the key" and after completing withdrawal he stayed at the hospital for three weeks before voluntarily signing out, although the required period of treatment for a medical discharge at the time was four and one-half months.]

This one kid who was a friend of mine came to me one night and said, "Let's get out of here." So I went and checked out too. Then I got to thinking, "I don't want to go home yet—I'm still sick—and what did I come down here for anyway." So I went up and got my papers back from the officer and tore them up. Then I found this kid and told him that I was staying and he said, "Oh we knew you weren't going to do it—we knew you'd chicken out." Then I went back and put my papers through again. I felt they were trying to "put me down."

When we got out I could have had a shot right away because one of these guys when we got to town said he knew a croaker who would fix us up, but I didn't go with them. I didn't care what they thought because I got to figuring that I had went this far and I might as well stay off.

When I got home I stayed off for two months but my mother was hollering at me all the time and there was this one family in the neighborhood that was always "chopping me up." I wanted to tell this woman off because she talked all right to my face but behind my back she said things like she was afraid I would turn her son on because I was hanging around with him. She would tell these things to my mother. I never turned anybody on! She didn't know that but I wanted to tell her. Finally I just got disgusted because nobody wanted to believe me and I went back on.

The experiences of this addict provide an interesting denial of the notion that addicts relapse because of association *per se* and support the thesis that relapse is a function of the kind of object ex-addicts make of themselves in the situations they face.

Relations with non-addicts as a prelude to relapse. While the ex-addict's interaction with addict groups is often a source of experiences which cause him to question the value to him of an abstainer identity, experiences with non-addict groups also play a vital role. In most instances the addict has established a status for himself in the eyes of non-addicts who may be acquainted with his case—members of his family, social workers, law enforcement officers, physicians and so forth. Through gestures, vocal and otherwise, these non-addicts make indications to the ex-addict concerning his membership and right to

Transforming Deviant Identity **405**

participation in their group, for example, the right to be believed when he attempts to indicate to the non-addict world that he believes in and subscribes to its values. In his contacts with non-addicts, the former addict is particularly sensitive to their cues.

During the early phases of an episode of abstinence the abstainer enters various situations with quite definite expectations concerning how he should be defined and treated. He indicates his desire for ratification of his new status in many ways, and finds it socially difficult when he sees in the conduct of others toward him a reference to his old identity as an addict. He is not unaware of these doubts about his identity.

My relatives were always saying things to me like "Have you really quit using that drug now?" and things like that. And I knew that they were doing a lot of talking behind my back because when I came around they would stop talking but I overheard them. It used to burn my ass.

On the other hand, the non-addicts with whom he has experience during this period have their own expectations concerning the abstainer's probable conduct. Based in part on the stereotypic thinking of non-addict society concerning addiction, in part on unfortunate previous experiences, they may exhibit some skepticism concerning the "cure" and express doubt about the abstainer's prognosis.[7]

The Social Psychological Meaning of Relapse

On an immediate concrete level, relapse requires that the individual reorient himself to the market conditions surrounding

the sale of illicit drugs. He must re-establish his sources of supply and, if he has been abstinent for very long, he may have to learn about new fads and fashions in drug use. He may learn, for example, that dolophin is more readily available than heroin at the moment of his return to drug use, that it requires less in the way of preparation, that it calls for such and such amount to safely secure a certain effect, what the effects will be, and so on.

But the ex-addict's re-entrance into the social world of addiction has much deeper meanings. It places demands and restraints upon his interactions and the meaningfulness of his experience. It requires a recommitment to the norms of addiction and limits the degree to which he may relate to non-addict groups in terms of the latter's values and standards. It demands participation in the old ways of organizing conduct and experience and, as a consequence, the readoption of the secondary status characteristics of addiction. He again shows a lack of concern about his personal appearance and grooming. Illicit activities are again engaged in to get money for drugs, and as a result the possibility of more firmly establishing the criminal aspect of his identity becomes a reality.

The social consequence of these experiences and activities is the re-establishment of the sense of social isolation from the non-addict group and a recaptured sense of the meaningfulness of experience in the social world of addiction. It is through these familiar meanings and the reapplication of the symbolic meanings of the addict world to his own conduct that identity and status as an addict are reaffirmed. The ex-addict who

[7] Family members may have been subjected to thefts by the addict, or other kinds of trickery, and they tend to be on their guard lest the experience be repeated. Interestingly, the matter of thefts of either money or small household objects (a radio or a clock) is often used by family members as an index as to whether "he's back on that stuff again" or not. His physical appearance is another gauge.

relapses is thus likely to comment, "I feel like one of the guys again," or as Street has put it, "It was like coming home." [8]

While repeated relapse on the addict's part may more firmly convince him that "once a junkie, always a junkie" is no myth but instead a valid comment on his way of life, every relapse has within it the genesis of another attempt at cure. From his however brief or lengthy excursions into the world of non-addiction, the relapsed addict carries back with him an image of himself as one who has done the impossible—one who has actually experienced a period when it was unnecessary to take drugs to avoid the dreaded withdrawal sickness. But these are not his only recollections. He recalls, too, his identification of himself as an abstainer, no matter how tentatively or imperfectly this may have been accomplished. He thinks over his experiences in situations while he occupied the status of abstainer and speculates about the possible other outcomes of these situations had he acted differently.

[Originally from Chicago, he experienced the only voluntary period of abstinence in a long career of addiction while living with his wife in Kansas City, Missouri. After an argument with his wife, during which she reminded him of his previous addiction and its consequences for her, he left her and returned to Chicago, where he immediately relapsed. After three weeks he was using about $12 worth of morphine daily.] He reports on his thoughts at the time as follows:

Now and then I'm given to rational thinking or reasoning and somehow I had a premonition that should I remain in Chicago much longer, shoplifting and doing the various criminal acts I did to get money for drugs, plus the criminal act of just using the drug, I would soon be in jail or perhaps something worse, for in truth one's life is at stake each day when he uses drugs. I reflected on the life I had known in Kansas City with Rose in contrast to the one I had returned to. I didn't know what Rose thought had become of me. I thought that more than likely she was angry and thoroughly disgusted and glad that I was gone. However, I wanted to return but first thought it best to call and see what her feelings were.

[At his wife's urging he returned to Kansas City and undertook a "cold turkey" cure in their home. He remained abstinent for a considerable period but subsequently relapsed again when he returned to Chicago.]

Reflections of the above kind provide the relapsed addict with a rich body of material for self-recrimination and he again evaluates his own conduct in terms of what he believes are the larger society's attitudes toward addicts and addiction. It is then that he may again speculate about his own potential for meaningful experiences and relationships in a non-addict world and thus set into motion a new attempt at cure.

Summary

Addiction to narcotic drugs in our society commits the participant in this activity to a status and identity that has complex secondary characteristics. These develop through shared roles and common interpersonal and institutional experience, and as a consequence addicts develop perspectives about themselves and about non-addict values. They evaluate social situations, and in turn are evaluated by the other participants in these situations, in these terms, often with the result that the value of the addict's identity relative to the social world of addiction is brought into question. When this happens the identification of oneself as an addict, committed to the values and statuses of the addict group, is contrasted

[8] Leroy Street (pseudonym) and D. Loth, *I Was A Drug Addict*, Pyramid Books (New York: Random House, 1953), p. 71.

with new or remembered identities and relationships, resulting in a commitment to cure with its implications of intense physical suffering. In the period following physical withdrawal from heroin, the addict attempts to enact a new social reality which coincides with his desired self-image as an abstainer, and he seeks ratification of his new identity from others in the situations he faces.

But the abstainer's social expectations during a period when he is off drugs are frequently not gratified. Here again, socially disjunctive experiences bring about a questioning of the value of an abstainer identity and promote reflections in which addict and non-addict identities and relationships are compared. The abstainer's realignment of his values with those of the world of addiction results in the redefinition of self as an addict and has as a consequence the actions necessary to relapse. But it should be noted that the seeds of a new attempt at abstinence are sown, once addiction has been reestablished, in the self-recriminations engaged in upon remembrance of a successful period of abstinence.

Differential Association and the Rehabilitation of Drug Addicts *

RITA VOLKMAN AND DONALD R. CRESSEY

In 1955 Cressey listed five principles for applying Edwin Sutherland's theory of differential association to the rehabilitation of criminals.[1] While this article is now frequently cited in the sociological literature dealing with group therapy, "therapeutic communities," and "total institutions," we know of no program of rehabilitation that has been explicitly based on the principles. The major point of Cressey's article, which referred to criminals, not addicts, is similar to the following recommendation by the Chief of the United States Narcotics Division: "The community should restore the former addict to his proper place in society and help him avoid associations that would influence him to return to the use of drugs."[2]

Cressey gives five rules (to be reviewed below) for implementing this directive to "restore," "help," and "influence" the addict. These rules, derived from the sociological and social-psychological literature on social movements, crime prevention, group therapy, communications, personality change, and social change, were designed to show that sociology has distinctive, non-psychiatric, theory that can be used effectively by practitioners

* Reprinted from *The American Journal of Sociology*, Vol. 69, No. 2 (September, 1963), pp. 129–142, by permission of the authors and The University of Chicago Press. Copyright 1963 by The University of Chicago.
    [1] Donald R. Cressey, "Changing Criminals: The Application of the Theory of Differential Association," *American Journal of Sociology*, LXI (September, 1955), 116–20 (see also Cressey, "Contradictory Theories in Correctional Group Therapy Programs," *Federal Probation*, XVIII [June, 1954], 20–26).
    [2] Harry J. Anslinger, "Drug Addiction," *Encyclopaedia Britannica*, VII (1960), 677–79.

seeking to prevent crime and change criminals. Sutherland also had this as a principal objective when he formulated his theory of differential association.[3]

Assuming, as we do, that Cressey's principles are consistent with Sutherland's theory and that his theory, in turn, is consistent with more general sociological theory, a test of the principles would be a test of the more general formulations. Ideally, such a test would involve careful study of the results of a program rationally designed to utilize the principles to change criminals. To our knowledge, such a test has not been made.[4] As a "next best" test, we may study rehabilitation programs that use the principles, however unwittingly. Such a program has been in operation since 1958. Insofar as it is remarkably similar to any program that could have been designed to implement the principles, the results over the years can be viewed as at least a crude test of the principles. Since the principles are interrelated, the parts of any program implementing them must necessarily overlap.

"Synanon," an organization of former drug addicts, was founded in May, 1958, by a member of Alcoholics Anonymous with the assistance of an alcoholic and a drug addict. In December, 1958, Volkman (a non-addict) heard about the two dozen ex-addicts living together in an abandoned store, and she obtained permission of the Synanon Board of Directors[5] to visit the group daily and to live in during the weekends. In July, 1959,

she moved into the girls' dormitory of the group's new, larger quarters and continued to reside at Synanon House until June, 1960. Cressey (also a non-addict) visited the House at Volkman's invitation in the spring of 1960; for one year, beginning in July, 1960, he visited the organization on the average of at least once a week. He deliberately refrained from trying to influence policy or program, and his theory about the effects of group relationships on rehabilitation were unknown to the group. Most of the interview material and statistical data reported below were collected by Volkman during her 1959–60 period of residence and were used in the thesis for her Master's degree, prepared under the direction of C. Wayne Gordon.[6] As both a full-fledged member of Synanon and as a participant observer, Volkman attended about three hundred group sessions, a few of which were recorded. She was accorded the same work responsibilities, rights, and privileges as any other member, and she was considered one of Synanon's first "graduates."

The Subjects

Background data were available on only the first fifty-two persons entering Synanon after July, 1958. These records were prepared by a resident who in July, 1959, took it upon himself to interview and compile the information. We have no way of determining whether these fifty-two persons are representative of all addicts. However, we believe they are

---

[3] Edwin H. Sutherland and Donald R. Cressey, *Principles of Criminology* (6th ed.; Philadelphia: J. B. Lippincott Co., 1960), pp. 74–80.

[4] See, however, Joseph A. Cook and Gilbert Geis, "Forum Anonymous: The Techniques of Alcoholics Anonymous Applied to Prison Therapy," *Journal of Social Therapy*, III (First Quarter, 1957), 9–13.

[5] The Board at first was composed of the three original members. It is now made up of the founder (an ex-alcoholic but a non-addict) and seven long-term residents who have remained off drugs and who have demonstrated their strict loyalty to the group and its principles.

[6] Rita Volkman, "A Descriptive Case Study of Synanon as a Primary Group Organization" (unpublished Master's thesis, Department of Education, University of California, Los Angeles, 1961).

TABLE 1

Age and Sex *

Age (In Years)	Males		Females		Total	
	No.	Per Cent	No.	Per Cent	No.	Per Cent
18–20	0	0	1	7	1	2
21–30	17	44	11	79	28	54
31–40	18	48	2	14	20	38
41–50	1	3	0	0	1	2
51–60	2	5	0	0	2	4
Total	38	100	14	100	52	100

* Median ages: males, 31.0; females, 27.5.

similar to the 215 persons who have resided at Synanon for at least one month.

Age and sex distributions are shown in Table 1: 44 per cent of the fifty-two were Protestant, 35 per cent Catholic, 8 per cent Jewish.[7] Racially, 27 per cent were Negro, and there were no Orientals; 19 per cent of the Caucasians were of Mexican origin and 13 per cent were of Italian origin. Educational attainment is shown in Table 2. Although the data on early family life are poor because the resident simply asked "What was your family like?" it may be noted that only five of the fifty-two indicated satisfaction with the home. Words and phrases such as "tension," "arguing," "bickering," "violence," "lack of warmth," "went back and forth," and "nagged" were common.[8]

The sporadic and tenuous occupational ties held by the group are indicated in Table 3. This table supports the notion that addicts cannot maintain steady jobs because their addiction interferes with the work routine; it suggests also that these members had few lasting peer group contacts or ties, at least so far as work associations go. In view of their poor em-

TABLE 2

Educational Attainment

	No.	Per Cent
Part grade school	1	2
Completed grade school .	3	6
Part high school	24	46
Completed high school ..	11	21
Part college	13	25
Completed college	0	0
Total	52	100

TABLE 3

Length and Continuity of Employment

No. of Years on One Job	Unsteady (Discontinuous or Sporadic)	Steady (Continuous)	Total
Under 1.	36 *	4	40
2–3	3	2	5
4–5	1	3	4
6 or over	2	1	3
Total	42	10	52

* Of this category 67 per cent defined their work as "for short periods only."

[7] In May, 1961, 20 per cent of the residents were Jewish.
[8] Cf. Research Center for Human Relations, New York University, *Family Background as an Etiological Factor in Personality Predisposition to Heroin Addiction* (New York: the Author, 1956).

ployment records, it might be asked how the addicts supported their addictions, which cost from $30 to $50 a day and sometimes ran to $100 a day. Only four of the men reported that they obtained their incomes by legitimate work alone; thirty (79 per cent) were engaged in illegitimate activities, with theft, burglary, armed robbery, shoplifting, and pimping leading the list. One man and seven women were supplied with either drugs or money by their mates or families, and five of these females supplemented this source by prostitution or other illegitimate work. Five of the fourteen women had no income except that from illegitimate activities, and none of the women supported themselves by legitimate work only.

Institutional histories and military service histories are consistent with the work and educational histories, indicating that the fifty-two members were not somehow inadvertently selected as "easy" rehabilitation cases. The fifty-two had been in and out of prisons, jails, and hospitals all

TABLE 4

Confinements in Institutions

No. of Con- finements	No.		
	Male	Female	Total *
1– 3 ...	9	6	15
4– 6 ...	12	7	19
7– 9 ...	8	0	8
10–12 ...	0	1	1
13–15 ...	2	0	2
Total con- fine- ments	166	59	225

* Three males indicated "numerous arrests," and four supplied no information. These seven were not included in the tally.

over the United States. Table 4 shows that ten men and one woman had been confined seven or more times; the mean number of confinements for males was 5.5 and for females 3.9. The table seems to indicate that whatever value confinement in institutions might have had for this group, it clearly did not prevent further confinements.

In sum, the pre-Synanon experiences of the fifty-two residents seems to indicate non-identification with pro-legal activities and norms. Neither the home, the armed services, the occupational world, schools, prisons, nor hospitals served as links with the larger and more socially acceptable community. This, then, is the kind of "raw material" with which Synanon has been working.[9]

The Program

ADMISSION

Not every addict who knocks on the door of Synanon is given admission. Nevertheless, the only admission criterion we have been able to find is *expressed willingness* to submit one's self to a group that hates drug addiction. Use of this criterion has unwittingly implemented one of Cressey's principles:

If criminals are to be changed, they must be assimilated into groups which emphasize values conducive to law-abiding behavior and, concurrently, alienated from groups emphasizing values conducive to criminality. Since our experience has been that the majority of criminals experience great difficulty in securing intimate contacts in ordinary groups, special groups whose major common goal is the reformation of criminals must be created.

This process of assimilation and alienation begins the moment an addict arrives

[9] Of the fifty-two members 60 per cent first heard about Synanon from addicts on the street or in jails, prisons, or hospitals; about a fourth heard about it on television or read about it in a magazine; and the remainder were told of it by members or past members.

at Synanon, and it continues throughout his stay. The following are two leaders' comments on admission interviews; they are consistent with our own observations of about twenty such interviews.

1. When a new guy comes in we want to find out whether a person has one inkling of seriousness. Everybody who comes here is what we call a psychopathic liar. We don't take them all, either. We work off the top spontaneously, in terms of feeling. We use a sort of intuitive faculty. You know he's lying, but you figure, "Well, maybe if you get a halfway positive feeling that he'll stay. . . ." We ask him things like "What do you want from us?" "Don't you think you're an idiot or insane?" "Doesn't it sound insane for you to be running around the alleys stealing money from others so's you can go and stick something up your arm?" "Does this sound sane to you?" "Have you got family and friends outside?" We might tell him to go do his business now and come back when he's ready to do business with us. We tell him, "We don't need you." "You need *us*." And if we figure he's only halfway with us, we'll chop off his hair.

It's all in the *attitude*. It's got to be positive. We don't want their money. But we may just tell him to bring back some dough next week. If he pleads and begs—the money's not important. If he shows he really cares. If this attitude is good. It's all in the attitude.

2. Mostly, if people don't have a family outside, with no business to take care of, they're ready to stay. They ain't going to have much time to think about themselves otherwise. . . . Now, when he's got problems, when he's got things outside, if he's got mickey mouse objections, like when you ask him "How do you feel about staying here for a year?" and he's got to bargain with you, like he needs to stay with his wife or his sick mother—then we tell him to get lost. If he can't listen to a few harsh words thrown at him, he's not ready. Sometimes we yell at him, "You're a goddamned

liar!" If he's serious he'll take it. He'll do anything if he's serious.

But each guy's different. If he sounds sincere, we're not so hard. If he's sick of running the rat race out there, or afraid of going to the penitentiary, he's ready to do anything. Then we let him right in. . . .

This admission process seems to have two principal functions. First, it forces the newcomer to admit, at least on a verbal level, that he is willing to try to conform to the norms of the group, whose members will not tolerate any liking for drugs or drug addicts. From the minute he enters the door, his expressed desire to join the group is tested by giving him difficult orders—to have his hair cut off, to give up all his money, to sever all family ties, to come back in ten days or even thirty days. He is given expert help and explicit but simple criteria for separating the "good guys" from the "bad guys"—the latter shoot dope. Second, the admission process weeds out men and women who simply want to lie down for a few days to rest, to obtain free room and board, or to stay out of the hands of the police. In the terms used by Lindesmith, and also in the terms used at Synanon, the person must want to give up drug *addiction*, not just the drug *habit*.[10] This means that he must at least *say* that he wants to quit using drugs once and for all, in order to realize his potentials as an adult; he must not indicate that he merely wants a convenient place in which to go through withdrawal distress so that he can be rid of his habit for a short time because he has lost his connection, or for some other reason. He must be willing to give up all ambitions, desires, and social interactions that might prevent the group from assimilating him completely.

If he says he just wants to kick, he's no good. Out with him. Now we know nine

[10] Alfred R. Lindesmith, *Opiate Addiction* (Bloomington: Principia Press, 1947), pp. 44–66.

out of ten lie, but we don't care. We'd rather have him make an attempt and *lie* and then get him in here for thirty days or so—then he might stick. It takes months to decide to stay.

Most fish [newcomers] don't take us seriously. We know what they want, out in front. A dope fiend wants dope, nothing else. All the rest is garbage. We've even taken that ugly thing called money. This shows that they're serious. Now this guy today was sincere. We told him we didn't want money. We could see he would at least give the place a try. We have to find out if he's sincere. Is he willing to have us cut off his curly locks? Imagine cutting his hair off makes him take us seriously. . . .

Although it is impossible to say whether Synanon's selective admission process inadvertently admits those addicts who are most amenable to change, no addict has been refused admission on the ground that his case is "hopeless" or "difficult" or that he is "unreachable." On the contrary, before coming to Synanon, twenty-nine of the fifty-two addicts had been on drugs for at least ten years. Two of these were addicted for over forty years, and had been in and out of institutions during that period. The average length of time on drugs for the fifty-two was eleven years, and 56 per cent reported less than one month as the longest period of time voluntarily free of drugs after addiction and prior to Synanon.

Indoctrination.—In the admission process, and throughout his residence, the addict discovers over and over again that the group to which he is submitting is antidrug, anticrime, and antialcohol. At least a dozen times a day he hears someone tell him that he can remain at Synanon only as long as he "stays clean," that is, stays away from crime, alcohol, and drugs. This emphasis is an unwitting implementation of Cressey's second principle:

The more relevant the common purpose of the group to the reformation of crim-

inals, the greater will be its influence on the criminal members' attitudes and values. Just as a labor union exerts strong influence over its members' attitudes toward management but less influence on their attitudes toward say, Negroes, so a group organized for recreation or welfare purposes will have less success in influencing criminalistic attitudes and values than will one whose explicit purpose is to change criminals.

Indoctrination makes clear the notion that Synanon exists in order to keep addicts off drugs, not for purposes of recreation, vocational education, etc. Within a week after admission, each newcomer participates in an indoctrination session by a spontaneous group made up of four or five older members. Ordinarily, at least one member of the Board of Directors is present, and he acts as leader. The following are excerpts from one such session with a woman addict. The rules indicate the extreme extent to which it is necessary for the individual to subvert his personal desires and ambitions to the antidrug, anticrime group.

Remember, we told you not to go outside by yourself. Whenever anybody leaves this building they have to check in and out at the desk. For a while, stay in the living room. Don't take showers alone or even go to the bathroom alone, see. While you're kicking, somebody will be with you all the time. And stay away from newcomers. You got nothing to talk to them about, except street talk, and before you know it you'll be splitting [leaving] to take a fix together. Stay out of the streets, mentally and physically, or get lost now.

No phone calls or letters for a while—if you get one, you'll read it in front of us. We'll be monitoring all your phone calls for a while. You see, you got no ties, no business out there any more. You don't need them. You never could handle them before, so don't start thinking you can do it now. All you knew how to do was shoot dope and go to prison.

You could never take care of your daughter before. You didn't know how to be a mother. It's garbage. All a dope fiend knows how to do is shoot dope. Forget it.

There are two obvious illustrations of the antidrug and anticrime nature of the group's subculture. First, there is a strong taboo against what is called "street talk." Discussion of how it feels to take a fix, who one's connection was, where one took his shot, the crimes one has committed, or who one associated with is severely censured. One's best friend and confidant at Synanon might well be the person that administers a tongue lashing for street talk, and the person who calls your undesirable behavior to the attention of the entire group during a general meeting.

Second, a member must never, in any circumstances, identify with the "code of the streets," which says that a criminal is supposed to keep quiet about the criminal activities of his peers. Even calling an ordinary citizen "square" is likely to stimulate a spontaneous lecture, in heated and colorful terms, on the notion that the people who are *really* square are those that go around as bums sticking needles in their arms. A person who, as a criminal, learned to hate stool pigeons and finks with a passion must now turn even his closest friend over to the authorities, the older members of Synanon, if the friend shows any signs of nonconformity. If he should find that a member is considering "sneaking off to a fix somewhere," has kept pills, drugs, or an "outfit" with him when he joined the organization, or even has violated rules such as that prohibiting walking alone on the beach, he must by Synanon's code relinquish his emotional ties with the violator and expose the matter to another member or even to the total membership

at a general meeting. If he does not do so, more pressure is put upon him than upon the violator, for he is expected to have "known better." Thus, for perhaps the first time in his life he will be censured for *not* "squealing" rather than for "squealing." [11] He must identify with the law and not with the criminal intent or act.

The sanctions enforcing this norm are severe, for its violation threatens the very existence of the group. "Guilt by association" is the rule. In several instances, during a general meeting the entire group spontaneously voted to "throw out" both a member who had used drugs and a member who had known of this use but had not informed the group. Banishment from the group is considered the worst possible punishment, for it is stressed over and over again that life in the streets "in your condition" can only mean imprisonment or death.

That the group's purpose is keeping addicts off drugs is given emphasis in formal and informal sessions—called "haircuts" or "pull ups"—as well as in spontaneous denunciations, and in denunciations at general meetings. The "synanon," discussed below, also serves this purpose. A "haircut" is a deliberately contrived device for minimizing the importance of the individual and maximizing the importance of the group, and for defining the group's basic purpose— keeping addicts off drugs and crime. The following is the response of a leader to the questions, "What's a haircut? What's its purpose?"

When you are pointing out what a guy is doing. We do this through mechanisms of exaggeration. We blow up an incident so he can really get a look at it. The Coordinators [a coordinator resembles an officer of the day] and the Board members and sometimes

---

[11] See Lewis Yablonsky, "The Anti-Criminal Society: Synanon," *Federal Probation,* XXVI (September, 1962), 50–57; and Lewis Yablonsky, *The Violent Gang* (New York: Macmillan Co., 1962), pp. 252–63.

an old timer may sit in on it. We do this when we see a person's attitude becoming negative in some area.

For a *real* haircut, I'll give you myself. I was in a tender trap. My girl split. She called me on the job three days in a row. I made a date with her. We kept the date and I stayed out all night with her. Now, she was loaded [using drugs]. I neglected— or I refused—to call the house. By doing this I ranked everybody. You know doing something like that was no good. They were all concerned. They sent three or four autos looking for me because I didn't come back from work. You see, I was in Stage II.

X found me and he made me feel real lousy, because I knew he worked and was concerned. Here he was out looking for me and he had to get up in the morning. Well, I called the house the next morning and came back. I got called in for a haircut.

I sat down with three Board members in the office. They stopped everything to give the haircut. That impressed me. Both Y and Z, they pointed out my absurd and ridiculous behavior by saying things like this— though I did not get loaded, I associated with a broad I was emotionally involved with who was using junk. I jeopardized my *own* existence by doing this. So they told me, "Well, you fool, you might as well have shot dope by associating with a using addict." I was given an ultimatum. If I called her again or got in touch with her I would be thrown out.

("Why?")

Because continued correspondence with a using dope fiend is a crime against *me*— it hurts *me*. It was also pointed out how rank I was to people who are concerned with me. I didn't seem to care about people who were trying to help me. I'm inconsiderate to folks who've wiped my nose, fed me, clothed me. I'm like a child, I guess. I bite the hand that feeds me.

To top that off, I had to call a general meeting and I told everybody in the building what a jerk I was and I was sorry for acting like a little punk. I just sort of tore myself down. Told everyone what a phony I had been. And then the ridiculing questions began. Everybody started in. Like, "Where

do you get off doing that to us?" That kind of stuff. When I was getting the treatment they asked me what I'd do—whether I would continue the relationship, whether I'd cut it off, or if I really wanted to stay at Synanon and do something about myself and my problem. But I made the decision before I even went in that I'd stay and cut the broad loose. I had enough time under my belt to know enough to make that decision before I even came back to the house. . . .

Group cohesion.—The daily program at Synanon is consistent with Cressey's third principle, and appears to be an unwitting attempt to implement that principle:

The more cohesive the group, the greater the members' readiness to influence others and the more relevant the problem of conformity to group norms. The criminals who are to be reformed and the persons expected to effect the change must, then, have a strong sense of belonging to one group: between them there must be a genuine "we" feeling. The reformers, consequently, should not be identifiable as correctional workers, probation or parole officers, or social workers.

Cohesion is maximized by a "family" analogy and by the fact that all but some "third-stage" members live and work together. The daily program has been deliberately designed to throw members into continuous mutual activity. In addition to the free, unrestricted interaction in small groups called "synanons," the members meet as a group at least twice each day. After breakfast, someone is called upon to read the "Synanon Philosophy," which is a kind of declaration of principles, the day's work schedule is discussed, bits of gossip are publicly shared, the group or individual members are spontaneously praised or scolded by older members. Following a morning of work activities, members meet in the dining room after lunch to discuss some concept or quotation that has been written on a blackboard. Stress is on participation and expression; quotations are selected by Board members to provoke controversy and examination of the meaning, or lack of meaning, of words. Discussion sometimes continues informally during the afternoon work period and in "synanons," which are held after dinner. In addition, lectures and classes, conducted by any member or outside speaker who will take on the responsibility, are held several times a week for all members who feel a need for them. Topics have included "semantics," "group dynamics," "meaning of truth," and "Oedipus complex."

There are weekend recreational activities, and holidays, wedding anniversaries, and birthdays are celebrated. Each member is urged: "Be yourself," "Speak the truth," "Be honest," and this kind of action in an atmosphere that is informal and open quickly gives participants a strong sense of "belonging." Since many of the members have been homeless drifters, it is not surprising to hear frequent repetition of some comment to the effect that "This is the first home I ever had."

Also of direct relevance to the third principle is the *voluntary* character of Synanon. Any member can walk out at any time; at night the doors are locked against persons who might want to enter, but not against persons who might want to leave. Many do leave.

Holding addicts in the house once they have been allowed to enter is a strong appeal to ideas such as "We have all been in the shape you are now in," or "Mike was on heroin for twenty years and *he's* off." It is significant, in this connection, that addicts who "kick" (go through withdrawal distress) at Synanon universally report that the sickness is not as severe

as it is in involuntary organizations, such as jails and mental hospitals. One important variable here, we believe, is the practice of not giving "kicking dope fiends" special quarters. A newcomer kicks on a davenport in the center of the large living room, not in a special isolation room or quarantine room. Life goes on around him. Although a member will be assigned to watch him, he soon learns that his sickness is not important to men and women who have themselves kicked the habit. In the living room, one or two couples might be dancing, five or six people may be arguing, a man may be practicing the guitar, and a girl may be ironing. The kicking addict learns his lesson: These others have made it. This subtle device is supplemented by explicit comments from various members as they walk by or as they drop in to chat with him. We have heard the following comments, and many similar ones, made to new addicts lying sick from withdrawal. It should be noted that none of the comments could reasonably have been made by a rehabilitation official or a professional therapist.

"It's OK boy. We've all been through it before."

"For once you're with people like us. You've got everything to gain here and nothing to lose."

"You think you're tough. Listen, we've got guys in here who could run circles around you, so quit your bull——."

"You're one of us now, so keep your eyes open, your mouth shut and try to listen for a while. Maybe you'll learn a few things."

"Hang tough, baby. We won't let you die."

Status ascription.—Cressey's fourth principle is:

Both reformers and those to be reformed must achieve status within the group by exhibition of "pro-reform" or anti-criminal values and behavior patterns. As a novitiate . . . he is a thera-

peutic parasite and not actually a member until he accepts the group's own system for assigning status.

This is the crucial point in Cressey's formula, and it is on this point that Synanon seems most effective. The house has an explicit program for distributing status symbols to members in return for staying off the drug and, later, for actually displaying antidrug attitudes. The resident, no longer restricted to the status of "inmate" or "patient" as in a prison or hospital, can achieve any staff position in the status hierarchy.

The Synanon experience is organized into a career of roles that represent stages of graded competence, at whose end are roles that might later be used in the broader community. Figure 1 shows the status system in terms of occupational roles, each box signifying a stratum. Such cliques as exist at Synanon tend to be among persons of the same stratum. Significantly, obtaining jobs of increased responsibility and status is almost completely dependent upon one's attitudes toward crime and the use of drugs. To obtain a job such as Senior Coordinator, for example, the member must have demonstrated that he can remain free of drugs, crime, and alcohol for at least three to six months. Equally important, he must show that he can function without drugs in situations where he might have used drugs before he came to Synanon. Since he is believed to have avoided positions of responsibility by taking drugs, he must gradually take on positions of responsibility without the use of drugs. Thus, he cannot go up the status ladder unless his "attitudes" are right, no matter what degree of skill he might have as a workman. Evaluation is rather casual, but it is evaluation nevertheless— he will not be given a decent job in the organization unless he relinquishes the

role of the "con artist" and answers questions honestly, expresses emotions freely, co-operates in group activities, and demonstrates leadership. In a letter to a public official in May, 1960, the founder explained the system as follows:

Continued residence [at Synanon], which we feel to be necessary to work out the problem of interpersonal relationships which underlie the addiction symptom is based on adherence by the individual to standards of behavior, thinking, and feeling acceptable to our culture. There is much work to be done here, as we have no paid help, and each person must assume his share of the burden. Increased levels of responsibility are sought and the experience of self-satisfaction comes with seeking and assuming these higher levels and seems to be an extremely important part of emotional growth.[12]

An analogy with a family and the development of a child also is used. Officially, every member is expected to go through three "stages of growth," indicated by Roman numerals in Figure 1. Stage I has two phases, "infancy" and "adolescence." In the "infancy" phase (I-A) the member behaves like an infant

TABLE 5

Length of Residence and "Stage" of Members, June, 1962

Length of Residence (In Months)	Stages				
	I	II	III	No.	Per Cent
1– 3	20	0	0	20	19
4– 6	15	0	0	15	14
7– 9	7	3	0	10	9
10–12	2	0	0	2	2
13–15	3	4	0	7	7
16–18	3	0	2	5	5
19–21	4	1	0	5	5
22–24	0	4	1	5	5
25 and over ..	0	12	24	36	34
Total	54	24	27	105	100

[12] See Volkman, *op. cit.,* pp. 90–96.

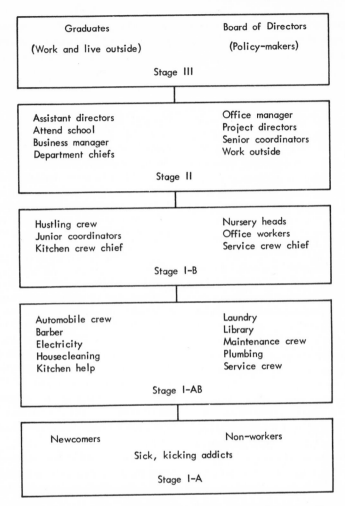

Fig. 1. Division of labor and stratification system, Synanon, June, 1962.

and is treated as one; as he kicks the habit "cold turkey" (without the aid of drugs) in the living room, he is dependent on the others, and he is supervised and watched at all times. When he is physically and mentally able, he performs menial tasks such as dishwashing and sweeping in a kind of "preadolescent" stage (I-AB) and then takes on more responsible positions (I-B). In this "adolescence" phase he takes on responsibility for maintenance work, participates actively in group meetings, demonstrates a

concern for "emotional growth," mingles with newcomers and visitors, and accepts responsibilities for dealing with them. In work activities, for example, he might drive the group's delivery truck alone, watch over a sick addict, supervise the dishwashing or cleanup crews, or meet strangers at the door.

Stage II is called the "young adult stage." Here, the member is in a position to choose between making Synanon a "career," attending school, or going to work at least part time. If he works for

Synanon, his position is complex and involves enforcing policy over a wide range of members. In Stage III, "adult," he moves up to a policy-making position in the Board of Directors or moves out of Synanon but returns with his friends and family for occasional visits. He can apparently resist the urge to resort to drugs in times of crisis without the direct help of Synanon members. One man described this stage by saying, "They go out, get jobs, lose jobs, get married, get divorced, get married again, just like everyone else." However, the group does maintain a degree of control. Graduates are never supposed to cut off their ties with their Synanon "family," and they are expected to return frequently to display themselves as a "dope fiend made good."

From Table 5 it is apparent that seniority in the form of length of residence (equivalent to the number of "clean" days) is an important determinant of status. As time of residence increases, responsibilities to the group, in the forms of work and leadership, tend to increase. In June, 1962, twenty-seven of the 105 members of Synanon were in Stage III. It should be noted that while stage is associated with length of residence, advancement through the stages is not automatic. The longer one lives at Synanon, the "cleaner" he is, the more diffuse the roles he performs, and the higher his status.

It is also important to note that high status does not depend entirely upon one's conduct within the house. Before he graduates to Stage III a member must in some way be accorded an increase in status by the legitimate outside community. This is further insurance that status will be conferred for activities that are antidrug in character. In early 1960, the members began to take an active part in legitimate community activities, mostly in the form of lectures and discussion groups. Since Synanon's inception, more than 350 service groups, church groups, political groups, school and college classes, etc.,

have been addressed by speakers from Synanon. Such speeches and discussions gain community support for the organization, but they further function to give members a feeling of being important enough to be honored by an invitation to speak before community groups. Similarly, members are proud of those individuals who have "made good" in the outside community by becoming board members of the P.T.A., Sunday-school teachers, college students, and members of civic and service organizations. Over thirty-five Synanon members are now working full or part time in the community, holding a wide range of unskilled (janitor, parking attendant), skilled (truck driver, carpenter, electrician), white-collar (secretary, photographer), and executive (purchasing agent) posts.

Further, the legitimate status of the *group* has increasingly risen during the last two years. Since the summer of 1960, an average of 100–150 guests have attended open-house meetings, and the guests have included distinguished persons from all walks of legitimate life. Well-known psychiatrists, correctional workers, businessmen, newspapermen, and politicians have publicly praised the work of the group. There have been requests for Synanon houses and for Synanon groups from several communities, and Synanon projects are now being conducted at Terminal Island Federal Prison and the Nevada State Prison. Recently, the group has been featured in films, on television and radio shows, and in national magazines. At least two books and a movie are being written about it. Over five hundred citizens have formed an organization called "Sponsors of Synanon." Even strong attacks from some members of the local community and complicated legal battles about zoning ordinances have served principally to unite the group and maximize the *esprit de corps.*

The "synanon."—Synanon got its name

from an addict who was trying to say "seminar." The term "Synanon" is used to refer to the entire organization, but when it is spelled with a lower-case *s* it refers only to the meetings occurring in the evenings among small groups of six to ten members. Each evening, all members are assigned to such groups, and membership in the groups is rotated so that one does not regularly interact with the same six or ten persons. The announced aim of these meetings is to "trigger feelings" and to allow what some members refer to as "a catharsis." The sessions are not "group therapy" in the usual sense, for no trained therapist is present. Moreover, the emphasis is on enforcing anticriminal and antidrug norms, as well as upon emotional adjustment.[13] These sessions, like the entire program, constitute a system for implementing Cressey's fifth principle, although they were not designed to do so.

The most effective mechanism for exerting group pressure on members will be found in groups so organized that criminals are induced to join with noncriminals for the purpose of changing other criminals. A group in which criminal A joins with some noncriminals to change criminal B is probably most effective in changing criminal A, not B; in order to change criminal B, criminal A must necessarily share the values of the anticriminal members.

In the house, the behavior of all members is visible to all others. What a member is seen to do at the breakfast table, for example, might well be scrutinized and discussed at his synanon that evening. The synanon sessions differ from everyday honesty by virtue of the fact that in these discussions one is expected to *insist on* the truth as well as to tell the truth. Any weapon, such as ridicule, cross-examination, or hostile attack, is both permissible and expected. The sessions seem to provide an atmosphere of truth-seeking that is reflected in the rest of the social life within the household so that a simple question like "How are you?" is likely to be answered by a five-minute discourse in which the respondent searches for the truth. The following discussion is from a tape recording of a synanon session held in June, 1961. It should be noted that an "innocent" question about appearance, asked by an older member who has become a non-criminal and a non-addict, led to an opportunity to emphasize the importance of loyalty to the antidrug, anticrime group.

"What are you doing about losing weight?"

"Why? Is that your business?"

"I asked you a question."

"I don't intend to answer it. It's not your business."

"Why do you want to lose weight?"

"I don't intend to answer it."

"Why?"

"Because it's an irrelevant and meaningless question. You know I had a baby only three weeks ago, and you've been attacking me about my weight. It's none of your business."

"Why did you call your doctor?"

"Why? Because I'm on a diet."

"What did he prescribe for you?"

"I don't know. I didn't ask him."

"What did you ask for?"

"I didn't. I don't know what he gave me."

"Come on now. What kind of pills are they?"

"I don't know. I'm not a chemist. Look the doctor knows I'm an addict. He knows I live at Synanon. He knows a whole lot about me."

"Yeah, well, I heard you also talking to him on the phone, and you sounded just like any other addict trying to cop a doctor out of pills."

"You're a goddamned liar!"

[13] See Cressey, "Contradictory Theories in Correctional Group Therapy Programs," *op. cit.*

"Yeah, well X was sitting right there. Look, does the doctor know and does the Board know?"

"I spoke to Y [Board member]. It's all been verified."

"What did Y say?"

"I was talking to . . ."

"What did Y say?"

"Well, will you wait just a minute?"

"What did Y say?"

"Well, let her talk."

"I don't want to hear no stories."

"I'm not telling stories."

"What did Y say?"

"That it was harmless. The doctor said he'd give me nothing that would affect me. There's nothing in it. He knows it all. I told Y."

"Oh, you're all like a pack of wolves. You don't need to yell and scream at her."

"Look, I heard her on the phone and the way she talked she was trying to manipulate the doctor."

"Do you resent the fact that she's still acting like a dope fiend and she still sounds like she's conning the doctor out of something? She's a dope fiend. Maybe she can't talk to a doctor any differently."

"Look, I called the doctor today. He said I should call him if I need him. He gave me vitamins and lots of other things."

"Now wait a minute. You called to find out if you could get some more pills."

"Besides, it's the attitude they heard over the phone. That's the main thing."

"Yeah, well they probably projected it onto me."

"Then how come you don't like anyone listening to your phone calls?"

"Are you feeling guilty?"

"Who said?"

"Me. That's who. You even got sore when you found out X and me heard you on the phone, didn't you? You didn't like that at all, did you?"

"Is that so?"

(*Silence.*)

"I don't think her old man wants her back."

"Well, who would? An old fat slob like that."

"Sure, that's probably why she's thinking of leaving all the time and ordering pills."

"Sure."

(*Silence.*)

"My appearance is none of your business."

"Everything here is our business."

"Look, when a woman has a baby you can't understand she can't go back to normal weight in a day."

"Now *you* look. We're really not interested in your weight problem now. Not really. We just want to know why you've got to have pills to solve the problem. We're going to talk about that if we want to. That's what we're here for."

"Look, something's bugging you. We all know that. I even noticed it in your attitude toward me."

"Yeah, I don't care about those pills. I want to know how you're feeling. What's behind all this? Something's wrong. What is it?"

(*Silence.*)

"Have you asked your old man if you could come home yet?"

(*Softly.*) "Yes."

"What did he say?"

(*Softly.*) "He asked me how I felt. Wanted to know why I felt I was ready to come home. . . ."

(*Silence.*)

(*Softly.*) "I did it out of anger. I wasn't very happy. (*Pause.*) A day before I tried [telephoning him] and he wasn't there. (*Pause.*) Just this funny feeling about my husband being there and me here. My other kid's there and this one's here. (*Pause.*) A mixed-up family."

"Why do you want to stay then? Do you want to be here?"

"No. I don't want to be here. That's exactly why I'm staying. I need to stay till I'm ready."

"Look, you've got to cut them loose for a while. You may not be ready for the rest of your life. You may not ever be able to be with those people."

(*Tears.*)

"I know. . . ."

After the synanon sessions, the house is always noisy and lively. We have seen members sulk, cry, shout, and threaten to leave the group as a result of conversation in the synanon. The following comments, every one of which represents the expression of a pro-reform attitude by the speaker, were heard after one session. It is our hypothesis that such expressions are the important ones, for they indicate that the speaker has become a reformer and, thus, is reinforcing his own pro-reform attitudes every time he tries to comfort or reform another.

"Were they hard on you?"
"I really let him have it tonight."
"I couldn't get to her. She's so damned blocked she couldn't even hear what I was trying to tell her."
"Hang tough, man; it gets easier."
"One of these days he'll drop those defenses of his and start getting honest."
"Don't leave. We all love you and want you to get well."

At Synanon, disassociating with former friends, avoiding street talk, and becoming disloyal to criminals are emphasized at the same time that loyalty to non-criminals, telling the truth to authority figures, and legitimate work are stressed. We have no direct evidence that haircuts, synanons, and both formal and spontaneous denunciations of street talk and the code of the streets have important rehabilitative effects on the actor, as well as (or, perhaps even "rather than") on the victim. It seems rather apparent, however, that an individual's own behavior must be dramatically influenced when he acts in the role of a moral policeman and "takes apart" another member. It is significant that older members of Synanon like to point out that the "real Synanon" began on "the night of the big cop out" (confession). In its earliest days, Synanon had neither the group cohesiveness nor the degree of control it now has. Some participants remained as addicts while proclaiming their loyalty to the principle of antiaddiction, and other participants knew of this condition. One evening in a general meeting a man spontaneously

stood up and confessed ("copped out") that he had sneaked out for a shot. One by one, with no prompting, the others present rose to confess either their own violations or their knowledge of the violations of their friends. From that moment, the Board of Directors believe, the organization became a truly antidrug group; there has been no problem of drug use since.

The Results

Of the fifty-two residents described earlier, four are "graduates" of Synanon, are living in the community, and are not using alcohol or drugs. Twenty-three (44.2 per cent) are still in residence and are not using alcohol or drugs. Two of these are on the Board of Directors and eleven are working part or full time. The remaining twenty-five left Synanon against the advice of the Board and the older members.

Information regarding the longest period of voluntary abstinence from drugs after the onset of addiction but prior to entering Synanon was obtained on forty-eight of the fifty-two persons. Eleven reported that they were "never" clean, six said they were continuously clean for less than one week, ten were continuously clean for less than one month. Thirty-nine (81 per cent) said they had been continuously clean for less than six months, and only two had been clean for as long as a one-year period. Twenty-seven (52 per cent) of the fifty-two residents have now abstained for at least six months; twelve of these have been clean for at least two years and two have been off drugs continually for over three years.

Between May, 1958 (when Synanon started), and May, 1961, 263 persons were admitted or readmitted to Synanon. Of these, 190 (72 per cent) left Synanon against the advice of the Board of Directors and the older members. Significantly, 59 per cent of all dropouts occurred within the first month of residence, 90 per cent within the first three months. Synanon is not adverse to giving a person a second chance, or even a third or fourth chance: of the 190 persons dropping out, eighty-three (44 per cent) were persons who had been readmitted. The dropout behavior of persons who were readmitted was, in general, similar to first admissions; 64 per cent of their dropouts occurred within the first month, 93 per cent within the first three months after readmission.

Of all the Synanon enrolees up to August, 1962, 108 out of 372 (29 per cent) are known to be off drugs. More significantly, of the 215 persons who have remained at Synanon for at least one month, 103 (48 per cent) are still off drugs; of the 143 who have remained for at least three months, 95 (66 per cent) are still non-users; of the 87 who have remained at least seven months, 75 (86 per cent) are non-users. These statistics seem to us to be most relevant, for they indicate that once an addict actually becomes a member of the antidrug community (as indicated by three to six months of participation), the probability that he will leave and revert to the use of drugs is low.

Conclusions

Synanon's leaders do not claim to "cure" drug addicts. They are prone to measure success by pointing to the fact that the organization now includes the membership of forty-five persons who were heroin addicts for at least ten years. Two of these were addicted for more than thirty years and spent those thirty years going in and out of prisons, jails, the U.S. Public Service Hospital, and similar institutions. The leaders have rather inadvertently used a theory of rehabilitation that implies that it is as ridiculous to try to "cure" a man of drug addiction as it is to try to "cure" him of sexual intercourse. A man can be helped to stay away from drugs, however, and this seems to be the contribution Synanon is making. In this regard, its "success" rate is higher than that of those institutions officially designated by society as places for the confinement and "reform" of drug addicts. Such a comparison is not fair, however, both because it is not known whether the subjects in Synanon are comparable to those confined in institutions, and because many official institutions do not concentrate on trying to keep addicts off drugs, being content to withdraw the drug, build up the addicts physically, strengthen vocational skills, and eliminate gaps in educational backgrounds.[14]

We cannot be certain that it is the group relationships at Synanon, rather than something else, that is keeping addicts away from crime and drugs. However, both the times at which dropouts occur and the increasing antidrug attitudes displayed with increasing length of residence tend to substantiate Sutherland's theory of differential association and Cressey's notion that modifying social relationships is an effective supplement to the clinical handling of convicted criminals. Drug addiction is, in fact, a severe test of Sutherland's sociological theory and Cressey's sociological principles, for addicts have the double problem of criminality and the drug habit. The statistics on dropouts suggest that the group relations method of rehabilitation does not begin to have its effects until newcomers are truly integrated into the antidrug, anticrime group that is Synanon.

[14] Cf. Harrison M. Trice, "Alcoholism: Group Factors in Etiology and Therapy," *Human Organization,* XV (Summer, 1956), 33–40 (see also Donald R. Cressey, "The Nature and Effectiveness of Correctional Techniques," *Law and Contemporary Problems,* XXIII [Fall, 1958], 754–71).